CURRICULUM FOR WALES

MATHEMATICS AND NUMERACY

Masteri Mathematics

FOR 11–14 YEARS

Linda Mason, Jonathan Agar,
Laszlo Fedor

BOOK 1

Boost

HODDER EDUCATION
AN HACHETTE UK COMPANY

The Publishers would like to thank the following for permission to reproduce copyright material.

Photo credits

p. 2 © cunaplus - stock.adobe.com; **p. 16** *l–r* © Africa Studio - Fotolia.com, © viperagp - stock.adobe.com, © yvdavid - Fotolia.com, © artkox - stock.adobe.com; **p. 19** © AGB Photo Library / Alamy Stock Photo; **p. 22** © robertharding / Alamy Stock Photo; **p. 34** © moonrun/Fotolia.com; **p. 48** *t* © igor - Fotolia.com, *ml* © ismailgazel - stock.adobe.com, *mr* © creativica - stock.adobe.com; **p. 157** © Elaine Lambert (Hodder Education); **p. 285** © Sue Hough; **p. 313** *t* © Wojciech Boruch - stock.adobe.com, *b* © prapann - stock.adobe.com; **p. 315** *t–b* © Su Nitram - stock.adobe.com, © Wojciech Boruch - stock.adobe.com, © Elena Milevska - stock.adobe.com, © technicolors - stock.adobe.com, © chartcameraman - Fotolia.com; **p. 326** © Spiroview Inc./stock.adobe.com; **p. 331** © stocksolutions - stock.adobe.com.

Acknowledgements

Every effort has been made to trace all copyright holders, but if any have been inadvertently overlooked, the Publishers will be pleased to make the necessary arrangements at the first opportunity.

Although every effort has been made to ensure that website addresses are correct at time of going to press, Hodder Education cannot be held responsible for the content of any website mentioned in this book. It is sometimes possible to find a relocated web page by typing in the address of the home page for a website in the URL window of your browser.

This book is based on material written for and published in *Key Stage 3 Mastering Mathematics: Book 1*, Second Edition (978 1 3983 0839 8) by Sophie Goldie, Luke Robinson, Andrew Ginty and Heather Davis, with Series Editor Steve Cavill. The publisher would like to thank them for permission to re-use their work in the present volume.

Hachette UK's policy is to use papers that are natural, renewable and recyclable products and made from wood grown in well-managed forests and other controlled sources. The logging and manufacturing processes are expected to conform to the environmental regulations of the country of origin.

Orders: please contact Hachette UK Distribution, Hely Hutchinson Centre, Milton Road, Didcot, Oxfordshire, OX11 7HH. Telephone: +44 (0)1235 827827. Email education@hachette.co.uk Lines are open from 9 a.m. to 5 p.m., Monday to Friday. You can also order through our website: www.hoddereducation.co.uk

ISBN: 978 1 3983 4445 7

© Hodder & Stoughton Limited 2022

First published in 2022 by
Hodder Education,
An Hachette UK Company
Carmelite House
50 Victoria Embankment
London EC4Y 0DZ

www.hoddereducation.co.uk

Impression number   10 9 8 7 6 5 4 3 2 1

Year   2026 2025 2024 2023 2022

All rights reserved. Apart from any use permitted under UK copyright law, no part of this publication may be reproduced or transmitted in any form or by any means, electronic or mechanical, including photocopying and recording, or held within any information storage and retrieval system, without permission in writing from the publisher or under licence from the Copyright Licensing Agency Limited. Further details of such licences (for reprographic reproduction) may be obtained from the Copyright Licensing Agency Limited, www.cla.co.uk

Cover photo © Vitaliy - stock.adobe.com

Illustrations by Aptara, Inc.

Typeset in India by Aptara, Inc.

Produced by DZS Grafik, printed in Bosnia & Herzegovina.

A catalogue record for this title is available from the British Library.

Contents

The curriculum vi
How to use this book vii

1 Probability 1
1.1 Introduction to probability 1
1.2 Single events 5
Review exercise 12

2 Working with shapes 15
2.1 Properties of 2-D shapes 16
2.2 Line symmetry 22
2.3 Rotational symmetry 28
Review exercise 34

3 Coordinates and transformations 36
3.1 Coordinates 37
3.2 Translations 41
3.3. Reflections and rotations 48
Review exercise 57

Consolidation 1 61

4 Types of number 66
4.1 Multiples 67
4.2 Factors and primes 70
4.3 Powers and roots 76
Review exercise 80

5 Calculations 82
5.1 Multiplying and dividing whole numbers 83
5.2 Solving word problems 88
5.3 BIDMAS 92
Review exercise 97

6 Using letter symbols 99
6.1 Word formulas 100
6.2 Using letters 103
6.3 Simplifying expressions 110
6.4 Equations 114
Review exercise 122

7 Sequences 125
7.1 Working with sequences 125
7.2 Generating sequences 133
Review exercise 142

Consolidation 2 146

8 Fractions 152
8.1 Equivalent fractions 153
8.2 Adding and subtracting fractions 160
8.3 Finding a fraction of an amount 165
8.4 Dividing an integer by a fraction 169
Review exercise 177

9 Place value and rounding 180
9.1 Understanding decimals 181
9.2 Rounding 188
9.3 Rounding decimals 192
Review exercise 198

Consolidation 3 201

10 Averages and range 204
10.1 Mode, median and range 205
10.2 The mean 211
10.3 Using averages and range 214
Review exercise 220

11 Displaying data 224
11.1 Using tables and charts 224
11.2 Vertical line charts 231
Review exercise 237

Consolidation 4 240

12 Working with decimals 244
12.1 Multiplying and dividing by powers of 10 244
12.2 Adding and subtracting decimals 249
12.3 Multiplying and dividing decimals 255
Review exercise 261

13 Percentages 264
13.1 Understanding percentages 264
13.2 Percentages of amounts 270
13.3 Converting between fractions, decimals and percentages 275
Review exercise 282

14 Ratio and proportion 285
14.1 Understanding ratios 285
14.2 Sharing in a given ratio 292
14.3 Proportion 298
Review exercise 303

Consolidation 5 306

15 Measurements 311
15.1 The metric system 311
15.2 Converting units of length 322
Review exercise 326

16 Area and perimeter 328
16.1 Area and perimeter 328
16.2 Area of a triangle 331
16.3 Compound shapes 335
Review exercise 341

17 Angles 344
17.1 Angle facts 344
17.2 Angles in a triangle 349
17.3 Angles in a quadrilateral 352
Review exercise 357

Consolidation 6 361

Glossary 364

The curriculum

A Curriculum for Wales

The Curriculum for Wales has been developed in Wales, by practitioners for practitioners, bringing together educational expertise with wider research and evidence. Our resources are designed to reflect the Welsh context and to help develop your identity as a citizen of Wales and the world.

We have worked in collaboration with University of Wales Press to produce this resource. They have reviewed it to make sure it is tailored to the new curriculum and explores Welsh culture and heritage in an authentic way. Find out more about University of Wales Press and their resources in Welsh and English languages by visiting their websites www.uwp.co.uk and www.gwasgprifysgolcymru.org

Our authors have a wealth of experience teaching, examining and working in education in Wales:

- **Laszlo Fedor** has 20 years' experience of working in state-funded schools in Wales. He teaches Mathematics to children of all abilities in secondary and sixth-form education.
- **Jonathan Agar** has been teaching in South Wales for over a decade, including time spent as head of department, assistant headteacher and principal examiner. He has a particular interest in pupils' misconceptions in Mathematics and has completed a Research Masters in Mathematics Education.
- Series Editor **Linda Mason** has many years of experience as teacher, adviser, curriculum consultant and principal examiner in Wales, including work across North Wales and with WJEC.

We would also like to thank the teachers from schools across Wales who helped to plan and review this title, including:

- Llanishen High School, Cardiff
- Cefn Hengoed Community School, Swansea
- Bishop Hedley High School, Merthyr Tydfil

How to use this book

▶ How to get the most from this book

Hodder Education's Mathematics resources support the learning and experience of Mathematics for years 7–9 and comprise:
- three books to support the Wales National Curriculum for ages 11–14
- Boost online content.

Our Book 1 material is split into 17 chapters, and each chapter comprises two, three or four units. In total there are 49 units in the book. The material across all three books, and the editable course planner, is designed to be used whenever the teacher feels it is appropriate for the class; for example, some content in Book 2 or even Book 3 may be suitable for some teaching in year 7. Similarly, our scheme of work is designed to be flexible.

The book contains indication of five proficiencies: **conceptual understanding, communication using symbols, fluency, logical reasoning** and **strategic competence**.

These five proficiencies are intertwined, so no individual proficiency is developed in isolation. Consequently, in general, many of the proficiencies could be highlighted in activities, examples and exercises throughout the book.

As an aid, the best fit or a principle proficiency is flagged as guidance only, to raise awareness of a particular proficiency for the learner. We have chosen to highlight good examples of conceptual understanding and communication using symbols as relevant alongside various mathematical explanations, activities and worked examples. Fluency, logical reasoning and strategic competence are highlighted in relation to individual questions in our exercises, reviews and consolidation sections. All of these indicators are intended as guidance to aid the learner in understanding their own proficiency development.

- Fluency
- Logical reasoning
- Strategic competence
- Conceptual understanding
- Communication using symbols

In summary, the five proficiencies capture a learner's developing understanding of the multi-faceted nature of their learning.

- **Conceptual understanding** allows learners to develop their ability to connect ideas through increasing depth of knowledge. Understanding the way in which concepts are connected aids learner development.
- Through progression in **communication using symbols**, learners develop understanding of conventions and abstract representation.
- With experience, learners will develop **fluency** in remembering facts, relationships and techniques.
- Learners develop **logical reasoning**, including justification and proof, in understanding the relationship between concepts.
- In developing **strategic competence**, learners show independence in applying ideas within a problem, and recognise mathematical structure.

All exercise questions that relate to finance are indicated with this symbol.

Each **chapter** includes:
- *Coming up* – a list of learning objectives that will be tackled in the chapter
- a *Starter* problem – either an activity or a puzzle – to engage the students with a new topic and designed to be used before the first lesson, or at the start of the first lesson in that topic

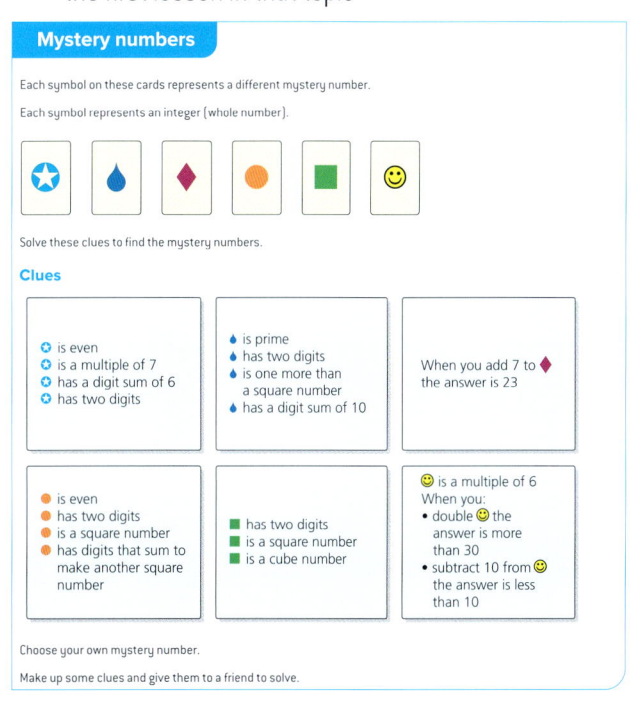

Mystery numbers

Each symbol on these cards represents a different mystery number.
Each symbol represents an integer (whole number).

⭐ 💧 ♦ 🟠 🟩 🙂

Solve these clues to find the mystery numbers.

Clues

⭐ is even ⭐ is a multiple of 7 ⭐ has a digit sum of 6 ⭐ has two digits	💧 is prime 💧 has two digits 💧 is one more than a square number 💧 has a digit sum of 10	When you add 7 to ♦ the answer is 23
🟠 is even 🟠 has two digits 🟠 is a square number 🟠 has digits that sum to make another square number	🟩 has two digits 🟩 is a square number 🟩 is a cube number	🙂 is a multiple of 6 When you: • double 🙂 the answer is more than 30 • subtract 10 from 🙂 the answer is less than 10

Choose your own mystery number.
Make up some clues and give them to a friend to solve.

- activities, investigations and whole-class discussion points
- a *Review exercise* at the end of the chapter; this encompasses all of the units covered in the chapter.

Each of the **individual units** within the chapter includes:

- a *Skill checker* – simple diagnostic questions to test basic understanding in preparation for the unit

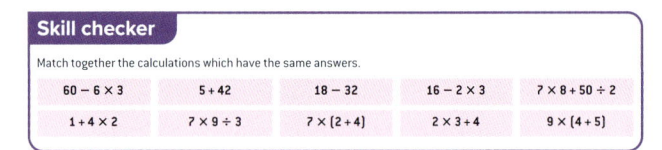

Skill checker

Match together the calculations which have the same answers.

$60 - 6 \times 3$	$5 + 42$	$18 - 32$	$16 - 2 \times 3$	$7 \times 8 + 50 \div 2$
$1 + 4 \times 2$	$7 \times 9 \div 3$	$7 \times (2 + 4)$	$2 \times 3 + 4$	$9 \times (4 + 5)$

- a clear and detailed explanation of the topic
- plenty of worked examples with solutions
- a focus on fluency, with a carefully structured approach that takes into account cognitive load theory
- helpful hints and guidance on misconceptions and pitfalls to watch out for
- *Now try these* exercise questions, which:
    ▸ develop conceptual understanding and communication using symbols
    ▸ are split up into three bands of increasing demand: Band 1 questions are for those students who are working towards age-related expectations, Band 2 are for those at age-related expectations, and Band 3 are for those working beyond age-related expectations. Most students will engage with Band 2 questions and either Band 1 or Band 3, depending on which is most appropriate
    ▸ are carefully calibrated to enable the whole class to understand each question and answer before moving on
    ▸ give the opportunity to apply skills, including working systematically, modelling, breaking problems down into stages, visualising, working backwards, and trial and improvement.

Non-calculator questions are indicated.

- a list of key words (highlighted in the text). These are fully explained in a glossary at the back of the book.

There are six sets of consolidation questions throughout the book, each of which appears after a sequence of two or three chapters. These are designed to cover approximately half a term's work.

The book encourages learners to use physical equipment (manipulatives) and representations as well as visual and abstract representations, for example using cards, bar model diagrams and physical number lines to aid the development of understanding.

Opportunities to link with Science and Technology, Humanities, Expressive Arts, Health and Well-being, Languages, Literacy and Communication teaching and learning are included in the *Cross-curricular activities* panels. Scattered throughout the books are examples that we hope will encourage exploration of historical Welsh mathematicians and contexts.

All answers are provided online at **www.hoddereducation.co.uk/MasteringMathematicsWales** and are freely accessible. You can also find an editable course planner here, with lesson suggestions and time built in for consolidation, assessment and application lessons. A suggestion for how content in these resources can be mapped to the Wales curriculum's What Matters statements and Progression Steps has been included in an editable format, to enable schools to create their own structure, as well as a full set of links to other areas of the curriculum across all subjects.

1 Probability

Coming up...

- Carrying out simple probability experiments
- Understanding chance, randomness and fairness
- Understanding equally and unequally likely outcomes
- Using the 0–1 probability scale
- Understanding that the probabilities of all possible outcomes sum to 1
- Calculating the probability of a single event

A dicey problem

Make a copy of this grid and play this dice game with a partner.

You will need two counters and a dice.

Rules

1. Choose a start position from A to F and place a counter on it.
2. Roll a dice. If you roll a:
   - 1 or 2: move one square left ←
   - 3, 4 or 5: move two squares right → →
   - 6: move one square down ↓
3. If you move off the board to the left or right, you lose.
4. The winner is the first person to move their counter to the bottom of the board.

What is the best starting position?

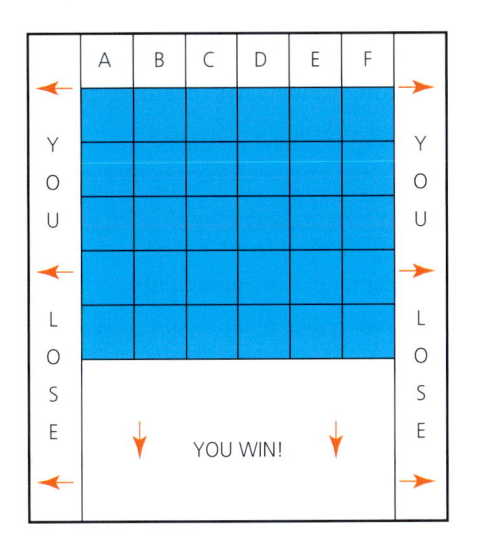

1.1 Introduction to probability

Skill checker

1. a Write down the number that each arrow is pointing to.
   b Write each number as:
      i   a fraction
      ii a percentage.

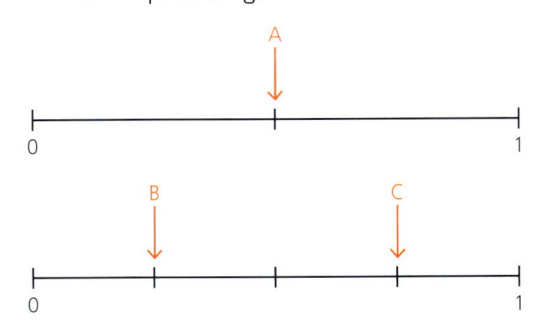

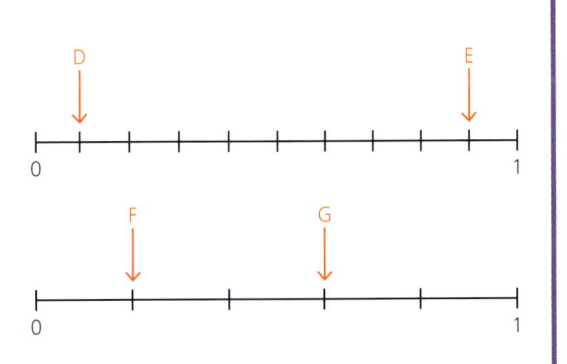

Curriculum for Wales **Mastering Mathematics: Book 1**

② Play this game with a partner.

Each player needs to draw out five boxes on a piece of paper.

☐ ☐ ☐ ☐ ☐

How to play:

Roll a ten-sided dice or run a similar computer simulation.

Each player records the number in one of their boxes.

Roll the dice four more times.

Each time record the roll in a different box.

☐ ☐ 6 ☐ ☐

Lilia rolled a 6 first, so she put a 6 in the middle. Is this the best place for it to go?

Your five rolls give you a five-digit number.

The person who has recorded the higher five-digit number wins.

What strategy did you use?

Many things in real life are not certain, but you can describe the likelihood or chance of a particular event happening using **probability**.

When you roll a dice or flip a coin you have carried out an **experiment**.

An **outcome** is the result from carrying out the experiment.

For example, the possible outcomes when you flip a coin are 'heads' and 'tails'.

Discussion activity

Give an example of an outcome of an experiment that:

a   is impossible
b   is certain
c   is unlikely
d   is likely
e   has an even chance of happening.

Probability tells you how likely an event is to occur and the probability of an event is given as either a decimal or fraction. Sometimes in real life a percentage is used.

A **probability scale** is used to compare probabilities.

The probability scale goes from impossible (probability 0) to certain (probability 1).

Impossible — Unlikely — Even chance — Likely — Certain
0 — — 0.5 — — 1
Highly unlikely   Highly likely

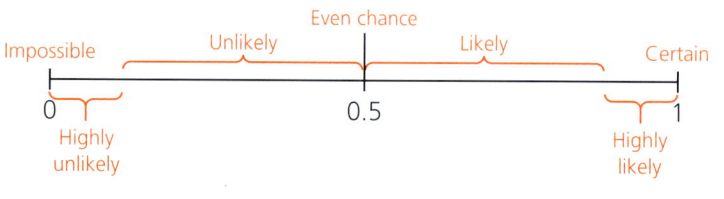

You are certain to get either heads or tails when you flip a coin.

It is impossible to roll a '7' on an ordinary six-sided dice.

An event that is **certain** to occur has a probability of 1 or 100%.

An event that is **impossible** has a probability of 0 or 0%.

The closer the probability of an event is to 1, the **more likely** the event is to happen.

The closer the probability of an event is to 0, the **less likely** the event is to happen.

An outcome with a probability of $\frac{1}{2}$, 0.5, or 50%, is equally likely to happen or not happen.

This is sometimes called an even chance.

Conceptual understanding

1 Probability

Worked example

Write these values in the correct position on the probability scale.

0   1   0.75 $\frac{1}{2}$ 0.25

Solution

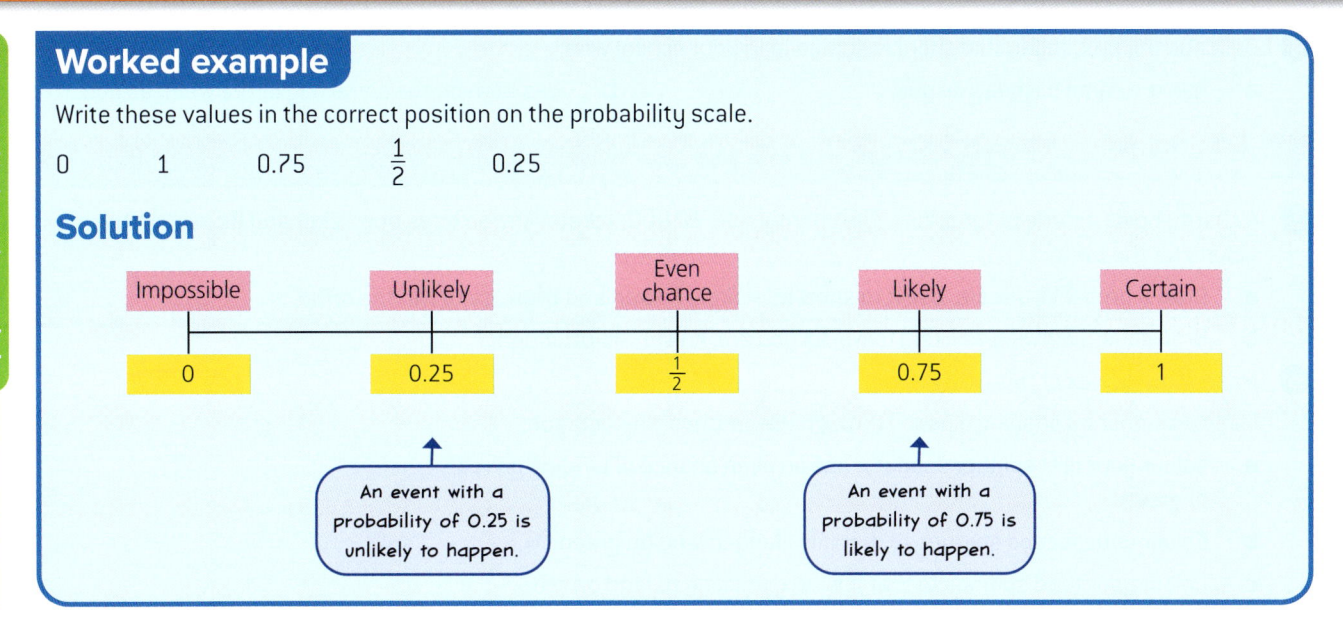

Impossible	Unlikely	Even chance	Likely	Certain
0	0.25	$\frac{1}{2}$	0.75	1

An event with a probability of 0.25 is unlikely to happen.

An event with a probability of 0.75 is likely to happen.

1.1 Now try these

Band 1 questions

1. Match each word/phrase to its definition.

   likely   impossible   unlikely   certain   even chance

   - Has an equal chance of happening or not happening
   - Will definitely happen
   - Will never happen
   - Will probably not happen
   - Will probably happen

2. Match the statements with the words below.
   a A coin will land on heads.
   b You will see a yeti if you visit Snowdonia.
   c The sun will set tonight.
   d I will roll a 6 when I roll a dice.
   e You will fly to Phobos, one of the moons of Mars.
   f Someone will win the lottery jackpot of £100 000 000 this weekend.
   g You will live to be 70 years old.

   certain   likely   even chance   unlikely   impossible

3. Place the following events in the correct places on a copy of the probability scale.

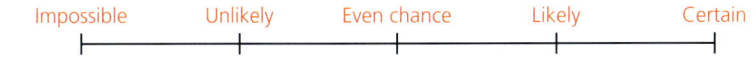

   Impossible   Unlikely   Even chance   Likely   Certain

   a The winning ticket in a raffle will be an odd number.
   b The sun will rise tomorrow.
   c A paraglider will land on the school.
   d The temperature will drop below 0 °C in December.
   e You will meet a live dinosaur tomorrow.

3

Curriculum for Wales **Mastering Mathematics: Book 1**

4 Describe the probability that there is someone in your school who:

    a   has the same birthday as you   b   was born on the same day of the week as you.

Band 2 questions

5 A charity holds a raffle to fundraise. The charity sells 10 000 tickets. Anwen buys one ticket and Bryn buys two tickets for the raffle.

    a   Draw a probability scale. Use it to show how likely Anwen and Bryn are to win the raffle.

    b   Bryn says, 'I'm twice as likely to win as you are, Anwen.' Is Bryn right?

6 Make three copies of this octagon.

Make a spinner by pushing a pencil through the centre of the octagon.

    a   Colour your first spinner so that it has an even chance of landing on red or green.

    b   Colour your second spinner so that it is likely to land on green.

    c   Colour your third spinner so that it is very unlikely to land on red.

7 On 18 September it rained.

Jac says, 'I'm glad it's raining today because I have to go out tomorrow and now it's more likely to be dry.'

    a   Is Jac right or wrong? Explain your answer.

    b   Would your answer change if the date was 18 June or 18 December?

8 Rhys is an athlete. He has won half of his races this season.

Rhys says, 'The chance of me winning my next race is even.'

Do you think Rhys is right? Explain why.

Band 3 questions

9 Sara and Megan each think of a whole number less than 100.

    a   Describe how likely it is that they are thinking of the same number.

Sara and Megan go into their classroom. Everyone in the class of 30 students thinks of a number less than 100.

    b   Describe how likely it is that two people are thinking of the same number.

    c   Describe how likely it is that someone is thinking of the same number as Megan.

The class go into an assembly with other classes. There are 150 children in the school hall.

Everyone thinks of a number less than 100.

    d   Describe how likely it is that two people are thinking of the same number.

    e   Describe how likely it is that someone is thinking of the same number as Megan.

10 Benjamin Franklin famously said, 'In this world nothing is certain except death and taxes.' Most people take out insurance policies to cover themselves against life's uncertainties – if you are insured and something goes wrong then the insurance company will pay you some money to try and put things right.

    a   Here is a list of different sorts of events that might happen to you this year for which you can take out an annual (yearly) insurance policy.

        Place each one on a probability scale.

        i   You miss your flight when you are going on holiday.   ii   Your pet needs an operation.

        iii   Your family's five-year-old dishwasher breaks down.   iv   You break your mobile phone.

        v   You fall over on holiday and break your leg.   vi   Your house is burgled.

    b   Compare your answers with other students. Discuss why you have put each one where you have.

    c   Why might someone buy insurance for an event that is unlikely to happen?

1.2 Single events

Skill checker

① Jac takes a marble at random from one of these bags.

a Match the bags to the probability that Jac draws a red marble.

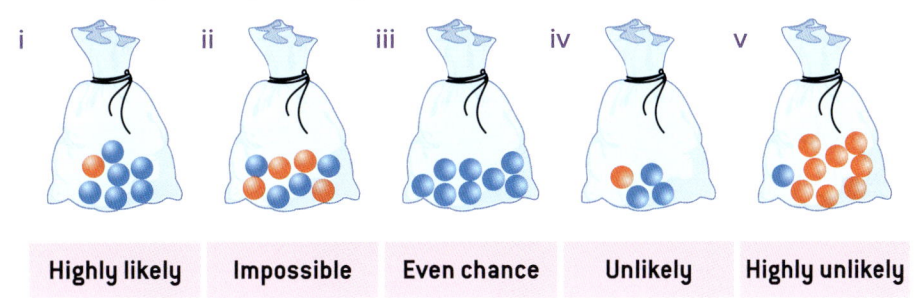

i   ii   iii   iv   v

Highly likely   **Impossible**   **Even chance**   **Unlikely**   **Highly unlikely**

b Draw a bag to match each of these labels.

Likely   **Certain**

② Match these dominoes to complete the rectangle.

1	$\frac{1}{2}$	Unlikely	99%	1.25	1 in 2	Likely	Certain
Certain	$\frac{1}{4}$	Impossible	0.01	Highly likely	100%	Even chance	0.5
Highly unlikely	75%	Highly likely	50%

| 0 | 0.95 |

One of the dominoes is incorrect. Which domino is wrong and why?

Remember that the result of an experiment or a situation involving uncertainty is called an outcome, like the score on a dice. The word **event** is used to describe a combination of outcomes, like scores 5 or 6 on a dice. So an **event** is **one or more outcomes** from an experiment.

For any event with **equally likely outcomes**, the probability of an event happening can be found using the formula:

$$P(\text{event happening}) = \frac{\text{total number of ways event can happen}}{\text{total number of possible outcomes}}$$

Worked example

Nihar throws a fair dice. He makes a list of all the possible outcomes:

1, 2, 3

a   Copy and complete Nihar's list.
b   What is meant by the word 'fair'?
c   Find the probability that Nihar gets:
   i   5
   ii   not a 5
   iii an even number
   iv   5 or more
   v   less than 5.

Solution

a   All possible outcomes: 1, 2, 3, 4, 5, 6
b   'Fair' means there is the same chance of rolling each number.
c   i $P(6) = \frac{1}{6}$ — One possible roll out of six equally likely outcomes.
    ii $P(\text{not a 5}) = \frac{5}{6}$ — Five possible rolls (1, 2, 3, 4 and 6) out of six equally likely outcomes.
    iii $P(\text{even}) = \frac{3}{6} = \frac{1}{2}$ — Three possible rolls: 2, 4 and 6.
    iv $P(\text{5 or more}) = \frac{2}{6} = \frac{1}{3}$ — Two possible rolls: 5 and 6.
    v $P(\text{less than 5}) = \frac{4}{6} = \frac{2}{3}$ — Four possible rolls: 1, 2, 3 and 4.

A dice that isn't fair is said to be biased.

Communication using symbols

Activity

Are these two probability games fair?
Play each game with a partner and record your results.

① Decide who is Player 1 and who is Player 2.

   Flip two coins.

   •   Two heads   Player 1 WINS
   •   Two tails   Player 1 WINS
   •   One head and one tail   Player 2 WINS

   Play the game a few times.
   Is the game fair? Why/why not?

② Three snails, Steffan, Sioned and S-Car-Go are having a race.

Choose a snail and put a counter on its START square.

Roll two dice.

When the total matches the number your snail is on then it moves forward one space.

Play the game a few times.

Is the game fair? Why/why not?

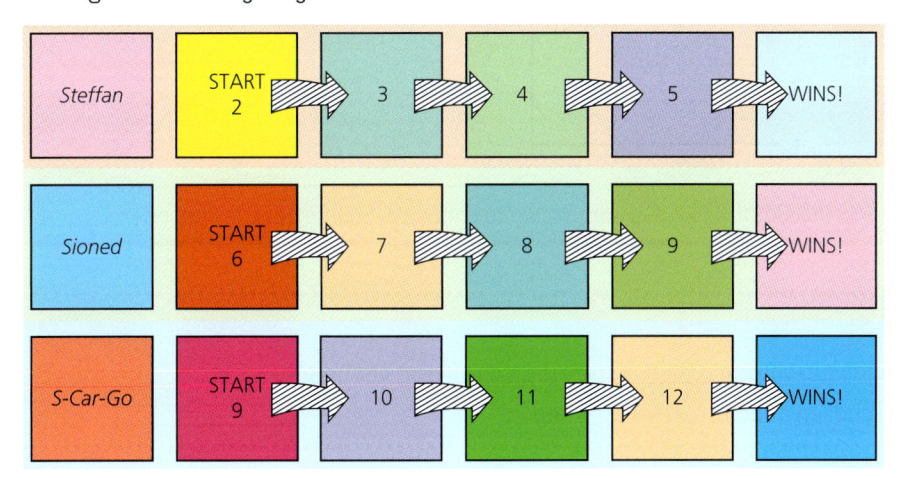

Steffan	START 2	3	4	5	WINS!
Sioned	START 6	7	8	9	WINS!
S-Car-Go	START 9	10	11	12	WINS!

Mutually exclusive events are events that cannot happen together. For example, you cannot roll a 2 and a 5 at the same time on one dice.

The probabilities of all mutually exclusive outcomes of an event add up to 1.

For example, when you flip a coin you are **certain** to get **either** heads **or** tails.

So you can say that P(heads) + P(tails) = 1.

Any event is certain to either happen OR not happen so:

P(event happening) + P(event not happening) = 1

You can rearrange this formula to give:

P(event not happening) = 1 − P(event happening)

For example, a weatherman says that the probability that it will rain tomorrow is 0.8.

The probability that it will not rain is

1 − 0.8 = 0.2

> It is certain to either rain or not rain tomorrow.
> So P(rain) + P(not rain) = 1
> Check: 0.8 + 0.2 = 1 ✓

Worked example

A letter is picked at random from the word PROBABILITY.

a What is meant by the phrase 'at random'?

b Find:

   i   P(letter B is chosen)

   ii P(a vowel is not chosen)

   iii P(letter C is chosen).

Solution

a 'At random' means that all the individual letters have equal chance of being chosen.

7

b i P(letter B is chosen) = $\frac{\text{total number of letter Bs}}{\text{total number of letters}} = \frac{2}{11}$ ← There are two Bs out of 11 letters in PROBABILITY.

ii There are four vowels out of the 11 letters in the word PROBABILITY, and seven letters that are not vowels.

P(a vowel is chosen) = $\frac{\text{total number of vowels}}{\text{total number of letters}} = \frac{4}{11}$

P(a vowel is not chosen) = 1 − P(a vowel is chosen)

$= 1 - \frac{4}{11}$

This is the same as:

P(a vowel is not chosen) = $\frac{\text{total number of non-vowels}}{\text{total number of letters}}$

$= \frac{7}{11}$

$= \frac{7}{11}$

iii The letter C does not occur in PROBABILITY so it is impossible to choose it. So P(letter C is chosen) = 0.

Discussion activity

Sometimes it is useful to get randomly chosen numbers from your calculator or device.
Find a way of getting randomly chosen numbers between 1 and 20.

1.2 Now try these

Band 1 questions

1 Lowri takes a shape from this box at random.
Find the probability that the shape she takes is:
   a a star
   b a circle
   c a square
   d a triangle
   e a shape with straight edges.

2 Tomos takes one of these cards without looking.

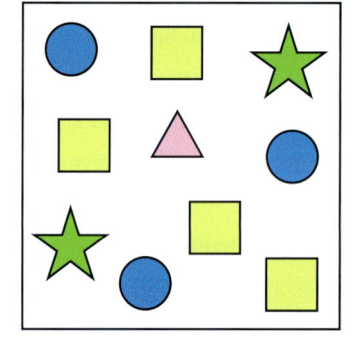

Find the probability that he takes:
   a the jack of spades
   b a queen
   c a heart
   d a card with a number on it.

3 Each of the 11 letters in the word ABRACADABRA are written on a card and put in a hat.

A B R A C A D A B R A

1 Probability

A card is taken at random from the hat. Work out the probability that the letter is:
a   an A
b   not an A
c   a B or a D
d   an E
e   an A, B, C, D or R.

4 Baz takes one of these cards without looking.

   | 2 | 4 | 3 | 8 | 2 | 9 | 6 | 3 |

a   Work out the probability that Baz takes:
    i   a 3
    ii   a number in the four times table
    iii an even number
    iv   an odd number.
b   Add your answers to part **a i** and **ii** together. Explain your answer.
c   Which two numbers have the same probability of being chosen?

Band 2 questions

5 Sajiid goes to a rescue centre to choose a kitten. There are three white kittens, two black ones and one tabby kitten. He chooses one without looking.
   Find the probability he chooses:
   a   a white kitten
   b   a black kitten
   c   a tabby kitten.

6 Make five copies of this spinner. Label your spinners a, b, c, d and e.

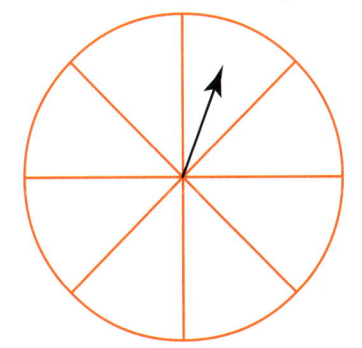

   Write numbers on each of your spinners so that the probability of getting:
   a   a '3' is impossible
   b   an odd number is certain
   c   an even number is more likely than an odd number
   d   an odd number is $\frac{1}{4}$
   e   a number less than 4 is $\frac{1}{2}$.

9

7 Ami says that the probability that she is late for school is 110%.

Bryn says that the probability that he is late is 4 in 5.

Explain why both Ami and Bryn are wrong.

Band 3 questions

8 The Hendy-Gwyn Journal claims that the probability that Hendy-Gwyn Town will win their next rugby match is $\frac{13}{20}$ and the probability they will lose is $\frac{3}{20}$.

What is the probability that the match will be a draw, according to the Hendy-Gwyn Journal?

9 A six-sided dice is biased. The table shows the probabilities for each score.

Score	1	2	3	4	5	6
Probability	0.05	0.1	0.15	0.2	0.25	?

   a What is the probability of rolling a 6?

   b Find the probability of rolling:

      i an even number

      ii an odd number.

   c Check that your answers to part **b i** and **ii** add up to 1. Why is this?

10 a There is a lucky dip stall at a local village fair.

     There are 70 prizes that are identically wrapped so that each prize is equally likely to be picked.

     A customer pays a fee and picks one of the prizes that they then keep.

     There are 40 packets of mints, 28 packets of bubble gum and two £2 coins as the prizes at the start of the lucky dip.

     What is the probability of the first customer:

      i picking a packet of mints

      ii picking a packet of bubble gum

      iii picking a £2 coin

      iv picking a packet of mints or bubble gum

      v not picking a £2 coin?

   b The first customer wins £2. Find the probability that the second customer gets:

      i £2

      ii a packet of mints

      iii a packet of bubble gum.

   c The second customer also wins £2. Find the probability that the third customer gets:

      i £2

      ii a packet of mints

      iii a packet of bubble gum.

   d The fee to play the game is 50p.

     A packet of mints costs 10p and a packet of bubble gum costs 15p.

     How much profit will the village fair make from this lucky dip if all the tickets are sold?

11 The scores on a biased dice have these probabilities.

Score	1	2	3	4	5	6
Probability	☐	2×☐	3×☐	4×☐	5×☐	6×☐

a   Iona writes the **same** fraction in each box (☐).
Work out the fraction that Iona writes.

b   Find the probability of scoring:
   i   4
   ii less than 4
   iii more than 4.

12 A farmer has a field with some black sheep and some white sheep in it.
The farmer chooses a sheep at random.
The probability she chooses a white sheep is $\frac{2}{3}$.
Two white sheep leave the field.
The probability that the farmer chooses a white sheep is now $\frac{3}{5}$.
Two black sheep enter the field.
The probability that the farmer chooses a black sheep is now $\frac{1}{2}$.
How many sheep were in the field originally?

Key words

Here is a list of the key words you met in this chapter.

Biased	Certain	Chance	Equally likely
Even chance	Event	Experiment	Fair
Impossible	Likely	Mutually exclusive events	Probability scale
Random	Unlikely	Probability	

Use the glossary at the back of this book to check any you are unsure about.

Curriculum for Wales Mastering Mathematics: Book 1

Review exercise: probability

Band 1 questions

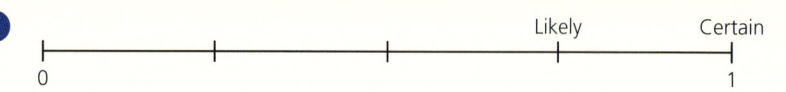

Fluency

①
```
|---|---|---|---|---|
0       Likely    Certain
                    1
```

a   Copy the probability scale and fill in the missing words.

b   Add in the missing decimal and fraction probability values at the marked points.

c   Mark each of these outcomes on the probability scale.

   i   You throw an ordinary dice and it comes up 2.

   ii   You will go on holiday sometime in the next two years.

   iii When you throw two dice, the total will be 16.

   iv   The longest day next year will be 21 March.

   v   You will pass your driving test first time.

   vi   The sun will rise tomorrow.

② Amir, Bethan, Carwyn, Dai, Efa and Ffion play snakes and ladders. Snakes and ladders is a game of chance and there is only ever one winner. Use the words 'impossible', 'unlikely', 'even chance', 'likely' or 'certain' to describe these outcomes.

a   Amir wins.

b   Amir doesn't win.

c   Carwyn is in the first three to finish.

d   Ffion comes last.

e   Dai comes seventh.

f   Bethan, Efa or Ffion wins.

g   One of the group of six wins.

h   Gruff wins.

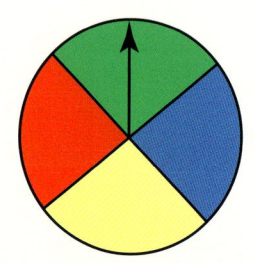

Logical reasoning

③

Spinner A   **Spinner B**

Jac says that Spinner B is more likely to land on green than Spinner A because the area of green is bigger on spinner B.

Aya says that Spinner A is more likely to land on green than Spinner B because the arrow on Spinner A is shorter.

Dafydd says that both spinners have an equal chance of landing on green.

Who is right? Explain your answer fully.

1 Probability

Band 2 questions

4 Jabir throws a 12-faced dice numbered 1 to 12.
  a What is the probability that he gets a 6?
  b What is the probability that he gets a number less than 6?
  c What is the probability that he gets a number greater than 6?
  d i Add up the probabilities in parts **a**, **b** and **c**.
     ii Explain your answer.

5 In the National Lottery, balls numbered from 1 to 59 are selected at random by a machine.
  Work out the probability that the first ball selected is:
  a the number 4
  b odd
  c greater than 30
  d a number in the three times table
  e not a number in the three times table
  f a number containing the digit 3
  g a number not containing the digit 3
  h an even number greater than 20.

Band 3 questions

6 Carys and Pedr are playing a game with cards numbered from 1 to 25. Carys takes a card at random.
  a Pedr says, 'You win if you choose a prime number. Otherwise I win.'
     Is Pedr's game fair? Explain your answer.
  b Carys says, 'I win if I get a prime number, you win if you get a multiple of 4 or a square number. Otherwise it's a draw.'
     Is Carys's game fair? Explain your answer.

7 Sparkle Chocs sweets come in five colours.

Colour	Red (Coch)	Purple (Porffor)	Orange (Oren)	Yellow (Melyn)	Blue (Glas)
Probability	0.15	?	0.25	0.2	0.05

Sara takes a sweet at random.
  a What is the probability that Sara gets a purple sweet?
  b Which is the most likely colour of sweet?
  c In a tube of 40 sweets, how many sweets of each colour would you expect?
  d Every minute, the Sparkle Chocs factory produces 50 blue sweets.
     i How many of each of the other colours are produced each minute?
     ii The factory runs ten hours a day, five days a week. How many sweets does it produce every week?

8 A bag contains red, blue and green counters. A counter is picked at random.
  The table shows the probability of picking each colour.

Colour	Red (Coch)	Blue (Glas)	Green (Gwyrdd)
Probability	0.35	0.25	?

  a Work out the probability that a green counter is picked.
  b Explain why the number of blue counters cannot be eight.
  c If there are eight green counters, how many red counters are there?

13

d If there are over 40 counters in the bag, how many might there be of each different colour?

e What is the smallest number of counters there could be in the bag?

9 Each of these five cards has a different number from 1 to 10 on one side.

A card is taken at random.

Use these clues to work out the numbers on the cards.
- The probability that the card is odd is $\frac{2}{5}$.
- The probability that the card is in the three times table is $\frac{3}{5}$.
- The probability that the card is in the five times table is $\frac{1}{5}$.
- The probability that the card is prime is $\frac{2}{5}$.

10 A bag contains some tiles.

Each tile is either a triangle, a square or a pentagon.

A tile is taken at random from the bag.

The probability that the shape is a pentagon is the same as the probability that the shape is a square.

The probability that the shape is a triangle is half the probability that the shape is a square.

The shapes in the bag have 63 sides altogether.

How many triangles are in the bag?

2 Working with shapes

Coming up...
▶ Recognising types of angle
▶ Naming common 2-D shapes
▶ Classifying types of triangle
▶ Recognising reflection symmetry
▶ Recognising rotation symmetry

Optical illusions

① Decide which angle in each pair is bigger.

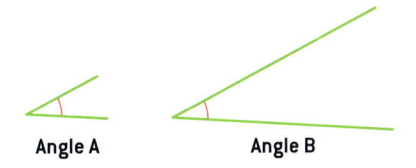

a Angle A   Angle B

b Angle A   Angle B

② a Which of these **vertical** lines is longer?

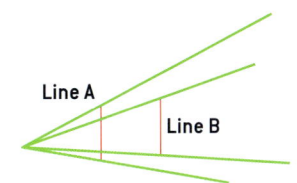

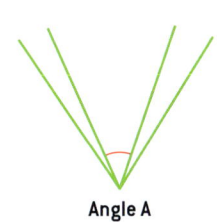

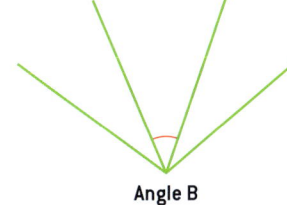

Line A   Line B

b Which of these **horizontal** lines is longer?

Line A   Line B

③ a Are the red vertical lines **parallel**?

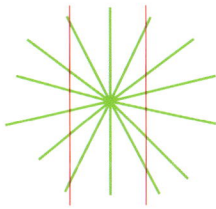

b Are the horizontal lines parallel?

④ Use the internet to find more examples of optical illusions and the famous artists who created them.

Make a poster of your favourite illusion.

Remember
Parallel lines are lines which never meet; they are always the same distance apart.

15

Curriculum for Wales **Mastering Mathematics: Book 1**

2.1 Properties of 2-D shapes

Skill checker

① Copy and complete this table by sorting these shapes into 2-D and 3-D shapes.

cylinder (silindr)   square (sgwâr)   sphere (sffêr)   cuboid (ciwboid)   hexagon (hecsagon)   pyramid (pyramid)   cube (ciwb)   triangle (triongl)   circle (cylch)   rectangle (petryal)

2-D shapes	3-D shapes

② Give the mathematical name for the shape of each of these objects.

a   b   c   d

③ a Copy the diagram and label the parts of this circle.
   b Insert the two missing words to complete this statement about circles.

   _____ = 2 × _____

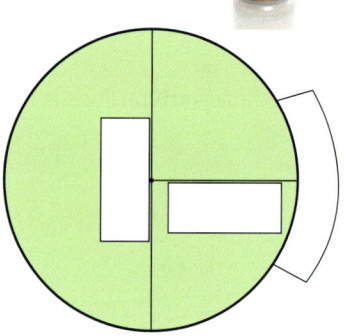

▶ Describing shapes

To describe a shape, you need to think about its:
- angles
- sides.

An **angle** is a turn; it is measured in degrees.

You need to know these words to describe angles.

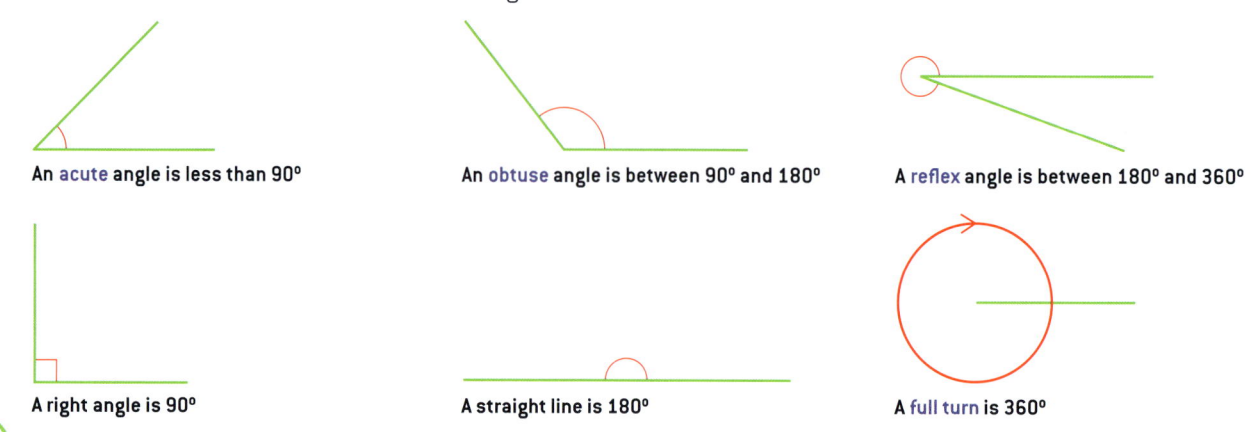

An <u>acute</u> angle is less than 90°   An <u>obtuse</u> angle is between 90° and 180°   A <u>reflex</u> angle is between 180° and 360°

A right angle is 90°   A straight line is 180°   A <u>full turn</u> is 360°

16

2 Working with shapes

You can use the following words to describe the **sides** of a shape.

| parallel | perpendicular | equal |

Remember:

❶ Parallel lines run in the same direction.

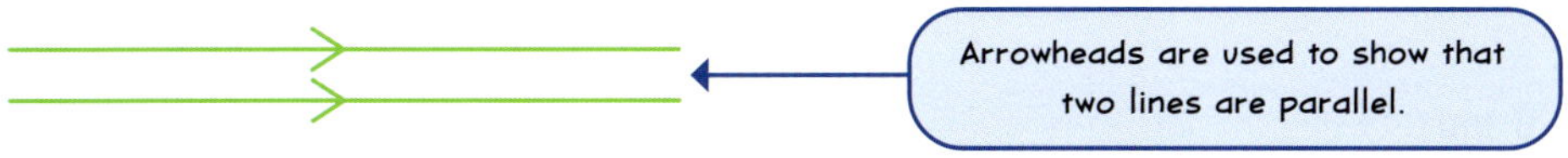

Arrowheads are used to show that two lines are parallel.

❷ Perpendicular lines are at right angles.

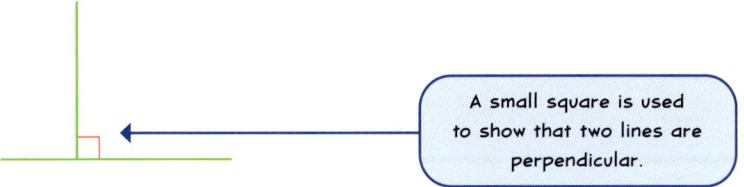

A small square is used to show that two lines are perpendicular.

❸ Equal sides have the same length.

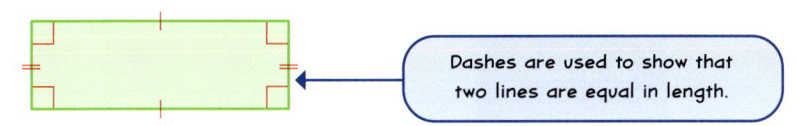

Dashes are used to show that two lines are equal in length.

> **Note**
> Did you know that, in mathematics, a line is infinitely long? It carries on forever in both directions. Often, 'line' is used to mean 'line segment' which is a section of a line that has a beginning and an end. In points 2 and 3 above, the lines are actually line segments.

A **triangle** is a 2-D shape with three straight sides.
You need to know the names of these special triangles.

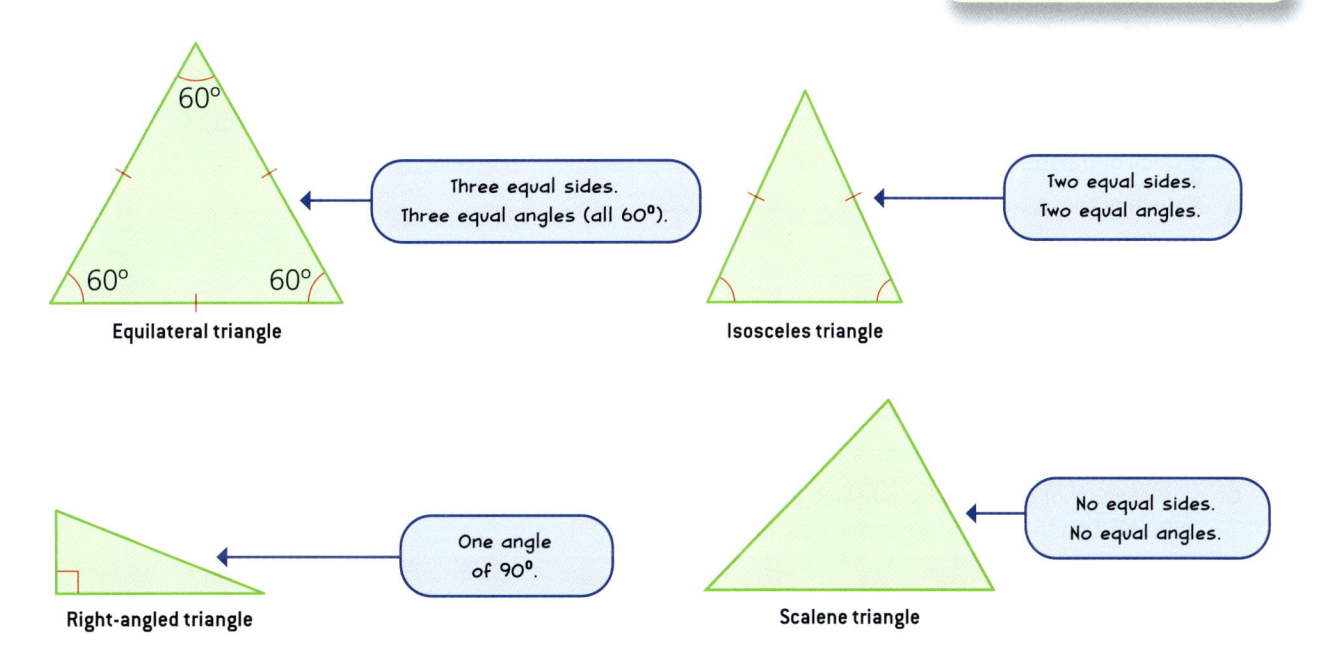

Three equal sides.
Three equal angles (all 60°).

Equilateral triangle

Two equal sides.
Two equal angles.

Isosceles triangle

One angle of 90°.

Right-angled triangle

No equal sides.
No equal angles.

Scalene triangle

17

Curriculum for Wales Mastering Mathematics: Book 1

Worked example

a Name the vertices and the sides of this triangle.
b Describe the shape of the triangle.
c Describe the angles of the triangle.

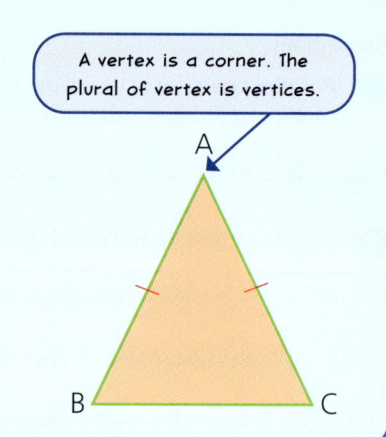

Solution

a The three vertices are A, B and C.
The three sides are AB, BC and AC.

b Sides AB and AC are equal.
The triangle is isosceles.

c All three angles are acute so ABC is an acute-angled triangle.
The angles B and C are also equal.

A vertex is a corner. The plural of vertex is vertices.

When naming 2-D shapes you need to think about the number of sides and **vertices** (corners).

Polygons are (closed) 2-D shapes with straight sides.

A **regular polygon** has all sides equal and all angles equal.

Name	Number of sides	Number of vertices
Triangle	3	3
Quadrilateral	4	4
Pentagon	5	5
Hexagon	6	6
Heptagon	7	7
Octagon	8	8
Nonagon	9	9
Decagon	10	10

Activity

① **a** Which of these shapes is a pentagon?
b Which of these shapes is regular?

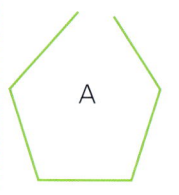

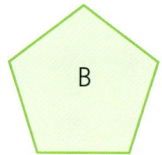

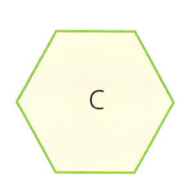

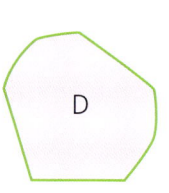

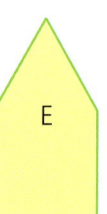

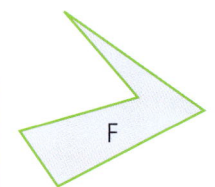

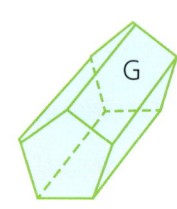

② **a** Name these special quadrilaterals.
b Describe each shape as fully as you can.
c Choose one of your descriptions and give it to a friend. Can they name the shape you have described?

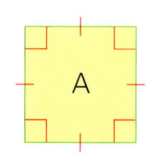

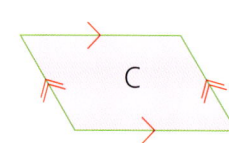

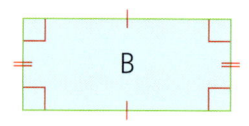

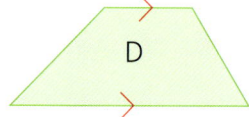

18

2 Working with shapes

Discussion activity

Look at this self-portrait by Edouard Vuillard. What shape is this painting? Do you think this is unusual?

Congruent shapes are exactly the same shape and size.

Worked example

a Match the pairs of congruent shapes.

b What is the mathematical name of these L-shapes?

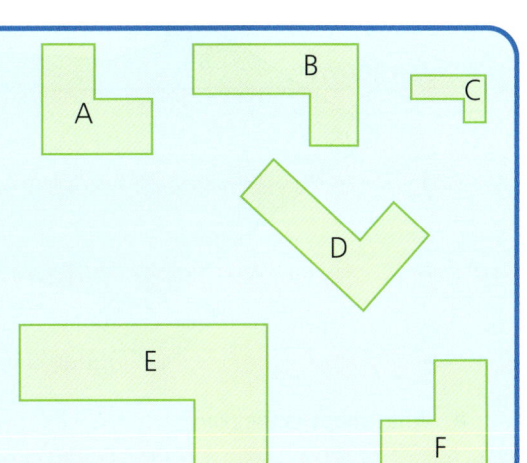

Solution

a A and F are exactly the same shape and size so they are congruent.

B and D are exactly the same shape and size so they are congruent.

C and E are the same shape, but different sizes so they are not congruent.

b The L-shapes have six sides, so they are hexagons.

2.1 Now try these

Band 1 questions

1 Write these angles in order of size, smallest first.

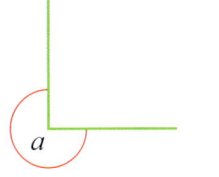

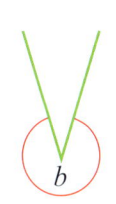

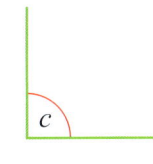

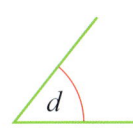

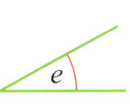

2 Look at these angles.
Which angles are:
a acute
b obtuse
c reflex?

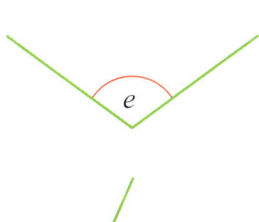

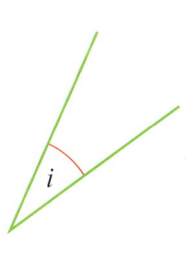

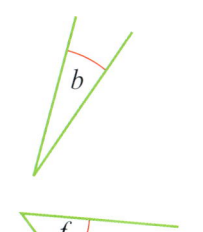

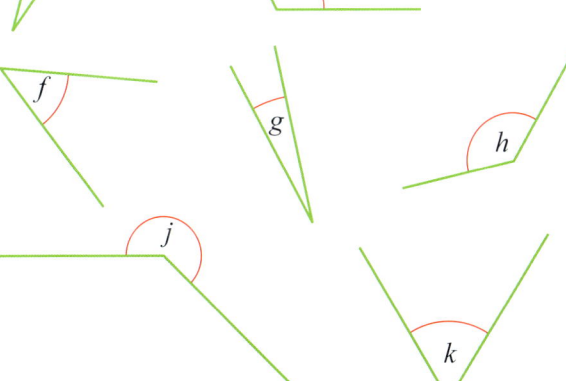

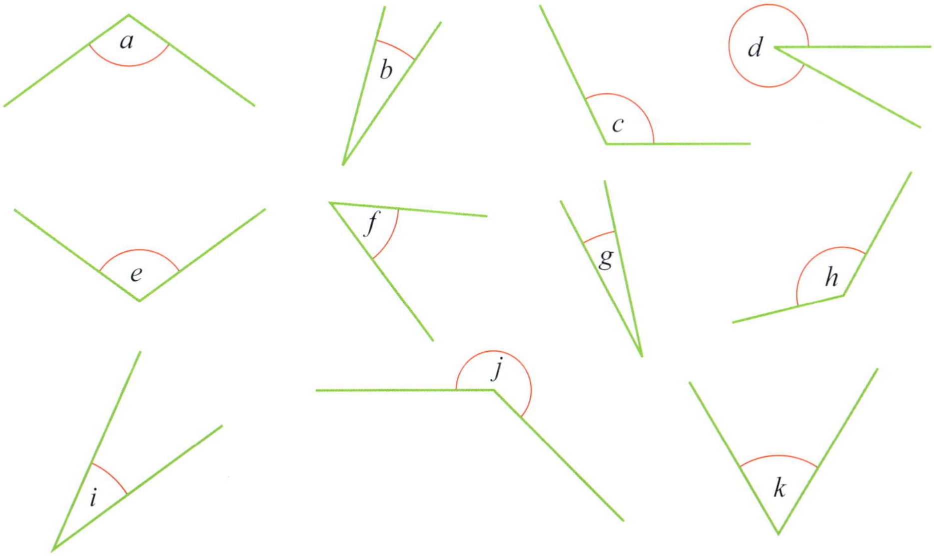

3
a How many right angles make angle x? 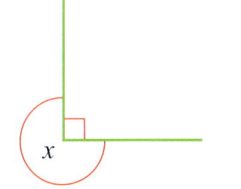
b How many right angles make a whole turn?

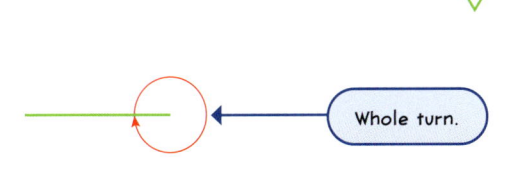

Whole turn.

19

Curriculum for Wales **Mastering Mathematics: Book 1**

Fluency

4 Cai is a tour guide at a castle.
He draws a plan of the castle to help the visitors.
Look at the plan below.

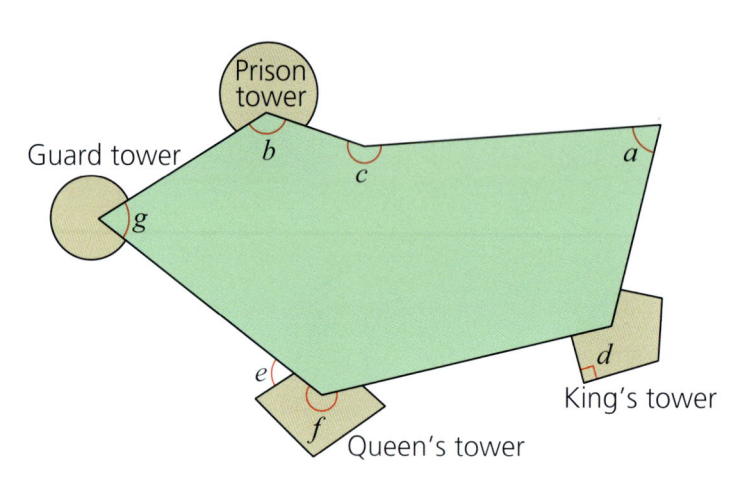

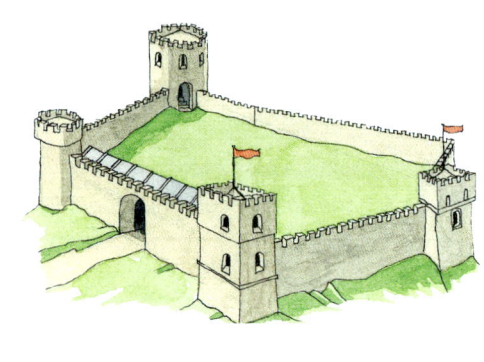

a What shape is the plan?

b The angle *a* is acute.
What are the special names for the other marked angles?

Logical reasoning

5 Put each of these triangles in the correct position in this table.
Triangles A and F have been done for you.

Type of triangle	Equilateral	Isosceles	Scalene
Acute-angled	A		
Obtuse-angled			
Right-angled		F	

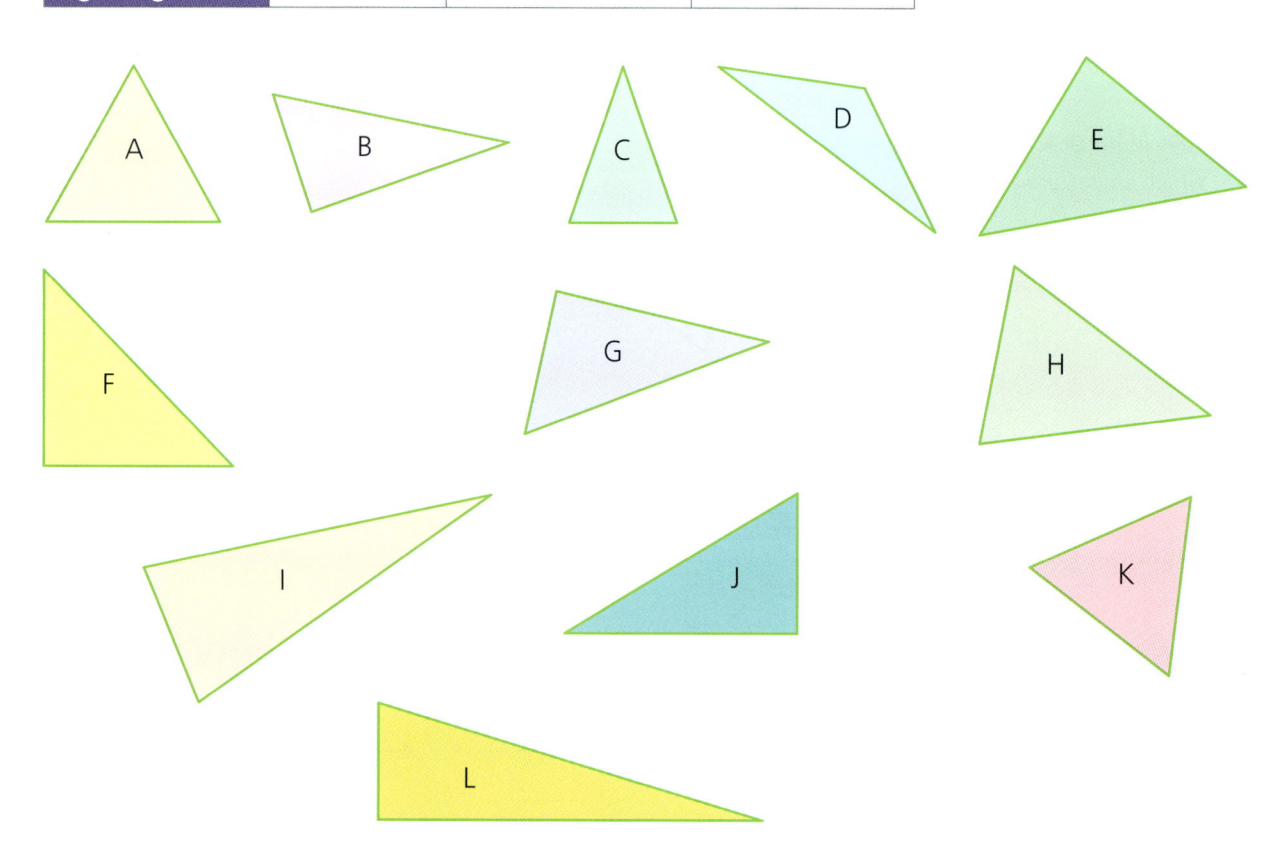

2 Working with shapes

Band 2 questions

6 a Look at this rectangle.

It is divided into four triangles.

  i Describe the triangles as fully as you can.

  ii Which triangles are congruent?

b A square is divided up the same way.

Describe the triangles as fully as you can.

7 Look at this diagram.

  a How many squares are there?

  b How many rectangles that are not squares are there?

  c How many rectangles are there altogether?

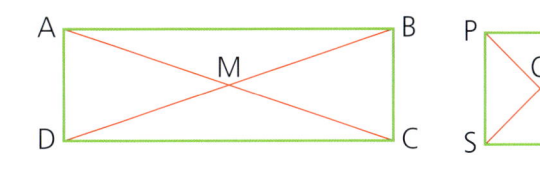

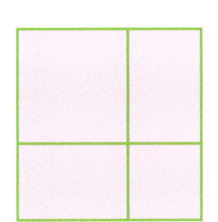

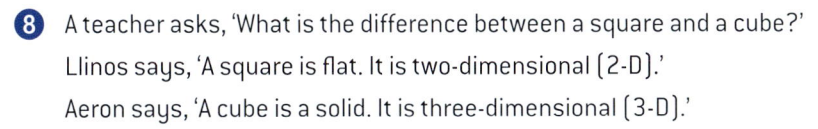

8 A teacher asks, 'What is the difference between a square and a cube?'

Llinos says, 'A square is flat. It is two-dimensional (2-D).'

Aeron says, 'A cube is a solid. It is three-dimensional (3-D).'

  a Are Llinos and Aeron right?

  b Describe the difference between a rectangle and a cuboid.

  c What is the 2-D equivalent of a sphere?

Band 3 questions

9 This card is used on a machine.

ABCD is a square with sides 4 cm long.

The other shapes are semicircles.

Find the height and width of the card.

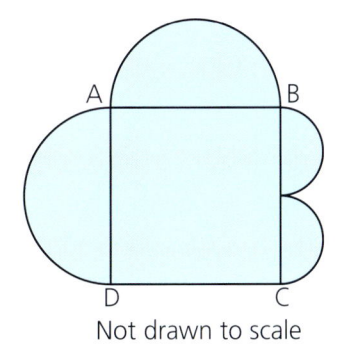

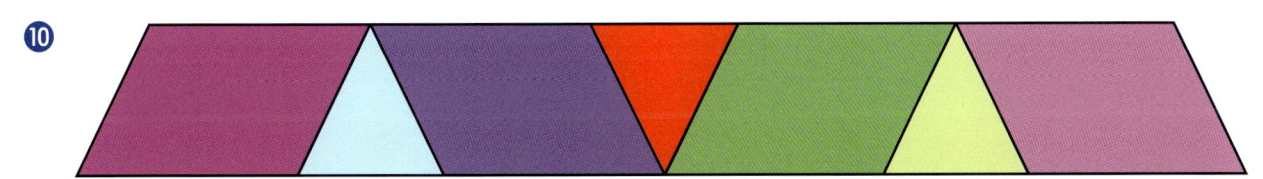

Not drawn to scale

10

  a Measure, in millimetres, the sides of the seven main shapes in this diagram.

  b Name the seven shapes.

  c Is it true that they are all congruent?

  d If you cut out the shapes, is it possible to make a square out of some or all of them? (No folding allowed!)

Curriculum for Wales Mastering Mathematics: Book 1

Logical reasoning

11 Which of these statements are true and which are false?
   a   A triangle must have an obtuse internal angle.
   b   A triangle must have an acute internal angle.
   c   A quadrilateral must have four sides.
   d   The number of sides of a polygon is always the same as the number of vertices.
   e   The radius of a circle is twice the diameter.
   f   Parallel lines never meet.

Strategic competence

12 Look at this circle.
   The 12 points marked on the circumference are equally spaced.
   a   Measure AG.
       Write down the radius of the circle.
   b   Join AE, EI and IA.
       What shape have you drawn?
   c   Starting at A, join up points to form:
       i   a square
       ii   a rectangle that is not a square
       iii a regular hexagon
       iv   a triangle that is isosceles but is not equilateral.

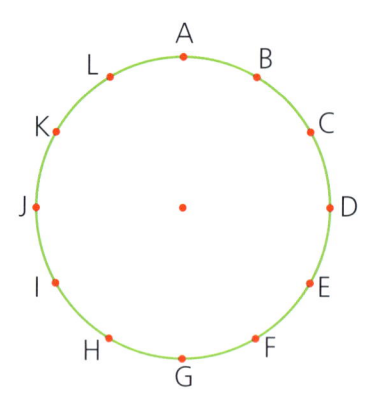

2.2 Line symmetry

Skill checker

① Name these regular polygons.

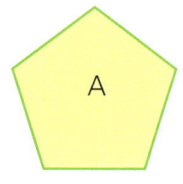

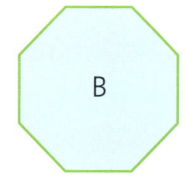

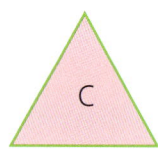

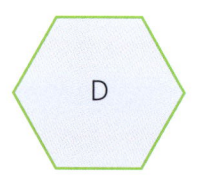

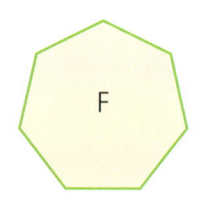

② Here is a photograph of the Welsh Parliament ('Senedd'), in Cardiff. It was designed by Richard Rogers who was a famous British architect. The building looks symmetrical, but can you find three things in this picture that are *not* symmetrical?

22

2   Working with shapes

Imagine folding a shape.

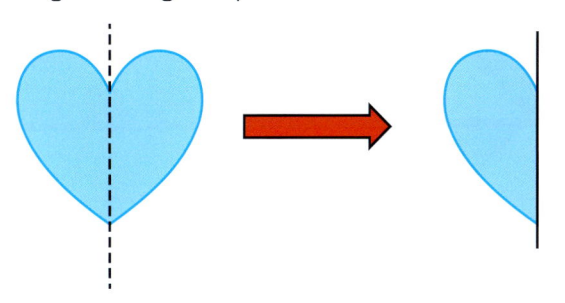

If the shape folds precisely onto itself, then that fold is a line of symmetry and the shape has **line symmetry** (or **reflective, reflection** or **mirror symmetry**).

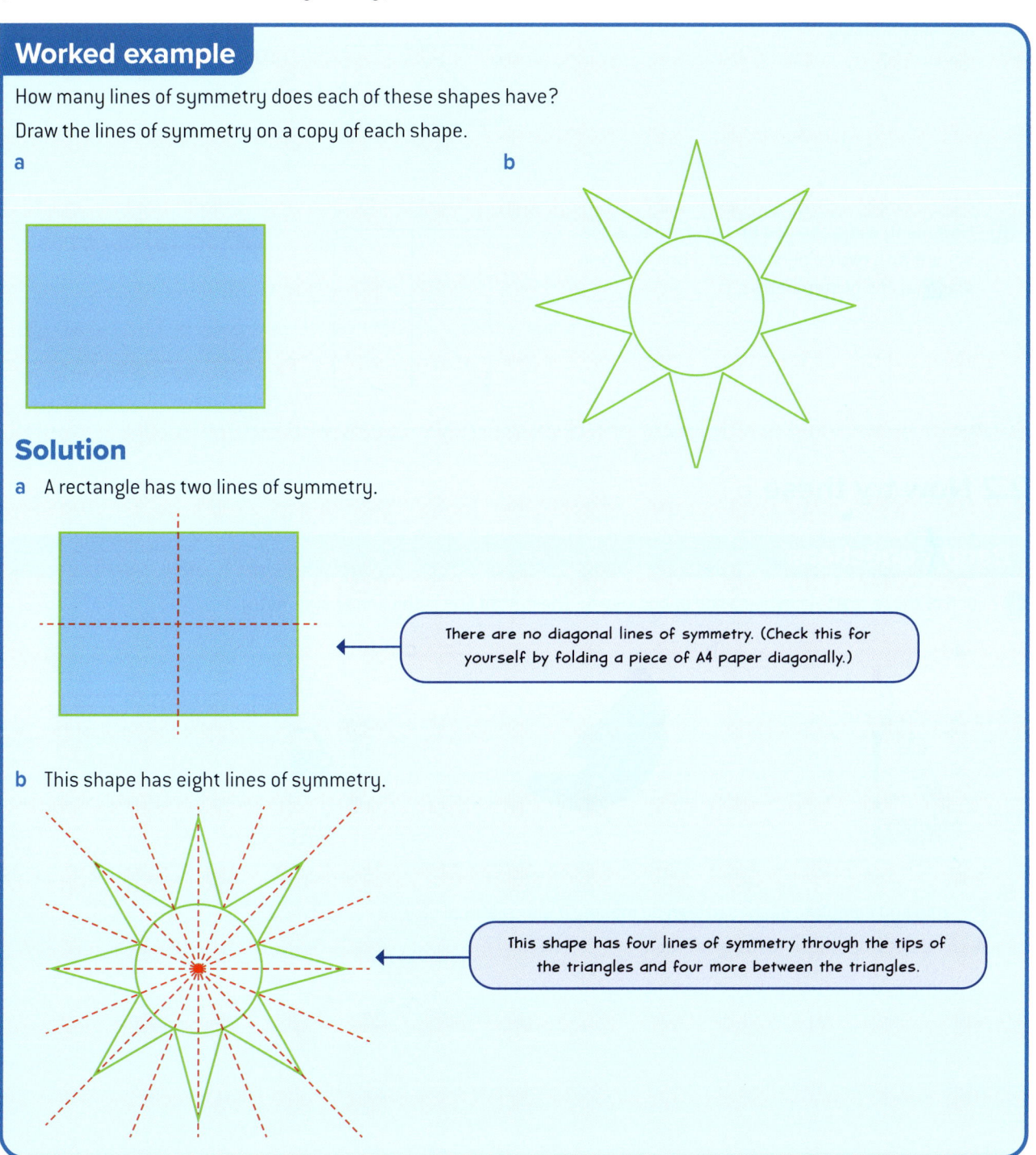

Conceptual understanding

Worked example

How many lines of symmetry does each of these shapes have?
Draw the lines of symmetry on a copy of each shape.

a

b

Solution

a   A rectangle has two lines of symmetry.

> There are no diagonal lines of symmetry. (Check this for yourself by folding a piece of A4 paper diagonally.)

b   This shape has eight lines of symmetry.

> This shape has four lines of symmetry through the tips of the triangles and four more between the triangles.

23

Curriculum for Wales Mastering Mathematics: Book 1

Activity

① How many lines of symmetry does this square have?

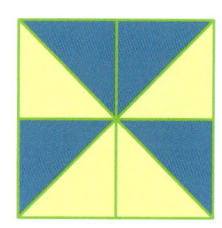

② Find as many ways as you can of shading in the square using **two** colours so that it has one vertical line of symmetry.

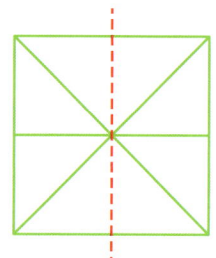

③ How many ways can you find of shading in the square with **two** colours so that it only has one diagonal line of symmetry?

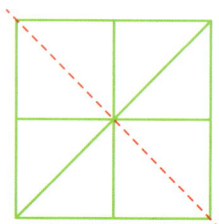

2.2 Now try these

Band 1 questions

❶ Each of these road signs has a line of symmetry. The dotted line is the line of symmetry.

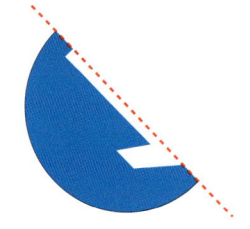

a   b   c

i Copy and complete each road sign by making it symmetrical.
ii Find out what these road signs mean.

2   Working with shapes

2 Copy and complete each shape so that the dotted line is a line of symmetry.

a   b 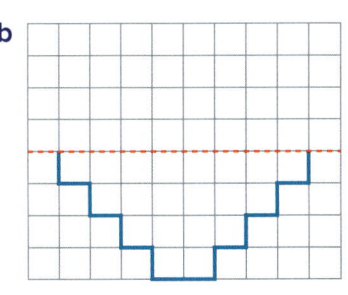   c

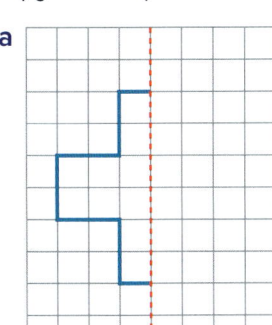

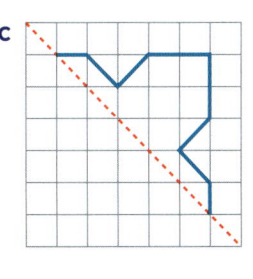

3 Copy each of these shapes carefully.

a   b 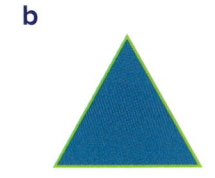   c 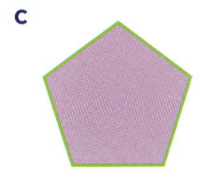   d 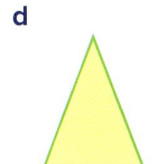   e

   i   Write down the name of each of these shapes.
   ii Draw all the lines of symmetry on each shape.
   iii How many lines of symmetry does each shape have?

Band 2 questions

4 Which of these road signs have line symmetry?

a   b    c 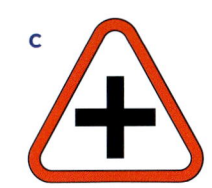   d    e

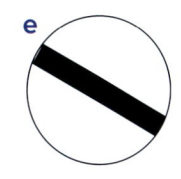

5 Copy these capital letters carefully and draw their lines of symmetry.

A B C D E F G H

6 Look at this circle.

25

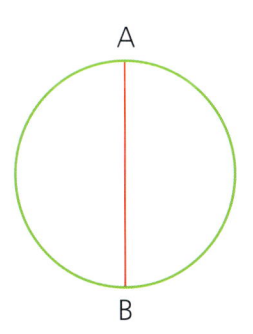

a Copy and complete this statement.

Line AB is a ▢ of the circle.

It cuts the circle into ▢ equal parts.

It is a ▢ of ▢.

b How many diameters does a circle have?

c How many lines of symmetry does a circle have?

7 a Draw an isosceles triangle like this one.

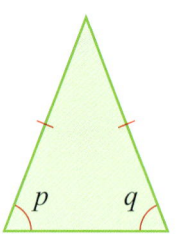

b Draw the line of symmetry.

c What does the line of symmetry tell you about the angles p and q?

Band 3 questions

8 This sports club logo has two lines of symmetry. Copy and complete the design.

The letters have all been put in for you.

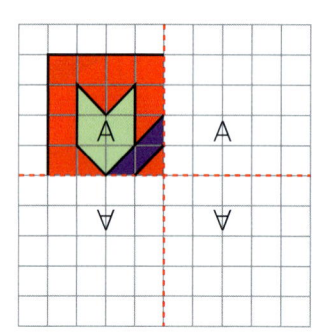

9 a This shape is almost symmetrical. On a copy of the shape, add one square to make it symmetrical.

b Look at the shapes on the next page.

  i Add one square to a copy of each of these shapes to make them symmetrical.

  Draw the line of symmetry each time.

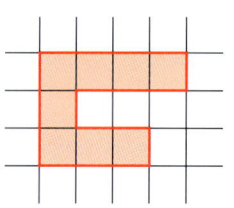

2 Working with shapes

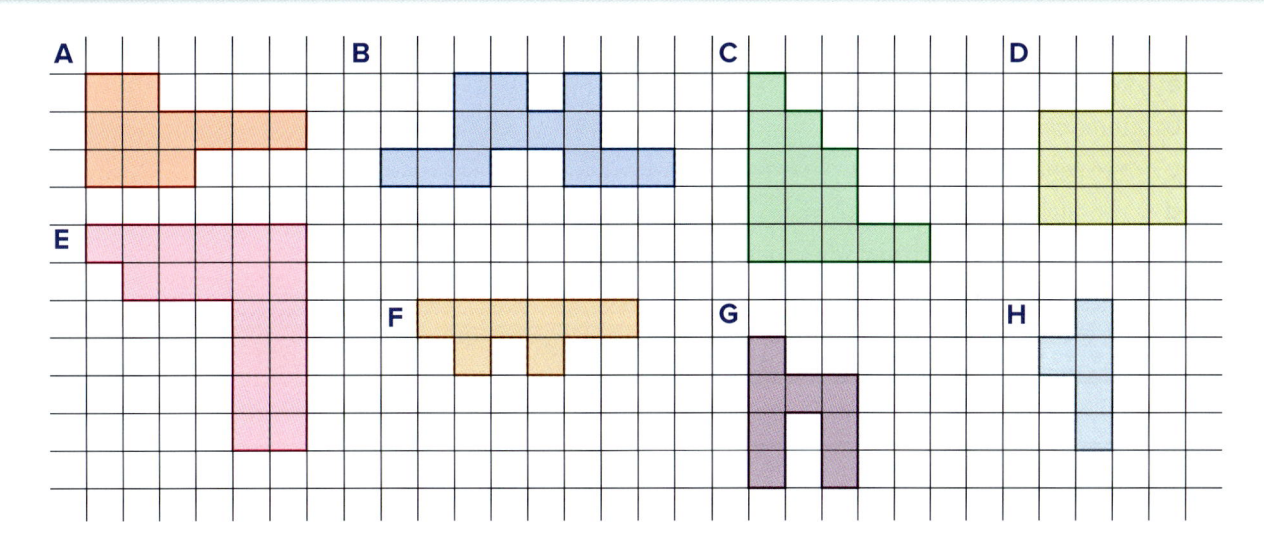

ii There are three different answers for one of the shapes. Which one?
iii Now make each of the shapes symmetrical by removing one square.

10 There are six square sheets of paper, each one folded twice.

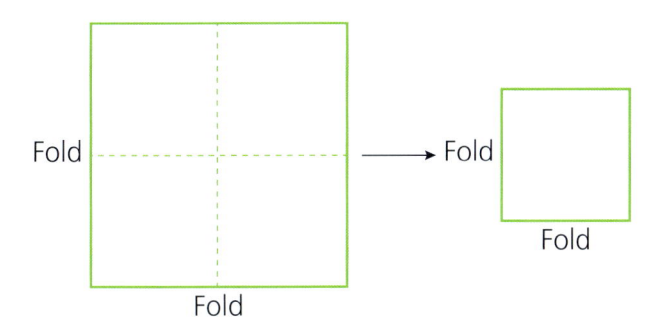

Peter makes cuts in them so that when the paper is unfolded each sheet contains holes.
Some of the holes are circles, some are squares and some are other shapes.

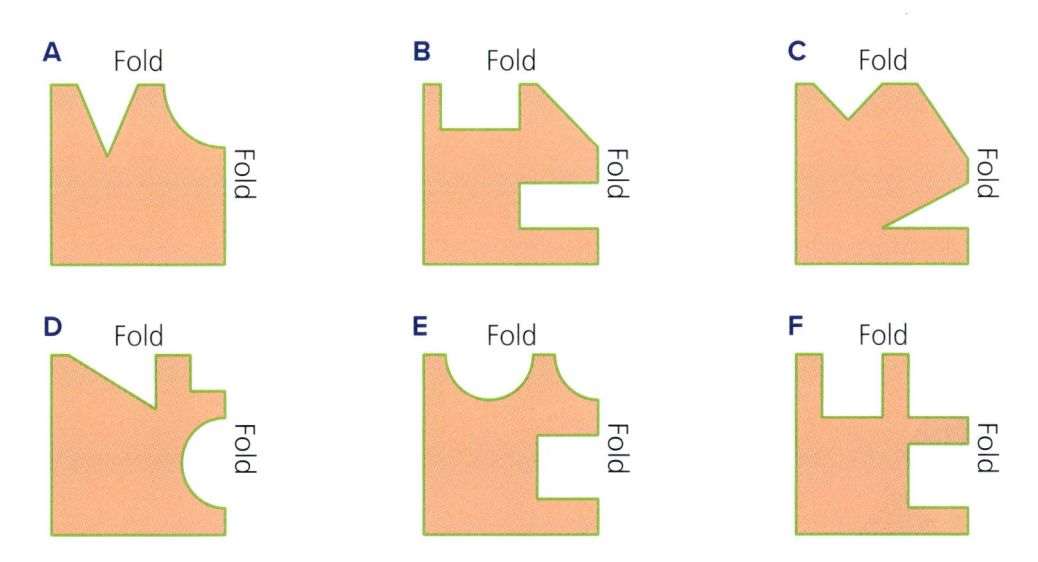

27

Logical reasoning

Which sheet of paper (if any) has three of its holes as follows:
- a two rectangles and a square
- b three circles
- c two squares and a triangle
- d two circles and a rectangle?

Find two answers for each part where possible.

2.3 Rotational symmetry

Skill checker

1. Write down the number of degrees in:
   - a a full turn
   - b a quarter turn
   - c a half turn.

2. Copy these diagrams. On each diagram colour in more tiles so that the pattern has the required number of lines of symmetry.
   - a Shade two squares to make two lines of symmetry.

   - b Shade two squares to make four lines of symmetry.

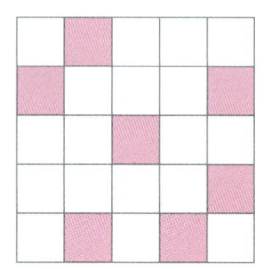

   - c Shade three triangles to make three lines of symmetry.

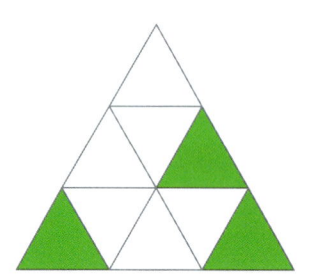

d Shade two triangles to make one line of symmetry.

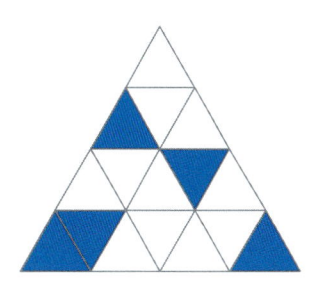

When a rectangle is rotated (turned) through 360° it looks the same twice.

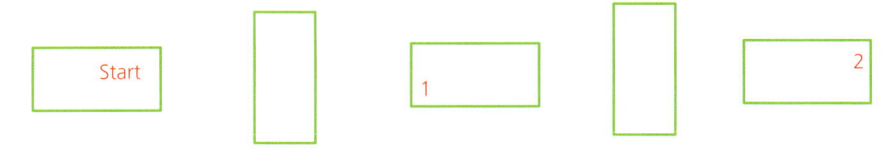

Start   1   2

It has rotational symmetry of order 2.

The order of rotational symmetry is the number of times that a shape will fit onto itself in one complete turn.

If a shape fits onto itself only once in one turn then it has rotational symmetry of order 1. This means that it has no rotational symmetry.

Start   1

This arrow has rotational symmetry of order 1.

Activity

① Look at these numbers.

| 11 | 96 | 88 | 86 |
| 19 | 33 | 52 | 18 |

Write down the numbers which have:
a line symmetry
b rotational symmetry
c exactly one line of symmetry
d rotational symmetry but no lines of symmetry
e rotational symmetry and two lines of symmetry.

Hint
Use tracing paper to help you work out the order of rotational symmetry. Trace an outline of the shape and then rotate the tracing paper over the original image.

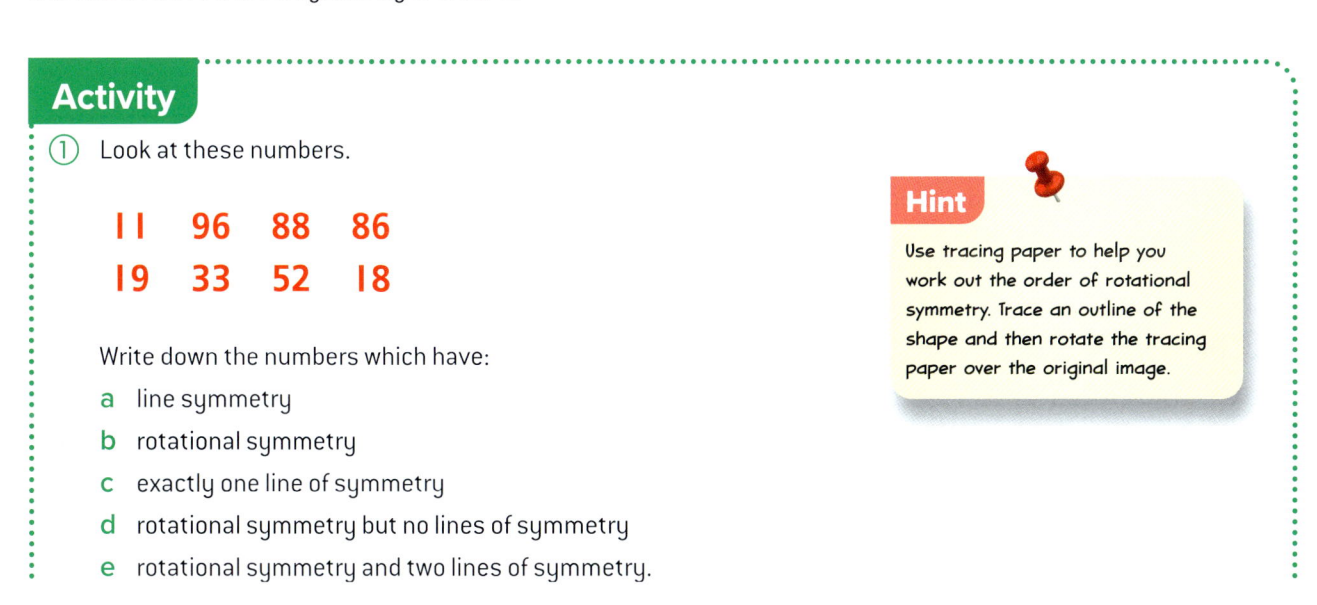

Curriculum for Wales **Mastering Mathematics: Book 1**

② Complete the magic square.

96			
88		91	
	86	18	
19	98	66	81

Hint
Each row, column and long diagonal has the same total.

What is special about the magic square?

The **centre of rotational symmetry** is the point about which the shape has to be rotated in order for it to fit on to itself. This is usually just called the **centre of rotation**.

Worked example

a What is the order of rotational symmetry of this shape?

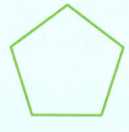

b Mark the centre of rotation with a cross.

Solution

a The pentagon will fit onto itself five times in one turn, so the order of rotational symmetry is 5.
b The centre of rotation is at the centre of the pentagon.

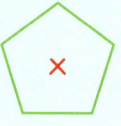

Discussion activity

Look at the list of key words at the end of this chapter. Can you think of where you might use some of these key words in other subjects in school?

2.3 Now try these

Band 1 questions

① Which of these dominoes have rotational symmetry?

a   b 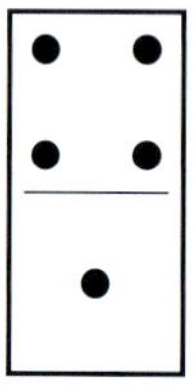   c 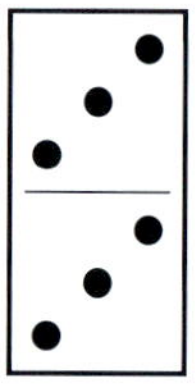   d 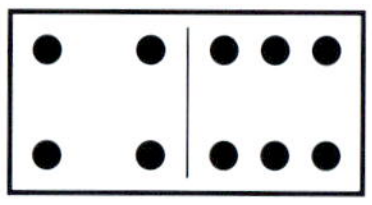   e

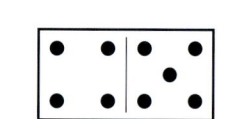

30

2 Working with shapes

2 Write down the order of rotational symmetry of each of these shapes.

a b 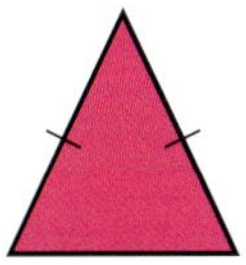 c  d

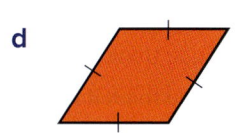

e  f  g  h

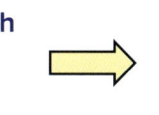

3 Copy each of these shapes carefully.

a b 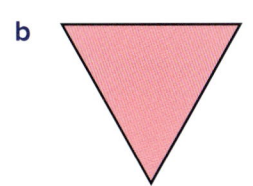 c 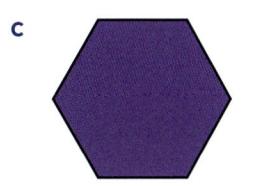 d

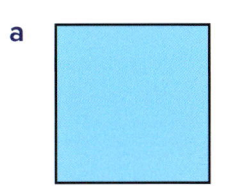

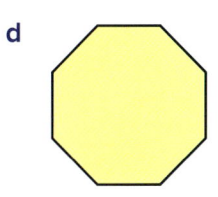

i Write down the name of each shape.
ii Write down the order of rotational symmetry of each shape.
iii Mark the centre of rotation of each shape with a cross.

Band 2 questions

4 These are diagrams of car hubcaps.

a b 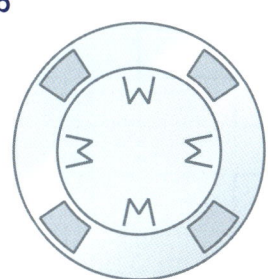 c

i Write down the order of rotational symmetry of each hubcap.
ii Draw a sketch of each hubcap.
   Mark the centre of rotational symmetry of each hubcap with a cross.

5 Some of the shapes below have line symmetry, some have rotational symmetry and some have both. Describe fully the symmetry of each shape.

a b 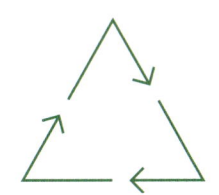 c 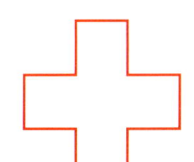 d

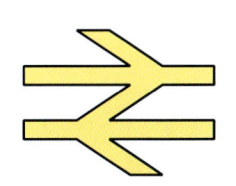

31

6 Is it *always* true, *sometimes* true or *never* true that a shape with rotational symmetry of order 3 will also have three lines of reflection symmetry? Write a paragraph explaining your answer.

If you think it is *always* true, explain how you can be so certain.

If you think it is *never* true, explain how you can be so certain.

If you think it is *sometimes* true, explain when it *is* and when it *isn't* true.

7 Here are parts of shapes which have two lines of symmetry.

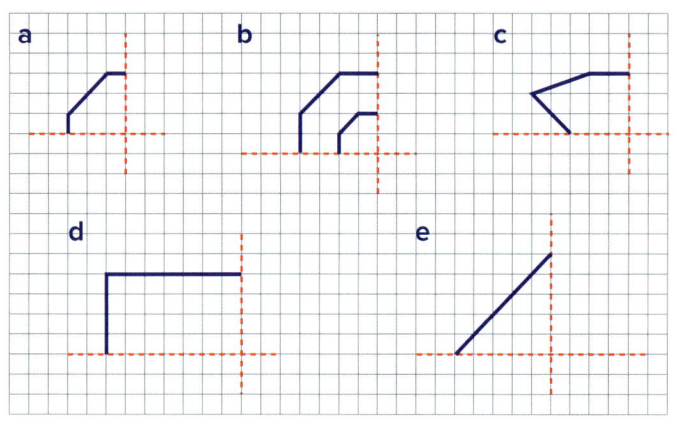

   i   Copy them and draw in the rest of the shape.
   ii Write down the order of rotational symmetry of each shape.

Band 3 questions

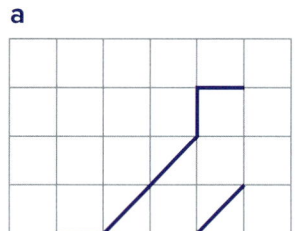

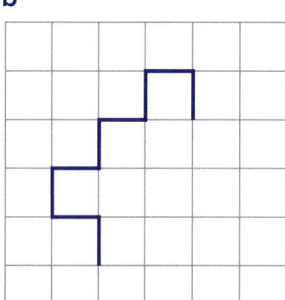

8   a   b

   i   Copy and complete these shapes so that they have both line and rotational symmetry.
       Mark the centre of rotational symmetry with a cross.
   ii For each one write down how many lines of symmetry it has and the order of rotational symmetry.

9 Copy this table, then draw a shape to fit into each section.

	Has rotational symmetry	Has no rotational symmetry
Has at least one line of symmetry		
Has no lines of symmetry		

10 Snow is made when water vapour freezes to form crystals. The crystals are usually shaped as regular hexagons.

They combine to form snowflakes with rotational symmetry of order 6.

Here is a snowflake drawn on isometric paper.

Design five more snowflakes.

Make them as large or as small as you like.

They can be very intricate, but remember that each one must have rotational symmetry of order 6.

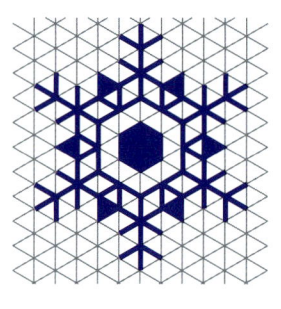

Key words

Here is a list of the key words you met in this chapter.

Acute	Angle	Circle	Circumference
Congruent	Diameter	Equilateral	Hexagon
Horizontal	Isosceles	Line segment	Obtuse
Octagon	Parallel	Parallelogram	Pentagon
Perpendicular	Polygon	Quadrilateral	Radius
Rectangle	Reflection	Reflex	Regular polygon
Right angle	Rotation	Scalene	Square
Symmetry	Triangle	Vertex	Vertical

Use the glossary at the back of this book to check any you are unsure about.

Curriculum for Wales **Mastering Mathematics: Book 1**

Review exercise: working with shapes

Band 1 questions

Fluency

① Look at this diagram.

There are seven coloured angles.

For each colour, state whether the angle is acute, obtuse, reflex, a right angle or a straight line.

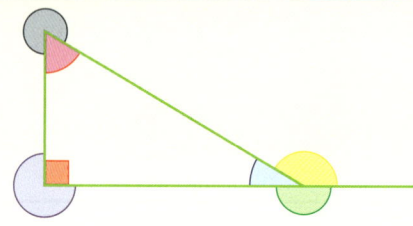

② i State how many lines of symmetry each of these national flags has.
   ii What is the order of rotational symmetry of each flag?

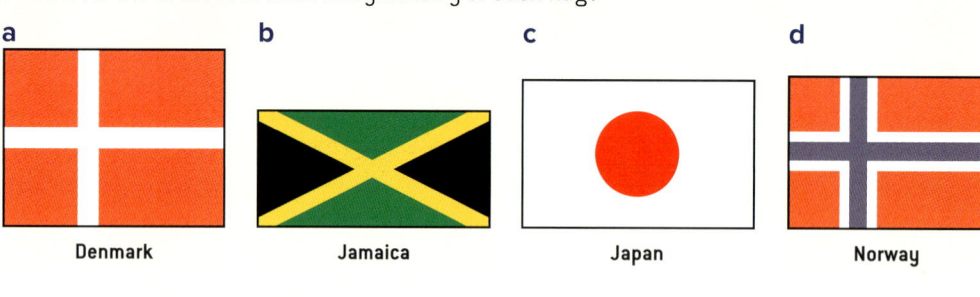

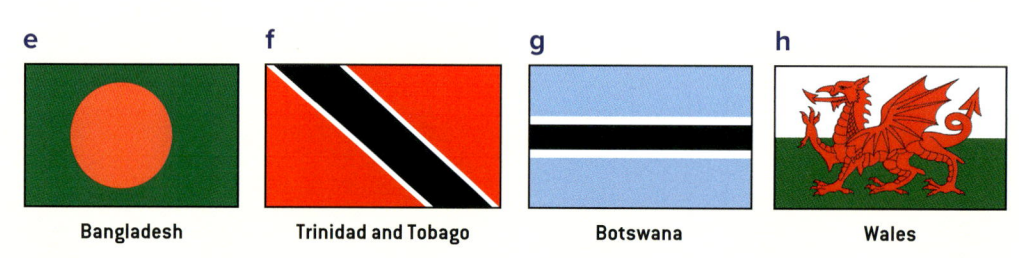

   a Denmark
   b Jamaica
   c Japan
   d Norway
   e Bangladesh
   f Trinidad and Tobago
   g Botswana
   h Wales

③ Write down the order of rotational symmetry of each of these shapes.

   a    b    c    d    e

Strategic competence

④ Describe the symmetry of each of these shapes.

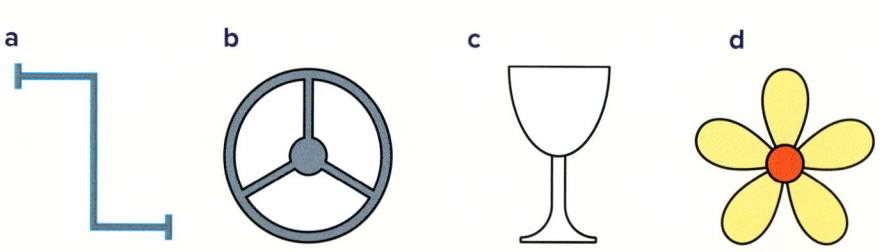

   a   b   c   d

Band 2 questions

Logical reasoning

⑤ Look at this diagram.
   a i Rhodri says that there are 12 equilateral triangles in this diagram, but Joshua says there are more. Who is correct? Explain your answer fully.
     ii Sketch the triangles which are congruent to each other.
   b Name another regular polygon in the diagram.

6 a Describe the symmetry in each of each of these words below.

TOT   DECIDED   TWT
SWIMS   NOON

b Find some other words in English or Welsh that are symmetrical.

Band 3 questions

7 Which of these statements are true and which are false?
If false, say why.
- **a** A triangle can have two parallel sides.
- **b** All squares are congruent.
- **c** The letter M is a quadrilateral.
- **d** All rectangles are parallelograms.
- **e** All pentagons have five lines of symmetry.
- **f** A square is a special sort of rectangle.

8 Look at this regular octagon.
- **a** On one copy of the diagram, join four vertices together to make a square.
  What other vertices could you join to make a square?
- **b** On a second copy of the diagram, join four vertices together to make a rectangle.
  What other vertices could you join to make a rectangle?

9 Draw quadrilaterals that have:
- **a** at least one pair of parallel sides
- **b** at least one pair of parallel sides and two pairs of equal angles
- **c** at least one pair of parallel sides, two pairs of equal angles and one line of symmetry.

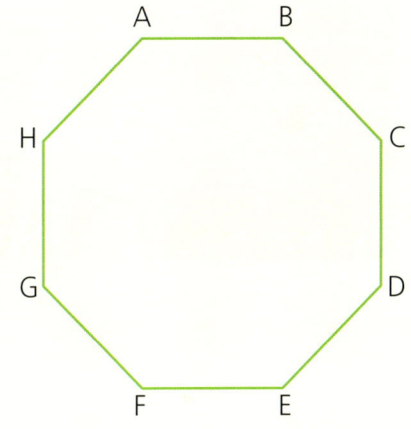

Cross-curricular activity

1 In your art lessons, think of ways you could include symmetry in your artwork.

2 Use drawing software to design a logo which exhibits both line and rotational symmetry.

3 Coordinates and transformations

Coming up...

- Using coordinates in all four quadrants
- Translating shapes
- Reflecting shapes
- Rotating shapes
- Recognising the transformations: translations, reflections and rotations
- Understanding the terms 'object' and 'image'

Battlestars

The winner is the first person to eliminate their opponent's starport, spaceships and shuttles.

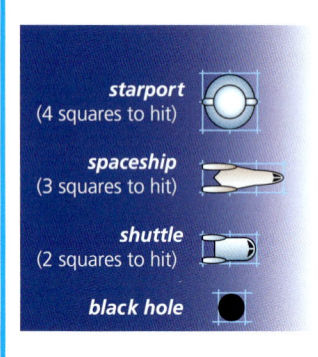

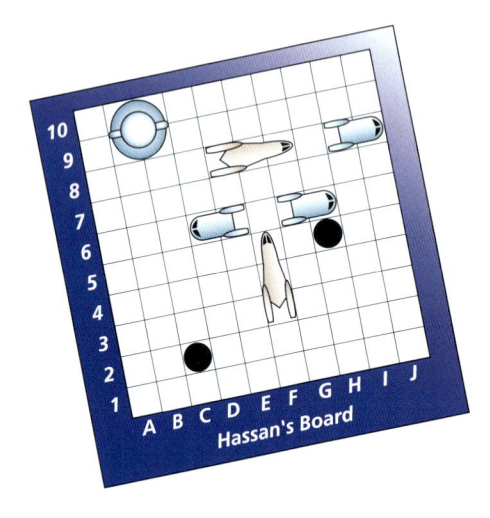

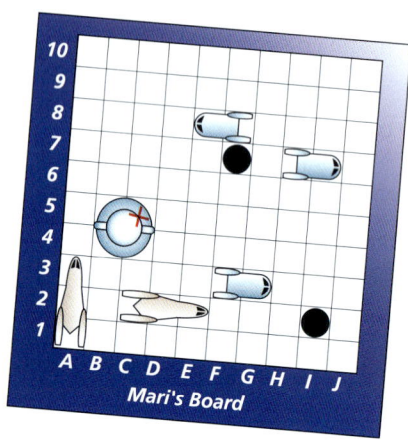

starport (4 squares to hit)
spaceship (3 squares to hit)
shuttle (2 squares to hit)
black hole

You lose if you hit both of your opponent's black holes.

① Hassan and Mari take it in turns to name a square to eliminate on the other's board.
Hassan goes first and chooses square C5. He hits part of a starport on Mari's board.
   a What other squares should Hassan hit to eliminate the starport completely?
If a player hits the two black holes on their opponent's board, they lose the game.
   b Which two squares contain black holes on Mari's board?
   c What is contained in square D6 on Hassan's board?
② Play a game of Battlestars with a partner.
What strategies did you use?

3 Coordinates and transformations

3.1 Coordinates

Skill checker

① Write down the number that each arrow is pointing to.

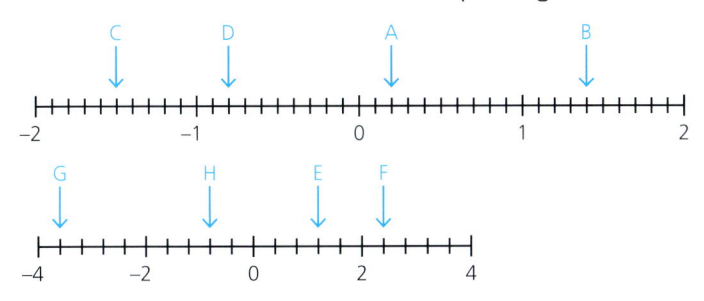

C   D   A   B
↓   ↓   ↓   ↓
├┼┼┼┼┼┼┼┼┼┼┼┼┼┼┼┼┼┼┼┼┼┼┼┼┼┤
-2   -1   0   1   2

G   H   E   F
↓   ↓   ↓   ↓
├┼┼┼┼┼┼┼┼┼┼┼┼┼┼┼┼┤
-4   -2   0   2   4

② Copy the number line and mark on these points.

A $1\frac{1}{2}$ B $2\frac{1}{4}$ C $\frac{3}{4}$ D $-\frac{1}{2}$ E $-1\frac{3}{4}$

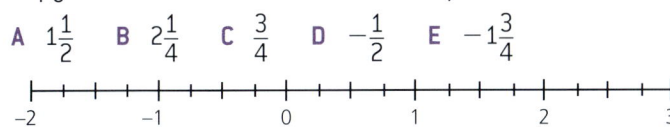

├┼┼┼┼┼┼┼┼┼┼┼┼┼┼┼┼┼┼┼┼┤
-2   -1   0   1   2   3

▶ Using coordinates in the first quadrant

Remember that the position of a point on a grid can be given by its coordinates.

For example, the point P is **three squares to the right** of the origin O and **two squares up**.

You say that P has the coordinates (**3**, **2**).

3 is the *x*-coordinate and **2** is the *y*-coordinate.

Remember that the *x*-coordinate comes before the *y*-coordinate.

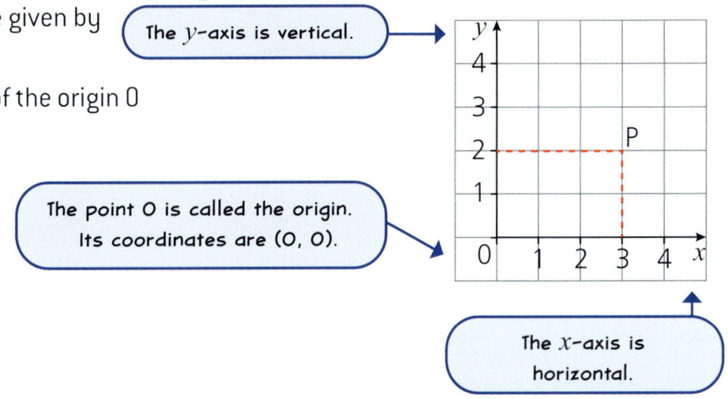

> The *y*-axis is vertical.

> The point O is called the origin. Its coordinates are (0, 0).

> The *x*-axis is horizontal.

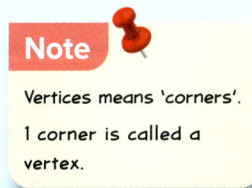

Worked example

a Draw a pair of axes from 0 to 5.
   Plot the points A(2, 5), B(5, 5), C(5, 2) and D(2, 2) and join them in order.

b What shape have you drawn? Justify your answer.

c What are the coordinates of the centre of the shape?

Note

Vertices means 'corners'.
1 corner is called a vertex.

Solution

a A, B, C and D are the vertices of the shape.

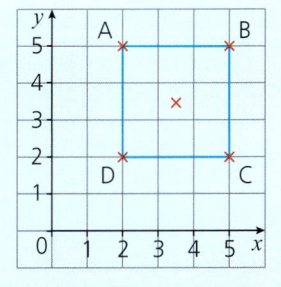

b AB = BC = CD = DA = 3 units
   AB and DC are horizontal. AD and BC are vertical, so all angles are right angles.
   Therefore ABCD is a square.

c The centre of the square is at $\left(3\frac{1}{2}, 3\frac{1}{2}\right)$.

Communication using symbols

37

Curriculum for Wales Mastering Mathematics: Book 1

▶ Using coordinates in all four quadrants

You can extend the x and y axes to include negative numbers.

This makes four regions called **quadrants**.

2nd quadrant   1st quadrant

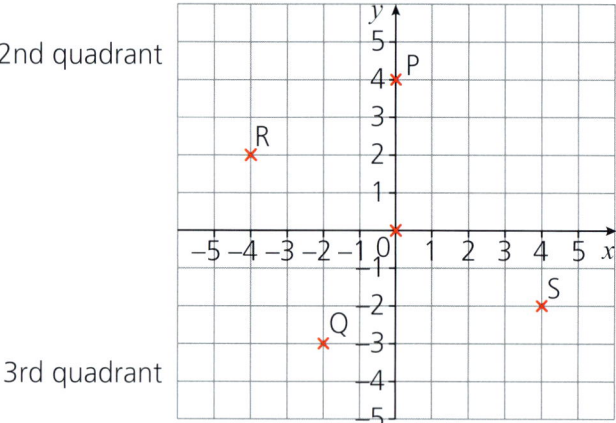

3rd quadrant   4th quadrant

Note

P has coordinates (0, 4).
Q has coordinates (−2, −3).
R has coordinates (−4, 2).
S has coordinates (4, −2).

Worked example

The diagram shows a star, with points A, B, C, D and E.
Write down the coordinates of the points A, B, C, D and E.

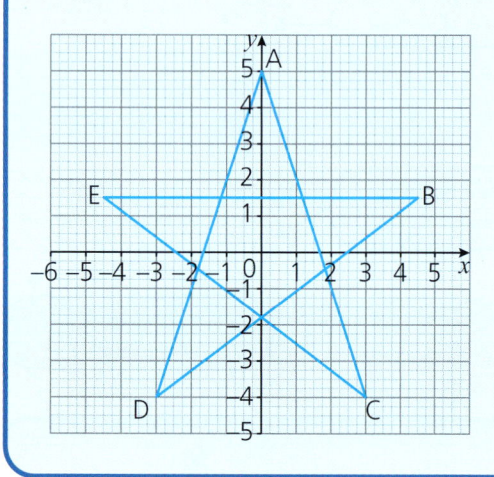

Solution

A is at (0, 5). ← A is 5 up from the origin.

B is at $\left(4\frac{1}{2}, 1\frac{1}{2}\right)$.

C is at (3, −4). ← C is 3 right and 4 down from O.

D is at (−3, −4). ← D is 3 left and 4 down from O.

E is at $\left(-4\frac{1}{2}, 1\frac{1}{2}\right)$.

3.1 Now try these

Band 1 questions

1 **a** Use the letter square to find out what these messages say.

The first word has been done for you.

	A	B	C	D	E	F	G	H
8	a	c	r	j	b	w	k	g
7	j	z	v	h	b	f	y	h
6	o	n	a	g	s	u	a	o
5	q	g	b	j	p	l	x	e
4	i	y	f	k	d	f	v	c
3	s	i	e	t	i	c	z	p
2	w	q	n	e	k	x	d	m
1	d	i	l	m	r	t	u	h

38

3 Coordinates and transformations

i H2, C3, H5, F1 / D1, H5 / A8, D3 / F1, D7, C3 / E6, H1, A6, E5, E6.

Meet

ii D1, G6, D3, H7, A3 / B3, E6 / F3, H6, A6, F5!
iii F3, A6, D1, C3 / D3, A6 / H2, G7 / E5, A8, E1, D3, B4.
iv D1, G7 / E4, A6, H8 / B1, E6 / B8, C6, C1, F5, H5, E4 / H2, G6, F2.

b Use the letter square to write your own message. (Try writing something in Welsh.)
Give the message to a friend to solve.

2 Write down the coordinates of each of the points plotted below.

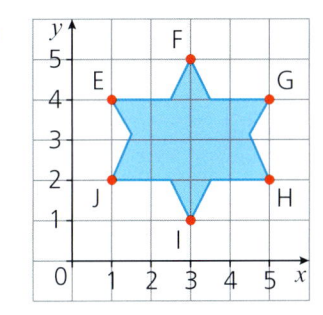

a [square ABCD plot]   b [star plot EFGHIJ]   c [triangle KLM plot]

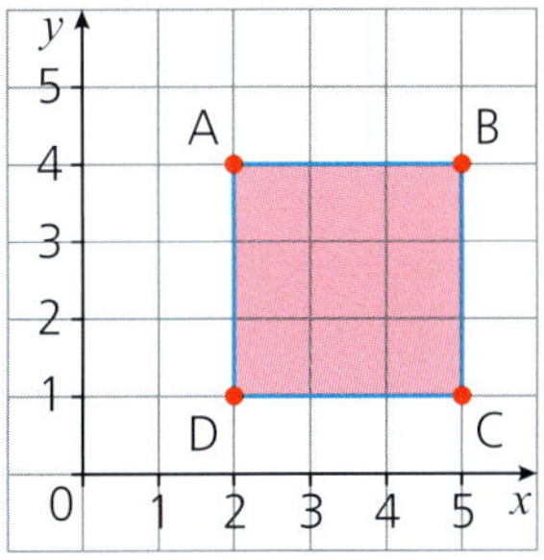

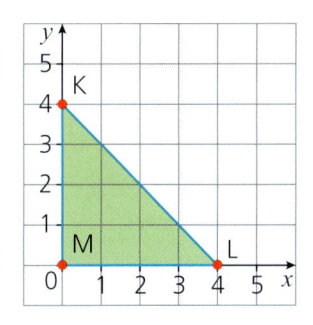

3 Draw a pair of axes from 0 to 10.

a Plot these points and join them in order.
(3, 4), (2, 2), (0, 0), (1, 0), (3, 2), (2, 0), (3, 0), (4, 2), (4, 3), (6, 3), (7, 4), (7, 2), (6, 0), (8, 0), (8, 1), (9, 0), (10, 1), (10, 2), (9, 5), (7, 6), (5, 6), (4, 7), (4, 8), (3, 7), (2, 8), (2, 7), (1, 6), (0, 6), (1, 5), (2, 5), (3, 4), (3, 2)

b Plot these points and join them up as you go.
(7, 0), (8, 2), (8, 1), (8, 3), (9, 4), (9, 5)

c Now put dots at (2, 6) and (0, 6). What have you drawn?

4 Draw a pair of axes from 0 to 6.

a Plot the points (1, 2), (4, 2) and (4, 5).
b Mark a fourth point to make a square. What are the coordinates of this point?

Band 2 questions

5 Here is a map showing seven towns and the roads between them.

The distances along the axes are in kilometres.

Cwmisel is at the point (10, 30).

Meidrwm is at (25, 0).

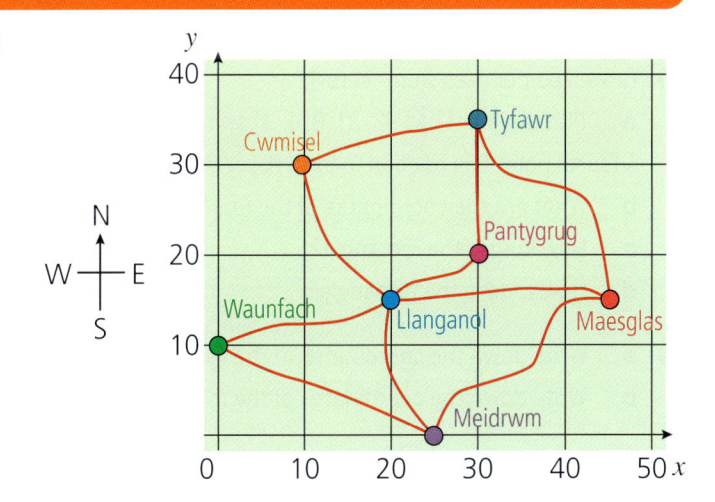

a What are the coordinates of:
 i Waunfach
 ii Llanganol?
b How far is it from:
 i Tyfawr to Pantygrug
 ii Llanganol to Maesglas?
c A new town is to be built at (45, 35).
 i How far will the new town be from Tyfawr?
 ii How far will the new town be from Maesglas?

6 Write down the coordinates of the points which make this bow tie.

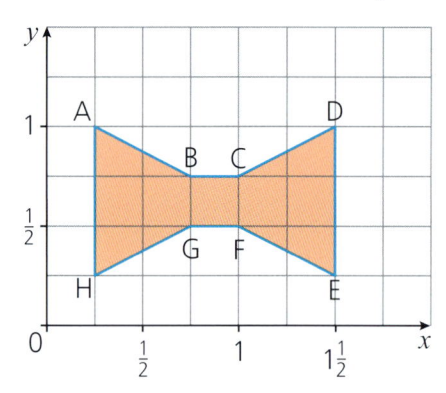

7 Draw a pair of axes from 0 to 6.
  a Plot these points and join them in order.
  $\left(3, 3\tfrac{1}{2}\right), \left(5\tfrac{1}{2}, 3\tfrac{1}{2}\right), \left(3\tfrac{1}{2}, \tfrac{1}{2}\right), \left(1, \tfrac{1}{2}\right)$ and back to $\left(3, 3\tfrac{1}{2}\right)$
  b What shape have you drawn?
  Justify your answer.

8 Draw axes using values of −6 to 6 for both x and y.
  a Plot these points and join them in order:
  A(4, 6), B(6, 0), C(4, −6), D(−4, −6), E(−6, 0), F(−4, 6) then back to A.
  b Are all the sides the same length?
  c Are all the angles exactly equal?
  d Describe the shape you have drawn.

Band 3 questions

9 The point (1, 3) is in the first quadrant.
  In which quadrants are these points?
  a (−3, −6)
  b (5, −10)
  c (−3, 8)
  d (100, 100)

10 Draw a pair of axes from −4 to 4.
  a Plot the points A (−2, 3), B (4, 3) and C (4, −2).
  A fourth point D is needed to form the rectangle ABCD.
  b What are the coordinates of the fourth point of the rectangle?
  c How long is the rectangle?
  d How wide is the rectangle?

Remember
The vertices of a shape are the corners.

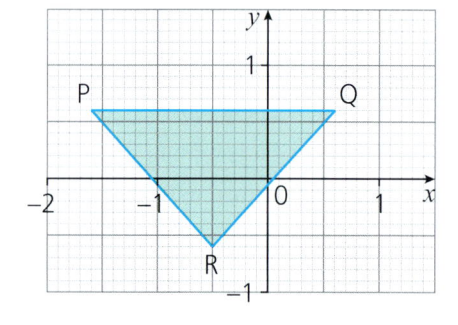

11 a Write down the coordinates of the vertices of triangle PQR.
  b Write down the coordinates of the midpoint of PQ.

12 **a** Write down the coordinates of A, B and C.
 b A fourth point, D is added to the diagram to form a rectangle.
   Write down the coordinates of D.

13 Draw axes with values for both x and y from −5 to 5.
   Plot these points and join them in order.
   A(−3, 1), B(0, 5), C(4, 2)
   These are three vertices of the square ABCD.
   a What are the coordinates of D?
   b What are the coordinates of the midpoint of each side of the square?

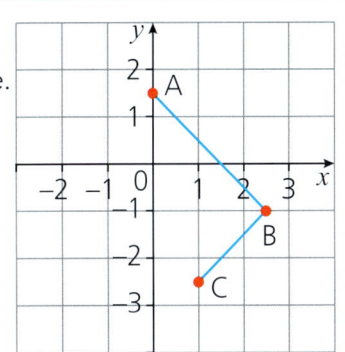

3.2 Translations

Skill checker

① Write down the coordinates of the vertices of the triangle ABC.

② Lloyd joins three points on the grid.
   He makes a triangle which is **congruent** to the triangle ABC.
   Which points did Lloyd join? Write down their coordinates.
   Find as many different answers as you can.

Remember
Congruent means 'exactly the same shape and size'.

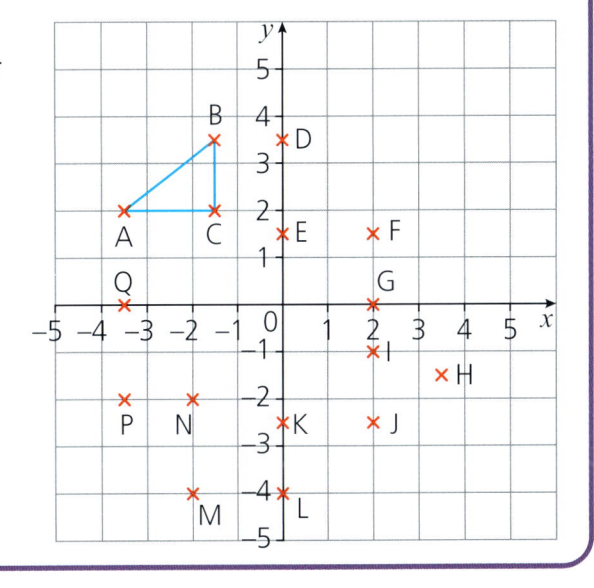

③ Lloyd makes a cardboard cut-out of triangle ABC.
   He slides the cardboard triangle on top of one of the other triangles he has drawn.
   Lloyd doesn't turn the triangle when he slides it.
   Write down the vertices of the triangle ABC is moved to.
   Find two different answers.

41

Translating a shape

Activity

Chen and Mia are playing a game of Robot Wars.

Here is Mia's grid.

Mia hides her robot at $(-2, 3)$.

If Chen places his robot on top of Mia's robot, he wins.

Chen places his robot at $(4, -2)$.

Mia says he is 11 steps away.

Chen now guesses $(0, 5)$.

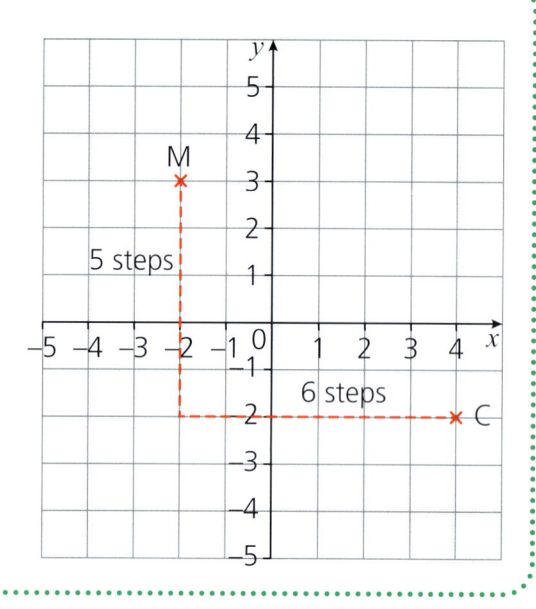

① a Why is this a sensible guess?
   b How many steps away is Chen now?
   c Name all the points that would be a sensible next guess.
      How far away from Mia's robot is each guess?

② Play your own game of Robot Wars with a partner.
   What strategies did you use?

You can use **transformations** to change (transform) a shape.

In maths there are four types of transformation:

- **translation** (sliding the shape)
- **reflection** (flipping the shape over)
- **rotation** (turning the shape round)
- **enlargement** (making the shape bigger or smaller).

You will find out more about enlargements in Book 3.

When you slide a shape without turning it round or turning it over, you have **translated** the shape.

You can **describe** a translation by saying how many squares **horizontally** (left/right) and **vertically** (up/down) you have moved the shape.

Worked example

Triangle P is translated onto triangle Q.

a Describe the **translation**.
b Describe the **transformation** that moves shape Q back onto shape P.

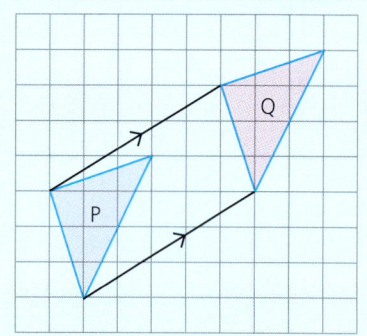

Note

- The transformed shape is called the **image**.
- The original shape is called the **object**.
- Use lines joining corresponding (matching) vertices on the object and image to help you work out how far the object has moved in each direction.

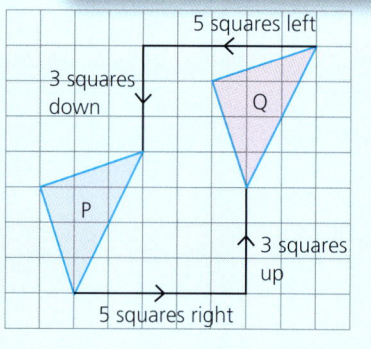

Solution

a P is translated five squares right and three squares up to Q.
b Q is translated five squares left and three squares down back onto P.

The transformation is a translation.
You must say what type of transformation it is in your answer.

42

3 Coordinates and transformations

When a shape is translated, the shape and its image are exactly the same shape and size: they are **congruent**.
You say that the object is **mapped** onto its image.

In the worked example on page 42, P is mapped onto Q.

Sometimes translations are carried out on a coordinate grid.

Worked example

Copy this grid.
a Translate A five squares left and two up.
   Label this triangle B.
b Translate B four squares right and two up.
   Label this triangle C.

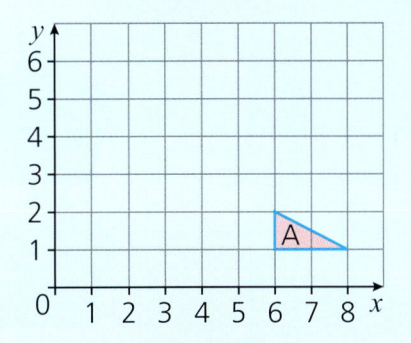

Solution

a Translating A five squares left results in triangle 1.
   Translating triangle 1 two squares up results in image B.

b Translating B four squares right results in triangle 2.
   Translating triangle 2 two squares up results in image C.

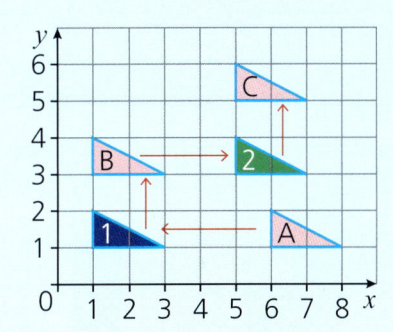

Discussion activity

Investigate how to write translations using a column vector.

Upwards movements are positive and moving to the right is positive. Why do you think this is?

3.2 Now try these

Band 1 questions

1 For each diagram, describe the **translation** which:
  i   maps shape A onto shape B
  ii maps shape B onto shape A.

a

b

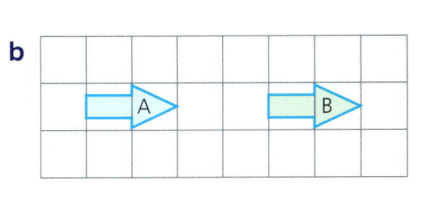

c

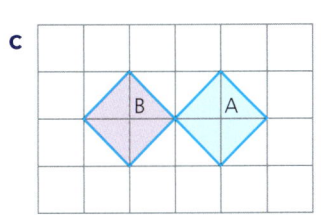

Curriculum for Wales Mastering Mathematics: Book 1

2 For each diagram, describe the **transformation** which:
  i maps shape A onto shape B
  ii maps shape B onto shape A.

  a **b** 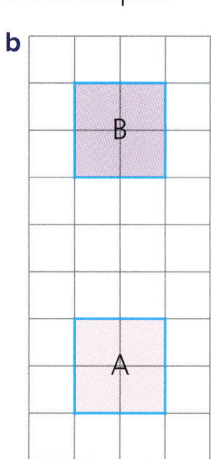 **c**

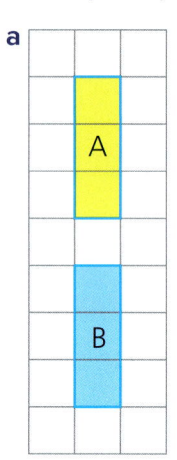

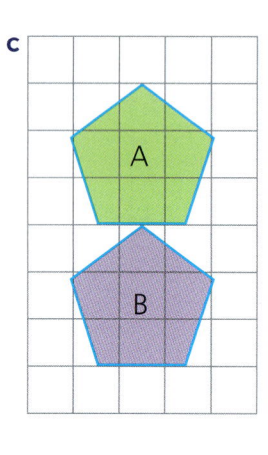

3 For each diagram, describe the translation which maps shape A onto shape B.

  a **b** 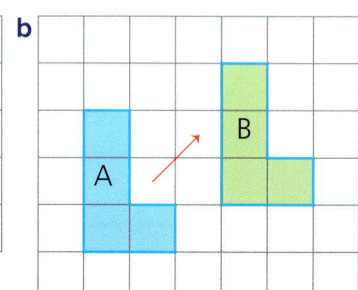 **c**

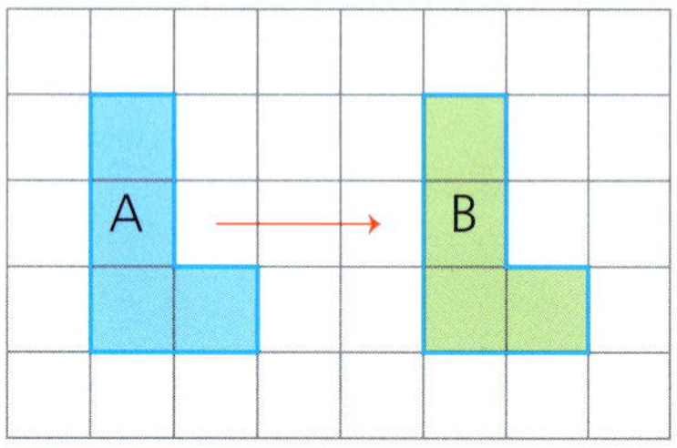

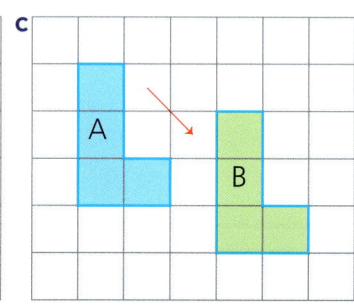

  d 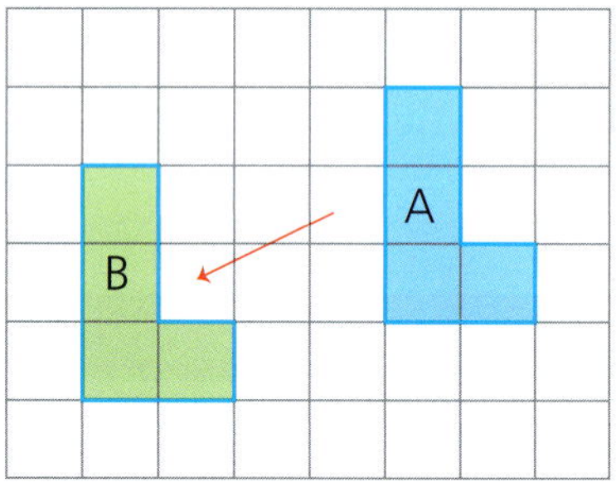 **e** 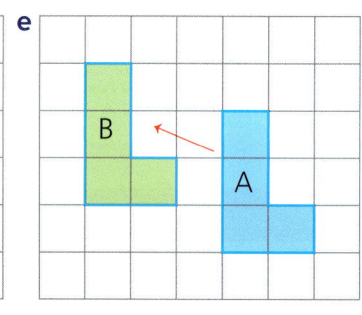 **f**

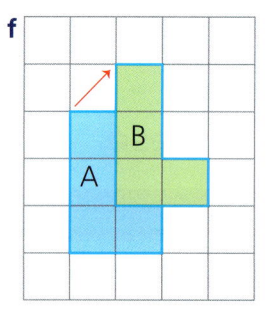

4 Which of these diagrams shows a translation? Explain your reasoning fully.

  a **b**

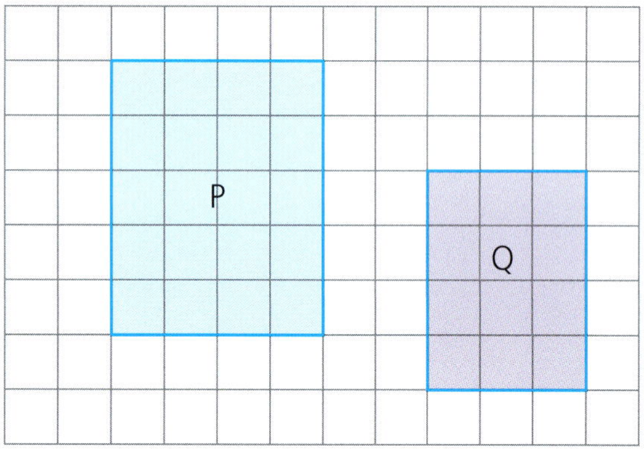

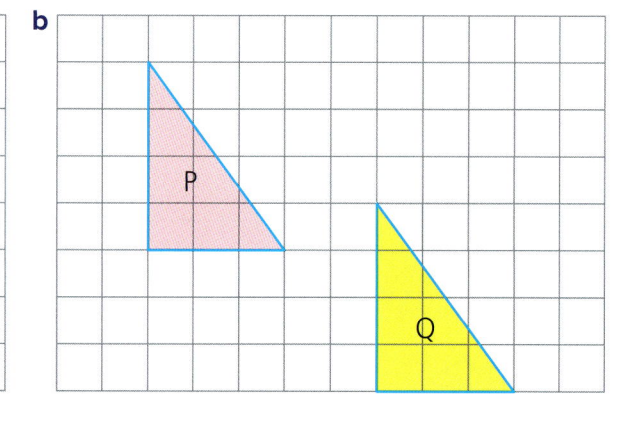

44

3 Coordinates and transformations

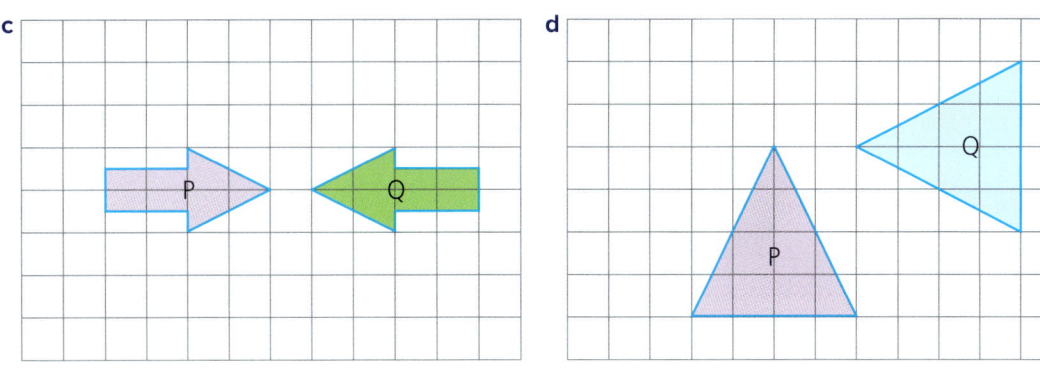

c
d

5 Hanna is playing a computer game. She is shooting down aeroplanes with a gun (G).

She moves the gun three squares right and two squares up to shoot down A.

From A she moves the gun to B, C, D and E.

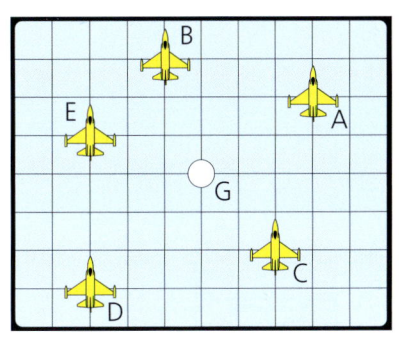

a   Describe the moves from:

   i   A to B   ii   B to C   iii   C to D   iv   D to E.

b   In what order should Hanna shoot the aeroplanes to minimise the distance her gun travels?

Band 2 questions

6 a   Anya says that to map shape A onto shape B you should translate it one square to the right.

   Is Anya correct? Explain your answer.

b   Describe the translation which maps:

   i   C onto D
   ii D onto E
   iii C onto E.

c   Joshua says that the same translation maps A onto E as maps B onto D. Is Joshua correct?

   Explain your answer.

7 Copy the diagram on the right.

Draw the triangle after:

a   a translation of four squares to the right and one square up

b   a translation of two squares to the left

c   a translation of three squares down

d   a translation of six squares to the left and six squares down.

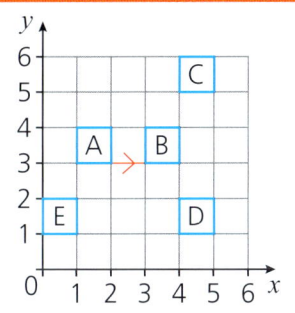

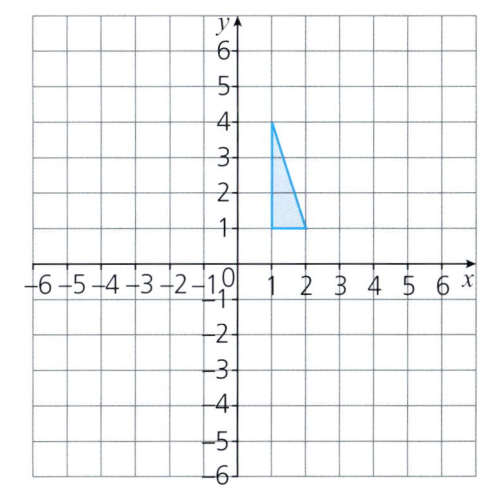

Curriculum for Wales Mastering Mathematics: Book 1

8 Describe the transformation which maps:

   a A onto B   **b** B onto C   **c** A onto C   **d** C onto A.

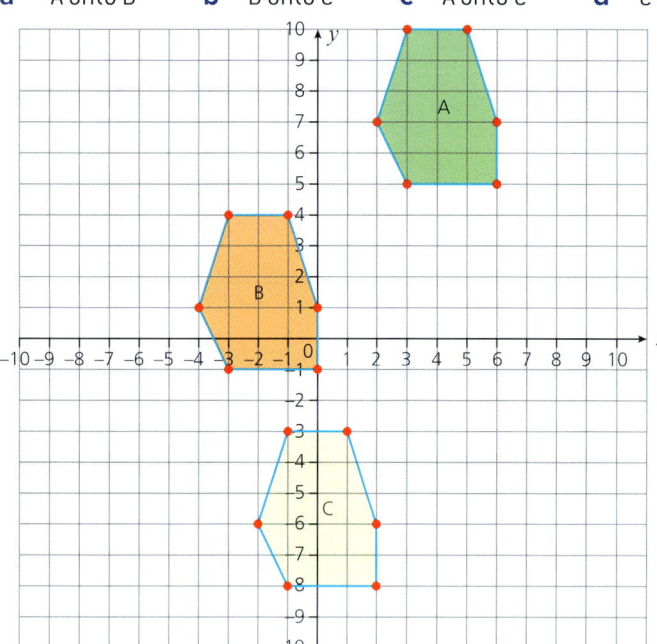

9 a Describe these transformations fully.
- **i** C to B
- **ii** A to B
- **iii** D to A
- **iv** C to D
- **v** B to D
- **vi** D to C
- **vii** B to C

  b How could you work out the answers for parts **vi** and **vii** using your answers for parts **i** to **v**?

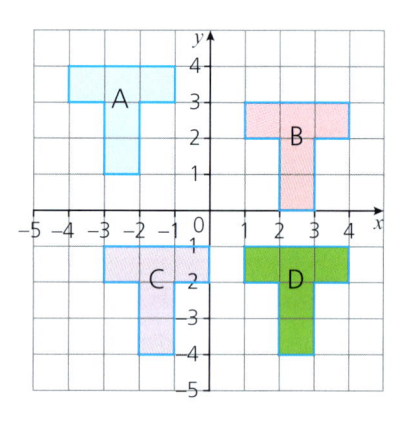

Band 3 questions

10 Copy this diagram, extending the grid as necessary.

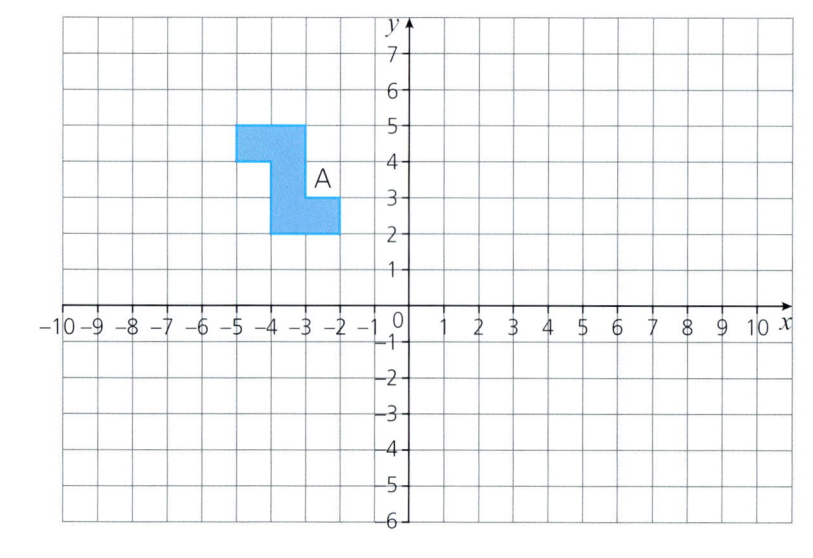

a Draw the shapes B to H described by the translations in the table. Label each of the images.

Translation	Left/right	Up/down
A → B	3 right	1 up
A → C	8 right	3 down
A → D	2 left	5 down
C → E	4 left	4 down
C → F	5 left	1 up
F → G	8 right	4 down
B → H	7 left	2 down

b Explain how you can use the **table only** to work out the translation for:
   i A to H
   ii A to G.

11 a Draw and label an x-axis from −9 to 9 and a y-axis from 0 to 9.
Plot the following points and join them to make a triangle.
(−8, 2), (−6, 7), (−3, 2)
Label this triangle W.

b Translate triangle W 11 squares to the right and two squares up.
Label the new triangle X.

c What translation will map X onto W?

12 Elin draws a shape on a grid and labels it A.
She translates shape A four squares left and five squares up onto shape B.

a Write down the translation which maps shape B onto shape A.

b Write down a sequence of three translations so that the shape returns to its original position.

13 Jerin plots the points A(3,1), B(−2, 3) and C(1, −4) on a grid.
She joins the points to make a triangle.
Jerin translates the triangle five squares right and three squares down onto triangle A'B'C'.

You say this as A dash, B dash, C dash.

a Work out the coordinates of the vertices of triangle A'B'C'.

Jerin translates ABC onto A"B"C". *A double dash*

The coordinates of A" are (−3, 5).

Note
We can use a column vector to write this translation. $\begin{pmatrix} 5 \\ -3 \end{pmatrix}$

b Describe the translation that maps triangle ABC onto triangle A"B"C".

c Describe the translation that maps triangle A'B'C' onto triangle A"B"C".

Curriculum for Wales Mastering Mathematics: Book 1

3.3 Reflections and rotations

Skill checker

1. A kaleidoscope is a toy which uses beads and mirrors to make patterns. The pattern below is made in a kaleidoscope. Describe its symmetry.

2. Describe the symmetry in each of the words below.

3. An **ambigram** is a word that can be read in different ways, like the words in question **2**.
   Use the internet to find out how to draw ambigrams. Can you design an ambigram of your name?

4. Symmetry has been used by artists. The famous Dutch artist MC Escher is well known for his mathematically inspired artwork. Can you find any of his work that exhibits symmetry? Are there any other artists who use symmetry as a basis for their art?

▶ Reflecting a shape

A **reflection** is a type of transformation.

When an **object** is reflected in a line, its **image** is formed on the other side of the line. The image is the same distance from the mirror line as the object is.

The red line is called the **mirror line** or the **line of reflection.**

The image and the original object are **congruent**.

> They are the same shape and the same size. The image has been flipped over.

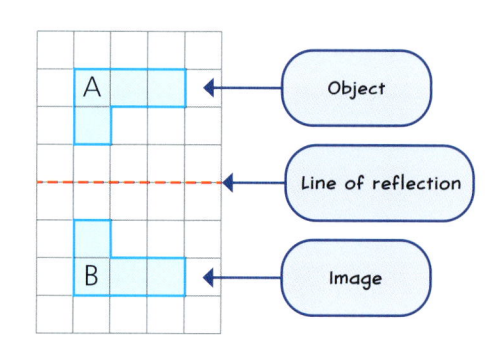

48

3 Coordinates and transformations

Worked example

Copy the diagram.

Draw the image of the shape after it is reflected in the red mirror line.

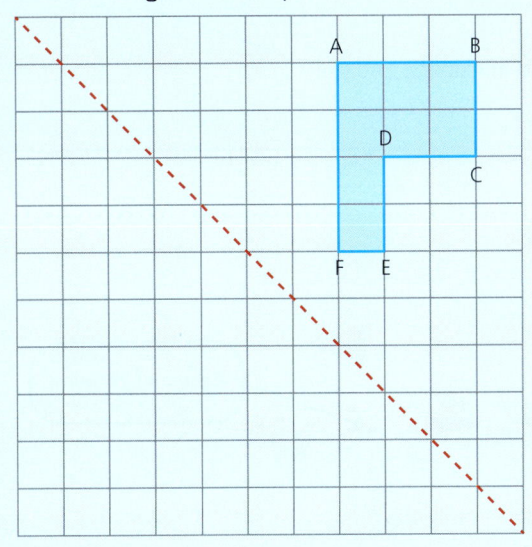

Solution

Rotate your page so that the mirror line is vertical. Construct the image and then turn your page back.

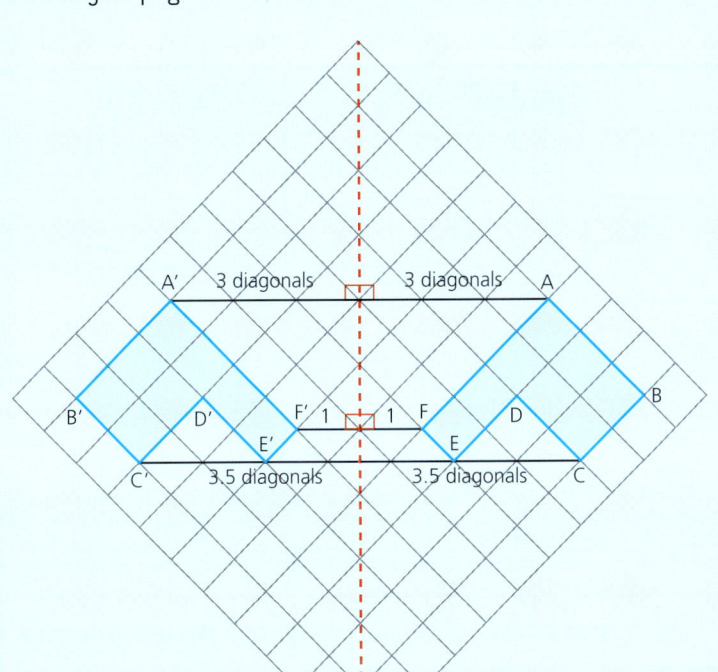

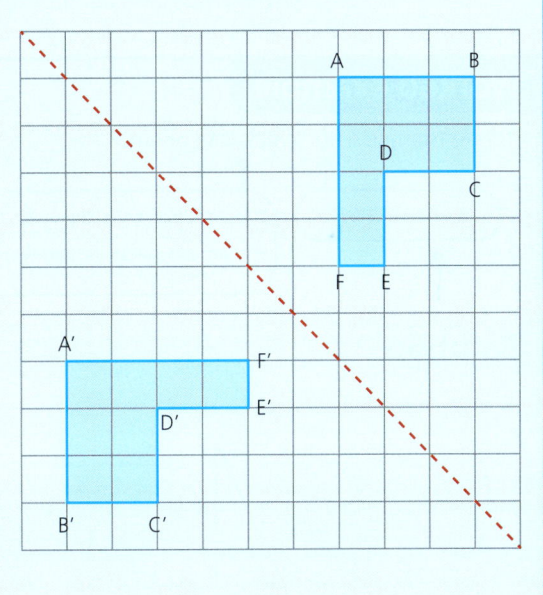

Curriculum for Wales Mastering Mathematics: Book 1

> **Activity**
> ① Draw a 6 cm × 6 cm square.
> Mark the four lines of symmetry with dotted lines as shown.
> ② Draw these four blue lines in one corner.
> Reflect these blue lines in the horizontal mirror line, the vertical mirror line and the diagonal mirror line.
> This is called a **Rangoli pattern**.
> ③ Design a Rangoli pattern of your own.

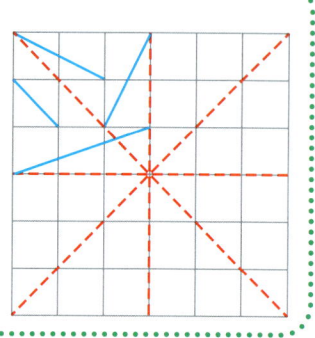

▶ Rotating a shape

Another type of transformation is a **rotation**.

Rotation is a movement made by turning an object.

The flag here has been rotated four times, each time by a quarter turn.

A full turn is 360°, so:

- a quarter turn is 90° (a right angle)
- a half turn is 180°
- a three-quarter turn is 270°.

The flag has been rotated by holding the end of the stick still.

This is the **centre of rotation**.

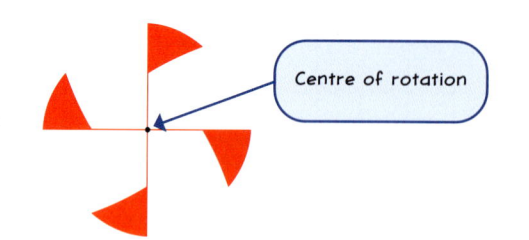

Worked example

Rotate triangle A 90° clockwise about P.

A quarter turn.

Clockwise is this way:
Anticlockwise is this way:

Solution

Step 1: Make sure your tracing paper is lined up like this.
Write a 'T' at the top of your tracing paper.
Trace the shape onto your tracing paper.

Step 2: Place your pencil tip on the centre of rotation.
This makes a pivot point.

Step 3: Carefully turn your tracing paper $\frac{1}{4}$ of a turn clockwise.
Stop when your 'T' is on the east (right).

50

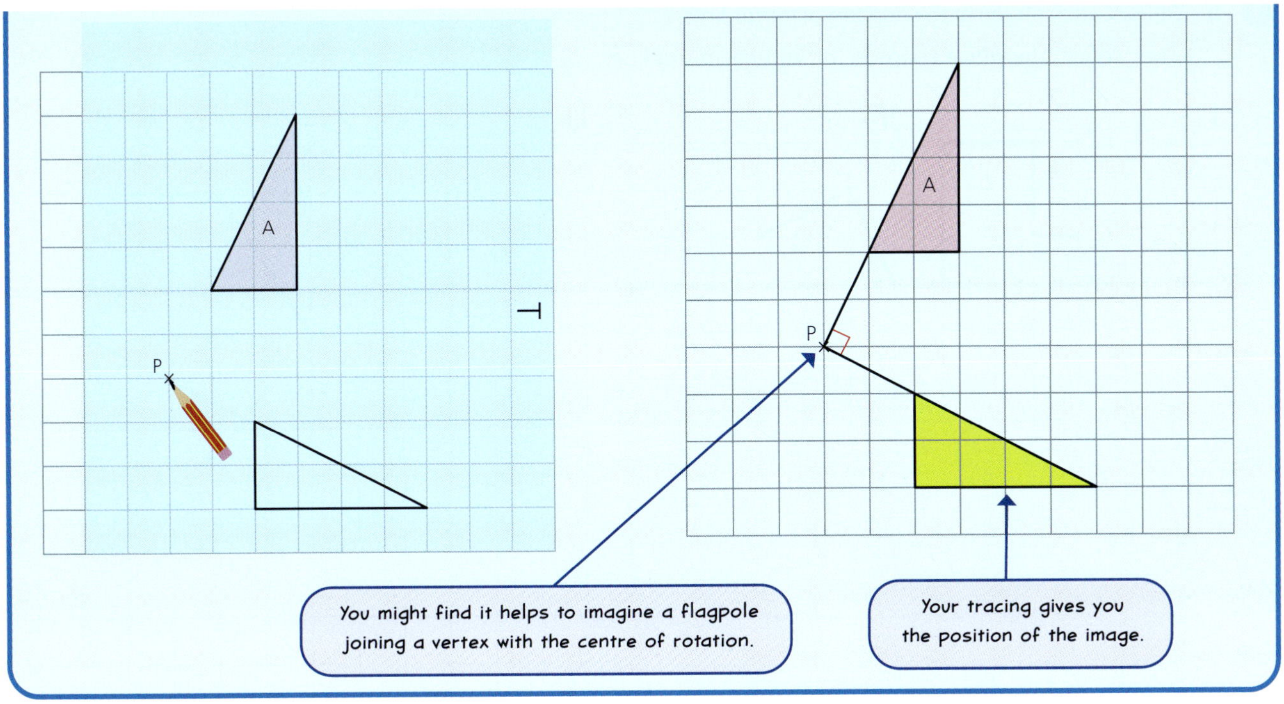

3 Coordinates and transformations

> You might find it helps to imagine a flagpole joining a vertex with the centre of rotation.

> Your tracing gives you the position of the image.

Sometimes you need to describe a rotation. When you do:
- Always use tracing paper to help you with rotations.
- Always give the **centre of rotation**.
- Say whether the rotation is **clockwise** or **anticlockwise**.

3.3 Now try these

Band 1 questions

1 Copy each diagram.

Draw the image of each shape after it is reflected in the red mirror line.

a

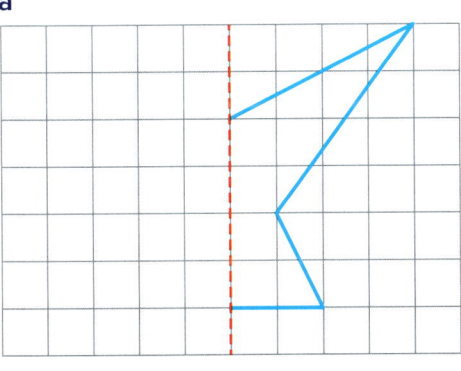

b

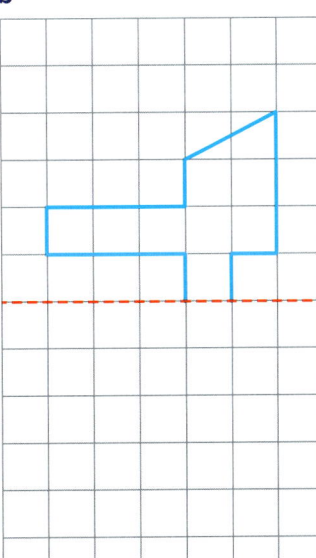

c

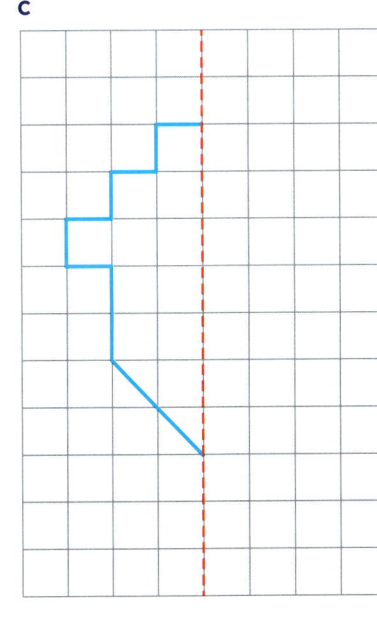

Curriculum for Wales Mastering Mathematics: Book 1

Logical reasoning

2 a Reflect each shape in the horizontal mirror line.
Then reflect the whole shape in the vertical mirror line.

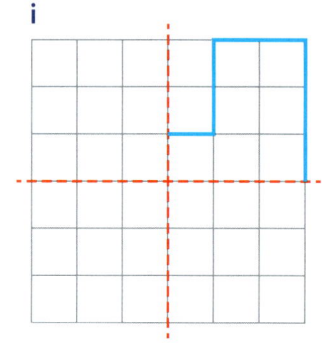

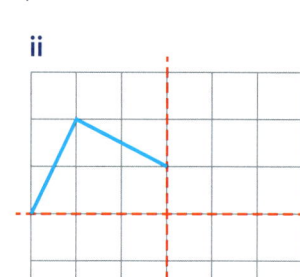

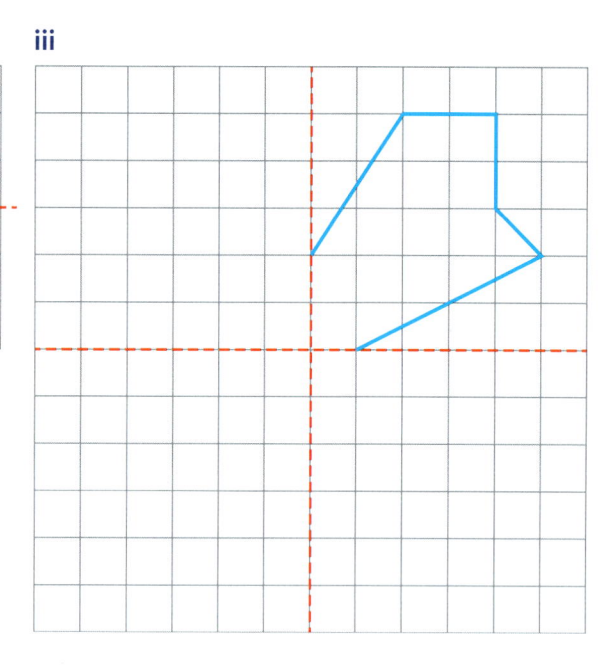

i   ii   iii

b Would your answers be the same if you had reflected in the vertical mirror line first?
Explain your answer.

Fluency

3 Match these arrows with the descriptions below.

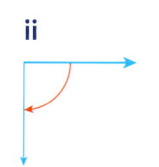

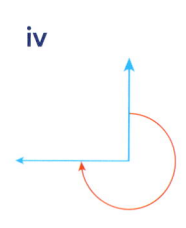

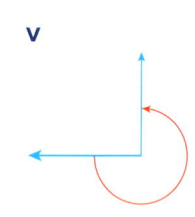

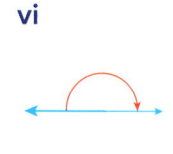

i   ii   iii   iv   v   vi

a   A quarter turn clockwise
b   A three-quarter turn anticlockwise
c   A half turn anticlockwise
d   A quarter turn anticlockwise
e   A half turn clockwise
f   A three-quarter turn clockwise

4 Make a copy of each shape on squared paper and then use tracing paper to help you rotate it.
  a   Rotate the parallelogram $\frac{1}{4}$ of a turn clockwise about P.
  b   Rotate the triangle $\frac{1}{4}$ of a turn anticlockwise about P.

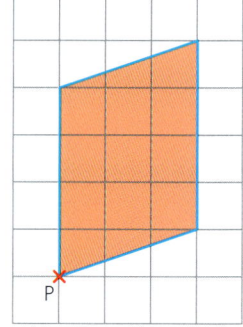

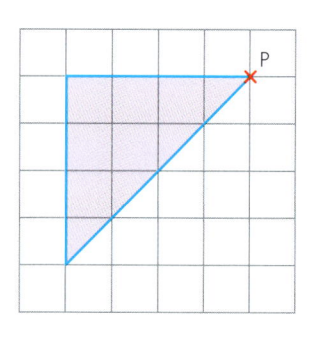

5 a i Rotate the trapezium $\frac{1}{2}$ a turn clockwise about P.

ii Rotate the T shape $\frac{1}{2}$ a turn anticlockwise about P.

b Amir says that a rotation of $\frac{1}{2}$ a turn clockwise is the same as a rotation of $\frac{1}{2}$ a turn anticlockwise.
Is Amir correct? Explain your answer.

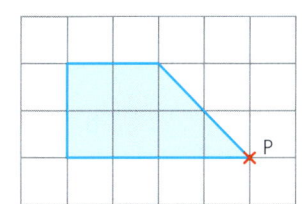

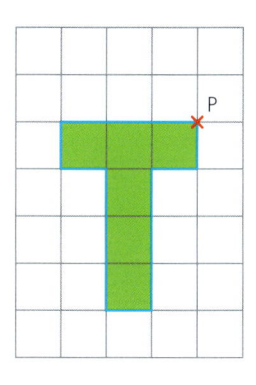

Band 2 questions

6 Copy each diagram.

Draw the image of each shape after it is reflected in the red mirror line.

a

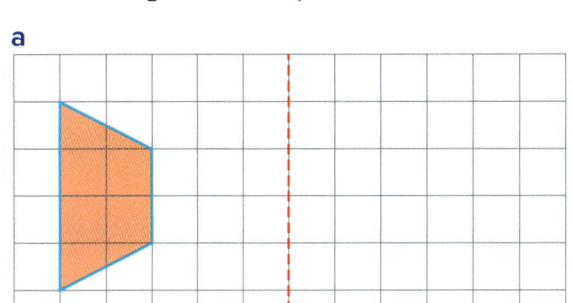

b

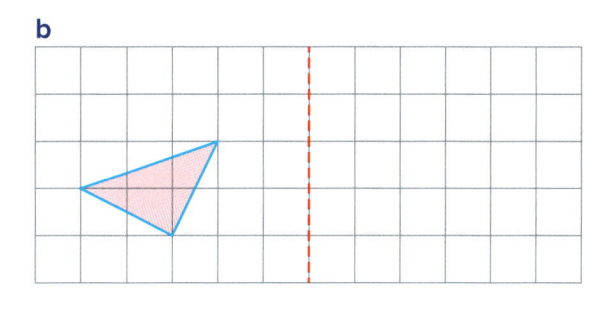

7 Copy each diagram.

Draw the image of each shape after it is reflected in the red mirror line.

a

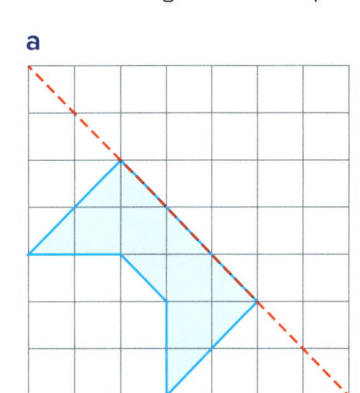

b

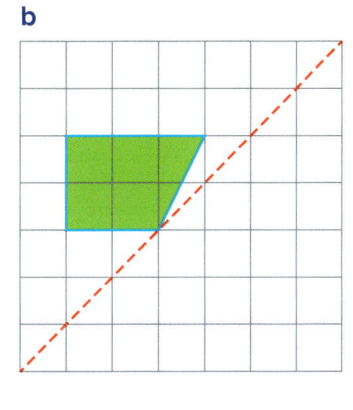

c

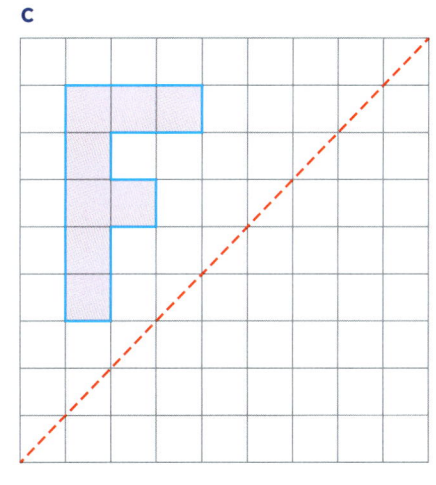

Curriculum for Wales Mastering Mathematics: Book 1

8 Which of these diagrams shows a reflection?
Explain your reasoning fully.

a

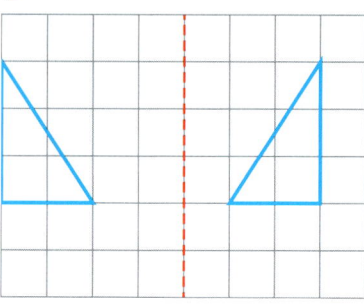

b

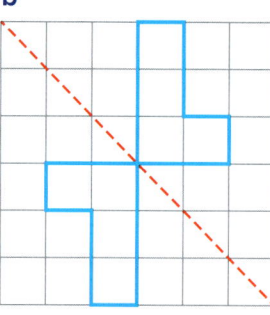

c

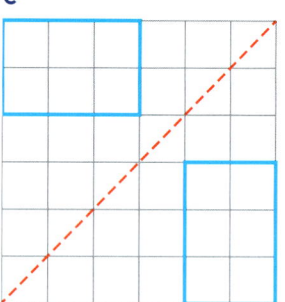

d

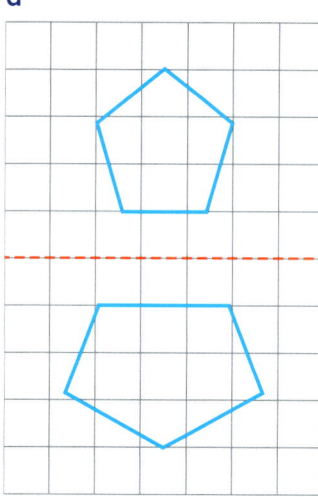

9 Make a copy of each shape on squared paper and then use tracing paper to help you rotate it.
In each part, label the image B.

a Rotate A 90° clockwise about P.

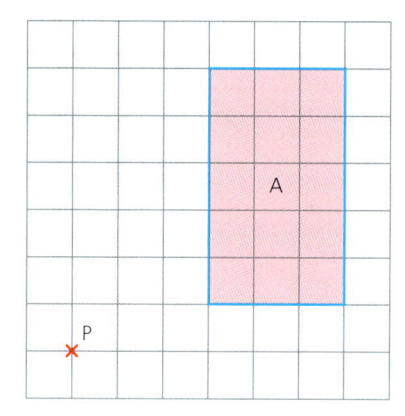

b Rotate A 90° anticlockwise about P.

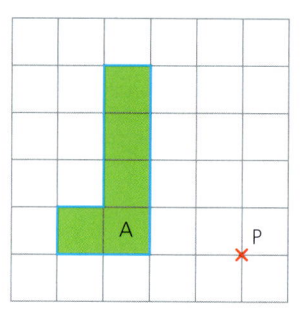

c Rotate A 180° about P.

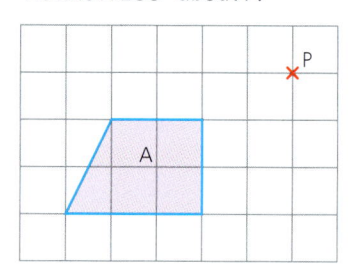

d Rotate A 270° clockwise about P.

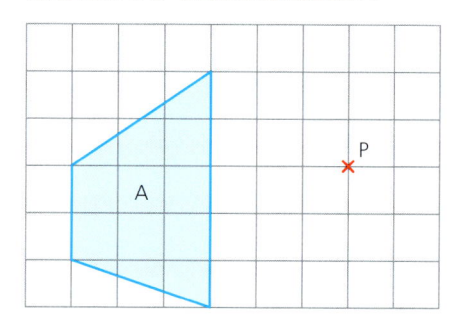

54

Band 3 questions

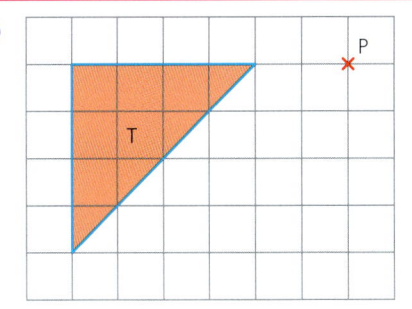

10

a Rotate triangle T 90° clockwise about P.

b Rotate triangle T 270° anticlockwise about P.

What do you notice?

11 For each part in question 9, describe fully the single transformation that maps shape B back onto shape A.

Is it possible to give two answers for each part?

12 a Copy this diagram of an E shape on the left-hand side of mirror line m_1, on squared paper.

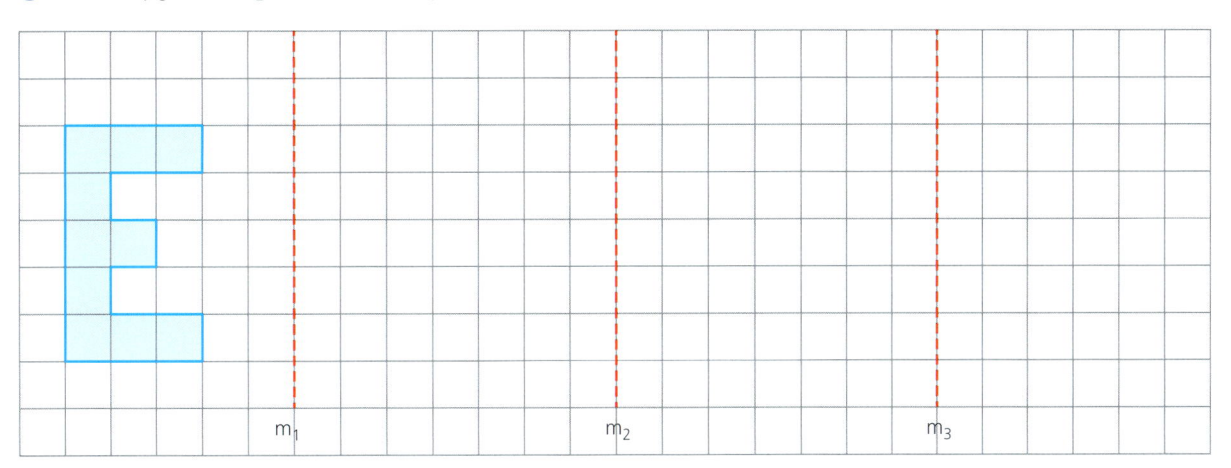

Reflect the E shape in m_1.

Reflect the image in m_2.

Reflect the new image in m_3.

Investigate what happens when other shapes are reflected successively in the parallel mirror lines m_1, m_2 and m_3.

b Can the resulting combined transformation be described by:

  i   a translation followed by a reflection

  ii   a reflection followed by a translation

  iii a single reflection?

Curriculum for Wales Mastering Mathematics: Book 1

Strategic competence

13 In each diagram, shape A is rotated onto shape B.
   i   On a copy of each grid, mark the centre of rotation.
   ii Describe the rotation fully.
   iii Write down the transformation which maps shape B back onto shape A.

   a
   b
   c

Logical reasoning

14 a Rotate shape A by 90° clockwise, centre (0, 0).
       Label the image B.
    b Rotate shape A by 180°, centre the origin.
       Label the resulting image C.
       Why does the direction not matter for this rotation?
    c Reflect shape A in the x-axis. Label the resulting image D.
    d Which transformation maps shape D onto shape C?

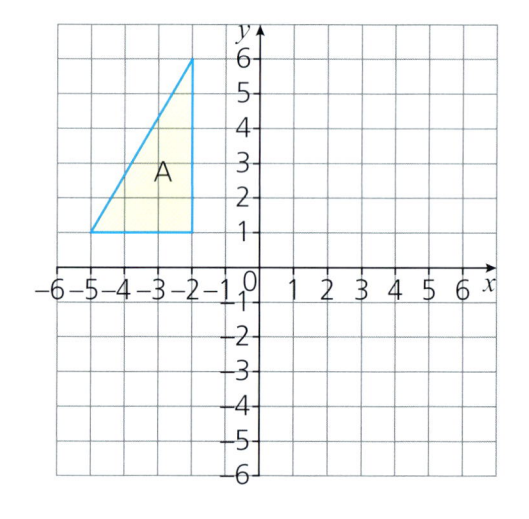

Key words

Here is a list of the key words you met in this chapter.

Axes	Centre of rotation	Congruent	Coordinates
Image	Mirror line	Object	Quadrant
Reflection	Rotation	Transformation	Translation
Trapezium	Vertex	x-coordinate	y-coordinate

Use the glossary at the back of this book to check any you are unsure about.

56

3 Coordinates and transformations

Review exercise: coordinates and transformations

Band 1 questions

1 Write down the coordinates of each of the points plotted below.

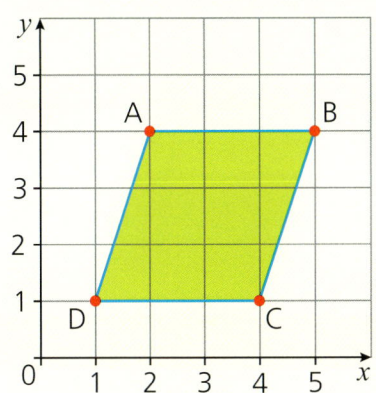

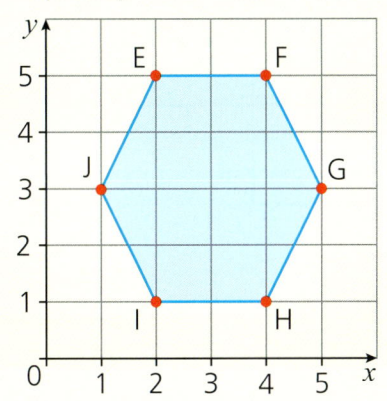

2 Look at this wallpaper pattern of repeated cars.

Car A is mapped to C by a translation of four squares right and one down.

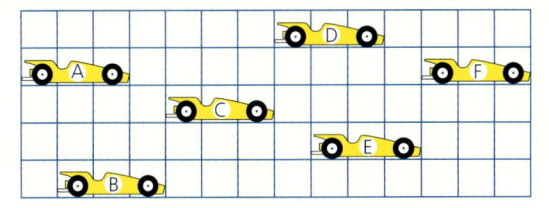

a Describe the translations which map:

- i   A to B
- ii A to D
- iii C to D
- iv E to D
- v   C to B
- vi B to E
- vii F to E
- viii F to A.

b Two of these translations are the same translation as D to C. Which are they?

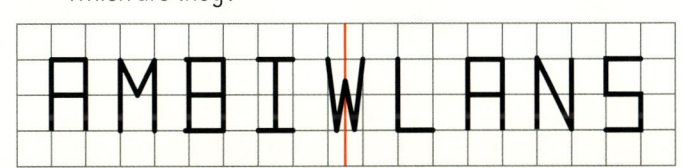

3

AMBIWLANS

a Copy this word onto squared paper in pencil.
b Now draw its reflection in the red line in ink.
c Why do emergency vehicles have reflected writing like this on the front?

Curriculum for Wales **Mastering Mathematics: Book 1**

Fluency

4 Copy these diagrams.

Reflect each shape in the line shown to complete a symmetrical shape.

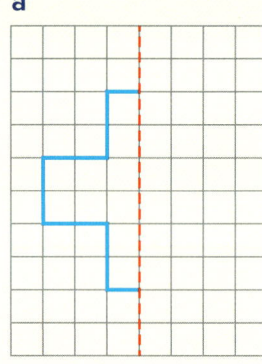

a

b

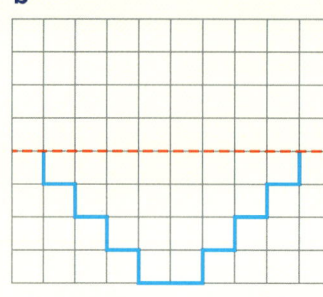

Band 2 questions

Logical reasoning

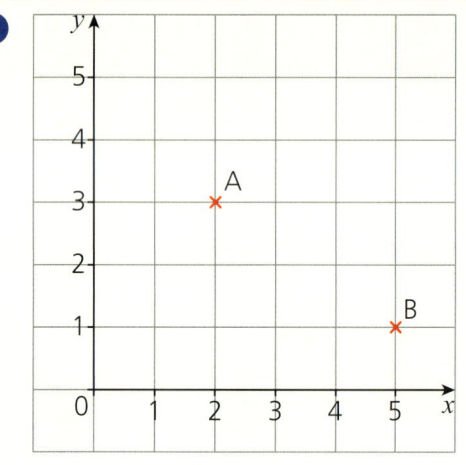

5

a Copy the diagram and mark:
  i three points with the same x-coordinate as A
  ii three points with the same y-coordinate as B.
b What do you notice?

Fluency

6

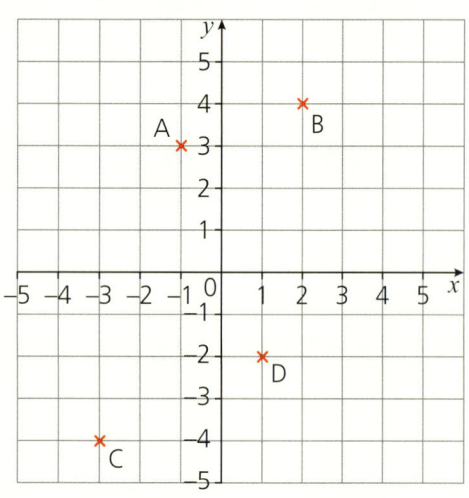

a Write down the coordinates of points A, B, C and D.
b Which point is in the third quadrant?
c Which point is in the fourth quadrant?

58

3   Coordinates and transformations

7 Which diagram correctly shows a reflection in the mirror line?

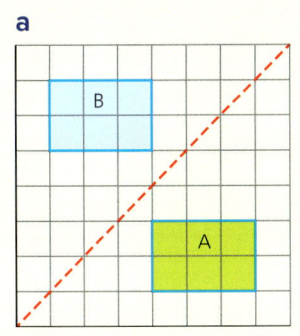

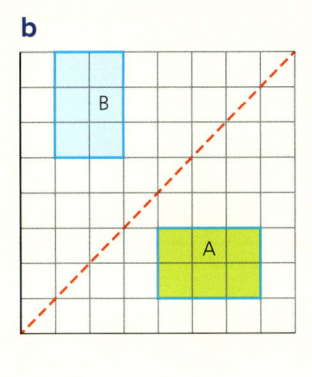

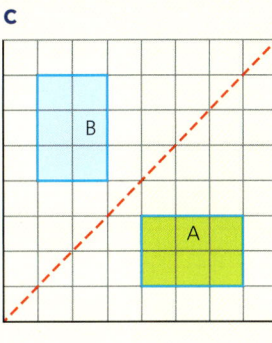

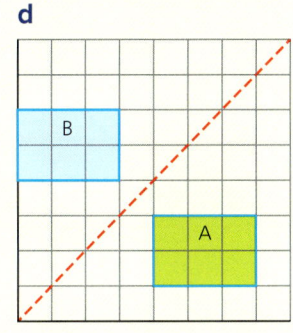

a   b   c   d

8 a Copy the diagram.
  b Shape A is translated two squares left and four squares up.
     Draw the image of shape A. Label it B.
  c Shape B is translated three squares left and two squares down.
     Draw the image of shape B. Label it C.
  d What single translation maps shape A onto shape C?

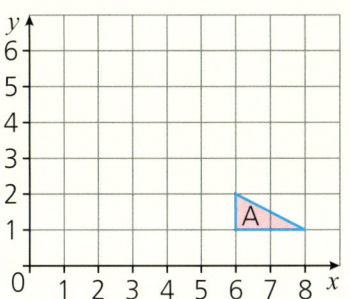

9 a Draw x- and y-axes, each from -5 to 5 using the same scale.
  b Plot the points $(-1, 4)$, $(-2, 2)$, $(1, -2)$ and $(1, 3)$.
  c Join the points in order, and join the last point to the first.
  d What shape have you drawn?

10 Elaine is designing a patchwork pattern.
  a Copy the diagram.
  b Reflect the pattern in the vertical mirror line.
     Now reflect the total pattern in the horizontal mirror line.
  c How can you extend the pattern further?

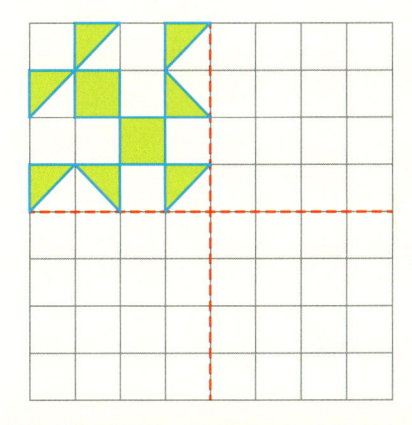

Band 3 questions

11 The diagram shows some coordinates plotted on a grid.
  a Which point is at $(-5, -2)$?
  b Write down the coordinates of E.
  c Which point is the midpoint of AD?
  d Which point has the greatest y-coordinate?
  e Which point has the lowest x-coordinate?
  f Which point(s) have the same x- and y-coordinates?
  g Which point has a y-coordinate of 1?
  h i   Which point lies on the y-axis?
     ii Madi says that this point is in the first quadrant.
         Is Madi correct?

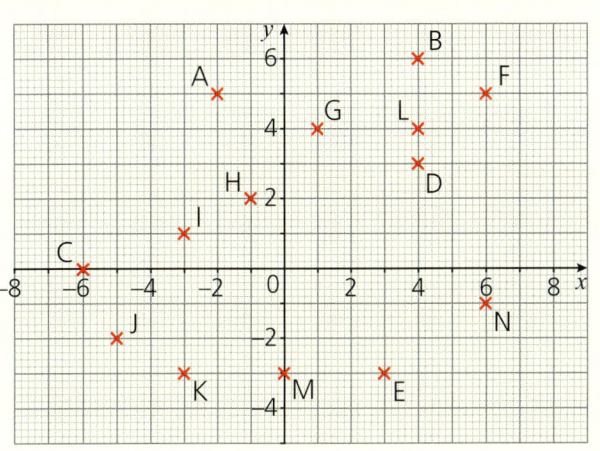

59

Curriculum for Wales Mastering Mathematics: Book 1

12 a Write down the coordinates of the vertices of the trapezium ABCD.

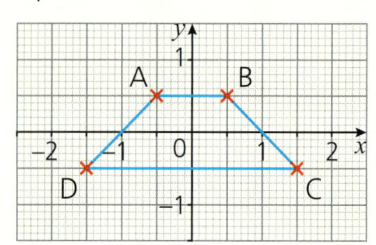

b Romesh says that ABCD has a line of symmetry along the x-axis.
Is Romesh correct? Give a reason for your answer.

13 a Copy this diagram.
b Reflect the shape in the y-axis.
c Now reflect both shapes in the x-axis.
d Describe the symmetry of the pattern you have made as clearly as you can.

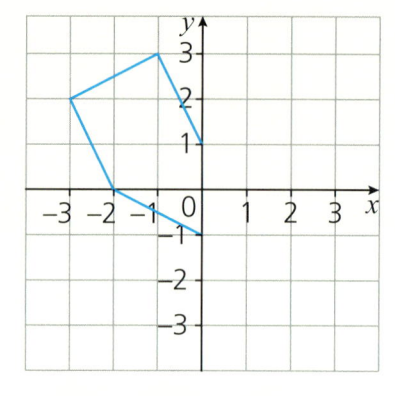

14 Describe fully these transformations.
State whether each of the transformations is a rotation, translation or reflection.
In each case give full details of the transformation.

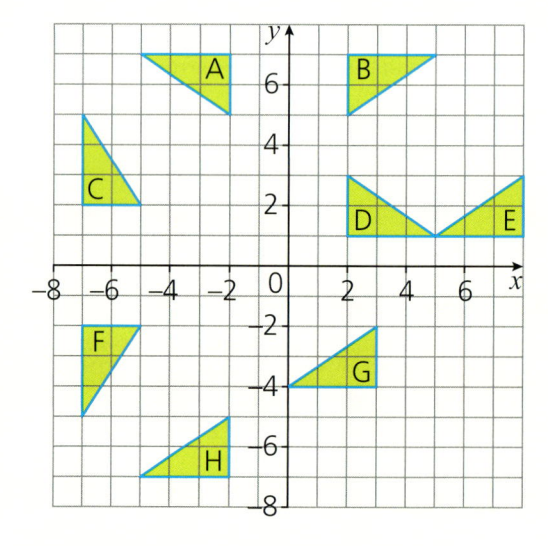

a A → B
b A → H
c G → E
d C → B
e G → H
f A → F
g B → H

Cross-curricular activity

Scratch is a simple programming language in which you can program characters to move around the screen (and do lots more!). Find out about Scratch and learn how to use it. Ask your technology teacher for help.

Consolidation 1: Chapters 1–3

Band 1 questions

1 Match the angles in the oval boxes to the descriptions in the rectangular boxes.

- Obtuse angle — Smaller than a right angle
- Reflex angle — Larger than two right angles
- Acute angle — Larger than a right angle, smaller than two right angles

2 Name each of these shapes. (What are their names in Welsh?) Write down how many lines of symmetry each shape has.

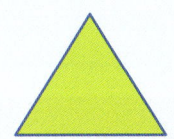

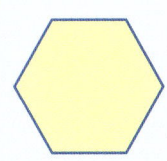

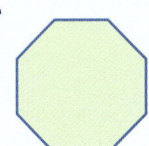

a (triangle)

b (square)

c (pentagon)

d (hexagon)

e (octagon)

3 Write down the number on the probability scale that means:

a certain

b impossible.

4 Sian and Alun are playing a game of Find the Gold.

They each place four gold bars on their grid.

The winner is the first person to find the hidden gold.

Here is Sian's grid.

a Alun guesses the point (2, 4). Does Sian answer 'Yes' or 'No'?

b Next turn, Alun guesses the point (4, 3). What does Sian answer?

c Alun tries a point next to (4, 3). List the four possible points. For each one say 'Yes' or 'No'.

d Write down the coordinates of all the points with gold.

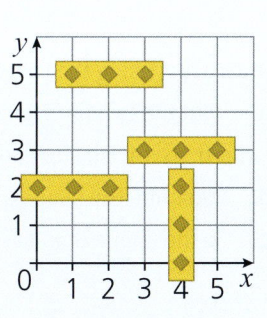

61

5 In this puzzle the S has been translated four squares right and two squares up. 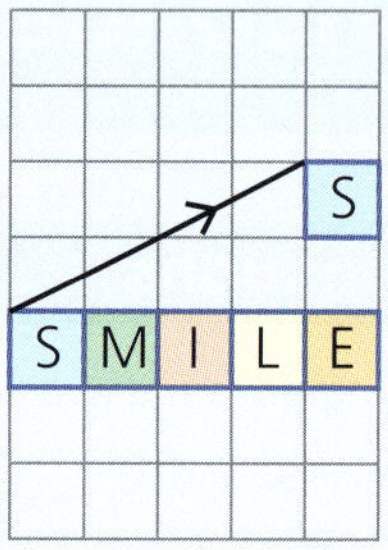
  a Draw the remaining tiles after these translations.
     • Translate M by one square right and two squares up.
     • Translate I by one square left and two squares up.
     • Translate L by three squares left and two squares up.
     • Translate E by one square left and two squares up.
     What word have you made?
  b Write down the translations which move the letters in this word to make another anagram of SMILE in the bottom row.
     Ask a partner to check your anagram.

6 Carry out the following transformations on shape A.
  a Rotate A 180° about P.
  b Reflect A in the mirror line.

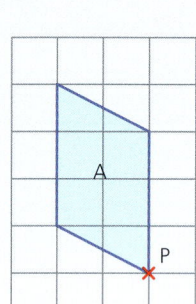

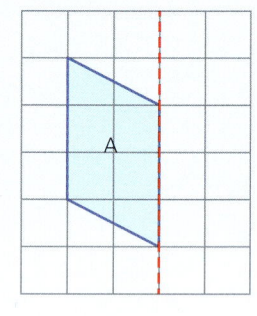

Band 2 questions

7 a Describe each of these translations.
      i   A to D
      ii   B to A
      iii E to C
      iv   C to E
      v   F to E
      vi   D to B
   b Why is A to C impossible?

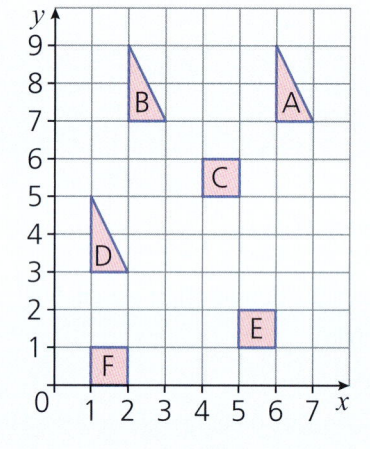

8 Draw axes, using the values of 0 to 14 for x and 0 to 6 for y.
   a Plot these points and join them in order:
      (0, 3), (4, 6), (9, 6), (13, 3), (9, 0), (4, 0) and back to (0, 3).
   b Describe the shape you have drawn.
   c Is the shape regular? Explain your answer fully.

9

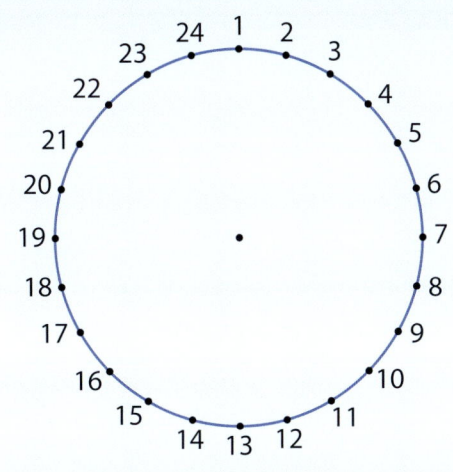

a Measure the diameter of this circle. What is its radius?
b On a copy of the diagram, join points 1, 7, 13, 19 and back to 1. What shape do you get?
c What other regular polygons can you draw using the points on this circle? List the points that you would join.

10 a For each shape, write down the order of rotational symmetry.
b Sketch the shape and mark the centre with a cross.
c Explain how you found the centres of rotational symmetry.

i ii  iii 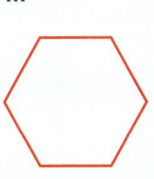 iv

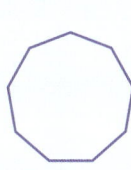

11 A fair six-sided dice is rolled.
On a copy of the probability scale, mark the probability that the number rolled is:

a odd
b 2
c less than 7
d greater than 3
e 8
f a factor of 12.

Part **a** has been done for you.

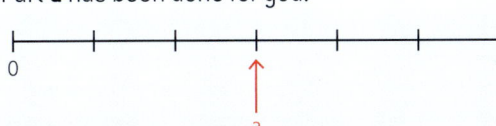

12 Geraint picks a card from a standard pack of 52 playing cards.
Find the probability that his card is:

a the five of spades
b a queen
c not a five
d a heart
e not a heart
f a king, queen or jack.

Curriculum for Wales Mastering Mathematics: Book 1

13 Write down the coordinates of the points A, B, C and D.

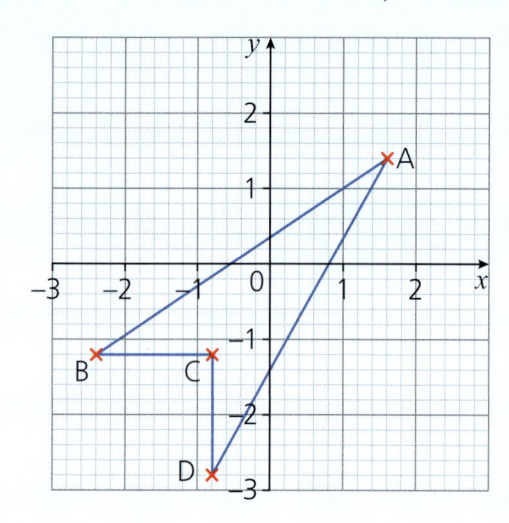

14 Twenty thousand people audition for a television talent show.

Ioan says, 'I'm going to audition too. I've got just as much chance as anyone else of winning.'

Do you think that Ioan is right? Explain your reasoning.

15 On a copy of the diagram, carry out the following transformations on the kite K.

a Reflection in the mirror line.

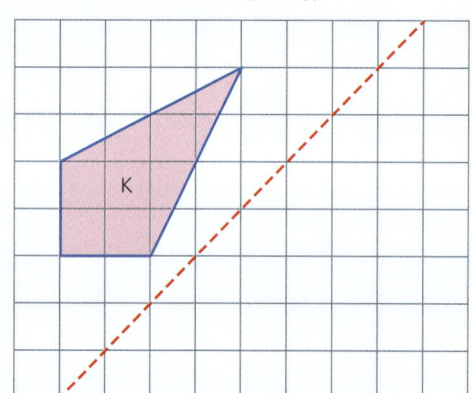

b Rotation of 90° anticlockwise about point P.

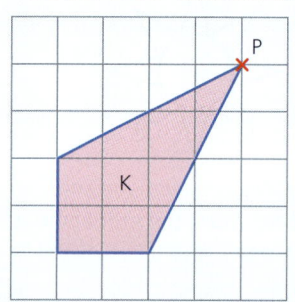

Band 3 questions

16 a Describe these transformations.

i   C → A   ii   A → B

iii C → B

b Compare your answer to **iii** in part **a** to those for **i** and **ii** together. What do you notice?

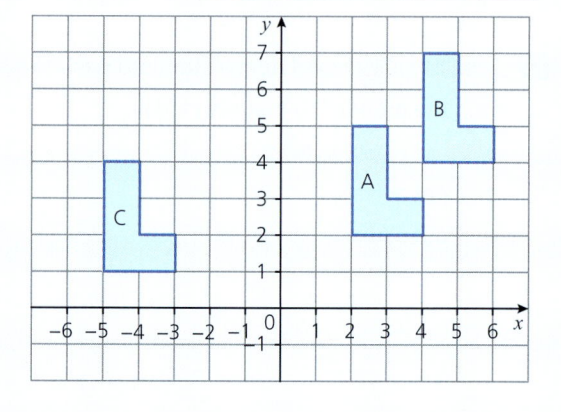

64

Consolidation 1

17 Pedr folds a square of paper twice.

He then cuts out some shapes so that it looks like this diagram.

Which of the diagrams below shows what the paper will look like when Pedr opens it out again?

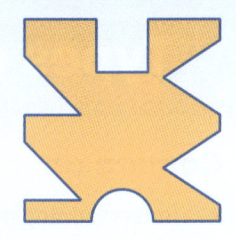

a    b    c    d

18 Usha is playing a game at the school fete. Each turn costs 50 pence.

She draws a ticket from a bucket. Each ticket has one of four symbols on it.

She wins £20 if she gets a star.

She loses if she gets an apple, a banana or a pear.

Symbol	Probabilities
Apple	0.3
Banana	0.4
Pear	0.25
Star	?

a What is the probability of getting a star?

b Usha plays the game 40 times. How much does she spend?

c How many times should she expect to win £20?

d Has the school made a sensible decision for the value of the prize money? Explain your answer.

19 Rhian has a bag containing red, blue and green counters.

The probability of picking a red counter, at random, is $\frac{3}{10}$.

a From this information, what is the smallest number of counters there could be in the bag?

The probability of picking a blue counter is $\frac{1}{4}$.

b What is the probability of picking a green counter?

c What is the smallest number of counters there could be in the bag?

There are 60 red counters.

d How many blue counters and how many green counters are there in the bag?

20 The diagram shows six congruent trapeziums.

a Describe a transformation that maps shape:

  i   P to R
  ii R to S
  iii Q to U
  iv S to P.

b Shape P is rotated onto shape U.

Find the coordinates of the centre of rotation. Describe the rotation fully.

c Shape R is rotated onto shape T.

Find the coordinates of the centre of rotation. Describe the rotation fully.

65

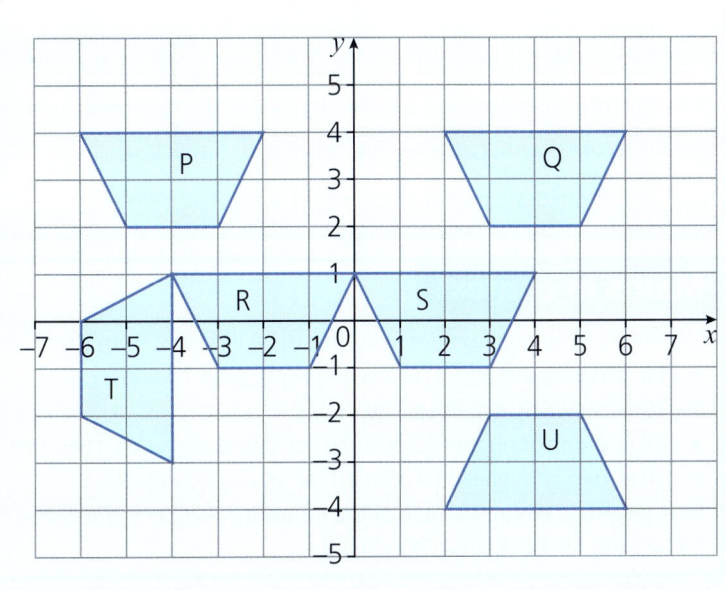

4 Types of number

Coming up...
- Understanding multiples
- Understanding factors
- Finding prime numbers
- Using powers and roots

Last one standing!

Mr Lloyd has 30 students in his maths class.

He gives each student a card with a number from 1 to 30 on it.

All the students start off by sitting down.

Mr Lloyd asks everyone in the one times table to stand up – everyone stands up.

Mr Lloyd asks everyone holding a card in the two times table to sit down.

① Which students sit down? Who is left standing up?

When a student changes their position, they:
- sit down if they were standing
- stand up if they were sitting.

Mr Lloyd asks everyone holding a card in the three times table to change their position.

② Which students are now standing up?

Use a copy of this table to help you. (In Welsh, 'up' is 'i fyny' and 'down' is 'i lawr'.)

1	2	3	4	5	6	7	8	9	10
Up	Up Down	Up	Up Down	Up	Up Down	Up	Up	Up	Up
11	12	13	14	15	16	17	18	19	20
Up	Up	Up	Up	Up	Up	Up	Up	Up	Up
21	22	23	24	25	26	27	28	29	30
Up	Up	Up	Up	Up	Up	Up	Up	Up	Up

Mr Lloyd then asks everyone holding a card in the four times table to change their position.

He carries on like this until he reaches the 30 times table.

③ Which children are left standing up at the end? Why?

Maths in context

The Welsh language number system can be different from the English language number system.
- 18 is 'deunaw' (two 9s) or 'un deg wyth' (one 10 and 8).
- 20 is 'ugain' or 'dau ddeg' (two 10s).
- 25 is 'pump ar hugain' (5 onto 20) or 'dau ddeg pump' (two 10s and 5).
- 30 is 'deg ar hugain' (10 onto 20) or 'tri deg' (three 10s).

Find two ways of saying each of the following numbers in Welsh:
34, 40, 42, 50, 56, 60, 64, 70, 80, 90.

4 Types of number

4.1 Multiples

Skill checker

Answer as many of these as you can in 1 minute.

① 3 × 5	② 6 × 2	③ 7 × 8	④ 4 × 7
⑤ 11 × 10	⑥ 4 × 8	⑦ 10 × 7	⑧ 9 × 9
⑨ 8 × 3	⑩ 9 × 12	⑪ 10 × 12	⑫ 9 × 8
⑬ 6 × 6	⑭ 2 × 5	⑮ 9 × 2	⑯ 9 × 6
⑰ 3 × 7	⑱ 4 × 11	⑲ 5 × 7	⑳ 3 × 9
㉑ 2 × 8	㉒ 3 × 6	㉓ 8 × 6	㉔ 11 × 3
㉕ 6 × 5	㉖ 11 × 12	㉗ 8 × 5	㉘ 9 × 7
㉙ 4 × 2	㉚ 7 × 7	㉛ 12 × 12	㉜ 3 × 4
㉝ 2 × 6	㉞ 5 × 11	㉟ 9 × 3	㊱ 4 × 12
㊲ 3 × 10	㊳ 2 × 11	㊴ 6 × 9	㊵ 8 × 8

Mark your answers and write down how many you answered correctly in 1 minute.
Try to improve your score by answering these questions again.

▶ Using multiples

The **multiples** of 7 are the numbers in the seven times table.

1 × 7 = 7
2 × 7 = 14
3 × 7 = 21
4 × 7 = 28
5 × 7 = 35

So the first five multiples of 7 are:

7, 14, 21, 28, 35, …

Note
You can carry on writing multiples forever.
There is an infinite number of multiples.

Worked example

Find the **lowest** number that is a multiple of both 8 and 12.

Solution

Write down the first few multiples of 8 and 12.

Multiples of 8 are: 8   16   ㉔   32   40   ㊽   56   64   ㊴72   80 …

Multiples of 12 are: 12   ㉔   36   ㊽   60   ㊴72   84 …

24, 48, 72, … are multiples of **both** 8 and 12.
So, 24 is the lowest number that is a multiple of both 8 and 12.

24, 48 and 72 are called **common multiples** of 8 and 12.
24 is the lowest of these common multiples.
You say that 24 is the **lowest common multiple** (or LCM) of 8 and 12.

67

Curriculum for Wales **Mastering Mathematics: Book 1**

> **Activity**
>
> ## Fizz-buzz
>
> Play a game of 'fizz-buzz' in a small group.
>
> Count up from 1, with each player in turn saying one number.
>
> When you get to a multiple of 3 say 'fizz'.
>
> When you get to a multiple of 5 say 'buzz'.
>
> When the number is a multiple of 3 and of 5 say 'fizz-buzz'.
>
> The first person to make a mistake loses the game!
>
> One Two Fizz Four Buzz Fizz Seven

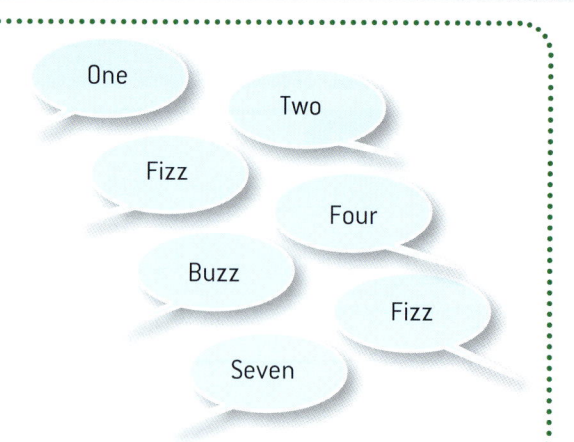

4.1 Now try these

Band 1 questions

Fluency

1 Write down the first five multiples of:

  a 4   b 5   c 9   d 10

Logical reasoning

2 a List the first ten multiples of 6.
   b List the first five multiples of 12.
   c What is the relationship between the lists in part **a** and part **b**?

Fluency

3 Write down:
   a all the multiples of 8 between 11 and 30
   b all the multiples of 12 between 100 and 200
   c all the multiples of 7 between 15 and 50.

Strategic competence

4 Parinda thinks of a number.

   She writes down some multiples of her number.

   8   32   64

   What number could Parinda be thinking of?
   Find three different answers.

Band 2 questions

Fluency

5 Find the answers to the following calculations.
   a The third multiple of 3 plus the second multiple of 20.
   b The seventh multiple of 2 multiplied by the second multiple of 7.
   c The third multiple of 3 subtracted from the fourth multiple of 4.
   d The tenth multiple of 7 divided by the seventh multiple of 5.

68

6 Copy all the numbers from the box below.

6	4	20	35	10	25
18	9	15	8	12	21
45	27	60	24	28	16

a Draw a circle around each multiple of 3.
b Draw a square around each multiple of 4.
c Draw a triangle around each multiple of 5.
d Which numbers need two shapes?
e Which number needs three shapes?
   Is this the smallest number that would need three shapes?
   Give a reason for your answer.

7 a What are the first ten multiples of 5?
b What are the first ten multiples of 6?
c What is the lowest common multiple (LCM) of 5 and 6?

8 Find the lowest common multiple (LCM) of each of these pairs of numbers.
a 3 and 4   b 6 and 9   c 6 and 10
d 10 and 20   e 10 and 15   f 20 and 25

9 Danesh says that the lowest common multiple of 12 and 15 is 180 as 12 × 15 = 180.
Amir says that Danesh is wrong.
Who is correct? Explain your answer fully.

10 Alys and Ffion play a game of 'fizz-buzz'.
They manage to get up to 100.

See the Activity on page 68 for the rules.

a How many times did someone say 'fizz'?
b How many times did someone say 'buzz'?
c How many times did someone say 'fizz-buzz'?

Band 3 questions

11 Alys and Ffion play a game called 'fizz-buzz-bang'.
The rules are the same as for 'fizz-buzz' but now, if the number is a multiple of 7, they say 'bang'.
What's the first number that is reached where someone says:
a 'fizz-bang'
b 'buzz-bang'
c 'fizz-buzz-bang'?

12 Copy and complete this multiplication grid.

×				
	15			
		2	11	
		20		40
	30		66	

69

13 Aki thinks of a number.

It is in the five times table and the nine times table.

Aki's number is less then 200.

What could Aki's number be? How many possible answers are there?

14 Work out the lowest common multiple of:

a 2, 3 and 8

b 8, 10 and 12.

15 Lewys and Carlos have a car race. They each drive multiple laps around a race track.

Lewys's car completes the race in 5 minutes and Carlos's car takes 7 minutes.

a How long is it before Lewys overtakes Carlos when they pass through the starting position?

b When this happens, how many laps has each car completed?

c Does Lewys overtake Carlos anywhere else on the circuit?

d If so, where does this happen and after how long?

4.2 Factors and primes

Skill checker

Answer as many of these as you can in 1 minute.

① 20 ÷ 4   ② 36 ÷ 6   ③ 18 ÷ 2   ④ 30 ÷ 5
⑤ 56 ÷ 7   ⑥ 32 ÷ 8   ⑦ 42 ÷ 6   ⑧ 72 ÷ 8
⑨ 24 ÷ 3   ⑩ 144 ÷ 12 ⑪ 11 ÷ 11   ⑫ 12 ÷ 4
⑬ 81 ÷ 9   ⑭ 20 ÷ 5   ⑮ 9 ÷ 3   ⑯ 18 ÷ 3
⑰ 72 ÷ 9   ⑱ 24 ÷ 8   ⑲ 56 ÷ 8   ⑳ 63 ÷ 9
㉑ 45 ÷ 5   ㉒ 21 ÷ 7   ㉓ 16 ÷ 4   ㉔ 77 ÷ 11
㉕ 42 ÷ 7   ㉖ 18 ÷ 9   ㉗ 99 ÷ 9   ㉘ 80 ÷ 8
㉙ 32 ÷ 4   ㉚ 40 ÷ 8   ㉛ 132 ÷ 11 ㉜ 8 ÷ 2
㉝ 54 ÷ 6   ㉞ 49 ÷ 7   ㉟ 25 ÷ 5   ㊱ 60 ÷ 5
㊲ 8 ÷ 4   ㊳ 6 ÷ 6   ㊴ 35 ÷ 7   ㊵ 44 ÷ 11

Mark your answers and write down how many you answered correctly in 1 minute.

Try to improve your score by answering these questions again.

▶ Finding factors

A **factor** is a number that divides into another number **exactly**.

A factor is always a whole number.

The factors of 12 are:

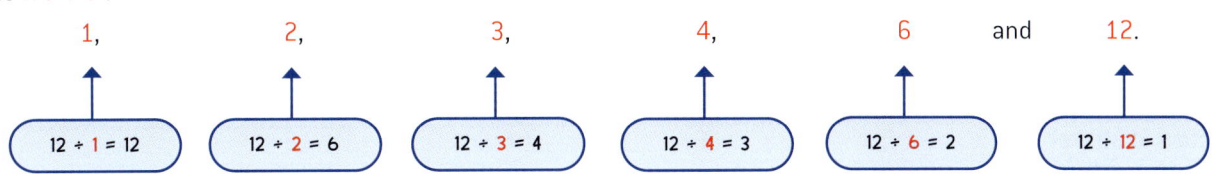

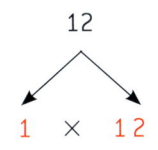

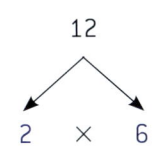

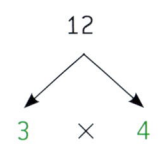

1,   2,   3,   4,   6   and   12.

12 ÷ 1 = 12   12 ÷ 2 = 6   12 ÷ 3 = 4   12 ÷ 4 = 3   12 ÷ 6 = 2   12 ÷ 12 = 1

12
1 × 12

12
2 × 6

12
3 × 4

Note

Factors come in pairs.

Every number has 1 and itself as factors.

Worked example

Find all the factors of 30.

Solution

Use factor pairs and work systematically so you don't miss any factors.

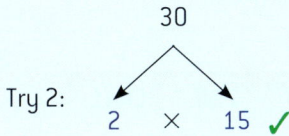

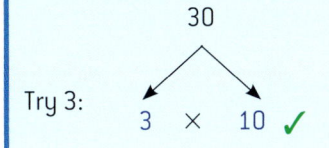

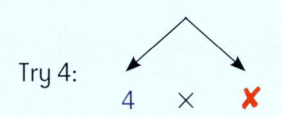

Try 1:   30 → 1 × 30 ✓

Try 2:   30 → 2 × 15 ✓

Try 3:   30 → 3 × 10 ✓

Try 4:   30 → 4 × ✗   4 is not a factor as 30 isn't divisible by 4.

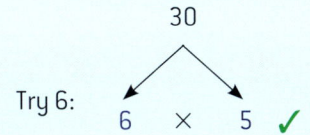

Try 5:   30 → 5 × 6 ✓

Try 6:   30 → 6 × 5 ✓   You've already found this pair so you can stop.

List all the factors in order: 1, 2, 3, 5, 6, 10, 15 and 30.

Curriculum for Wales **Mastering Mathematics: Book 1**

> **Worked example**
>
> Find the **highest** number that is a factor of both 12 and 30.
>
> **Solution**
>
> Write down the factors of 12 and 30.
>
> Factors of 12 are: ① ② ③ 4 ⑥ 12
>
> Factors of 30 are: ① ② ③ 5 ⑥ 10 15 30
>
> 1, 2, 3 and 6 are factors of **both** 12 and 30.
>
> So, 6 is the highest number that is a factor of both 12 and 30.

1, 2, 3 and 6 are called **common factors** of 12 and 30.

6 is the highest of these common factors.

You say that 6 is the **highest common factor** (or HCF) of 12 and 30.

Activity

Divisibility tests

You can often tell if a number is divisible by another number by looking at its digits.

Use your calculator to help you find the rules for divisibility tests.

① Which of these numbers are divisible by 2?

| 42 | 103 | 3078 | 96 | 2114 | 500 | 796 | 8641 |

Copy and complete this statement.

A number is divisible by 2 if its last digit is _____.

② Which of these numbers are divisible by 10?

Which of these numbers are divisible by 5?

| 45 | 650 | 1090 | 65 | 702 | 20 | 70 | 785 |

Copy and complete these two statements.

A number is divisible by 10 if its last digit is _____.

A number is divisible by 5 if its last digit is _____.

③ a Write out your three times table.

Add up the digits in each answer. What do you notice?

b Which of these numbers are divisible by 3?

| 83 | 258 | 4196 | 102 | 1137 | 200 | 736 |

c Copy and complete this statement.

A number is divisible by 3 if its digits _____.

④ a Write out your nine times table.

Add up the digits in each answer. What do you notice?

72

b Which of these numbers are divisible by 9?

| 108 | 7135 | 103 | 284 | 243 | 8226 |

Copy and complete this statement.

A number is divisible by 9 if its digits _____.

⑤ Can you find divisibility tests for 4, 6 and 8?

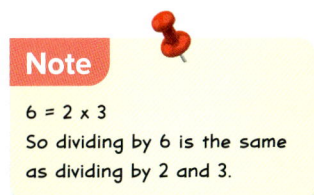

Note
6 = 2 × 3
So dividing by 6 is the same as dividing by 2 and 3.

▶ Prime numbers

A **prime number** has exactly two factors: 1 and itself.

For example, 13 is prime because the only factors of 13 are 1 and 13.

The first 5 prime numbers are 2, 3, 5, 7 and 11.

2 is the **only even prime** number.

1 is **not** a prime number as it only has one factor – itself!

Worked example

a Is 27 a prime number?

b Is 19 a prime number?

Solution

a From your times tables: 1 × 27 = 27 and 3 × 9 = 27.

27 has 1, 3, 9 and 27 as factors and so it is not prime.

b 19 is prime as its only factors are 1 and 19.

> 19 isn't the answer to any multiplication other than 1 × 19 and 19 × 1.

Discussion activity

Investigate where prime numbers are used in science and technology.

4.2 Now try these

Band 1 questions

1 a Write down all the factors of each of these numbers.

  i 3 **ii** 4 **iii** 5 **iv** 6 **v** 7 **vi** 8 **vii** 9 **viii** 10

  b Which of the numbers in part **a** are prime?

2 Eight oranges can be packed into rectangular boxes in two different ways.

How many different ways can you pack these numbers of oranges into rectangular boxes?

  a 12 oranges   **b** 18 oranges
  c 15 oranges   **d** 20 oranges
  e 7 oranges   **f** 17 oranges

What do you notice about your answers?

1 by 8

2 by 4

3 a Copy and complete these number sentences.

　　i $1 \times \square = 24$　　**ii** $2 \times \square = 24$　　**iii** $3 \times \square = 24$　　**iv** $4 \times \square = 24$

b List the factors of 24.

c Explain why 24 is not a prime number.

4 a Which factor pair is missing for the number 40?

　　1×40　　2×20　　4×10

b List all the factors of 40.

5 a Which factor pair is wrong for the number 56?

　　1×56　　2×28　　4×14　　6×9　　7×8

b List all the factors of 56.

6 Mr Gharaati says that you can make any even number greater than 2 by adding together two prime numbers.

For example:

$10 = 3 + 7$ or $10 = 5 + 5$

Copy and complete the table to show Mr Gharaati is right for even numbers up to 20.

Number	4	6	8	10	12	14	16	18	20
Prime sum				3 + 7 or 5 + 5					

Which numbers have two different answers?

Band 2 questions

7 Use factor pairs to help you to find all the factors of each of these numbers.

　a 36　　**b** 55　　**c** 60　　**d** 72

8 List all the prime numbers between 1 and 30.

9 a Is 45 a prime number?

　　Give a reason for your answer.

b Explain why 23 518 is not a prime number.

10 a Use factor pairs to find all the factors of:

　　i 18　　**ii** 30

b Write down the common factors of 18 and 30.

c Write down the highest common factor of 24 and 30.

11 Find the highest common factor of each of these pairs of numbers.

　a 4 and 6　　**b** 8 and 16　　**c** 12 and 15

　d 20 and 30　　**e** 10 and 15　　**f** 24 and 40

4   Types of number

12 Solve each of these puzzles to find the four mystery numbers.

a
- ☆ is a prime number
- ☆ is a factor of 49

b
- ◎ is a common factor of 12 and 18
- ◎ is even
- ◎ is not prime

c
- ✻ is even and has 2 digits
- ✻ is a factor of 72
- ✻ is a multiple of 3
- ✻ is one more than a multiple of 5

d
- ○ is a factor of 15
- ○ is a factor of 21
- ○ is a prime number

Band 3 questions

13 Find the highest common factor of each of these pairs of numbers.
- a 36 and 60
- b 30 and 72
- c 40 and 100
- d 90 and 210

14 Find:
- a a three-digit number that doesn't have 2 as a factor
- b a three-digit number that doesn't have 2 or 3 as a factor
- c a three-digit number that doesn't have 2, 3 or 5 as a factor
- d a four-digit number that doesn't have 2, 3, 5, 7 or 11 as a factor
- e a four-digit number with exactly three factors.

15 The Sieve of Eratosthenes is an ancient method used to find prime numbers.

2	3	4	5	6	7
8	9	10	11	12	13
14	15	16	17	18	19
20	21	22	23	24	25
26	27	28	29	30	31
32	33	34	35	36	37
38	39	40	41	42	43
44	45	46	47	48	49
50	51	52	53	54	55
56	57	58	59	60	61
62	63	64	65	66	67
68	69	70	71	72	73
74	75	76	77	78	79
80	81	82	83	84	85
86	87	88	89	90	91
92	93	94	95	96	97

This grid shows steps 1 to 4.

All the multiples of 6 are in this column.

Strategic competence

Here is how it works:

Step 1: Make a list of numbers starting with 2.
Step 2: Circle 2. ← *This is the first prime number.*
Step 3: Cross out all the multiples of 2.
Step 4: Circle 3. ← *This is the next prime number.*
Step 5: Cross out all the multiples of 3.
Step 6: Circle the next number which hasn't been crossed out.
Cross out all the multiples of this number. ← *All the multiples of 4 (including 4) have been crossed out as they are all even.*
Step 7: Repeat **Step 6** until all the numbers on the grid are circled or crossed out.

All the circled numbers are prime numbers.

Which columns are all the primes in? Why does this happen?

Cross-curricular activity

Discuss with your teacher how to write a computer program that could test whether a number up to 100 is prime or not.

16 Rhiannon has some sweets that she wants to share with her friends.

She has 112 toffees and 72 marshmallows.

Rhiannon wants all of her friends to have an equal number of each type of sweet.

  a   What is the greatest number of friends Rhiannon can share the sweets with?
       How many sweets do they each get?

Rhiannon eats two toffees and two marshmallows.

Rhiannon says, 'Now I can share my sweets equally with more people!'

  b   Is Rhiannon right? Explain your answer.

4.3 Powers and roots

Skill checker

① Check how much your times tables have improved by answering the questions in the Skill checkers on pages 67 and 70.

② Work out these.
   a $2 \times 3 \times 3$
   b $2 \times 7 \times 5$
   c $4 \times 3 \times 5$
   d $5 \times 4 \times 2$
   e $2 \times 2 \times 2$
   f $4 \times 4 \times 4$

③ Write down the first five multiples of 5.

④ List all the factors of 100.

▶ Square numbers

Conceptual understanding

A **square number** is the result of multiplying an integer by itself.

The first five square numbers are:

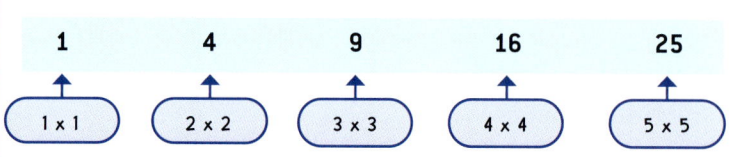

1	4	9	16	25
1 × 1	2 × 2	3 × 3	4 × 4	5 × 5

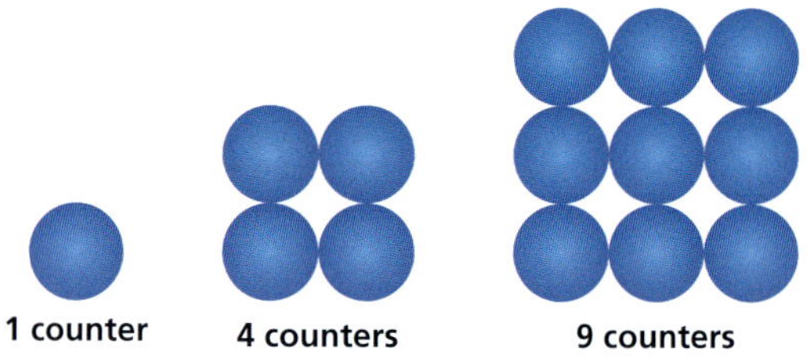

Square numbers get their name because you can arrange them into squares.

1 counter   4 counters   9 counters

You use a small 2 to show that you are squaring a number like this:

$3^2 = 3 \times 3 = 9$

Say '3 squared equals 3 times 3 equals 9'.

The opposite of squaring is **square rooting**.

You use the symbol $\sqrt{}$ to show that you are square rooting.

$\sqrt{9} = 3$

Say 'the square root of 9 equals 3 because 3 times 3 is 9'.

Activity

Find out how to square and square root numbers on your calculator.

The button to square numbers may look like this: x^2.

The button to square root numbers may look like this: $\sqrt{\Box}$.

Use your calculator to work out these.

a 17^2
b 23^2
c $\sqrt{2500}$
d $\sqrt{1296}$

▶ Cube numbers

A **cube number** is the result of multiplying an integer by itself twice.

The first five cube numbers are:

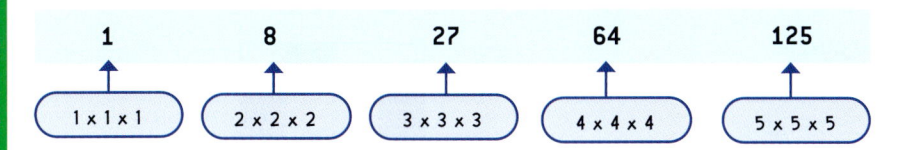

1	8	27	64	125
1 x 1 x 1	2 x 2 x 2	3 x 3 x 3	4 x 4 x 4	5 x 5 x 5

Cube numbers get their name because you can arrange them into cubes.

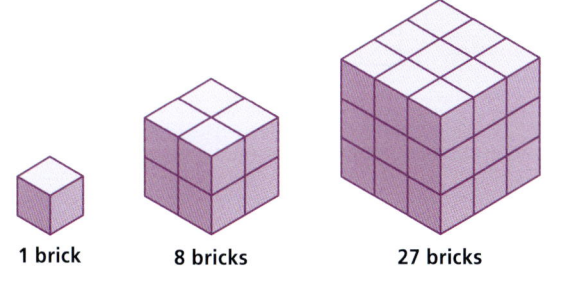

1 brick   8 bricks   27 bricks

You use a small 3 to show that you are cubing a number like this:

$2^3 = 2 \times 2 \times 2 = 8$

Say '2 cubed equals 2 times 2 times 2 equals 8'.

The opposite of cubing is **cube rooting**.

You use the symbol $\sqrt[3]{}$ to show that you are cube rooting.

$\sqrt[3]{8} = 2$

Say 'the cube root of 8 equals 2 as 2 times 2 times 2 is 8'.

4.3 Now try these

Band 1 questions

Fluency

1. Write down the first ten square numbers.
2. Write down the first six cube numbers.
3. Find the square root of:
   - a 16
   - b 25
   - c 100
4. Find the cube root of:
   - a 1
   - b 27
   - c 125

Strategic competence

5. Efa thinks of a number.

   She says, 'My number is a square number. It is less than 100. It is also a cube number.'

   What number is Efa thinking of? Find two possible answers.

Band 2 questions

Fluency

6. Copy and complete these.
   - a $9 = \square^2$
   - b $25 = \square^2$
   - c $100 = \square^2$
7. Work out these.
   - a $\sqrt{16}$
   - b $\sqrt{81}$
   - c $\sqrt{144}$
8. Work out these.
   - a $\sqrt[3]{64}$
   - b $\sqrt[3]{8}$
   - c $\sqrt[3]{216}$

Strategic competence

9. Copy and complete this cross-number puzzle.

   Across
   1. 4^2
   4. 7^2
   5. The square root of 25
   8. The cube root of 8
   9. 11^3

   Down
   2. 4^3
   3. $\sqrt{9}$
   6. 11^2
   7. The square root of 169

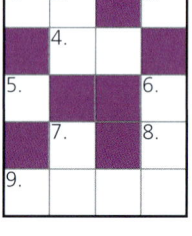

10. Enfys has 50 counters.

    Can she arrange them **all** into:
    - a 1 square
    - b 2 squares
    - c 3 squares
    - d 4 squares?

    For each part, either show how Enfys should arrange them or explain why it is impossible.

Band 3 questions

Fluency

11. Calculate the difference between each pair.
    - a 3^2 and 2^3
    - b 5^2 and 4^2
    - c 5^3 and 4^3

78

12 Petra is a gardener. She has 100 flowers to plant in a bed.

There are 48 red flowers, 32 yellow flowers, 12 blue flowers and 8 white flowers.

The garden designer has said that each colour of flower should be planted to make a rectangle and that all four rectangles should be arranged to make a square. Petra has to use all of the flowers.

   a   How many flowers will be along each side of the square?

   b   What size will each of the four rectangles need to be in order to make the square?

13 A tiler uses 100 square tiles to tile two square panels.

The tiler doesn't cut any of the tiles.

   a   Is it possible for the panels to be the same size? Explain why/why not.

   b   How many tiles does he use for each panel?

14 Dafydd has 80 toy bricks. Can he arrange them **all** into:

   a   one cube

   b   two cubes

   c   three cubes?

Explain your answers fully.

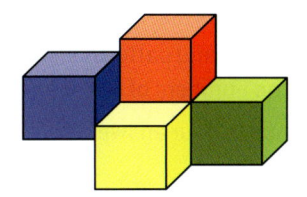

Key words

Here is a list of the key words you met in this chapter.

Cube	Cube root	Factor
Highest common factor (HCF)	Integer	Lowest common multiple (LCM)
Multiple	Prime	Sum
Square	Square number	Square root

Use the glossary at the back of this book to check any you are unsure about.

Curriculum for Wales Mastering Mathematics: Book 1

Review exercise: types of number

Band 1 questions

1 Write down:
- a the fifth multiple of 3
- b the eighth multiple of 16
- c the third multiple of 72.

2 Idris makes buns. He sells them in packs of four.

a Copy and complete the table.

Number of packs	1	2	3	4	5	10
Number of buns	4					

b Describe any patterns that you can see in the numbers of buns.

c Shade in your answers on a copy of this grid.

d Shade in the numbers of buns for six, seven, eight and nine packs onwards. What patterns are there?

1	2	3	4	5	6	7	8	9	10
11	12	13	14	15	16	17	18	19	20
21	22	23	24	25	26	27	28	29	30
31	32	33	34	35	36	37	38	39	40
41	42	43	44	45	46	47	48	49	50
51	52	53	54	55	56	57	58	59	60
61	62	63	64	65	66	67	68	69	70
71	72	73	74	75	76	77	78	79	80
81	82	83	84	85	86	87	88	89	90
91	92	93	94	95	96	97	98	99	100

3 Which of these numbers are:
- a square numbers
- b cube numbers?

  6   8   9   22   25   45   64   100

4
- a List the factors of 16.
- b Which of the factors in part **a** are:
  - i square numbers
  - ii prime numbers
  - iii cube numbers?

5
- a Find all the factors of 35.
- b Find all the factors of 36.
- c Find all the factors of 37.
- d i Which of the numbers 35, 36 and 37 is a prime number?
  - ii How can you tell from its factors?
- e i Which of the numbers 35, 36 and 37 is a square number?
  - ii How can you tell from its factors?

6 Which of these numbers are prime?

  5   19   27   37   39   46

Band 2 questions

7 Copy and complete this table.

Number	1	2	3	4	5	6	7	8	9	10
Number of factors	1	2	2							

- a i List the numbers which have only two factors.
  - ii What type of numbers are these?
- b i List the numbers with an odd number of factors.
  - ii What type of numbers are these?

8 a List the factors of 96.
   b Identify the factors of 96 that are:
      i odd numbers   **ii** prime numbers   **iii** multiples of 4
      iv cube numbers   **v** the product of two of the other factors.

> The result of two numbers multiplied together is called the 'product' of those numbers.

9 Say whether each of these statements is true or false.
   a All multiples of 2 are even numbers.
   b All multiples of 3 are odd numbers.
   c Apart from 1 and 12, the number 12 is a multiple of three other numbers.
   d Apart from 1 and 17, the number 17 is not a multiple of any number.
   e If you add two odd numbers, your answer is a multiple of 2.

10 Find all the square numbers between 27 and 56.

Band 3 questions

11 Here is a list of the first six multiples of a number. Each of the digits has been replaced by a coloured shape. What digit does each shape represent? Explain how you know.

12 Find:
   a two square numbers that add to give another square number
   b three square numbers that add to give another square number
   c two prime numbers that add to give another prime number
   d three prime numbers that add to give another prime number
   e two prime numbers that add to give a square number
   f two square numbers that add to give a prime number.

13 Kwame says that it is possible to make every square number between 4 and 100 by adding two prime numbers.
   a Show that Kwame is correct.
   b Is it possible to make any square number by adding two prime numbers? Explain your answer.

> **Note** Try making some square numbers that are greater than 100.

14 How many squares are there on a chess board?

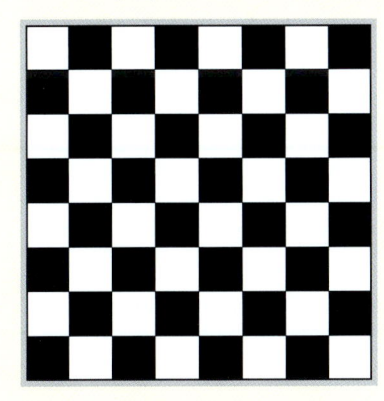

> **Note** There are more than 64. Work systematically so you don't miss any!

5 Calculations

Coming up...
- Multiplying and dividing whole numbers
- Understanding remainders
- Solving word problems
- Using BIDMAS

Number cards

Nerys has some number cards.

| 2 | 6 | 9 | 1 | 5 |

① How should Nerys arrange the five number cards so they show the
  i greatest   ii least
  possible number?

② How should Nerys arrange the number cards so that these calculations have the
  i greatest   ii least
  possible positive answers?

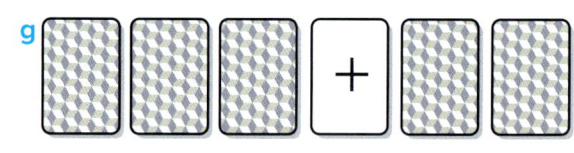

a ☐ + ☐

b ☐ − ☐

c ☐ × ☐

d ☐☐ + ☐☐

e ☐☐ − ☐☐

f ☐☐ × ☐☐

g ☐☐ + ☐☐☐

h ☐☐☐ − ☐☐

i ☐☐ × ☐☐☐

Maths in context

Robert Recorde (1512–1558) was a Welsh mathematician. He invented the equal sign '='. He also introduced the already existing plus sign and addition symbol '+' to our nation.

Find out about other symbols and mathematical operations. When were they first used? Who invented them?

5 Calculations

5.1 Multiplying and dividing whole numbers

Skill checker

① Find the **sum** of these pairs of numbers.

> The sum is the answer when you add numbers.

    a   63 and 22   b   145 and 251   c   205 and 473
    d   149 and 38   e   576 and 47   f   603 and 98

② Work out these.

    a 3×10 b 5×100 c 8×1000
    d 17×100 e 20×10 f 90×1000

③ Work out these.

    a i 4×6 ii 6×4
    b i $43 + 65$ ii $65 + 43$
    c i $2 \times 3 \times 4 \times 5$ ii $2 \times 4 \times 3 \times 5$ iii $5 \times 2 \times 4 \times 3$
    d i $76 + 125 + 342$ ii $125 + 342 + 76$ iii $176 + 325 + 42$

What do you notice? Is this always true?

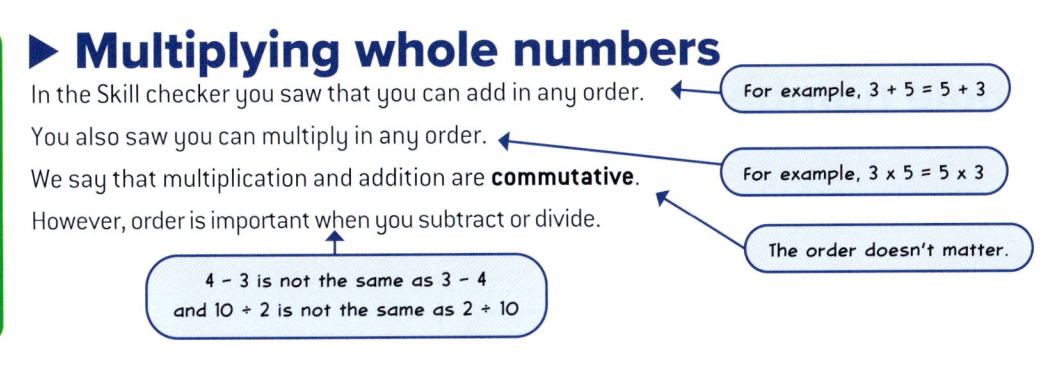

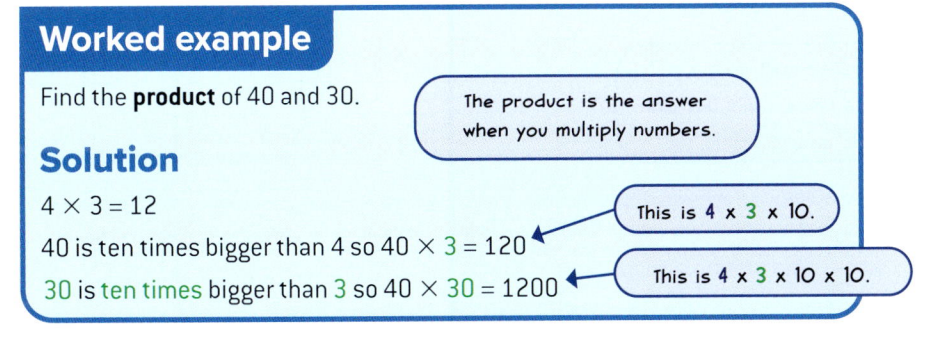

▶ Multiplying whole numbers

In the Skill checker you saw that you can add in any order.

> For example, $3 + 5 = 5 + 3$

You also saw you can multiply in any order.

We say that multiplication and addition are **commutative**.

> For example, $3 \times 5 = 5 \times 3$
> The order doesn't matter.

However, order is important when you subtract or divide.

$4 - 3$ is not the same as $3 - 4$
and $10 \div 2$ is not the same as $2 \div 10$

Worked example

Find the **product** of 40 and 30.

> The product is the answer when you multiply numbers.

Solution

$4 \times 3 = 12$

40 is ten times bigger than 4 so $40 \times 3 = 120$ *This is $4 \times 3 \times 10$.*

30 is ten times bigger than 3 so $40 \times 30 = 1200$ *This is $4 \times 3 \times 10 \times 10$.*

The next example shows you two methods you can use to multiply two whole numbers. Make sure you understand each method.

Worked example

Work out 123×26.

Solution

Method 1: Column method

```
      1  2  3
   ×     2  6
   ─────────────
   2  4  6  0    ← 123 × 20
      7₁ 3₁ 8    ← 123 × 6
   ─────────────
   3  1  9  8
   1
```

Method 2: Grid method

Write 123 as $100 + 20 + 3$ and 26 as $20 + 6$

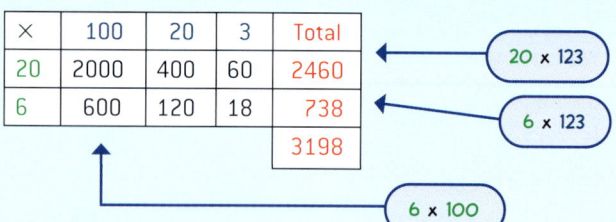

×	100	20	3	Total
20	2000	400	60	2460	← 20 × 123
6	600	120	18	738	← 6 × 123
				3198

↑ 6 × 100

Check: You can use estimation to check that your answer is about right.

Round the numbers to make them easier to multiply.

123×26 is roughly $100 \times 30 = 3000$ which is close to the answer of 3198.

Discussion activity

Are there any other methods that you have encountered before for multiplying large numbers?

▶ Dividing whole numbers

The **inverse** (opposite) of multiplication is division.

For example, $4 \times 5 = 20$ so you can say $20 \div 5 = 4$.

> You can also say $5 \times 4 = 20$ so $20 \div 4 = 5$.

The next example shows you two methods that you can use for division. Make sure you understand each method.

Worked example

Short division

```
       4  6
   6 ) 2 7 ³6
```

← 6 into 2 doesn't go.
6 into 27 goes 4 times with 3 left over.
6 into 36 goes 6 times.

Long division

```
          4 6
      6 ) 2 7 6
         −2 4
         ─────
            3 6
           −3 6
           ─────
              0
```

Check: You can use multiplication to check a division.

$6 \times 46 = 6 \times 40 + 6 \times 6$

$\qquad = 240 + 36$

$\qquad = 276$ ✔

> Since $276 \div 46 = 6$ then $6 \times 46 = 276$.

Conceptual understanding

5 Calculations

Division doesn't always give a whole number answer. Sometimes you are left with a remainder.

Worked example

Work out 371 ÷ 14.

Solution

Finding a remainder

1 × 14 = 14   5 × 14 = 70
2 × 14 = 28   6 × 14 = 84
3 × 14 = 42   7 × 14 = 98
4 × 14 = 56

```
      2 6 r 7
14 ) 3 7 ⁹1
```

14 into 37 goes 2 times with 9 left over.
14 into 91 goes 6 times with 7 left over.

So 371 ÷ 14 = 26 remainder 7.

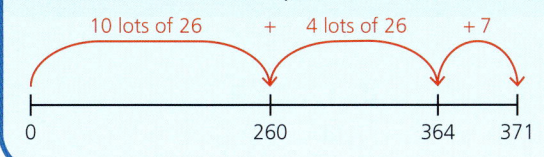

Note

It helps to note down the times table of the number you are dividing by.

Using a decimal

You can carry on the division by adding zeros after the decimal point.

So write 371 as 371.0

Continue the division in the same way as before.

```
      2 6 . 5
14 ) 3 7 ⁹1.⁷0
```

14 into 70 goes 5 times.

You can add as many zeros as you need to!

So 371 ÷ 14 = 26.5

Check: You can use multiplication as a check.

10 lots of 26   +   4 lots of 26   + 7

0   260   364   371

Activity

Multiplication and division short cuts

Number	Multiply	Divide
4	Double and then double again	Halve and then halve again
5	Halve and then multiply by 10	Divide by 10 and then double
8	Double, double and then double again	Halve, halve and then halve again

Look at how Tomos works out these.

1. To find 37 × 4
   Double 37 is 74
   Double 74 is 148
   So 37 × 4 = 148

2. To find 46 × 5
   Half of 46 is 23
   10 × 23 is 230
   So 46 × 5 = 230

3. To find 425 ÷ 5
   425 ÷ 10 = 42.5
   Double 42.5 is 85
   So 425 ÷ 5 = 85

85

① Use the shortcuts to work out these.

    a   172 ÷ 4   **b**   37 × 4   **c**   225 ÷ 5

    d   43 × 8   **e**   2345 ÷ 5   **f**   8 × 17

    g   208 ÷ 8   **h**   432 × 5   **i**   4 × 123

Why do these shortcuts work?

Multiplying by numbers that are near multiples of 10

② Look at how Petra works out these.

1. To find 19 × 7	2. To find 31 × 9
20 × 7 = 140	30 × 9 = 270
subtract 1 × 7 = 7	add 1 × 9 = 9
19 × 7 = 133	31 × 9 = 279

Use Petra's method to work out these.

    a   39 × 7   **b**   51 × 9   **c**   79 × 3

    d   71 × 6   **e**   91 × 7   **f**   61 × 9

    g   199 × 12   **h**   301 × 15   **i**   2998 × 8

5.1 Now try these

Band 1 questions

Fluency

① Work out these.

    a   **i**   3 × 4   **b**   **i**   5 × 7   **c**   **i**   6 × 8   **d**   **i**   7 × 9

         ii   3 × 40   **ii**   5 × 70   **ii**   60 × 8   **ii**   70 × 9

         iii   3 × 400   **iii**   5 × 700   **iii**   600 × 8   **iii**   700 × 9

② Work out these.

    a   5 × 30   **b**   30 × 40   **c**   50 × 20

    d   80 × 50   **e**   400 × 3   **f**   70 × 40

Logical reasoning

③ Work out these calculations.

Explain how you can use your answers to parts **i** and **ii** to answer part **iii**.

    a   **i**   5 × 7   **b**   **i**   3 × 9   **c**   **i**   4 × 8   **d**   **i**   6 × 9

         ii   10 × 7   **ii**   20 × 9   **ii**   30 × 8   **ii**   40 × 9

         iii   15 × 7   **iii**   23 × 9   **iii**   34 × 8   **iii**   46 × 9

Fluency

④ Work out these.

    a   **i**   17 × 4   **b**   **i**   239 × 8   **c**   **i**   69 × 7

         ii   17 × 400   **ii**   239 × 8000   **ii**   69 × 70

⑤ Calculate these.

    a   138 ÷ 3   **b**   245 ÷ 5   **c**   156 ÷ 2

    d   234 ÷ 3   **e**   530 ÷ 5   **f**   186 ÷ 6

    g   528 ÷ 4   **h**   756 ÷ 6   **i**   176 ÷ 8

5 Calculations

6 Zoltan works out that 414 ÷ 18 = 23.
    a Use Zoltan's answer to find the answer to 18 × 23.
    b Explain how you know.

Band 2 questions

7 Decide whether the following statements are always true, sometimes true or never true.
    Give examples to explain your reasoning.
    a An even number multiplied by an even number is even.
    b An even number multiplied by an odd number is odd.
    c An odd number multiplied by an odd number is odd.
    d An odd number divided by an odd number is odd.

8 Find the product of each pair of numbers.
    a 43 and 35   **b** 621 and 78   **c** 507 and 93
    d 477 and 23   **e** 517 and 88   **f** 4091 and 238

9 Look at how Luciana works out 19 × 24.

> I know that 10 lots of 24 is 240
> So 20 lots of 24 is 480
> So 19 lots of 24 is 480 − 24
> So 19 × 24 = 456

Work these out using Luciana's method.
    a 29 × 15   **b** 11 × 23   **c** 9 × 47
    d 21 × 33   **e** 43 × 19   **f** 37 × 17

10 Work out these.
    a 985 ÷ 15 = ☐ remainder ☐
    b 460 ÷ 19 = ☐ remainder ☐
    c 315 ÷ 8 = ☐ remainder ☐
    d 170 ÷ 12 = ☐ remainder ☐
    e 350 ÷ 23 = ☐ remainder ☐
    f 300 ÷ 21 = ☐ remainder ☐

11 Tomos and Luciana have each worked out 236 × 48.
Tomos writes: 236 × 48 = 1328
Luciana writes: 236 × 48 = 11 329
Without working out the exact answer, explain why both Tomos and Luciana are wrong.

12 Work out these. Write each of your answers as a decimal.
    a 156 ÷ 24   **b** 248 ÷ 20   **c** 204 ÷ 15
    d 280 ÷ 25   **e** 231 ÷ 28   **f** 171 ÷ 24

Band 3 questions

13 Look at these arithmagons.

a

```
    24
13     21
    15
```

b

```
     7
112     
    336  819
```

c

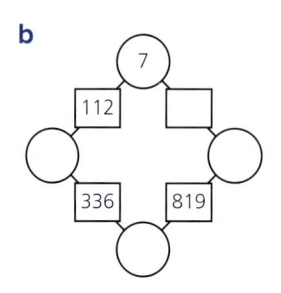

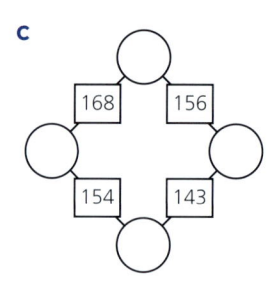

```
     
168     156
   154   143
```

The number in each square is the product of the numbers in the circles adjacent to it.
Fill in the missing numbers.

> Adjacent means 'next to'.

14 In each of these calculations, the letters (A, B, etc.) stand for different single digits (but not zero).
Work out what they could be.
Find two possible answers for parts **a** and **b**.

a
```
   A
 × A
 ───
  BA
```

b
```
   C
 × C
 ───
  D6
```

c
```
  2LM
 ×  M
 ────
 LMNL
```

15 In these calculations each box stands for a missing digit. Can you find them?

a $35 \times 57 = 1\square\square5$

b $\square3 \times 59 = 767$

c $1\square\square \times 23 = 3013$

d $36 \times 4\square = 169\square$

e $56 \times 7\square = 4\square32$

f $48 \times \square7 = 2\square\square6$

g $1\square \times \square9 = 4\square6$

h $\square3 \times \square7 = 41\square\square$

i $\square7 \times \square3 = 1591$

5.2 Solving word problems

Skill checker

Speed test!

See how quickly you can answer these. Can you answer them all in less than 5 minutes?

① a $736 + 203 = \square$ b $14 + 23 + 17 = \square$ c $99 + 98 = \square$ d $230 - 96 = \square$

   e $300 - 97 = \square$ f $180 - 153 = \square$ g $\square \times 7 = 56$ h $421 \times 5 = \square$

   i $72 \div \square = 8$ j $324 \div 4 = \square$ k $6 \times 12 = \square$ l $7 \times 7 = \square$

② a $25 + 60 + 18$ b $41 + 173 + 68$ c $514 + 307 + 266$ d $399 + 28 + 514$

   e $19 - 8$ f $65 - 32$ g $236 - 197$ h $1050 - 688$

   i 403×6 j 589×7 k 327×63 l 516×38

   m $210 \div 6$ n $2891 \div 7$ o $832 \div 8$ p $900 \div 25$

Remainder bingo

Play a game of remainder bingo with a partner.

8	5	7
1	3	11
9	0	14

Each of you needs to:
- Draw a 3 × 3 grid like the one above.
- Choose nine numbers from 0 to 14 and write them anywhere in your grid.

Take turns to choose one of these questions.

| 223 ÷ 15 | 153 ÷ 16 | 46 ÷ 3 | 183 ÷ 12 | 188 ÷ 15 | 515 ÷ 21 | 78 ÷ 8 | 241 ÷ 18 |
| 514 ÷ 20 | 137 ÷ 11 | 184 ÷ 13 | 192 ÷ 16 | 612 ÷ 30 | 108 ÷ 14 | 46 ÷ 7 |

Both of you should answer the question and cross out the remainder if it appears in your grid.

The first person to cross out a line of three wins the game.

The line can be vertical, horizontal or diagonal.

▶ Solving word problems

You often need to use the operations +, −, × and ÷ to solve word problems.

Look out for these key words:
- sum ⎫
- total ⎭ Add the numbers together.
- difference ← Subtract the smaller number from the larger.
- product ← Multiply the numbers together.

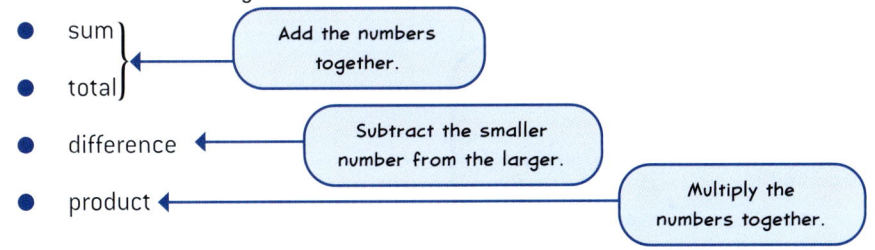

Worked example

Antal travels to school 39 weeks a year.

A weekly travel pass costs £13.

Antal decides to buy an annual pass for £465.

How much money does Antal save?

Annual means 'yearly'.

Solution

Work out how much Antal would spend in a year using weekly passes.

```
      39
   ×  13
   ─────
     390
     117
       2
   ─────
     507
       1
```

The cost of 39 weekly passes is £507.

Find the difference between the prices: £507 − £465 = £42

Antal saves £42.

Note

Remember to write a sentence to answer the question.

Curriculum for Wales Mastering Mathematics: Book 1

▶ Working with remainders

Sometimes when you divide one number by another there is a remainder.

You have to think carefully about what to do with this remainder.

Activity

① Work out 41 ÷ 4.

Write your answer:

    a   as a decimal

    b   using a remainder

    c   as a fraction.

② Solve these problems. How should you deal with the remainder in each case?

    a   Four friends share £41. How much should they each get?

    b   41 bath bombs are packed into boxes.

        Each box contains four bath bombs. How many boxes are there altogether?

    c   A group of 41 students go to a concert. They decide to travel to the concert by car.

        Each car can take four students. How many cars do they need?

    d   Four children share 41 sweets. How many sweets do they each get?

    e   Harri has 41 quarter slices of pizza left over from a party. How many pizzas is this altogether?

Worked example

Mia is making some bracelets.

Each bracelet needs 24 beads. Mia has 320 beads.

How many bracelets can she make?

Solution

It helps to write the times table of the number you are dividing by.

$$24 \overline{)3\,2^{8}0}\quad \begin{array}{c}1\ 3\,r\,8\end{array}$$

1 × 24 = 24

2 × 24 = 48

3 × 24 = 72

4 × 24 = 96

So Mia can make 13 bracelets and will have eight beads left over.

Check that your answer is about right: 320 ÷ 24 is about 300 ÷ 20 = 15

> 24 into 32 goes 1 time with 8 left over.
> 24 into 80 goes 3 times with 8 left over.

> You have to round down because Mia doesn't have enough beads for 14 bracelets.

5 Calculations

5.2 Now try these

Band 1 questions

1. A coach trip costs £65 per person. How much does a trip for a family of five people cost?
2. Three friends share £156 between them. How much should they each get?
3. Four friends share some takeaway pizza. The takeaway costs £68. How much should each friend pay?
4. Four mountain bikes cost £599, £649, £700 and £859. What is the total cost of the bikes?
5. What is the difference in price between a car costing £15 995 and a car costing £10 925?

Band 2 questions

6. Bethan is planning a trip to the Space Museum for her Youth Group. She has £430 to spend. How many people can go?

   SPACE MUSEUM
   Tickets £15 per person

7. The chart shows the distances between some UK airports.

   Maira is a pilot.

   On Monday, she flies from Aberdeen to Leeds Bradford airport and then from Leeds Bradford to Heathrow.

   On Tuesday, she flies from Heathrow to Birmingham International and then from Birmingham International to Aberdeen.

   On which day did Maira fly further? How much further did she fly that day?

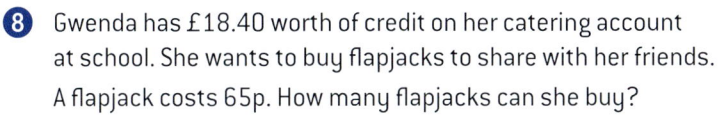

Aberdeen				
551	Heathrow			
437	139	Birmingham International		
130	390	306	Edinburgh	
333	203	118	206	Leeds Bradford

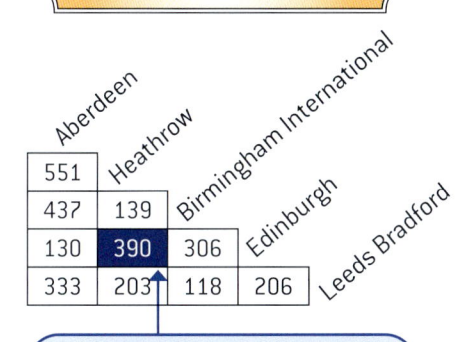

   The distance between Heathrow and Edinburgh is 390 miles.

8. Gwenda has £18.40 worth of credit on her catering account at school. She wants to buy flapjacks to share with her friends. A flapjack costs 65p. How many flapjacks can she buy?

9. 326 students sign up for a school trip. Each minibus can take 16 people.
   How many minibuses are needed?

Band 3 questions

10. Mrs Jones has a budget of £6000 to spend on laptops. Each laptop costs £325.
    Mrs Jones orders as many laptops as her budget allows. How much money does Mrs Jones have left over?

11. A cinema has 16 rows of seats. Each row seats 25 people.

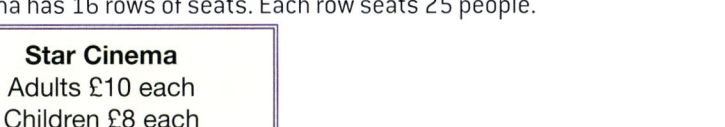

    Star Cinema
    Adults £10 each
    Children £8 each

    For the screening of the latest summer blockbuster, the cinema is full. It sold 145 child tickets.
    How much does the cinema make from the ticket sales?

12 Ysgol Afonffordd orders new tables for the dining hall. There is a choice of two designs.

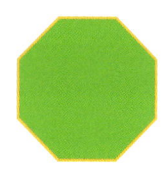

Seats: 6 students
Price: £99 each

Seats: 8 students
Price: £130 each

The dining hall needs to seat 336 students.

Which design of table is cheaper for the school to order?

How much cheaper is this design for the school?

13 In one very strange cricket match, the scores of all 11 batsmen are consecutive numbers.
- a What is the smallest total they could have scored?
- b What are the scores of the batsmen if the total is:
   - i 121 runs
   - ii 374 runs
   - iii 616 runs?
- c Could the total be:
   - i 84 runs
   - ii 95 runs?

> Consecutive numbers follow each other in order.

14 Seimon wins a million pounds in a lottery. He spends:
- £35 000 on a new car
- £17 000 on a holiday.

He spends half of the remaining money on a new house.

How much was Seimon's house?

5.3 BIDMAS

Skill checker

Work out these.

① a 3^2
  b 4^2
  c 12^2

② a 2^3
  b 5^3
  c 10^3

③ a $\sqrt{100}$
  b $\sqrt{49}$
  c $\sqrt{400}$

④ a $\sqrt[3]{1}$
  b $\sqrt[3]{64}$
  c $\sqrt[3]{27}$

5 Calculations

Activity

Jeevika and Nico compare their answers for their maths homework.

Jeevika
1. $3 + 4 \times 2 = 7 \times 2$
   $= 14$
2. $10 - 2 \times 3 = 10 - 6$
   $= 4$
3. $2 \times 4^2 = 8^2$
   $= 64$
4. $7 + 6 - 2 + 3 = 13 - 5$
   $= 8$

Nico
1. $3 + 4 \times 2 = 3 + 8$
   $= 11$
2. $10 - 2 \times 4 = 8 \times 4$
   $= 32$
3. $2 \times 4^2 = 2 \times 16$
   $= 32$
4. $7 + 6 - 2 + 3 = 13 - 2 + 3$
   $= 11 + 3$
   $= 14$

Who is right?

Is it possible that they are **both** correct? Why/why not?

It is important that there is only one correct answer to a calculation like $3 + 4 \times 2$ so mathematicians have agreed on the order in which operations should be carried out.

The order is:

- **B**rackets
- **I**ndices
- **D**ivision
- **M**ultiplication
- **A**ddition
- **S**ubtraction

This means powers (such as squares and cubes) and roots (such as square roots and cube roots).

Discussion activity

Why do we all need to follow the same rules of BIDMAS?

You can use the word BIDMAS to help you remember the right order.

When there is a mixture of + and −, you work from left to right. This is also true when there is a mixture of ÷ and ×.

Worked example

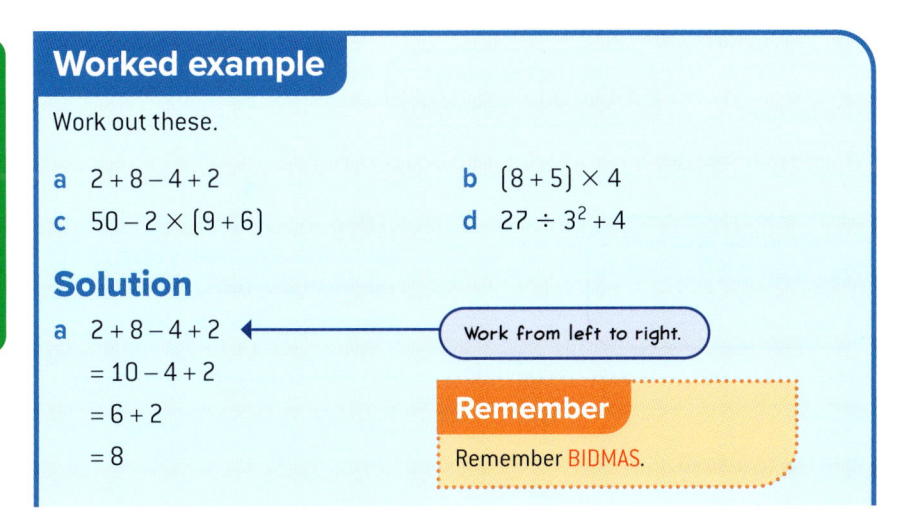

Work out these.

a $2 + 8 - 4 + 2$
b $(8 + 5) \times 4$
c $50 - 2 \times (9 + 6)$
d $27 \div 3^2 + 4$

Solution

a $2 + 8 - 4 + 2$ ← *Work from left to right.*
   $= 10 - 4 + 2$
   $= 6 + 2$
   $= 8$

Remember

Remember BIDMAS.

Conceptual understanding

93

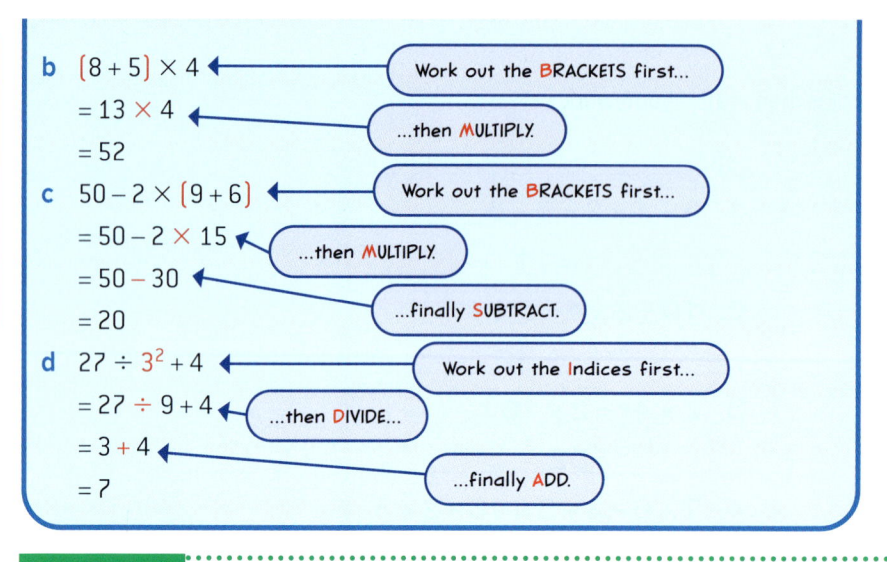

Curriculum for Wales Mastering Mathematics: Book 1

Conceptual understanding

b $(8 + 5) \times 4$ ← Work out the BRACKETS first...
   $= 13 \times 4$ ← ...then MULTIPLY.
   $= 52$

c $50 - 2 \times (9 + 6)$ ← Work out the BRACKETS first...
   $= 50 - 2 \times 15$ ← ...then MULTIPLY.
   $= 50 - 30$ ← ...finally SUBTRACT.
   $= 20$

d $27 \div 3^2 + 4$ ← Work out the Indices first...
   $= 27 \div 9 + 4$ ← ...then DIVIDE...
   $= 3 + 4$ ← ...finally ADD.
   $= 7$

Activity

One, two, three, four...

Jac has some number cards.

| 1 | 2 | 3 | 4 |

Jac uses all four cards, brackets and the operations +, −, ÷ and × to make numbers.

Jac arranges the cards like this:

| 3 | × | (| 4 | − | 1 |) | − | 2 |

What number has Jac made?

Show how you can make all the numbers from 1 to 20.

Conceptual understanding

Some calculations are written as a fraction.

For example, $\dfrac{6 \times 8}{14 - 2}$.

The fraction bar is called a 'vinculum'.

The fraction bar means 'divide' and acts like a bracket.

So $\dfrac{6 \times 8}{14 - 2}$ is the same as $(6 \times 8) \div (14 - 2)$ and you can say:

$\dfrac{6 \times 8}{14 - 2} = (6 \times 8) \div (14 - 2)$

$= 48 \div 12$

$= 4$

You may like to write it like this: $\dfrac{6 \times 8}{14 - 2} = \dfrac{48}{12} = 4$

Note

This is how a fraction is used to represent a division.

Discussion activity

From your discussions, can you now explain the following:
- Why is multiplication carried out before addition?

> Hint: Think about the order in which addition can be done, e.g. 5 + 6 = 6 + 5.
>
> Remember: Addition is commutative.
>
> - Why are calculations inside brackets carried out before other calculations?
>
> Hint: Think about the order in which multiplication can be done, e.g. 5 × 6 = 6 × 5.
>
> Remember: Multiplication is commutative.

5.3 Now try these

Band 1 questions

1 Work out these.
- a 3 × 10 + 4
- b 3 × 100 + 4
- c 3 × (10 + 100) + 4

2 Work out these.
- a (2 + 3) × 5
- b (3 − 2) × 100
- c (2 + 1) × 10
- d 5 × (8 − 4)
- e (10 + 2) ÷ 3
- f (7 + 3) ÷ 2
- g (4 − 1) ÷ 3
- h (10 + 10) × 5
- i (6 ÷ 3) × 5

3 Work out these.
- a (2 + 3) × 6
- b 2 × 6 + 3 × 6
- c (2 + 3) × (5 + 1)
- d 2 × (5 + 1) + 3 × (5 + 1)
- e (2 + 3) × 5 + (2 + 3) × 1
- f 2 × 5 + 2 × 1 + 3 × 5 + 3 × 1

4 Noah and Sofia have been set some maths homework. When they compare their answers, they find that they disagree on every question!

Work out who has got each question right.

Where has the other gone wrong?

Noah
- a 2 + 3 × 4 = 14
- b 1 + 5² = 36
- c 4 + 3 − 1 + 2 = 4
- d 16 + 12 ÷ 4 + 2 = 21
- e 72 ÷ 9 − 1 = 7
- f (4 + 2) × (3 + 5) = 15

Sofia
- a 2 + 3 × 4 = 20
- b 1 + 5² = 26
- c 4 + 3 − 1 + 2 = 8
- d 16 + 12 ÷ 4 + 2 = 9
- e 72 ÷ 9 − 1 = 9
- f (4 + 2) × (3 + 5) = 48

Band 2 questions

5 Work out these.
- a (5 + 4) × (9 − 7)
- b (9 − 1) × (8 − 1)
- c (100 − 10) ÷ (2 + 1)
- d (7 − 1) − (8 − 6)
- e (36 ÷ 3) ÷ (18 ÷ 9)
- f (17 + 3) ÷ (8 − 3)
- g (12 − 6) − (6 − 4)
- h (12 ÷ 6) ÷ (6 ÷ 3)
- i (9 ÷ 3) × (5 − 2)

6 Add brackets to make each of these equations correct.

You may need more than one set of brackets.
- a 5 + 2 × 8 = 56
- b 9 + 42 − 6 ÷ 3 = 21
- c 14 − 8 ÷ 2 + 1 = 2

95

Curriculum for Wales Mastering Mathematics: Book 1

7 Here is a message in a code. Each number represents a letter in the alphabet: A = 1, B = 2 and so on.
What does the message say?

| $3 \times 2 - 5$ | $(2+1) \times (7-1)$ | $2 \times 2^3 \div 4$ | $6 \div 2 + 1$ | $3^2 - 2^2$ |
| $3 \times 12 \div 2$ | $2 + 2 \div 2$ | $(2+2) \times 2$ | $3 \times (4+1)$ | $12 \div 4 + 2 \times 2$ |

8 Sioned and Geraint are contestants in a number quiz.
  a Sioned's target number is 358.
  The numbers she has are 100, 10, 8, 6, 4 and 3.
  She can use the operations +, −, ÷ and × and brackets as many times as she wishes.
  How can she make the target number? Write down the calculation using brackets.
  b Geraint's target number is 278.
  The numbers he has are 75, 50, 8, 4, 3 and 2.
  How can he make the target number? Write down the calculation using brackets.

Band 3 questions

9 Work out these.
  a $4 \times 10^2 + 5 \times 10 + 1$
  b $4 \times 10^2 + 5 \times 10$
  c $4 \times 10^2 + 1$
  d $3 \times 10^3 + 4 \times 10^2 + 6 \times 10 + 9$
  e $3 \times 10^3 + 6 \times 10 + 9$
  f $3 \times 10^3 + 4 \times 10^2 + 9$
  g $3 \times 10^3 + 9$
  h $3 \times 10^3 + 4 \times 10^2 + 6 \times 10$
  i $3 \times 10^3 + 4 \times 10^2$

10 Work out these.
  a $\dfrac{160-120}{5 \times 8}$
  b $\dfrac{(16-13) \times 10}{3+2}$
  c $\dfrac{2^2 \times (15-3)}{10-4}$

11 Work out these.
  a $\left(\sqrt[3]{16} + \sqrt{9}\right)$
  b $\sqrt{64} - \sqrt[3]{64}$
  c $\sqrt[3]{125} + 3^2$

12 Add brackets to make each of these equations correct.
You may need more than one set of brackets.
  a $7 + 3 \times 4 - 31^2 = 81$
  b $7 - 5^2 - 1^3 = 27$
  c $6 - 2 \times 8 - 3 = 20$
  d $3 \times 5 + 4 - 8 + 12 \div 6 - 1 = 23$

13 Find the correct operation (+, −, ÷ or ×) to replace ◯ and ▢ in these equations.
  a $17 \bigcirc 17 \square 17 = 306$
  b $38 \bigcirc 47 \square 58 = 49$
  c $(47 \bigcirc 53) \square 10 = 1000$
  d $27 \bigcirc (5 \square 5) = 675$

Key words

Here is a list of the key words you met in this chapter.

Addition (add)   BIDMAS   Brackets   Commutative
Difference   Division (divide)   Indices   Inverse
Multiplication (multiply) Operations   Product   Powers
Subtraction (subtract) Sum   Total

Use the glossary at the back of this book to check any you are unsure about.

96

5 Calculations

Review exercise: calculations

Band 1 questions

1. Find the product of each pair of numbers.
   a   3 and 90
   b   30 and 90
   c   30 and 900

2. Work out these.
   a   56 × 3
   b   56 × 30
   c   56 × 33

3. Work out these.
   a   455 ÷ 7
   b   150 ÷ 6
   c   518 ÷ 14
   d   1445 ÷ 17

4. Work out these.
   a   (9 + 1) × 10
   b   (12 − 2) × 4
   c   (6 + 6) × 3
   d   9 × (11 − 10)
   e   (5 + 2) ÷ 7
   f   (16 − 2) ÷ 7

5. Look at this maze.
   Which route from START to FINISH has the lowest total?
   Find a route from START to FINISH that totals exactly 100.

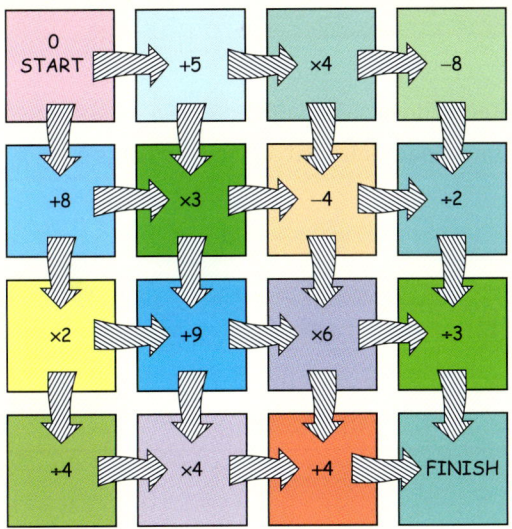

   Row 1: 0 START → +5 → ×4 → −8
   Row 2: +8 → ×3 → −4 → +2
   Row 3: ×2 → +9 → ×6 → +3
   Row 4: +4 → ×4 → +4 → FINISH

6. A group of friends go to an Adventure Park. How many are in the group?

   Afonffordd Adventure Park
   £24 per person
   Total: £336

Band 2 questions

7. Work out these.
   a   (3 + 2) × (2 + 3)
   b   (5 − 4) × (9 − 8)
   c   (6 + 6) × (5 + 5)
   d   (3 − 2) × (4 + 1)
   e   (6 − 2) × (8 − 3)
   f   (9 − 4) × (8 − 6)

8. An ounce is approximately 28 grams.
   A muffin weighs 4 ounces. How much would six muffins weigh in grams?

97

Curriculum for Wales Mastering Mathematics: Book 1

Logical reasoning

⑨ A holiday company offers the following prices per person for return flights.

> Montego Bay for £290
> Bermuda for £419

Cerys wants to book flights for five people. She has a budget of £2000.

a How much does she have left if she books the flights to Montego Bay?

b Without carrying out the exact multiplication, explain how you know that she can't afford to book flights to Bermuda.

Strategic competence

⑩ A train has 12 standard class coaches and four first class coaches.

Each standard class coach seats 64 people and each first class coach seats 24 people.

How many people can be seated in the train?

Band 3 questions

⑪ Steffan is a delivery driver; he works five days a week.

Here are Steffan's journeys over one week. Steffan drives:

- 126 km on Monday
- Twice as far on Tuesday as he did on Monday
- 40 km less on Wednesday than he did on Tuesday
- Four times further on Thursday than he did on Wednesday.

Steffan has driven 1850 km by the end of Friday. How far does Steffan drive on Friday?

Logical reasoning

⑫ Cerys has made a mess of her homework. Work out the number under each ink splat and rewrite Cerys's homework for her.

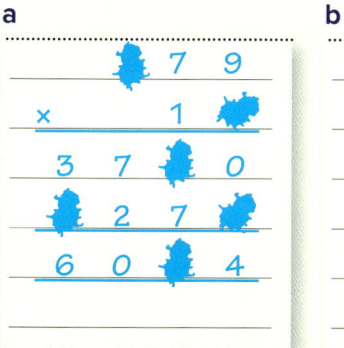

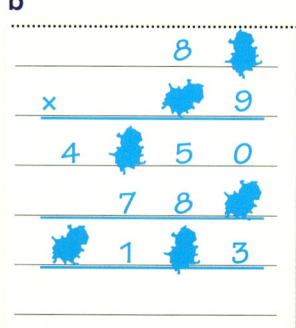

a
```
      7 9
  ×   1 ▉
    3 7 0
    2 7 ▉
    6 0 4
```

b
```
      ▉ 8
  ×     9
    4 ▉ 5 0
      7 8 ▉
      1 ▉ 3
```

c
```
         1 ▉
    1▉) 2 5 ⁷▉
```

d
```
            ▉ 4
      2▉) 6 2 ¹⁰▉
```

Strategic competence

⑬ Meike has some number cards.

Meike uses all four cards, brackets, squares and square roots, and the operations +, −, ÷ and ×
to make numbers.

Show how Meike can make all the numbers from 1 to 10.

| 4 | 4 | 4 | 4 |

Challenge: Use four 4s to make all the numbers up to 100.

98

6 Using letter symbols

Coming up...
- ▶ Using word formulas
- ▶ Using letters in formulas and expressions
- ▶ Simplifying expressions
- ▶ Solving equations

Mystery numbers

Each symbol on these cards represents a different mystery number.

Each symbol represents a whole number.

Solve these clues to find the mystery numbers.

Clues

- ✪ is even
- ✪ is a multiple of 7
- ✪ has a digit sum of 6
- ✪ has two digits

- 💧 is prime
- 💧 has two digits
- 💧 is one more than a square number
- 💧 has a digit sum of 10

When you add 7 to ♦ the answer is 23

- ● is even
- ● has two digits
- ● is a square number
- ● has digits that sum to make another square number

- ■ has two digits
- ■ is a square number
- ■ is a cube number

- ☺ is a multiple of 6
- When you:
  • double ☺ the answer is more than 30
  • subtract 10 from ☺ the answer is less than 10

Choose your own mystery number.

Make up some clues and give them to a friend to solve.

99

6.1 Word formulas

Skill checker

Match together the calculations which have the same answers.

| $60 - 6 \times 3$ | $5 + 4^2$ | $18 - 3^2$ | $16 - 2 \times 3$ | $7 \times 8 + 50 \div 2$ |
| $1 + 4 \times 2$ | $7 \times 9 \div 3$ | $7 \times (2 + 4)$ | $2 \times 3 + 4$ | $9 \times (4 + 5)$ |

▶ What is a formula?

A **formula** is a rule for working something out. It can be written in words or symbols.

For example, the time needed to roast a turkey is 50 minutes plus an extra 30 minutes per kilogram.

You can write this using the formula:

Cooking time in minutes = 50 + 30 × mass in kg

The words in a formula can be replaced with numbers that you know. This is called **substituting**.

Note

In this book, we are using 'formulas' as the plural of 'formula', but 'formulae' can also be used.

Worked example

Rhodri is cooking a 5 kg turkey.

His recipe book has the formula:

Cooking time in minutes = 50 + 30 × mass in kg

Rhodri wants dinner to be ready for 1 p.m.

At what time should he put the turkey in the oven?

Solution

Cooking time in minutes = 50 + 30 × mass in kg
$\qquad$ = 50 + 30 × 5 ← Substitute 5 into the formula.
$\qquad$ = 50 + 150
$\qquad$ = 200 minutes

Change 200 minutes to hours:

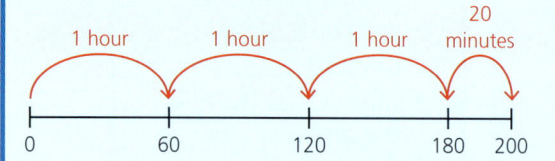

1 hour, 1 hour, 1 hour, 20 minutes
0 — 60 — 120 — 180 — 200

So 200 minutes = 3 hours 20 minutes.

Count back from 1 p.m.:

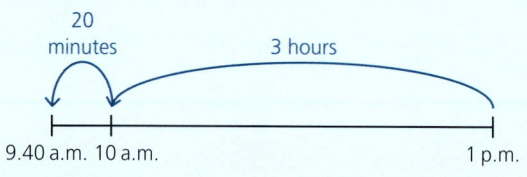

20 minutes, 3 hours
9.40 a.m.   10 a.m.   1 p.m.

Rhodri should put the turkey in the oven at 9.40 a.m.

6 Using letter symbols

6.1 Now try these

Band 1 questions

1. To convert metres to centimetres you use the formula:

    Length in centimetres = 100 × length in metres

    Convert the following measurements to centimetres.
    - a Tallest giraffe: 6 m
    - b Largest big cat (Siberian tiger): 3 m
    - c Longest python: 14.85 m
    - e Length of smallest dog: 0.15 m
    - d Tallest man: 2.72 m
    - f Length of a stag beetle: 0.05 m

2. Eve sees this sign at the supermarket.

    Apples only 45p each

    - a Work out the cost of:
        - i two apples
        - ii ten apples
        - iii 20 apples.
    - b Copy and complete this formula.

        Cost in pence = ☐ × number of apples

3. A fitness trainer uses the formula:

    Maximum safe heart rate (beats per minute) = 220 − age (in years)

    to work out if her clients are exercising safely.
    - a Work out the maximum safe heart rate of the following people.
        - i Mabon, aged 65 years
        - ii Bethan, aged 40 years
        - iii Gwenda, aged 77 years
    - b The fitness trainer works out that Dilys has a maximum safe heart rate of 190 beats per minute. How old is Dilys?

4. Rhian is two years older than Eira. Which of these rules is correct?
    - A Rhian's age in years + 2 = Eira's age in years
    - B Eira's age in years + 2 = Rhian's age in years

Band 2 questions

5. A railway company works out its fares using this formula:

    Fare (£) = Length of journey in kilometres ÷ 10 + 5

    Calculate the fare for a journey of:
    - a 50 km
    - b 100 km
    - c 200 km
    - d 5 km.

6. A bowling alley uses the following formula to work out how much to charge customers:

    Cost (in pounds) = 6 × number of games + 5

    Ten Pin Bowling
    £6 per game
    £5 for shoe hire

    - a Work out how much it costs for:
        - i one game
        - ii two games
        - iii three games.
    - b Sayeed has £40. He wants to play as many games as possible. How many games can he play?

7. Aliyah has £40 which she uses to buy some magazines for the school library.

    She works out how much change she should have from £40 using the following formula:

    Change (in pounds) = 40 − 3 × number of magazines

    - a Work out how much change Aliyah has if she buys:
        - i two magazines
        - ii three magazines
        - iii five magazines.
    - b i What is the maximum number of magazines that she can buy?
       ii How much money does she have left?

Curriculum for Wales Mastering Mathematics: Book 1

Logical reasoning

8 A paperback book costs twice as much as an eBook. Which of these rules is correct?
  A Cost (£) of paperback × 2 = cost (£) of eBook
  B Cost (£) of eBook ÷ 2 = cost (£) of paperback
  C Cost (£) of eBook × 2 = cost (£) of paperback

Fluency

9 Here is part of a price list for hiring tools:
The total cost is made up of a fixed cost and a charge for each day the item is hired for.
The hire shop uses this formula to work out the cost of hiring an extension ladder:

Item	Fixed cost	Daily charge
Extension ladder	£10	£20
Wheelbarrow	£8	£20
Concrete mixer	£12	£30
Chainsaw	£15	£30

Total cost (£) of hiring ladder = ☐ + ☐ × number of days hired

  a Copy and complete the formula for the cost of hiring a ladder.
  b Write down a formula for hiring each of the other tools.
  c Use your formulas to work out the cost of hiring:
    i a ladder for four days
    ii a wheelbarrow for two days
    iii a concrete mixer for one day
    iv a chainsaw for two days.
  d Dafydd is giving his garden a makeover at the weekend. He needs a chainsaw, a concrete mixer and a wheelbarrow.
    How much does it cost him to hire them all for two days?

Band 3 questions

10 A car hire company uses the following formula to work out the hire cost:

  Hire cost (£) = 30 × number of hire days + 0.1 × number of miles driven

  a Work out how much each of the following customers is charged for hiring a car:
    i Pedr hires a car for four days and drives 100 miles.
    ii Tegwen hires a car for seven days and drives 500 miles.
    iii Haydn hires a car for ten days and drives 1040 miles.
  b Find how much the company charges for:
    i each day of car hire
    ii each mile driven.

Logical reasoning

11 A health visitor uses this formula to work out how much sleep a child needs:

  Number of hours sleep = (30 − age of child in years) ÷ 2

  a Work out how much sleep each of these children should have each day.
    i Molly, aged 1
    ii Theo, aged 10
    iii Abdul, aged 6
  b Can the health visitor use the formula for teenagers? Explain your answer.

12 Zahir uses a formula to work out the total points for each football team in his local league:

  Total points = 3 × number of wins + number of draws

  a Find how many points are awarded for each:
    i win
    ii draw
    iii loss.
  b Zahir's team wins six games, loses three games and has one draw.
    How many points does his team score?
  c Gwen's team plays ten games and has three draws.
    What is the
    i highest
    ii lowest
    number of points Gwen's team could have scored?
  d Is it possible for Gwen's team to score exactly 20 points?
    Explain your answer fully.

6 Using letter symbols

13 Jac writes down some formulas about time.

> Number of seconds = number of minutes × 60
> Number of days = number of years × 365

a i How many seconds are there in four minutes?

   ii How many days are there in ten years?

b Copy and complete these formulas:

   Number of days = number of weeks × ☐

   Number of seconds = number of minutes × ☐

c Write one number in the box to complete this formula:

   Number of minutes = number of days × ☐

d Jac is 12 years, 8 weeks and 3 days old.

   Use the formulas to work out Jac's age in seconds.

e Work out how old you are in seconds.

f Abdul says that one of Jac's formulas is not quite right.

   Is Abdul correct? Explain your answer fully.

g Write one number in the box to complete this formula:

   Number of days = number of seconds ÷ ☐

h Baby Kwame was born at 9 a.m. exactly.

   Today he is 1 million seconds old.

   i How many days old is Kwame?

   ii At what time today does he become 1 million seconds old?

6.2 Using letters

Skill checker

① A plumber uses this formula to work out how much to charge a customer:

   Cost (£) = 40 + 25 × number of hours worked

a Work out how much the plumber should charge a customer for a job that takes:

   i 4 hours   ii 6 hours   iii 9 hours.

b The plumber charges one customer £90.

   How many hours did he work?

② A designer charges £28 per hour.

   She is offering a discount of £50 to attract new customers.

a The designer uses a formula to work out how much she should charge her customers.

   Copy and complete the formula:

   Cost (£) = ☐ × number of hours worked ☐ 50

b How much should the designer charge a customer for a project that takes 20 hours?

c Should the designer offer a discount to a customer for a project which takes 2 hours?

   Give a reason for your answer.

103

▶ Using letters to write a formula

Sometimes formulas are written down using **letter symbols** instead of words. This makes the formula quicker to write. The symbols must always represent **numbers**.

A cinema uses the following formula to work out how much to charge its customers:

Price (£) = 12 × number of adults + 8 × number of children

This can be written in symbols as:

$P = 12a + 8c$

You don't need to write the 'x' signs. So $8c$ means '8 × c' or '8 lots of c'.

where:

- P stands for 'price in pounds'
- a stands for 'the number of adults'
- c stands for 'the number of children'.

It is important to say what each of the letters in a formula stands for.

The letters stand for numbers. They are not abbreviations for words.

c = children ✗
c = number of children ✓

The letters used in a formula are called **variables**.

They represent numbers which can change (or vary).

The value of c depends on how many children go to the cinema.

You can replace the letters in the formula with values. This is called **substitution**.

Five Stars Cinema
★★★★★
Adult £12
Child £8

Worked example

Work out the cost of two adults and four children seeing a film at Five Stars Cinema.

Solution

Substitute $a = 2$ and $c = 4$ into the formula:

$P = 12a + 8c$

So:

$P = 12 × 2 + 8 × 4$
  $= 24 + 32$
  $= 56$

Don't forget to write in the 'x' signs.

So the cost is £56.

Remember

Remember BIDMAS: multiply first, then add.

▶ Using letters to write an expression

Here are some bags of counters.

The red bag has x counters in it.

The blue bag has y counters in it.

The total number of counters in the bags is $x + y$.

$x + y$ is called an **expression**. It has no = sign.

You can substitute values into the expression to **evaluate** it. *Work it out.*

For example, when $x = 12$ and $y = 15$ then:

$x + y$
$= 12 + 15$
$= 27$

x counters y counters

When you use letter symbols you are using **algebra**. Make sure you know the rules for using algebra.

> **Remember**
> Letter symbols in algebra are known as variables.

Worked example

Tosin has some counters.

Bags all come with x counters and boxes all come with y counters.

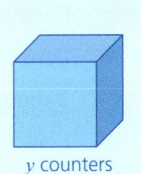

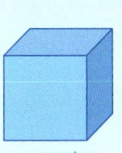

x counters x counters x counters y counters y counters

He removes four counters from one of the bags.

a i Write an expression for the total number of counters Tosin has left.
   ii Work out how many counters Tosin has if $x = 7$ and $y = 5$.
b Tosin empties out half of the counters from a red bag with x counters in it.
   i Write down an expression for the number of counters Tosin has left in the bag.
   ii Work out how many counters are left in the bag if $x = 10$.

Solution

a i Total number of counters is:
      $3 \times x + 2 \times y - 4$
      $= 3x + 2y - 4$
   ii Substitute $x = 7$ and $y = 5$ into $3x + 2y - 4$.
      $3 \times x + 2 \times y - 4$
      $= 3 \times 7 + 2 \times 5 - 4$
      $= 21 + 10 - 4$
      $= 27$
      Tosin has 27 counters.

b i Tosin has $\frac{x}{2}$ counters.
   ii Substitute $x = 10$ into $\frac{x}{2}$.
      $\frac{x}{2} = \frac{10}{2}$
      $= 5$
      There are five counters left in the bag.

Don't forget the rules!

1 Don't use a $\times$ symbol or a $\div$ symbol.
   - $6n$ ✓ $6 \times n$ ✗   (6 lots of n)
   - $\frac{n}{2}$ ✓ $n \div 2$ ✗   (n divided by 2)
2 Write numbers first, then letters.
   - $6a$ ✓ $a6$ ✗
3 Write letters in alphabetical order.
   - xyz ✓ zxy ✗
4 x^2 means '$x \times x$'.   (Say 'x squared'.)
5 y^3 means '$y \times y \times y$'.   (Say 'y cubed'.)
6 Don't use decimals.
   - $\frac{1}{2}x$ ✓ $0.5x$ ✗

Curriculum for Wales Mastering Mathematics: Book 1

Communication using symbols

Activity

Lowri thinks of a number.

She calls her number n.

Match together the following statements and expressions where n represents Lowri's number.

$\dfrac{n}{3}$ $n + 3$ $\dfrac{3}{n}$ $3 - n$ n^3 $n - 3$ $3n$

a 3 lots of Lowri's number
b Lowri's number add 3
c Lowri's number subtract 3
d Lowri's number subtracted from 3
e Lowri's number multiplied by 3
f 3 more than Lowri's number
g 3 less than Lowri's number
h Lowri's number divided by 3
i Lowri's number cubed
j 3 divided by Lowri's number

How can you use substitution to check you are right?

Worked example

Evaluate each of these expressions when $x = 4$ and $y = 2$.

a $xy + 2$ b $x^2 + y^3$ c $5(x + y)$

Evaluate means 'work out'.

Solution

Substitute $x = 4$ and $y = 2$ into each expression.

a $xy + 2 = 4 \times 2 + 2$
    $= 8 + 2$
    $= 10$

xy means '$x \times y$'.

b $x^2 + y^3 = 4^2 + 2^3$
    $= 16 + 8$
    $= 24$

x^2 means '$x \times x$' and y^3 means '$y \times y \times y$'.

c $5(x + y) = 5 \times (4 + 2)$
    $= 5 \times (6)$
    $= 30$

Remember

Remember BIDMAS: Work out the bracket first.

Maths in context

$E = mc^2$ is one of the world's most famous equations.

Who discovered this?

What nationality was he?

When was he born?

6 Using letter symbols

6.2 Now try these

Band 1 questions

1. Work out the value of $x + 7$ when:
   a. $x = 1$
   b. $x = 2$
   c. $x = 3$

2. Work out the value of $9m$ when:
   a. $m = 1$
   b. $m = 2$
   c. $m = 3$

   Remember
   $9m$ means '$9 \times m$' or '9 lots of m'.

3. Work out the value of $15 - p$ when:
   a. $p = 1$
   b. $p = 2$
   c. $p = 3$

4. Evaluate
   a. $b + 7$
   b. $10b$
   c. $12 - b$

   when:
   i. $b = 2$
   ii. $b = 3$
   iii. $b = 4$

   Remember
   Evaluate means 'work out'.

5. When $n = 4$, work out the value of:
   a. $n + 5$
   b. $n - 1$
   c. $2n$
   d. $3n$
   e. $12 - n$
   f. $\dfrac{n}{2}$ ← n divided by 2

6. Work out the value of $2x + 4$ when:
   a. $x = 2$
   b. $x = 3$
   c. $x = 5$

7. Benji works out his weekly pay using the formula:
   $$W = 12h$$
   where W = weekly pay in pounds and h = number of hours worked.
   a. Benji works 25 hours in one week. How much should he be paid?
   b. Work out the value of W when $h = 38$.

Band 2 questions

8. Rewrite the following correctly.
   a. $5 \times a$
   b. $b \times 4$
   c. $c7$

9. Work out the value of $3a + 2b$ when:
   a. $a = 2$ and $b = 3$
   b. $a = 4$ and $b = 5$
   c. $a = 4$ and $b = 1$
   d. $a = 0$ and $b = 7$

10. When $r = 2$, $s = 3$ and $t = 5$ work out the value of:
    a. $r + s + t$
    b. $2rs$
    c. $4rs + t$
    d. $3s + st$
    e. $3r + 2s - rt$
    f. $5rs - 4st + 3rt$

107

Logical reasoning

11 Ben is x years old.
Katrina is $(2x + 4)$ years old.
Ruby is $(x - 3)$ years old.
Sam is $2x$ years old.
   a Who is the oldest? How do you know?
   b Work out how old each person is when $x = 5$.

12 Group together matching expressions.

2 more than n	2 plus n	2n	2 less than n	n added to n	twice n
2 × n	n × 2	$n - 2$	$2 + n$	$n + n$	$n + 2$

13 a A school shop sells calculators for £6 each.
   i The shop sells five calculators.
      How much money has the shop received?
   ii A formula is used to work out the takings at the end of the day.
      c stands for the number of calculators sold.
      T stands for the amount of money received in pounds.
      Which of these formulas is correct?

   $T = c \div 6$ $T = c + 6$ $T = 6c$

   b The shop also sells geometry sets for £3 each.
   g stands for the number of geometry sets sold.
   Write an expression for the amount of money received for geometry sets.
   c What is the formula $T = 6c + 3g$ used to work out?

Fluency

14 Dai works for Rise and Shine Window Cleaners.

> **Rise and Shine**
> Window Cleaners
> £5 plus £3 per window

   a Write a formula to help Dai calculate the cost of cleaning any number of windows.
   Use w to stand for the number of windows and c to stand for the total cost in pounds.
   b Find the value of c when $w = 10$.

15 Jeans cost j pounds per pair.
T-shirts cost t pounds each.
   a Write down an expression for:
      i the cost of three T-shirts
      ii the cost of one pair of jeans and three T-shirts
      iii how much more a pair of jeans costs than a T-shirt.
   b $j = 35$ and $t = 12$
   Work out the value of each expression found in part **a**.

Band 3 questions

16 Evaluate the following when $a = 3$ and $b = 4$.

a $6(a + 2)$ b $9(b - 1)$ c $2(a + b)$
d $7(1 + 2a)$ e $3(2b - a)$ f $b(5a - 10)$

Remember

Remember BIDMAS. Work out the bracket first!

17 a Carwyn says that when $x = 2$, then $3x^2$ is 36.
Llinos says that when $x = 2$, then $3x^2$ is 12.
Who is right? Explain your answer fully.

b Work out the value of $3x^2$ when $x = 4$.

18 A bicycle shop uses this formula to calculate the cost of hiring bicycles:

$$C = \frac{3h}{2} + 20$$

where C stands for cost in pounds and h stands for the number of hours.
Calculate the cost of hiring a bicycle for:

a 2 hours   b 6 hours   c 9 hours.

19 When $y = 5$, work out the value of:

a y^2 b $y^2 + 4$ c $4y^2$
d $40 - y^2$ e y^3 f $2y^3$
g $5 + 4y^3$ h $y^3 + y^2$ i $2(y^2 - y)$

20 The formula to find the number, h, halfway between two numbers n and m is:

$$h = \frac{n + m}{2}$$

a Use the formula to work out the number halfway between these pairs of numbers.
  i 6 and 10   ii 35 and 237   iii 15 and 40

b Amir, Beca, Cai and Delyth all live on the same road.
Amir lives at number 34 and Cai lives at number 242.
Beca lives halfway between Amir and Cai.
Delyth lives halfway between Beca and Cai.
What number does Delyth live at?

21 Work out the value of $\frac{a + b}{a}$ when:

a $a = 3$ and $b = 9$ b $a = 2$ and $b = 10$
c $a = 4$ and $b = 8$ d $a = 5$ and $b = 0$

22 'Super Savers' Bank uses the following formula to work out how much interest a customer earns in a year:

$$I = \frac{PR}{100}$$

where:
- I is the amount of interest earned
- P is the amount of money invested
- R is the percentage interest rate.

Catherine invests £2000 at an interest rate of 2%.
Ibrahim invests £1000 at an interest rate of 3%.
Owen invests £5000 at an interest rate of 0.5%.

a Which customer earns the most interest after one year?
b Calculate the difference between the highest and lowest amount of interest earned.

6.3 Simplifying expressions

Skill checker

Can you rewrite each of the following as a single multiplication?

You may only use whole numbers.

You may **not** use the number 1.

① $5 \times 2 - 3 \times 2$ ② $4 \times 7 + 7 \times 3$ ③ $6 \times 11 + 11$ ④ $17 \times 5 - 8 \times 7$
⑤ $6 \times 3 - 3$ ⑥ $7 \times 10 - 3 \times 13$ ⑦ $7 \times 11 + 3 \times 4$ ⑧ $13 \times 6 - 2 \times 13$

Why is it impossible to rewrite some of these as a single multiplication?

▶ Combining like terms

You can write $4 + 4 + 4 + 4 + 4$ as 5×4 or 5 lots of 4.

In the same way, you can write the expression $n + n + n + n + n$ as $5n$.

You have **simplified** the expression.

> $5n$ means '5 × n' or '5 lots of n'.

Worked example

Simplify:

a $a + 2a + 3a$
b $7b - 4b$

> a means '1 lot of a' or '$1a$'.
> So 1 lot of a + 2 lots of a + 3 lots of a = 6 lots of a.

Solution

a $a + 2a + 3a$
   $= 6a$
b $7b - 4b$
   $= 3b$

You can **simplify** an expression by combining **like terms**.

Like terms contain exactly the same letter symbols (variables).

Worked example

Simplify these.

a $3a + 8b - 2a - 7b + a$
b $6x + 5 + 3 - 4x - 1$

> $1a$ is written as a.

Solution

a Simplify $3a + 8b - 2a - 7b + a$
   $= 3a - 2a + a + 8b - 7b$
   $= 2a + b$

> Collect like terms.
> Keep the sign ('+' or '−') with the term that follows it.

You cannot simplify this any further because a and b are unlike terms.

$2a + b$ is the **simplest form**.

b $6x + 5 + 3 - 4x - 1$
   $= 6x - 4x + 5 + 3 - 1$
   $= 2x + 7$

> Collect together like letter terms and constant (number) terms.

6 Using letter symbols

Activity

You can use algebra tiles to help you simplify expressions.

Group like tiles together.

Example

These tiles show that $3x + 2 + 2x + 1 = 5x + 3$.

You can group together tiles which make a zero pair (cancel).

These tiles make zero pairs.

They cancel each other out.

Example

These tiles show that $3x + 3 - x - 2 = 2x + 1$.

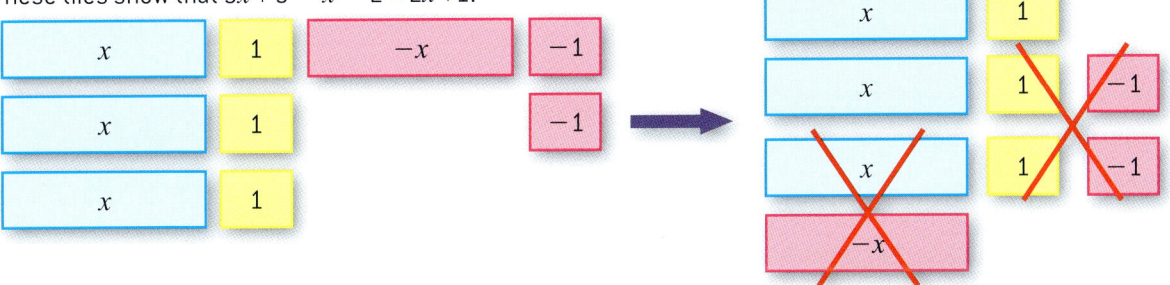

① Use algebra tiles to help you simplify these expressions.

  a $x + x + x + x + x + x$
  b $x + 3 + x + 2$
  c $2x + 4 + 4x + 2$
  d $3x + 4 - x - 3x + 4x - 2$
  e $5x - 3x + 7 - 2x - 6$
  f $x - 1 - 2x + 2 + 3x - 3 - 4x + 4$

② Use algebra tiles to make your own expression to simplify.

Give your expression to a partner to simplify.

Do you both get the same answer?

If you disagree, how can you check who is right?

You can simplify more complicated expressions in the same way.

> **Worked example**
>
> Simplify these expressions.
>
> **a** $6xy - 2x + 4xy + 5x$
>
> **b** $7x + x^2 - 2x + 3x^2$
>
> **Solution**
>
> **a** $6xy - 2x + 4xy + 5x$
>
> $= 6xy + 4xy - 2x + 5x$ *(Collect like terms.)*
>
> $= 10xy + 3x$
>
> You can't simplify this any further as xy and x are not like terms.
>
> **b** $7x + x^2 - 2x + 3x^2$ *(x and x^2 are not like terms.)*
>
> $= 7x - 2x + x^2 + 3x^2$
>
> $= 5x + 4x^2$

6.3 Now try these

Band 1 questions

1 Simplify these expressions:

    a $a + a + a + a + a + a$ **b** $b + b$ **c** $c + c + c + c + c + c + c$

    d $d + d + d$ **e** $e + e + e + e$ **f** $f + f + f + f + f$

2 a Find the values of $2c$, $3c$ and $5c$ when:

    i $c = 2$ **ii** $c = 3$ **iii** $c = 4$.

  b For each value of c, show that $2c + 3c$ is the same as $5c$.

3 Simplify these expressions.

    a $m + 2m + 3m$ **b** $2h + 5h + 3h$ **c** $3a + 5a + 7a + 9a$

    d $x + 2x + 3x + 4x$ **e** $3g + 2g + 4g + g$ **f** $5j + 2j + j + 3j$

4 Simplify:

    a $7r - 2r$ **b** $12s - 3s + 5s$ **c** $12t + 5t - 4t$

    d $19u - 5u + 7u - 11u$ **e** $5v - 3v - v + 2v$ **f** $8w - 5w - 4w + 3w$

5 a Work out the value of these expressions when $a = 3$, $b = 4$ and $c = 5$.

    i $5a - 4a$ **ii** $6b - 5b$ **iii** $10c - 4c - 5c$

    What do you notice?

  b Simplify the expressions given in part **a**.

6 A box contains wooden building blocks of two different lengths: x cm and 4 cm as shown.

    | x cm | | 4 cm |

Molly puts some of the blocks together.

a Write down an expression for the total length of the blocks.

   i | x | x | x | 4 | 4 |

   ii | x | 4 | x | 4 | 4 |

   iii | x | 4 | x | 4 |

b Does changing the order in which the blocks are placed change the total length?

c Simplify each of your expressions in part **a**.

7 Simplify:
- **a** $5p + 2p + 3 + 1$
- **b** $7q - 2q + 5 - 2$
- **c** $4r - 3r - 2 + 7$
- **d** $4s + 5 - 3s - 4 - s$
- **e** $4 + 4t + 5 - 3t$
- **f** $2 + 9u + 1 - 7u - 3$

Band 2 questions

8 Myfanwy has a bag of counters.

An expression for the total number of counters is $12n + 18$.

- **a** Myfanwy puts the counters into two piles.

  The number of counters in one pile is $4n + 12$.

  Write down an expression for the number of counters in the other pile.

- **b** Myfanwy puts the counters into two equal piles.

  Write down an expression for the number of counters in one pile.

- **c** Given that $n = 5$, how many counters does Myfanwy have?

9 Simplify these expressions.
- **a** $2c + 5d + 2c + d$
- **b** $a + 2b + 4b + 3a + 3b$
- **c** $3x + 2y - 3x + 4y$
- **d** $2g + 3f - g + 5f - g$
- **e** $3m + 2n + 4n$
- **f** $6p - 2q + 3 + 3p + 5q + 2$

10 Selwyn, Rhodri and Tarek are adding up the number of goals they scored in the football season:
- Selwyn scored x goals.
- Rhodri scored three more goals than Selwyn.
- Tarek scored twice the number of goals that Rhodri did.

Write down and simplify an expression for the total number of goals scored by all three players.

11 Write these expressions as simply as possible.
- **a** $3 \times f$
- **b** $n \times n$
- **c** $p \times r$
- **d** $a \times 2 \times c$
- **e** $d \times 3 \times e$
- **f** $x \times 3 \times x$

12 Which of these expressions does not simplify to $10rv$? Explain your answer.
- **a** $5r \times 5v$
- **b** $2r \times 5v$
- **c** $r \times 10v$

Band 3 questions

13 Simplify these expressions.
- **a** $a^2 + 2a^2 + 3a^2$
- **b** $ab + 2a^2 + 3ab + a^2$
- **c** $b^2 + 2c^2 - 3b^2 + c^2$
- **d** $4d^2 + d - d^2 + 5d$
- **e** $e^2 + 3ef - 2ef + 3e^2$
- **f** $3fg + 2g - 2fg + 3g - 2f + f$
- **g** $g^2 + 2g^2 - 3g^2 + g^2$
- **h** $4g^2 + 2g^2 - 3h^2 + 2h^2$

113

14 Try this mind-reading trick.

    a Think of a number   **b** Double it
    c Add 12   **d** Divide by two
    e Subtract the number you first thought of   **f** The answer is 6!

How does this trick work?

Can you design your own puzzle?

15 The expression in each brick in these walls is found by adding the expressions in the two bricks beneath it. Copy the walls and fill in the missing expressions in each brick.

a Bricks shown: $4n - m$, $5n - m$, $2n$, $n + 2m$

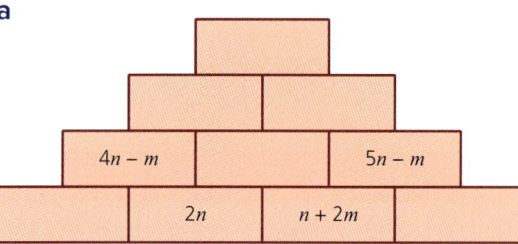

b Bricks shown: $x - y$ (top), $2x - y$, x, y, $x - 2y$

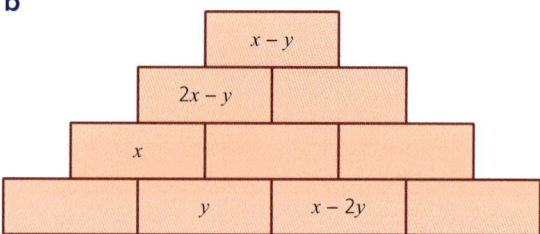

6.4 Equations

Skill checker

1 Use the bar model method to find the missing numbers.

    a 5 more than ☐ is 9.

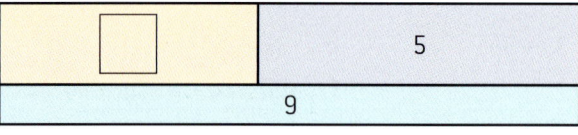

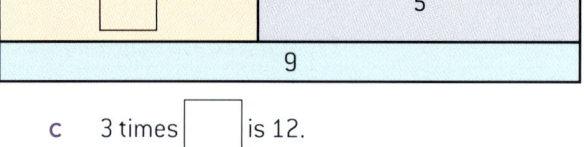

    b 20 less than ☐ is 15.

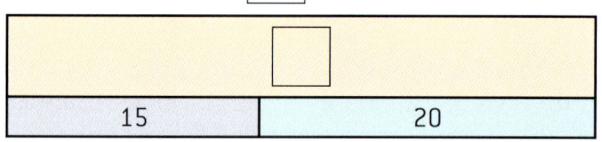

    c 3 times ☐ is 12.

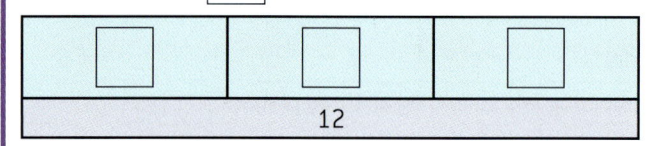

2 Simplify these expressions.

    a $x + x + x$

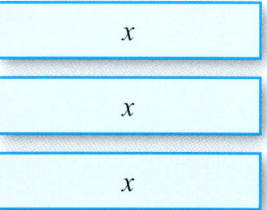

    b $3x + 4 + 2x - 2$

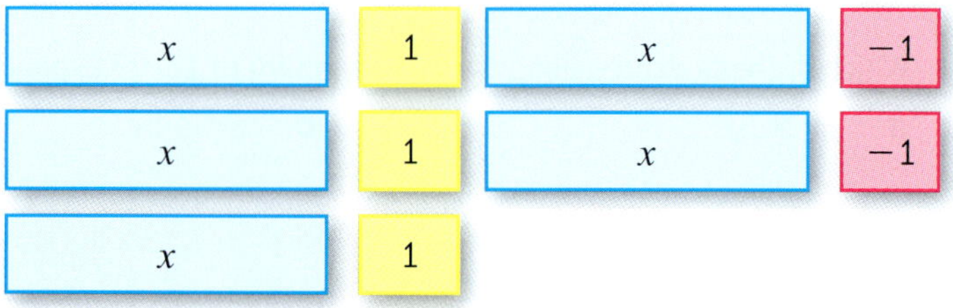

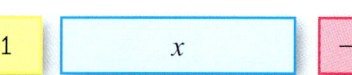

    c $2x + 4x - 3x$

    d $4x - 2 + 3x + 7 - 10x$

3 When $x = 3$, find the value of:

    a $3x$ **b** $5x + 2$ **c** $7 - 2x$

6 Using letter symbols

▶ Solving equations

An **equation** says that one expression is equal to another. For example: $2x + 3 = 11$.

Solving an equation means finding the value of x that makes the equation true.

x is called an **unknown** as you don't know its value until you solve the equation.

You can use a bar model method to help you solve an equation.

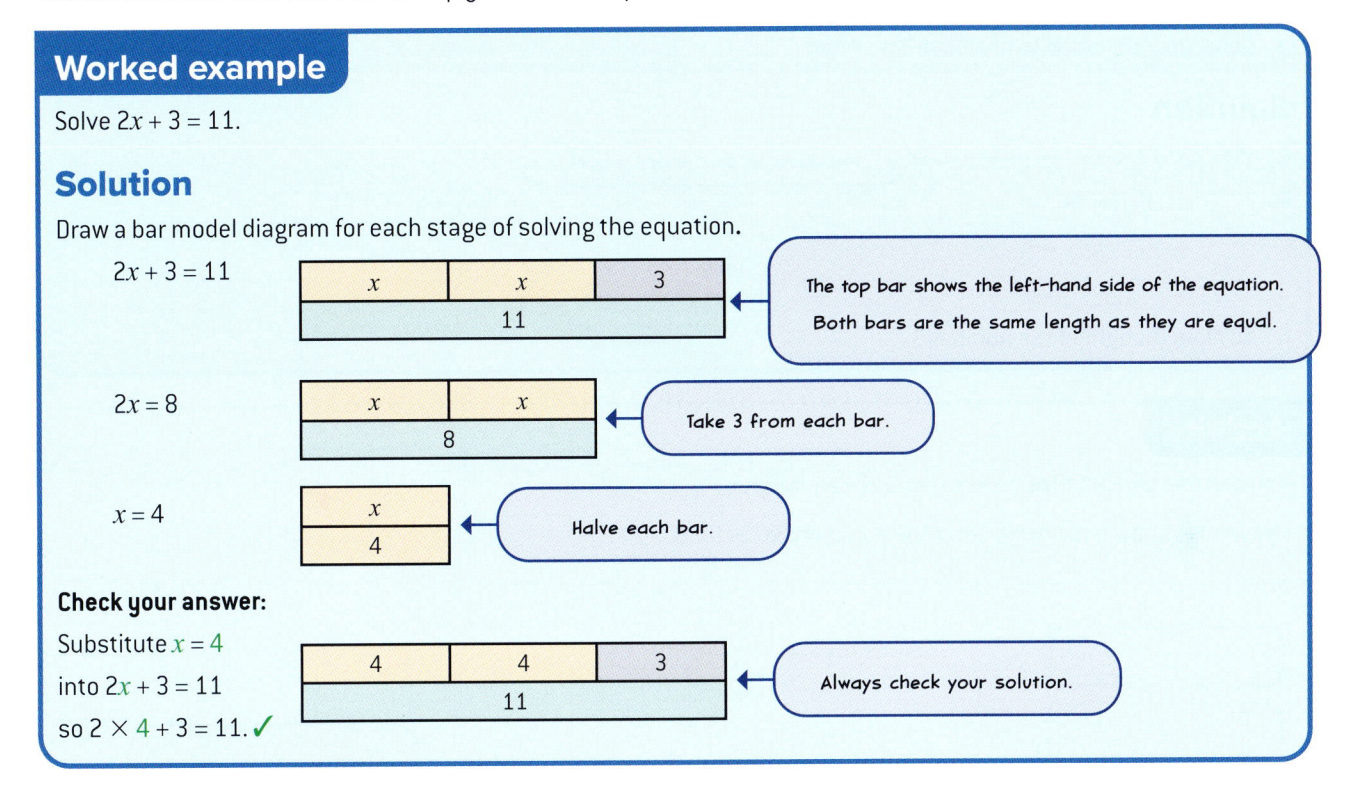

Worked example

Solve $2x + 3 = 11$.

Solution

Draw a bar model diagram for each stage of solving the equation.

$2x + 3 = 11$

The top bar shows the left-hand side of the equation. Both bars are the same length as they are equal.

$2x = 8$

Take 3 from each bar.

$x = 4$

Halve each bar.

Check your answer:
Substitute $x = 4$
into $2x + 3 = 11$
so $2 \times 4 + 3 = 11$. ✓

Always check your solution.

▶ The balance method

Imagine a pair of scales. To keep them balanced you have to add or subtract the same amount to both sides.

The first set of scales show two identical parcels and 1 kg balancing with 5 kg.

To find the mass of the parcel:

Subtract 1 from both sides.   Divide both sides by 2.

So one parcel is 2 kg.

In the same way, to keep an equation balanced, you must apply the same operation to both sides.

You can write this using algebra:

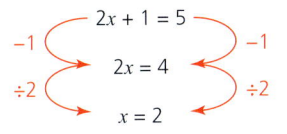

$2x + 1 = 5$ −1
$2x = 4$ ÷2
$x = 2$

−1
÷2

115

Curriculum for Wales Mastering Mathematics: Book 1

Worked example

Akim thinks of a number.

He multiplies it by 7 and subtracts 6.

The result is 29.

a Write down an equation for Akim's number.
b Solve your equation to find Akim's number.

Solution

a $7a - 6 = 29$ ← The unknown can be any letter!

b
$$7a - 6 = 29$$
$$+6 \quad \quad +6$$
$$7a = 35$$
$$\div 7 \quad \quad \div 7$$
$$a = 5$$

Check: $7 \times 5 - 6 = 29$ ✓

So Akim thought of the number 5.

Activity

You can use algebra tiles to help you solve equations.

These tiles show you how to solve the equation $3x - 1 = 8$.

Step 1:

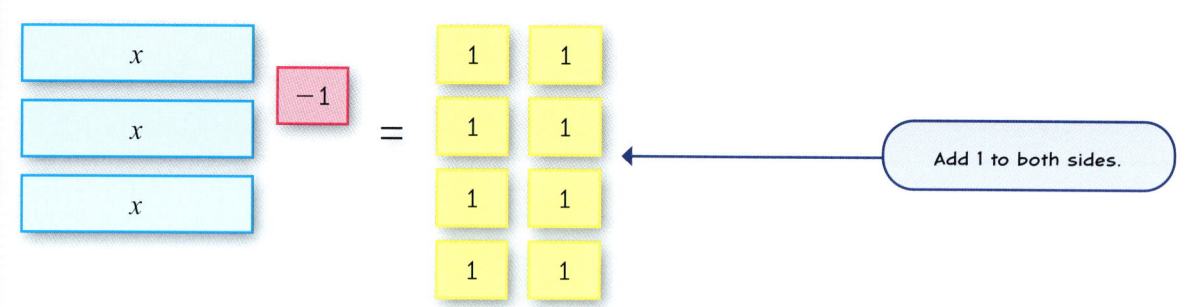

Add 1 to both sides.

Step 2:

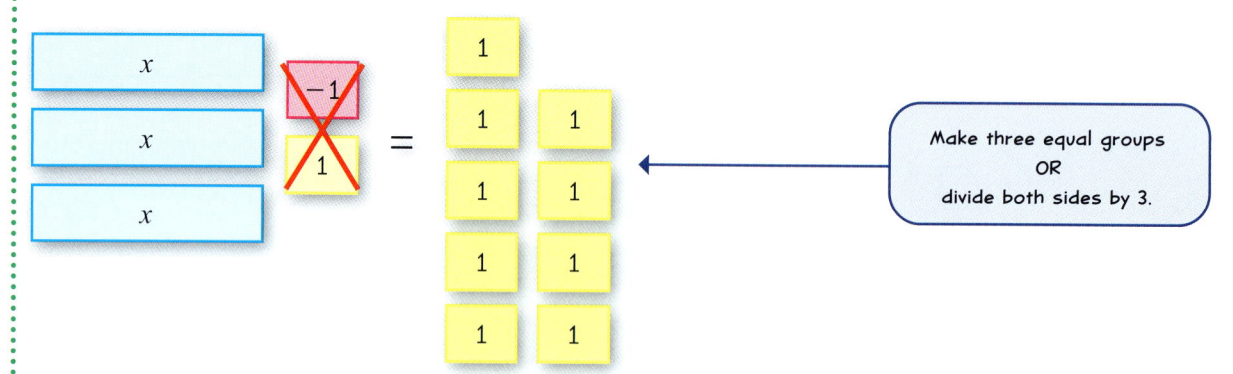

Make three equal groups
OR
divide both sides by 3.

Step 3:

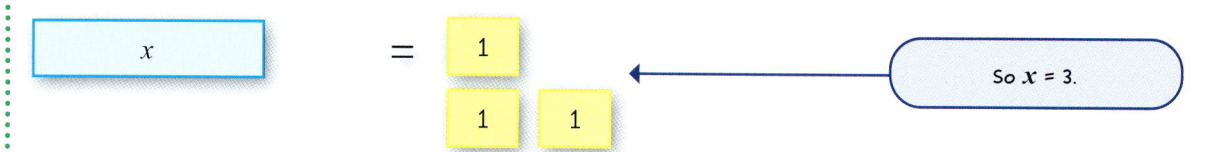

So $x = 3$.

So the algebra tiles show that $x = 3$.

Use algebra tiles to solve these equations.

① $x + 6 = 10$ ② $4x = 12$ ③ $x - 3 = 2$
④ $2x + 3 = 7$ ⑤ $5x - 2 = 13$ ⑥ $4 = 1 + 3x$
⑦ $10 - x = 6$ ⑧ $12 - 2x = 4$ ⑨ $5 = 7 - 2x$

▶ The function machine method

We can use the idea of number machines to solve equations. They are called function machines.
To use function machines, we must know the **inverses** of operations.
An inverse returns you to where you started.

Worked example

a Solve the equation $x + 2 = 11$ using a function machine.
b Solve the equation $3x + 7 = 22$.

Solution

a Input → x → $+2$ → 11 → Output

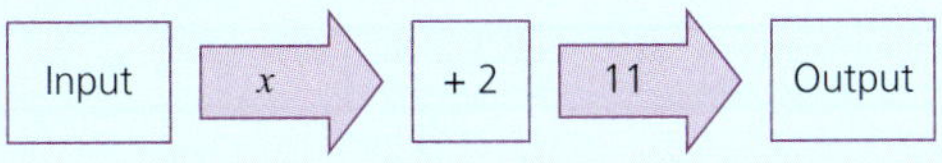

The inverse function machine is:

Output ← 9 ← -2 ← 11 ← Input

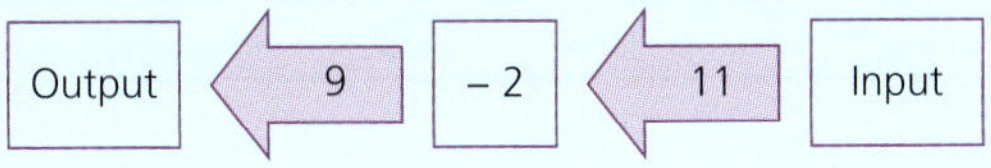

Addition (+) and subtraction (−) are inverses of each other.

$x = 9$

b Input → x → $\times 3$ → $3x$ → $+7$ → 22 → Output

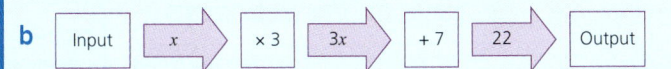

The inverse function machine is:

Output ← 5 ← $\div 3$ ← 15 ← -7 ← 22 ← Input

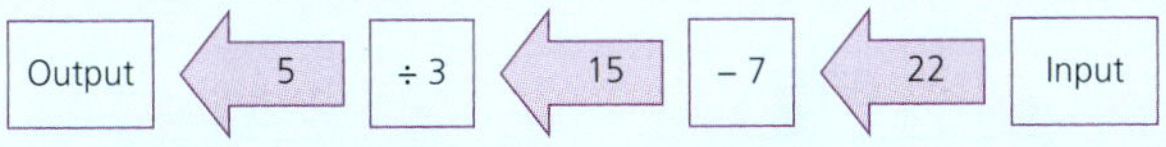

Division (÷) and multiplication (×) are inverses of each other.

$x = 5$

Curriculum for Wales Mastering Mathematics: Book 1

> **Activity**
>
> Use function machines to solve these equations.
>
> ① $x + 4 = 7$ ② $3x = 21$ ③ $x - 7 = 13$
>
> ④ $4x + 1 = 21$ ⑤ $5x - 3 = 27$ ⑥ $1 + 2x = 9$

6.4 Now try these

Band 1 questions

1 Find the value of the missing numbers.

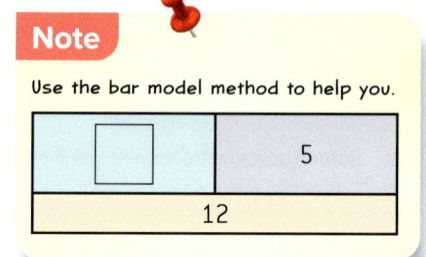

a ☐ + 5 = 12   b 10 + ☐ = 15

c 27 = ☐ + 10   d ☐ − 3 = 10

e 4 × ☐ = 20   f 21 = ☐ × 3

Note

Use the bar model method to help you.

☐	5
12	

2 Find the value of each variable.

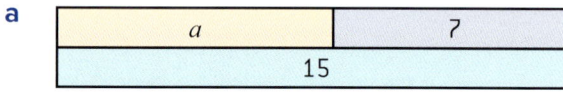

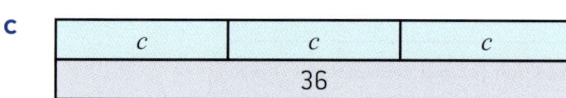

a | a | 7 |
   |---|---|
   | 15 ||

b | 4 | b |
   |---|---|
   | 7 ||

c | c | c | c |
   |---|---|---|
   | 36 |||

d | d | d | d | d |
   |---|---|---|---|
   | 28 ||||

3 Find the mass of each parcel.

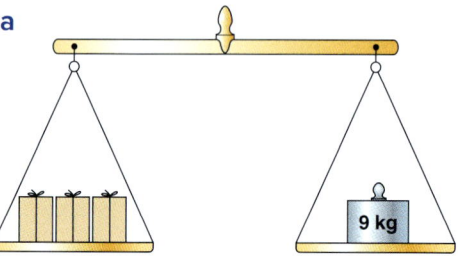

a (balance: 3 parcels = 9 kg)

b (balance: parcel + 4 kg = 10 kg)

Do the same to both sides!

4 Solve these equations.

a $m + 4 = 11$ b $a + 11 = 15$ c $6 + b = 8$

d $x + 5 = 15$ e $y + 7 = 17$ f $z + 15 = 115$

5 Solve these equations.

a $p - 6 = 10$ b $d - 7 = 13$ c $a - 4 = 4$

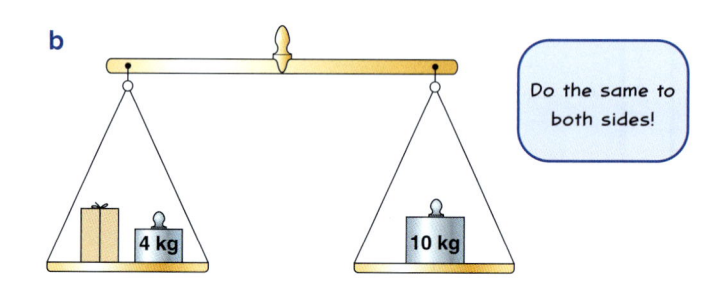

d $q - 5 = 15$ e $s - 9 = 15$ f $t - 25 = 97$

Add the same amount to both sides.

6 Solve these equations.

a $2a = 6$ b $4b = 12$ c $3m = 15$

d $4a = 16$ e $3s = 18$ f $5r = 20$

Divide both sides by the same number.

118

6 Using letter symbols

Band 2 questions

7 Solve these equations.
- a $\quad 5p = 20$
- b $\quad 6 + f = 7$
- c $\quad 8a = 32$
- d $\quad g - 2 = 8$
- e $\quad m - 11 = 21$
- f $\quad 9h = 36$
- g $\quad 12x = 72$
- h $\quad y - 8 = 22$
- i $\quad 8s = 24$

8 Solve each of the equations represented in these diagrams. For each one:
- i write down an equation for the problem
- ii draw scales and write out a new equation for each stage of your solution
- iii show how you checked your solution.

a

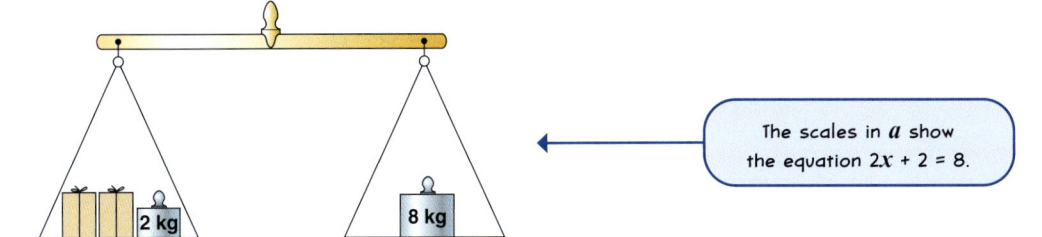

The scales in a show the equation $2x + 2 = 8$.

b

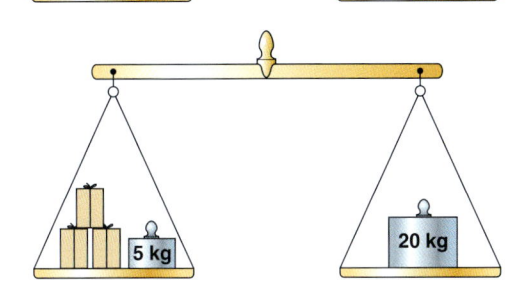

c

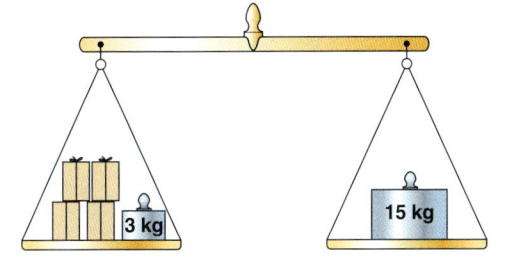

d

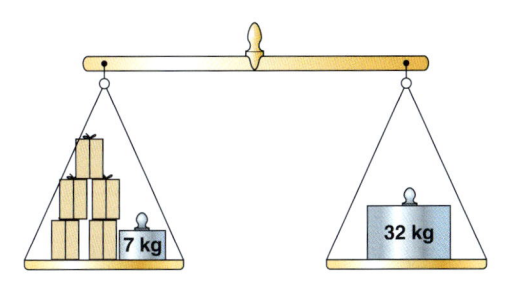

9 Use a bar model to help you solve the following equations. The first two have been started for you.

a $\quad 2a + 4 = 12$

a	a	4
12			

b $\quad 3b + 8 = 23$

b	b	b	8
23			

- c $\quad 5c + 3 = 18$
- d $\quad 5 + 3d = 11$
- e $\quad 1 + 7e = 15$
- f $\quad 10 + 3f = 16$

10 Solve these equations.
- a $\quad a - 2 = 10$
- b $\quad 2a - 2 = 10$
- c $\quad 3a - 2 = 10$
- d $\quad 4a - 2 = 10$

119

Curriculum for Wales **Mastering Mathematics: Book 1**

Logical reasoning

11   Here is Zachary's maths homework.

1. $5x - 3 = 7$
    $5x - 3 + 3 = 7 + 3$
    $5x = 10$
    $5x \div 5 = 10 \div 5$
    $x = 2$

2. $2x - 4 = 14$
    $2x - 4 + 4 = 14 - 4$
    $2x = 10$
    $2x \div 2 = 10 \div 2$
    $x = 5$

3. $3x - 1 = 26$
    $3x - 1 + 1 = 26 + 1$
    $3x = 27$
    $3x \div 3 = 27 \div 3$
    $x = 9$

4. $4x + 3 = 24$
    $4x \div 4 + 3 = 24 \div 4$
    $x + 3 - 3 = 6 - 3$
    $x = 3$

   a   Check Zachary's homework.
   b   Zachary got some of the questions wrong.
   Show the correct working and answer for any he has got wrong.

12   Meena and Alun are having an argument.

> The answer to $5x - 12 = 18$ is $x = 5$.

> No, it isn't. It's $x = 3$.

   a   Who is right?
   b   How can you tell whether an answer is wrong without solving the equation?
   c   What is the right answer?

Band 3 questions

Fluency

13   Junko thinks of a number as shown.
   a   Write down an equation for Junko's number.
   b   Solve your equation to work out Junko's number.

> I multiply my number by 4 and add 6. My answer is 30.

14   Cledwyn thinks of a number as shown.
   a   Write down an equation for Cledwyn's number.
   b   Solve your equation to work out Cledwyn's number.

> I multiply my number by 2 and subtract 4. My answer is 8.

Logical reasoning

15   **a**   Match each of these equations with its solution.
   i $3x - 2 = 10$ **ii** $5x - 1 = 24$
   iii $4x + 11 = 17$ **iv** $2x + 5 = 10$
   v $3x - 33 = 0$

   $x = 5$ $x = 2\frac{1}{2}$ $x = 1\frac{1}{2}$ $x = 3$ $x = 2$ $x = 11$ $x = 4$

   b   Which **two** values of x are not used?
   Write your own equations with these values of x as their solutions.

16 Taran buys five pens in a shop for £4.20.

    a Write an equation for this information using p pence as the cost of one pen.   *Work in pence.*

    b Solve your equation to find the cost of one pen.

17 Catrin buys two apples, at 48p each, and four bananas.

She spends £2.56 altogether.

    a Write an equation for this information, using b pence as the cost of one banana.

    b Solve your equation to find the cost of one banana.

18 One cinema ticket costs £c.

Dani buys five tickets.

She gets £2.50 change from £50.

    a Write an equation for c and solve it.

    b How much is one cinema ticket?

19 Three friends run a relay race.

Altogether their time is 65 seconds.

Harri takes 4 seconds longer than Dafydd.

Manon takes 5 seconds less than Dafydd.

How many seconds does each person take?

20 Anwen is six years older than her brother Dilwyn.

In 16 years, the sum of their ages will be 100 years.

Suppose that Anwen is x years old now.

    a Copy and complete the table.

	Anwen's age (years)	Dilwyn's age (years)
Now	x	$x - 6$
In 16 years		

    b Form an equation and solve it.

    c How old are Anwen and Dilwyn now?

Key words

Here is a list of the key words you met in this chapter.

Equation	Evaluate	Expression	Formula
Simplify	Solve	Substitute	Unknown
Variable			

Use the glossary at the back of this book to check any you are unsure about.

Review exercise: using letter symbols

Band 1 questions

1 Ali has 20 fewer books than Teleri.
   - **a** Who has more books?
   - **b** Which of these rules is correct?
     - **i** Number of Ali's books + number of Teleri's books = 20
     - **ii** Number of Ali's books + 20 = number of Teleri's books
     - **iii** Number of Ali's books − 20 = number of Teleri's books

2 Look at this advert.
   - **a** Copy and complete this formula.

     Cost of hire (£) = ☐ × number of hours

     Speedy Boats
     £15 per hour
   - **b** Work out the cost of hiring a boat for:
     - **i** 2 hours
     - **ii** 3 hours
     - **iii** 12 hours.

3 Simplify these expressions.
   - **a** $4g + 2 - 3g + 5$
   - **b** $2d + 4 + 5d + 7 + 3d$
   - **c** $4m - 2 + 4m - 3$
   - **d** $2x + 3 - x + 2 + 4x$
   - **e** $3c + 2 - 2c - 1$
   - **f** $3y + 5 - y + 3 + 2y - 8$

4 Solve these equations.
   - **a** $c - 7 = 10$
   - **b** $5 + d = 7$
   - **c** $g - 5 = 5$
   - **d** $u + 5 = 19$
   - **e** $h - 8 = 42$
   - **f** $j + 125 = 1125$
   - **g** $7n = 42$
   - **h** $10x = 70$
   - **i** $12y = 132$

5 Jo has a pencils and Humza has b pencils.
   Write in words the meaning of each of these equations.
   - **a** $a = 8$
   - **b** $a + b = 12$
   - **c** $a = 2b$

Band 2 questions

6 Simplify these expressions.
   - **a** $a + 2b + 4 + 5a$
   - **b** $4x + 5y - 2x + y$
   - **c** $2x - 3y + 6y + 7$
   - **d** $9x + 6y - 5x - 4$
   - **e** $3p - 4q + 7 - 3p$
   - **f** $4p - 5 + 3q - 4$
   - **g** $9r - 3s - 8r + 3s$
   - **h** $7h - 2i - 4h + 6i$
   - **i** $5x + 2y + 3x - 6y - 8x$

7 Work out the value of $2a + 4b - 5c$ when:
   - **a** $a = 2, b = 3$ and $c = 1$
   - **b** $a = 9, b = 7$ and $c = 2$
   - **c** $a = 1, b = 0$ and $c = 0$
   - **d** $a = 4, b = 3$ and $c = 4$.

8 Jon and Raj are co-pilots in a jet that flies from London to New York.
   The journey is 3500 miles long.
   They share the flying.
   - **a** Raj flies the first 2200 miles.
     How far does Jon fly?
   - **b** On another trip, Jon flies 1800 miles.
     How far does Raj fly?

6   Using letter symbols

c   Copy and complete this formula.

   Distance (in miles) flown by Raj = 3500 ☐

d   Write another formula that gives the same information in a different way.

9   Write algebraic expressions for the following:
   a b added to 2
   b   6 lots of b
   c   2 subtracted from b
   d   2 lots of b
   e   6 less than b
   f   7 more than b
   g b multiplied by 3
   h b squared
   i a lots of b.

10   A clothes shop has a sale.
   a   Use j for the number of pairs of jeans.
      Use t for the number of T-shirts.
      Copy and complete this formula:
      Cost (£) = 30 ☐ + ☐ t

      Jeans £30
      T-shirts £10
      Great value!

   b   Work out the cost of four pairs of jeans and three T-shirts.

11   Pens cost p pence each and rulers cost r pence each.
   Write down an expression for the cost of:
   a   one pen and one ruler
   b   three pens
   c   four pens and five rulers
   d p pens.

12   Solve these equations.
   a $2a + 1 = 5$
   b $3b + 6 = 27$
   c $5c - 4 = 16$
   d $3 + 7d = 10$
   e $10g - 22 = 38$
   f $3h - 6 = 0$

13   Solve these puzzles by finding the value of each symbol.
   The numbers give the row and column totals.
   a
   b

Band 3 questions

14   Simplify these expressions.
   a $x^2 + 3x^2$
   b $x^2 + 2x^2 - 3x - 4x$
   c $4x + 2xy - 3x - 4xy$
   d $6xy + 2y - 3y - 4xy - xy + 5y$

Curriculum for Wales Mastering Mathematics: Book 1

15 All the lengths marked on this rectangle are in centimetres.

Find an expression for the missing lengths in this rectangle.

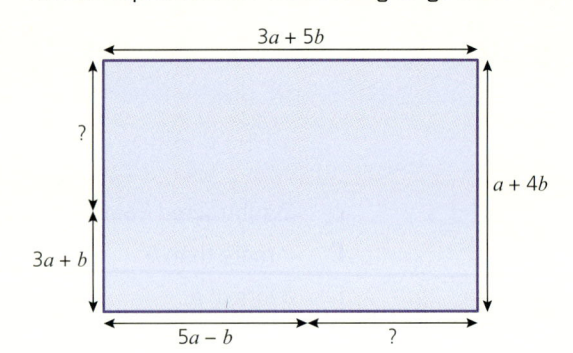

Top: $3a + 5b$
Right: $a + 4b$
Left: ?
Bottom-left: $3a + b$
Bottom: $5a - b$, ?

16 The formula to convert a temperature in degrees Fahrenheit, F, to a temperature in degrees Celsius, C, is:

$$C = \frac{5(F - 32)}{9}$$

Someone with a fever has a temperature above 37.8 °C.

Dai has a temperature of 99 °F.

Does Dai have a fever? Give a reason for your answer.

17 Three friends play a computer game.

Between them they score 530 points.

Rhys scores 30 more points than Bethan.

Mair scores twice as many points as Rhys.

How many points does each friend score?

18 a Copy this arithmagon.

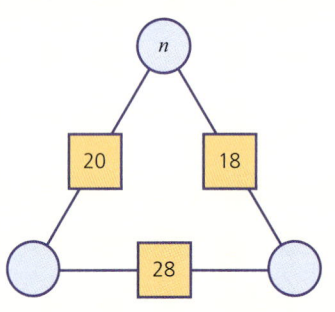

(Arithmagon with top circle n, squares 20, 18, 28)

The number in the square is the sum of those in the two circles on either side.

Fill in the bottom circles in terms of n.

b Use your answers to part **a** to write an equation in terms of n and the number 28.

c Solve your equation to find n.

Check your answer in the arithmagon.

d Copy and complete this arithmagon.

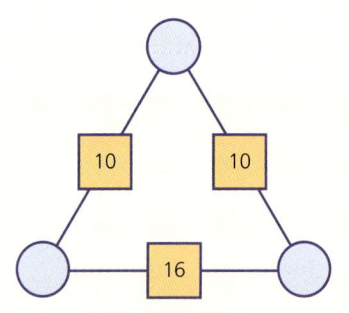

(Arithmagon with squares 10, 10, 16)

124

7 Sequences

Coming up...
▶ Working with sequences
▶ Generating sequences

Whatever next!

What comes next in each of these patterns?
Explain how you know.

①	←	↑	→	↓	←	↑	→
②	Z	Y	X	W	V		
③	A	C	E	G	I	K	M
④	M	T	W	T	F	S	
⑤	M	V	E	M	J	S	U
⑥	J	F	M	A	M	J	J
⑦	Q	W	E	R	T		
⑧	1 Ƨ Ɛ ƕ 5 6 7						

7.1 Working with sequences

Skill checker

Write down the first five:
a even numbers
b square numbers
c cube numbers
d multiples of 6
e prime numbers.

▶ Number sequences

A **sequence** is a set of numbers, letters or shapes which follow a rule.
The sequence 1, 3, 5, 7, 9, ... is the sequence of **odd numbers**.
A **term** is a particular number in a sequence.

125

Term number:

① ② ③ ④ ⑤
1, 3, 5, 7, 9, ...

↑ ↑ ↑
1st term 2nd term 5th term

> The dots '...' show that the sequence carries on like this forever – it is infinite.

You can **generate** the terms in a sequence using its **rule**.

Some rules tell you:
- one term in the sequence
- how to work out the next term.

So in the sequence of odd numbers the rule is:
- the first term is 1
- to find the next term, add 2.

> This is called a 'term-to-term rule'. It tells you how to get from one term to the next.

By using the rule for moving from one term to another, you can predict the next or missing terms.

In this sequence, the rule is 'the first term is 11, add 2 to get the next term'.

11, 13, 15, 17, 19, ... ← The next term is 19 + 2 = 21.

In this sequence, the rule is 'the first term is $\frac{1}{2}$, add 1 to the denominator (bottom of the fraction) to get the next term'.

$\frac{1}{2}, \frac{1}{3}, \frac{1}{4}, \frac{1}{5}, ...$ ← The next term is $\frac{1}{6}$.

You can often work out the pattern or rule that a sequence is using by looking at the **differences** between the terms.

In an **arithmetic** sequence, there is the **same difference** between each pair of terms.

Here is an arithmetic sequence:

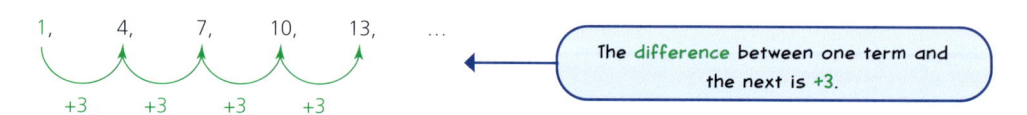

1, 4, 7, 10, 13, ...
 +3 +3 +3 +3

> The **difference** between one term and the next is **+3**.

The term-to-term rule is:
- the first term is 1
- to find the next term, add 3.

Each term is 3 more than the one before, so the next term is 13 + 3 = 16.

Here is another arithmetic sequence:

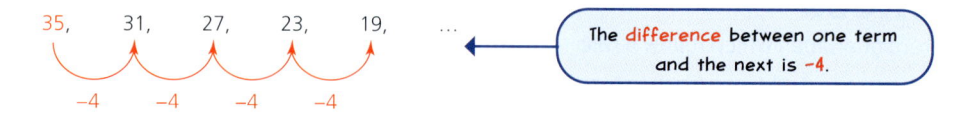

35, 31, 27, 23, 19, ...
 −4 −4 −4 −4

> The **difference** between one term and the next is **−4**.

Each term is 4 less than the one before, so the next term is 19 − 4 = 15.

The term-to-term rule is:
- the first term is 35
- to find the next term, subtract 4.

7 Sequences

Worked example

Find the missing terms in these arithmetic sequences.

> There is the same difference between each pair of terms.

a 3, 7, 11, ☐, 19, ☐, 27, …

b 100, 93, 86, 79, ☐, ☐, …

Solution

a The sequence 3, 7, 11, … has the rule 'the first term is 3, add 4 to the previous term'.

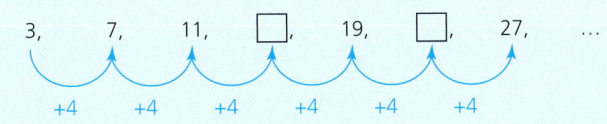

3, 7, 11, ☐, 19, ☐, 27, …
+4 +4 +4 +4 +4 +4

So the missing terms are 15 and 23.

b The sequence 100, 93, 86, … has the rule 'the first term is 100, subtract 7 from the previous term'.

100, 93, 86, 79, ☐, ☐,
−7 −7 −7 −7 −7

So the missing terms are 72 and 65.

The rule to get from one term to the next doesn't have to be 'add' or 'subtract'.

Worked example

The first term of a sequence is 512.

To find the next term, **divide by 2**.

a Write down the first four terms in the sequence.
b What is the last whole number in this sequence?
c Is this an arithmetic sequence? Explain your answer.

Solution

a Term number:

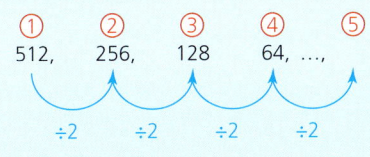

① ② ③ ④ ⑤
512, 256, 128, 64, …,
÷2 ÷2 ÷2 ÷2

b Term number:

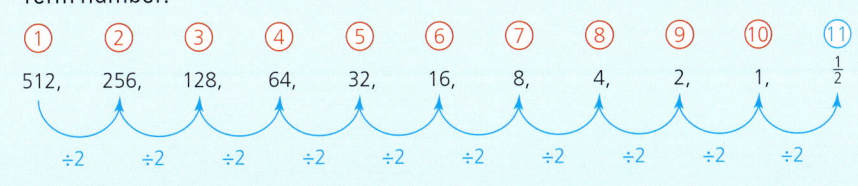

① ② ③ ④ ⑤ ⑥ ⑦ ⑧ ⑨ ⑩ ⑪
512, 256, 128, 64, 32, 16, 8, 4, 2, 1, $\frac{1}{2}$
÷2 ÷2 ÷2 ÷2 ÷2 ÷2 ÷2 ÷2 ÷2 ÷2

So the last **whole number** is the tenth term, which is 1.

c Look at the differences between terms.

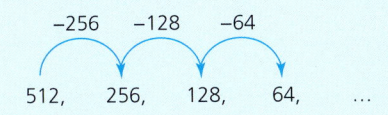

−256 −128 −64
512, 256, 128, 64, …

The differences between the terms are **not the same** so the sequence is **not arithmetic**.

127

Curriculum for Wales **Mastering Mathematics: Book 1**

▶ Picture sequences

Sequences can be made from patterns.

Worked example

Leila uses some tiles to make patterns.

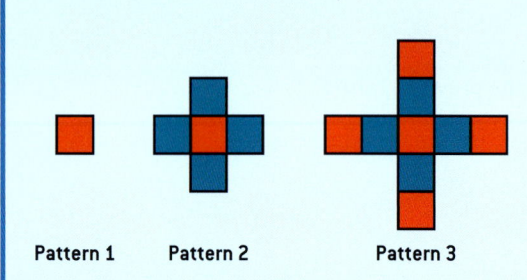

Pattern 1   Pattern 2   Pattern 3

a Draw the next pattern in the sequence.

b Copy and complete the table.

Pattern number	1	2	3	4
Number of squares	1	5		

c Without drawing any more patterns, work out how many squares are needed for Pattern 5.

Solution

a

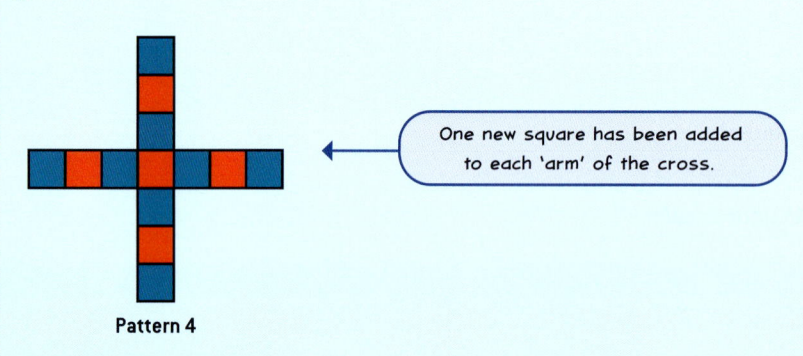

Pattern 4

One new square has been added to each 'arm' of the cross.

b Count the number of squares used to make each pattern.

Pattern number	1	2	3	4
Number of squares	1	5	9	13

c You need to add four new squares to make the next pattern.

So Pattern 5 needs 13 + 4 = 17 squares.

7 Sequences

Activity

Glyn makes some patterns out of counters.

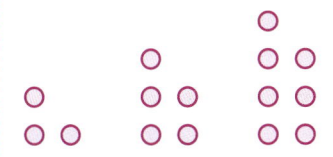

Pattern 1   Pattern 2   Pattern 3

Pattern number	1	2	3	4	5
Number of counters	3	5	7		

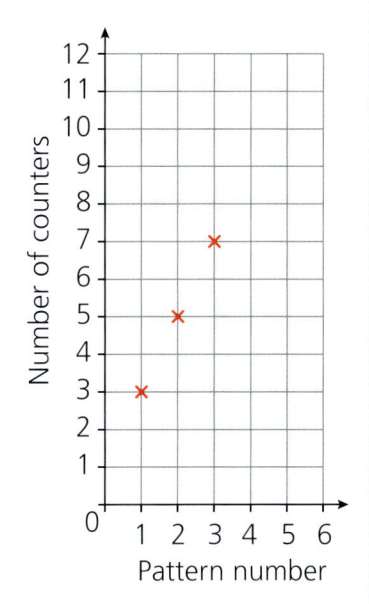

1. Copy and complete Glyn's table.
2. Glyn draws a graph to show the number of counters used for each pattern.
    a Copy and complete Glyn's graph.
    b What do you notice about the points?
       Is Glyn's sequence arithmetic?
    c Do you think you should join the points?
       Why/why not?
3. Draw a table and graph like Glyn's for each of these patterns.
    a   b
    Pattern 1 Pattern 2 Pattern 3   Pattern 1 Pattern 2 Pattern 3
4. Make your own counter pattern.
    Make sure that you add the **same number** of counters each time to make the next pattern.
    Draw a table and graph for your pattern.
5. Why do you think sequences like these are sometimes called **linear**?

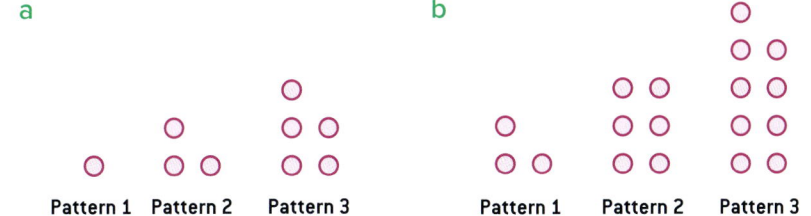

7.1 Now try these

Band 1 questions

1. Find the next three terms in each of these sequences.
    a 7, 10, 13, 16, 19, ___, ___, ___
    b 5, 11, 17, 23, 29, ___, ___, ___
    c 15, 23, 31, 39, 47, ___, ___, ___

2. Find the next three terms in each of these sequences.
    a 99, 90, 81, 72, 63, ___, ___, ___
    b 1000, 975, 950, 925, 900, ___, ___, ___
    c 43, 38, 33, 28, 23, ___, ___, ___

Curriculum for Wales Mastering Mathematics: Book 1

3 Look at this sequence:

1, 7, 13, 19, 26, 33, 40, 47

Write down the:

a   first term
b   fifth term
c   eighth term.

4 Copy the term-to-term rule and copy and complete each sequence.

The sequence in part **a** has been done for you.

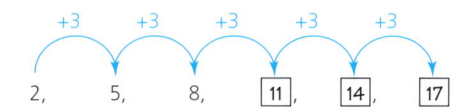

a   Add three

   +3 +3 +3 +3 +3
2,   5,   8,   11, 14, 17

b   Add five   4,   9,   14,   ☐, ☐, ☐
c   Subtract four   20,   16,   12,   ☐, ☐, ☐
d   Divide by three 729, 243, 81,   ☐, ☐, ☐
e   Multiply by four 1,   4,   16,   ☐, ☐, ☐

5 Mo uses tiles to make patterns.

Pattern 1   Pattern 2   Pattern 3

a   Draw Pattern 4 and Pattern 5.

b   i   Copy and complete the table.

Pattern number	1	2	3	4	5
Number of tiles	2	4			

   ii   What type of numbers has Mo made?

c   Can you arrange an odd number of rectangles in pairs to make rectangles?

   Why do you think 1, 3, 5, 7, … are called 'odd'?

Band 2 questions

6 For each sequence, copy and complete these sentences with appropriate numbers.

   i   The first term is _____ .
   ii   To find the next term add _____ .

   a   1,   5,   9,   13,   17,   …
   b   3,   5,   7,   9,   11,   …
   c   5,   8,   11,   14,   17,   …

7 a   For each of these sequences, find the differences between the terms.

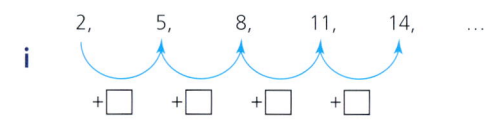

   i
       2,   5,   8,   11,   14,   …
         +☐   +☐   +☐   +☐

130

ii

20, 18, 16, 14, 32, ...

−☐ −☐ −☐ −☐

iii

1, 3, 7, 15, 31, ...

+☐ +☐ +☐ +☐

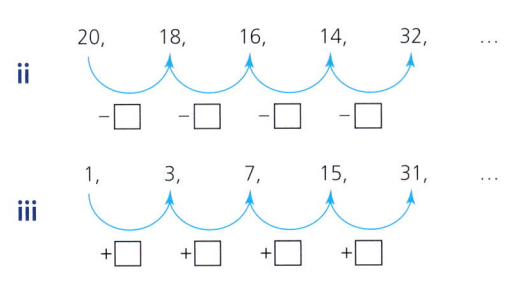

b Which sequence is **not** arithmetic? Give a reason for your answer.

8 Write down the first five terms of each of these sequences.

	The first term is ...	To find the next term you ...
a	18	add 2
b	20	subtract 3
c	0.1	multiply by 10
d	1024	divide by 4

9 Find the missing terms in each of these arithmetic sequences.
   a 2, 4, ☐, 8, 10, 12, ☐, 16
   b ☐, 90, 80, 70, ☐, 50, 40, ☐
   c ☐, ☐, ☐, 19, 24, 29, 34, ☐

10 Dewi writes down a sequence.

He says, 'the term-to-term rule for my sequence is add 5'.

Explain why you can't write down Dewi's sequence.

11 Haf uses some matchsticks to make patterns.
   a Draw the next two patterns.
   b Copy and complete this table for the first five patterns.

Pattern 1   Pattern 2   Pattern 3

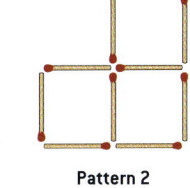

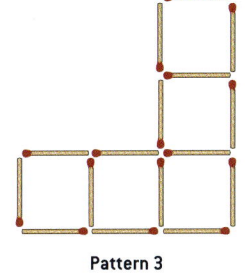

Pattern	1	2	3	4	5
Number of squares	1	3			
Number of matchsticks	4	10			

   c i How many squares are added to make the next pattern?
   ii How many more matchsticks does Haf need to make Pattern 6?
   d i Work out how many matchsticks Haf needs to make Pattern 8.
   ii How many squares are in Pattern 8?
   e Is it possible for one of Haf's patterns to have 100 squares?
   Give a reason for your answer.

12 For each of these sequences:
  i find the next two terms
  ii give the term-to-term rule.

  a 2, 4, 8, 16, …
  b 5, 9, 13, 17, …
  c 81, 27, 9, 3, …
  d 3, 11, 18, 24, …
  e 42, 36, 30, 24, …
  f 3, 6, 12, 24, …

Band 3 questions

13 For each of these sequences:
  i work out the differences between the terms
  ii write down the next three terms
  iii explain how to work out the next term.

  a 1, 3, 6, 10, 15, …
  b 1, 3, 7, 13, 21, …
  c 100, 99, 97, 92, 85…
  d 1, 1, 2, 3, 5, 8…

14 Lili uses some counters to make square patterns.

She starts with one counter and then adds counters to make the next pattern.

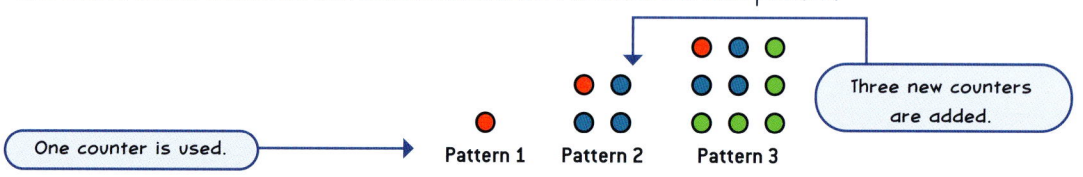

One counter is used. Pattern 1 Pattern 2 Pattern 3 Three new counters are added.

  a How many counters are in each pattern?
  b Copy and complete the table.

Pattern number	1	2	3	4	5
Number of new counters added	1	3			
Total number of counters	1	4			

  c Work out how many counters are in:
   i Pattern 6
   ii Pattern 10
   iii Pattern 20
   iv Pattern n.
  d Explain how you can use Lili's pattern to work out these.
   i 1 + 3
   ii 1 + 3 + 5
   iii the sum of the first ten odd numbers
   iv the sum of the first 100 odd numbers
   v the sum of the first n odd numbers

15 Amir writes down this arithmetic sequence:

  4, 7, 10, 13, …

He says, 'The tenth term is $4 + 9 \times 3 = 31$, as you have to add on 3 nine times.'
  a Show that Amir is right.
  b Use Amir's method to find the 100th term.
  c Without writing out the full sequence, work out the 100th term of each of these sequences.
   i 6, 10, 14, 18, …
   ii 3, 8, 13, 18, …

16 Erin and Jacinda are talking about their plans to get fit.

Erin says, 'I'm going to do 10 press-ups one day, then 15 the next and then 20 the next and so on.'

Jacinda says, 'I'll do 30 press-ups one day, then 33 the next and then 36 the next and so on.'

a Carry on the sequence to show how many press-ups Erin does over one week.

Day	1	2	3	...
Number of press-ups	10	15	20	...

b How many press-ups does
   i Erin   **ii** Jacinda
   do altogether in the first seven days?

c One day Erin and Jacinda do the same number of press-ups.
   Work out which day this is.

d Who does the most press-ups if they keep this up for a month?
   Give a reason for your answer.

17 a This sequence is called a 'look-and-say' sequence. Can you see why?

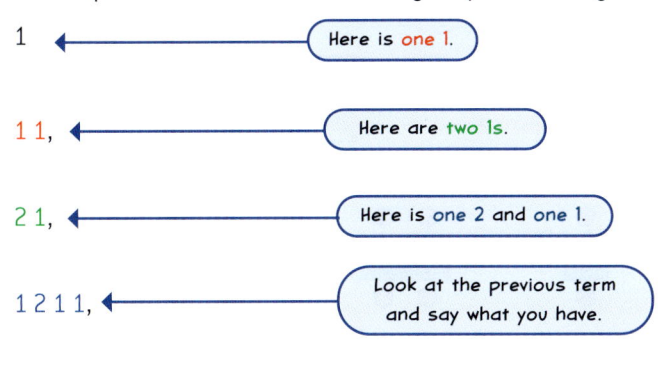

1 ← Here is one 1.

1 1, ← Here are two 1s.

2 1, ← Here is one 2 and one 1.

1 2 1 1, ← Look at the previous term and say what you have.

1 1 1 2 2 1, ...

b What is the next term in the sequence?

c Will the digit '4' ever appear in this look-and-say sequence?
   Explain your answer fully.

d A similar sequence starts with 2 instead of 1.
   After the second term, how will each term end?

e Can you find a look-and-say sequence where every term is the same?

7.2 Generating sequences

Skill checker

1 Write down the next three terms in each of these sequences.

a 1, 3, 5, 7, 9, ☐, ☐, ☐

b 21, 18, 15, 12, 9, ☐, ☐, ☐

c 1, 5, 9, 13, 17, ☐, ☐, ☐

d 60, 53, 47, 40, 33, ☐, ☐, ☐

② The rules show how to get from one term to the next in these three sequences.
For each sequence, the first term is 10.
Write down the next three terms.
 a **Rule 1:** Multiply by 2 then subtract 5.
 b **Rule 2:** Add 6 then divide by 2.
 c **Rule 3:** Subtract 8 then multiply by 10.

③ Work out the value of $3n$ when:
 a $n = 1$
 b $n = 2$
 c $n = 3$.

④ Work out the value of $4n + 1$ when:
 a $n = 1$
 b $n = 2$
 c $n = 3$.

▶ Position-to-term rules

Activity

New tables are needed for the school canteen.

Here are some seating arrangements.

'When three square tables are joined together, eight people can be seated.'

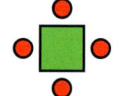

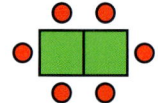

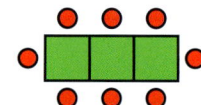

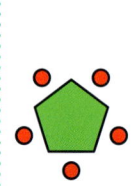

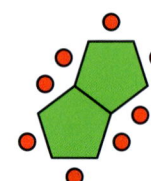

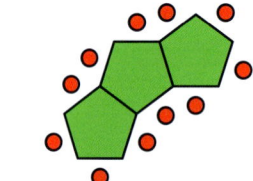

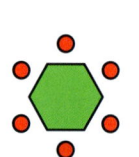

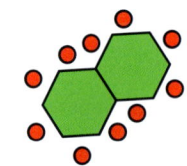

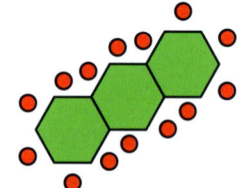

Jol wants to work out how many people can be seated when 20 tables are joined together.

Jol has found some rules:

To work out the number of people who can be seated you …

… multiply the number of tables by 4 and then add 2

… add 2 to the number of tables

… multiply the number of tables by 2 and then add 2.

 a Match each of Jol's rules with the correct table shape.
 b Write down the missing rule.
 c Find your own rules for heptagonal (seven-sided) and octagonal (eight-sided) tables.

Investigate further.

Remember that each number in a sequence has a term number.
In this sequence, each term is 2 × the term number.

Term number   ①   ②   ③   ④   ⑤
Sequence   2   4   6   8   10   ← This is the two times table.

You can use the term number to generate a sequence.

Worked example

The rule for a sequence is:

   4 × the term number − 1

Find the first four terms in the sequence.

Solution

Use the rule: 4 × the term number − 1
The 1st term is: 4 × 1 − 1 = 4 − 1 = 3
The 2nd term is: 4 × 2 − 1 = 8 − 1 = 7
The 3rd term is: 4 × 3 − 1 = 12 − 1 = 11
The 4th term is: 4 × 4 − 1 = 16 − 1 = 15
So the sequence is:

Term number   ①   ②   ③   ④   ← Notice that each term is four
Term   3   7   11   15   more than the term before.

When you use the term number to work out the terms in a sequence, you are using a **position-to-term** rule.

Usually a position-to-term rule is written in terms of the general term number, n.

So in the example above, the nth term is $4n - 3$.   ← Think 'any' term!

Worked example

The rule for the nth term of a sequence is $2n + 1$.

a Find the first three terms in the sequence.
b Find the 100th term.

Solution

a Use the rule: nth term = $2n + 1$
   The 1st term is when $n = 1$.   1st term = 2 × 1 + 1 = 3
   The 2nd term is when $n = 2$.   2nd term = 2 × 2 + 1 = 5
   The 3rd term is when $n = 3$.   3rd term = 2 × 3 + 1 = 7
b The 100th term is when $n = 100$.   100th term = 2 × 100 + 1 = 201

Curriculum for Wales Mastering Mathematics: Book 1

You can use the rule for the nth term to help you with sequences that come from patterns.

Worked example

A farmer has sections of fencing with four bars between each pair of posts.
He puts them together to make a fence.

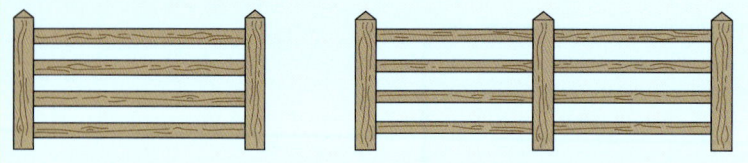

Fence 1   Fence 2

a Draw Fence 3 and Fence 4.

b Copy and complete this table.

Fence number, n	Number of posts (p)	Number of bars (b)
1	2	4
2	3	
3		
4		

c Show how to work out how many

  i posts

  ii bars

are needed for Fence 10.

d Complete these rules.

  i The number of posts = fence number + ☐   So $p = n +$ ☐

  ii The number of bars = ☐ × fence number   So $b =$ ☐ n

Solution

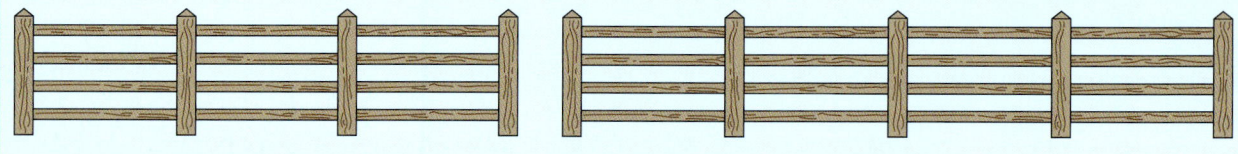

Fence 3   Fence 4

b

Fence number, n	Number of posts (p)	Number of bars (b)
1	2	4
2	3	8
3	4	12
4	5	16

c There is one more post used than the fence number, so Fence 10 needs 11 posts.

Each section of fencing needs four bars, so Fence 10 needs 4 × 10 = 40 bars.

d i The number of posts = fence number + 1   So $p = n + 1$

  ii The number of bars = 4 × fence number   So $b = 4n$

7.2 Now try these

Band 1 questions

1 The rule for a sequence is:

    the term number + 3

  a What is the first term in the sequence?

  b What is the second term in the sequence?

  c What is the third term in the sequence?

  d What is the tenth term in the sequence?

2 Find the first five terms of each of these sequences.

  a The rule for the sequence is:

    the term number − 1

  b The rule for the sequence is:

    the term number + 8

  c The rule for the sequence is:

    5 × the term number

  d The rule for the sequence is:

    10 × the term number

Hint

Replace 'the term number' with 1, 2, 3, 4 and 5 to work out each term.

3 Match each of these sequences with its rule.

3, 6, 9, 12, 15 …	Rule: 5 × term number
4, 5, 6, 7, 8 …	Rule: term number × 3
6, 7, 8, 9, 10 …	Rule: term number + 3
5, 10, 15, 20, 25 …	Rule: term number + 5

4 Look at this number machine.

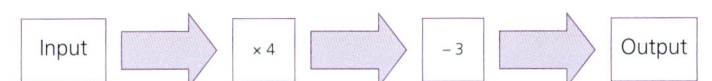

Input → × 4 → − 3 → Output

  a Copy and complete this table for the number machine. The first line has been done for you.

Input	Calculation	Output
1	1 × 4 − 3	1
2		
3		
4		
5		

  b What pattern can you see in the output column?

  c Write down the first ten terms of the output sequence.

5 **a** Find the missing terms in these sequences.

    i 8, 16, 24, 32, ☐, ☐, 56, …

    ii 11, ☐, 17, 20, ☐, ☐, 29, …

    iii 11, 19, ☐, 35, ☐, ☐, 59, …

b One of the sequences in part **a** comes from this number machine. Which sequence is it?

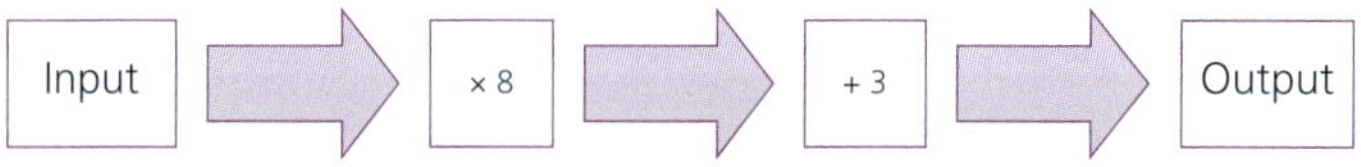

Input → × 8 → + 3 → Output

Band 2 questions

6 a Write down the first five terms of the sequences with these position-to-term rules.

   i nth term = $4n$ **ii** nth term = $8n$

   iii nth term = $n + 5$ **iv** nth term = $n + 7$

b Write down the first number and give the term-to-term rule for each sequence.

7 a Draw the next pattern in each of these sequences.

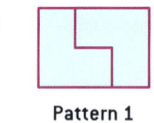

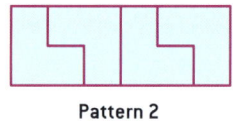

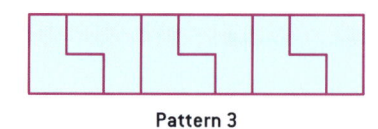

   i Pattern 1, Pattern 2, Pattern 3

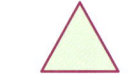

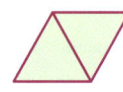

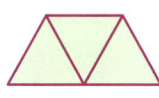

   ii Pattern 1, Pattern 2, Pattern 3

   iii Pattern 1, Pattern 2, Pattern 3

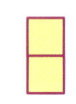

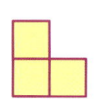

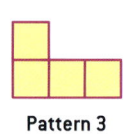

b Copy and complete the table for the patterns in part **a**.

Pattern number	1	2	3	4	5
Number of triangles					
Number of L shapes					
Number of squares					

c Copy and fill numbers in the boxes to complete the rules:
- Number of triangles = ☐
- Number of L shapes = ☐ × pattern number
- Number of squares = pattern number + ☐

8 Write down the first five terms of the sequences with these position-to-term rules.

   a nth term = $2n - 1$ **b** nth term = $5n + 2$

   c nth term = $3n + 4$ **d** nth term = $10n - 9$

9 Write down the first five terms of the sequences with these position-to-term rules.

   a nth term = $10 - n$ **b** nth term = $10 - 2n$

   c nth term = $20 - 4n$ **d** nth term = $50 - 3n$

7 Sequences

10 a Look at this tiling pattern.
Draw Pattern 4.

Pattern 1   Pattern 2   Pattern 3

b Copy and complete the following table.

Pattern number	1	2	3	4	5
Number of red tiles					
Number of blue tiles					
Total number of tiles					

c Without drawing, work out the number of
  i red tiles   **ii** blue tiles   **iii** tiles in total
in the tenth pattern.

d Complete these rules.
Number of red tiles = _____
Number of blue tiles = pattern number + ☐
Total number of tiles = ☐ × pattern number + ☐

Band 3 questions

11 Write down the first five terms of the sequences with these position-to-term rules.
  a nth term = $n^2 + 3$
  b nth term = $n^2 - 1$
  c nth term = $2n^2$
  d nth term = $2n^2 - 3$

12 Match the sequences on the left with the position-to-term formulas on the right.

4, 8, 12, 16, 20, …	$2n - 6$
2, 3, 4, 5, 6, ..	$3n + 2$
−4, −2, 0, 2, 4, …	n^2
5, 8, 11, 14, 17, …	$4n$
1, 4, 9, 16, 25, …	$n + 1$

Cross-curricular activity

Use a spreadsheet to generate the sequences in question 12.

Could you also write a simple computer program to generate these sequences?

(If you are more advanced at programming, could you develop your program to generate any sequence by giving its position-to-term rule?)

13 a Draw the next pattern in the following sequence.

Pattern 1   Pattern 2   Pattern 3

b Copy and complete the following table.

Pattern number	1	2	3	4	5
Number of purple squares					
Number of white squares					
Total number of squares					

c Write down how many purple squares are needed to make the twelfth pattern.
Explain how you know.

d Work out how many white squares are needed to make the twelfth pattern.
Explain how you know.

14 Dafydd is organising a tombola for his Youth Club.

Each member of the club draws a ticket with a number on it out of a hat.

To win a prize, the number on the ticket must be a term in one of these sequences.

Sequence	Prize
nth term $= n^2 + 1$	Chocolates
The first term is 1. The next term is double the previous term.	Cuddly toy
The first two terms are both 1. The next term is the sum of the previous two terms.	Cinema tickets
nth term $= 2n^2 - 1$	Book token

Which prizes will these tickets win?

17   20   19   13   45   12

50   7   64   36   91   56

15 Iona is making patterns using matchsticks.

The rule to find the number of matchsticks, m, needed for pattern n is:

$m = 9n - 5$

a How many matchsticks does Iona need to make the twentieth pattern?

b Iona has 130 matchsticks. Show whether she can use all of them to make a single pattern.

c Gareth has 230 matchsticks. Show whether he can use all of them to make a single pattern.

16 Bethan is using some coins to make patterns.

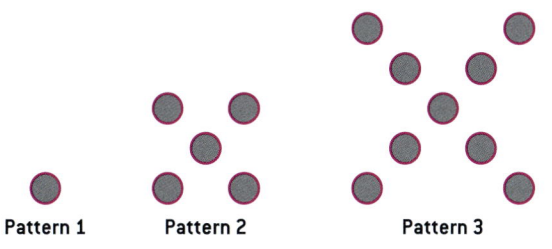

Pattern 1   Pattern 2   Pattern 3

a Draw Pattern 4.
b Bethan says that the number of coins used for each pattern follows the rule:

   $4n - 3$

   Show that Bethan's rule is true for the first four patterns.
c Bethan has 150 coins. She wants to use them to make just one pattern.
   i   Which is the highest pattern number she can make?
   ii How many coins does she have left over?
d Bethan now uses her 150 coins to make as many different patterns as she can.
   i   What pattern number can she make up to?
   ii How many coins does she have left over?

> **Key words**
>
> Here is a list of the key words you met in this chapter.
>
> | | | |
> |---|---|---|
> | Arithmetic sequence | Difference | Even |
> | Graph | Heptagon | Odd |
> | Position-to-term rule | Sequence | Term |
> | Term number | Term-to-term rule | |
>
> Use the glossary at the back of this book to check any you are unsure about.

Review exercise: sequences

Band 1 questions

1 Write down the next three terms in each of these sequences.
   a 5, 8, 11, 14, ☐, ☐, ☐
   b 15, 13, 11, 9, ☐, ☐, ☐
   c 12, 17, 22, 27, ☐, ☐, ☐
   d 100, 95, 90, 85, ☐, ☐, ☐
   e 70, 63, 56, 49, ☐, ☐, ☐
   f 7, 11, 15, 19, ☐, ☐, ☐
   g 88, 91, 94, 97, ☐, ☐, ☐

2 Look at this sequence:

   | 3, | 7, | 11, | 15, | 19, ... |

   a What is the first term of the sequence?
   b What is the third term of the sequence?
   c Copy and complete the following.
      Each term is ☐ more than the one before.
      So the difference between the terms is ☐.

3 For each of these sequences, explain how to find the next term and then write down the next three terms.
   a 1, 4, 7, 10, ...
   b 28, 24, 20, 16, ...
   c 5, 10, 20, 40, ...

4 Find numbers to go in ◇ and ☐ to make a rule for these sequences.
   • The first term is ◇.
   • To find the next term add ☐.
   a 9,   14,   19,   24,   29, ...
   b 5,   12,   19,   26,   33, ...
   c 3,   11,   19,   27,   35, ...

5 This is the rule for a sequence.
   • The first term is ◇.
   • To find the next term add ☐.
   Find numbers to go in ◇ and ☐ so the sequence has only:
   a even numbers
   b odd numbers
   c the numbers in the five times table
   d numbers which have a 7 as the final digit.

Band 2 questions

6 Each of these sequences is arithmetic. Copy each sequence and fill in the missing numbers.
   a ☐, 6, 9, ☐, ☐, 18
   b 11, ☐, 15, ☐, 19, 21
   c 6, 11, ☐, ☐, 26, 31
   d ☐, ☐, ☐, 27, 36, 45
   e ☐, 20, ☐, 12, ☐, 4

7 Write down the term-to-term rule for each of these sequences.
   a 2, 5, 8, 11, 14, …
   b 3, 7, 11, 15, 19, …
   c 50, 47, 44, 41, 38, …
   d 9, $10\frac{1}{2}$, 12, $13\frac{1}{2}$, …
   e 1, 2, 4, 8, 16, …
   f 1, 10, 100, 1000, …
   g 1, 3, 7, 15, …
   h 32, 16, 8, 4, 2, …
   i 2, 6, 18, 54, …

8 a Find the first five terms of each of these sequences.
   i nth term = $4n - 1$
   ii nth term = $n + 1$
   iii nth term = $14 - 5n$
   iv nth term = $2n + 5$
   b Find the tenth term of each of the sequences in part **a**.

9 Look at these patterns.

   Pattern 1   Pattern 2   Pattern 3

   a Draw the next pattern in the sequence.
   b Copy and complete this table.

Pattern number	1	2	3	4	5
Number of blue squares					
Number of green squares					
Total number of squares					

   c Find numbers to go in the boxes to complete these rules.
   • Number of blue squares = ☐
   • Number of green squares = pattern number ☐ − ☐
   • Total number of squares = ☐ × pattern number ☐ − ☐

10 Meena uses counters to make patterns.

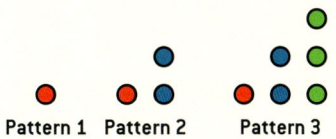

   Pattern 1   Pattern 2   Pattern 3

   a Draw the next pattern.
   b How many counters are there in each pattern?
   c Work out how many counters are needed for pattern 5.
   d i   The numbers 1, 3, 6, 10 … are called the **triangle numbers**.
          Why do you think they have this name?
      ii Write down the first ten triangle numbers.
      iii Write down the differences between the terms.
   e Write down two triangle numbers that are also square numbers.

143

11 Look at these matchstick patterns.

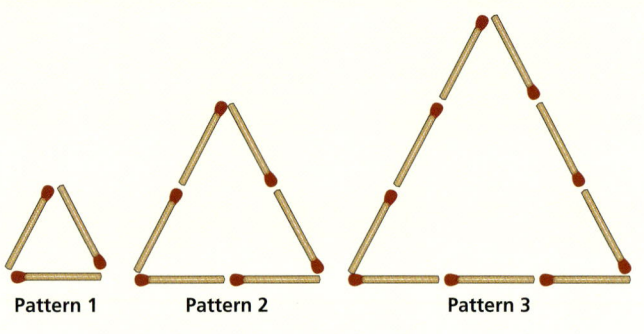

Pattern 1   Pattern 2   Pattern 3

a   Draw the next pattern in the sequence.
b   Copy and complete this table.

Pattern number, n	1	2	3	4	5
Number of matchsticks, m	3				

c   Complete this rule for the sequence.

$m = \square \times n$

Explain why your rule works.

d   Copy and complete the graph on the right.

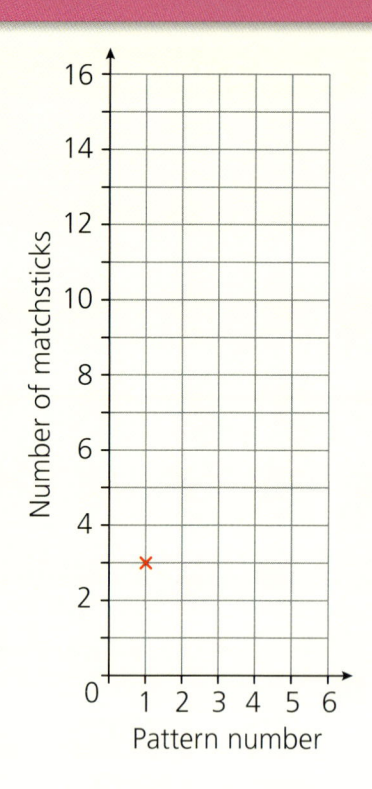

Band 3 questions

12   Humza writes down the first two numbers in a sequence.

   1, 4, …

Continue the sequence for Humza.
How many different sequences can you find?
Write down the rule for each of your sequences.

13   Jon says that this sequence is arithmetic because the difference between the terms is constant.

   2, 3, 2, 3, 2, 3

Is Jon correct? Explain your answer.

14   Matchsticks are used to make a sequence of patterns.
The number of matches, m, used in the nth pattern is given by the formula:

$m = 4n + 1$

a   How many matches are needed to make the fifth pattern?
b   How many matches are needed **altogether** to make the first three patterns?
c   Which pattern needs 81 matches?

7 Sequences

15 Which option, A or B, would you rather have?

Option A For one month only: £1 a day every day.

Option B For one week only: 30p on Monday and then double the amount of the previous day for the rest of the week.

Explain your reasoning fully.

16 Patterns are made using black and white hexagonal tiles.

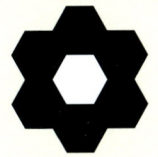

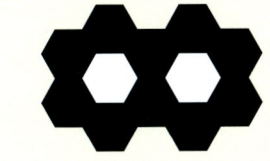

Pattern 1   Pattern 2   Pattern 3

a How many white tiles need to be added to make the next pattern?
b How many white tiles are needed for Pattern 10?
c How many black tiles need to be added to make the next pattern?
d How many black tiles are needed for Pattern 10?
e Copy and complete these rules for the nth pattern.

Number of black tiles = ☐ × n + ◇

Total number of tiles = ☐ × n + ◇

17 A snail is crawling up a tree. The tree is 21 m tall.

Every day the snail crawls up 4 m but every night it falls back 2 m.

a Write down the first six terms in the number sequence that describes the snail's height at the start of each day.
b How long does it take for the snail to reach the top of the tree?

Cross-curricular activity

1 The Fibonacci sequence (1, 1, 2, 3, 5, …), although not a linear sequence, occurs in nature and has important uses in art.

In your art and science lessons, investigate the importance of this sequence in those subjects.

2 Can you find any sequence which has applications in the real world, for example in finance?

145

Consolidation 2: Chapters 4–7

Band 1 questions

1
  a Write down all the multiples of 5 between 34 and 61.
  b Write down all the multiples of 4 between 27 and 45.
  c Write down all the multiples of 9 between 35 and 82.

2 Copy this diagram. Extend your diagram to include all the whole numbers up to 30.

  a For each number along the bottom, shade or colour the boxes to show the factors.

    The first three numbers have been done for you.

  b What do you notice about the bottom row? Why does this happen?

  c What do you notice about the diagonal? Why does this happen?

  d Which have more factors, odd numbers or even numbers? Give a reason for your answer.

  e Which number(s) have exactly
    i one factor   **ii** two factors?
    What is special about these numbers?

  f What type of number has an odd number of factors? Why?

3 A gardener plants 13 rows of 25 tulip bulbs and 15 rows of 17 daffodil bulbs.

  How many bulbs does he plant altogether?

4 The rules in the table below show how to get from one term to the next in four sequences.

Write down the next three terms in each sequence.

Write down the name of each sequence.

Rule	1st term	2nd term	3rd term	4th term	5th term	Name of sequence
Add 2	2	4				
Add 2	1	3				
Add 5	5					Multiples of …
Add 7	7					

5 Samir has a rule for estimating the height of a person.

- Measure around your head.
- Multiply your answer by 3.
- This gives your height.

146

Consolidation 2

a Estimate the height of each of these people.

	Distance around head
Becky	50 cm
Harry	43 cm
George	64 cm

b Write down a formula for estimating a person's height using Samir's rule.

c Does Samir's rule work?

Measure yourself and some friends to find out.

6 The box shows the cost of tickets for visiting a theme park.

> Family £105
> Adult £37
> Child £26

Two adults and two children visit the theme park.

They buy a family ticket.

How much more would it cost to buy two adult tickets and two child tickets?

7 A meal in a restaurant costs the same for each person.

For a group of 14 people, the cost is £364.

What is the price per person?

8 Simplify these.

a $4a - 3a + 2a - a$ b $10b + 5b - 4b$ c $7c - 3c - 4c$ d $8d - 6d + 3d - 4d$

Band 2 questions

9 Work out these.

a $3 + 4 \times 7$ b $(3 + 4) \times 7$ c $20 \div 5 - 3$
d $20 \div (5 - 3)$ e $9 + 3 \times 9 - 3$ f $(9 + 3) \times (9 - 3)$

10 Look at the numbers in this box.

| 5 | 7 | 25 | 6 | 40 | 1 | 64 | 36 | 8 | 19 | 2 | 21 | 24 | 125 | 48 |

Write down all the numbers from the box which are:

a multiples of 5
b square numbers
c multiples of both 5 and 10
d prime numbers
e cube numbers
f multiples of both 4 and 6
g factors of 42
h both square numbers and cube numbers.

11 Put brackets in the right places to make these calculations correct.

a $25 - 2 + 3 \times 4 = 5$ b $20 \times 4 + 1 - 10 = 90$
c $10 - 2 \div 4 + 1 = 3$ d $12 + 6 \times 5 - 2 = 30$

12 A teacher hires some coaches for a school trip.

450 students want to go on the trip. Each coach costs £120 to hire and can carry 68 students.

What is the total cost of the coaches?

147

13
a List the first eight multiples of:
  i 30
  ii 24.
b Write down the lowest common multiple (LCM) of 30 and 24.
c List the factors of:
  i 30
  ii 24.
d Write down the highest common factor (HCF) of 30 and 24.

14 John, Megan, Humza and Lucy have to get through the multiples maze.
They can only move up, down, left or right.

		John			Exit A		
9	97	18	26	31	84	91	13
17	29	27	33	9	77	47	59
Lucy	7	14	63	49	21	70	5	85	Exit D
	2	42	56	1	3	50	32	40	Exit B
Megan	4	36	23	19	15	55	20	71
	43	44	8	48	60	16	28	67
Exit C	6	24	12	30	35	25	45	10	Humza

- John follows multiples of 3.
- Megan follows multiples of 4.
- Humza follows multiples of 5.
- Lucy follows multiples of 7.

a i Write down the numbers in the route that each person follows.
   ii At which exit does each person come out?
b i Which number do John, Megan and Humza all use?
   ii You can change this number to stop them getting through the maze.
      Give a possible number you can change it to.

15 Simplify these.
a $4e + 3 + 2e + 5$
b $6 + 3f + 1 - 2f - 4$
c $8g + 4 - 5g - 3 + 2g$
d $7h - 4h + 3 - 2h - 3$
e $6s + 3t + 5t - 4s$
f $12u + 4v + 6u + 3v - 2v$
g $w + 2x + 3w + 4x + 5w$
h $6y + 8z - 4y + 3y - 5z - 3z$

16 An online discount store is having a half-price sale.
Some of these formulas are correct. Which are they?
a Sale price = regular price × 2
b Sale price = regular price ÷ 2
c Regular price = sale price × 2
d Regular price ÷ sale price = 2
e Sale price ÷ regular price = 2

17 Solve these equations.
a $3x - 4 = 5$
b $5x - 7 = 13$
c $4t + 3 = 15$
d $9x + 3 = 30$
e $8p - 5 = 59$
f $6x + 8 = 8$

18 Marc writes down this sequence.

> 2, 4, 6, 8, 10, …

a How does Marc work out the next number in his sequence?
b What is the tenth term in Marc's sequence?
c Copy and complete this formula for the value of the nth term in Marc's sequence.

nth term = ☐ × term number

d Meinir changes Marc's sequence into:

> 3, 5, 7, 9, 11, …

What has Meinir done to each term in Marc's sequence to make her sequence?
e Write a formula for the nth term of Meinir's sequence.
f Write a formula for the nth term of the sequence 1, 3, 5, 7, 9, …

Band 3 questions

19 Work out these.

a $3^2 - 2^2$
b $3^3 - 2^3$
c $\sqrt{49} - \sqrt{4}$
d $\sqrt[3]{1000}$

20 Sort these numbers into the correct boxes in the table.

| 25 | 6 | 80 | 60 | 72 | 40 | 120 | 12 | 30 | 55 |

	Multiple of 6	NOT a multiple of 6
Multiple of 10		
NOT a multiple of 10		

21 Simplify these.

a $a^2 + a^2 + a^2 + a^2$
b $4b - 3b + 2b^2 + 5b^2$
c $3c^2 - 2d - 2c^2 - d$
d $7de + 5e - 3de - 6e + 2de$
e $4e^2 + 3 - 2e - 3e^2 - 4 + 3e$
f $9h^2 - hi - 2hi - 6h^2 + 3hi$

22 For each of these patterns:

i Draw the next pattern in the sequence.
ii Copy and complete the table.

Pattern number, n	1	2	3	4	5
Number of matchsticks, m					

iii Work out how many matchsticks are in Pattern 10.
iv Complete the formula for the number of matchsticks, m, in pattern n.

Curriculum for Wales Mastering Mathematics: Book 1

a

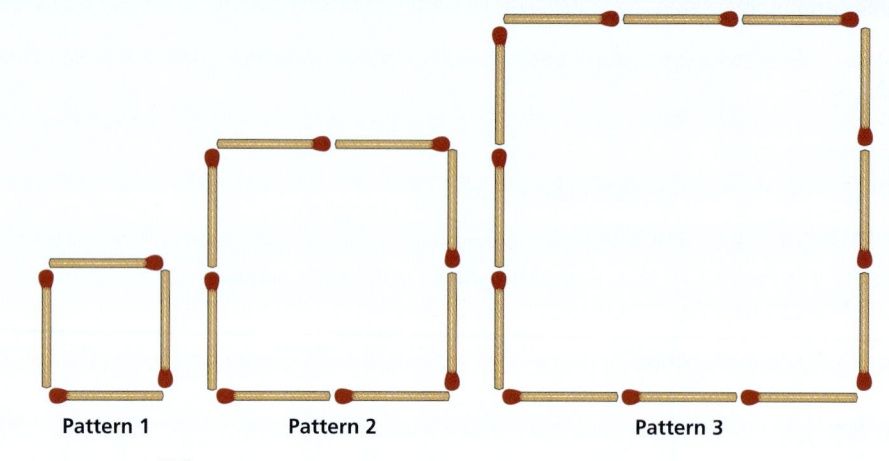

Pattern 1   Pattern 2   Pattern 3

Formula: $m = \square \times n$

b

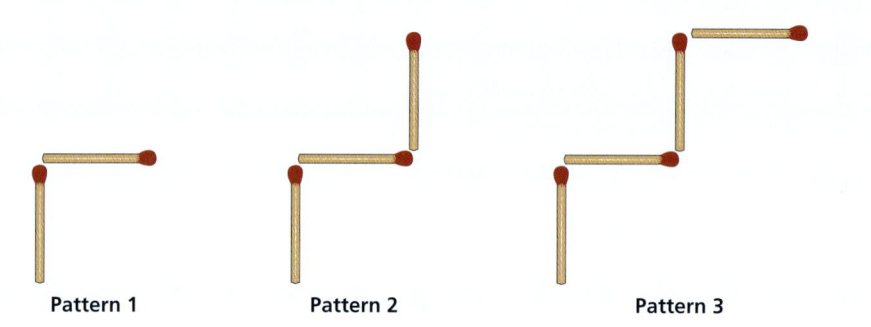

Pattern 1   Pattern 2   Pattern 3

Formula: $m = n + \square$

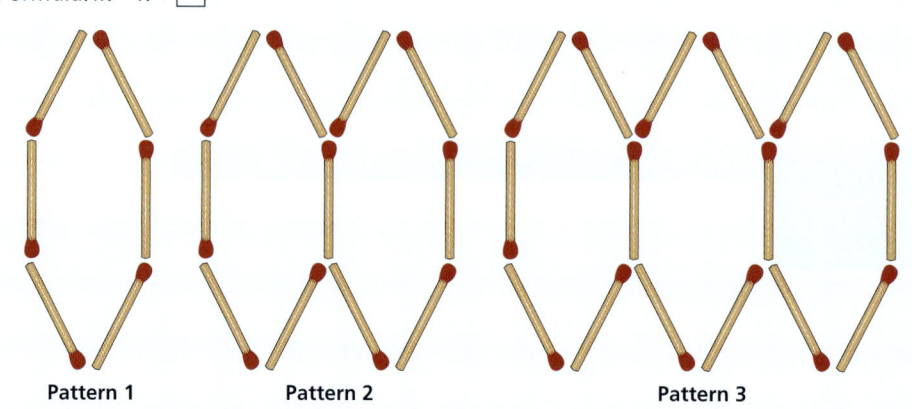

c

Pattern 1   Pattern 2   Pattern 3

Formula: $m = \square n + \square$

23 The lock on Catrin's bike has a three-digit code.

Each digit is either 5, 6, 7, 8 or 9.

Solve these clues to work out Catrin's combination code.
- The whole number is a multiple of 5.
- The second digit is odd.
- The number made by the last two digits is a multiple of 3.
- The first digit is even.
- The whole number is a multiple of 3.

150

24 The lock on Aeron's mountain bike also has a three-digit code.

Each digit is either 1, 2, 3, 4 or 5.

Solve these clues to work out Aeron's combination code.
- The code is even.
- The number made by the last two digits is a multiple of 9.
- The whole number is a multiple of 6.

25 A tree has three sets of coloured lights on it.
- The red lights flash every 5 seconds.
- The green lights flash every 7 seconds.
- The blue lights flash every 4 seconds.

a The red and green lights flash at the same time.

How many seconds will it be before they flash at the same time again?

b All three sets of lights flash at the same time.

How many seconds will it be before they flash at the same time again?

26 Madog has a set of four steps.

The tread is twice the riser.

Madog has a 108 cm length of carpet that covers the steps exactly.

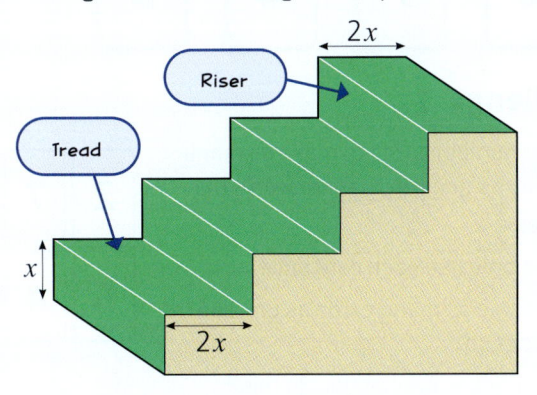

a Write an equation to show this information.

b Solve the equation to find:

　i　the height of the riser　　　ii　the width of the tread.

27 Three prizes are given from a prize fund, with these conditions.
- The first prize is twice the third prize.
- The second prize is £5 more than the third prize.

a Find the values of the prizes when the total prize money is:

　i　£65　　　ii　£37.

b It is decided that the first prize must be at least £5 more than the second prize.

What is the smallest amount of prize money needed to meet all three conditions?

8 Fractions

Coming up...

- Arranging fractions in order
- Using the number line for ordering fractions
- Using the symbols =, ≠, <, >, ≤, ≥
- Using addition and subtraction applied to proper fractions
- Multiplying and dividing integers and proper fractions
- Calculating fractions of amounts
- Using a calculator to calculate results accurately and then interpreting them appropriately
- Expressing one quantity as a fraction of another, where the fraction is less than 1

Make some fractions

Here are some number cards.

| 1 | 2 | 3 | 4 | 5 | 6 | 7 | 8 | 9 |

Challenge 1

Use the number cards to make as many fractions as you can that are worth the same as $\frac{1}{2}$.

You can only use each card once.

You can only use two cards for each fraction.

In how many ways can you do this?

$$\frac{1}{2}$$

Challenge 2

Use the number cards to make as many fractions as you can that are worth the same as $\frac{1}{2}$.

You can only use each card once.

You can only use three cards for each fraction.

In how many ways can you do this?

$$\frac{6}{12}$$

Challenge 3

Use the number cards to make as many fractions as you can that are worth the same as $\frac{1}{2}$.

You can only use each card once.

You can use as many cards as you like for each fraction.

In how many ways can you do this?

Can you find a way that uses all the cards?

$$\frac{27}{54}$$

8 Fractions

8.1 Equivalent fractions

Skill checker

① What fraction of each of these flags is blue?

a   b

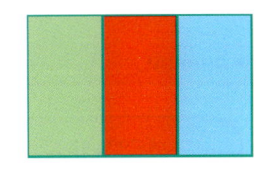

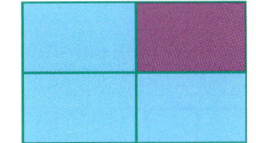

c 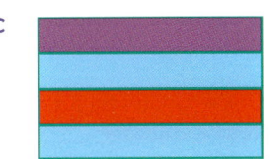   d

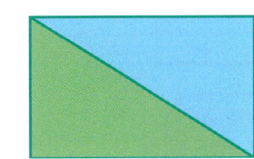

② Match each diagram to one of the fractions below.

a   b    c    d 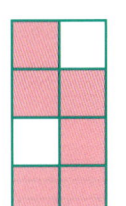   e 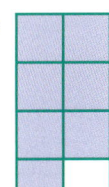   f

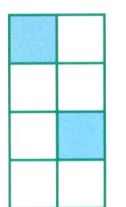

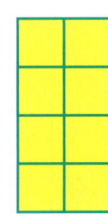

$\frac{7}{8}$ $\frac{1}{4}$ $\frac{3}{4}$ $\frac{5}{8}$ 1 $\frac{1}{2}$

③ Write down all of the factors of each number.
   a 6   b 15   c 30   d 18

④ Which of these numbers are multiples of 3?
   16   26   36   43   51   64

Activity

Look at these diagrams.

a   b 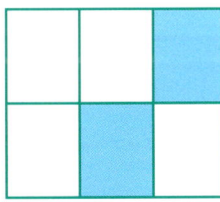   c

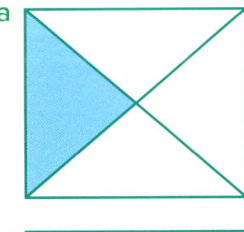

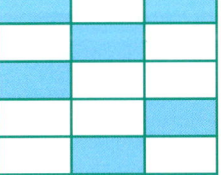

d    e 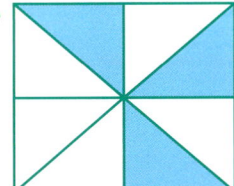   f

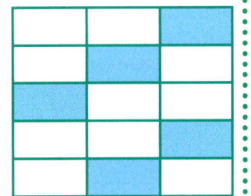

① Discuss which ones have one third shaded and write them down.
② Write down the fraction that is shaded for each drawing.
③ Write down the fractions that represent $\frac{1}{3}$.

Note

See Chapter 4 for a reminder of factors and multiples.

Curriculum for Wales Mastering Mathematics: Book 1

You have seen that $\frac{1}{3}$, $\frac{2}{6}$ and $\frac{5}{15}$ all represent one third.

> numerator
> denominator

They have different **numerators** and different **denominators** but they are worth the same.

They all represent one out of three equal parts.

Look at the fractions and the diagrams that represent one third. You can use them to write down other fractions that represent one third, such as $\frac{3}{9}$, $\frac{4}{12}$ and $\frac{10}{30}$.

$\frac{1}{3}$, $\frac{2}{6}$, $\frac{3}{9}$, $\frac{4}{12}$, $\frac{5}{15}$ and $\frac{10}{30}$ are **equivalent** fractions. They look different but are worth the same amount.

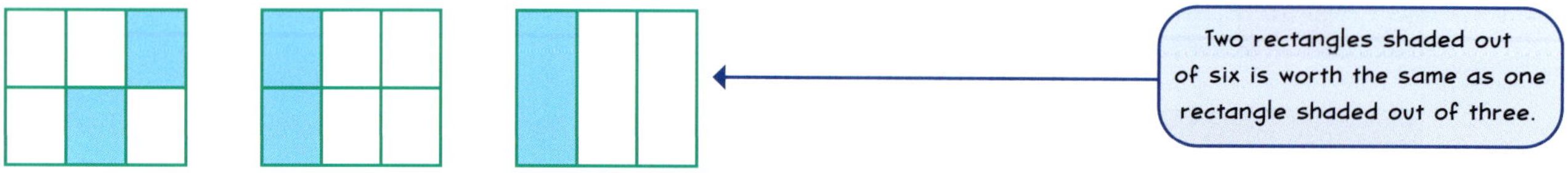

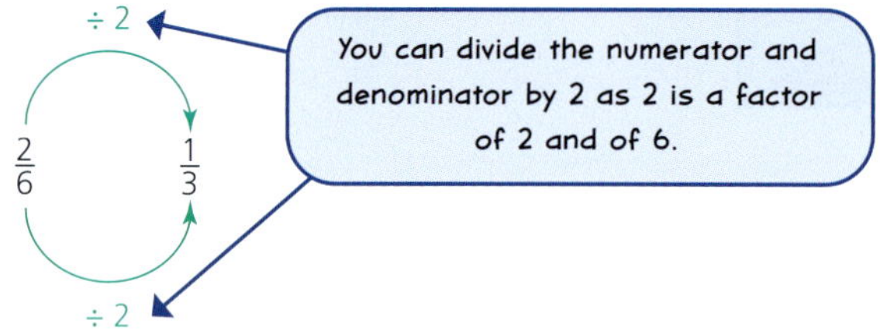

Conceptual understanding

> Two rectangles shaded out of six is worth the same as one rectangle shaded out of three.

$\frac{2}{6}$ ÷ 2 → $\frac{1}{3}$
÷ 2

> You can divide the numerator and denominator by 2 as 2 is a factor of 2 and of 6.

Remember
The numerator is the top number and the denominator is the bottom number.

You can write this as $\frac{2}{6} = \frac{2 \times 1}{2 \times 3} = \frac{1}{3}$.

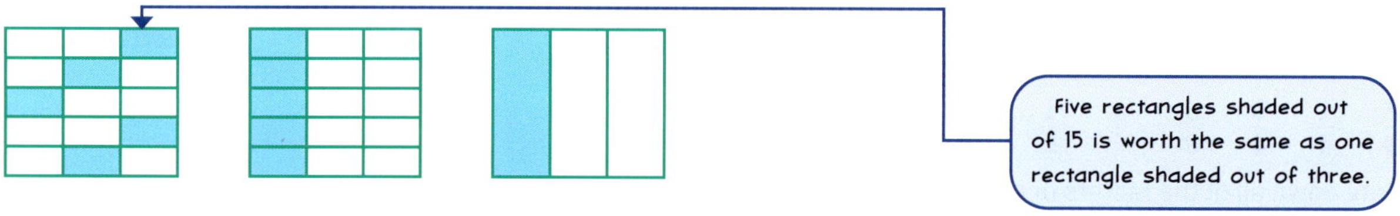

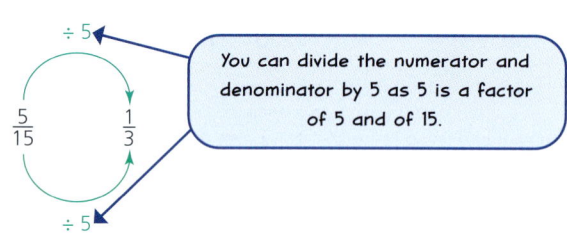

> Five rectangles shaded out of 15 is worth the same as one rectangle shaded out of three.

$\frac{5}{15}$ ÷ 5 → $\frac{1}{3}$
÷ 5

> You can divide the numerator and denominator by 5 as 5 is a factor of 5 and of 15.

Fractions are usually written in their simplest form, so you write all of the fractions equivalent to one third as $\frac{1}{3}$.

Writing fractions in their simplest form is called **cancelling** or **simplifying**.

Worked example

Simplify $\frac{24}{30}$.

Solution

2 is a factor of both 24 and 30, so you can divide both the numerator and the denominator by 2.

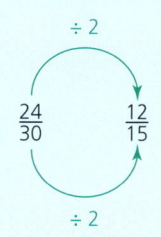

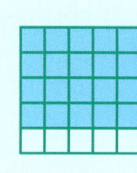

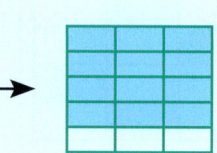

$\frac{24}{30}$ ÷ 2 → $\frac{12}{15}$
÷ 2

154

3 is a factor of both 12 and 15, so divide 12 and 15 by 3.

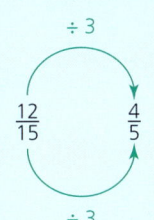

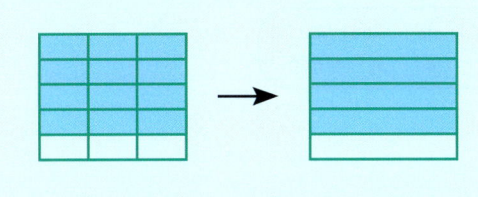

$\frac{12}{15} \xrightarrow{\div 3} \frac{4}{5}$ (÷ 3)

Note
You could do this in one step by dividing both the numerator and the denominator by 6.

$\frac{4}{5}$ is in its simplest form. 4 and 5 don't have a common factor so you can't simplify this further.

Activity
Show that $\frac{2}{3} < \frac{3}{4}$ in as many different ways as you can.

Sometimes you need to rewrite a fraction by multiplying both the numerator (top) and the denominator (bottom) by the same number. This is useful when comparing or combining fractions.

Worked example
Show that $\frac{2}{3} < \frac{3}{4}$.

Remember
< means 'less than'.
> means 'greater than'.

Solution
You can write both fractions as twelfths because both denominators (3 and 4) are factors of 12.

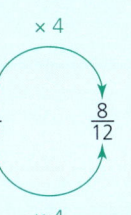

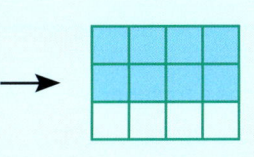

$\frac{2}{3} \xrightarrow{\times 4} \frac{8}{12}$

The multiplier of 4 turns thirds into twelfths.

You can write this as $\frac{2}{3} = \frac{4 \times 2}{4 \times 3} = \frac{8}{12}$.

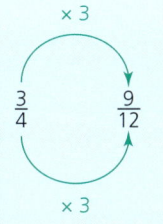

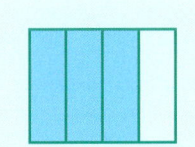

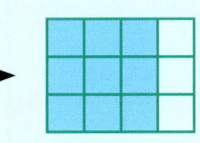

$\frac{3}{4} \xrightarrow{\times 3} \frac{9}{12}$

The multiplier of 3 turns quarters into twelfths.

You can write this as $\frac{3}{4} = \frac{3 \times 3}{3 \times 4} = \frac{9}{12}$

and $\frac{8}{12} < \frac{9}{12}$, so $\frac{2}{3} < \frac{3}{4}$.

Fractions must be written using whole numbers.

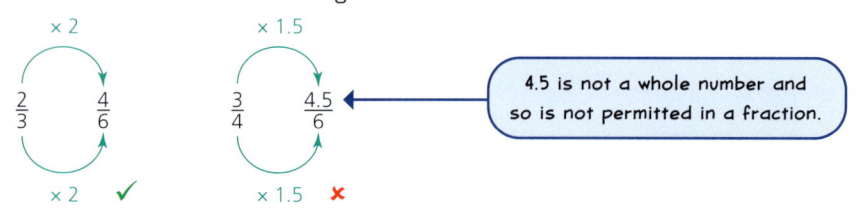

$\frac{2}{3} \xrightarrow{\times 2} \frac{4}{6}$ ✓

$\frac{3}{4} \xrightarrow{\times 1.5} \frac{4.5}{6}$ ✗

4.5 is not a whole number and so is not permitted in a fraction.

Worked example

Harri ran $\frac{3}{10}$ of a mile and Catrin ran $\frac{4}{15}$ of a mile. Who ran further?

Solution

Rewrite the fractions so that they both have the same denominator.

The denominator must be a multiple of 10 and of 15.

$10 \times 15 = 150$ so you could write both denominators as 150 but it is easier to use the lowest denominator possible.

The lowest common multiple of both 10 and 15 is 30.

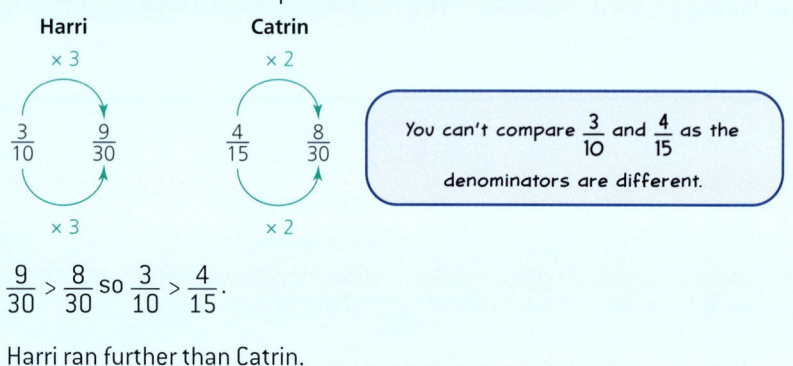

Harri: $\frac{3}{10} \xrightarrow{\times 3} \frac{9}{30}$

Catrin: $\frac{4}{15} \xrightarrow{\times 2} \frac{8}{30}$

You can't compare $\frac{3}{10}$ and $\frac{4}{15}$ as the denominators are different.

Note: 30 is called the 'lowest common denominator'.

$\frac{9}{30} > \frac{8}{30}$ so $\frac{3}{10} > \frac{4}{15}$.

Harri ran further than Catrin.

Equivalent fractions can be used when you write one number as a fraction of another.

Note: For a reminder of lowest common multiples, see Chapter 4.

Worked example

Aled gets 48 marks out of 80 in his maths test.
What fraction of the marks does Aled get?

Solution

Write this as $\frac{48}{80}$.

This is the number of marks that Aled gets.

This is the total number of marks available.

$\frac{48}{80} \xrightarrow{\div 16} \frac{3}{5}$

Hint: You could have simplified in two or more steps.

This shows that $\frac{48}{80} = \frac{3}{5}$.

Therefore, the fraction of the marks that Aled gets is $\frac{3}{5}$.

8 Fractions

8.1 Now try these

Band 1 questions

1 Which of these badges are coloured correctly?

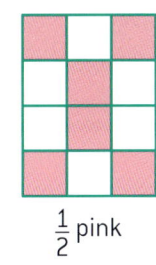

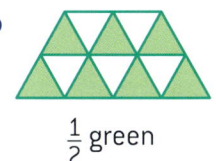

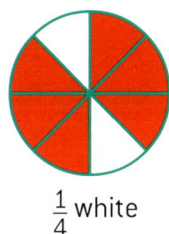

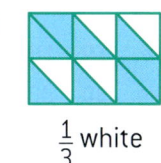

a $\frac{1}{2}$ pink

b $\frac{1}{2}$ green

c $\frac{1}{4}$ white

d $\frac{1}{3}$ white

2 A packet of coloured sweets is emptied.

a Copy and complete the table.

Colour	Red	Blue	Brown	Yellow	Pink	Green
Number						

b What fraction of the packet is:

  i blue
  ii brown
  iii green
  iv red or green
  v blue or yellow
  vi not red?

3 Use this diagram to write the fractions below it in order, with the smallest first.

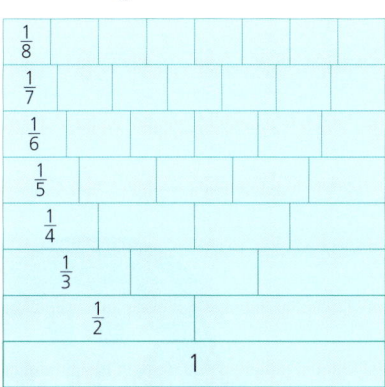

$\frac{2}{5}$ $\frac{1}{2}$ $\frac{1}{8}$ $\frac{3}{7}$ $\frac{5}{6}$ $\frac{2}{3}$ $\frac{3}{4}$

4 Place the symbol < or > between each pair of fractions to make true statements.

a $\frac{3}{11}$ $\frac{2}{11}$

b $\frac{5}{12}$ $\frac{1}{12}$

c $\frac{1}{2}$ $\frac{1}{4}$

d $\frac{1}{3}$ $\frac{1}{2}$

5. Match the fractions in the first box to the fractions of equal value in the second box.

| $\frac{4}{8}$ | $\frac{2}{6}$ | $\frac{6}{8}$ | $\frac{3}{12}$ | $\frac{2}{10}$ |

| $\frac{1}{5}$ | $\frac{1}{4}$ | $\frac{1}{3}$ | $\frac{1}{2}$ | $\frac{3}{4}$ |

6. Which of these fractions are equivalent to one third $\left(\frac{1}{3}\right)$?

$\frac{2}{6}$ $\frac{15}{25}$ $\frac{6}{18}$ $\frac{14}{20}$ $\frac{8}{10}$ $\frac{8}{24}$ $\frac{10}{30}$ $\frac{10}{20}$ $\frac{12}{16}$ $\frac{16}{20}$ $\frac{7}{21}$ $\frac{24}{30}$ $\frac{17}{51}$ $\frac{24}{28}$ $\frac{16}{48}$

7. Copy and complete.

a $\frac{1}{10} = \frac{\Box}{20}$
b $\frac{2}{5} = \frac{\Box}{20}$
c $\frac{1}{4} = \frac{\Box}{20}$

d $\frac{3}{5} = \frac{\Box}{20}$
e $\frac{3}{4} = \frac{\Box}{20}$
f $\frac{3}{10} = \frac{\Box}{20}$

Band 2 questions

8. Copy and complete.

a $\frac{1}{2} = \frac{3}{\Box} = \frac{\Box}{14}$
b $\frac{1}{3} = \frac{\Box}{9} = \frac{5}{\Box}$
c $\frac{1}{4} = \frac{\Box}{8} = \frac{6}{\Box}$

d $\frac{2}{3} = \frac{4}{\Box} = \frac{\Box}{12}$
e $\frac{3}{4} = \frac{\Box}{16} = \frac{24}{\Box}$
f $\frac{2}{5} = \frac{8}{\Box} = \frac{\Box}{15}$

9. a Write $\frac{5}{6}$ and $\frac{3}{4}$ as equivalent fractions with a denominator of 12.
   b Which fraction is bigger, $\frac{5}{6}$ or $\frac{3}{4}$?

10. The table shows the points scored by the football teams in the Premier League in one year.

Manchester United	83	Hull	49
Arsenal	78	Crystal Palace	49
Newcastle	69	Stoke	48
Chelsea	67	Fulham	48
Liverpool	64	Swansea	47
Norwich	60	Aston Villa	45
Everton	59	Cardiff	44
Southampton	52	West Ham	42
Manchester City	51	West Bromwich	26
Tottenham	50	Sunderland	19

What fraction of the teams scored more than 60 points?

11. A dartboard is a circle divided into 20 sectors numbered 1 to 20.
    a i What fraction of the sectors are even numbers?
       ii What fraction are odd numbers?
    b What fraction of the sectors are multiples of 5?
    c i What fraction of the sectors are prime numbers?
       ii What fraction of the sectors are not prime numbers?
    d Add the numbers on the black sectors and the numbers on the white sectors.
       What fraction of the total is the total of the black sectors?

8 Fractions

12 Which of these fractions are equivalent to $\frac{9}{15}$?

$\frac{18}{30}$ $\frac{12}{18}$ $\frac{21}{35}$ $\frac{6}{12}$ $\frac{6}{10}$ $\frac{15}{25}$

13 **a** Sahid wants to rewrite all of these fractions so that they have the same denominator.
What is the lowest denominator he can use?

$\frac{2}{5}$ $\frac{3}{10}$ $\frac{1}{2}$ $\frac{7}{25}$

  b Now write the fractions in order of size, starting with the smallest.

14 For each option below, write the first amount as a fraction of the second amount. Simplify your answer.
  a 24, 48
  b £10, £100
  c 24 kg, 80 kg
  d 15 km, 35 km
  e 96 cm, 144 cm

15 For each pair of fractions, replace 'and' with =, < or > to make true statements.
  a $\frac{1}{2}$ and $\frac{1}{3}$
  b $\frac{1}{3}$ and $\frac{5}{12}$
  c $\frac{2}{9}$ and $\frac{5}{18}$
  d $\frac{2}{5}$ and $\frac{12}{30}$
  e $\frac{1}{4}$ and $\frac{3}{10}$
  f $\frac{4}{5}$ and $\frac{5}{6}$
  g $\frac{5}{8}$ and $\frac{2}{3}$
  h $\frac{3}{4}$ and $\frac{5}{7}$

16 For each fraction:
  a write the fraction in its simplest form
  b show how you can reach the simplest form in one step.

  i $\frac{6}{8}$
  ii $\frac{4}{16}$
  iii $\frac{9}{12}$
  iv $\frac{12}{18}$
  v $\frac{10}{30}$
  vi $\frac{18}{24}$

17 Lucy, Michelle and Ali share £36. Lucy gets £18. Michelle gets £12. Ali gets £6.
What fraction of £36 does each person get?
Write each fraction in its simplest form.

Band 3 questions

18 Find a fraction that lies between each of the following pairs of fractions.
  a $\frac{1}{2}$ and $\frac{3}{4}$
  b $\frac{1}{2}$ and $\frac{1}{4}$
  c $\frac{1}{2}$ and $\frac{1}{3}$
  d $\frac{1}{2}$ and $\frac{2}{3}$
  e $\frac{1}{4}$ and $\frac{2}{5}$
  f $\frac{3}{8}$ and $\frac{3}{4}$

19 Anya gets £12 pocket money. This is how she spends it.

Magazines   £4.50
Sweets   £1.50
Music   £5

  a What fraction does she spend on magazines?
  b Anya saves any money she has left. What fraction of her pocket money does she save?

159

Logical reasoning

20 Decide whether each statement is true or false, justifying your answer.

a $\frac{5}{6} < \frac{7}{10}$

b $\frac{4}{5} \leq \frac{9}{10}$

c $\frac{9}{21} > \frac{8}{20}$

d $\frac{13}{39} \neq \frac{12}{36}$

e $\frac{15}{18} \geq \frac{50}{60}$

f $\frac{3}{7} < \frac{5}{9} < \frac{7}{12}$

Strategic competence

21 Bethan wants to cut some ribbon to make a bow.

She cuts 85 cm for the bow from 2.5 m of ribbon.

What fraction of the ribbon does she have left?

Fluency

22 a Write each of these fractions with a denominator of 100.

i $\frac{4}{5}$ ii $\frac{7}{10}$ iii $\frac{3}{4}$ iv $\frac{11}{20}$ v $\frac{9}{50}$ vi $\frac{3}{25}$

b Write each of the fractions in part **a** as a percentage.

c Write each of the fractions in part **a** as a decimal.

d Place the fractions in order, starting with the smallest.

Strategic competence

23 Here are Eko's end of term test results.

a In which subject did Eko do best?

b Which was Eko's worst subject?

School report	
Name	Eko Jones
Test results	

Subject	Result	Total
Welsh	15	20
English	25	40
Geography	44	80
Maths	48	60

8.2 Adding and subtracting fractions

Skill checker

1 Write these fractions in their simplest form.

a $\frac{6}{8}$

b $\frac{14}{21}$

c $\frac{36}{48}$

d $\frac{150}{210}$

2 Which of these fractions are equivalent to $\frac{3}{5}$?

$\frac{6}{10}$ $\frac{8}{10}$ $\frac{13}{15}$ $\frac{36}{60}$ $\frac{35}{55}$ $\frac{39}{52}$

3 Place < or > between the two fractions to make a true statement.

$\frac{3}{7}$ $\frac{7}{15}$

4 In a class of 20 students, 16 play an instrument. What fraction of the class play an instrument?

5 Work out:

a $\frac{1}{3} + \frac{1}{3}$

b $\frac{2}{7} + \frac{3}{7}$

c $\frac{7}{9} - \frac{2}{9}$

8 Fractions

Activity

1. What fraction of the whole square is represented by A, B, C, D and E?
2. Use your answers to part **a** to write a sum with an answer of 1.
3. Use your answers to part **a** to write a sum with an answer of $\frac{1}{2}$.
4. Write your answers for A, D and E using different denominators. Write down as many different sums as you can using some or all of the fractions for A, B, C, D and E.

Remember

Sum means 'add'.

One of the sums you may have found in the activity above is $\frac{1}{4} + \frac{1}{16} + \frac{1}{16} + \frac{1}{8} = \frac{1}{2}$.

You can use the diagram to write each fraction as sixteenths.

You can only add or subtract fractions when they all have a **common** (same) **denominator**.

You can write the sum as $\frac{4}{16} + \frac{1}{16} + \frac{1}{16} + \frac{2}{16} = \frac{8}{16}$

16 is the lowest number that is a multiple of 2, 4, 8 and 16.

16 is the largest denominator you have used and it is called the **lowest common denominator**.

Worked example

Jac and Lowri have a cake.
Jac eats $\frac{1}{4}$ of the cake and Lowri eats $\frac{1}{6}$ of the cake. How much of the cake do they eat altogether?

Solution

The denominators are 4 and 6. They are both factors of 12.

The fractions can be converted to twelfths.

Change each fraction to an equivalent fraction with 12 as the denominator.

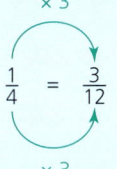

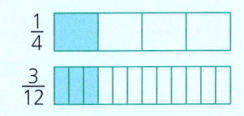

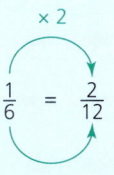

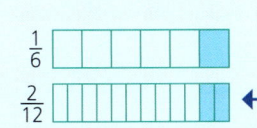

$\frac{1}{4} = \frac{3}{12}$ (× 3)

$\frac{1}{6} = \frac{2}{12}$ (× 2)

Once the denominators are the same, you can add the numerators.

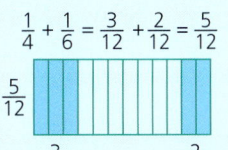

$\frac{1}{4} + \frac{1}{6} = \frac{3}{12} + \frac{2}{12} = \frac{5}{12}$

They eat $\frac{5}{12}$ of the cake.

The same approach is used when subtracting fractions.

> **Worked example**
>
> Jac has $\frac{7}{12}$ of his cake left.
>
> He gives half of the original cake to his mother. How much is left now?
>
> **Solution**
>
> Jac has $\frac{7}{12} - \frac{1}{2}$ left.
>
> $\frac{1}{2} = \frac{6}{12}$ (× 6)
>
> $\frac{1}{2}$ and $\frac{6}{12}$ are equivalent fractions.
>
> 12 is the lowest common denominator of 12 and 2.
>
> $\frac{7}{12} - \frac{1}{2} = \frac{7}{12} - \frac{6}{12} = \frac{1}{12}$
>
> Once the denominators are the same, you can subtract the numerators.
>
> $\frac{1}{12}$ of the cake is left.

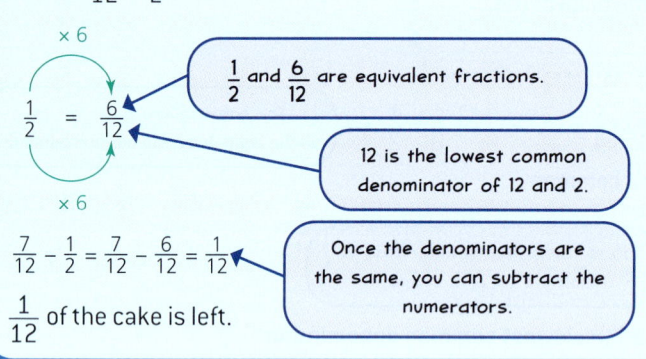

You can use a calculator to check answers. Some calculators have a button that looks like this:

Other calculators have a button that looks like this: a^b/c

8.2 Now try these

Band 1 questions

1 Work out:

a $\frac{1}{3} + \frac{1}{3}$

b $\frac{1}{5} + \frac{2}{5}$

c $\frac{2}{7} + \frac{4}{7}$

d $\frac{2}{9} + \frac{5}{9}$

2 Work out these fractions, simplifying your answer if possible.

a $\frac{5}{8} - \frac{3}{8}$

b $\frac{5}{7} - \frac{2}{7}$

c $\frac{3}{4} - \frac{1}{4}$

d $\frac{5}{9} - \frac{2}{9}$

3 Work out the missing fractions.

a $\frac{1}{7} + \frac{\square}{\square} = \frac{3}{7}$

b $\frac{4}{5} - \frac{\square}{\square} = \frac{1}{5}$

c $\frac{1}{10} + \frac{\square}{\square} - \frac{3}{10} = \frac{7}{10}$

d $\frac{\square}{\square} + \frac{3}{4} = 1$

e $\frac{7}{8} - \frac{\square}{\square} = \frac{1}{4}$

8 Fractions

④ a Match the calculations represented by the fraction bars with options **i** to **iv**.

  i $\frac{1}{2} - \frac{1}{3}$ ii $\frac{1}{2} + \frac{1}{6}$ iii $\frac{3}{5} - \frac{3}{10}$ iv $\frac{2}{3} + \frac{1}{4}$

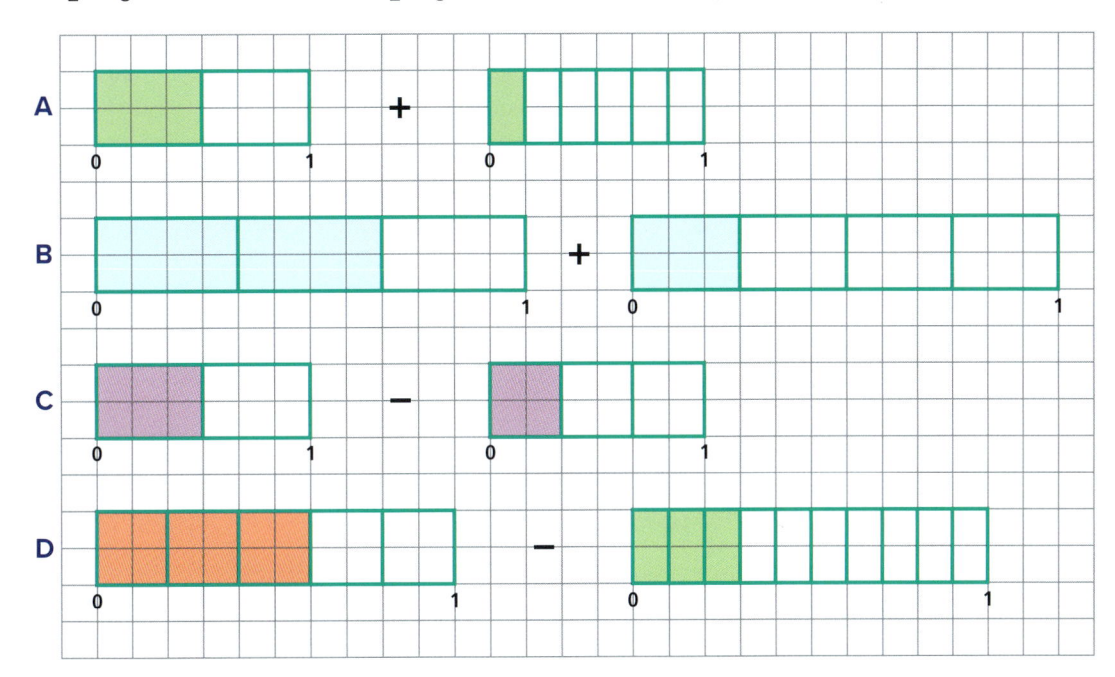

  A +

  B +

  C −

  D −

  b Match these answers to each calculation in part **a**.

  $\frac{3}{10}$ $\frac{2}{3}$ $\frac{11}{12}$ $\frac{1}{6}$

⑤ Copy and complete these.

  a $\frac{1}{7} + \frac{\square}{\square} = 1$ b $\frac{3}{\square} + \frac{\square}{4} = 1$ c $\frac{\square}{3} + \frac{2}{\square} = 1$ d $\frac{2}{\square} + \frac{1}{5} + \frac{2}{\square} = 1$

⑥ Copy and complete these.

  a $\frac{1}{2} + \frac{1}{4} + \frac{1}{8} = \frac{\square}{8}$ b $\frac{1}{2} + \frac{\square}{\square} = \frac{3}{4}$ c $\frac{\square}{\square} + \frac{5}{7} = \frac{13}{14}$ d $\frac{1}{6} + \frac{\square}{8} = \frac{13}{\square}$

Band 2 questions

⑦ Draw fraction bars to represent these additions and subtractions.
  Use them to work out the answers.

  a $\frac{1}{2} + \frac{1}{3}$ b $\frac{1}{3} + \frac{1}{4}$ c $\frac{2}{3} - \frac{1}{4}$ d $\frac{5}{6} - \frac{1}{3}$

⑧ a Copy and complete these equivalent fractions.

  i $\frac{1}{5} = \frac{\square}{10} = \frac{\square}{20}$ ii $\frac{2}{5} = \frac{\square}{10} = \frac{\square}{20}$

  b Use your answers to part **a** to work these out.

  i $\frac{3}{10} - \frac{1}{5}$ ii $\frac{3}{10} + \frac{2}{5}$ iii $\frac{1}{5} - \frac{1}{20}$ iv $\frac{7}{20} + \frac{2}{5}$ v $\frac{2}{5} - \frac{7}{20}$

Curriculum for Wales Mastering Mathematics: Book 1

Fluency

9 Look at the following pairs of fractions.
  a Find the lowest common denominator for each pair.
  b Add each pair of fractions.
  i $\frac{2}{5}$ and $\frac{1}{5}$
  ii $\frac{3}{4}$ and $\frac{1}{8}$
  iii $\frac{1}{3}$ and $\frac{1}{5}$
  iv $\frac{1}{6}$ and $\frac{3}{8}$

10 Work out these.
  a $\frac{3}{7} - \frac{2}{7}$
  b $\frac{10}{19} - \frac{3}{19}$
  c $\frac{2}{5} - \frac{1}{10}$
  d $\frac{2}{5} + \frac{3}{10}$
  e $\frac{3}{4} - \frac{5}{12}$

11 Work out these.
  a $\frac{2}{3} + \frac{1}{4}$
  b $\frac{8}{9} - \frac{3}{4}$
  c $\frac{3}{10} + \frac{5}{9}$
  d $\frac{5}{6} - \frac{4}{9}$
  e $\frac{1}{3} + \frac{1}{4} + \frac{1}{5}$
  f $\frac{6}{7} - \frac{3}{4} + \frac{1}{6}$

Strategic competence

12 Savid receives money for his birthday.
He spends $\frac{3}{7}$ of his money on a jumper and $\frac{5}{14}$ of his money on some T-shirts.
He saves the rest of his money.
What fraction does he save?

Band 3 questions

Logical reasoning

13 Copy and complete, writing all fractions in their simplest form.
  a $\frac{3}{4} + \frac{\square}{\square} = \frac{11}{12}$
  b $\frac{\square}{\square} - \frac{3}{20} = \frac{19}{40}$
  c $\frac{\square}{\square} + \frac{1}{7} = \frac{26}{35}$
  d $\frac{7}{12} - \frac{\square}{\square} = \frac{1}{4}$
  e $\frac{2}{3} - \frac{\square}{\square} + \frac{1}{4} = \frac{19}{24}$

Strategic competence

14 Darren, Paul and Marc are standing for team captain.
$\frac{3}{10}$ of the votes are for Darren.
Paul gets $\frac{3}{8}$ of the votes.

Votes for Team Captain
Darren	Paul	Marc
$\frac{3}{10}$	$\frac{3}{8}$	?

  a What fraction of the class votes for Marc?
  b Which is the largest fraction?
  c Who is chosen as team captain?

15 $\frac{3}{5}$ of a garden is lawn and $\frac{2}{9}$ is used for growing vegetables.
What fraction is left for other uses?

16 Three identical shampoo bottles are $\frac{1}{5}$ full, $\frac{1}{4}$ full and $\frac{1}{3}$ full respectively.
Can all of the shampoo in the three bottles be put into one bottle?

17 A cook has $\frac{5}{8}$ of a litre of buttermilk left over after cooking on Wednesday.

She uses $\frac{2}{5}$ of a litre of buttermilk on Thursday and buys another half-litre of buttermilk.

How much buttermilk does she have?

18 Musa can buy two different types of fruit salads. He likes grapes best.
 a In Fruit Salad A, he finds that $\frac{1}{5}$ of the fruit pieces are red grapes and $\frac{1}{4}$ are green grapes.
    What fraction of the fruit pieces in Fruit Salad A are grapes?
 b In Fruit Salad B, $\frac{3}{10}$ of the fruit pieces are apple, $\frac{1}{4}$ are pear and the rest are grapes.
    What fraction of Fruit Salad B are grapes?
 c Fruit Salad A costs £5 and holds approximately 20 pieces of fruit. Fruit Salad B costs £3 and holds approximately 15 pieces of fruit.
    Which fruit salad would Musa buy?

19 A train sets off from Newport station $\frac{1}{3}$ full.

At the first stop, $\frac{1}{5}$ of the capacity of the train get off and $\frac{7}{12}$ of the train's capacity get on.

At the second stop, nobody gets off but a further $\frac{1}{6}$ of the train's capacity get on.

At the next stop, $\frac{1}{20}$ of the train's capacity get off. What fraction of the train's capacity remain on board?

8.3 Finding a fraction of an amount

Skill checker

① What fraction is:
 a white   b green
in these flags?
 i Ireland   ii Nigeria

② Halve each of these numbers.
 a 8   b 16   c 20   d 100

③ Work out a quarter of each of these numbers.
 a 8   b 16   c 20   d 100

④ Work out three-quarters of each of these numbers.
 a 8   b 16   c 20   d 100

Remember
- To halve a number, you divide by 2.
- To find a quarter of a number, you divide by 4.
- To find three-quarters of a number, you divide by 4 and multiply by 3.

Worked example

Find $\frac{2}{5}$ of 60.

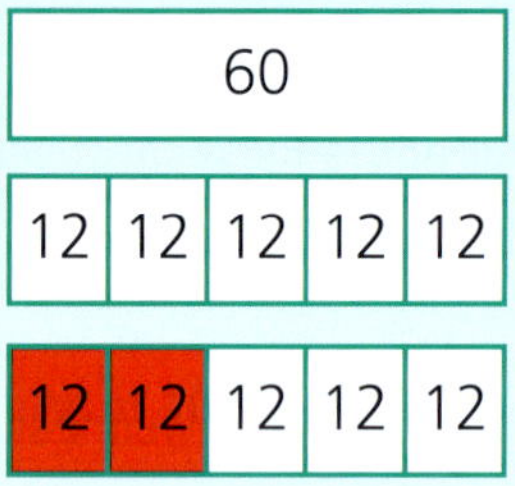

Solution

$\frac{1}{5}$ of 60 = 12 ← 60 ÷ 5 = 12

So $\frac{2}{5}$ of 60 = 2 × 12 = 24

60

| 12 | 12 | 12 | 12 | 12 |

| 12 | 12 | 12 | 12 | 12 |

Remember

Finding $\frac{1}{5}$ is the same as dividing by 5.

Finding $\frac{2}{5}$ means multiplying that by 2.

Cross-curricular activity

You will look at money management in your PSE lessons.

Make a list of what you spend your pocket money on each week.

Calculate what fraction of your total pocket money you spend on each item/activity.

Could you spend your pocket money more wisely?

Activity

① Work out $\frac{3}{5}$ of 40 using this diagram.

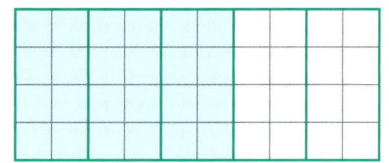

② Use a calculator to work out:
 a 3 × 40 ÷ 5
 b 40 ÷ 5 × 3
 c 3 ÷ 5 × 40
 d 40 × 3 ÷ 5

③ What do you notice about the calculations in question **2**? Can you explain why this happens?

④ Use a calculator to work out:
 a 5 ÷ 3 × 40
 b 40 ÷ 3 × 5
 c 3 × 5 × 40
 d 5 × 3 ÷ 40

⑤ Explain why the calculations in question **4** do not give you the same answers as question **2**.

Worked example

Work out $8 \times \frac{3}{4}$.

Solution

$8 \times \frac{3}{4}$ is 8 lots of $\frac{3}{4}$.

Use a number line to help you.

0   1   2   3   4   5   6

8 lots of $\frac{3}{4} = \frac{24}{4}$ and $\frac{24}{4} = 6$.

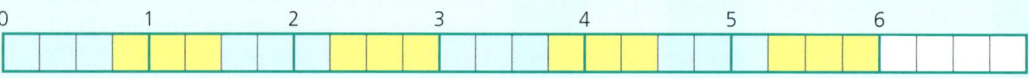

So $8 \times \frac{3}{4} = 6$.

You can multiply in any order, so $\frac{3}{4} \times 8$ is also 6.

We know 2 × 5 = 5 × 2 so the order doesn't matter when multiplying numbers.

$\frac{3}{4}$ of 8 is 6 so 'of' in mathematics means that you multiply.

Communication using symbols

Discussion activity

In this chapter, we consider adding, subtracting, multiplying and dividing fractions.

Which is the most difficult to do and why?

Which is the easiest?

8 Fractions

8.3 Now try these

Band 1 questions

1 Match the bar model diagrams to the calculations and work out the answers.

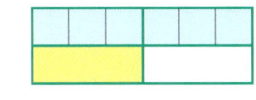

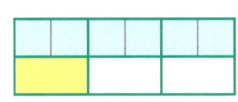

a   b

c   d

    i $\frac{1}{3}$ of 9   ii $\frac{1}{5}$ of 10   iii $\frac{1}{2}$ of 6   iv $\frac{1}{3}$ of 6

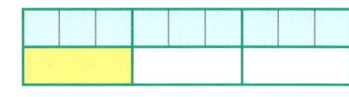

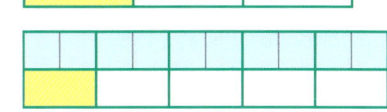

2 Work out:

a $\frac{1}{2}$ of 12   b $\frac{1}{3}$ of 12   c $\frac{2}{3}$ of 12   d $\frac{1}{4}$ of 12   e $\frac{1}{6}$ of 12

3 Copy and complete:

$\frac{1}{2}$ of 100 = $\frac{1}{4}$ of ☐

4 Work out these.

a $\frac{1}{3}$ of 15   b $\frac{2}{3}$ of 15   c $\frac{1}{4}$ of 20   d $\frac{3}{4}$ of 20

e $\frac{1}{5}$ of 20   f $\frac{2}{5}$ of 20   g $\frac{3}{5}$ of 20   h $\frac{4}{5}$ of 20

5 Work out these.

a $\frac{1}{4}$ of 100 cm   b $\frac{1}{3}$ of 45 minutes   c $\frac{1}{5}$ of 60 minutes   d $\frac{1}{4}$ of 64 kg

e $\frac{2}{3}$ of 18 kg   f $\frac{3}{4}$ of 32 ounces   g $\frac{3}{7}$ of 28 days   h $\frac{4}{9}$ of 360°

6 Tim, Mark and Humza share £30. Tim gets $\frac{1}{3}$. Mark gets $\frac{1}{5}$. Humza gets $\frac{1}{6}$.

    a   How much money does each person get?

    b   i   How much is left over?   ii   What fraction is left over?

Band 2 questions

7 Work out:

a $\frac{3}{4}$ of 24   b $\frac{2}{5}$ of 20   c $\frac{5}{9}$ of 27   d $\frac{2}{15}$ of 30

e $\frac{4}{7}$ of 28   f $\frac{3}{10}$ of £2.50   g $\frac{2}{3}$ of £3.99   h $\frac{4}{5}$ of £3.60

Curriculum for Wales Mastering Mathematics: Book 1

Fluency

8 Work out:

a $\dfrac{1}{8} \times 56$ b $\dfrac{2}{3} \times 12$ c $\dfrac{3}{4} \times 20$ d $\dfrac{3}{5} \times 35$ e $\dfrac{2}{7} \times 42$ f $\dfrac{4}{9} \times 63$

Strategic competence

9 Calculate the following offer prices.

a A litre bottle of cola costs 99p.
A special offer bottle has $\dfrac{1}{3}$ off the normal price. What is the offer price?

b A laptop normally sells at £450.
There is a special offer of $\dfrac{1}{5}$ off. What is the offer price?

Fluency

10 Work out:

a $6 \times \dfrac{1}{2}$ b $20 \times \dfrac{1}{10}$ c $15 \times \dfrac{2}{5}$ d $21 \times \dfrac{3}{7}$ e $100 \times \dfrac{4}{5}$ f $18 \times \dfrac{1}{4}$

Logical reasoning

11 Copy and complete:

a $\dfrac{1}{3} \times \square = 4$ b $\dfrac{2}{3} \times \square = 12$ c $\dfrac{\square}{5} \times 40 = 24$

d $\dfrac{5}{\square} \times 42 = 30$ e $\dfrac{\square}{\square} \times 60 = 45$ f $\dfrac{7}{\square} \times 48 = 42$

Strategic competence

12 Jani eats $\dfrac{1}{5}$ of a packet that contains 20 biscuits.

Tomos has a packet that contains 24 biscuits.

What fraction of his packet must Tomos eat so that he has the same number of biscuits remaining as Jani?

Logical reasoning

13 Copy and complete:

a $\square \times \dfrac{1}{4} = 10$ b $\square \times \dfrac{3}{4} = 33$ c $\square \times \dfrac{1}{2} = 2\dfrac{1}{2}$

d $\square \times \dfrac{3}{5} = 21$ e $60 \times \dfrac{\square}{12} = 25$ f $100 \times \dfrac{\square}{\square} = 5$

Strategic competence

14 Half of Melissa's marbles are red.

Emyr has 12 marbles. A third of Emyr's marbles are red.

He gives half of his red marbles to Melissa.

She now has 11 red marbles.

How many marbles does Melissa now have altogether?

Band 3 questions

Logical reasoning

15 Peter says, 'To multiply $\dfrac{2}{5}$ by 10 you have to multiply the 2 by 10 and the 5 by 10.'

a Explain why Peter is wrong.   b What calculation should you do?

c Work out $\dfrac{2}{5}$ multiplied by 10.

16 a Work out $\dfrac{1}{3}$ of £36.   b Work out $\dfrac{1}{3}$ off £36.

c Explain why your answers to parts **a** and **b** are different.

8 Fractions

17 Work out:

a $\frac{1}{100} \times 10\,000$ b $\frac{1}{10} \times 560$ c $\frac{3}{10} \times 40$

d $\frac{12}{100} \times 400$ e $\frac{111}{1000} \times 5000$ f $\frac{7}{100} \times 60$

18 Place the digits 2, 3 and 9 in the boxes so that the answer is 6.

$\square \times \dfrac{\square}{\square}$

19 Copy and complete:

a $\frac{2}{3} \times \square = \frac{1}{3} \times \square = 32$ b $\frac{3}{4} \times \square = \square \times \frac{1}{4} = 120$

c $\frac{2}{5} \times 42 + \frac{1}{10} \times 42 = \square$ d $\frac{11}{12} \times 72 - \frac{1}{4} \times 72 = \dfrac{\square}{\square} \times 72$

20 A clothes shop advertises '$\frac{1}{4}$ off' all prices in a sale.

After a week, they advertise '$\frac{1}{3}$ off' all sale prices in a flash sale.

A pair of jeans costs £36 before the sale. What is its price in the flash sale?

8.4 Dividing an integer by a fraction

Skill checker

1 a How many thirds are in one whole?
b How many tenths are in one whole?
c How many twenty-sixths are in one whole?

2 Simplify:

a $\frac{4}{8}$ b $\frac{6}{10}$ c $\frac{24}{36}$

3 Work out:

a $\frac{1}{4} \times 12$ b $\frac{1}{3} \times 15$ c $\frac{2}{3} \times 15$

4 Work out:

a $10 \div 5$ b $24 \div 3$ c $21 \div 7$

169

Activity

Use a calculator to explore what happens when you replace the box with a whole number.

☐ ÷ $\frac{1}{7}$

Note: Use the fraction button to input the fractions.

① Use a calculator to work out $4 \div \frac{1}{7}$.
② Work out $28 \times \frac{1}{7}$.
③ Write $4 \div 28$ as a fraction.
④ Use a calculator to work out $4 \div \frac{2}{7}$.
⑤ Work out $14 \times \frac{2}{7}$.
⑥ What do you notice?

Discussion activity

[Number line from 0 to 4 divided into sevenths, with $\frac{1}{7}$ labelled]

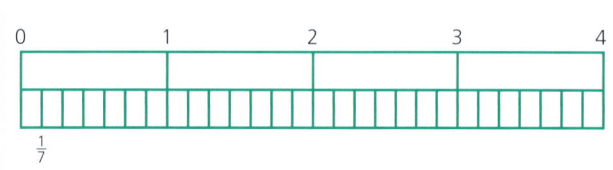

① Discuss how to use this diagram to work out the following.
  a How many sevenths are there in 1?
  b Why is $1 \div \frac{1}{7} = 1 \times 7$?
  c Why is $2 \div \frac{1}{7} = 2 \times 7$?
  d Why is $4 \div \frac{1}{7} = 4 \times 7$?

② Explain how this diagram also represents $28 \times \frac{1}{7} = 4$.
③ Explain how this diagram also represents $4 \div 28 = \frac{1}{7}$.

Worked example

Use a bar model diagram to find:

a $4 \div \frac{1}{5}$
b $4 \div \frac{2}{5}$
c $4 \div \frac{4}{5}$

Solution

a $4 \div \frac{1}{5}$ can be represented by:

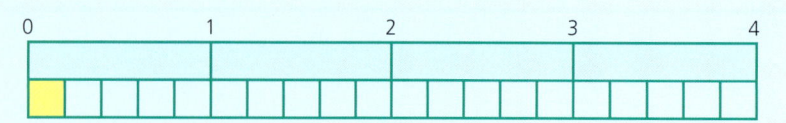

[Number line from 0 to 4 divided into fifths]

> There are five lots of $\frac{1}{5}$ in each whole one. Dividing by $\frac{1}{5}$ is the same as multiplying by 5.

8 Fractions

Conceptual understanding

There are 20 lots of $\frac{1}{5}$ in four whole ones.

So, $4 \div \frac{1}{5} = 20$.

b $4 \div \frac{2}{5}$ can be represented by:

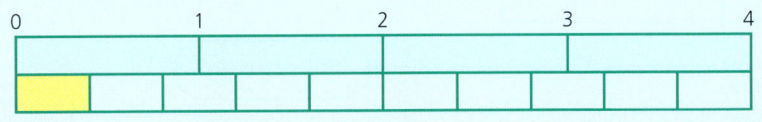

There are ten lots of $\frac{2}{5}$ in four whole ones.

$1 \div \frac{1}{5} = 5$

So, $4 \div \frac{1}{5} = 20$.

So, $4 \div \frac{2}{5} = 10$.

c $4 \div \frac{4}{5}$ can be represented by:

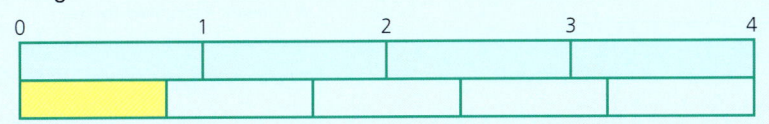

There are five lots of $\frac{4}{5}$ in four whole ones.

$1 \div \frac{1}{5} = 5$

So, $4 \div \frac{1}{5} = 20$.

So, $4 \div \frac{2}{5} = 10$.

So, $4 \div \frac{4}{5} = 5$.

Activity

① What do you get when you divide half by 2?
② What do you get when you divide a fifth by 2?
③ What do you get when you divide a quarter by 2?

Worked example

Use a bar model diagram to find:

a $\frac{1}{5} \div 4$ **b** $\frac{2}{5} \div 4$ **c** $\frac{4}{5} \div 4$

Solution

a $\frac{1}{5} \div 4$ can be represented by:

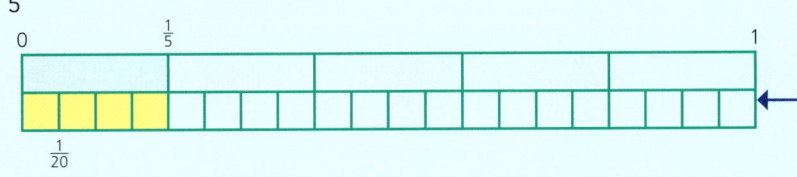

There are five lots of $\frac{1}{5}$ in a whole.

$\frac{1}{5}$ is divided into four equal parts. There are $4 \times 5 = 20$ of these parts in a whole.

So, $\frac{1}{5} \div 4 = \frac{1}{20}$.

171

b $\frac{2}{5} \div 4$ can be represented by:

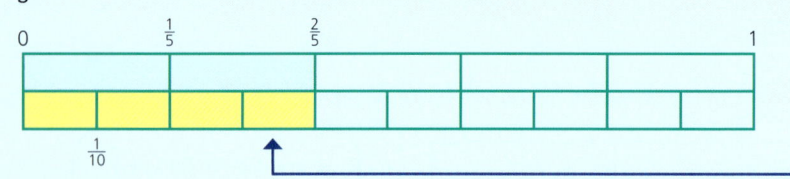

When $\frac{2}{5}$ is divided into four equal parts, each one is $\frac{1}{10}$.

So, $\frac{2}{5} \div 4 = \frac{1}{10}$.

> Half of $\frac{1}{5}$ is $\frac{1}{10}$.

c $\frac{4}{5} \div 4$ can be represented by:

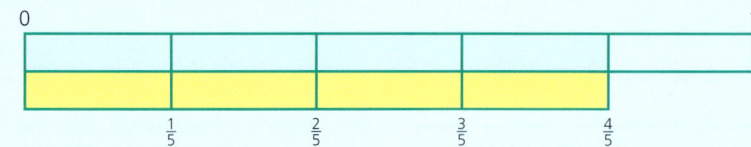

When $\frac{4}{5}$ is divided into four equal parts, each one is $\frac{1}{5}$.

So, $\frac{4}{5} \div 4 = \frac{1}{5}$.

The **reciprocal** of 4 is $\frac{1}{4}$.

The reciprocal of $\frac{1}{4}$ is 4.

The reciprocal of $\frac{2}{5}$ is $\frac{5}{2}$ and the reciprocal of $\frac{5}{2}$ is $\frac{2}{5}$.

> $4 \times \frac{1}{4} = 1$
>
> $\frac{1}{4} \times 4 = 1$

> **Note**
> A number multiplied by its reciprocal gives the answer 1.

Conceptual understanding

Worked example

Write down the reciprocal of:

a 10

b $\frac{3}{7}$

Solution

a The reciprocal of 10 is $\frac{1}{10}$.

> 10 can be written as $\frac{10}{1}$.

b The reciprocal of $\frac{3}{7}$ is $\frac{7}{3}$.

Discussion activity
Is there a quick way you can write down a reciprocal of a number?

Remember
Units 8.3 and 8.4 show how a fraction is used as an operator.

You have already worked with a fraction used to represent division when learning about the importance of BIDMAS in unit 5.3.

8.4 Now try these

Band 1 questions

1
  a How many halves are in 3?
  b How many halves are in 10?
  c How many thirds are in 2?
  d How many tenths are in 10?

2 Write down the reciprocals of these numbers.
  a 4   b $\frac{1}{5}$ c $\frac{1}{4}$ d $\frac{1}{7}$ e 5   f 10

3 This bar model diagram illustrates $4 \div \frac{1}{2} = 8$.

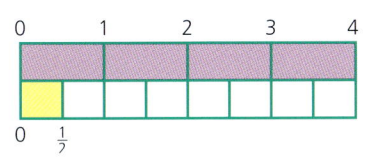

State the division calculation represented by each of the following bar model diagrams.

  a

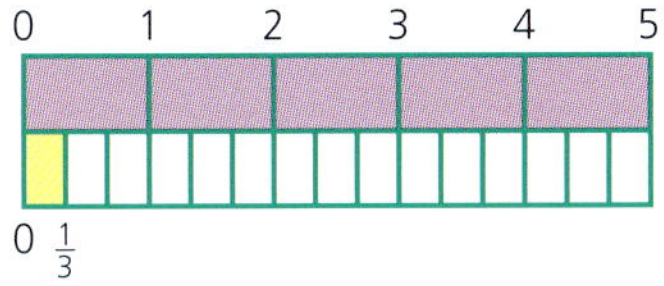

  b

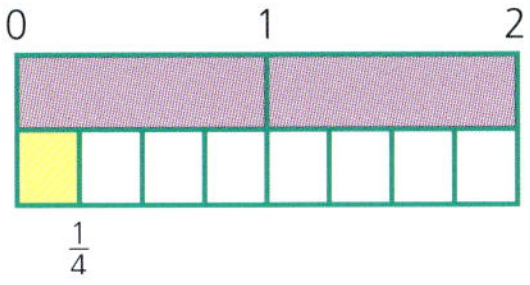

  c

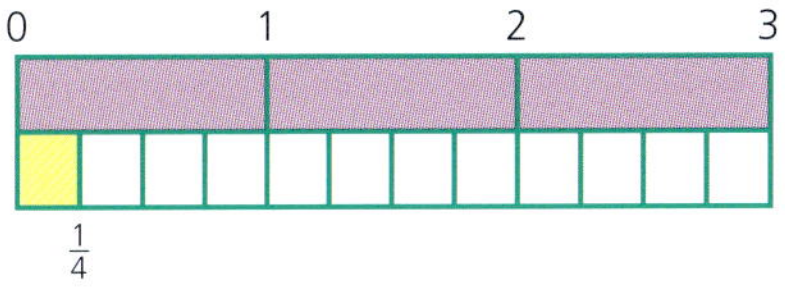

4 Draw a bar model diagram for each calculation to work out:
  a $\frac{1}{2} \div 2$ b $\frac{1}{3} \div 2$ c $\frac{1}{5} \div 3$ d $\frac{1}{4} \div 5$

5 a Which **two** of the calculations are represented by the bar model diagram?

$\frac{1}{18} \times 3$ $3 \div 6$ $\frac{1}{3} \div 6$ $\frac{1}{6} \div 3$ $\frac{1}{6} \times 3$

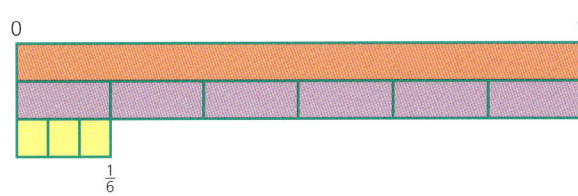

b Which **three** of the calculations are represented by the bar model diagram?

$$\frac{1}{3} \times 5 \qquad 15 \times \frac{1}{5} \qquad 3 \times 15 \qquad 3 \div 15 \qquad 3 \div \frac{1}{5}$$

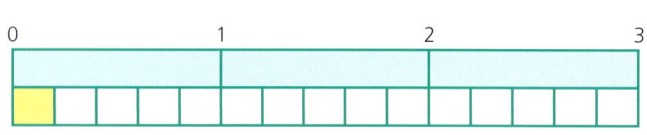

6 Jac prepares for a party.

He thinks that each person will eat $\frac{1}{4}$ of a pizza.

How many people does he expect to feed with five pizzas?

Band 2 questions

7 Anna shares $\frac{1}{4}$ of her birthday cake between five people.

What fraction of the cake does each person get?

8 State the division calculation represented by each of the following bar model diagrams.

a

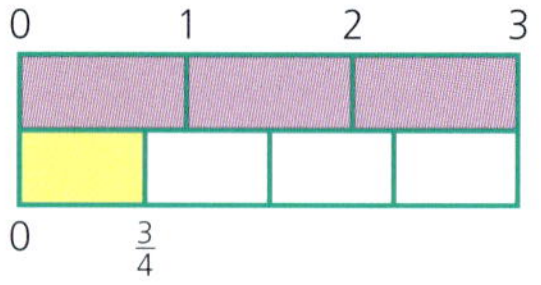

b

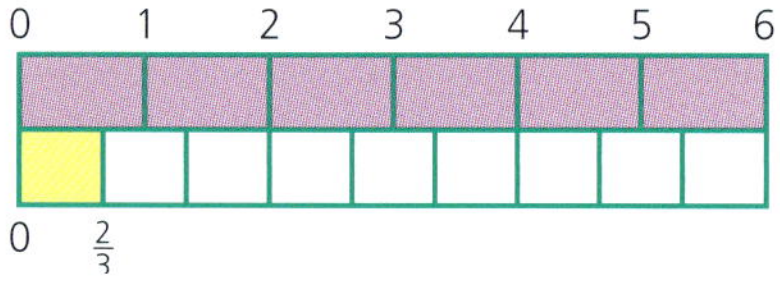

9 a Which **three** of the calculations are represented by the bar model diagram?

$$4 \div 6 \qquad 4 \div \frac{2}{3} \qquad 6 \times 4 \qquad \frac{2}{3} \div 4 \qquad 6 \times \frac{2}{3} \qquad 6 \div \frac{2}{3}$$

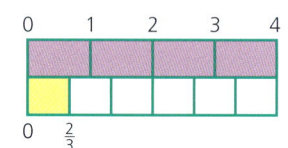

b Which **three** of the calculations are represented by the bar model diagram?

$$10 \div 12 \qquad 12 \times \frac{5}{6} \qquad 12 \div 10 \qquad 10 \div \frac{5}{6} \qquad \frac{5}{6} \div 10$$

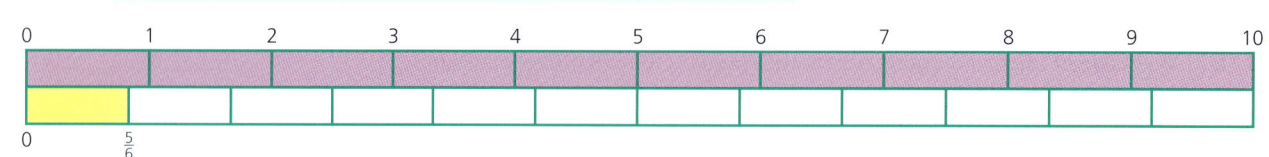

c Which **four** of the calculations are represented by the bar model diagram?

$$2 \times \frac{3}{8} \qquad \frac{3}{4} \times 2 \qquad \frac{3}{4} \div 2 \qquad \frac{3}{4} \div \frac{3}{8} \qquad \frac{3}{8} \times 2 \qquad 2 \div \frac{3}{4}$$

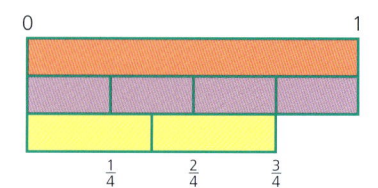

8 Fluency

10 Write down the reciprocals of these numbers.
  a $\frac{4}{3}$ b $\frac{2}{5}$ c $\frac{3}{4}$ d $\frac{2}{7}$ e $\frac{5}{2}$ f $\frac{15}{8}$

11 Draw a bar model diagram to represent each of the divisions and work out the answer.
  a $\frac{5}{6} \div 4$ b $\frac{2}{5} \div 5$ c $\frac{3}{5} \div 3$ d $\frac{4}{7} \div 2$ e $\frac{6}{7} \div 3$

12 Work out:
  a $16 \div \frac{1}{3}$ b $16 \div \frac{1}{5}$ c $\frac{1}{4} \div 3$ d $\frac{1}{6} \div 2$

13 Copy and complete:
  a $\frac{1}{5} \div 6 = \frac{\square}{30}$ b $\frac{1}{7} \div 2 = \frac{1}{\square}$ c $8 \div \frac{1}{\square} = 24$ d $\square \div \frac{1}{4} = 28$

14 Karl has read $\frac{1}{5}$ of his book in two days.
  a What fraction is this per day?
  b What fraction has he still not read?
  c He must return the book to the library in six days' time. What fraction must he now read each day?

Band 3 questions

15 Copy and complete:
  a $\frac{2}{\square} \div 3 = \frac{2}{15}$ b $\frac{3}{8} \div \square = \frac{1}{8}$ c $\square \div \frac{2}{3} = 18$ d $15 \div \frac{\square}{6} = 18$

16 Work out:
  a $2 \div \frac{2}{5}$ b $8 \div \frac{2}{5}$ c $8 \div \frac{4}{5}$ d $\frac{2}{3} \div 3$ e $\frac{3}{4} \div 7$ f $\frac{3}{7} \div 4$
  g $12 \div \frac{2}{7}$ h $12 \div \frac{4}{7}$ i $\frac{7}{10} \div 6$ j $\frac{9}{10} \div 6$ k $\frac{9}{10} \div 3$

17 What number is the reciprocal of itself?

18 Medwyn Miller the millionaire left his fortune to be divided between his children and his grandchildren.
  a A quarter of his money is to be divided equally between his four children.
     What fraction does each receive?
  b The remainder is divided equally between his ten grandchildren.
     What fraction is this for each grandchild?
  c His fortune was £4 million.
     Calculate the amount that went to each child and each grandchild.

19 Work out:
  a $48 \div \frac{16}{17}$ b $\frac{20}{23} \div 4$ c $48 \div \frac{3}{11}$ d $\frac{25}{29} \div 5$ e $48 \div \frac{4}{15}$ f $\frac{81}{100} \div 9$

175

Strategic competence

20 A fish weighs 10 kg plus a third of its weight.
How much does the fish weigh?

Logical reasoning

21 a Work out $20 \div \frac{4}{5}$.
  b Work out $\frac{4}{5} \div 20$.
  c What do you notice about your answers to parts **a** and **b**?
  d Find another **two** calculations that have the same property.

22 a Work out $1 \div \frac{1}{10}$ and use your answer to work out $1 \div 0.1$.
  b Work out $9 \div \frac{1}{10}$ and use your answer to work out $9 \div 0.1$.
  c Work out $9 \div \frac{9}{10}$ and use your answer to work out $9 \div 0.9$.
  d Work out $9 \div \frac{3}{10}$ and use your answer to work out $9 \div 0.3$.
  e Explain how you would work out $6 \div 0.1$.

Key words

Here is a list of the key words you met in this chapter.

Cancel	Common denominator	Common factor	Denominator
Division	Equal	Equivalent	Factor
Inverse	Multiple	Multiplication	Multiplier
Numerator	Reciprocal	Simplify	

Use the glossary at the back of this book to check any you are unsure about.

8 Fractions

Review exercise: fractions

Band 1 questions

1
  a. Nia takes three pieces of pizza. What fraction of the pizza does she take?
  b. Mohsen takes two pieces of pizza. What fraction of the pizza does he take?
  c. What fraction of the pizza is left? Simplify your answer.

2 Tim has 36 marbles.
  a. $\frac{1}{3}$ of the marbles are blue. How many marbles are blue?
  b. $\frac{1}{6}$ of the marbles are red. How many marbles are red?
  c. 3 of the marbles are green. What fraction of the marbles are green?
  d. The rest of the marbles are yellow. What fraction of the marbles are yellow?

3
  a. What fraction of the chocolate bar is one square?
  b. How many squares are there in five of these chocolate bars?

4 Copy and complete:
  a. $\frac{3}{7} + \frac{1}{7} = \frac{\square}{7}$
  b. $\frac{\square}{9} - \frac{5}{9} = \frac{2}{9}$
  c. $\frac{1}{4} + \frac{1}{4} \square \frac{3}{4}$
  d. $\frac{1}{\square}$ of 27 = 3
  e. $\frac{1}{2} \square \frac{1}{5}$
  f. $\frac{1}{5}$ of $\square$ = 4

5 A box contains 3 kg of washing powder.
One machine wash uses $\frac{1}{8}$ kg of washing powder.
How many washes will you get from a full box?

6 Match these fractions to the points on the number line.

$\frac{3}{5}$ $\frac{1}{2}$ $\frac{1}{10}$ $\frac{19}{20}$ $\frac{1}{4}$

0 — B — E — A — C — D — 1

Band 2 questions

7 Mr Brown starts his journey with $\frac{1}{2}$ a tank of petrol. He uses $\frac{1}{3}$ of a tank.
How much petrol has he left?
What fraction must he put in his tank to fill it up?

8 Work out:

a $\frac{1}{3} + \frac{1}{4}$
b $7 \div \frac{1}{3}$
c $\frac{1}{2} - \frac{1}{5}$
d the reciprocal of 6

e $\frac{1}{3} \div 7$
f $\frac{1}{6} \times 24$
g the reciprocal of $\frac{2}{3}$
h $24 \times \frac{1}{8}$

9 £48 is shared between Emyr, Andy and John.

Emyr gets £16. Andy gets £12. John gets the rest.

What fraction of the money does each person get?

Write the fractions in their simplest form.

10 Copy and complete with a number, fraction, or sign.

a $\frac{2}{7}$ of $\square = 14$
b $\square \div \frac{1}{6} = 72$
c $\frac{5}{12} \square \frac{1}{3}$

d $\square + \frac{1}{4} = \frac{3}{4}$
e $\frac{1}{3} \square 5 = \frac{1}{15}$
f $\square - \frac{1}{3} = \frac{1}{12}$

g $\frac{3}{5} \div \square = \frac{3}{10}$
h $\frac{11}{60} \square \frac{1}{5}$
i $\frac{2}{5} - \square = \frac{3}{20}$

11
a What fraction of an hour is 15 minutes?
b What fraction of a week is two days?
c Work out $\frac{2}{3}$ of 48 kg.
d How many quarter pounds are there in 3 pounds?
e Which is greater, $\frac{1}{3}$ of 6 kg or $\frac{1}{6}$ of 12 kg?

12 Sion says that $20 \div \frac{2}{5}$ is 8 because $\frac{1}{5}$ of 20 is 4 so $\frac{2}{5}$ of 20 must be 8.

Explain why Sion is wrong.

13 Is it always, sometimes, or never true that a reciprocal is not a whole number? Justify your answer.

Band 3 questions

14
a What fraction of a quarter of an hour is 5 minutes?
b What fraction of four weeks is three days?
c Work out $\frac{2}{7}$ of eight weeks.
d Which is greater, $\frac{3}{1000}$ of a metre or $\frac{3}{10}$ of a centimetre?
e How many $\frac{1}{100}$ of a metre are in 1 kilometre?

15 Work out:

a $\frac{5}{6} \times 18$
b $\frac{11}{15} - \frac{2}{3}$
c $7 \div \frac{1}{13}$

d the reciprocal of $\frac{13}{5}$
e $\frac{3}{5} + \frac{2}{7}$
f $143 \times \frac{12}{13}$

178

16 Copy and complete with a number, fraction, or sign.

a $\frac{3}{5} \div \square = \frac{1}{10}$
b $\frac{6}{7} - \square = \frac{3}{28}$
c $\frac{3}{11} \square \frac{1}{4}$
d $12 \div \square = 28$

e $\square \times \frac{4}{5} = 36$
f $\frac{12}{18} \square \frac{40}{60}$
g $\frac{2}{9} \times \square = 16$
h $\frac{4}{5} \square 2 = \frac{2}{5}$

17 What number is four times its reciprocal?

18 A crocodile measures 3 m plus $\frac{2}{7}$ of its length.
How long is the crocodile?

19 What fraction is halfway between $\frac{3}{7}$ and $\frac{5}{9}$?

20 $\frac{2}{5}$ is halfway between two fractions.
One of them is $\frac{1}{12}$.
What is the other fraction?

9 Place value and rounding

Coming up...

▶ Understanding and using place value for decimals
▶ Arranging decimals in order
▶ Using the number line for ordering decimals
▶ Using the symbols =, ≠, <, >, ≤, ≥
▶ Working interchangeably with terminating decimals and their corresponding fractions (such as 0.375 and $\frac{3}{8}$)
▶ Using standard units of mass, length, time, money, and other measures, including with decimal quantities
▶ Appreciating the infinite nature of the set of real numbers
▶ Rounding numbers and measures to an appropriate degree of accuracy (e.g. to a number of decimal places)

Make some numbers

Here are some number cards.

| 1 | 2 | 3 | 4 | 5 | 6 | 7 | 8 | 9 |

Place them side by side to make numbers.

Challenge 1

a Using four of the digits 1 to 9, make the largest number that you can.
b Using four of the digits 1 to 9, make the smallest whole number that you can.
c Using four of the digits 1 to 9, make the largest odd number that you can.
d Using four of the digits 1 to 9, make the smallest odd number that you can.

Challenge 2

a Using four of the digits 1 to 9, and a decimal point, make the smallest number that you can.
b Using two of the digits 1 to 9, and a decimal point, make the number nearest to ten that you can.
c Using four of the digits 1 to 9, and a decimal point, make the number nearest to ten that you can.

Challenge 3

a Using four of the digits 1 to 9, make the number nearest to 3000 that you can.
b Using the digits 1 to 4, make the number nearest to 3000 that you can.
c Using the digits 1 to 4, make the number nearest to 5000 that you can.
d Using the digits 1 to 4, make the number nearest to 2500 that you can.

9 Place value and rounding

9.1 Understanding decimals

Skill checker

1. The number 325 can be thought of as three hundreds, two tens and five ones, or 300 + 20 + 5.
   So 325 = 300 + 20 + 5.
   Write these numbers in the same way.

   a 498
   b 694
   c 703
   d 310
   e 87
   f 1034
   g seven thousand, three hundred and fifty-eight
   h two thousand and thirty-four

2. In each part, which one of <, > or = should go in the box?

   a 704 ☐ 740
   b 2 031 010 ☐ 2 million, three hundred thousand
   c twenty thousand and fifty ☐ 20 050
   d 8300 ☐ eight thousand and thirty-one
   e fifty thousand ☐ 5000

3. Write each set of numbers in order from smallest to largest.

   a 2345, 3245, 5324, 2543, 3425, 4235
   b 2098, 9802, 9820, 9280, 2089, 2890, 2980, 8092, 9082

4. Look at these number cards.

   5 1 7 0 3 8

   a What is the largest two-digit number you can make with these cards?
   b What is the smallest two-digit number you can make with these cards?
   c What is the largest three-digit number you can make with these cards?
   d What is the smallest three-digit number you can make with these cards?
   e What is the largest five-digit number you can make with these cards?
   f What is the smallest five-digit number you can make with these cards?

Although the base 10 system existed before the thirteenth century, it was in the thirteenth century that Leonardo of Pisa introduced it for whole numbers to Europe. Three centuries later, Simon Stevin thought of extending the base 10 system to parts of a whole number.

Discussion activity

Where did the base 10 system originate from?

Note

Leonardo of Pisa is more commonly known as Fibonacci.

Activity

Conceptual understanding

Moving from hundreds to tens, you divide by 10. Moving from tens to units, you divide by 10.

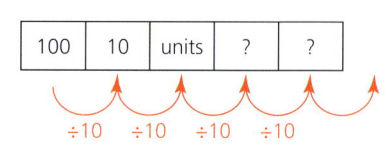

| 100 | 10 | units | ? | ? |

↑÷10 ↑÷10 ↑÷10 ↑÷10

① What do you get when you divide 1 by 10?

② Work out:

   a $\quad \dfrac{1}{10} \div 10$ b $\quad \dfrac{1}{100} \div 10$ c $\quad \dfrac{1}{1000} \div 10$

③ What calculation do you do to move in the opposite direction?

④ Work out:

   a $\quad 1 \times 10$ b $\quad \dfrac{1}{10} \times 10$ c $\quad \dfrac{1}{100} \times 10$ d $\quad \dfrac{1}{1000} \times 10$

⑤ What goes in the last two boxes of the diagram above?

The pattern of dividing by 10 gives tenths and then hundredths and then thousandths, and so on forever.

A dot, the **decimal point**, separates the whole numbers from the parts of a whole.

The parts of a whole are called **decimal places**.

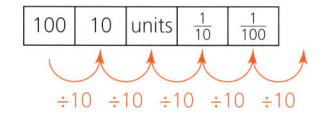

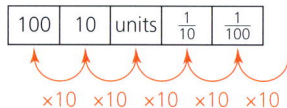

| 100 | 10 | units | $\frac{1}{10}$ | $\frac{1}{100}$ |

÷10 ÷10 ÷10 ÷10 ÷10

| 100 | 10 | units | $\frac{1}{10}$ | $\frac{1}{100}$ |

×10 ×10 ×10 ×10 ×10

> **Note**
> You will learn more about multiplying and dividing by powers of 10 in Chapter 12.

Multiplying by 10 moves in the opposite direction, from hundredths to tenths to units to tens to hundreds, and so on forever.

The number 58.31 is $50 + 8 + \dfrac{3}{10} + \dfrac{1}{100}$ using fraction notation.

> You say this number as 'fifty-eight point three one'.

100	10	units	$\frac{1}{10}$	$\frac{1}{100}$
	5	8	3	1

Using decimal notation, 58.31 is $50 + 8 + 0.3 + 0.01$.

The 3 is worth $\dfrac{3}{10}$ and the 1 is worth $\dfrac{1}{100}$.

units	$\frac{1}{10}$	$\frac{1}{100}$	$\frac{1}{1000}$
0	8	0	7

The 8 in 0.807 is worth $\dfrac{8}{10}$, the following 0 indicates zero hundredths and the 7 is worth 7 thousandths.

> You say this number as 'zero point eight zero seven'.

There are 807 thousandths in 0.807.

$\dfrac{8}{10} + \dfrac{0}{100} + \dfrac{7}{1000} = \dfrac{807}{1000}$

9 Place value and rounding

Worked example

Place these numbers in order, from smallest to largest.

0.3   0.31   0.7   0.13   0.71   0.07

Solution

A place-value table can help to show which digits represent the greatest value.

units		$\frac{1}{10}$	$\frac{1}{100}$
0	.	3	
0	.	3	1
0	.	7	
0	.	1	3
0	.	7	1
0	.	0	7

Both numbers have 3 in the tenths position so you have to look at the hundredths.

There is nothing in the hundredths for 0.3 and a 1 for 0.31 so 0.3 is smaller than 0.31.

0.13 has 1 in the tenths position so comes after 0.07.

0.07 has zero in the tenths position so is the smallest number.

All of the numbers have zero in the units position so this makes no difference to the order of the numbers.

Similarly, 0.7 is smaller than 0.71.

The final order is 0.07, 0.13, 0.3, 0.31, 0.7, 0.71.

Remember

These are all decimals.

Some fractions cannot be written as terminating decimals.

They are infinite or recurring decimals.

Activity

For each decimal in the table, find the fraction in the table that matches its value.

$\frac{7}{100}$	0.023	$\frac{1}{10}$	0.07
0.1	$\frac{1}{1000}$	0.7	$\frac{23}{100}$
0.23	$\frac{7}{10}$	$\frac{23}{1000}$	0.001

Explain how you know that they are worth the same amount.

Worked example

Convert these decimals into fractions.

0.31   0.6   0.07   0.75   0.135

Note

The place value gives the fractions.

Solution

$0.31 = 0 + 0.3 + 0.01$

$= 0 + \frac{3}{10} + \frac{1}{100}$

$= \frac{30}{100} + \frac{1}{100}$

$= \frac{31}{100}$

3 is in the tenths position so is worth 3 tenths.

1 is in the hundredths position so is worth 1 hundredth.

The fractions are added using the common denominator of 100.

The table shows the method for the other examples.

units	$\frac{1}{10}$	$\frac{1}{100}$	$\frac{1}{1000}$		Decimal partition		Fraction partition		Answer
0 •	6			=	0 + 0.6	=	$0 + \frac{6}{10}$	=	$\frac{6}{10} = \frac{3}{5}$
0 •	0	7		=	0 + 0.0 + 0.07	=	$0 + \frac{0}{10} + \frac{7}{100}$	=	$\frac{7}{100}$
0 •	7	5		=	0 + 0.7 + 0.05	=	$0 + \frac{7}{10} + \frac{5}{100} = \frac{70}{100} + \frac{5}{100}$	=	$\frac{75}{100} = \frac{3}{4}$
0 •	1	3	5	=	0 + 0.1 + 0.03 + 0.005	=	$0 + \frac{1}{10} + \frac{3}{100} + \frac{5}{1000} = \frac{100}{1000} + \frac{30}{1000} + \frac{5}{1000}$	=	$\frac{135}{1000} = \frac{27}{200}$

Worked example

Write these fractions as decimals.

a $\frac{17}{100}$ b $\frac{13}{20}$ c $\frac{3}{8}$

Solution

a $\frac{17}{100}$ has a denominator that is a **power of 10**
and so is already in a form that uses the place value columns.

$\frac{17}{100}$ is equivalent to 0.17.

$\frac{17}{100} = \frac{10}{100} + \frac{7}{100} = \frac{1}{10} + \frac{7}{100} = 0.17$

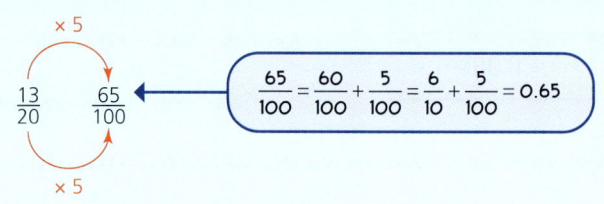

Note

The powers of 10 are 10, 100, 1000, …

b **Method 1:** Converting to a denominator that is 10, 100, 1000, …

$\frac{13}{20}$ is not in a form with a power of 10 as the denominator.

It is rewritten as an equivalent fraction with 100 as the denominator.

× 5

$\frac{13}{20} \rightarrow \frac{65}{100}$

× 5

$\frac{65}{100} = \frac{60}{100} + \frac{5}{100} = \frac{6}{10} + \frac{5}{100} = 0.65$

Note

For a reminder of equivalent fractions, see Chapter 8.

Remember

0.65 is a **terminating** decimal. A terminating decimal ends.

Method 2: Using short division

$\frac{13}{20}$ represents the calculation 13 ÷ 20.

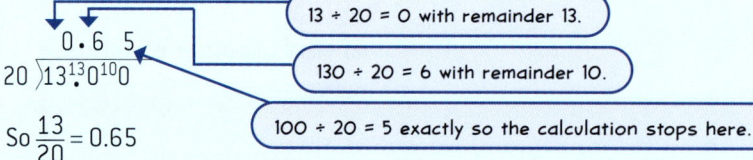

$0 \cdot 6\ 5$
$20\overline{)13.^{13}0^{10}0}$

13 ÷ 20 = 0 with remainder 13.
130 ÷ 20 = 6 with remainder 10.
100 ÷ 20 = 5 exactly so the calculation stops here.

So $\frac{13}{20} = 0.65$

c **Method 1:** Converting to a denominator that is 10, 100, 1000, …

$\frac{3}{8}$ is not yet in a form with a denominator that is a power of 10.
It is rewritten as an equivalent fraction with a denominator of 1000.

Remember

0.375 is a terminating decimal.

9 Place value and rounding

Conceptual understanding

$$\frac{3}{8} \xrightarrow{\times 125} \frac{375}{1000} \leftarrow \frac{375}{1000} = \frac{300}{1000} + \frac{70}{1000} + \frac{5}{1000} = \frac{3}{10} + \frac{7}{100} + \frac{5}{1000} = 0.375$$

$$\times 125$$

So $\frac{3}{8} = 0.375$

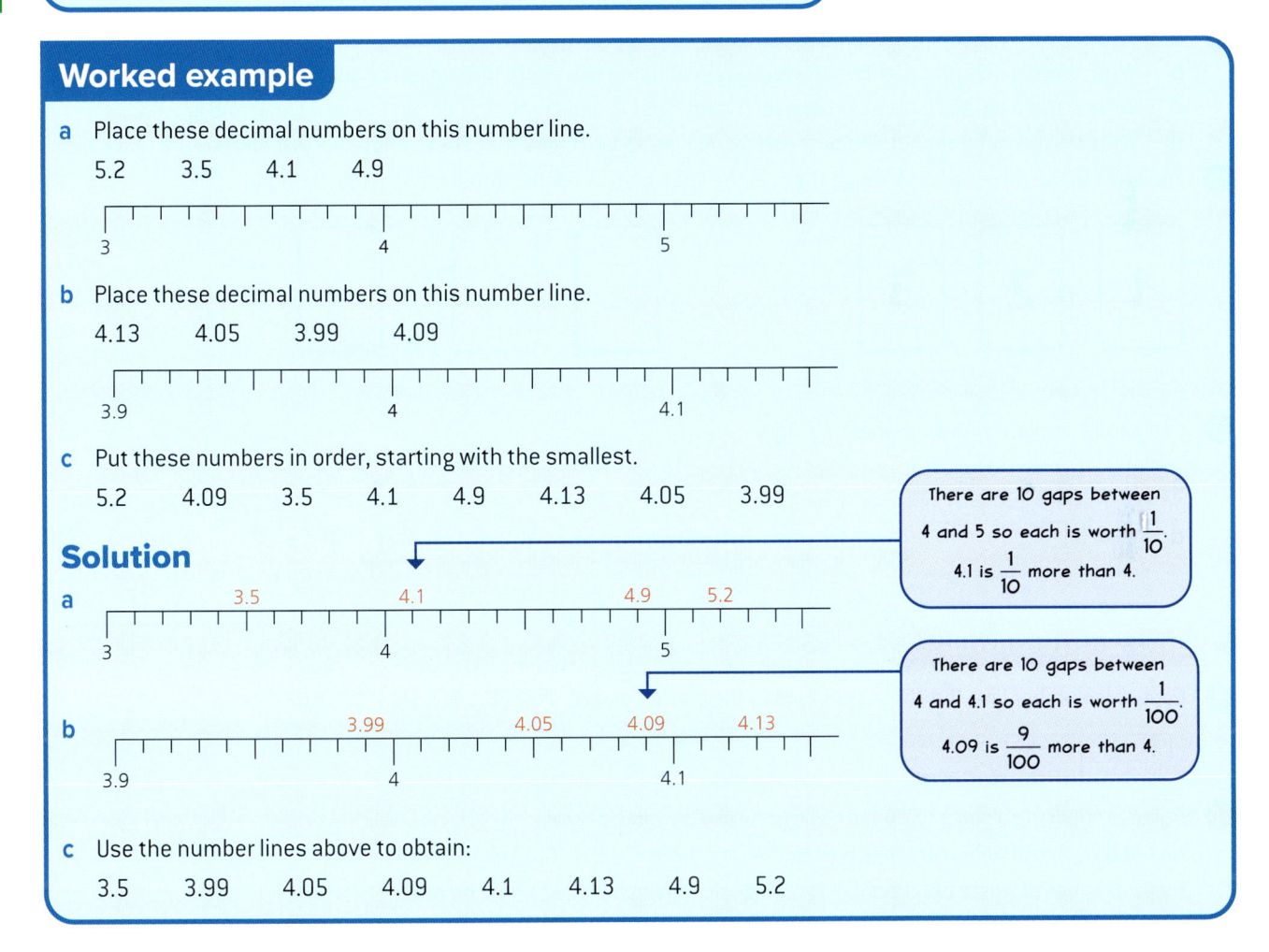

Method 2: Using short division

$\frac{3}{8}$ represents the calculation $3 \div 8$.

$$\begin{array}{r} 0.375 \\ 8\overline{)3.^30^60^40} \end{array}$$

← 40 ÷ 8 = 5 exactly so the calculation stops here.

So $\frac{3}{8} = 0.375$

Worked example

a Place these decimal numbers on this number line.

   5.2   3.5   4.1   4.9

   [number line from 3 to 5]

b Place these decimal numbers on this number line.

   4.13   4.05   3.99   4.09

   [number line from 3.9 to 4.1]

c Put these numbers in order, starting with the smallest.

   5.2   4.09   3.5   4.1   4.9   4.13   4.05   3.99

Solution

a [number line from 3 to 5 with 3.5, 4.1, 4.9, 5.2 marked]

> There are 10 gaps between 4 and 5 so each is worth $\frac{1}{10}$.
> 4.1 is $\frac{1}{10}$ more than 4.

b [number line from 3.9 to 4.1 with 3.99, 4.05, 4.09, 4.13 marked]

> There are 10 gaps between 4 and 4.1 so each is worth $\frac{1}{100}$.
> 4.09 is $\frac{9}{100}$ more than 4.

c Use the number lines above to obtain:

   3.5   3.99   4.05   4.09   4.1   4.13   4.9   5.2

9.1 Now try these

Band 1 questions

1 What is the value of the green digit in each number?

a 16.3

b 4.7

c 319.4

d 181.3

Curriculum for Wales Mastering Mathematics: Book 1

Fluency

② Look at the number line on the right. What decimal numbers do the arrows point to?

③ Look at the number line to the right. What fractions do the letters refer to?

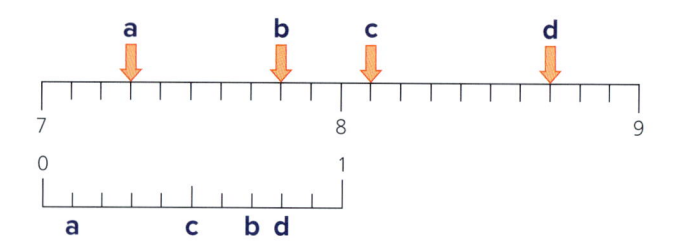

Logical reasoning

④ Match each of the fractions to one of the decimals.

| $\frac{7}{10}$ | $\frac{1}{5}$ | $\frac{9}{10}$ | $\frac{1}{2}$ | $\frac{3}{5}$ |

| 0.5 | 0.6 | 0.9 | 0.7 | 0.2 |

⑤ Arrange these numbers in order, starting with the smallest.

| 2.7 | 0.3 | $\frac{7}{10}$ | 1.5 | 6 |

⑥ a Write down a number between 6 and 7 using two digits.
   b Write down a different number between 6 and 7 using two digits that doesn't have a 5 in it.
   c Write down a different number between 6 and 7 using two digits that doesn't have a 5 in it and is > 6.2.
   d Write down a different number between 6 and 7 using two digits that doesn't have a 5 in it and is > 6.2 and < 6.6.

Strategic competence

⑦ You have these three cards. Arrange them in the spaces to make the smallest possible number.

[1] [2] [3]   ☐ ☐ . ☐

Logical reasoning

⑧ Copy and complete with a number or a sign.

a $0.1 = \frac{\square}{10}$ b $0.3 \square 0.2$ c $1.2 \square 2.1$

d $\frac{3}{10} = 0.\square$ e $\frac{1}{\square} = 0.5$ f $0.4 = \frac{\square}{5}$

Band 2 questions

Fluency

⑨ Copy this number line. Put these numbers in the correct places: 7.05, 7.14, 7.19, 7.16, 7.02

7.0   7.1   7.2

Strategic competence

⑩ Dylan is choosing a piece of ribbon to go around a birthday cake.
He needs 0.8 m of ribbon and has pieces that are 0.79 m, 0.9 m, 0.83 m and 0.08 m long.
He prefers not to waste any ribbon if he can avoid it. Which piece should he use?

⑪ Copy and complete:

a $0.83 = 0.\square + 0.03$ b $0.83 = \frac{\square\square}{100}$ c $\frac{9}{100} = 0.0\square$

d $0.75 = \frac{\square}{\square}$ e $\frac{3}{20} = 0.\square\square$ f $\frac{7}{\square\square} = 0.28$

Logical reasoning

⑫ Ieuan tries to put decimals in ascending order. Which of his answers is correct?
Explain to Ieuan what he has done wrong.

a 0.2, 0.12, 0.21, 0.22
b 1.06, 1.6, 1.66, 6.1

186

9   Place value and rounding

13 Write each of these decimals as fractions. Simplify your answers.
   a 0.03   b 0.12   c 0.25   d 0.08   e 0.45   f 0.64

14 Write each of these fractions as decimals.
   a $\frac{1}{4}$ b $\frac{1}{20}$ c $\frac{11}{20}$ d $\frac{9}{50}$ e $\frac{1}{25}$ f $\frac{13}{25}$

15 Nadiya has a choice of different weights of bags of flour to buy.
    They are 0.8 kg, 1.5 kg, $\frac{3}{4}$ kg and 0.85 kg.
    She wants to buy the smallest amount of flour. Which bag should she buy?

Band 3 questions

16 a What numbers are shown by **i**, **ii**, **iii** and **iv** on the number line to the right?
    b Write each number as a fraction.

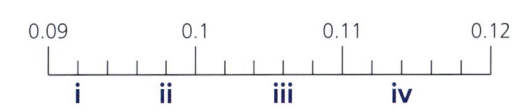

    0.09   0.1   0.11   0.12
      i   ii   iii   iv

17 Copy the diagram. Write these numbers in the boxes so that all four inequalities are true.

    □ > □
    > <
    □ > □

    0.940   0.409   0.490   0.904

18 Write these decimals as fractions in their simplest form.
    a 0.8   b 0.45   c 0.105   d 0.085
    e 0.04   f 0.004   g 0.075   h 0.376

19 Write these fractions as decimals.
    a $\frac{3}{10\,000}$ b $\frac{1}{25}$ c $\frac{12}{250}$ d $\frac{1}{400}$
    e $\frac{17}{250}$ f $\frac{31}{40}$ g $\frac{3}{16}$ h $\frac{51}{80}$

20 Make some cards with the digits 0, 1, 2, 3, 4, 5, 6, 7, 8 and 9 written on them.

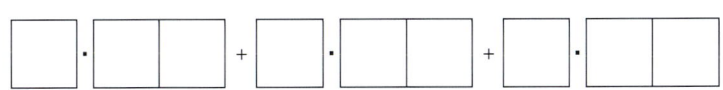

    □.□□ + □.□□ + □.□□

    Place the cards into the boxes to make three three-digit numbers (you'll have one card left over!) so that the total is:
    a i   as large as you can make it.   ii as small as you can make it.
    b Explain how you know that your solution is correct without having to work out the calculation.

21 Convert $\frac{3}{7}$ to a decimal.
    What happens? Explain why it happens.

22 Which of these fractions can be written as a terminating decimal?

    $\frac{3}{5}$ $\frac{2}{3}$ $\frac{3}{400}$ $\frac{2}{7}$ $\frac{7}{250}$ $\frac{9}{80}$ $\frac{4}{99}$

9.2 Rounding

Skill checker

① Round these numbers to the nearest 10.
    a 69   b 121   c 9980   d 1 324 175

② Round these numbers to the nearest 100.
    a 169   b 121   c 9990   d 1001

③ Copy this number line from 300 to 1200.

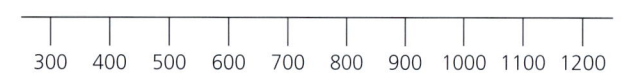

300 400 500 600 700 800 900 1000 1100 1200

    a Mark each of these numbers on it.

        524 620 902 982 1120

    b Round each number to the nearest 100.

④ What is the value of the green digit in each number?
    a 563   b 2065   c 2140   d 11 111

Discussion activity

Daily News

2 million watch as First Minister addresses the nation

Did exactly 2 million people watch the First Minister?

Another newspaper states, 'The actual number was 2 193 703.'

    a How could they know the actual number?
    b Do you think exactly 2 193 703 watched?
    c What would make you think that the number 2 193 703 was made up?
    d What rounding did the first newspaper use?
    e Why do you think they rounded to that accuracy?

9 Place value and rounding

Worked example

Round 185 642 to:

a the nearest 1000

b the nearest 10 000.

Solution

a The multiples of 1000 near to 185 642 are 184 000, 185 000, 186 000 and 187 000.

184 000   185 000   186 000   187 000

185 642 is between 185 000 and 186 000.

6 is in the hundreds position, worth 600, showing 185 642 is nearer 186 000.

185 642 is nearer 186 000 than 185 000 and so 185 642 rounds to 186 000 to the nearest 1000.

b The multiples of 10 000 near 185 642 are 170 000, 180 000, 190 000 and 200 000.

170 000   180 000   190 000   200 000

5 is in the thousands position, worth 5000, so 185 000 is halfway between 180 000 and 190 000.

185 642 is between 180 000 and 190 000.

642 means that 185 642 is nearer 190 000.

When you round 185 642 to the nearest 10 000 you get 190 000.

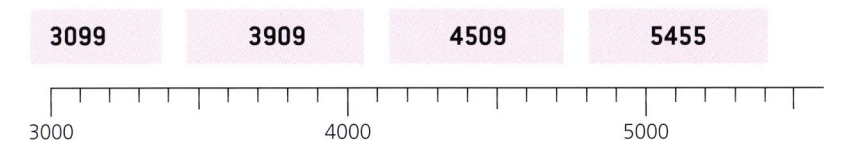

Cross-curricular activity

In geography – and other subjects – you will sometimes need to rank data in order of population size or some other measure.

There are 22 counties in Wales.

What are the largest and smallest counties in Wales, in terms of population?

Write each population to the nearest thousand.

Remember

You always round up in mathematics when the number is exactly halfway.

9.2 Now try these

Band 1 questions

1 Use the number line to round these numbers to the nearest thousand.

3099   3909   4509   5455

3000   4000   5000

2 Which of these numbers are rounded to the nearest thousand?

1000   2100   5065   6000   11 000   29 500

3 Write each of these numbers to the nearest thousand.

a 2135
b 4697
c 8052
d 7904
e 87 241
f 43 278
g 45 649
h 145 625

189

Curriculum for Wales Mastering Mathematics: Book 1

Strategic competence

④ The map shows the area (in square kilometres) of some European countries.

Write each area correct to the nearest thousand square kilometres and list the countries in order of size.

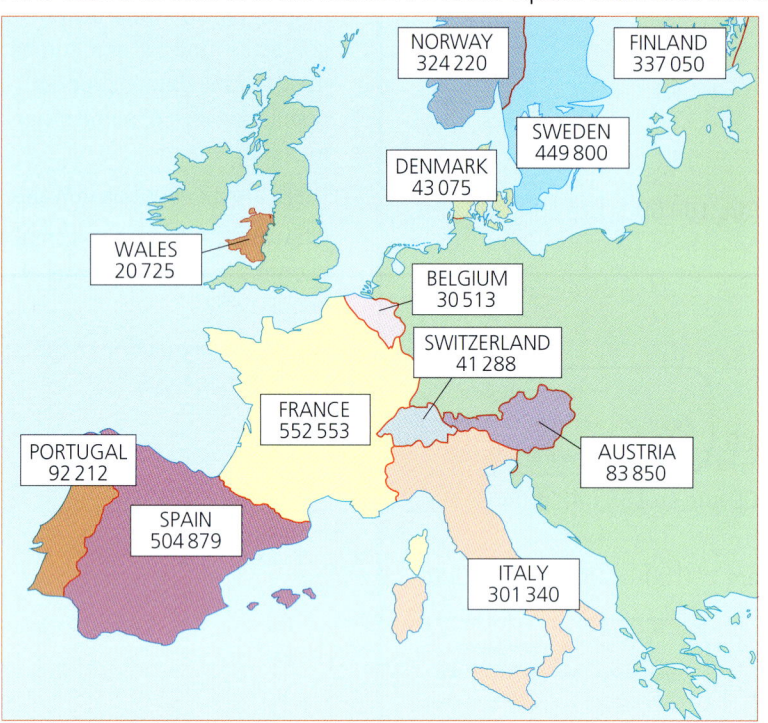

- NORWAY 324 220
- FINLAND 337 050
- SWEDEN 449 800
- DENMARK 43 075
- WALES 20 725
- BELGIUM 30 513
- SWITZERLAND 41 288
- FRANCE 552 553
- PORTUGAL 92 212
- AUSTRIA 83 850
- SPAIN 504 879
- ITALY 301 340

⑤ Find this four-digit number.
- It rounds to 7000 to the nearest thousand.
- It rounds to 6500 to the nearest hundred.
- It ends in 1.
- Its digits add up to 14.

Logical reasoning

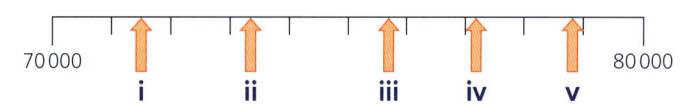

⑥ Look at the number line.

70 000 — i — ii — iii — iv — v — 80 000

a Round the numbers indicated by the arrows to the nearest 10 000.
b Round the numbers indicated by the arrows to the nearest 1000.

Band 2 questions

Fluency

⑦ Write each of these numbers to the nearest ten thousand.
a 45 649 **b** 743 278 **c** 6 804 452
d 7 956 604 **e** 3 999 000

Logical reasoning

⑧ Give a sensible approximation to the number in each of the following statements.

In each case, state the level of rounding you are using.

a The distance from the Earth to the Moon is 384 432 km.
b The vineyard produced 6720 bottles of its best wine.

Fluency

⑨ Round the equatorial radius of each planet to the nearest 10 000 km.
a Jupiter 71 492 km **b** Uranus 25 559 km
c Saturn 60 268 km **d** Earth 6378.1 km

190

9 Place value and rounding

10 Which of the following numbers round to 3 000 000 to the nearest 100 000?

| 2 087 032 | 2 876 423 | 3 034 562 | 3 456 321 | 2 999 999 | 2 945 777 |

11 Rhodri plans to do a walk for charity.

He knows that he can walk 28 km per day.

He plans to walk from Lands' End to John o' Groats, a distance of 1407 km.

He has 1 month for his challenge.

Show, by rounding, that Rhodri cannot complete his challenge in that time.

Band 3 questions

12 Write each of these numbers to the nearest million.
   a 2 718 355
   b 18 447 241
   c 100 425 197
   d 145 625 333

13 Give a sensible approximation to the number in each of the following statements.

In each case, state the level of rounding you are using.

   a The pathologist's sample indicated that there were 42 675 755 bacteria in the swimming pool.
   b The orchard packed 1 972 355 grams of apples for the drinks company.

14 Write newspaper headlines for each of these facts. You will need to decide a suitable style of reporting and the level of rounding that you use.

   a Police report that 281 cars per hour were heading to Rhyl.
   b A bush fire in California spreads across 2 197 acres of land.
   c A cyclist takes 5 days to cover 355 km from Llandudno to Cardiff.
   d Scientists say that our solar system is located 26 835 light years from the centre of the Milky Way.

15 Round the distances of these planets from the Sun to the nearest hundred million kilometres.

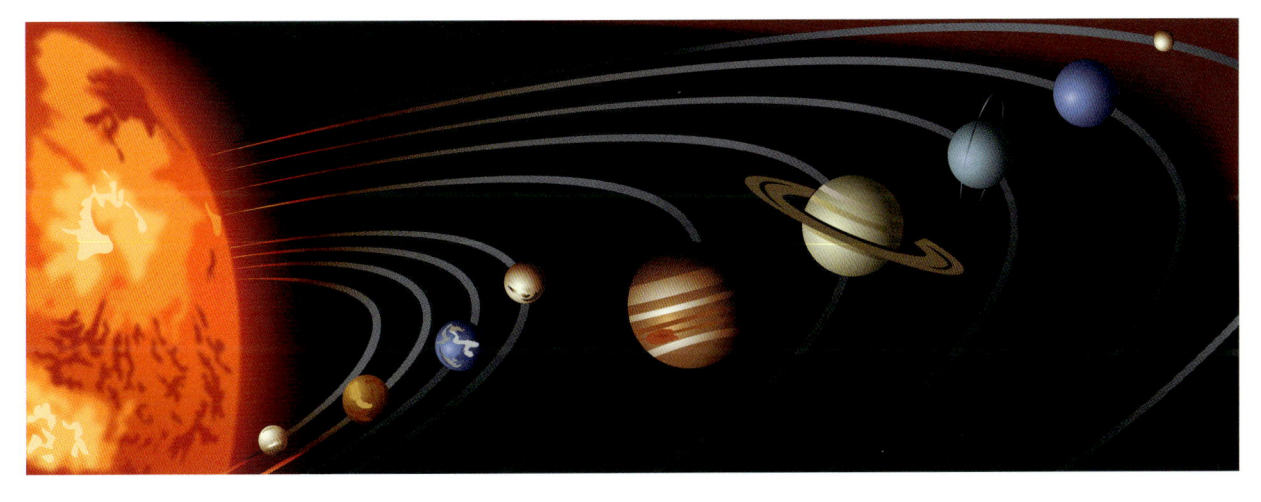

   a Jupiter: 778 330 000 km
   b Saturn: 1 429 400 000 km
   c Uranus: 2 870 990 000 km
   d Neptune: 4 504 300 000 km

Strategic competence

16. Think of numbers that round to 2 000 000. For example, 1 876 009 rounds to 2 000 000 to the nearest million.
    a Match the cards:

Numbers that round to 2 000 000 to the nearest 1000	Numbers that round to 2 000 000 to the nearest million	Numbers that round to 2 000 000 to the nearest 100 000
Numbers that round to 2 000 000 to the nearest 10 000	Between 1 999 500 and 2 000 500 but not including 2 000 500	Between 1 500 000 and 2 500 000 but not including 2 500 000

    $1\,995\,000 \leq N < 2\,005\,000$ $1\,950\,000 \leq N < 2\,050\,000$

    b How many numbers round to 2 000 000 to the nearest whole number?

17. The average speed of the Apollo spacecraft was 39 896 kilometres per hour.
    a Round this speed to the nearest 10 000 kilometres per hour.
    b Estimate how far the spacecraft travelled in one day. Round your answer to the nearest million kilometres.
    c The Apollo spacecraft would have taken two years to reach Mars. Estimate how far it would have travelled.

Logical reasoning

18. Using the number 25 832 500, investigate the connection between **A**, **B** and **C**.
    A The digits which tell you whether to round up or round down.
    B The number of zeros at the right-hand end of the rounded number.
    C The degree of rounding (e.g. to the nearest hundred, thousand, ten thousand, hundred thousand, million).

9.3 Rounding decimals

Skill checker

1. Round these to the nearest whole number.
   a 4.3   b 1.5   c 2.9

2. Round these to the nearest whole number.
   a 27.5   b 108.1   c 0.2   d 9.9

3. Round these to the nearest whole number.
   a 7.45   b 8.15   c 9.26   d 9.89

4. Copy this number line.

   0 1 2 3 4 5 6 7 8 9 10

   a Mark these numbers on your copy of the number line.
      i   3.2   ii 7.8   iii 9.1
      iv 1.9   v   0.2
   b Round each number to the nearest whole number.

5. What is the value of the green digit in each of these numbers?
   a 203   b 56.81   c 2.07   d 0.002

9 Place value and rounding

Activity

Conceptual understanding

① What is the same and what is different about these three number lines?

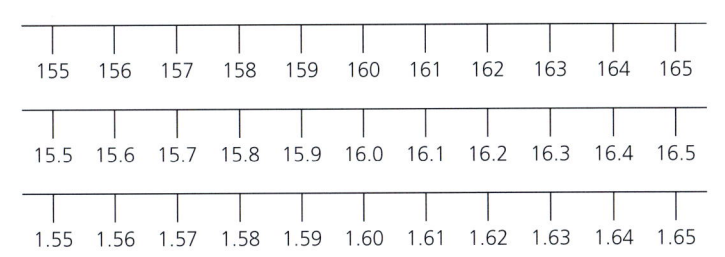

```
155  156  157  158  159  160  161  162  163  164  165

15.5  15.6  15.7  15.8  15.9  16.0  16.1  16.2  16.3  16.4  16.5

1.55  1.56  1.57  1.58  1.59  1.60  1.61  1.62  1.63  1.64  1.65
```

② Use the first number line to round 158.1 to the nearest whole number.

③ Use the second number line to decide which of the marked numbers is closest to 15.81.

④ Use the third number line to decide which of the marked numbers is closest to 1.581. What do you notice?

Worked example

Round 3.141 59 to:

a the nearest tenth **b** two decimal places **c** three decimal places.

Solution

a Rounding to the nearest tenth is called rounding to **one decimal place**.

The tenths on each side of 3.141 59 are 3.1 and 3.2.

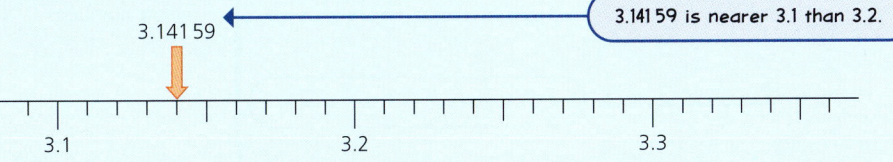

3.141 59

3.141 59 is nearer 3.1 than 3.2.

```
3.1          3.2          3.3
```

3.141 59 rounds to 3.1 to one decimal place.

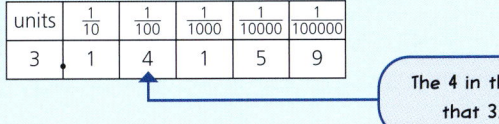

units	$\frac{1}{10}$	$\frac{1}{100}$	$\frac{1}{1000}$	$\frac{1}{10000}$	$\frac{1}{100000}$
3 .	1	4	1	5	9

The 4 in the hundredths column tells you that 3.141 59 is nearer 3.1 than 3.2.

Tenths are the first decimal place. The second decimal place shows whether to round up or down.

b Rounding to **two decimal places** is the same as rounding to the nearest hundredth.

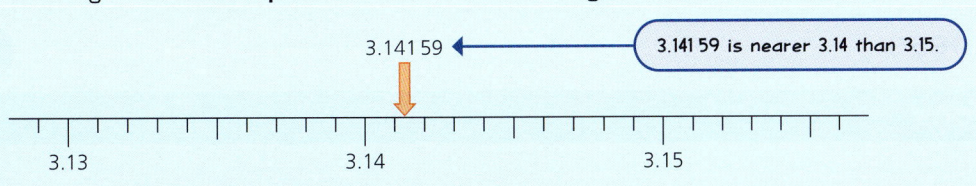

3.141 59

3.141 59 is nearer 3.14 than 3.15.

```
3.13          3.14          3.15
```

3.141 59 rounds to 3.14 to two decimal places.

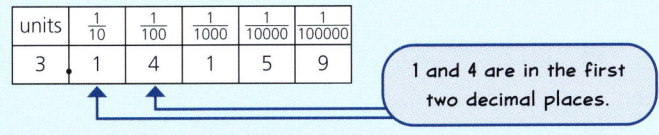

units	$\frac{1}{10}$	$\frac{1}{100}$	$\frac{1}{1000}$	$\frac{1}{10000}$	$\frac{1}{100000}$
3 .	1	4	1	5	9

1 and 4 are in the first two decimal places.

The 1 in the thousandths column tells you that 3.141 59 is nearer 3.14 than 3.15.

c Rounding to **three decimal places** is the same as rounding to the nearest thousandth.

3.141 59 is nearer 3.142 than 3.141.

3.141 59 rounds to 3.142 to three decimal places.

units	$\frac{1}{10}$	$\frac{1}{100}$	$\frac{1}{1000}$	$\frac{1}{10000}$	$\frac{1}{100000}$
3 .	1	4	1	5	9

This 1 is in the third decimal place.

The 5 in the ten-thousandths column tells you that 3.141 59 is about halfway between 3.141 and 3.142.

The 9 in the hundred-thousandths column tells you that 3.141 59 is nearer 3.142 than 3.141.

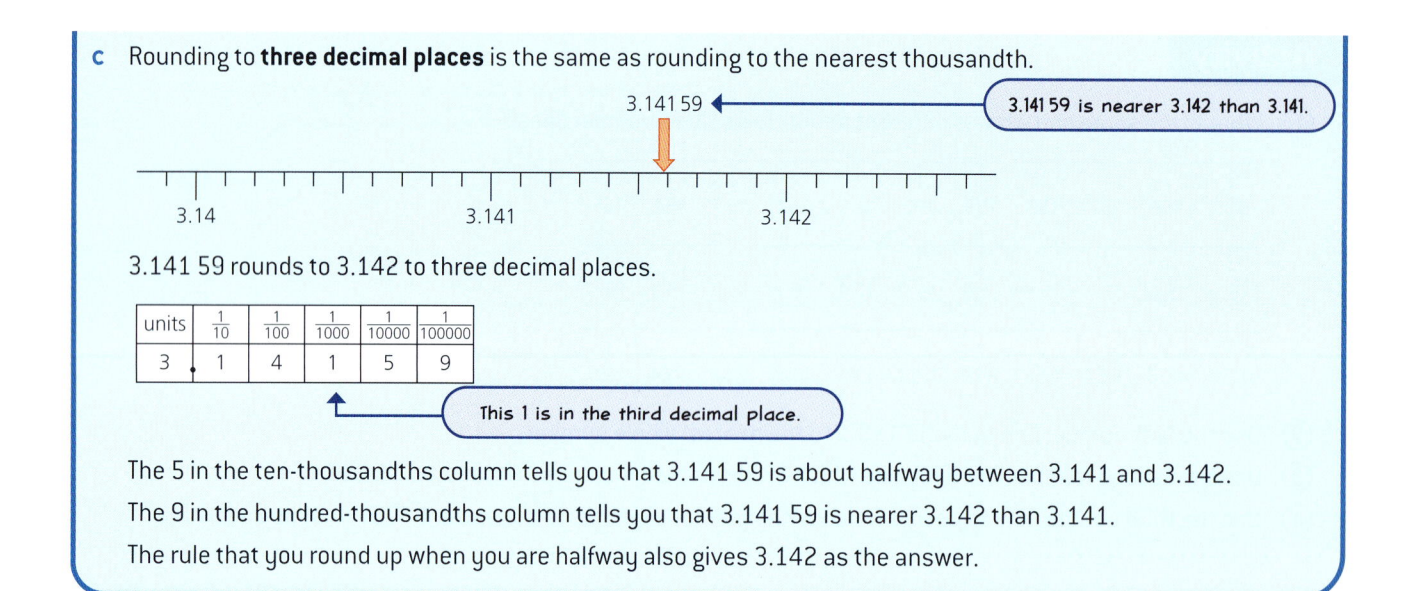

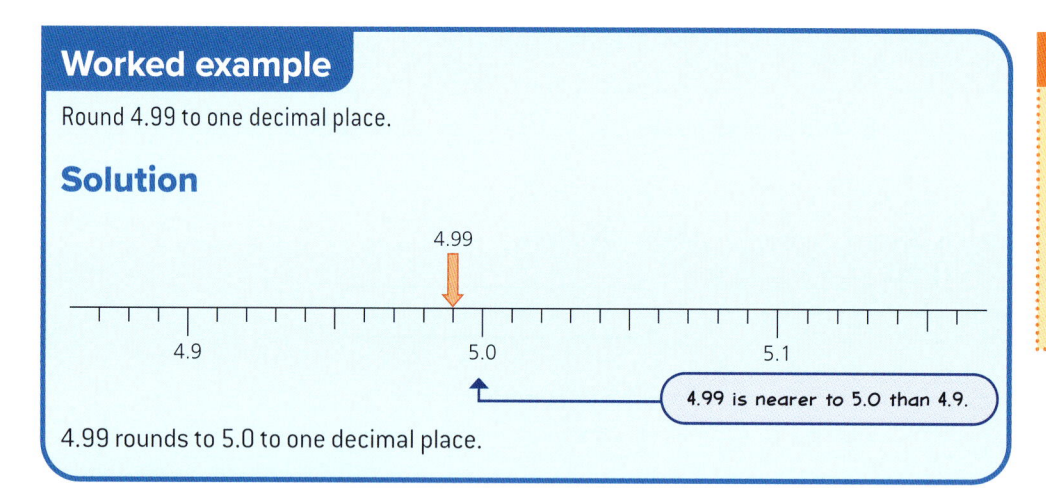

The rule that you round up when you are halfway also gives 3.142 as the answer.

Worked example

Round 4.99 to one decimal place.

Solution

4.99 is nearer to 5.0 than 4.9.

4.99 rounds to 5.0 to one decimal place.

Remember

Usually you write 5.0 as 5.

Writing 5.0 shows that the number has been rounded to one decimal place, not the nearest whole number.

Discussion activity

In this chapter, we have looked at rounding decimals to three different levels of accuracy: to one decimal place, two decimal places and three decimal places.

Would rounding to four decimal places be more difficult? Explain your reasoning.

9.3 Now try these

Band 1 questions

1 **a** Add 0.1 to:
　　　i 4　　　**ii** 7.6　　　**iii** 10　　　**iv** 2.9　　　**v** 9.9

　　b Subtract 0.1 from:
　　　i 8.4　　　**ii** 0.6　　　**iii** 0.12　　　**iv** 10　　　**v** 100

　　c Write down the number that is 0.01 more than:
　　　i 6.48　　　**ii** 12.33　　　**iii** 0.02　　　**iv** 0.09　　　**v** 9.99

　　d Write down the number that is 0.01 less than:
　　　i 7.56　　　**ii** 0.04　　　**iii** 3.452　　　**iv** 0.1　　　**v** 1

9 Place value and rounding

2 Write down a number that is:
  a more than 10, and is given to two decimal places
  b between 6 and 7, and is given to one decimal place
  c between 100 and 101, and is given to one decimal place
  d between 10 and 10.1, and is given to three decimal places.

3 Which of these numbers round to 10 to the nearest whole number?

| 10.3 | 10.45 | 9.45 | 9.19 | 9.8 | 8.5 | 11 | 9.99 |

4 Look at the number line.

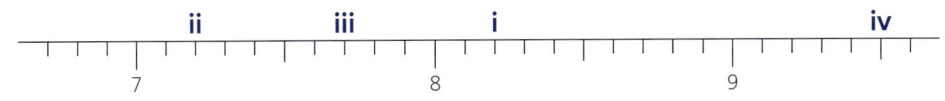

(number line from 7 to 9 with marks ii, iii, i, iv)

  a Write down the numbers marked.
  b Round them to the nearest whole number.

5 Mari buys a magazine costing £3.95, a drink for £1.80 and a sandwich for £2.75. She only has a £10 note. Round the amounts to the nearest pound to see if she has enough money.

6 Copy this number line.

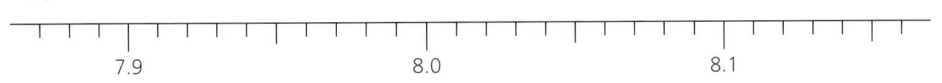

(number line from 7.9 to 8.1)

  a Place these numbers on your number line.
    i   8.14
    ii 7.93
    iii 8.01
    iv 8.05
    v   7.89
  b Round these numbers to one decimal place and circle your answers on your number line.
    i   8.14
    ii 7.93
    iii 8.01
    iv 8.05
    v   7.89

Band 2 questions

7 a Continue this sequence until you reach 2.32.
         2.20, 2.21, 2.22, 2.23, ...
  b Round these numbers to two decimal places (the answers are all in the sequence in part **a**).
    i   2.213
    ii 2.294
    iii 2.301
    iv 2.207
    v   2.3156

8 Copy this number line.

(number line: 4.55 4.56 4.57 4.58 4.59 4.60 4.61 4.62 4.63 4.64 4.65)

  a Put each of these numbers in the correct place on your line.
    i   4.632
    ii 4.576
    iii 4.645
    iv 4.602
  b Round each of the numbers in part **a** to two decimal places and circle the rounded numbers on your number line.
  c Write the numbers in part **a** in order, starting with the smallest.

Curriculum for Wales **Mastering Mathematics: Book 1**

9 Write each of these numbers to two decimal places.
   a   12.6723
   b   1.4038
   c   0.695 17
   d   0.076 08
   e   1.0359
   f   4.0032
   g   9.951 98
   h   0.9999

10 a   Find a number that lies between:
   i   2.95 and 2.96
   ii   3.99 and 4.01
   iii   0.23 and 0.37
   b   Find the number that is exactly halfway between each pair of numbers in part **a**.
   c   How many numbers lie between 2.95 and 2.96?

11 Suja has several lengths of wood and wonders if she has enough for a project that requires 6 m of wood.
Estimate whether the lengths of 1.476 m, 0.873 m, 2.034 m, 1.609 m are enough.
Justify your answer and decide whether it is helpful in this case.

12 Round the numbers on these calculator displays to one decimal place.
   a   56.489243
   b   21.874399
   c   7.8945265

13 Rhys buys a sandwich for £2.89 and three drinks, costing £1.75 each.
Use rounding to find out if £10 is enough money to pay for them.

Band 3 questions

14 Write each of these numbers to three decimal places.
   a   12.6723
   b   1.4038
   c   0.695 17
   d   0.076 08
   e   1.0359
   f   4.0032
   g   9.951 98
   h   0.9999

15 Steffan buys two shirts for £12.75 and a pair of trousers for £24.50.
Use rounding to the nearest pound to estimate whether £50 is enough money to pay for them.
Why does this give the wrong answer?

16 Which of the following round to:
   a   0.03
   b   0.030
   c   neither.

   0.29 to one decimal place
   0.0301 to three decimal places
   0.0299 to two decimal places
   0.0299 to three decimal places
   0.0311 to two decimal places
   0.025 to two decimal places
   0.0349 to three decimal places
   0.029 999 to one decimal place

17 a   Round £7.8264 to the nearest penny.
   b   Round 23.7649 metres to the nearest centimetre.
   c   Round 34.345 cm to the nearest millimetre.
   d   Round 750 millilitres to the nearest litre.

AQ: questio 13 and are very similar in close proximi Is this okay?

196

18 This question is about two different ways of rounding 8.446.

   a Directly: round 8.446 to the nearest whole number.

   b In stages:

      i round 8.446 to two decimal places

      ii round your answer to part **i** to one decimal place

      iii round your answer to part **ii** to the nearest whole number.

   c The two methods above give different answers. Which one is correct?

19 Mia is building an extension to her house. She measures the plot ready to order the materials.

She measures in metres and rounds her measurements.

Advise her on what rounding to use.

Justify your choice and your rejection of other options.

Key words

Here is a list of the key words you met in this chapter.

Decimal place	Decimal point	Denominator	Digit
Divide	Equivalent	Fraction	Hundreds
Hundredths	Millions	Place value	Power of 10
Tens	Tenths	Terminating decimal	Thousands
Thousandths	Units		

Use the glossary at the back of this book to check any you are unsure about.

Curriculum for Wales Mastering Mathematics: Book 1

Review exercise: place value and rounding

Band 1 questions

1 a What numbers are shown on the number line?

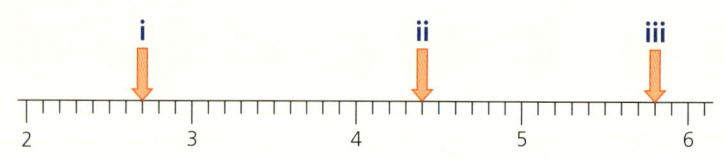

[Number line from 2 to 6 with arrows labelled i (between 2 and 3), ii (between 4 and 5), iii (between 5 and 6)]

  b Write the numbers in order, starting with the largest.
  c Round each number to the nearest whole number.
  d Write each number as a mixed number (a whole number followed by a fraction).

2 Match the fractions and decimals.

| $\frac{3}{10}$ | 0.5 | 0.1 | $\frac{1}{2}$ | 0.2 | $\frac{4}{5}$ | 0.3 | 0.8 | $\frac{1}{5}$ | $\frac{1}{10}$ |

3 Insert <, > or = between each pair of numbers to make true statements.

  a 0.1 ☐ 0.01
  b 0.2 ☐ $\frac{1}{2}$
  c $\frac{1}{5}$ ☐ 0.5
  d $\frac{3}{5}$ ☐ 0.6
  e 0.3 ☐ 0.31

4 Arrange the amounts in order of size, with the smallest first.

  a £0.70, £7, £70, £0.71, £0.07
  b 36 kg, 0.36 kg, 3.6 kg, 0.036 kg, 0.63 kg
  c 45 m, 0.45 m, 0.54 m, 0.04 m, 0.005 m
  d 1.11 km, 0.13 km, 1.3 km, 1.01 km, 0.31 km

5 Suja buys items costing £3.75, £11.99 and £4.20.

Round the amounts to the nearest pound to estimate how much she spent altogether.

6 Some of these numbers round to 2.1 to the nearest tenth. Which ones?

| 2.01 | 2.07 | 1.09 | 1.99 | 2.11 | 2.15 | 2.05 | 2.13 |

Band 2 questions

7 What is the value of the highlighted digit in each of these numbers?

  a 3**5**.71
  b 215.6**7**
  c 1920.0**4**
  d 0.00**9** 416

8 Rewrite these sentences using suitably rounded numbers.

  a The batting average of a top Glamorgan batsman is 41.64.
  b The average gate at Wrexham's football league matches is 5088.37.
  c In a typical year, Fishguard Council spends £89 187 on games fields.
  d In a typical year, Glamorgan County Cricket Club teams score 15 893 runs.

9 Write these fractions as decimals.

  a $\frac{3}{100}$
  b $\frac{21}{100}$
  c $\frac{17}{20}$
  d $\frac{16}{25}$

9   Place value and rounding

10 These are answers to questions involving money in pounds.
Round them to the nearest penny.

a 1.8745597

b 0.476589324

c 0.87587587

11 Write each of these numbers to one decimal place and to two decimal places.
a 0.333   b 1.038   c 5.303   d 5.093   e 2.099
f 0.065   g 10.056 h 5.555   i 5.006   j 5.999

12 Which of these statements are true and which are false?
a 30.031 < 30.301
b $\frac{1}{4} > 0.35$
c $0.006 \leq \frac{1}{250}$
d $\frac{9}{20} = 0.45$
e 299 009 rounds to 300 000 to the nearest 10 000.
f $0.08 \geq \frac{2}{25}$

Band 3 questions

13 Write these decimals as fractions.
a 0.04   b 0.325   c 0.084   d 0.0025

14 a Estimate the numbers being indicated on this number line from 100 000 to 110 000.

   100 000   110 000
        i   ii   iii   iv   v

b Write each number to the nearest thousand.

15 Write these fractions as decimals.
a $\frac{3}{1000}$ b $\frac{7}{50}$ c $\frac{503}{1000}$
d $\frac{7}{40}$ e $\frac{3}{200}$ f $\frac{7}{8}$

16 One of the following statements is wrong. Which one?
a 83 860, rounded to the nearest 1000, is 84 000.
b 8386, rounded to the nearest 100, is 8400.
c 8 386 500, rounded to the nearest million, is 8 000 000.
d 8 386 500, rounded to the nearest ten thousand, is 8 380 000.

17 Use rounding to estimate the weight of shopping when the following items are purchased:
- Three items weighing 250 g each
- Four items weighing 330 g each
- Two items weighing 1.5 kg each
- One item weighing 1.786 kg
- Two items weighing 28 g each.

Is your estimate an overestimate or an underestimate?

18 Sophie is thinking of a number.

Clue 1: It rounds to 0.045 to three decimal places.
Clue 2: It has a 7 in the hundred thousandths position.
Clue 3: It is a terminating decimal.
Clue 4: It is greater than 0.0453.
Clue 5: When multiplied by 100 000, it is a whole number.
Clue 6: It is the smaller of the two remaining possibilities.

a   What is Sophie's number?
b   How many numbers satisfy Clues 1 and 2?
c   How many numbers satisfy Clues 1, 2 and 3?
d   How many numbers satisfy Clues 1, 2, 3 and 4?

Consolidation 3: Chapters 8–9

Band 1 questions

1
a. What is 2 worth in 5.2?
b. Work out $\frac{1}{10} \times 60$.
c. Round 45.87 m to the nearest metre.
d. Round 4970 to the nearest 1000.

2
a. What are the next two terms of this sequence?
   4.1   4.4   4.7   ?   ?
   Use the number line to help you.
b. What is the tenth term of the sequence?

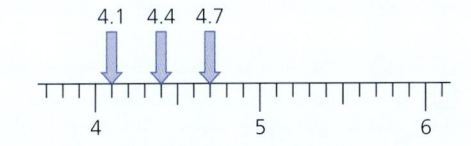

3 Joseff buys a watermelon. He cuts it into twelfths.
a. How many pieces does he cut the watermelon into?
b. Joseff eats three of the pieces. What fraction of the watermelon is that?
c. Ffion eats four pieces. What fraction of the watermelon is that?
d. What fraction of the watermelon is left?
e. Sam eats four pieces of watermelon. What fraction is left now?
f. Joseff and Sam decide to share what is left. What fraction of the watermelon do they each get?

4 Stella has 175 megabytes (MB) of free storage space on her computer memory stick.
She wants to copy these folders onto her memory stick.
- Sketchpad folder 34.78 MB
- Music folder 54.81 MB
- Photo folder 80.62 MB
- Drawing template 0.91 MB
- Design template 3.67 MB

a. Round each size to the nearest whole number.
b. Use the rounded numbers to estimate whether Stella's memory stick has space for them all.
c. Do you get the same result using the unrounded sizes?

5 Suja has £16 pocket money.
a. She saves £2. What fraction of her pocket money is that?
b. She spends $\frac{1}{4}$ of her pocket money on flowers for her nain. How much is that?
c. How much of her pocket money does Suja have left?
d. She now spends £1.75 on a magazine, £4.99 on a calculator for school and £1.35 on a snack. Use rounding to estimate whether she has enough money left for the £1 bus fare home.

6 Copy and complete with a number or sign.

a. $0.4 = \frac{4}{\Box}$
b. $0.25 = \frac{1}{\Box}$
c. $\frac{6}{7} - \Box = \frac{2}{7}$
d. $\frac{1}{7} \Box \frac{1}{8}$
e. $\frac{3}{5} + \Box = \frac{4}{5}$
f. $5 \div \Box = 30$
g. $\frac{1}{9}$ of $\Box$ = £2
h. $\frac{3}{\Box} = 0.03$
i. $\frac{1}{3} \div \Box = \frac{1}{15}$
j. $0.07 \Box 0.7$

Band 2 questions

7 Write down the reciprocals of:
   a 12
   b $\frac{1}{5}$
   c $\frac{4}{5}$
   d $\frac{7}{3}$
   e $\frac{3}{5}$

8 Here is a sequence: $\frac{1}{9}$ $\frac{1}{3}$ $\frac{5}{9}$ ...
   Write down the next two terms.

9 Xavier says that $0.2 = \frac{1}{2}$. Explain why he is wrong.

10 a Round 5.905 to two decimal places.
   b Write $\frac{37}{100}$ as a decimal.
   c Write 0.4 as a fraction in its simplest form.
   d Round 29.999 to two decimal places.
   e Write 0.85 as a fraction in its simplest form.
   f Work out $\frac{1}{2} + \frac{1}{4} - \frac{5}{8}$.
   g Work out $100 \times \frac{3}{20}$.
   h Work out $\frac{5}{9} \div 2$.

11 Sian has 1 metre of ribbon. She uses 20 cm.
   a What fraction of the ribbon does she use?
   b What fraction is left?

12 Chris works out 56.381×2.8018 on a calculator and gets 59.1828.
   Use rounding to show that the answer is wrong.

13 Copy and complete with a number or a sign.
   a $0.36 \,\square\, 0.306$
   b $\frac{2}{3}$ of $\square = 16$
   c $\frac{2}{3} \,\square\, \frac{3}{4}$
   d $\frac{2}{\square} \times 20 = 8$
   e $\square \div \frac{2}{3} = 21$
   f $\frac{\square}{9} \times 72 = 56$

Band 3 questions

14 Work out:
   a $\frac{5}{9}$ of 36
   b $\frac{3}{7} + \frac{4}{9}$
   c $\frac{1}{4} + \frac{1}{5} - \frac{1}{10}$
   d $39 \times \frac{4}{13}$
   e $\frac{6}{7} \div 3$

15 Carys has 330 stickers in her sticker collection.
   $\frac{4}{15}$ of her stickers are black.
   How many non-black stickers does she have?

16 Raoul scores 30 out of 70. Cecile scores 40 out of 90.
Whose score is better? Justify your answer.

17 Order the following from smallest to largest.

0.81 $\frac{3}{8}$ $\frac{17}{20}$ 0.075 $\frac{9}{40}$ 0.425

18 The length of Neptune's orbit is 28.2429 billion km. Its speed is 5.43 km per second.
Use rounding to estimate the length of Neptune's year in Earth years.

19 What number is halfway between $\frac{2}{13}$ of 52 and $45 \times \frac{5}{9}$?

20 What number is halfway between $\frac{3}{8} \div 6$ and 0.0075?

10 Averages and range

Coming up...
- Using mode, median and range
- Using the mean
- Identifying outliers
- Comparing data sets

What are my numbers?

Solve these clues to find the numbers on the cards.

Each card has a **whole number** on it from 1 to 10. The cards are in order, with the smallest number first.

①
The middle card is 7.

The total of the cards is 20.

The difference between the highest and lowest cards is 7.

②
The middle card is 5.

The total of the cards is 28.

Only two of the cards are the same.

The difference between the highest and lowest cards is 7.

Most of the cards are odd numbers.

Can you find more than one answer?

③ Make up your own set of 3 or 5 numbers.

Write clues for the numbers.

Challenge a friend to work out your numbers.

10 Averages and range

10.1 Mode, median and range

Skill checker

1. **a** Find the **difference** between 7 and 32.

   To find the difference between two numbers, subtract the lower from the higher.

   b In this list of colours, what is the **frequency** of the colour green?

yellow	green	red	yellow	blue
green	red	red	orange	purple

   Frequency means 'how many'.

2. Twenty children were asked to name their favourite sport. The results were:

Football	Netball	Cricket	Football	Rounders	Rugby	Football	Netball	Basketball	Hockey
Football	Rugby	Netball	Cricket	Football	Basketball	Rounders	Football	Hockey	Hockey

   Anna has begun to complete a tally chart. So far, she has only recorded the first five of the sports listed above.

   a Copy and complete Anna's tally chart to show this data.

Sport	Tally	Number of children
Football	||	
Netball	|	
Cricket	|	
Rounders	|	
Total:		

   b Which sport has the highest frequency?

3. Find the middle value of this list.

   3   5   5   7   8   9   10

4. Can you find the middle value of this list?

   3   5   6   6   7   8   11   12

▶ Finding averages and range

You will sometimes need to summarise a set of data.

You can do this by giving a value that is representative or typical of all the values in the data set.

A typical value is called an average. Two averages are mode and median.

The **mode** is the most common.

A mode can be non-numerical. For example, in question **2** of the Skill checker, the most popular sport was football. You say that the **modal** sport is football.

The **median** is the middle value when a set of numbers is written in order of size.

A median must be numerical.

You can also describe how spread out the data is. One measure of spread is range.

The **range** is the difference between the highest and the lowest values.

> **Worked example**
>
> Each morning, for a week, Sandra records the number of birds on a patch of grass.
>
> | Day | Monday | Tuesday | Wednesday | Thursday | Friday | Saturday | Sunday |
> |---|---|---|---|---|---|---|---|
> | No. of birds | 6 | 2 | 6 | 6 | 5 | 4 | 5 |
>
> a Write down the modal number of birds.
> b Find the median number of birds.
> c Work out the range of the number of birds.
>
> ## Solution
>
> First, write the numbers in order:
>
> 2   4   5   5   6   6   6
>
> a There is one 2, one 4, two 5s, and three 6s.
>
>   There are more 6s than any other number, so the mode is 6.
>
> b 2   4   5   ⑤   6   6   6
>
>   5 is the middle number, so the median is 5.
>
> c Range = 6 − 2 = 4

For an even number of items, the median is halfway between the middle two values.

> **Worked example**
>
> A school football team plays 16 matches. Here are the numbers of goals they score.
>
> 1   0   5   3   6   0   2   4   3   0   4   0   5   3   2   1
>
> a Find the mode.
> b Find the median.
> c Work out the range.
> d Janos plays striker for the team. He is asked about the average number of goals the team scores.
>
>   Which average do you think Janos prefers to use?
>
> ## Solution
>
> First write the numbers of goals in order:
>
> 0   0   0   0   1   1   2   ②   3   3   3   4   4   5   5   6
>
> a The mode is 0.
> b There are two middle numbers: 2 and 3.
>
>   So the median is 2.5.
>
> c The range is 6 − 0 = 6.
> d Janos won't want to say that the average number of goals his team scores is 0.
>
>   So he won't use the mode. He will use the median as this is higher.

10   Averages and range

Use a **tally chart** to avoid counting errors.

Worked example

Seren goes ten-pin bowling.
Here are the numbers of pins she knocks down in each game.

Game 1   0 2 6 8 6 7 3 9 6 0

Game 2   5 7 6 7 5 0 2 3 6 8

Game 3   7 7 4 9 5 6 8 6

a Draw a tally chart and find the frequency of each score.
b Find the mode of Seren's scores.
c Work out the range of Seren's scores.
d Seren then has four more turns and scores 10 on each of them.
   How does this affect the mode and range of her scores?

Solution

a

Score	Tally	Frequency
0	|||	3
1		0
2	||	2
3	||	2
4	|	1
5	|||	3
6	𝍲 ||	7
7	𝍲	5
8	|||	3
9	||	2
Total:		28

A score of 6 has the highest frequency.

Remember
Frequency means 'how many'.

b The mode of Seren's scores is 6.
c The range is 9 − 0 = 9.

range = highest score − lowest score

d After Seren's extra turns, the frequency of 10 is 4.
   The mode is still 6 as she scored this seven times.
   The range is 10 − 0 = 10 so is now greater.

Curriculum for Wales **Mastering Mathematics: Book 1**

> **Activity**
>
> In groups of two, three or four students, write the numbers 1 to 12 on different pieces of card.
>
> | 1 | 2 | 3 | 4 | 5 | 6 |
> | 7 | 8 | 9 | 10 | 11 | 12 |
>
> Turn the cards over and mix them up. Then share the cards out randomly amongst the group.
>
> Roll a pair of dice and add the two numbers shown on the dice.
>
> Whichever student has that total, gets one point.
>
> Repeat 40 times, recording the results.
>
> The winner is the student with the highest number of points.
>
> a   Which total is the mode?
> b   Calculate the range of the totals.
> c   Find the median total.
> d   Compare your mode with other groups.
> e   Which totals are the best ones to have?
> f   Which total is the worst one to have?

10.1 Now try these

Band 1 questions

1 Here are nine jumbled cards. Match each blue card with one red card and one green card.

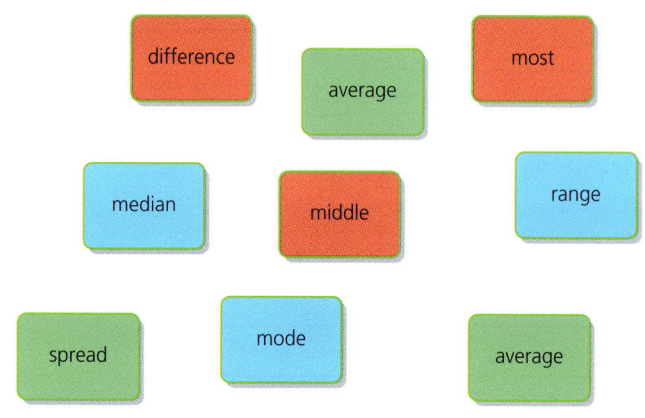

- difference (red)
- average (green)
- most (red)
- median (blue)
- middle (red)
- range (blue)
- spread (green)
- mode (blue)
- average (green)

2 a   Write down the mode of these four numbers: 2, 2, 2, 3.
    b   Write down the median of these five numbers: 1, 4, 6, 7, 9.

3 Find the mode of each of these data sets.
    a   3, 4, 4, 6, 7, 7, 8, 8, 8, 9
    b   11, 13, 14, 14, 14, 15, 15, 15, 15, 20
    c   10, 11, 12, 12, 14, 17, 19
    d   2, 5, 1, 2, 1, 4, 2, 3

4 Osian and Alun repeatedly throw a dart at a dartboard and record each score.
Osian's scores are: 8, 6, 26, 8, 22, 7, 5, 8, 9, 24.
Alun's scores are: 26, 4, 30, 7, 8, 5, 12, 7, 9.
    a   What is Osian's modal score?
    b   What is Alun's modal score?

5 Calculate the range of each of these data sets.
    a   50, 21, 25, 15, 35, 41, 44, 1, 4, 19, 23
    b   1, 3, 10, 5, 2, 12, 15, 19, 5, 20, 7, 11, 3
    c   45, 87, 200, 203, 4, 76
    d   1451, 67, 895, 895, 895, 1000

10 Averages and range

6 Find the median of each of these data sets.
  a 2, 7, 8, 10, 15
  b 9, 3, 1, 17, 8, 6, 11
  c 7, 9, 10, 16, 23, 31
  d 8, 4, 7, 16, 23, 18, 12, 9

7 Drawing pins are sold in small boxes. On each box is written:

> Average contents 50 pins

Hamza counts the pins in ten boxes:
53   49   51   50   53   48   54   55   51   51

Hamza says that the writing on the boxes is right. Do you agree?

8 Elwyn does seven times table tests.
His scores are: 5, 6, 10, 8, 10, 10, 9.
Elwyn claims that his average score is 10.
Do you agree?

Band 2 questions

9 Find the mode, median and range of these ten numbers.
1   −6   3   −8   −2   0   12   −5   −13   3

10 Margret lives in Reykjavík, Iceland.
She records the outside temperature twice on the first day of each month for a year.

Month	Jan	Feb	Mar	Apr	May	Jun	Jul	Aug	Sep	Oct	Nov	Dec
Midnight temp (°C)	−3	−2	−2	1	4	7	9	8	6	2	−1	−2
Noon temp (°C)	3	3	4	6	10	12	14	14	11	7	4	3

  a i   Write down the lowest temperature in the table.
     ii Write down the highest temperature in the table.
  b i   Find the modal midnight temperature.
     ii Find the median midnight temperature.
     iii Work out the range of the midnight temperatures.
  c i   Find the modal noon temperature.
     ii Find the median noon temperature.
     iii Work out the range of the noon temperatures.

11 a Mari says that modal is the same as median.
       Ceri says that modal is the same as mode.
       Only one of them is right.
       Who is right?
     b Thirty students sit a short test.
       All of the scores are collected in this tally chart.
       i   Copy the tally chart and fill in the frequencies.
       ii Write down the modal score.
       iii Work out the range of the scores.

Score	Tally	Frequency
0		
1		
2	IIII I	
3	IIII IIII	
4	IIII IIII I	
5	III	
	Total:	

209

Curriculum for Wales Mastering Mathematics: Book 1

Logical reasoning

12 **a** Is it possible for a set of numbers to have no mode?
   b Is it possible for a set of numbers to have more than one mode?
   c Give examples for each of your answers to parts **a** and **b**.

13 Elfyn calculates the range of these numbers: 12, 7, 2, 8, 13, 6.
   He writes his answer as −11.
   Teleri tells him his answer is wrong.
   Who is right?
   What mistake has been made?

14 Sandor is writing a maths test for his friends.
   He includes this question:

   > Here are eight boys' names:
   > Tomos, Ieuan, Hardeep, Cynan, Makut, Pedr, Ioan, Mabon
   > **a** Find the modal name.
   > **b** Find the median name.

   Comment on Sandor's question.

15 Bryn throws darts at a dartboard and records his scores:
   64   60   60   28   100   66   81
   Tomos calculates the median and range. Here is his answer.

   > 64, 60, 60, (28), 100, 66, 81
   > The median is 28.
   > The range is 81 − 64 = 17

   a Explain Tomos's mistake.
   b Find the correct median.
   c Work out the correct range.

Band 3 questions

Strategic competence

16 Sali and Alwena are shown these numbered cards and asked to work out what the number on the third card is.

   [6]   [9]   [?]

   They are told that the range of the three numbers is 4.
   Sali says that the third number must be 10 because 10 − 6 = 4.
   Alwena disagrees.
   Who is correct? Why?

210

17 a Three numbers have a mode of 4. What is the median of the three numbers?
  b Three different numbers have a median of −6 and a range of 9.
   i Find the lowest possible total of the three numbers.
   ii Find the greatest possible total of the three numbers.

18 Hania records the outside midday temperature four times during one winter.
The range of the four temperatures is 15 °C.
The median is 4 °C.
The mode is −3 °C.
Find the four temperatures that Hania recorded.

19 Linda writes numbers on five cards and puts them face down.
She tells Alun that the mode of the five numbers is −7.

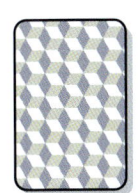

Linda then removes two of the cards.
She tells Alun that the mode of the remaining numbers is 9.
Calculate the total of the five numbers.

20 The median and mode of four numbers are both 8.
The total of the four numbers is 28.
  a Given that the range is 6, find the smallest number.
  b Given, instead, that the range is 16, find the smallest number.

10.2 The mean

Skill checker

1 A group of eight people on a school trip are aged 7, 6, 8, 6, 6, 8, 32 and 7.
  a Find the **sum** of their ages.
  b Which age is not typical for the group?

2 a Which two of these three calculations have the same answer?
   $12 + 8 + 6 \div 2 =$
   $(12 + 8 + 6) \div 2 =$
   $12 + 8 + (6 \div 2) =$
  b Write down the answers to each of the calculations.

Curriculum for Wales Mastering Mathematics: Book 1

▶ Finding the mean

Mean is another average.

It can be used to describe a typical value of a set of data.

The mean of a set of data is its total divided by the number of values.

> **Discussion activity**
>
> Think about equal sharing.
>
> Five friends have each collected some tokens.
>
> The friends decide it would be fair if they shared the tokens so they had the same number each.
>
> Discuss how they might do this.

> **Worked example**
>
> Find the mean of these ten test scores:
>
> 9   2   5   8   6   9   8   9   7   9
>
> **Solution**
>
> The total is 9 + 2 + 5 + 8 + 6 + 9 + 8 + 9 + 7 + 9 = 72.
>
> The mean is 72 ÷ 10 = 7.2.

An **outlier** is an item of data which is very different from the rest.

It can be the result of a mistake but may be just unusually large or small.

> **Activity**
>
> The following sets of data all contain an outlier.
>
> a   The ages of people on a school trip to Cardiff:
>
>   13   12   12   14   35   11   11   13   15   14   12
>
> b   The masses of ten bags of crisps:
>
>   24.9 g   25 g   24.7 g   25.5 g   13.2 g   24 g   26 g   25.7 g   26.1 g   23.9 g
>
> c   Mrs Jones's weekly shopping bills:
>
>   £35.60   £47.51   £102.96   £43.12
>
> d   The daily midday temperature for a week in April:
>
>   12 °C   10 °C   11 °C   9 °C   12 °C   9.5 °C   120.5 °C
>
> In each case, identify the outlier and decide whether or not to include it when calculating the mean.
>
> Give a reason for your decision.

10.2 Now try these

Band 1 questions

1. Ysgol Afonffordd are collecting money for a children's charity.

   The Year 7 classes collect these amounts:

   £5   £10   £10   £15   £15

   a   How much was collected?

   b   How many classes were there?

   c   What was the mean amount collected per class?

10 Averages and range

2 a Find the total of each of the data sets in **i**, **ii** and **iii**.
   b Find the mean of each of the data sets in **i**, **ii** and **iii**.
      i 4, 9, 11, 5, 6
      ii 1, 1, 2, 2, 2, 3, 3, 4
      iii 5, 0, 3, 10, 12, 6, 5, 1, 13, 8

3 These students collected money for an animal rescue shelter as shown in the table.
Find the mean amount of money collected per student.

Emily	Candice	Jay	Hal	Grant
£25	£18	£29	£31	£22

4 Ree measures the temperatures of five drinks.
20 °C   8 °C   38 °C   68 °C   11 °C
   a Calculate the mean temperature of the five drinks.
Ree measures the temperature of a sixth drink as 14 °C.
   b Calculate the mean temperature of all six drinks.

Band 2 questions

5 Timi sees a label on a packet of nails, which claims that the average contents is 25.
Timi counts the number of nails in ten packets. Here are his results.
21   24   26   22   27   27   28   26   24   23
   a Work out the mean number of nails per packet.
   b Do you agree with the label? Explain your answer.

6 Ami's average time for swimming 100 m breaststroke is 32 seconds.
She records her times (in seconds) in each of her next 12 training sessions.
33   32   32   34   32   32   31   33   31   31   32   31
   a Work out her mean time for these sessions.
   b Is Ami improving?

7 All these data sets include outliers.
   a Gwen's examination marks (%):
      25   70   30   152   40
   b Age of competitors at a skateboard contest:
      18   13   54   17   12
   c Total rolled on two dice:
      5   6   16   7   9   12
   For each data set:
      i state the value of the outlier
      ii decide whether you should remove the outlier and explain why
      iii calculate the range.

8 The mean number of pears in five bags is 8.
The first four bags contain nine, eight, seven and six pears.
How many pears are in the fifth bag?

9 The mean number of sweets in five packets is 28.
The numbers of sweets in four of the bags are 27, 30, 29, 32.
Find the number of sweets in the fifth bag.

Band 3 questions

Strategic competence

10 The mean price of nine items is £2.50.
A tenth item costs £3.50.
Calculate the mean of all ten items.

11 A list of five numbers has a mean of 42.
One of the numbers is removed from the list.
The mean of the remaining numbers is 40.
What number was removed?

12 Aled goes ten-pin bowling. Here is the number of pins he knocks down in each turn.
Game 1: 6, 0, 5, 7, 6, 7, 5, 0, 2, 3
Game 2: 6, 8, 7, 7, 4, 9, 5, 6, 9, 10, 6

a Work out the mean number of pins Aled knocks down in Game 1.
b Work out his mean in Game 2.

Aled wants to work out his overall mean, so he adds his two means and then divides by 2.
Nerys says he is wrong.

c Is Nerys right? Explain your answer.

13 a Mizhir plays cricket. He averages 32 runs per innings for seven innings.
After his eighth innings his average is 34.5 runs per innings.
How many runs did he score in his eighth innings?

> A batting average is the mean average.

b Tadeen has a batting average of 21 for his first eight innings. His batting average for the next four innings is 39.
Find his batting average for all 12 innings.

Logical reasoning

14 Alys runs a mean average of 7 km each day for 16 days.
She then runs a mean average of 13 km each day for the next 8 days.
Iwan tells Alys that her mean average over the 24 days is (7 + 13) ÷ 2 = 10 km.
Explain Iwan's error.
Calculate Alys's mean average distance over the 24 days.

Strategic competence

15 The mean of four numbers is 19.
The mean of the two smallest numbers is 10.
The mean of the three smallest numbers is 12.
Find the difference between the two highest numbers.

10.3 Using averages and range

Skill checker

Sharnaz measures the lengths of ten caterpillars:

31 mm   29 mm   32 mm   26 mm   30 mm   25 mm   26 mm   30 mm   28 mm   26 mm

a Find the modal length.
b Find the median length.
c Find the mean length.
d Find the range of the lengths.

▶ Comparing an average and the range

You can now start to compare two sets of data using an average and the range.

A higher range suggests the data is more spread out (more varied).

A smaller range suggests greater consistency.

Worked example

Use this data to compare the shoe sizes of boys and girls.

Shoe sizes (boys)	Shoe sizes (girls)
5, 7, 3, 6, 7, 9, 7, 5, 7, 4, 10	7, 5, 5, 6, 7, 4, 8, 5, 6

Solution

First, write each set in order.

Shoe sizes (boys)	Shoe sizes (girls)
3, 4, 5, 5, 6, ⑦, 7, 7, 7, 9, 10	4, 5, 5, 5, ⑥, 6, 7, 7, 8

Modes: boys ⑦ and girls ⑤
Medians: boys ⑦ and girls ⑥
Means: boys (70 ÷ 11 = 6.4) and girls (53 ÷ 9 = 5.9)
Ranges: boys (10 − 3 = 7) and girls (8 − 4 = 4)

On average, the boys have bigger shoe sizes than the girls, but the boys' shoe sizes are more varied (spread out).

Activity

① Calculate the mean, median and mode of each of these data sets.
② Describe the problems with each average.
③ Make a list of the advantages and disadvantages of each type of average.

  a 13, 14, 0, 12, 0, 11, 15, 18, 17
  b 10 g, 13 g, 17 g, 12 g, 15 g, 10 g, 17 g, 16 g
  c £23, £14, £18, £22, £19, £20, £16, £21
  d 6, 91, 5, 82, 3, 41, 85, 4, 90
  e 11 km, 9 km, 3 km, 6 km, 9 km, 8 km, 12 km, 1256 km

Cross-curricular activity

Spreadsheets are very useful when working out the averages of a set of data. Find out how to do this.

10.3 Now try these

Band 1 questions

1 a Which of these is the odd one out?

| mean | median | mode | range |

  b Give a mathematical reason for your choice.
  c Give a non-mathematical reason for your choice.

Curriculum for Wales Mastering Mathematics: Book 1

Fluency

2 Here are some midday temperatures in the resort of Costa Monica for ten consecutive days.

21 °C   23 °C   31 °C   29 °C   22 °C   32 °C   22 °C   27 °C   28 °C   25 °C

  a Find the range of the temperatures.
  b What is the mean temperature?
  c What is the mode?

3 Find the mean, median, mode and range of these five numbers.

4   7   4   10   5

Logical reasoning

4 Shraga's dad tells him he can have a treat if his average exam score is more than 50%. His exam scores are:

58%   49%   49%   53%   31%   57%

Which average should Shraga use when he tells his dad? Explain why.

5 Tecwyn and Pedr are training for a race. Here are their times, to the nearest minute, to run 2.5 kilometres.

Tecwyn: 15, 14, 15, 16, 17, 15, 13, 14, 15, 16

Pedr: 13, 11, 12, 13, 12, 13, 11, 12, 12, 11

  a Work out the mean time for:
    i Tecwyn
    ii Pedr.
  b Work out the range for:
    i Tecwyn
    ii Pedr.
  c Who is the faster runner?
  d Who has the more consistent times?

Band 2 questions

6 Here are the lifetimes of ten *Everglow* batteries.

15 hours, 19 hours, 12 hours, 15 hours, 10 hours, 17 hours, 6 hours, 16 hours, 9 hours, 8 hours

Everglow batteries last longer.

Average lifetime 15 hours.

  a Find the mean lifetime of the batteries.
  b Find the median lifetime of the batteries.
  c Is the Everglow claim correct? Explain why.

7 Jac and Dewi are comparing their end of term results.

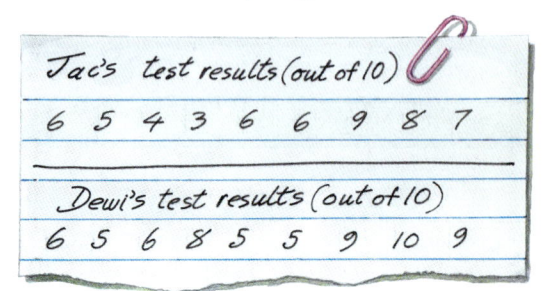

Jac's test results (out of 10)
6 5 4 3 6 6 9 8 7

Dewi's test results (out of 10)
6 5 6 8 5 5 9 10 9

  a Find the median score for Jac and Dewi.
  b Who has performed better? Explain your answer.

10 Averages and range

8 Magdolna is taking part in a skating competition.

There are seven judges.

Here are the scores that six of the judges give Magdolna.

6	6	8
4	5	3

a Find Magdolna's mode and median score so far.

b The final judge awards Magdolna two points. What will happen to her mean?

c Which average do you think Magdolna will use when she tells her friends her average score?

9 Osian uses two different fertilisers on his tomatoes. The table shows the mean and range for the number of tomatoes on his plants.

Fertiliser	Mean	Range
Grow-a-lot	21	13
Organic mix	19	5

a Which fertiliser gives the higher average number of tomatoes?

b Which fertiliser gives the lower range?

c Osian decides to use Grow-a-lot next year. Do you agree with his choice?

10 Anna, Beca and Carys each do five times table tests.

Anna's scores are: 8, 7, 9, 10, 7.

Beca's scores are: 7, 3, 10, 8, 10.

Carys's scores are: 1, 10, 9, 9, 2.

They all claim to have the best average score. Who is right? Explain your answer.

11 Mr Patel wants to compare the attendance rates of students from Pwllheli and students from Abersoch in his tutor group.

He has written the number of absences for one term on the board.

One of the Pwllheli students in the class has been in hospital for most of the term.

Pwllheli: 5 12 0 2 0 8 6 3 0 41 1 0 9 4

Abersoch: 3 2 5 1 8 2 6 10 9 5 4 3 9 8 6

a Identify the absence rate for the Pwllheli student who has been in hospital. Decide whether to include it or not and give a reason why.

b Find the mean for the Pwllheli students and the mean for the Abersoch students.

c Find the median for the Pwllheli students and the median for the Abersoch students.

d Which do you think is the best measure to use to compare these data sets?

e Find the range for the Pwllheli students and the range for the Abersoch students.

f What does the range tell you about the data?

Curriculum for Wales Mastering Mathematics: Book 1

Logical reasoning

12 Here are the points scored by two rugby teams in ten matches.

Team	Scores
Afonffordd Wanderers	11, 6, 9, 21, 15, 21, 16, 12, 3, 12
Blaenffordd Lions	0, 24, 7, 18, 5, 8, 9, 12, 9, 22

  a   Calculate the mean, median and modal scores for each team.
  b   Find the range for each team.
  c   Which team has the better scores? Give a reason for your answer.

In their next match, Afonffordd Wanderers score 16 points and Blaenffordd Lions score 11 points.

  d   Explain how the mean, median, mode and range will change when these scores are added to their records.

Band 3 questions

Fluency

13 Find the mean, median, mode and range of these eight temperatures:

−1 °C   − 5 °C   3 °C   7 °C   −4 °C   0 °C   4 °C   −4 °C

Logical reasoning

14 Below is a list of the salaries paid in a small company.

£17 000   £19 000   £17 000   £17 000   £19 000   £20 000   £25 000   £148 000

  a   The company director is trying to promote the excellent salary opportunities available in the company. Which average should she use?
  b   The union representative wishes to highlight poor pay. Which average should he use?

15 A doctor's receptionist records the waiting times, in minutes, for a group of patients one Monday in January.

12   15   6   2   17   10   4   8   21   32   45   4   6   20   17   12   7   4   34   37   45   10   12   14

Determine which, if any, of these statements are true.

If a statement is not true, write an alternative statement that is.

  a   The majority of patients wait less than 15 minutes.
  b   The average waiting time is 15 minutes.
  c   Patients never have to wait more than 20 minutes longer than the average waiting time.

Strategic competence

16 Here are some outside temperatures taken at noon over six days.

Monday (Dydd Llun)	Tuesday (Dydd Mawrth)	Wednesday (Dydd Mercher)	Thursday (Dydd Iau)	Friday (Dydd Gwener)	Saturday (Dydd Sadwrn)
5 °C	3 °C	−2 °C	4 °C	−1 °C	3 °C

  a   Find the modal noon temperature.
  b   Find the median noon temperature.
  c   Find the mean noon temperature.
  d   When Sunday's (Dydd Sul) noon temperature is included, none of the averages change. What was the noon temperature on Sunday?

17 Nadir tries to find the averages of these items of data. He gets them all wrong.

27   23   37   23   30

Here is his working.
What should the answers be?
Explain what Nadir has done wrong in each case.

mean = 27 + 23 + 37 + 23 + 30 ÷ 5
     = 116 ✗

mode = 2 ✗

median = 37 ✗

218

Strategic competence

18 The mean of five different positive whole numbers is 6.
One of the numbers has exactly one factor.
One of the numbers is an even prime.
Two of the numbers are square numbers.
Two of the numbers are cube numbers.
None of the numbers are multiples of 5.
Find the median of the five numbers.

Note
Revisit Chapter 4 for a recap of number types.

Key words

Here is a list of the key words you met in this chapter.

Average	Difference	Frequency	Mean
Median	Modal	Mode	Outlier
Range	Sum	Tally chart	Total

Use the glossary at the back of this book to check any you are unsure about.

Review exercise: averages and range

Band 1 questions

Fluency

1. Find the range of lengths in each of these data sets.
   a. 4 m, 6 m, 7 m, 11 m, 16 m, 23 m
   b. 12 cm, 6 cm, 19 cm, 35 cm, 11 cm
   c. 5.7 km, 9.2 km, 3.7 km, 5.3 km, 6.1 km, 8.3 km

2. Find the mode of each of these data sets.
   a. 2, 3, 4, 4, 5, 7, 8
   b. 12, −19, 25, 12, 9, −6, 8
   c. −6, 2, 3, −3, 3, −6, −6, 2, −3

3. Find the median temperature for each of these data sets.
   a. 8 °C, 11 °C, 13 °C, 19 °C, 28 °C
   b. 17 °C, −11 °C, 6 °C, −1 °C, −18 °C
   c. 4 °F, 18 °F, 13 °F, 7 °F

4. Find the mean price of each of these data sets.
   a. £5, £3.40, £2.64, £7.68, £1.98
   b. 72p, 34p, 8p, 17p, 19p, 48p
   c. €2.57, €2.78, €2.64, €5.13

5. Six friends each buy a new dress for a party. Here are the costs of the dresses.

   £16   £136   £35   £16   £55   £100

   a. Work out the mode and the median values.
   b. What is the difference between the most expensive dress and the least expensive dress?

6. These are the masses of 15 parcels.
   Convert the data into the same units and then answer the questions.

1.2 kg	40 g	250 g	2.1 kg	3.5 kg
0.7 kg	430 g	1.1 kg	300 g	0.2 kg
0.1 kg	350 g	250 g	0.5 kg	370 g

   a. What is the mode of the data?
   b. What is the range?
   c. What is the median?
   d. A post office worker says, 'Most parcels are over 0.5 kg'. Is that true for these parcels?

Logical reasoning

7. Three friends play a board game. The table shows their scores each time they rolled the dice.

Isaac	1, 3, 5, 6, 2, 4, 5, 2, 4, 4
Ellis	2, 3, 3, 4, 6, 1, 1, 5, 2, 3
Max	4, 5, 5, 6, 6, 1, 1, 2, 3, 4

   a. For each player, find:
      i. the mode
      ii. the median
      iii. the range.
   b. Do the differences in your answers in part **a** tell you anything about the three players?

8 A data set has five numbers. One of them is missing.

23   46   45   29   ☐

The list has a mode of 45.

a   What is the missing number?

b   Find the median of the complete data set.

c   Find the range of the complete data set.

Band 2 questions

9 Mr Davies and Mrs Evans want to compare how long it takes them to get to work.

They write down their journey times each day in minutes.

Monday (Dydd Llun)	Tuesday (Dydd Mawrth)	Wednesday (Dydd Mercher)	Thursday (Dydd Iau)	Friday (Dydd Gwener)	Saturday (Dydd Sadwrn)	Sunday (Dydd Sul)
34	36	35	31	35	21	18
32	34	31	34	30	–	–

a   Find the median time for:

  i   Mr Davies

  ii Mrs Evans.

b   Calculate the mean time for:

  i   Mr Davies

  ii Mrs Evans.

c   Find the range for:

  i   Mr Davies

  ii Mrs Evans.

d   Compare the range for Mr Davies and Mrs Evans.

Why do you think the range differs?

e   Who has the shorter average journey time?

State which average you have used and explain why.

10 The number of cars passing each hour in Ceri's vehicle survey is shown in the table.

Time	1st hour	2nd hour	3rd hour	4th hour	5th hour	6th hour
Cars	75	63	204	66	90	86

a   Find the mean number of cars passing per hour.

b   What is the range for the number of cars passing each hour?

c   The third hour is excluded from the data. How does this affect the range?

d   Why do you think the number of cars passing in the third hour is much higher than in the other hours?

11 Here are the five best javelin throws for three athletes.

Athlete	Length of throw (metres)
Ben Jason	61, 82, 73, 59, 81
Chris White	72, 70, 69, 64, 75
Mel Cox	63, 59, 58, 65, 69

a   Find the mean, median, mode and range for each athlete.

b   Chris White is chosen to represent the team. Explain why.

Curriculum for Wales Mastering Mathematics: Book 1

Strategic competence

12 Luciana sits seven exams. Her scores are:

| 55% | 68% | 72% | 87% | 48% | 96% | 78% |

Luciana sits an eighth exam.

Her mean score is now 71%.

What did Luciana score in the eighth exam?

Logical reasoning

13 Two friends attend a five-day introductory session at their local gym.

The table shows the distances, in kilometres, that they cover in ten minutes on the treadmill each day.

	Day 1	Day 2	Day 3	Day 4	Day 5
Ami	0.92	0.98	0.94	1.10	1.16
Blodwen	1.70	1.90	2.00	2.12	2.16

Cross-curricular activity

Try to do a similar activity to the one in question 13 with a friend, such as running or walking in a local park or your school field.

Perform the activity and use an app on a device (such as a mobile phone or a fitness tracker) to measure the distance.

a Who runs the greater distance?
b Who runs the shorter distance?
c Calculate the mean and range for Ami.
d Calculate the mean and range for Blodwen.
e Who makes the greater improvement in the five days?
   Give a reason for your answer.

14 Here are the weights of ten bags of crisps.

24.9g   25g   24.7g   25.5g   13.2g   24g   26g   25.7g   26.1g   23.9g

a Which value is an outlier?
b Harri calculates the mean weight of the crisps.
   Should Harri include the outlier in his calculation? Give a reason for your answer.
c Work out the mean weight of the crisp packets.
d Which other average might be better? Explain why.

Band 3 questions

15 The data set shows the internet service download speeds in megabits per second (Mbps) to different households in the borough of Abertaf from three different service providers.

The speeds were all taken at 8 p.m. on a Friday.

Lightning ISP	10.2, 8.9, 6.9, 12.2, 13.2, 9.3, 8.9, 11.0, 8.5, 13.3
Total Internet	11.3, 12.2, 10.3, 9.5, 12.0, 10.5, 11.6, 9.8, 8.6, 10.2, 8.9, 11.3
DataPlus	6.9, 7.5, 10.2, 11.9, 8.9, 5.9, 7.5, 9.5, 7.2

a On average, which provider offers the fastest download speeds? How do you know?
b Which internet service provider offers the most consistent internet speeds?
   How do you know?

DataPlus signs up another household in Abertaf.

It claims that it now provides an average download speed of at least 10 MBps.

c i   What is the minimum download speed it needs to provide to this household in order to make this claim true?
   ii Do you think it is likely that DataPlus can achieve this? Give a reason for your answer.

10 Averages and range

16 Niall, Jac and Lowri are racing drivers. The table shows their practice lap times for the Cwmtaf racing track.

Driver	Lap 1	Lap 2	Lap 3	Lap 4	Lap 5
Niall	2 m 34 s	2 m 32 s	2 m 30 s	2 m 31 s	2 m 29 s
Jac	2 m 4 s	2 m 25 s	2 m 39 s	2 m 24 s	2 m 42 s
Lowri	2 m 42 s	2 m 40 s	2 m 38 s	2 m 35 s	2 m 30 s

Emyr, owner of the Walliams racing team, must choose one main driver and one reserve driver to represent his team in a 50-lap race.

  a Emyr chooses Niall. Do you agree with this decision?
  Use statistical measures to help you decide.

  b Jac thinks he should be the reserve. Do you agree? Why?

  c Emyr eventually chooses Lowri to be his reserve driver. Why do you think he made this decision?

17 Guto Morton, champion diver, has achieved the following scores from five judges for three different types of dive.

Type of dive	Judge 1	Judge 2	Judge 3	Judge 4	Judge 5
Freestyle	5.9	6.0	5.7	5.8	5.9
Backflip	4.5	4.3	4.4	4.6	4.0
Bellyflop	2.5	4.1	5.9	3.9	5.8

  a Which dive did Guto perform best? Why do you think this?
  b Which dive did the judges disagree over the most? How can you tell?
  c Which judge gave Guto the best scores?

18 Two groups of six swimmers take part in a swimming relay.

The changeover times are given in this table.

Group 1 (minutes)	34	45	54	59	82	94
Group 2 (minutes)	25	42	61	77	89	100

  a Find the individual times of the 12 swimmers.
  b Complete a copy of this table.

	Group 1	Group 2
Mean		
Median		
Mode		
Range		

Cross-curricular activity

In your PE lesson, split your class into two groups to recreate question 18 for a running relay.

If your times are in minutes and seconds, how could you work out the mean?

  c Compare the results for each group. Which is the better group and why?

19 Three positive numbers have a mode of 5 and a range of 6.
Calculate the mean of the three numbers.

20 Three temperatures have a mean of −7 °C and a median of −4 °C.
Given the range is 15 °C, find the lowest of the three temperatures.

21 Four positive whole numbers have a mean of 18 and a median of 16.
What is the greatest possible range?

22 Four items are labelled with their prices.
  • The mean price is £2.52.
  • The price range is £1.42.
  • The median price is £2.78.
Find the price of the most expensive item.

23 In a class of 12 students, the mean score in a test is 78%.
In a second class, the mean score is 83%.
The overall mean for the two classes combined is 80%.
How many students are in the second class?

11 Displaying data

Coming up...

▶ Using and interpreting pictograms
▶ Using tally charts and frequency tables
▶ Drawing and interpreting bar charts
▶ Using and interpreting vertical line graphs

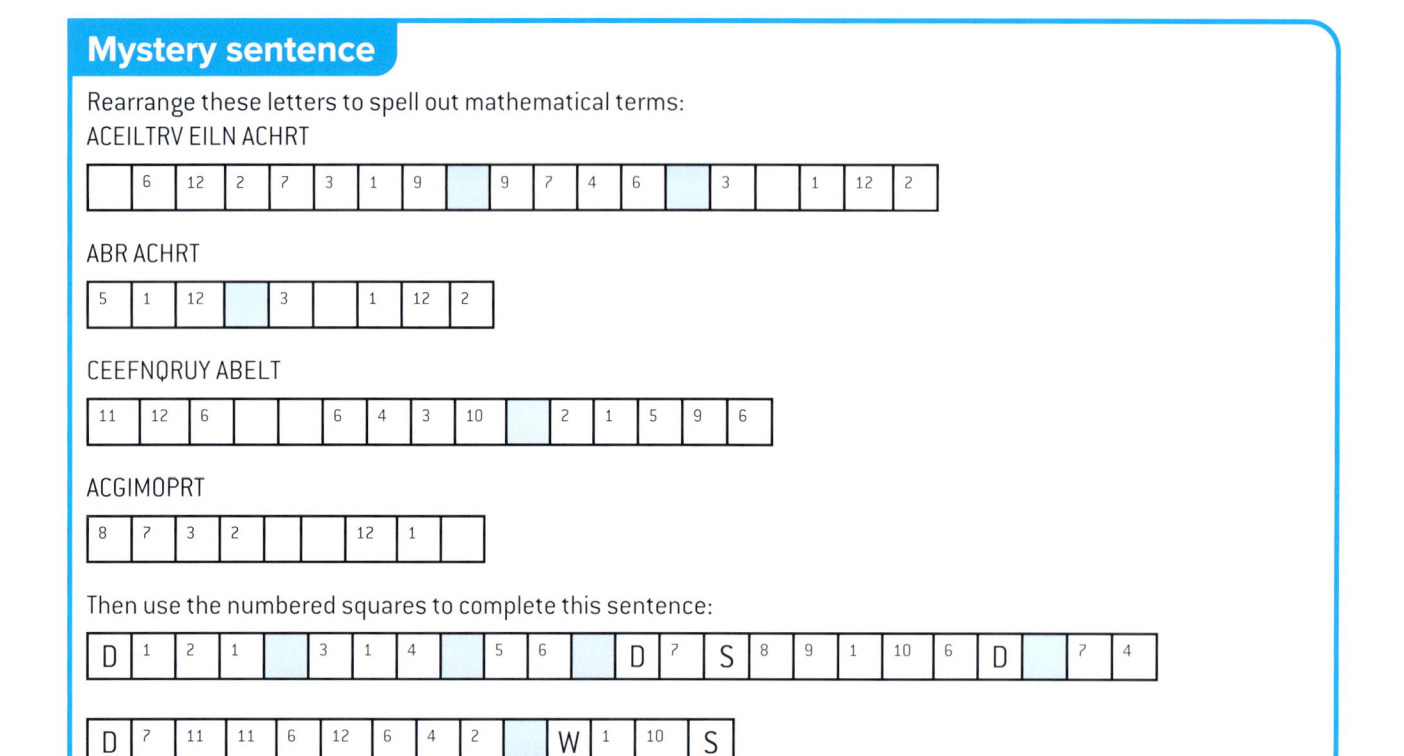

Mystery sentence

Rearrange these letters to spell out mathematical terms:

ACEILTRV EILN ACHRT

| | 6 | 12 | 2 | 7 | 3 | 1 | 9 | | 9 | 7 | 4 | 6 | | 3 | | 1 | 12 | 2 |

ABR ACHRT

| 5 | 1 | 12 | | 3 | | 1 | 12 | 2 |

CEEFNQRUY ABELT

| 11 | 12 | 6 | | 6 | 4 | 3 | 10 | | 2 | 1 | 5 | 9 | 6 |

ACGIMOPRT

| 8 | 7 | 3 | 2 | | | 12 | 1 | |

Then use the numbered squares to complete this sentence:

| D | 1 | 2 | 1 | | 3 | 1 | 4 | | 5 | 6 | | D | 7 | S | 8 | 9 | 1 | 10 | 6 | D | | 7 | 4 |

| D | 7 | 11 | 11 | 6 | 12 | 6 | 4 | 2 | | W | 1 | 10 | S |

11.1 Using tables and charts

Skill checker

① Count the tally marks in each of these.
   a ||||
   b ||||| ||
   c ||||| ||||| ||||| |

11 Displaying data

② If 🙂 represents two people, how many people are represented in each of these?

a 🙂 🙂 🙂

b 🙂 🙂 🙂 🙂 🙂 🙂

③ Find the modal colour in this list:

red   black   green   yellow   red   green   orange   green

Activity

① Count the number of marks inside each box.

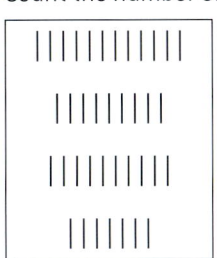

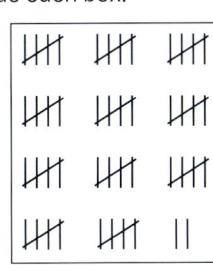

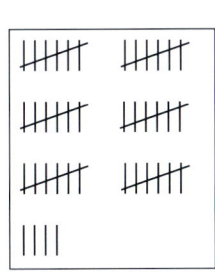

② Which box is the easiest to count?
③ Why do you think that tallies are collected in blocks of five?

▶ Frequency diagrams

You can use a **tally chart** when collecting data or organising existing data. Arrange the tallies in groups of five.

You can make a **frequency table** by adding a frequency column to a tally chart. The frequency tells you the number of times something happens.

Worked example

A group of people were asked about the types of film they like.

Film type	Tally	Frequency
Comedy	|||| |||| ||||	14
Factual	|||| ||	
Horror	|||| |||| ||	
Mystery	|||| ||||	
Science fiction		16
Romance		3
	Total:	62

$2 \times 5 + 4 = 14$

a How many people said they liked mystery films?
b Fill in the missing frequencies.
c Fill in the tallies for Romance and Science fiction.

Solution

a $2 \times 5 = 10$

b, c

Film type	Tally	Frequency
Comedy	⊁⊁⊁⊁ IIII	14
Factual	⊁ II	7
Horror	⊁⊁⊁ II	12
Mystery	⊁⊁⊁	10
Science fiction	⊁⊁⊁⊁⊁ I	16
Romance	III	3
	Total:	62

▶ Pictograms

You can use a **pictogram** when you want to make data more interesting or memorable, and the representation more appropriate.

Remember to include a **key** to explain what each symbol represents.

Worked example

Joe owns a village shop. He wants to know how many litres of each type of milk he should order.

This pictogram shows the number of litres of each type of milk that Joe sells one morning.

Full cream

Semi-skimmed

Skimmed

🍾 = 2 litres

a What does 🍾 mean?

b How many litres of each type of milk did Joe sell?

c How many litres of milk did Joe sell altogether?

Solution

a One bottle is equal to 2 litres. A half-bottle is 1 litre.

b Full cream: There are nine symbols. $9 \times 2 = 18$ litres

Semi-skimmed: There are 11 symbols. $11 \times 2 = 22$ litres

Skimmed: There are four whole symbols and one half symbol. $4 \times 2 + 1 \times 1 = 9$ litres

c Total: $18 + 22 + 9 = 49$ litres of milk sold altogether

The pictures used in pictograms can sometimes be difficult to subdivide.

You can draw a bar chart instead. Leave a gap between each category, ensuring that the gaps are all the same size.

Remember to include a title with any chart.

11 Displaying data

Worked example

Hanna is organising an end-of-year event for her year group.

She asks everyone in her class what they would like to do and records their suggestions in a table.

Activity	Disco	Theme park	Cinema	Zoo	Ice skating
Frequency	7	5	2	3	3

Draw a bar chart for Hanna's data.

Solution

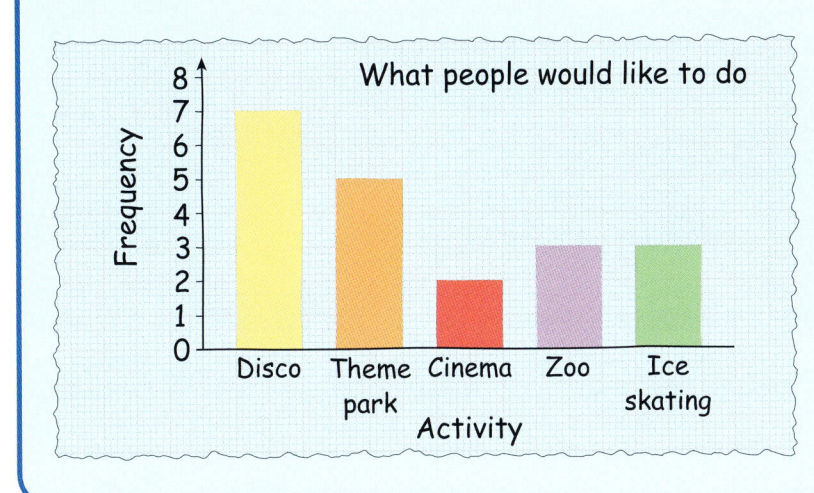

Remember
- Bars are the same width.
- Frequency goes on the vertical axis.
- It is usual to have spaces between the bars.

11.1 Now try these

Band 1 questions

1. This pictogram shows a football team's results for one season.

   ⚽ = 4 matches

   a. How many matches does ◐ stand for?
   b. How many matches did the team win?
   c. How many matches did they lose?
   d. How many matches did they draw?
   e. Copy these axes and then use them to draw a bar chart to show this data.

Curriculum for Wales Mastering Mathematics: Book 1

Fluency

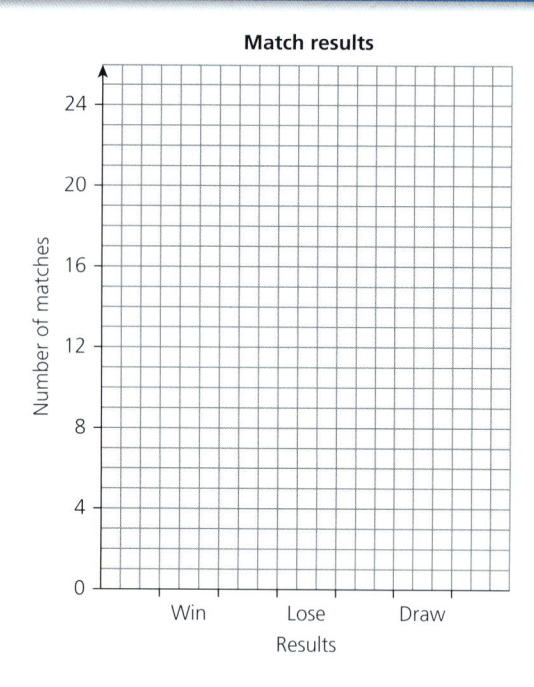

Match results

(Bar chart grid with y-axis "Number of matches" from 0 to 24, and x-axis "Results" with categories Win, Lose, Draw)

Logical reasoning

❷ Jo delivers newspapers. Here are the papers she delivers each day.

Cardiff Times	Cambrian News	Cambrian News	Western Mail	Cambrian News	Cambrian News	Mirror	Western Telegraph
Guardian	Mirror	Cardiff Times	Western Mail	Guardian	Mirror	Cardiff Times	Cambrian News
Mirror	Mirror	Carmarthen Journal	Western Telegraph	Carmarthen Journal	Independent	Western Mail	Cambrian News

  a Display this information in a tally chart.
  b Which is the most popular newspaper on Jo's round?
  c How many newspapers does Jo deliver?

❸ The list gives the soft drinks sold in a cinema kiosk one evening.

Cola	Cherryade	Cola	Lemonade	Cola	Cola	Cherryade	Orangeade
Cherryade	Lemonade	Cola	Orangeade	Cherryade	Cola	Cola	Cola
Cherryade	Cola	Cherryade	Cola	Orangeade	Cola	Cola	Lemonade

  a Use a tally chart to organise this data.
  b How many drinks were sold altogether?
  c Which was the most popular drink?
  d Draw a pictogram of the types of drink sold.
     Use 🥛 to represent two drinks in your pictogram.
  e The kiosk will need more stock soon.
     What advice would you give them about how much of each drink to buy?
     Give a reason for your answer.

11 Displaying data

Band 2 questions

4 A council is concerned about the traffic at a busy junction.

Dewi carries out a traffic survey for one hour between 5 a.m. and 6 a.m. one Monday morning. He notes down each type of vehicle using the junction.

car	car	lorry	bicycle	car	lorry
car	lorry	car	motorbike	car	bicycle
motorbike	car	car	car	motorbike	car
car	car	lorry	car	lorry	car
lorry	car	car	bicycle	car	car
car	car	lorry	car	car	lorry

a Draw a combined tally chart and frequency table for this data.
b Which was the most common vehicle type?
c How many vehicles did Dewi see?
d Draw a bar chart to show this data.
e Give a reason why Dewi's survey might not provide the council with enough information.

5 The pictogram shows how many people live in five different hamlets.

A hamlet is a small village.

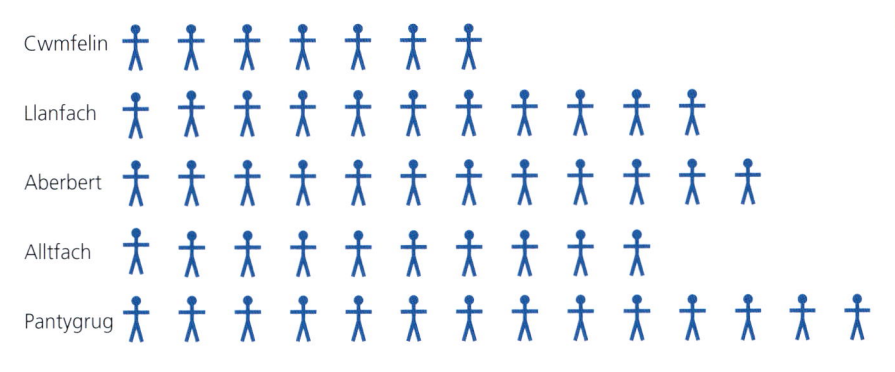

Cwmfelin: 7 figures
Llanfach: 10 figures
Aberbert: 11 figures
Alltfach: 8 figures
Pantygrug: 12 figures

Key: ⚊ represents 10 people

a What do you think ⅂ stands for?
b How many people live in:
   i Cwmfelin   ii Llanfach   iii Aberbert   iv Alltfach   v Pantygrug?
c Draw a pictogram to show the number of people who live in these four hamlets. Remember to include a key.

Gelli: 85 people
Penffordd: 100 people
Drelas: 135 people
Cwmgwaun: 110 people

Curriculum for Wales Mastering Mathematics: Book 1

Logical reasoning

6 Llinos has drawn a bar chart to show how the people in her class travelled to school one day.

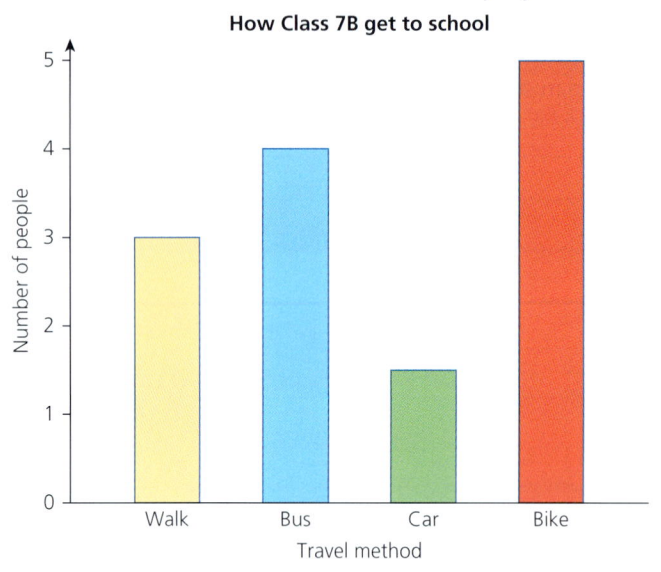

How Class 7B get to school

(Bar chart: Walk = 3, Bus = 4, Car = 1.5, Bike = 5; y-axis: Number of people; x-axis: Travel method)

a Which is the modal method of travel? How do you know?

b Llinos has made a mistake when drawing her bar chart.
Which bar has been drawn incorrectly? How do you know?

Band 3 questions

7 Mrs Jones teaches Geography to two Year 7 classes.
One day she gives both classes the same test.
She gives each student a grade: A, B, C, D or E.
Mrs Jones draws this bar chart to show the results.

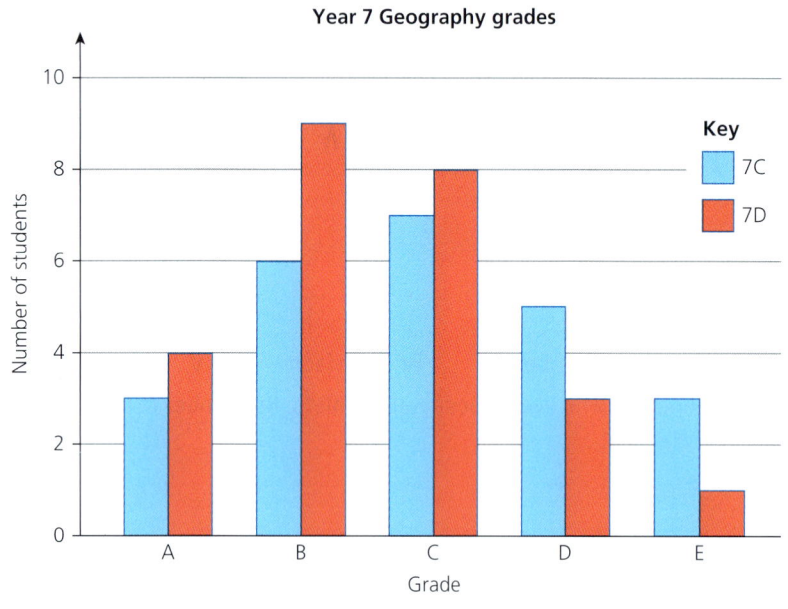

Year 7 Geography grades

(Dual bar chart with Key: 7C (blue), 7D (orange).
A: 7C = 3, 7D = 4
B: 7C = 6, 7D = 9
C: 7C = 7, 7D = 8
D: 7C = 5, 7D = 3
E: 7C = 3, 7D = 1)

a How is this dual bar chart different from the bar charts you have drawn in this chapter?

b Why do you think Mrs Jones has drawn it like this?

c How many students are there in Class 7C?

d How many students are there in Class 7D?

e Which class did better in the test? Explain your reasoning.

11 Displaying data

8 Anwen works in a hotel. She draws this compound bar chart to illustrate the ages of the guests one day.
Anwen explains that the bar chart shows there are 10 American guests between the ages of 31 and 60.

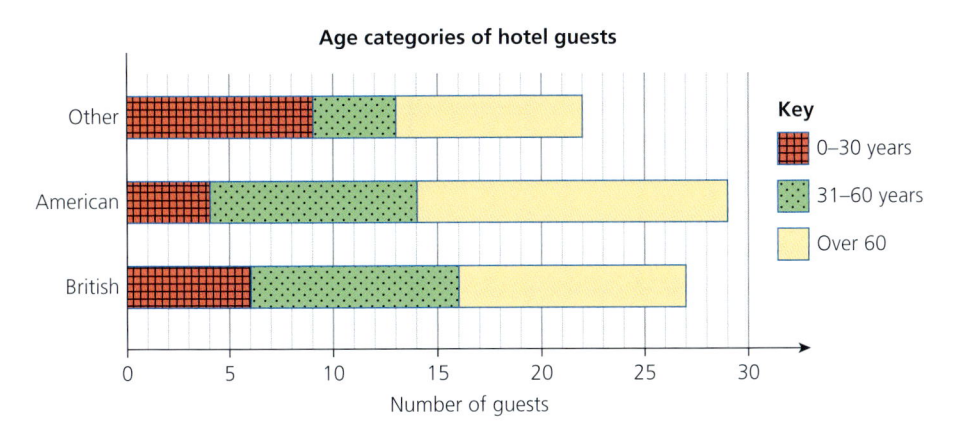

Age categories of hotel guests

Key:
- 0–30 years
- 31–60 years
- Over 60

Number of guests

a   How many of the guests are British and aged between 0 and 30?
b   How many of the guests are American?
c   How many of the guests are aged over 60?
d   What is the total number of guests staying in the hotel?

9 Using these clues, draw a bar chart to illustrate the number of each type of tree in a park.
- There are 98 trees in total and six different types of tree.
- There are more than 20 ash trees, but oak is the most common.
- The only elm tree is by the main entrance, and there is one pine tree at each corner of a football pitch.
- There are 23 willow trees, but the numbers of all the other trees are square numbers.
- There is an odd number of beech trees.

11.2 Vertical line graphs

Skill checker

Find the mode, median, mean and range of these numbers:
23, 25, 24, 23, 25, 26, 25, 23, 22, 36, 23

▶ Vertical line graphs

You can use **vertical line graphs** instead of bar charts. Vertical line graphs are also known as vertical line charts or vertical line diagrams.

The frequency axis is drawn vertically.

Plot the points, and then draw a vertical line from each point to the horizontal axis.

Curriculum for Wales Mastering Mathematics: Book 1

Worked example

Judith rolls a dice 30 times and records the results in a tally chart.

Dice roll	Tally	Frequency
1	⦀⦀ ⦀⦀	7
2	⦀⦀⦀⦀	4
3	⦀⦀⦀⦀ ⦀⦀⦀	8
4	⦀⦀⦀⦀	4
5	⦀⦀⦀⦀	5
6	⦀⦀	2
	Total:	30

Show this data on a vertical line graph.

Solution

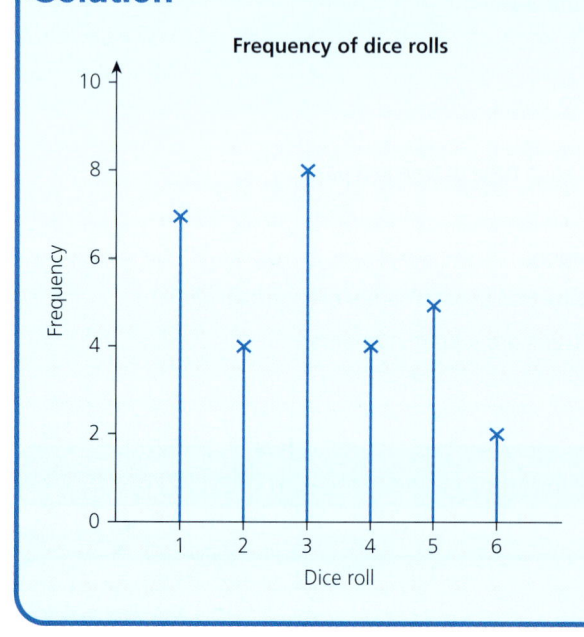

Frequency of dice rolls

(Vertical line graph with Dice roll on x-axis (1–6) and Frequency on y-axis (0–10). Points: 1→7, 2→4, 3→8, 4→4, 5→5, 6→2.)

Activity

Roll a pair of normal dice.

Calculate the difference between the two numbers rolled.

For example, rolling a 6 and a 2 gives a difference of 4. Record the difference.

What are the lowest and the highest possible differences?

Repeat 50 times, recording the difference on each roll.

Complete a tally chart for your results and find the frequency of each difference.

Draw a vertical line graph to illustrate your results.

Which differences have the lowest frequency? Explain why.

11 Displaying data

11.2 Now try these

Band 1 questions

1 Ffion plays two games of bowling. After each of her turns, she writes down the number of pins she knocks down. Her scores for each turn are shown here.

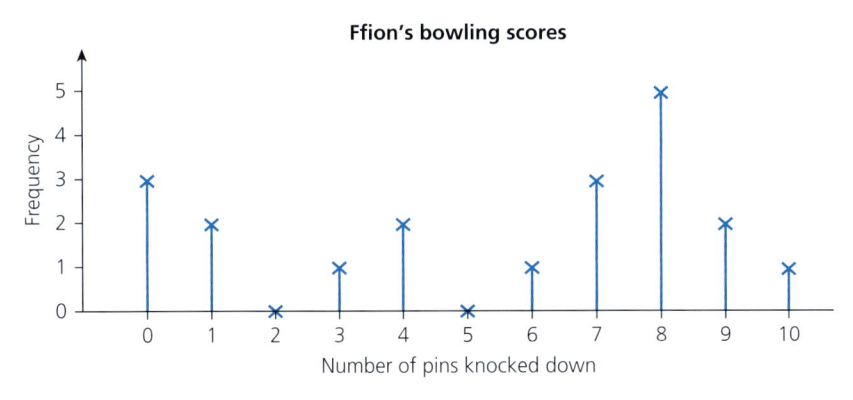

Ffion's bowling scores

a How many times did Ffion knock down all ten pins?
b How many times did she not knock down any pins?
c Which two scores did she not get in any of her turns?

2 Use this data to complete the vertical line graph. The first one has been done for you.

Score	Frequency
0	5
1	3
2	6
3	7
4	1
5	4

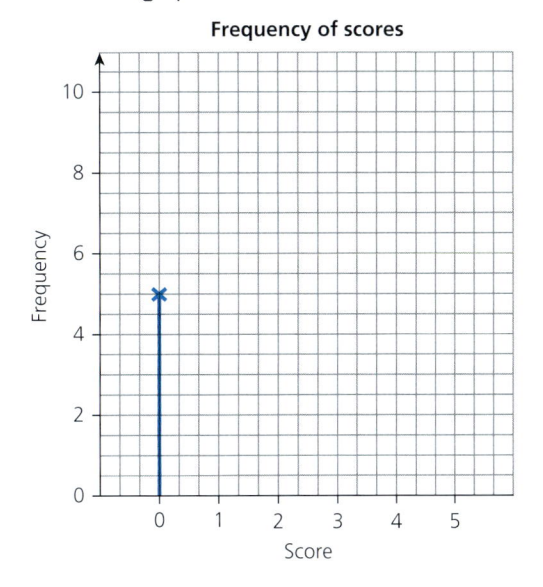

Frequency of scores

3 Each week, Elinor does a spelling test at school. Each test is out of 10.

Elinor's results for the last 20 tests are shown here.

a How many times did Elinor score 9?
b What is Elinor's highest score?
c What is Elinor's lowest score?
d Write down Elinor's modal score.

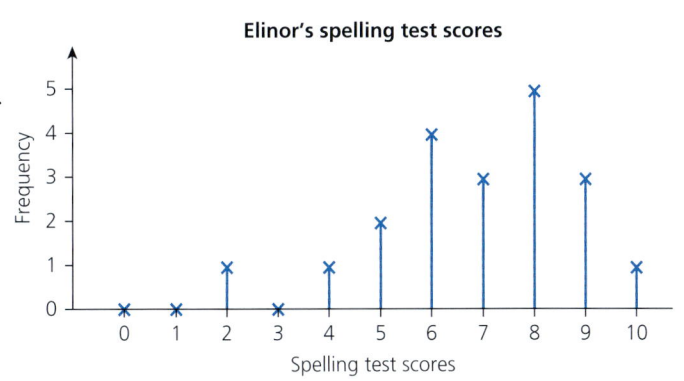

Elinor's spelling test scores

233

Curriculum for Wales Mastering Mathematics: Book 1

Band 2 questions

Logical reasoning

4 Arwyn records the number of birds on his bird-table each morning at 8 o'clock.

His results are shown on this vertical line diagram.

   a How many times did Arwyn see just one bird on the bird-table?

   b What is the greatest number of birds on the bird-table at any one time?

   c How many mornings are shown on the graph?

   d How many birds were counted to get this data?

      Does your answer tell you how many different birds Arwyn saw? Explain your answer.

5 Sioned counts the numbers of matches in 30 matchboxes. Her results are shown in the graph.

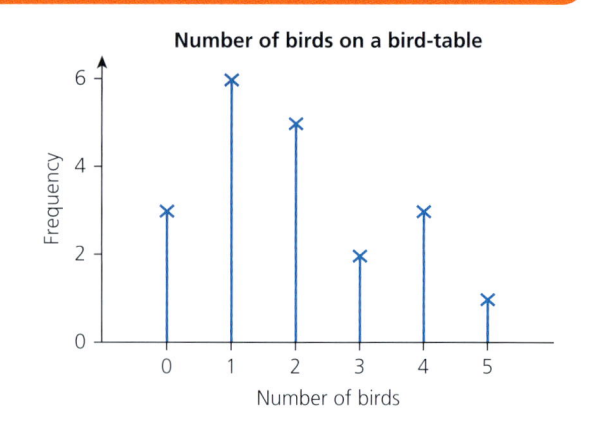

The graph shows that there were two boxes containing 48 matches and four boxes containing 49 matches.

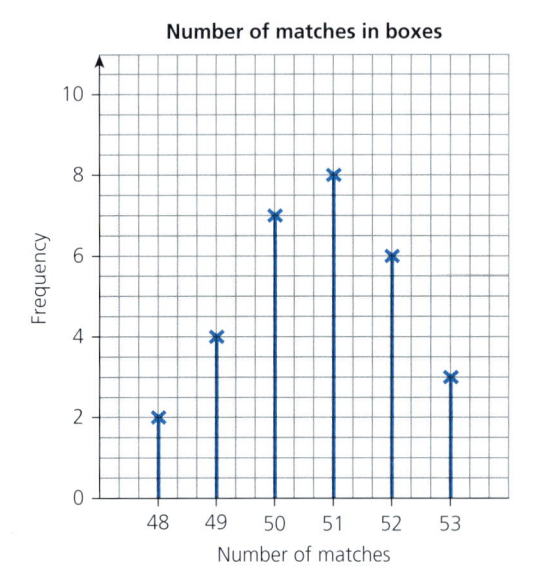

   a Write down the modal number of matches.

   b Sioned writes the numbers of matches in order of size:

      48, 48, 49, 49, 49, 49 …

      Complete Sioned's list.

   c Calculate the total number of matches.

   d How could Sioned have calculated the total without first listing all the different values?

Fluency

6 Dafydd recorded the numbers of goals his favourite football team scored in their last 20 games. His results are shown in the table.

Draw a vertical line graph to illustrate this data.

Number of goals	Frequency
0	4
1	5
2	7
3	3
4	0
5	1

234

Band 3 questions

7 Inez rolls a dice 20 times and records the scores.
The frequency of each score is shown in the graph.

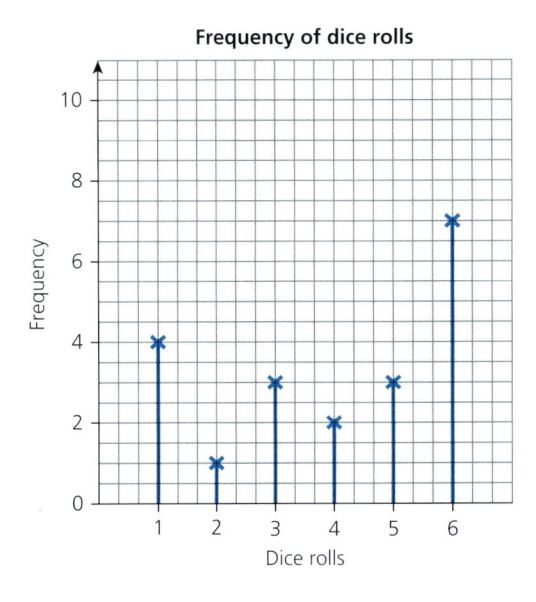

Frequency of dice rolls

(Vertical line graph: 1 → 4, 2 → 1, 3 → 3, 4 → 2, 5 → 3, 6 → 7)

a Find the range of the scores.
b Inez writes out the 20 scores in order of size: 1, 1, 1, 1, 2, …
Continue Inez's list.
c Calculate the median score.
d Calculate the total of all 20 dice rolls.
e Inez says that there are more 6s than any other score so the dice is biased. Do you agree?

8 In Abhi's school examinations, grade 1 is the lowest grade that can be achieved and grade 10 is the highest grade that can be achieved. Abhi records the 40 grades that Class 8C achieve in their science exams.
Half of the grades were higher than 5, and the total of all grades was 176.

a Explain why the frequency of grade 7 must be 7.
b Complete the vertical line graph for grades 7, 4 and 3.

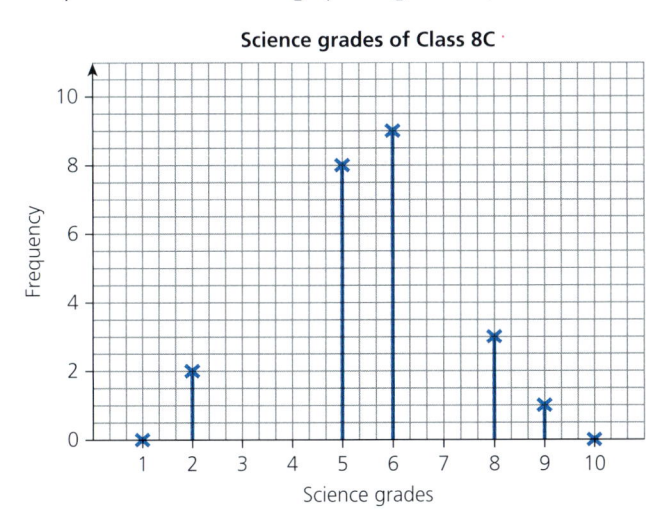

Science grades of Class 8C

(Vertical line graph: 1 → 0, 2 → 2, 5 → 8, 6 → 9, 8 → 3, 9 → 1, 10 → 0)

235

Curriculum for Wales Mastering Mathematics: Book 1

Strategic competence

9 Kaito and Efa surveyed the wildlife on a local river.

They recorded the number of eggs in some birds' nests before writing this puzzle, so that the data could be reconstructed.

> We checked 100 nests altogether.
> There were 15 nests with three eggs each.
> The number of nests with an odd number of eggs was 53.
> There were 14 nests with six eggs in each.
> There were 64 eggs in nests with four eggs in each.
> There were 425 eggs altogether.
> Exactly half of the nests had five or more eggs in them.
> The modal number of eggs was 5.
> There was a square number of nests with two eggs in them.
> The number of nests with a prime number of eggs was 55.
> There was a square number of nests with five eggs in them.
> Three nests had no eggs in them.
> There were no more than eight eggs in any of the nests.
> The number of nests with a square number of eggs was 23.

a Use the clues to find the frequency of each number of eggs.
b Draw a vertical line graph to illustrate the data.

Cross-curricular activity

Spreadsheets are very good at displaying data in different ways. Find out how to do this.

Key words

Here is a list of the key words you met in this chapter.

| Bar chart | Frequency table | Key |
| Tally chart | Vertical line graph | Pictogram |

Use the glossary at the back of this book to check any you are unsure about.

236

11 Displaying data

Review exercise: displaying data

Band 1 questions

1 The bar chart shows the favourite sports of Year 7.

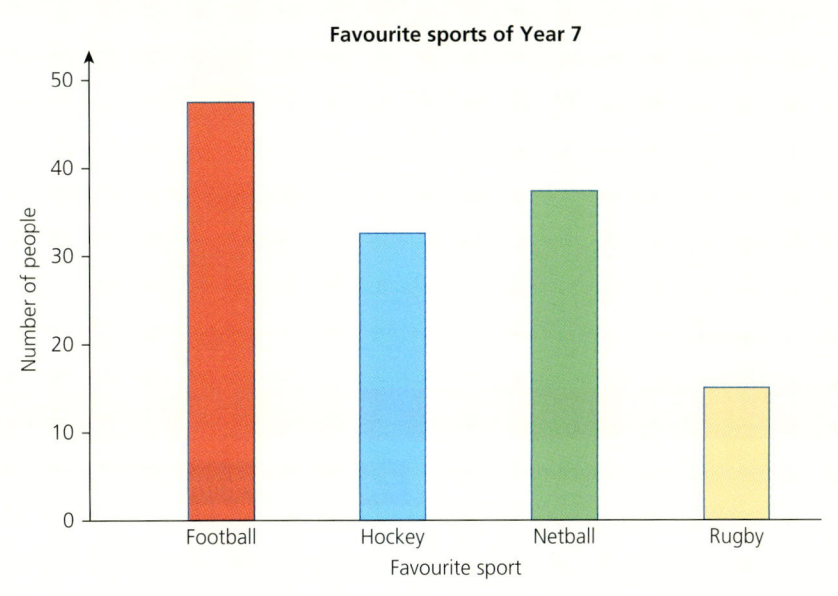

Favourite sports of Year 7

You could try this question in your class. Ask your classmates what their favourite sport is and draw a new bar chart.

    a Which sport is the most popular?

    b Which sport is the least popular?

2 The number of students in the Year 7 form-groups at Ysgol Hendy are shown in this graph.

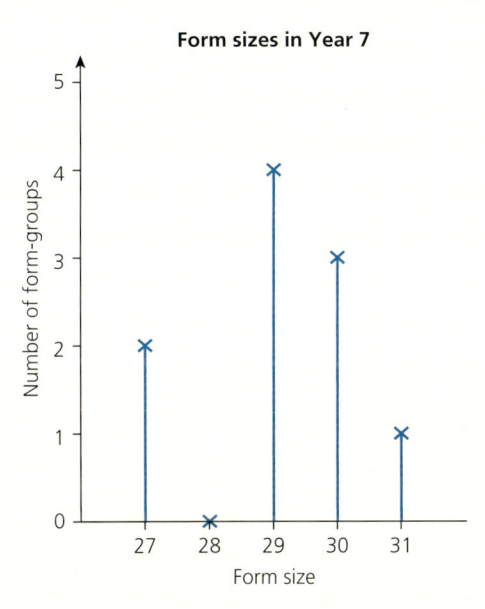

Form sizes in Year 7

    a How many of the forms have 29 students?

    b How many of the forms have more than 29 students?

237

Curriculum for Wales Mastering Mathematics: Book 1

Fluency

3 Luciana counts her rugby team's wins, draws and losses for a whole season. The pictogram shows her data.

Win: 🏉 🏉 🏉 🏉 🏉

Draw: 🏉 (half)

Lose: 🏉 🏉 (half)

Key: 🏉 represents two games

a How many games did the team win?

b How many games did they play in the season?

Band 2 questions

Logical reasoning

4 Cai asks ten of his friends, 'Which types of television programme do you enjoy watching?'

a Draw a bar chart to illustrate his results.

b Why is the frequency total more than the number of friends he asked?

Type of programme	Frequency
Comedy	3
Film	4
Soap	6
Game show	2
Drama	1
Sport	7
Other	2
Total:	25

Fluency

5 Lili asks her classmates about their shoe sizes. She records her results in a tally chart.

a Draw a vertical line chart to illustrate this data.

b Lili writes the shoe sizes in order: 3, $3\frac{1}{2}$, $3\frac{1}{2}$, 4, 4, 4, …

Copy and complete Lili's list.

c Find the median shoe size.

Shoe size	Tally
3	|
$3\frac{1}{2}$	||
4	⦀⦀ ||||
$4\frac{1}{2}$	⦀⦀ ||
5	⦀⦀
$5\frac{1}{2}$	||||
6	||

You could try questions 4 or 5 with information from your class!

6 **a** How many scores are represented in this vertical line chart?

b Find the median score in this vertical line chart. You may want to list the scores first.

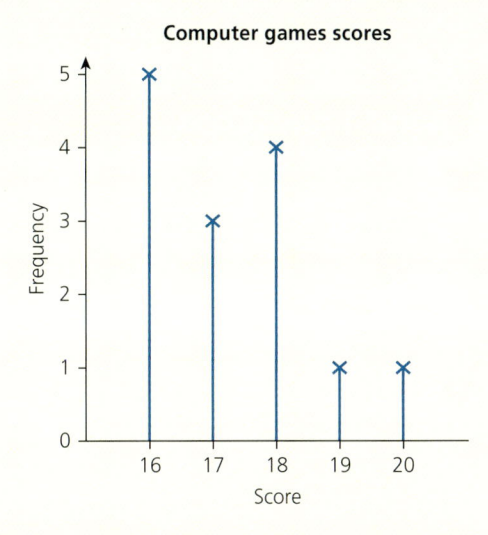

Computer games scores

Band 3 questions

7 Hazeema decides to use this symbol 👤 to represent five people when she draws a pictogram.

Tarfaan tells her that this symbol might be difficult to use.

a Why does Tarfaan think there might be a problem?

b Hazeema says that she has already looked at the frequencies in her data and that there won't be a problem. What could Hazeema have noticed?

8 Every evening, Shaima notices that some starlings sit on a telegraph wire.

She counts them at 8 o'clock every evening for 40 days.

The numbers of starlings on the wire are shown in the vertical line chart.

The total number of starlings counted is 152.

Two of the lines are missing from the vertical line chart.

Copy and complete the graph.

Number of starlings each evening

9 Tonwen's class does a short times-table test. Each student is given a whole number score out of 10.

Some of the results are shown in the vertical line graph.

The lowest score is 3, but no one scored 4.

Tonwen correctly calculates that when all the scores are added then the total is 118.

Exactly half of the students scored more than 5.

a Explain why the number of students must be 20.

b Explain why the frequency of a score of 3 cannot be zero.

c What is the modal score?

d Copy and complete the vertical line chart.

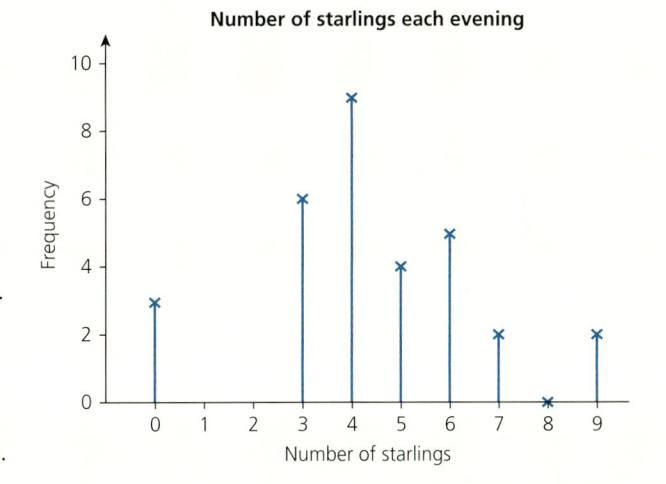

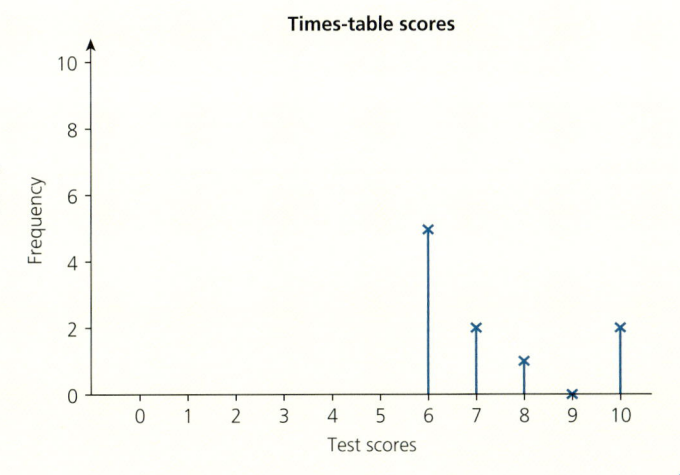

Times-table scores

239

Consolidation 4: Chapters 10–11

Band 1 questions

1. Janthine's shop sells sandwiches. These are the sandwiches sold one day:

   Chicken Salad Cheese Ham Beef Prawn Cheese Ham Ham Beef Salad Chicken Salad
   Ham Beef Chicken Ham Beef Salad Ham Salad Cheese Salad Cheese Ham Beef

   a   Draw a tally chart to show how many of each type of sandwich were sold.
   b   Draw a pictogram to illustrate the numbers of each sandwich. Use 🥪 to represent two sandwiches.

2. A pictogram uses the symbol ⚽ to represent four football matches. How many football matches would be represented by this row?

   ⚽ ⚽ ⚽ ◐

3. Dilwyn records the beak colours of the birds that visit his garden. What is the modal beak colour?

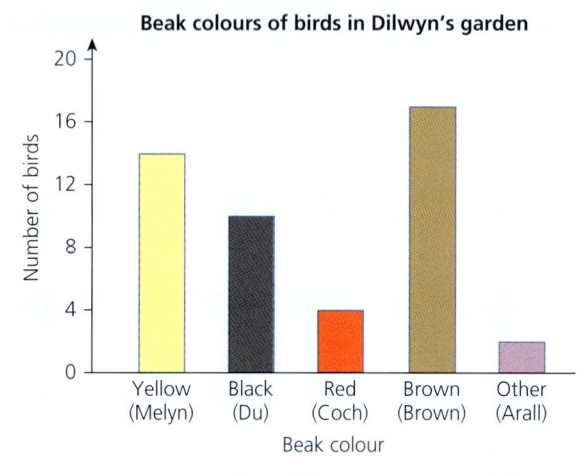

   Beak colours of birds in Dilwyn's garden

   Yellow (Melyn): 14
   Black (Du): 10
   Red (Coch): 4
   Brown (Brown): 17
   Other (Arall): 2

4. Ten students sit three examinations. Their marks, out of 40, are:

   Mathematics (Mathemateg):   20, 37, 30, 10, 22, 27, 29, 15, 16, 19
   English (Saesneg):   12, 18, 22, 27, 33, 25, 35, 15, 31, 39
   Science (Gwyddoniaeth):   15, 19, 21, 23, 25, 29, 32, 34, 5, 16

   a   Work out the range of marks for each exam.
   b   Work out the median for each exam.

5. The table shows Dafydd's marks for his end of year assessments. Find Dafydd's mean mark.

English (Saesneg)	History (Hanes)	Science (Gwyddoniaeth)	French (Ffrangeg)	Geography (Daearyddiaeth)	Maths (Mathemateg)	Art (Celf)
34	20	31	25	28	42	37

Consolidation 4

6 This vertical line graph shows some scores.
    a What is the modal score?
    b What is the range of the scores shown?
    c How many scores are shown on the graph?

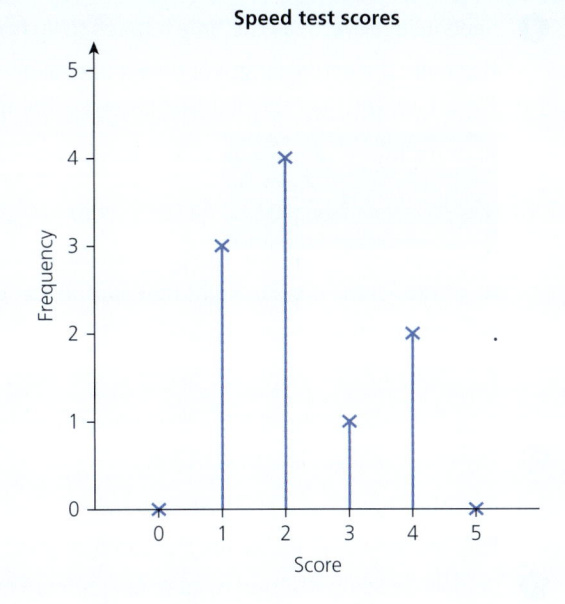

Speed test scores

Band 2 questions

7 Harri and Sali draw bar charts to show their holiday weather and compare them.
    a Who do you think had nicer holiday weather?
    b Comment on their categories. How could they be improved?

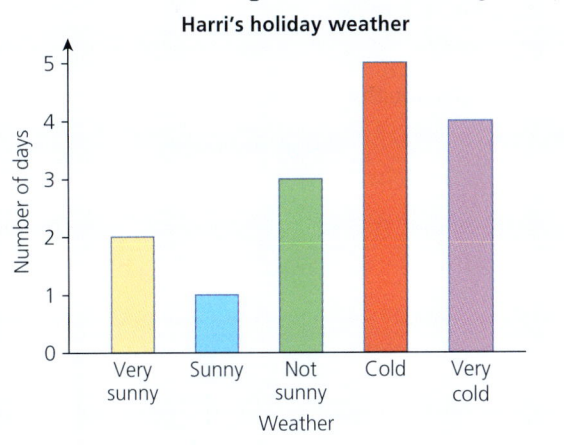

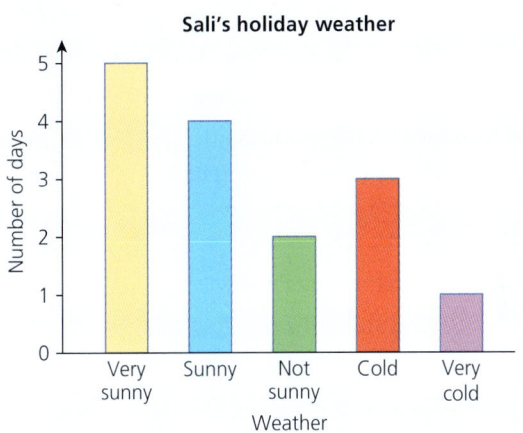

8 Anna throws a tennis ball ten times. She records the distance it travels on each throw.
    23 m   11 m   26 m   25 m   23 m   27 m   29 m   31 m   40 m   22 m
    a Write down the modal distance.
    b Find the median distance.
    c Calculate the mean distance.
    d Calculate the range of the distances.
    e Which of parts **a**–**c** gives the longest average distance?

Curriculum for Wales **Mastering Mathematics: Book 1**

9 SpeedyJet advertises the time it takes to fly from Gatwick Airport to Vienna Airport as 2 hours 30 minutes.

However, the actual length of time it has taken the airline to complete this flight, including delays at Gatwick Airport, for the past ten flights is shown in the table.

Flight number	1	2	3	4	5	6	7	8	9	10
Flight times, including delays (minutes)	155	150	148	162	175	165	210	160	154	173

a What is the median flight time for the last ten flights?

b What is the range of flight times?

c SpeedyJet claims that its flights are never more than ten minutes late.

Does the data support this claim? Explain your answer.

10 The mean of eight lengths is 15 m.

A ninth length of 18 m is then included.

Will the new mean be higher, the same, or lower than 15 m?

11 Jerin is deciding whether to go to Abercliff or Porthgwyn this summer.

The table shows the number of hours of sunshine at the two resorts in one week last August.

Resort	Sunshine hours
Abercliff	6, 10, 1, 7, 11, 3, 4
Porthgwyn	5, 8, 4, 6, 5, 6, 8

a Calculate the mean, median and modal sunshine hours for each resort.

b Find the range of sunshine hours for each resort.

c Jerin decides to go to Porthgwyn. Why do you think he has made this choice?

12 Mrs Lloyd records the marks her students achieve in their history test. The vertical line chart shows the results.

a Write down the modal mark.

b How many students' results have been recorded?

c Mrs Lloyd starts to list the marks in order: 3, 4, 4, 5, ...

Continue the list.

d Find the median mark.

e Find the mean mark.

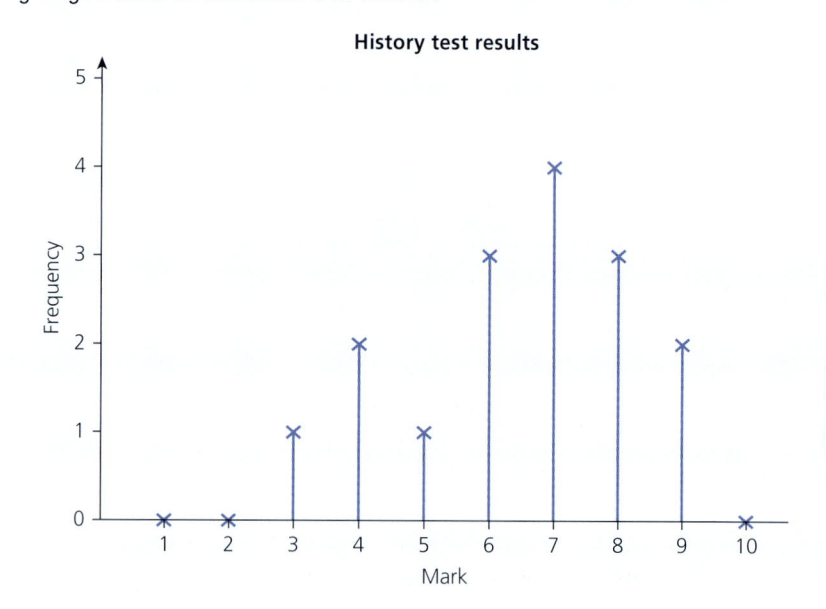

Band 3 questions

13 Every evening, Carwyn and Cerys walk through a field and count the number of rabbits they see.

Carwyn correctly calculates the mean, median and mode of the number of rabbits they've seen over the past 20 evenings. He tells Cerys that the three averages are 6.5, 7 and 6.3, but he can't remember which average is which.

Cerys says, 'I can't remember the data but I can work out which average is which.'

How does Cerys know which average is the mean, which one is the median, and which one is the mode?

242

Consolidation 4

14 Ioan asks his classmates about their preferred takeaway meals.

He asks them to choose from the list shown and records their choices.

Takeaway meal	Tally
Burger and chips	ⅢⅠ ⅢⅠ Ⅰ
Chinese	ⅢⅠ Ⅰ
Indian	ⅠⅠ
Pizza	ⅢⅠ ⅠⅠⅠ

a Draw a bar chart to show these results.
b Are there any other takeaway meals you think Ioan could have included in his survey?
c Suggest some improvements to the way Ioan carried out his survey.

15 During a school competition, Caradog records the distances during the shotput event.

He draws a graph to show the distances. Comment on the graph he uses.

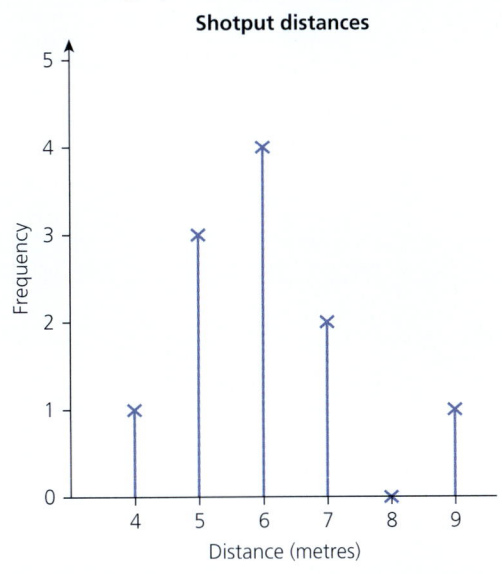

Shotput distances

(graph: Frequency vs Distance (metres); points at (4,1), (5,3), (6,4), (7,2), (8,0), (9,1))

16 A youth club collects the ages of its members from Caernarfon and from Bangor in this frequency table.

Some of the frequencies are missing.

The modal age of **all** members is 15.

The median age of the members from Bangor is 16.

What is the total number of all of the members from Caernarfon and Bangor?

> You might find it useful to list the ages of the members from Bangor, leaving gaps where necessary.

	Frequency	
Age	Caernarfon	Bangor
13	1	0
14	3	3
15		
16	3	7
17	2	1
Total:	16	

17 The mean of three prime numbers is 8.

Find the mean of the two biggest numbers.

18 The mean, median, mode and range of five whole numbers are all 5.

Alun says that the five numbers must be 2, 5, 5, 6, 7.

Linda says he is wrong.

Who is right?

> **Note**
> Revisit Chapter 4 for a recap of primes.

243

12 Working with decimals

Coming up...
- ▶ Multiplying by 10, 100 and 1000
- ▶ Dividing by 10, 100 and 1000
- ▶ Adding and subtracting decimals
- ▶ Multiplying and dividing decimals

Maze puzzle

Find your way through the maze. You can't visit the same box more than once.

① What is the biggest value you got at the end?

② What is the smallest value you got at the end?

③ How many different routes have you found through the maze?

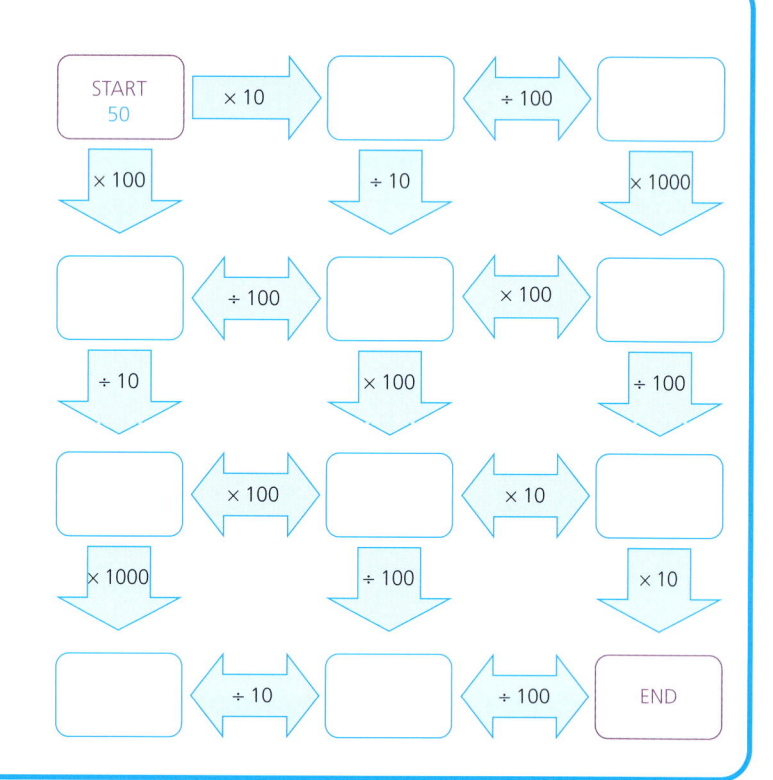

START 50 → × 10 → ☐ ← ÷ 100 → ☐
↓ × 100   ↓ ÷ 10   ↓ × 1000
☐ ← ÷ 100 → ☐ ← × 100 → ☐
↓ ÷ 10   ↓ × 100   ↓ ÷ 100
☐ ← × 100 → ☐ ← × 10 → ☐
↓ × 1000   ↓ ÷ 100   ↓ × 10
☐ ← ÷ 10 → ☐ ← ÷ 100 → END

12.1 Multiplying and dividing by powers of 10

Skill checker

① For each of the following numbers, copy and complete the sentences.

729	7 is in the hundredths column	__ is in the tens column	__ is in the ones column
48.5	4 is in the tens column	__ is in the ones column	__ is in the tenths column
3.62	3 is in the ____ column	__ is in the tenths column	2 is in the ____ column

② a In the number 62, which column is the 6 in?

b When the number 62 is multiplied by 100, which column does the 6 move to?

c When the number 62 is divided by 100, which column does the 6 move to?

Remember, when you:
- multiply by 10 you move all the digits one place to the left
- divide by 10 you move all the digits one place to the right.

This is true for decimals as well as integers.

> An integer is a positive or a negative whole number.

You can use a place-value diagram to work out 4.67×10.

T	O	.	t	h
	4	.	6	7
4	6	.	7	

> Only the decimal point is fixed.

You can use a place-value diagram to work out $4.67 \div 10$.

T	O	.	t	h	th
	4	.	6	7	
	0	.	4	6	7

> Again, the decimal point is fixed.

Worked example

Work out these.

a 3.2×100
b 0.32×1000
c $32 \div 10$
d $3.2 \div 100$

H	T	O	.	t	h	th
		3	.	2		
3	2	0	.	0		
		0	.	3	2	
3	2	0	.	0		
	3	2	.			
		3	.	2		
		3	.	2		
			.	0	3	2

> × 100 moves the digits two places to the left.

> When writing the answers down, these zeros are not needed.

Solution

Use a place-value diagram to help you.

a $3.2 \times 100 = 320$
b $0.32 \times 1000 = 320$
c $32 \div 10 = 3.2$
d $3.2 \div 100 = 0.032$

Activity

Construct a slider

① Copy this grid carefully onto cardboard and cut it out.

Th	H	T	O	.	t	h	th
		6	3	.	2		

2 cm   0.5 cm

② Cut three slits in the positions marked with the three red dashed lines.
③ Cut a long strip of card, about one centimetre wide and twice as long as the grid.
④ Feed the strip up through the first slit, down through the second (under the decimal point) and up through the third. Check that it slides smoothly through the slits.
⑤ Write in pencil a number in the middle line of the grid. For example, write **63.2**.
⑥ Write the same number onto your cardboard strip, with the digits lined up with the digits on the grid.
⑦ Now slide your cardboard strip one space to the right to divide by 10, or one space to the left to multiply by 10. Move two spaces to divide or multiply by 100.
⑧ Does it work well? What could be better?

Conceptual understanding

12 Working with decimals

245

Worked example

A length of wood is to be cut into ten equal pieces. The wood is 7.6 m long.

a How long is each piece of wood in metres?

b To change metres to millimetres, you multiply by 1000. Work out the length of one piece of wood in millimetres.

Solution

a To cut 7.6 m into ten equal pieces, the calculation is 7.6 ÷ 10.

Dividing by 10 moves all the digits one step to the right. So each piece of wood is 0.76 m long.

H	T	O	.	t	h	th
		7	.	6		
			.	7	6	

So 7.6 ÷ 10 = 0.76.

b There are 1000 mm in 1 m. To find the length of each piece of wood in mm, multiply 0.76 by 1000.

So each piece of wood is 760 mm long.

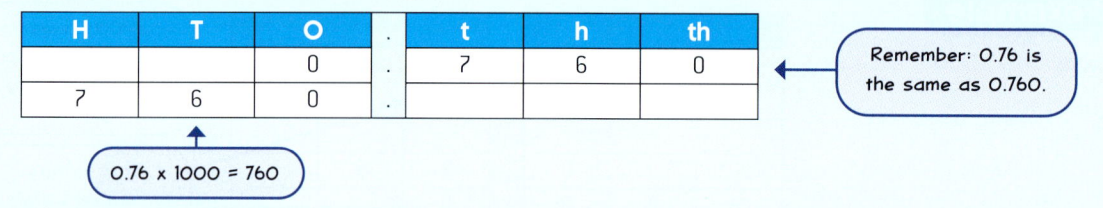

H	T	O	.	t	h	th
		0	.	7	6	0
7	6	0	.			

Remember: 0.76 is the same as 0.760.

0.76 × 1000 = 760

Worked example

a Work out 1.3 ÷ 0.1.

b Work out 4.67 ÷ 0.01.

Solution

a How many 0.1s are there in 1.3?

1.3												
1										0.3		
0.1	0.1	0.1	0.1	0.1	0.1	0.1	0.1	0.1	0.1	0.1	0.1	0.1

There are thirteen 0.1s in 1.3.

So 1.3 ÷ 0.1 = 13.

Th	H	T	O	.	t	h	th
			1	.	3		
		1	3	.			

Dividing by 0.1 has the same effect as multiplying by 10.

b Think about 4.67 ÷ 0.01 as 'how many 0.01s are there in 4.67?'

There are four hundred 0.01s in 4, sixty 0.01s in 0.6 and seven 0.01s in 0.07.

So 4.67 ÷ 0.01 = 467.

Th	H	T	O	.	t	h	th
			4	.	6	7	
	4	6	7	.			

Dividing by 0.01 has the same effect as multiplying by 100.

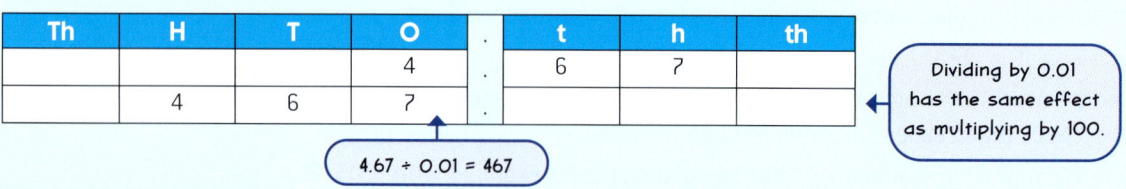

4.67 ÷ 0.01 = 467

Discussion activity

Apart from in Mathematics lessons, where else do you use decimals? This could be in other subjects at school or in your everyday lives.

12.1 Now try these

Band 1 questions

For questions 1 to 6, use a place-value table like this one.

TTh	Th	H	T	O	.	t	h	th	tth
			7	6	.				
					.				

1 Work out these.
  a 76 × 10
  b 192.025 × 10
  c 970 × 10
  d 65.003 × 10

2 Work out these.
  a 25.3 × 100
  b 6.723 × 100
  c 868.4 × 100
  d 26.023 × 100

Remember
- Dividing by 0.1 is the same as multiplying by 10.
- Dividing by 0.01 is the same as multiplying by 100.
- Multiplying by 0.1 is the same as dividing by 10.
- Multiplying by 0.01 is the same as dividing by 100.

3 Work out these.
  a 18.423 × 1000
  b 0.0021 × 1000
  c 651.36 × 1000
  d 10.2 × 1000

4 Work out these.
  a 76 ÷ 10
  b 192.025 ÷ 10
  c 970 ÷ 10
  d 65.003 ÷ 10

5 Work out these.
  a 25.3 ÷ 100
  b 6.723 ÷ 100
  c 868.4 ÷ 100
  d 26.023 ÷ 100

6 Work out these.
  a 18.423 ÷ 1000
  b 0.0021 ÷ 1000
  c 651.36 ÷ 1000
  d 10.2 ÷ 1000

7 Copy and complete these calculations.
  a 25.7 × 10 =
  b 0.257 × 100 =
  c 0.00257 × 1000 =
  d 2310 ÷ 10 =
  e 231 ÷ 100 =
  f 2.31 ÷ 1000 =

8 Elwyn multiplies the number 1.2 by 100.
His working is shown in the table. What has Elwyn done wrong?

Th	H	T	O	.	t	h	th
			1	.	2		
			0	.	0	1	2

Band 2 questions

9 Copy the diagram. Fill in each flag to show which operation you need to use.
Choose from × 10, × 100, × 1000, ÷ 10, ÷ 100, ÷ 1000.

7.4 →(× 10)→ 74 → 7400 → 7.4

0.0074 → 7.4 → 740 → 0.74

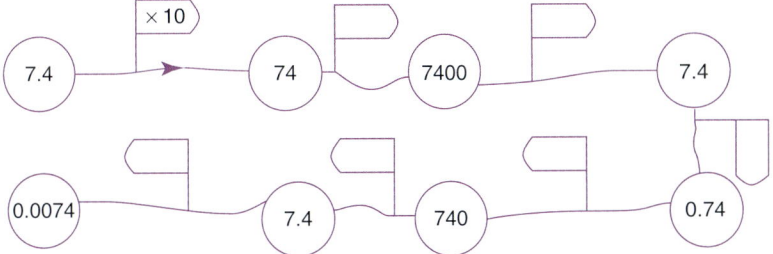

10 A whole number has three digits. It is put through this number chain.

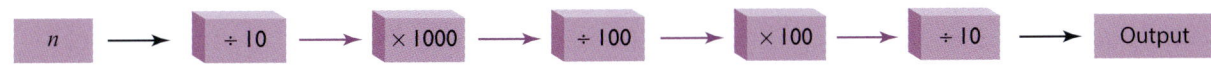

n → ÷ 10 → × 1000 → ÷ 100 → × 100 → ÷ 10 → Output

Which of these could be the output and which ones could not? How do you know?
  a 3250
  b 16700
  c 42.5
  d 0.034
  e 1.6

11 Heledd wants to change 6.8 into 0.068. She does it in two steps as follows:

6.8 ÷ 10 = 0.68

0.68 ÷ 10 = 0.068

How can Heledd change 6.8 into 0.068 using the operations × 10 and ÷ 10

  a in four steps

  b in eight steps?

  c Explain why Heledd can't solve the problem using three steps.

12 Two of these calculations are **not** correct. Which ones?

| 400 ÷ 10 = 40 | 400 ÷ 100 = 4 | 40 ÷ 10 = 0.4 | 40 ÷ 100 = 0.4 | 4 ÷ 10 = 0.04 | 4 ÷ 100 = 0.04 |

13 Fiona is in charge of a stall at the school fete.

She starts with a float of 10p coins.

How many 10p coins are needed for a float of

  a £5   **b** £10   **c** £12.50   **d** £19.90?

A float is money available at the start used for giving change.

14 The numbers in this table are found by multiplying or dividing the numbers in the middle row by 10, 100 or 1000. Copy and complete the table.

×1000				42 000 000
×100	2300		46 100	
×10	230		4610	
Number	23	3000		2750
÷10	2.3			
÷100	0.23		4.61	
÷1000		3		

15 Write down the answers to the following.

  a **i** How many 0.1s are there in 3?

   ii 3 ÷ 0.1 =

  b **i** How many 0.1s are there in 3.2?

   ii 3.2 ÷ 0.1 =

  c **i** How many 0.01s are there in 3?

   ii 3 ÷ 0.01 =

  d **i** How many 0.01s are there in 3.2?

   ii 3.2 ÷ 0.01 =

  e Complete the rules:

   i Dividing by 0.1 is the same as multiplying by _____.

   ii Dividing by 0.01 is the same as multiplying by _____.

Band 3 questions

16 Rhian and Suresh are playing a game with cards.

Rhian has these cards: × 1000 | ÷ 10 | × 100 .

Suresh has these cards: × 1 | ÷ 100 | × 100 .

The starting number is 10. The first person to reach the number 100 wins.

Rhian goes first.

  a Can Rhian win on her first go? Which card would she need?

Rhian plays her ÷10 card.

b What number does that give?

Now it is Suresh's turn. He carries on after Rhian.

c Which card should Suresh play to win on his first go?

Rhian and Suresh now start a new game. They have the same function cards as before.

This time Suresh goes first and he plays his ×1 card.

d What number does that give?

17 Owen has a set of cards like this:

×0.1   ÷0.1

There are lots of each card in the set.

Use these cards to fill in the boxes.

You don't have to use each card every time.

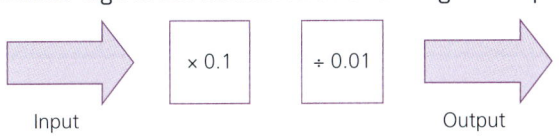

a 5.2 □□□ = 0.52
b 70.6 □□□ = 0.706
c 2 □□□ = 20
d 5.9 □□□ = 59

18 A three-digit whole number has no zero digits. It is put through this number machine:

Input → ×0.1 → ÷0.01 → Output

Which of these could be the output? How do you know?

a 41 300 **b** 13.4 **c** 0.026 **d** 5670 **e** 9.6

12.2 Adding and subtracting decimals

Skill checker

1 Find the two missing digits.

```
    1  7
+  4  □  6
─────────
    4  9
```

2 Find the two missing digits.

```
   5  2  1
-  3  6  □
─────────
      1  8
```

3 Find the three missing digits.

```
   4  □  5
+  3  4  □
─────────
      3  9
```

4 Find the three missing digits.

```
   9  □  □
-  3  9  7
─────────
      9  7
```

▶ Adding decimals

You can also use the column method to add and subtract decimals.

Make sure you keep the decimal points lined up.

Begin working with the column to the right and move towards the left.

Worked example

Find:

a 17.21 + 402.07

b 113.25 + 802.9

Remember
Ones are also called units.

Solution

a 17.21 + 402.07

```
     1 7 . 2 1
+    4 0 2 . 0 7
   ─────────────
   4 1 9 . 2 8
```

Keep the decimal points lined up.

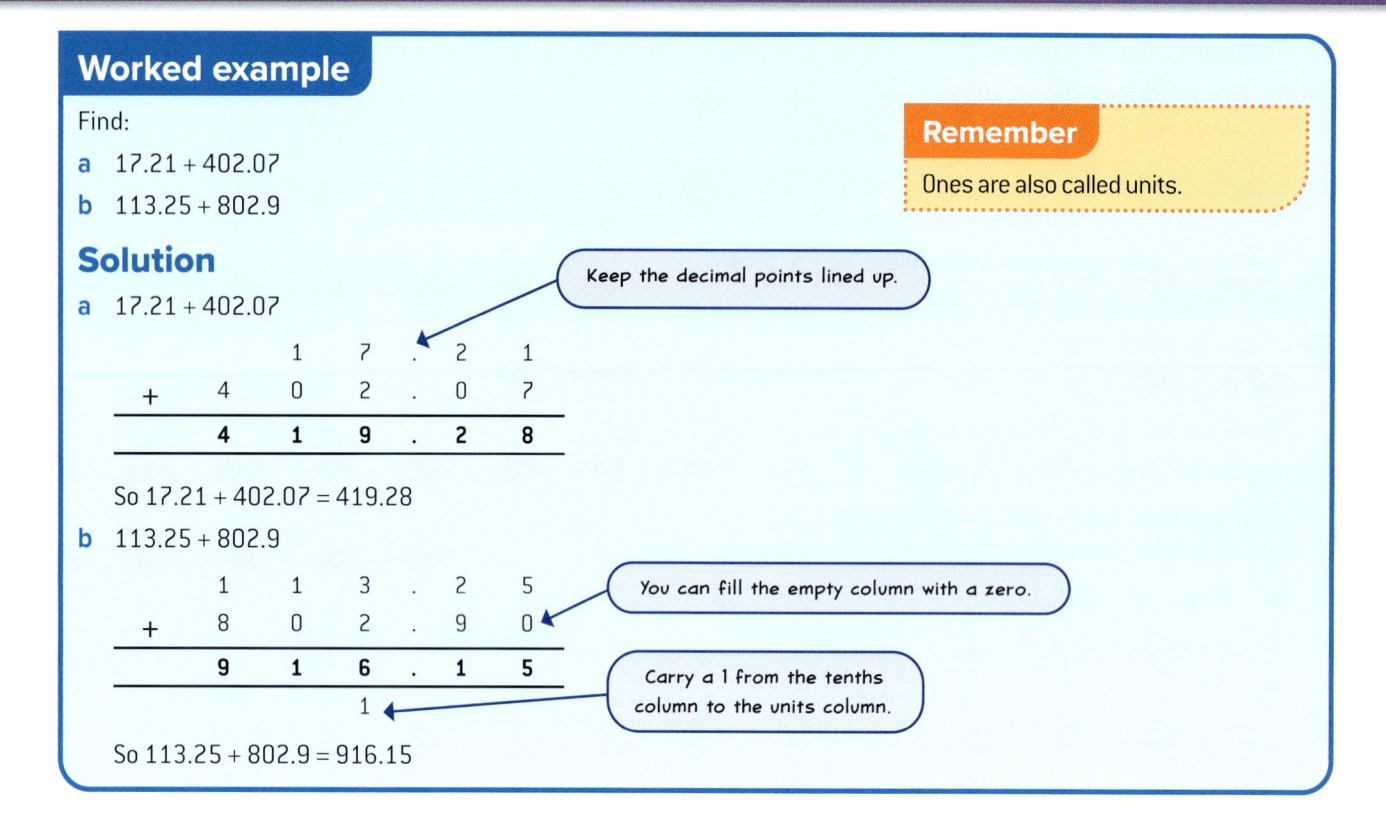

So 17.21 + 402.07 = 419.28

b 113.25 + 802.9

```
   1 1 3 . 2 5
+    8 0 2 . 9 0
   ─────────────
   9 1 6 . 1 5
         1
```

You can fill the empty column with a zero.

Carry a 1 from the tenths column to the units column.

So 113.25 + 802.9 = 916.15

▶ Subtracting decimals

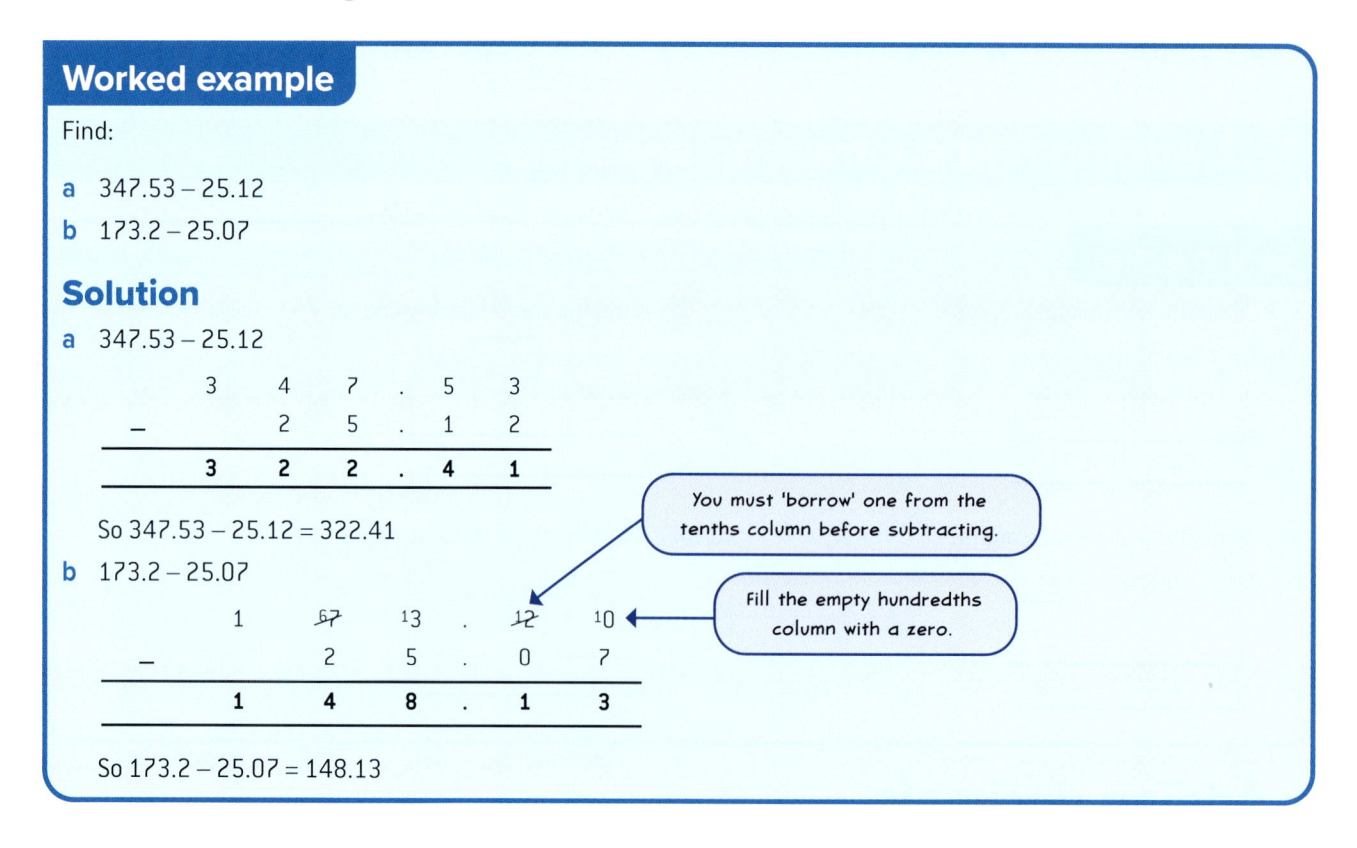

Worked example

Find:

a 347.53 − 25.12

b 173.2 − 25.07

Solution

a 347.53 − 25.12

```
   3 4 7 . 5 3
−    2 5 . 1 2
   ─────────────
   3 2 2 . 4 1
```

So 347.53 − 25.12 = 322.41

b 173.2 − 25.07

```
   1 ₆7 ¹³ . ₁2 ¹0
−      2 5 . 0 7
   ─────────────
   1 4 8 . 1 3
```

You must 'borrow' one from the tenths column before subtracting.

Fill the empty hundredths column with a zero.

So 173.2 − 25.07 = 148.13

12 Working with decimals

Worked example

Two teachers take ten students on a bus for a school trip.

The students' bus tickets cost £3.65 each. The teachers' tickets cost £7.10 each.

How much money do they spend altogether on the tickets?

Solution

Work out the cost of the students' tickets:

10 × 3.65 = 36.50

Money must have two decimal places, so this is £36.50.

Now include the two teachers. The calculation is:

36.50 + 7.10 + 7.10

Keep the decimal points lined up:

```
    3  6 . 5  0
+      7 . 1  0
       7 . 1  0
    ─────────────
    5  0 . 7  0
       2
```

The total cost is £50.70.

Remember

▶ Keep the decimal point lined up when you add or subtract decimals.

▶ If it helps, make sure the decimal numbers have the same number of decimal places by putting zeros in any blank columns.

12.2 Now try these

Band 1 questions

1 Work out these.

| a | 4.2 + 3.6 | b | 18.1 + 1.7 | c | 24.2 + 34.5 |
| d | 6.9 − 5.4 | e | 17.5 − 5.2 | f | 28.6 − 7.3 |

2 Work out these.

| a | 5.15 + 3.21 | b | 14.01 + 2.87 | c | 25.36 + 31.42 |
| d | 6.95 − 5.42 | e | 20.99 − 10.98 | f | 16.48 − 5.32 |

3 Work out these.

| a | 6.26 + 3.65 | b | 18.28 + 0.17 | c | 17.76 + 1.42 |
| d | 5.29 − 3.31 | e | 14.12 − 12.04 | f | 10.62 − 10.34 |

4 Mark Eli's homework. Write out the corrections for any answers that are wrong.

142.78 + 9.12 = 161   142.78 − 9.12 = 133.66

142.78 + 99.12 = 251   142.78 − 99.12 = 23.66

5 Rhys earns £6.50 washing windows for his parents.

At the Halloween school disco he spends £2.25 getting his face painted and 95p on an orange juice.

How much money does he have left?

6 Shena needs the following items before she goes back to school.

- Geometry set £4.25
- Pens and highlighters £6.95
- Calculator £9.95

a How much do the items cost altogether?

b Shena pays with two £10 notes and a £5 note. How much change should she receive?

251

Band 2 questions

7 Work out these.
  a 5.96 + 6.2
  b 78.5 + 0.56
  c 2.57 + 91.6
  d 16.81 − 12.9
  e 20.69 − 2.8
  f 1 − 0.99

8 Here is some of Aled's homework. What has he done wrong in each part?

  a
  ```
      5 . 9
  +   1 . 2
  ─────────
      4 . 7   ✗
  ```

  b
  ```
        1 . 2 3
  +     5 7 . 6
  ─────────────
        6 9 9    ✗
  ```

9 Megan has placed some very cold water in the sunshine in a science experiment.
The temperature of the water before and after the experiment is measured by a thermometer and is shown below.
By how much did the temperature of the water increase in the sunshine?

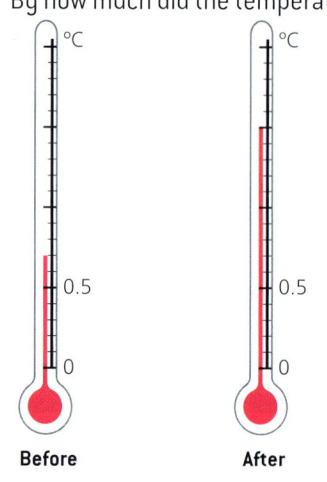

Before   After

10 Nine mats, shown in the diagram, are placed on the floor of a school hall for a game. The areas of eight of the mats are shown.

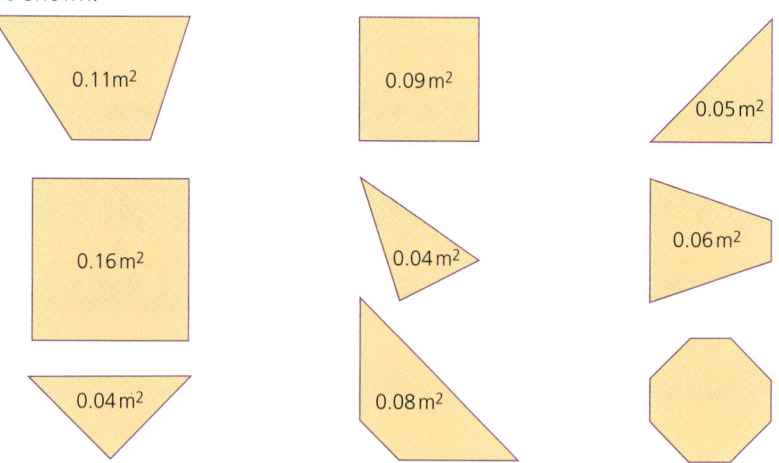

0.11 m²   0.09 m²   0.05 m²

0.16 m²   0.04 m²   0.06 m²

0.04 m²   0.08 m²

  a Find the sum of the areas of the trapezium-shaped mats.
  b Which is greater: the sum of the areas of the square mats or the sum of the areas of the triangular mats? By how much?
  c The sum of the areas of all the mats is 0.7 m². Find the area of the octagonal mat.

11 Rakhi has some cards.

She uses them to make calculations with an answer of 17.49.

| +10.67 | −1.6 | +2.67 | +12.27 | −5.72 | +17.99 |

Copy and complete these calculations.

a 6.82 ☐ = 17.49

b 6.82 ☐ ☐ = 17.49

12 The cities of Decimalia, Numberton and Calcuville all lie along a straight road, with Numberton in the middle.

In Decimalia there is a sign saying:

> Numberton 24.9 km
> Calcuville 37.8 km

a How far is it from Numberton to Calcuville?

b The distance from Decimalia to Numberton is greater than the distance from Numberton to Calcuville. By how much?

13 A scientist has seven beakers of liquids.

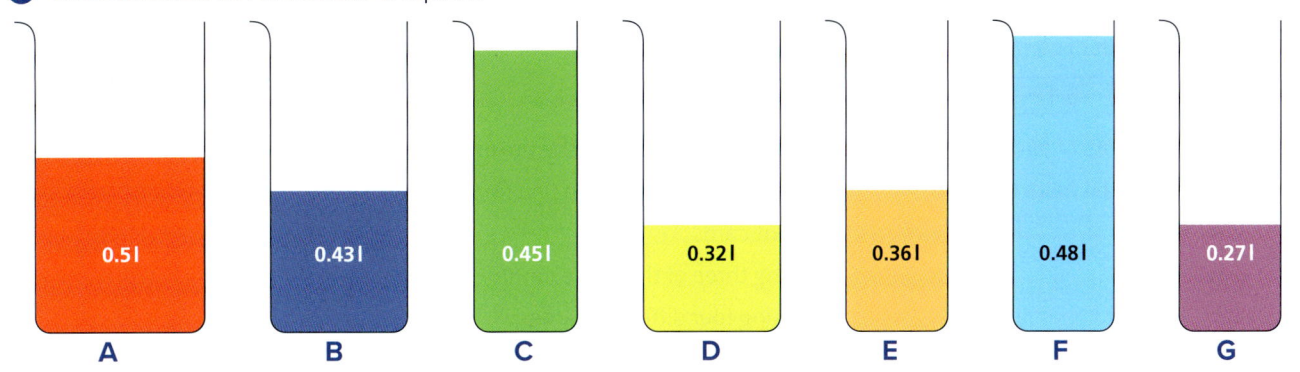

A: 0.5 l
B: 0.43 l
C: 0.45 l
D: 0.32 l
E: 0.36 l
F: 0.48 l
G: 0.27 l

She knows that:
- mixing liquids A and B will cause a huge explosion
- mixing liquids C and D will create a poisonous gas
- mixing liquids C and F will make a terrible smell
- mixing liquids F and G will form a solid.

Without mixing any of the liquids that would give her the problems listed above:

a How could she combine three of the liquids to make exactly 1.3 litres?

b How could she combine four of the liquids to make more than 1.65 litres?

14 Ceri orders her grocery shopping online.

a Copy and complete the missing amounts in all the blank spaces.

2 large bottles of milk at £1.55 each	£
3 cereal bars at 62p each	£
1 box breakfast cereal	£3.75
4 bread rolls at 36p each	£
1 box of 12 large eggs	£2.88
Order total	£
Delivery charge	£2.50
Total amount to pay	£

b Ceri has a budget of £20. How much money does she have left in her budget after paying for the shopping?

15 A sequence of nine numbers is:

| 0.1 | 0.2 | 0.3 | 0.4 | 0.5 | 0.6 | 0.7 | 0.8 | 0.9 |

Find a quick way to calculate the sum of all nine numbers.

Band 3 questions

16 Find:
- a 601.3 + 10.727
- b 6548.23 + 78.199
- c 12.466 + 7.534
- d 89.231 − 64.549
- e 942.11 − 54.23
- f 0.844 − 0.097

17 Suki's pen has leaked over her maths homework.

Copy her working and replace the ink splats with the correct numbers.

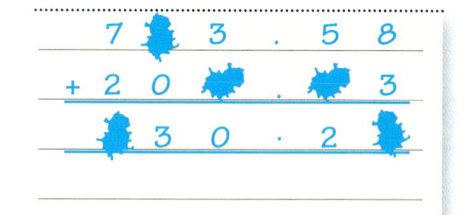

```
    7 ▓ 3 . 5 8
+   2 0 ▓ . ▓ 3
    ─────────────
    ▓ 3 0 . 2 ▓
```

18 Cai has a set of cards like this:

| +0.1 | +0.12 | +0.14 | +0.16 | +0.18 |

There are lots of each card in the set. Use these cards to fill in the boxes.

There may be more than one way to answer the questions. Can you find all the ways?

- a 1 ▢ ▢ = 1.3 using two different cards
- b 70.6 ▢ ▢ ▢ = 71.08 using three of the same cards
- c 2 ▢ ▢ ▢ ▢ = 2.6 using four different cards
- d 99.8 ▢ ▢ ▢ ▢ = 100.2 using four of the same cards

19 One house brick is in the shape of a cuboid. Its length is 0.25 m and its width is 0.1 m. Jac is building a wall for a small shed. He begins by laying ten of these house bricks end to end and an eleventh brick sideways, as shown.

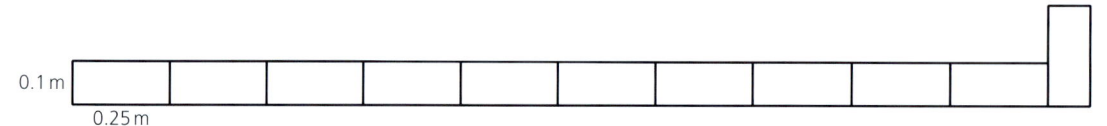

0.1 m
0.25 m

- a How long is this section of wall?
- b The height of a different type of brick is 0.075 metres. When Jac has put down ten layers of these bricks, he must add a layer of smaller bricks that are 0.05 metres in height. How tall is the wall at this stage?

20 In these arithmagons, the number in each square is the sum of the numbers in the circles it lies between. Copy and complete these arithmagons.

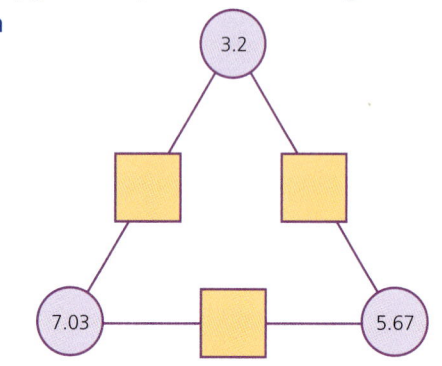

a

- Top circle: 3.2
- Bottom-left circle: 7.03
- Bottom-right circle: 5.67

b

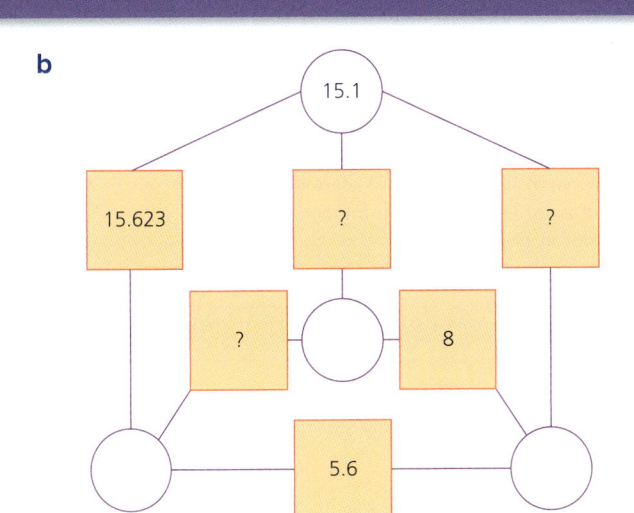

15.623 15.1 ? ?

? 8

5.6

c

1.97
8.3   6.25
13.36   9.95
12.7

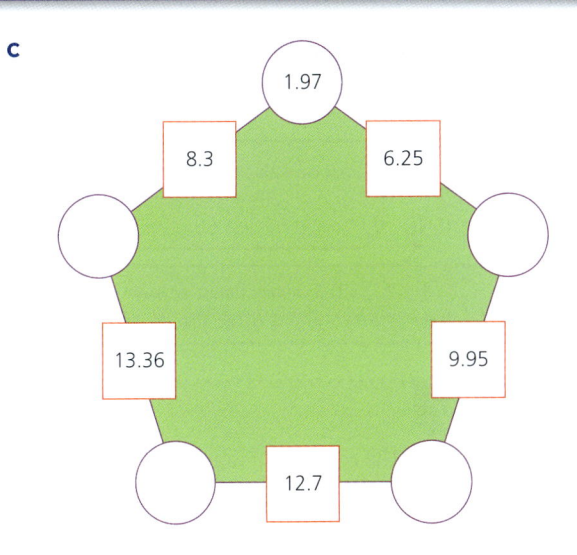

12.3 Multiplying and dividing decimals

Skill checker

① Find your way through the maze! Start on the green 12 and finish on the red 3. You can move up, down, left or right. You can't visit the same square more than once.

Start →

12	÷2	6	×4	48	÷4	12	×6	72	÷9
×9	8	÷8	24	×8	6	÷10	40	×5	8
96	÷2	3	×8	6	÷3	4	×5	80	÷5
×7	11	÷3	5	÷2	8	÷4	20	×6	6
6	÷4	1	×12	12	÷3	5	×12	5	÷9
×8	9	÷7	8	÷4	10	÷6	60	×11	10
2	÷8	16	×6	2	÷5	6	×6	36	÷4
×5	3	÷4	12	÷9	1	÷5	30	×8	9
10	÷3	1	×10	10	÷2	5	×6	3	÷3
×10	100	÷2	60	÷5	12	÷4	3	×1	3

← Finish

② Bryn the barber does adults' and childrens' haircuts.

He charges £12 for a haircut for an adult.

On Tuesday he does 20 haircuts and makes £207.

Nine of the haircuts were for adults and the rest were for children.

a How many children came in for a haircut?
b How much does Bryn charge for a child's haircut?

▶ Multiplying decimals

You can use the times tables to help you to multiply decimals.

12 × 3 = 36

1.2 × 3 = 3.6 ◀── 1.2 is ten times smaller than 12 so the answer to 1.2 × 3 is ten times smaller than 36. There is just one digit after the decimal point in the question, so one digit after the decimal point in the answer.

1.2 × 0.3 = 0.36
▲
└── 0.3 is ten times smaller than 3 so the answer to 1.2 × 0.3 is ten times smaller than 3.6. There are two digits after the decimal point in the question, so two digits after the decimal point in the answer.

Activity

Harri says that the number of digits after the decimal point in the answer is always the number of digits after the decimal point in the question.

1.2 × 3 = 3.6 has one digit after the decimal point.

1.2 × 0.3 = 0.36 has two digits after the decimal point.

Now answer these.

① 3 × 2 = 6
so 0.3 × 2 =
and 0.3 × 0.2 =

② 6 × 12 = 72
so 0.6 × 12 =
and 0.6 × 1.2 =
and 0.6 × 0.12 =

③ 12 × 11 = 132
so 1.2 × 11 =
and 1.2 × 1.1

④ 14 × 3 = 42
so 1.4 × 3 =
and 1.4 × 0.3 =

⑤ 5 × 2 = 10
so 0.5 × 2 =
and 0.5 × 0.2 =

Is Harri right?
Investigate this further by trying some on your calculator. Can you find examples of when Harri might be incorrect and explain why?

▶ Dividing decimals

Worked example

Find 2 ÷ 0.4.

Solution

Method 1

The bar model diagram below shows that there are five 0.4s in 2.

2				
0.4	0.4	0.4	0.4	0.4

0.4 + 0.4 + 0.4 + 0.4 + 0.4 = 2
so 2 ÷ 0.4 = 5

Method 2

To help you to divide by a decimal, use a similar calculation involving whole numbers.

20 ÷ 4 = 5
so 20 ÷ 0.4 = 50 ◀── 0.4 is 10 times smaller than 4.
and 2 ÷ 0.4 = 5 ◀── 2 is 10 times smaller than 20.

12 Working with decimals

> **Worked example**
>
> Find 5 ÷ 0.02.
>
> ### Solution
> **Method 1**
>
> You would need to add five 0.02s to make 0.1.
>
> | 0.1 | | | | |
> |---|---|---|---|---|
> | 0.02 | 0.02 | 0.02 | 0.02 | 0.02 |
>
> 0.02 + 0.02 + 0.02 + 0.02 + 0.02 = 0.1
>
> So you would need to add fifty 0.02s to make 1.
>
> So you would need to add 250 0.02s to make 5.
>
> **Method 2**
> Use a similar calculation involving whole numbers.
> You know that:
> 50 ÷ 2 = 25
> so 50 ÷ 0.2 = 250 ← *0.2 is 10 times smaller than 2.*
> and 50 ÷ 0.02 = 2500 ← *0.02 is 10 times smaller than 0.2.*
> and 5 ÷ 0.02 = 250 ← *5 is 10 times smaller than 50.*

> **Worked example**
>
> Use the bar model diagram below to complete the following:
>
> | 1.2 | | | |
> |---|---|---|---|
> | 0.3 | 0.3 | 0.3 | 0.3 |
>
> How many lots of 0.3 make 1.2?
>
> So 0.3 × _____ = 1.2
>
> and 1.2 ÷ 0.3 = _____
>
> ### Solution
> 4 lots of 0.3 make 1.2.
> So 0.3 × 4 = 1.2
> and 1.2 ÷ 0.3 = 4

> **Worked example**
>
> Find 0.6^2.
>
> ### Solution
> $0.6^2 = 0.6 \times 0.6$
>
> $= 0.36$ ← *You know that 6 × 6 = 36. So 0.6 × 0.6 = 0.36.*
>
> *There are two digits after the decimal point because altogether there are two digits after the decimal point in the numbers in the question.*
>
> **Remember**
> Squaring something means multiplying it by itself.

257

12.3 Now try these

Band 1 questions

Fluency

1. **a** Copy and complete this calculation.

   $8 \times 4 = $ _____

   b Copy the bar model diagram. Fill in the number in the top bar.

0.4	0.4	0.4	0.4	0.4	0.4	0.4	0.4

   c Copy and complete this calculation.

   $8 \times 0.4 = $ _____

Strategic competence

2. **a** Work out $24 \div 3$.
   b Work out $2.4 \div 3$.
   c A father shares £2.40 equally between his three children. How much does each child receive?

3. **a** Work out $42 \div 7$.
   b Work out $4.2 \div 7$.
   c A piece of wood of length 4.2 metres is cut into seven pieces of equal length. How long is each piece?

Logical reasoning

4. Work out these.

   a i 4×3 **b** i 5×2 **c** i 8×3

   ii 0.4×3 ii 0.5×2 ii 0.8×3

   iii 4×0.3 iii 5×0.2 iii 8×0.3

5. Work out these.

   a i $25 \div 5$ **b** i $72 \div 8$ **c** i $36 \div 3$

   ii $2.5 \div 5$ ii $7.2 \div 8$ ii $3.6 \div 3$

   iii $25 \div 0.5$ iii $72 \div 0.8$ iii $36 \div 0.3$

Band 2 questions

Fluency

6. Find the answers to these calculations.

   a i 3×2 **b** i 5×3 **c** i 1×9 **d** i 6×4 **e** i 8×7

   ii 3×0.2 ii 5×0.3 ii 0.1×9 ii 6×0.4 ii 0.8×7

   iii 0.3×0.2 iii 0.5×0.3 iii 0.1×0.9 iii 0.6×0.4 iii 0.8×0.7

7. Find the answers to these calculations.

   a i $16 \div 2$ **b** i $15 \div 3$ **c** i $18 \div 9$ **d** i $28 \div 4$ **e** i $35 \div 7$

   ii $16 \div 0.2$ ii $15 \div 0.3$ ii $1.8 \div 9$ ii $28 \div 0.4$ ii $3.5 \div 7$

   iii $1.6 \div 0.2$ iii $1.5 \div 0.3$ iii $1.8 \div 0.9$ iii $2.8 \div 0.4$ iii $3.5 \div 0.7$

8. Copy and complete the following calculations.

   a $2 \times 0.7 + 0.3 = $ **b** $0.8 \times 3 - 1 = $ **c** $2 + 3 \times 0.6 = $ **d** $4 - 0.5 \times 3 = $

   e $0.8 \div 4 + 1.7 = $ **f** $6 \div 0.2 + 2.1 = $ **g** $9 - 1.5 \div 3 = $ **h** $42 - 9 \div 0.3 = $

9. Copy and complete the following calculations.

   a $0.1^2 = $ **b** $0.2^2 = $ **c** $0.3^2 = $ **d** $0.4^2 = $

> You know that $1 \times 1 = 1$.
> 0.1^2 means '0.1×0.1'.
> So there will be two digits after the decimal point in your answer.

12 Working with decimals

10 Copy and complete the following calculations.

a $0.1^3 =$
b $0.2^3 =$
c $0.3^3 =$
d $0.4^3 =$

> You know that 1 × 1 × 1 = 1.
> 0.1^3 means '0.1 × 0.1 × 0.1'.
> So there will be three digits after the decimal point in your answer.

11 Copy and complete the following.

a 6 ÷ 2 = 3
   6 ÷ 0.2 =
   0.6 ÷ 0.2 =
   0.06 ÷ 0.2 =

b 24 ÷ 6 = 4
   24 ÷ 0.6 =
   2.4 ÷ 0.6 =
   0.24 ÷ 0.6 =

c 132 ÷ 12 = 11
   132 ÷ 1.2 =
   13.2 ÷ 1.2 =
   1.32 ÷ 1.2 =

Band 3 questions

12 Work out these.

a The square root of 0.01
b The square root of 0.16
c The square root of 0.25
d The square root of 0.36
e The square root of 0.49

13 Work out these.

a The cube root of 0.001
b The cube root of 0.008
c The cube root of 0.027
d The cube root of 0.064

14 Work out these.

a $\sqrt{0.36}$
b $\sqrt{0.49}$
c $\sqrt{0.81}$
d $\sqrt[3]{0.027}$

15 Work out these.

a $0.4 + \sqrt{0.36}$
b $\sqrt{1.44} + 1.2 \div 4$
c $1 - 2 \times \sqrt{0.49}$
d $\sqrt{0.81} + 3 \times 12$
e $6 \div 0.2 - \sqrt{1.21}$
f $2 - 0.6 \times \sqrt[3]{0.064}$

16 a Find the output for this function machine.

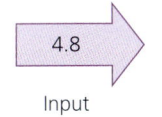

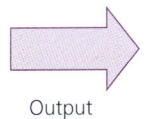

4.8 (Input) → ÷ 4 → × 5 → Output

b Find the input for this function machine.

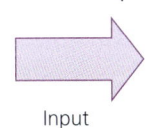

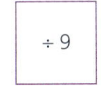

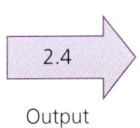

Input → ÷ 9 → × 12 → 2.4 (Output)

17 What a mess! This multiplication square has had ink spilt on it. Can you copy it out and fill in the squares with the correct numbers?

×	0.1	0.02		
0.2			0.1	
2				
3		0.06		24
				80

Logical reasoning

18 Given that 43 × 87 = 3741, use your knowledge of place value to work out the calculations below.

   a   43 × 8.7
   b   4.3 × 8.7
   c   43 × 0.87
   d   0.43 × 8.7
   e   0.43 × 0.87
   f   4300 × 0.87

Key words

Here is a list of the key words you met in this chapter.

Decimal	Decimal place	Decimal point
Hundreds	Hundredths	Ones
Place value	Tens	Tenths
Thousandths	Units	Thousands

Use the glossary at the back of this book to check any you are unsure about.

12 Working with decimals

Review exercise: working with decimals

Band 1 questions

1 Work out the answers to these calculations.
  a 14.1 + 5.6
  b 16.9 − 14.8
  c 26.26 + 468.2
  d 108.31 − 67.5
  e 34.654 + 29.78
  f 13.298 − 4.909

2 A painter is painting a bedroom pink.
  He has 1.8 litres of red paint in one tin and 2.3 litres of white paint in another.
  He mixes them both together in a large container to make pink paint.
  a How much pink paint does the painter end up with?
  b The painter uses 2.9 litres of paint. How much is left?

3 Copy the place-value table. Divide these numbers by 0.1, writing the answers below each of the original numbers.

Tth	Th	H	T	O	.	t	h	th	tth
			1	7	.				
					.				
		4	0	2	.	0	7	8	
					.				

4 Repeat question **3** but this time multiply by 0.1. Do you need to work the answer out on a calculator?

5 Pedr is making a rabbit hutch.
  He needs ten pieces of wood that are 0.4 m long and ten pieces that are 0.8 m long.
  He can buy wood in 3 m lengths.
  How many of these 3 m lengths of wood does Pedr need to buy?

6 Last year the price of a CoolPhone 1 was £245.95.
  This year the CoolPhone 2 is launched. It costs £279.98.
  The price of the CoolPhone 1 is reduced by £69.99.
  How much cheaper is it to buy a CoolPhone 1 than a CoolPhone 2?

7 The first and second place onions in a giant onion competition weigh 52.8 kg and 47.4 kg.
  One of the judges says, 'The combined weight of these two onions is more than 100 kg!'
  Is the judge correct? Justify your answer.

8 In an ice-dancing competition, Jayne and Christopher compete together as a pair.
  The five judges award marks out of 6.0.
  Two of the judges give Jayne and Christopher 6.0, two of them give 5.8 and one of them gives 5.6.
  a What is their total score?
  b Before Jayne and Christopher had danced, the pair in the lead had scored 5.7, 5.7, 5.8, 5.8 and 5.9.
     Do Jayne and Christopher go into the lead?

Band 2 questions

9 Copy the place-value table below and complete the answer line.

	H	T	O	.	t	h	th
		1	7	.	8		
+			6	.	3	7	
+	4	0	2	.	0	7	8
				.			

261

10 Copy the diagram.

a Fill in the blank spaces in the flags and the circles. The operation in each flag will be plus or minus a decimal number.

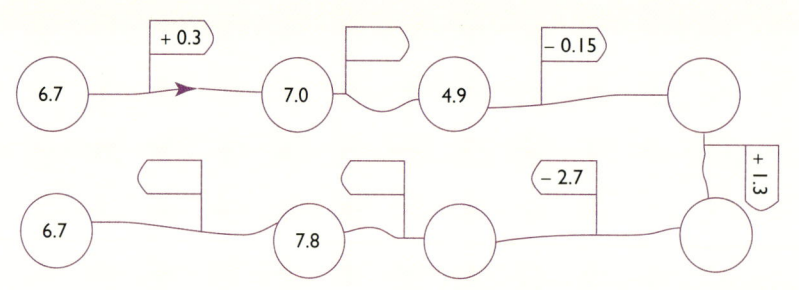

b The starting number is 6.7. After 7 operations the finishing number is also 6.7. Do you think that the finishing number would always be the same as the starting number if the operations were kept the same?

11 The decimal number 2.46 is put through this number chain.

2.46 → −0.35 → +0.521 → −1.89 → +0.4 → Output

a Without calculating the output, can you decide which one of the numbers below could be the output and which ones could not? How do you know?

3.25   3.779   4.25   1.141   1.6

b Calculate the output value to check your answer to part **a**.

12 Ariana and Llewellyn are in the pharmacy.

a Ariana buys some emery boards, cotton wool, nail scissors and nail polish.
  i How much does this cost altogether?
  ii How much change will she get from a £10 note?

b Llewellyn buys some hair gel, deodorant and soap.
  i How much does this cost altogether?
  ii How much change will he get from a £10 note?

Emery boards   99p
Cotton wool   £1.45
Nail scissors   £2.49
Nail polish   £4.50
Hair gel   £2.19
Deodorant   £2.29
Soap bar   £2.35

13 The Davies family consists of two adults and two children.
The family are planning a visit to Seren gym.

Gym price (per visit)	Member	Non-member
Adult	£4.97	£6.45
Child	£3.89	£4.48

a How much will a visit to the gym cost if all of the family are members?
b How much less do the family pay as members of the gym than they would if they were non-members?
c The Davies family always visit the gym together.
Gym membership costs them £39.98 a year.
How many times do the family have to visit the gym to make membership worthwhile?

Band 3 questions

14 Katie has a stack of ×0.1 cards and a stack of ÷0.1 cards.

She is trying to fill in the arrow below with cards that will change 4.2 into 0.042. She can use more than one card.

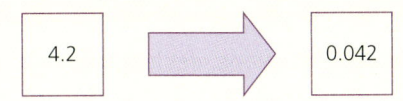

4.2 → 0.042

a Find a way to change 4.2 to 0.042:
   i using two cards
   ii using four cards
   iii using eight cards.
b Explain why Katie can't solve the problem using three cards.

15 A decimal number between 0.4 and 0.5 has three decimal places. It is put through this number machine.

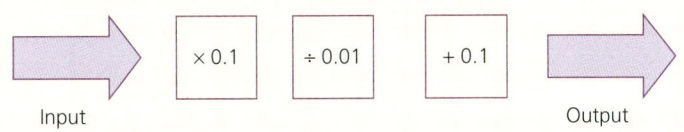

Input → ×0.1 → ÷0.01 → +0.1 → Output

Only one of the numbers below could be the output. Which one? How do you know?

3.899   5.201   4.25   4.05   0.455

16 Is it *always* true, *sometimes* true or *never* true that: when you add two decimal numbers between 0 and 1, the answer will be greater than 1?

- If you think *always*, explain how you can be so certain.
- If you think *never*, explain how you can be so certain.
- If you think *sometimes*, give two examples: one showing that it can be true and one showing that it can be false.

17 The Mountains of Mirth lie next to the ocean.

The highest peak is Mount Blackadder, marked with a B on the picture. Its peak is 7.86 km above sea level.

The table shows the heights of the mountains above sea level.

Peak name	Height above sea level (km)
Mount Atkinson (A)	3.75
Mount Blackadder (B)	7.86
Mount Cleese (C)	5.19
Mount Dibley (D)	4.71
Mount Everett (E)	4.58

The ocean is 1.1 km deep.

Beneath the sea surface lies Mountain Fawlty (marked F). It rises above the ocean floor exactly one tenth the height of Mount Blackadder.

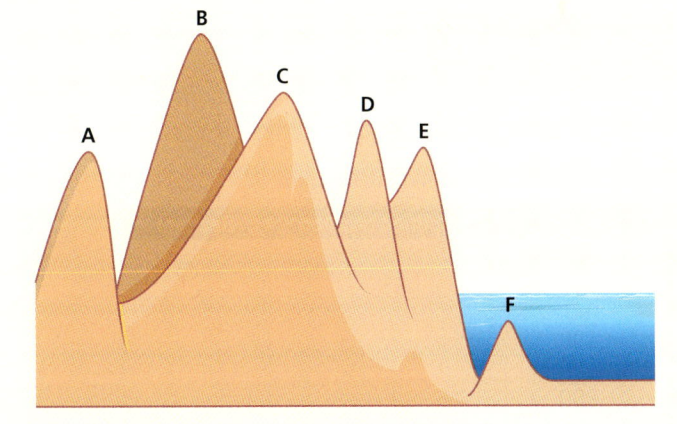

a On Saturday, a mountaineer climbs from sea level to the summit of Mount Atkinson and back down. The following day the mountaineer climbs Mount Cleese and back down to sea level.

How many kilometres, up and down, has the mountaineer climbed this weekend?

b A diver dives from the sea surface to the top of Mount Fawlty. How many kilometres has she dived?

c The diver is in radio contact with a climber at the top of Mount Everett. How high above the diver is the climber?

13 Percentages

Coming up...
- Understanding percentages
- Percentages of amounts
- Converting between fractions, decimals and percentages

Conceptual understanding

What's wrong with these signs and labels?

①
Materials
45% Wool
30% Cotton
25% Nylon
15% Polyester

②
0% OFF
ALL ITEMS
IN STORE TODAY!

③ In a packet of identically sized buttons there are five different colours, with the same number of each colour.

25% of the buttons are red.

④
Today only
Get 50% OFF
or half price
whichever is less.

13.1 Understanding percentages

Skill checker

Simplifying fractions and converting fractions to decimals are key skills in your work on percentages.

Copy and complete this table.

The first row has been done for you.

Fraction	Simplified fraction	Decimal
$\frac{45}{60}$	$\frac{3}{4}$	0.75
$\frac{90}{100}$		
$\frac{128}{200}$		
$\frac{24}{40}$		
$\frac{46}{50}$		
$\frac{16}{10}$		
$\frac{144}{120}$		

13 Percentages

The phrase 'per cent' means 'out of 100'. ◀── 'per' means 'out of'.

So, a percentage is a number of parts per hundred.

'cent' means '100'.

For example, 7% means 7 out of 100, or $\frac{7}{100}$.

Remember: the percentage sign means 'out of 100' so, for example:

30% = $\frac{30}{100}$, which **simplifies** to $\frac{3}{10}$.

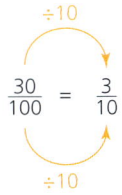

$\frac{30}{100} = \frac{3}{10}$ (÷10)

Simplifying a fraction is also called cancelling the fraction down.

Note
For a reminder of simplifying fractions, see Chapter 8.

The bar model diagram shows that 30% is three lots of 10%.

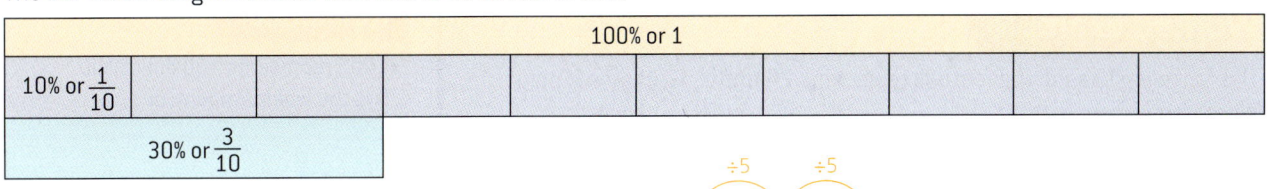

100% or 1										
10% or $\frac{1}{10}$									
30% or $\frac{3}{10}$									

As another example:

25% = $\frac{25}{100}$, which cancels down to $\frac{1}{4}$.

$\frac{25}{100} = \frac{5}{20} = \frac{1}{4}$ (÷5, ÷5)

The bar model diagram also shows that 25% is the same as $\frac{1}{4}$.

100% or 1			
25% or $\frac{1}{4}$	25% or $\frac{1}{4}$	25% or $\frac{1}{4}$	25% or $\frac{1}{4}$

Activity

① Fill in the blanks in this table.

Percentage	10%	20%	25%	30%	33$\frac{1}{3}$%	40%		60%	66$\frac{2}{3}$%		75%	80%	
Fraction	$\frac{1}{10}$		$\frac{1}{4}$	$\frac{3}{10}$			$\frac{1}{2}$			$\frac{7}{10}$			$\frac{9}{10}$

Try to remember these common percentages as fractions.

② Play this game in pairs. Make these percentage cards.

Deal five cards to each person.

Take it in turns to lay a card. Keep a running total of all the cards played.

The first player to take the total to exactly 100% wins the round. Or if a player takes the total above 100%, they lose the round.

Play three rounds.

1%	1%	1%	2%	2%
5%	5%	10%	10%	10%
20%	20%	25%	25%	30%
40%	50%	60%	70%	80%

▶ Percentages add up to 100%

Worked example

One season, a football team wins 35% of its games and draws 25%. What percentage of its games does the team lose?

Solution

100% − 35% − 25% = 40%

The team loses 40% of its games.

Note

Not all percentages add up to 100%. You will learn more about this in Book 2, Chapter 12.

▶ Expressing one quantity as a percentage of another

Worked example

The following season the football team wins 24 of the 40 games it plays. What percentage is this?

Remember

100% represents 100 out of 100. It is the whole amount, or 1.

Solution

The team has won $\frac{24}{40}$ of its games.

Calculator method

Firstly, turn the fraction of games won into a decimal:

$$\frac{24}{40} = 0.6$$

Type the fraction into your calculator, press $=$ then press $S \Leftrightarrow D$ to turn the fraction into a decimal.

Then turn the decimal into a percentage by multiplying by 100:

$$0.6 \times 100 = 60 = 60\%$$

Non-calculator method

$$\frac{24}{40} = \frac{6}{10} = \frac{60}{100} = 60\%$$

First cancel the fraction down, dividing top and bottom by 4. Then multiply top and bottom by 10 to make the denominator 100.

The team won 60% of its games.

Worked example

Ten children are playing in a park. Seven of them go home. What percentage of the children are left in the park?

Solution

Three of the ten children are left in the park.

$$\frac{3}{10} = \frac{30}{100} = 30\%$$

30% of the children are left.

Cross-curricular activity

The two official languages of Wales are English and Welsh.

In March 2021, the Office of National Statistics (ONS) reported on the number of Welsh speakers in Wales.

To the nearest hundred thousand, they found that 900,000 people over the age of 3 were able to speak Welsh, out of the three million people in Wales.

What percentage of people in Wales speak Welsh?

Worked example

Copy the line below and write a number in the space that makes the statement true.

15 is _____ % of 20.

Solution

15 out of 20 can be written as the fraction $\frac{15}{20}$, which cancels down to $\frac{3}{4}$.

So, 15 is $\frac{3}{4}$ of 20.

Now write it as a percentage:

15 is 75% of 20.

13.1 Now try these

Band 1 questions

1. A sweater is made of only two fabrics: acrylic and wool. The label inside the sweater is shown, but a part of it is missing. What percentage of the sweater is wool?

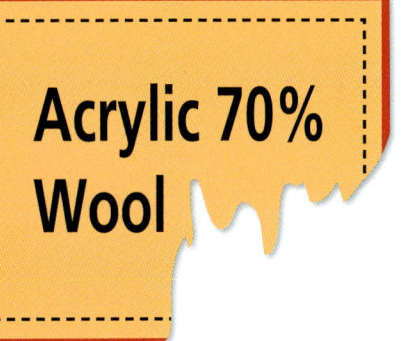

   Acrylic 70%
   Wool

2. Class 8E did a survey. They found that:
   - 15% of the class are vegetarians
   - 75% of the class caught a cold last year
   - 10% have no brothers or sisters.

   Find the percentage of the class that:

   a are not vegetarian

   b did not catch a cold last year

   c have at least one sibling.

3. In an election, 27% voted for Aled Atherton, 33% for Beca Bloor, 36% for Carys Campbell and the rest for Dylan Donaldson. What percentage voted for Dylan Donaldson?

4. Copy and complete the following.

   a 3 is _____ % of 30.

   b 20 is _____ % of 60.

   c 250 is _____ % of 1000.

   d 150 is _____ % of 600.

Curriculum for Wales Mastering Mathematics: Book 1

Fluency

5 The rectangles below are made up of squares of equal area.
What percentage of each rectangle is shaded?

a

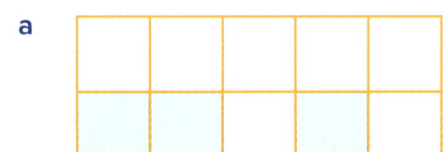

b

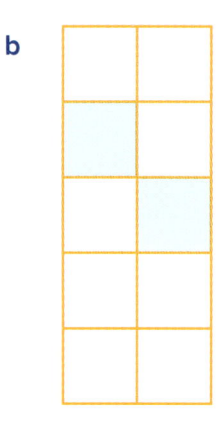

c

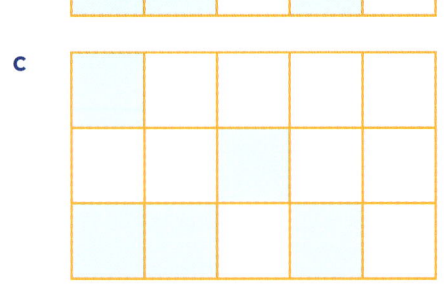

Band 2 questions

Logical reasoning

6 a What percentage of 160 is 120?
 b What percentage is 50 of 200?
 c What percentage of 120 is 40?
 d What percentage of 600 is 120?

7 Sioned earns £300 per month. Her rent is £180 per month.
What percentage of her income is spent on rent?

8 Some school friends decide to form a band. There are three boys and two girls.
 a What percentage of the band are girls?
 b Later, two boys leave the band and another girl joins. What percentage are girls now?

9 Mrs Brown has 24 pairs of shoes. At the moment she can only find 18 pairs.
What percentage of her shoes has she lost?

Strategic competence

10 Elis practises archery. He fires five arrows at the target and they land in the positions marked A, B, C, D and E in the diagram.

 a Work out Elis's total score.
 b What is the maximum score Elis could achieve with five arrows?
 c Work out what percentage of the maximum score Elis got.

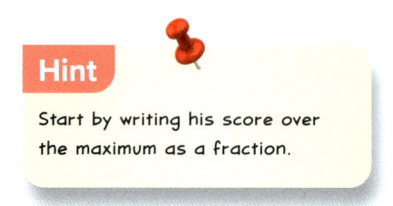

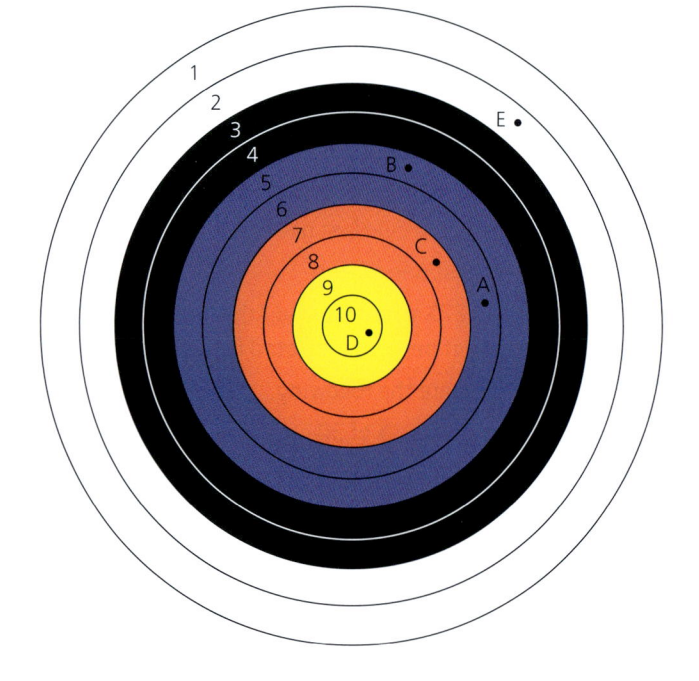

Hint
Start by writing his score over the maximum as a fraction.

268

Band 3 questions

11 a What percentage of 210 is 140?
   b What percentage is 70 of 350?
   c What percentage of 120 is 6?
   d What percentage of 450 is 108?

12 Lowri Moore and her mum are going on holiday.

Mrs Moore takes four suitcases with her. Lowri only takes one.

Each suitcase weighs the same amount when full.

What percentage of the total weight is made up of Lowri's belongings?

13 Dev is taking part in a quiz. Here are his scores in the three rounds:

QUIZ SCORES	
Emojis	7 out of 10
Pop music	15 out of 20
Capital cities	13 out of 20

   a Find Dev's score in the emojis round as a percentage.
   b Find Dev's score in the pop music round as a percentage.
   c Find Dev's score in the capital cities round as a percentage.
   d Find Dev's overall score as a percentage.

14 a On a trawler, the fishermen throw back 4% of the fish they catch because they are too small. What percentage of the fish do they keep?
   b On a different trawler, the fishermen reject 0.4 tons of fish out of a total catch of 80 tons. What percentage do they reject?

15 Dani has just finished her school exams.

Here is a part of her school report.

It shows her results from last year and this year.

Subject	Last year's score	This year's score
Welsh	20 out of 80	15 out of 50
Maths	24 out of 60	50 out of 80
English	14 out of 40	36 out of 60

   a In which subject did Dani do best this year?
   b In which subject did Dani improve the most from last year?

16 The students in two Year 10 tutor groups at Ysgol Hafod can choose to take music or drama or neither subject. The table shows what they chose.

	Music	Drama	Neither
Tutor group 10AD	18	12	10
Tutor group 10EJ	7	14	14

   a What percentage of 10AD chose to take drama?
   b What percentage of 10AD chose neither subject?
   c What percentage of 10EJ chose to take music?
   d What percentage of 10EJ chose neither subject?
   e What percentage of both tutor groups chose music?
   f What percentage of both tutor groups chose neither subject?

13.2 Percentages of amounts

Skill checker

Speed test! Can you answer all 12 parts in less than 2 minutes?

① Convert these percentages to fractions.
- a 10% = ☐
- b 25% = ☐
- c 40% = ☐
- d 60% = ☐
- e 75% = ☐
- f 90% = ☐

② Convert these fractions to percentages.
- a $\frac{1}{20}$ = ☐
- b $\frac{1}{5}$ = ☐
- c $\frac{3}{10}$ = ☐
- d $\frac{1}{2}$ = ☐
- e $\frac{7}{10}$ = ☐
- f $\frac{4}{5}$ = ☐

③ Work out the percentages of the items listed in the table.

	10%	25%	50%
20			
100 metres			
£16.48			
240 litres			

Remember

To find 10% or $\frac{1}{10}$ of a quantity, divide the quantity by 10.

To find 25% or $\frac{1}{4}$ of a quantity, divide the quantity by 4.

To find 50% or $\frac{1}{2}$ of a quantity, divide the quantity by 2.

Worked example

Copy the statement and write a number in the space that makes it true:

_____ is $33\frac{1}{3}$% of 15.

Solution

$33\frac{1}{3}$% is the same as $\frac{1}{3}$. So the question becomes:

_____ is $\frac{1}{3}$ of 15.

To find one third of 15, divide 15 by 3.

The answer is 5.

So 5 is $33\frac{1}{3}$% of 15.

For more difficult percentage questions, there is a choice of method.

The examples on the next page demonstrate a calculator method and two non-calculator methods.

13 Percentages

Worked example

Find 40% of 60.

Solution

Non-calculator method 1

Begin by finding 10% of 60, or $\frac{1}{10}$ of 60:

10% of 60 = 6

40% of 60 = 4 × 6 = 24

40% of 60 is 24.

Non-calculator method 2

Change 40% to a fraction.

$$40\% = \frac{40}{100} = \frac{4}{10} = \frac{2}{5}$$

So, to find 40% of a quantity, find $\frac{2}{5}$ of the quantity.

40% of 60 = $\frac{2}{5}$ of 60

= 24

> 40% of 60 is 24.

> To find $\frac{2}{5}$ of a number, divide it by 5 and multiply by 2

Calculator method

Change 40% to a decimal.

40% = 0.4

So, to find 40% of a quantity on the calculator, multiply by 0.4.

0.4 × 60 = 24

> **Note**
> You can always replace the word 'of' with a multiplication sign (×).

Worked example

Many questions – like this one – could be asked in either a calculator assessment or a non-calculator assessment. Harder ones like 43.7% of £216 are more likely to be asked in a calculator assessment.

Do not use non-calculator methods in a calculator assessment.

At an auction, a painting is sold for £3200.

The buyer must pay a deposit of 17% straight away and the rest when the painting is collected.

a How much does the buyer pay now?

b How much does the buyer pay when they collect the painting?

Solution

a You must find 17% of £3200.

Non-calculator method

Begin by finding 10% of £3200, or $\frac{1}{10}$ of £3200:

10% of £3200 = £320

Find 7%. First find 1%, which is $\frac{1}{10}$ of £320:

1% of £3200 = £32

7% of £3200 = 7 × 32 = £224

17% = 10% + 7%

17% of £3200 = 320 + 224 = £544

Calculator method

17% = 0.17

So 17% of £3200 = 0.17 × 3200 = £544.

The buyer must pay £544 now.

b The buyer must pay the rest of the money when they collect the painting. This is:

3200 − 544 = £2656

The buyer must pay £2656 when they collect.

Curriculum for Wales **Mastering Mathematics: Book 1**

> **Discussion activity**
>
> To work out 10% of any number, we can simply divide the number by 10.
>
> Why doesn't that work for any other percentage? For example, to work out 20% of a number, we don't divide the number by 20.

13.2 Now try these

Band 1 questions

Fluency

① Copy and complete each of these.
   a 50% of 60 is _____.
   b 25% of 80 is _____.
   c 40% of 50 is _____.
   d $66\frac{2}{3}$% of 36 is _____.

② Look at these computer download bars. In each case the total time is given.
   For each one work out:
   i   the time taken so far
   ii the time remaining for the download.

   a
   75% 100%
   Total download time: 8 minutes

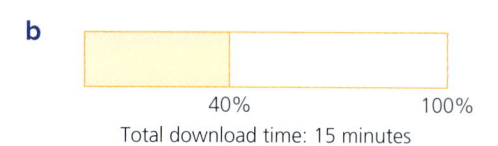

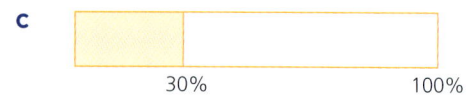

   b
   40% 100%
   Total download time: 15 minutes

   c
   30% 100%
   Total download time: 20 minutes

Logical reasoning

③ Sara's dad was organising the school raffle.
   By chance, Sara won 70% of the prizes.
   There were 30 prizes altogether.
   How many of them did Sara win?

④ An adult's train ticket from Cardiff to Llandudno costs £69.10.
   A child's ticket costs 65% of the adult's price. How much is a child's ticket?

⑤ A large bottle of lemonade holds 1.75 litres. A standard size bottle holds 0.75 litres.
   79% of the large bottle and 56% of the standard bottle have been drunk.
   Which bottle contains more lemonade and by how much?

13　Percentages

Band 2 questions

6 Match these red and blue cards in pairs.

a 50% of £10	b 1% of £7	c 10% of £1	£8.00	3p	20p
d 50% of £16	e 10% of £2	f 25% of £100	7p	25p	£3.00
g 100% of £15	h 100% of £6	i 10% of £4	£15.00	1p	£4.00
j 50% of £4	k 50% of £20	l 1% of £1	£5.00	£1.00	£10.00
m 10% of £6	n 25% of £1	o 100% of £4	40p	£25.00	50p
p 25% of £4	q 1% of £3	r 75% of £1	£6.00	10p	£2.00
s 75% of £4	t 25% of £2	u 75% of £2	£1.50	60p	75p

7 A shop buys 500 batteries. 2% of them are faulty.

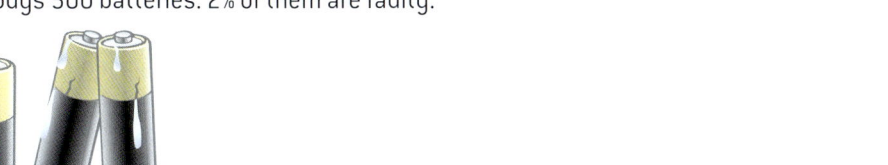

a　How many batteries are faulty?
b　How many batteries are in good condition?
c　What percentage of batteries are in good condition?

8 a　Linda and Cai share the cost of some takeaway food. Linda pays 25% of the cost. If the takeaway food cost £24.60, how much did Cai pay?

b　Neven and Heledd share the cost of some party food. Heledd pays 75% of the cost. If the cost of the food was £13.20, how much did Neven pay?

c　Tom and Megan share the cost of some golf balls. Megan pays 10% of the cost. If the golf balls were £16, how much did Tom pay?

9 31% of an orange drink is real fruit juice.

Work out the amount of real fruit juice in:

a　a 250 ml glass
b　a 1 litre carton
c　a 2.5 litre jug.

10 Kate is buying a house. The cost is £160 000.

She must pay a deposit of 12%. How much is the deposit?

273

Band 3 questions

11 A tax called VAT is added to many purchases.
  a If it is an extra 20% of the cost, find the VAT to be added to:
   i   a restaurant bill of £70
   ii a garage bill of £210.
  b On electricity, VAT is only paid at 5%. Find the VAT to be paid on an electricity bill of £90.

12 A school has 800 students.
  a 55% of these students are girls. How many are girls?
  b 5% of all students are left-handed. How many left-handed students are there?
  c There are 16 students for every member of staff. How many members of staff are there?
  d 60% of staff members are left-handed. Are there more left-handed students or left-handed staff members and by how many?

13 The final of the school's netball competition is taking place. The crowd watching is made up of men, women, boys and girls, as shown in the table.

	Males	Females	Total
Children		100	
Adults			250
Total	200		400

  a Copy the table and fill in the blank spaces.
  b What percentage of the children are boys?
  c What percentage of the adults are women?
  d What percentage of the males are adults?
  e What percentage of the females are children?
  f What percentage of all the people are adult males?

14 Any country's land can be split into four categories:
  • Arable: used to grow food, e.g. rice
  • Pasture: growing grass to feed animals
  • Forest: trees
  • Other: towns, deserts, mountains, etc.

  a Liechtenstein in central Europe is one of the smallest countries in the world, with an area of only 160 km^2. The pie chart shows how the land is used in Liechtenstein.

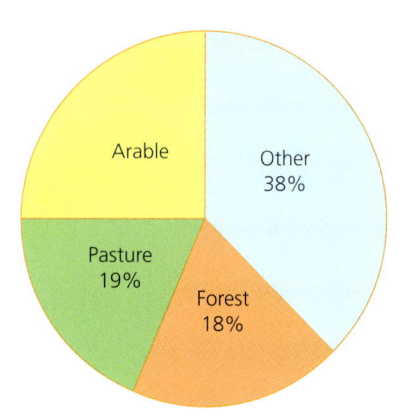

   i   What percentage of the land use in Liechtenstein is arable?
   ii What area of land is covered in forest? Give your answer in km^2.

b Portugal is a country in southern Europe with an area of 92 212 km².

The pie chart shows how the land is used in Portugal.

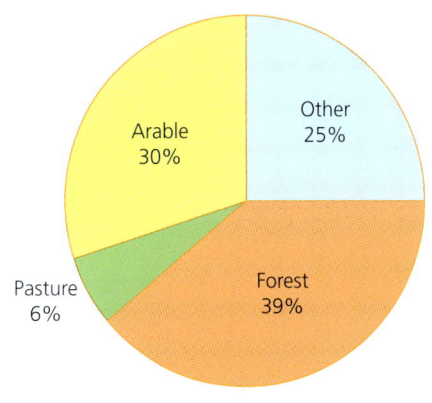

Pie chart: Arable 30%, Other 25%, Forest 39%, Pasture 6%

  i What area of land is covered in forest? Give your answer in km² to the nearest whole number.
  ii Which land use do you think uses roughly 23 000 km²?

c Look at this table showing the total area of England and Wales.

It also shows the percentage of each country covered by forest.

	Area (km²)	Percentage covered by forest
England	130 395	10%
Wales	20 735	15%

Which country has more forest, England or Wales, and by how much?

15 Suzanne buys a new car. It is priced at £9500, but Suzanne chooses to pay in instalments.

Firstly, she pays a deposit of 13% of the price. Then she makes 12 monthly payments of 8% of the price.

a How much is the deposit Suzanne pays?
b How much does she then pay each month?
c How much does Suzanne pay altogether?
d How much more than the price of £9500 does Suzanne pay?

13.3 Converting between fractions, decimals and percentages

Skill checker

Speed test! See how quickly you can answer these. Can you answer them all in less than 5 minutes?

① Convert these percentages to decimals.

  a 10% = ☐ **b** 25% = ☐ **c** 40% = ☐
  d 60% = ☐ **e** 75% = ☐ **f** 90% = ☐

② Convert these decimals to percentages.

  a 0.05 = ☐ **b** 0.2 = ☐ **c** 0.3 = ☐ **d** 0.5 = ☐ **e** 0.7 = ☐ **f** 0.8 = ☐

③ Convert these percentages to simplified fractions.

  a 15% = ☐ **b** 35% = ☐ **c** 45% = ☐ **d** 65% = ☐ **e** 22% = ☐ **f** 95% = ☐

④ Convert these fractions to percentages.

  a $\frac{1}{25}$ = ☐ **b** $\frac{2}{5}$ = ☐ **c** $\frac{6}{200}$ = ☐ **d** $\frac{27}{50}$ = ☐ **e** $\frac{28}{40}$ = ☐ **f** $\frac{108}{135}$ = ☐

▶ Converting percentages to decimals and fractions

Worked example

Write each percentage
i as a fraction
ii as a decimal.

a 80%   b 39%   c 45%   d 12.5%

Solution

a i As a fraction:

$$80\% = \frac{80}{100} = \frac{8}{10} = \frac{4}{5}$$

 ii As a decimal:

$$\frac{80}{100} = 0.80 \text{ or } 0.8$$

b i As a fraction:

$$39\% = \frac{39}{100}$$ ← This fraction cannot be simplified.

 ii As a decimal:

$$\frac{39}{100} = 0.39$$

c i As a fraction:

$$45\% = \frac{45}{100} = \frac{9}{20}$$ ← Simplify by dividing top and bottom by 5.

 ii As a decimal:

$$\frac{45}{100} = 0.45$$

d i As a fraction:

$$12.5\% = \frac{12.5}{100} = \frac{25}{200}$$ ← Multiply top and bottom by 2 to get whole numbers.

$$= \frac{5}{40} = \frac{1}{8}$$ ← Divide top and bottom by 5, then by 5 again.

 ii As a decimal:

$$\frac{12.5}{100} = \frac{125}{1000} = 0.125$$

▶ Converting fractions to percentages

Worked example

It is Francesca's birthday.

Her mum cuts a large pizza into 20 equal pieces.

Francesca eats three of the pieces.

a What fraction of the pizza has Francesca eaten?
b What percentage of the pizza has Francesca eaten?

Solution

a Francesca eats three out of 20 pieces.
   As a fraction, she eats $\frac{3}{20}$ of the pizza.
b Convert the fraction to a percentage:
   $$\frac{3}{20} = \frac{15}{100} = 15\%$$
   Multiply top and bottom of the fraction by 5 to get a denominator of 100.
   Francesca eats 15% of the pizza.

Worked example

Write $\frac{72}{75}$ as a percentage.

Solution

$$\frac{72}{75} = \frac{24}{25} = \frac{96}{100} = 96\%$$

Divide the numerator and denominator by 3.

Multiply the numerator and denominator by 4 to make the denominator 100.

▶ Converting decimals to percentages

Worked example

Write these decimals as percentages.

a 0.82   b 0.07   c 0.4   d 0.625   e 0.9975

Solution

a $0.82 = \frac{82}{100} = 82\%$

b $0.07 = \frac{7}{100} = 7\%$

c $0.4 = 0.40 = \frac{40}{100} = 40\%$

d $0.625 = \frac{625}{1000} = \frac{62.5}{100} = 62.5\%$

e $0.9975 = \frac{9975}{10\,000} = \frac{99.75}{100} = 99.75\%$

▶ Compare two quantities using percentages

Worked example

Put these quantities in order of size from smallest to largest.

$\frac{2}{3}$ 0.615 $\frac{3}{5}$ 65%

Solution

Write all the quantities as percentages:

$\frac{2}{3} = 66\frac{2}{3}\%$ $0.615 = \frac{615}{1000} = \frac{61.5}{100} = 61.5\%$

$\frac{3}{5} = \frac{6}{10} = \frac{60}{100} = 60\%$ 65% is already a percentage.

So the order from smallest to largest is $\frac{3}{5}$, 0.615, 65%, $\frac{2}{3}$.

13.3 Now try these

Band 1 questions

1. Convert these decimals to percentages.
   a 0.75   b 0.7   c 0.25   d 0.2   e 0.05

2. Convert these percentages to decimals.
   a 80%   b 15%   c 79%   d 68.5%   e 41.25%

3. Convert these fractions to percentages.
   a $\frac{1}{4}$ b $\frac{3}{5}$ c $\frac{2}{3}$ d $\frac{7}{10}$ e $\frac{3}{20}$
   f $\frac{36}{60}$ g $\frac{69}{75}$ h $\frac{26}{40}$ i $\frac{108}{120}$

4. Convert these percentages to fractions in their simplest form.
   a 75%   b 45%   c 27%   d 60%   e 80%   f 95%

5. Copy and shade the appropriate parts of these diagrams.
   a 70%   b $\frac{4}{5}$ 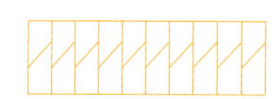   c 0.85 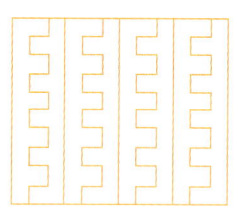
   d $\frac{2}{7}$ 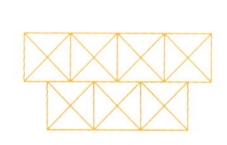   e 0.6    f 48% 
   g 0.72 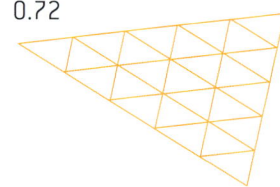   h 88% 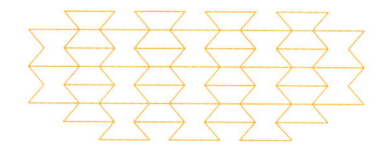   i $\frac{2}{3}$

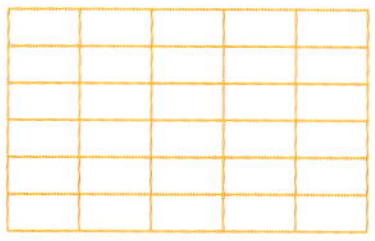

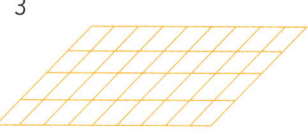

13 Percentages

Band 2 questions

6 Put the lists in parts **a**, **b** and **c** in order of size, from smallest to largest.
   a $\frac{1}{3}$ 0.31 0.287 $\frac{3}{10}$ 27%
   b 0.471 0.51 52% $\frac{1}{2}$ $\frac{47}{100}$
   c 0.199 0.19 18% $\frac{1}{5}$ $\frac{11}{50}$

7 Copy and complete these, putting the correct sign <, > or = between the numbers.
   a $\frac{3}{5}$ ☐ 60%   b 25% ☐ $\frac{1}{5}$ c 35% ☐ $\frac{2}{5}$ d $\frac{1}{7}$ ☐ $12\frac{1}{2}$%   e 0.3 ☐ 3%

8 Mrs Jones is driving from Trumpton to Camberwick Green. She sees this road sign in Trumpton.

   Chigley   14 km
   Camberwick Green   21 km

   a Arriving in Chigley, Mrs Jones thinks, 'I've travelled 75% of the way to Camberwick Green now!'
      Is Mrs Jones correct? Explain your answer.
   b Mrs Jones picks up flowers in Camberwick Green and drives back towards Trumpton. When she reaches Chigley:
      i   How many kilometres of her return journey has she travelled?
      ii What fraction of the return journey has she travelled?
      iii What percentage of the return journey is this?

9 Gwen scores 65% in her RE exam. The exam is marked out of 40.
   a How many marks did Gwen get out of 40?
   b Efa scores 24 marks in her Welsh exam.
      She says to Gwen, 'I didn't get as many marks as you, but my percentage score was still higher!'
      Is this possible? Explain your answer.

10 Eva keeps a record of the number of sunny days on her holidays. She writes them as fractions.
   By turning these fractions into percentages, write them in order from highest to lowest.
   a Tenby $\frac{3}{4}$ b Porthcawl $\frac{20}{25}$ c Florida $\frac{6}{10}$ d Mallorca $\frac{18}{20}$ e Home $\frac{39}{50}$

11 "58% is the same as $\frac{5}{8}$." Explain why Owain is incorrect.

Band 3 questions

12 a In the street where Rhiannon lives there are 360 houses. 240 of these houses have a garage.
         What percentage of houses in Rhiannon's street have no garage?
      b Of those houses that have a garage, 90% have a car parked in the garage.
         Find the number of houses that have a car parked in the garage.
      c What percentage of all the houses have a car parked in the garage?

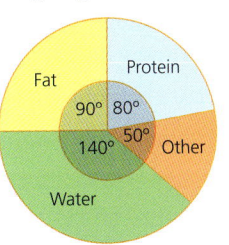

13 The pie charts show the constituent food types of cheese and eggs.
   a A café wants to give nutritional information on its menu. Copy and complete this information sheet for the café, giving your answers as percentages.

Food type	Cheese	Eggs
Fat	25%	
Water		
Protein		
Other		

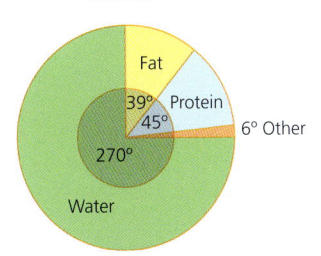

Cheese: Fat 90°, Protein 80°, Other 50°, Water 140°

Eggs: Fat 39°, Protein 45°, Other 6°, Water 270°

   b Which has more fat: 200 g of cheese or 200 g of eggs? Explain your answer.

279

14 The tables show Mikayla's marks for the autumn and summer terms.

a   In which term was Mikayla's English mark better?
b   What do you notice about her marks for Technology?
c   For which subject did she get a better mark in the autumn term than in the summer term?
d   In which subjects did she improve her marks from the autumn term to the summer term?
e   In which subject did she make the biggest improvement?

Autumn term	
Subject	Mark
Physical Education (Chwaraeon)	19 out of 25
English (Saesneg)	34 out of 50
Welsh (Cymraeg)	14 out of 20
History (Hanes)	17 out of 25
Geography (Daearyddiaeth)	15 out of 30
Mathematics (Mathemateg)	41 out of 50
Science (Gwyddoniaeth)	21 out of 30
Art (Celf)	28 out of 40
Music (Cerddoriaeth)	12 out of 24
Technology (Technoleg)	36 out of 40

Summer term	
Subject	Mark
Physical Education (Chwaraeon)	17 out of 20
English (Saesneg)	32 out of 40
Welsh (Cymraeg)	21 out of 25
History (Hanes)	8 out of 10
Geography (Daearyddiaeth)	13 out of 20
Mathematics (Mathemateg)	35 out of 40
Science (Gwyddoniaeth)	14 out of 20
Art (Celf)	17 out of 25
Music (Cerddoriaeth)	11 out of 20
Technology (Technoleg)	27 out of 30

15 For a school project, Marc is measuring the amount of rain that falls each day during a school week. The amounts of rainwater he measures are shown on the bar chart.

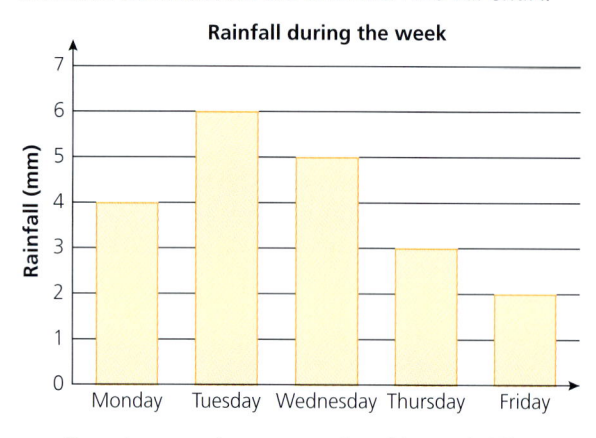

Rainfall during the week

Monday: 4 mm, Tuesday: 6 mm, Wednesday: 5 mm, Thursday: 3 mm, Friday: 2 mm

a   Tuesday was the wettest day this week. What percentage of the rain fell on Tuesday?
b   What percentage of the rain fell on Friday?

Marc continued his rainfall measurements for the entire month of April, including weekends. His measurements are shown in the bar chart.

This bar chart shows the number of times each amount of rain fell.

For example, there were six days when there was no rainfall, five days when there was 1 mm, etc.

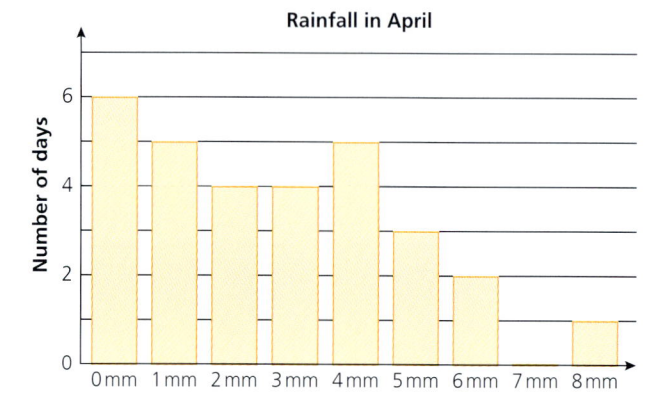

Rainfall in April

0 mm: 6 days, 1 mm: 5 days, 2 mm: 4 days, 3 mm: 4 days, 4 mm: 5 days, 5 mm: 3 days, 6 mm: 2 days, 7 mm: 0 days, 8 mm: 1 day

c What percentage of days were completely dry?

d On what percentage of days did 7 mm of rain fall?

e On what percentage of days did 5 mm of rain fall?

f On what percentage of days did more than 5 mm of rain fall?

16 Mr Watt has solar panels on the roof of his house. The solar panels generate electricity for him to use in the house.

If he doesn't use all the electricity, the electricity company buys it from him.

The table shows how much electricity the solar panels generate in a week. It also shows how much Mr Watt used.

Day	Generated	Used
Sunday (Dydd Sul)	21 units	7 units
Monday (Dydd Llun)	26 units	16 units
Tuesday (Dydd Mawrth)	28 units	21 units
Wednesday (Dydd Mercher)	39 units	13 units
Thursday (Dydd Iau)	35 units	17 units
Friday (Dydd Gwener)	31 units	5 units
Saturday (Dydd Sadwrn)	45 units	11 units

a What percentage of all the units generated were generated on Saturday of this week?

b What percentage of the units generated on Tuesday did Mr Watt use?

c How many units did the electricity company buy from Mr Watt on Wednesday? What percentage of the units generated was that?

d Overall, what percentage of the electricity generated did Mr Watt use?

> **Key words**
>
> Here is a list of the key words you met in this chapter.
>
> Decimal   Fraction   Percentage   VAT
>
> Use the glossary at the back of this book to check any you are unsure about.

Review exercise: percentages

Band 1 questions

Fluency

1. 'Silver' coins actually contain no silver. They are made of a combination of the metals copper and nickel.
   76% of a 'silver' coin is copper. What percentage is nickel?

2. Out of 25 kg of rubbish Mr Green produced one month, he could recycle 16 kg.
   a What fraction of his rubbish could Mr Green recycle?
   b What percentage of his rubbish could Mr Green recycle?

3. Write these amounts as percentages.
   a 16 out of 50
   b 5 kg out of 200 kg
   c 3 cm out of 12 cm
   d 4 litres out of 25 litres

4. a Stella scores 48 marks out of a possible 80 in a French test.
      What is this as a percentage?
   b Simon scores 40% in the same test. How many marks did he get out of 80?

Logical reasoning

5. Daniel counts the number of each letter of the alphabet on the front page of his local newspaper.
   There are 546 letters in total. 47 of them are the letter E.
   What percentage of the letters on the front page are E?

Band 2 questions

6. Twelve out of 60 calculators have flat batteries within two years.
   What percentage do not have flat batteries?

7. Four hundred cats were interviewed by their owners about which brand of cat food they preferred. Eight out of ten cats said they preferred Catty-Chops.
   a Write eight out of ten:
      i   as a fraction in its simplest form
      ii as a percentage.
   b How many cats said they preferred Catty-Chops?

Strategic competence

8. Elfed works in a fish shop called Coys-R-Us. This table shows the number of fish sold over one week. In total, 300 fish were sold this week.

Day	Number of fish sold
Sunday (Dydd Sul)	51
Monday (Dydd Llun)	30
Tuesday (Dydd Mawrth)	24
Wednesday (Dydd Mercher)	
Thursday (Dydd Iau)	36
Friday (Dydd Gwener)	39
Saturday (Dydd Sadwrn)	72

   a What percentage of fish were sold on Saturday?
   b Elfed works out that 16% of the fish sales took place on Wednesday. Work out how many fish were sold that day.

c The following week the total number of fish sold increased to 400.

16% of the sales were on Friday of this second week.

Find how many fish were sold on the Friday.

d In the second week, Elfed calculated that 13% of fish sales took place on the Wednesday.

Elfed's boss says that fish sales have fallen on Wednesdays. Is she right?

9 Put these in order of size, from smallest to largest.

$$\frac{1}{3} \quad 26\% \quad \frac{2}{5} \quad \frac{1}{4} \quad \frac{3}{10} \quad 33\%$$

10 In a TV talent show there were 300 000 votes.

Sui Lin received 14% of the vote.

Clare had 75 000 votes.

Rhodri had 96 000 votes.

Sioned had the rest.

a What percentage did each person get?

b Copy and complete this bar chart to show the voting.

Band 3 questions

11 Lara is doing some work on percentages for her homework. The questions are given below.

What's wrong with her working? Can you correct it?

a Work out 45% of 500.

$$45\% \text{ of } 500 = \frac{45}{100} \times 500 = \frac{5}{20} \times 500 = \frac{1}{4} \times 500 = 125$$

b Write 60 as a percentage of 300.

$$\frac{60}{300} = \frac{6}{30} = \frac{3}{10} = 30\%$$

Logical reasoning

⑫ In an autumn storm, 95% of the leaves came off a tall oak tree.

There were approximately 65 000 leaves on the tree before the storm.

Roughly how many leaves were left afterwards?

⑬ Look at the arithmagon.

For each square, find the percentage of the sum of the values in the two circles it lies between.

One of the squares has been done for you.

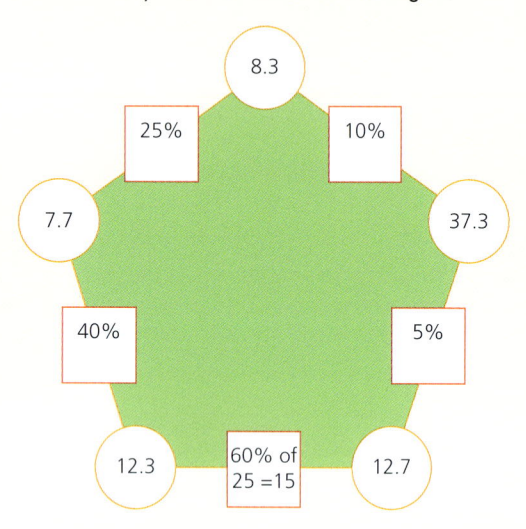

- 8.3
- 25%
- 10%
- 7.7
- 37.3
- 40%
- 5%
- 12.3
- 60% of 25 = 15
- 12.7

Strategic competence

⑭ Look at the numbers from 1 to 10:

1 2 3 4 5 6 7 8 9 10

Two of these numbers begin with the digit 1.

$$\frac{2}{10} = \frac{1}{5} = 20\%$$

So 20% of the numbers from 1 to 10 begin with a 1.

a What percentage of the numbers from 1 to 20 begin with a 1?

b What percentage of the numbers from 1 to 100 begin with a 1?

Logical reasoning

⑮ Liz did a survey of the students in her class.

She asked the question, 'Which supermarket does your family usually go to?'

The results are shown in the pie chart.

The same number of students said Stainberrys and Superstuff.

12.5% of students said Scrounders.

a What percentage said Scrimptons?

b There are 32 students in the class.

Find the number of students who said each of the four supermarkets.

⑯ *If you increase a number by 10%, then decrease your answer by 10%, you end up with your original number.*

Is Rhian correct? Explain your reasoning.

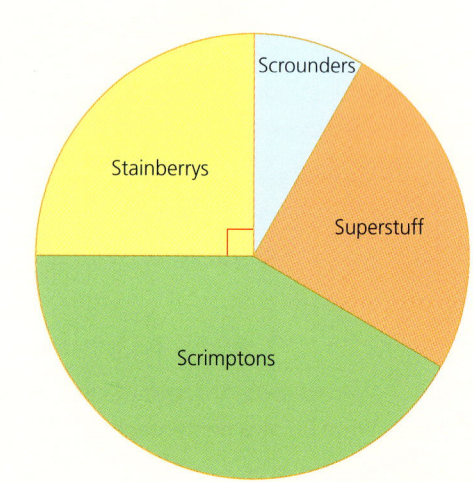

14 Ratio and proportion

Coming up...
- Understanding ratios
- Sharing in a given ratio
- Understanding proportion

Ratio pairs

Play this game in pairs.
Make these ratio cards.

1:10	1:5	1:4	1:3	1:2
2:3	2:5	3:4	3:5	4:5
8:10	2:6	6:8	2:10	4:6
4:8	6:10	3:12	20:50	10:100

Turn the cards upside-down.

The first player turns a card over and then another card.

If the ratios are **equivalent** they keep the pair of cards and have another go.

If the cards are not the same, they return them upside-down and the second player takes a turn.

When all the cards have gone, the player with the most pairs wins.

14.1 Understanding ratios

Skill checker

Put these fractions into pairs of equivalent fractions.
Which fraction is the odd one out, without a pair?

$\frac{42}{56}$ $\frac{30}{45}$ $\frac{4}{5}$ $\frac{3}{4}$ $\frac{160}{400}$ $\frac{24}{30}$

$\frac{3}{8}$ $\frac{4}{10}$ $\frac{45}{120}$ $\frac{27}{33}$ $\frac{99}{121}$

285

Curriculum for Wales Mastering Mathematics: Book 1

A child builds a stack of green and orange bricks, starting by putting a green brick on the ground.

The pattern is green, orange, orange / green, orange, orange / …

The ratio of green : orange bricks is 1 : 2.

It is also possible to see a green : orange ratio of 2 : 4 or 3 : 6.

The ratios 1 : 2, 2 : 4 and 3 : 6 are called **equivalent ratios**.

$\frac{1}{2}$, $\frac{2}{4}$ and $\frac{3}{6}$ are **equivalent fractions**.

Notice their similarity to equivalent ratios.

1 : 2 is called the **simplified ratio** of 2 : 4 and 3 : 6.

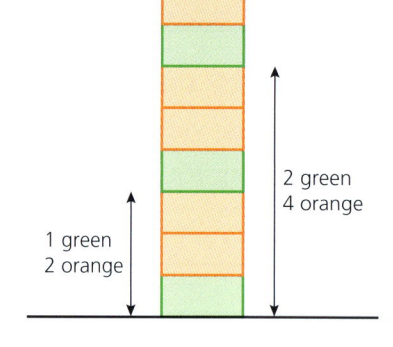

1 green 2 orange
2 green 4 orange

Worked example

In a bag of marbles there are 10 red marbles and 20 blue ones.

a Find the ratio of red : blue marbles.

b What fraction of the marbles is red?

Solution

a There are 10 red and 20 blue marbles.

So the ratio of red : blue is 10 : 20, or 1 : 2.

b Use the simplified ratio. For every red marble there are two blue marbles.

One out of every three marbles is red. The fraction that is red is $\frac{1}{3}$.

Note

You learnt about equivalent fractions in Chapter 8.

Cross-curricular activity

In your art lessons you will be used to mixing different coloured paints to create new colours. Mixing two primary colours in the ratio 1 : 1 produces a secondary colour.

What are the three secondary colours, and which primary colours are mixed to produce them?

Worked example

In a class, 12 students play sport and the other 16 students do not play sport.

a What is the ratio of students who play sport to those who do not play sport in its simplest form?

b In a group going on a school trip, the ratio of those who play sport to those who do not play sport is the same as in the whole class.

There are nine students on the trip who play sport. How many students are there on the trip that do not play sport?

c What fraction of students on the school trip play sport?

d What is the ratio of students who do not play sport to those who do play sport?

Remember

The order of the words matters!

286

Solution

a You can use a ratio table.

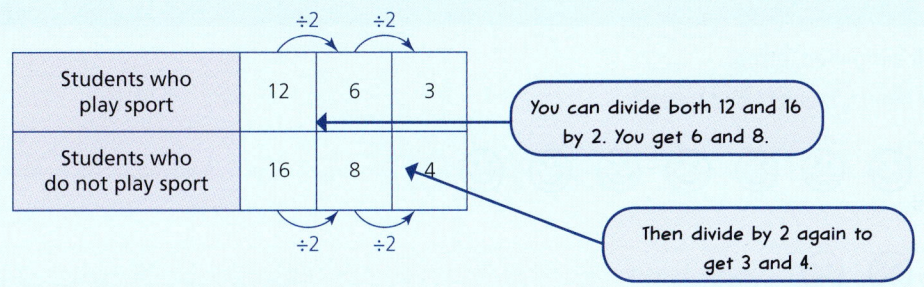

Students who play sport	12	6	3
Students who do not play sport	16	8	4

÷2, ÷2 across the top and bottom.

> You can divide both 12 and 16 by 2. You get 6 and 8.

> Then divide by 2 again to get 3 and 4.

In its simplest form, the ratio is 3 : 4.

b

Students who play sport	3	9
Students who do not play sport	4	12

×3

There are students on the trip who do not play sport.

c To work out what fraction of the students is the students who play sport, use the simplified ratio 3 : 4.

For every three students who play sport there are four who do not play sport.

This means that three out of seven students play sport.

So $\frac{3}{7}$ of the students play sport.

d The ratio of students who do not play sport to those who do play sport is 4 : 3.

Worked example

A ratio can have three or more parts.

In the picture of the necklace you can see a repeating pattern:

black, red, brown, brown, brown / black, red, brown, brown, brown / ...

The simplified ratio of black : red : brown is 1 : 1 : 3.

If there are seven black beads, how many brown beads are there?

Solution

The ratio 1 : 1 : 3 is equivalent to 7 : 7 : 21.

If there are seven black beads, there are seven red beads and 21 brown beads.

Discussion activity

One of the places where you commonly see ratios is on the label of a bottle of squash.

Why are ratios important when making squash? What would happen if the ratio wasn't there?

Remember

Multiplying or dividing each part of a ratio by the same number gives an equivalent ratio.

Ratios are usually given in their simplest form, with the smallest possible whole numbers.

14.1 Now try these

Band 1 questions

1 Find these ratios in their simplified forms.

   a What is the ratio of smiley faces to sad faces?

   b What is the ratio of thumbs to hearts?

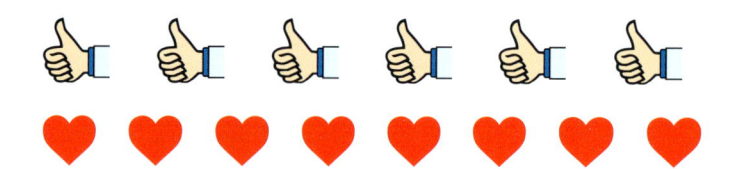

   c Can you draw two sets of emojis in the ratio 2 : 3?

   d Can you draw two different sets of emojis using the same ratio, but with different numbers of emojis?

2 Simplify these ratios:

   a 8 : 2   **b** 5 : 10   **c** 3 : 9   **d** 10 : 2   **e** 15 : 3

   f 9 : 15   **g** 14 : 4   **h** 36 : 30   **i** 81 : 54   **j** 34 : 51

3 Find the number that goes in the box to make an equivalent ratio.

   a 2 : 5 = ☐ : 40   **b** 2 : 3 = 6 : ☐   **c** 1 : 9 = ☐ : 36   **d** 3 : 2 = 9 : ☐

   e 5 : 3 = ☐ : 15   **f** 4 : 7 = 16 : ☐   **g** 14 : 9 = 42 : ☐   **h** 6 : 5 = ☐ : 30

   i 8 : 11 = ☐ : 99   **j** 32 : 7 = ☐ : 21

4 At Ysgol Harlech, Mr Owens, the caretaker, is painting the front door purple.

The instructions say mix red and blue paint in the ratio 1 : 2.

Mr Owens mixes 2 litres of red paint with 6 litres of blue.

Is he doing the right thing? Explain your answer.

5 In a box of tissues there are 20 pink tissues and 30 white tissues.

   a Write down the ratio of pink tissues : white tissues.

   b Simplify the ratio.

14 Ratio and proportion

Band 2 questions

6 Concrete is a mixture of cement, sand and gravel in the ratio 1 : 2 : 3.

How many bags of cement and gravel are needed when four bags of sand are used?

7 Steffan and Chloe are looking at these emojis.

They work out the ratio of lips to eyes.

Steffan says there are four lips and five eyes, so the ratio is 4 : 5.

Chloe says there are eight lips and ten eyes, so the ratio is 8 : 10.

Who is right? Explain your answer.

8 Simplify these ratios.

   a 8 : 2 : 4   **b** 5 : 10 : 20   **c** 12 : 3 : 9   **d** 10 : 8 : 2   **e** 3 : 15 : 3

   f 9 : 15 : 27   **g** 12 : 4 : 14   **h** 3 : 30 : 60   **i** 81 : 54 : 108   **j** 34 : 51 : 68

9 Find the number that goes in each box to make an equivalent ratio.

   a 2 : 3 : 5 = 16 : ☐ : 40   **b** 2 : 8 : 3 = 4 : 16 : ☐

   c 7 : 9 : 3 = 84 : ☐ : 36   **d** 3 : 4 : 2 = 9 : ☐ : ☐

   e 1 : 5 : 3 = ☐ : 15 : ☐   **f** 4 : 7 : 6 = 24 : ☐ : ☐

   g 2 : 9 : 5 = 12 : ☐ : ☐   **h** 6 : 5 : 4 = ☐ : 30 : ☐

   i 8 : 12 : 20 = ☐ : ☐ : 100   **j** 3 : 7 : 16 = ☐ : ☐ : 80

10 a One evening, a vet sees 12 dogs and 8 cats. Find the ratio of dogs : cats in its simplest form.

   b On a farm, the ratio of cows to sheep is 5 : 8. If there are 25 cows, how many sheep are there?

11 Aled, Ben and Catrin did some work for their uncle on his farm. They were paid in the ratio 2 : 1 : 4.

Catrin was paid £28. How much did Aled and Ben receive?

12 a In a primary school class, half of the children play a musical instrument. Which one of these ratios represents this fact?

      1 : 2   2 : 1   1 : 1   1 : 3   3 : 1

   b In a different class, three-quarters of the children play a musical instrument. Which one of these ratios is the correct ratio of children who do not play an instrument to those that do play an instrument?

      1 : 2   2 : 1   1 : 4   4 : 1   1 : 3   3 : 1

13 Cherry cola is made by mixing cherry cordial and cola in the ratio 2 : 9.

Vijay has 150 ml of cherry cordial.

   a How much cola does he need if he uses all the cordial?

   b How much cherry cola does he make?

289

14 Look at these flags.

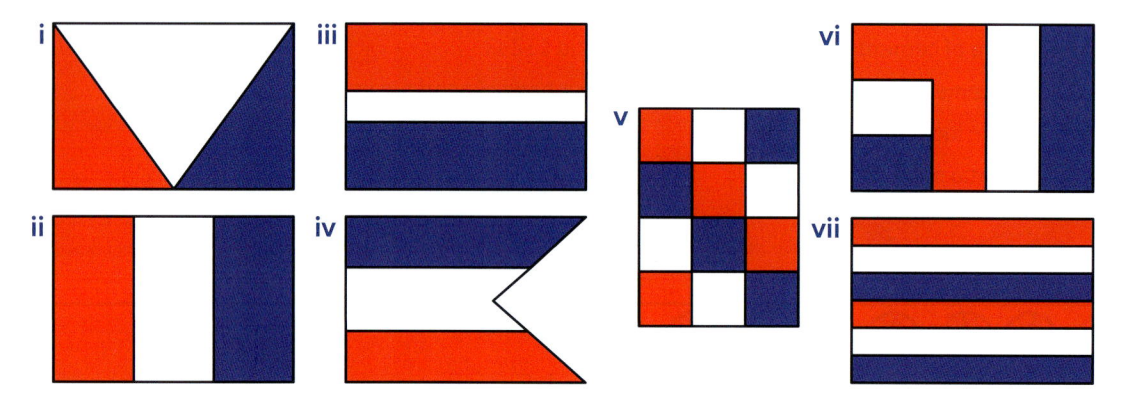

a Which of the flags has red, white and blue in the ratio 1 : 1 : 1? There may be more than one answer.

b Which of the flags has red, white and blue in the ratio 1 : 2 : 1?

Band 3 questions

15 Agata plays this word in a word game:

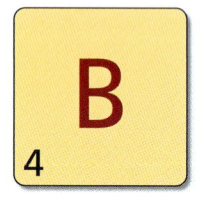

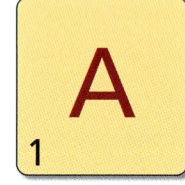

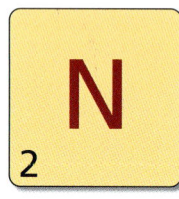

The number on each tile is the number of points scored for laying it.

This word scores 7 points.

The ratio of points scored by the three letters is 4 : 1 : 2.

The letter U scores 2 points.

If Agata had played BUN instead of BAN:

a How many points would Agata have scored?

b What is the ratio of points scored by the three letters of BUN? Give the ratio in its simplest form.

c The letter E scores 1 point.

   The letter K scores 6 points.

   The letter D scores 2 points.

   Which of the words below gives a simplified ratio of 2 : 1 : 1 : 3?

   BAND   BEND   BANE   BANK   BUNK

16 The length of this cuboid is 18 cm. Its width is 9 cm and its height is 6 cm.

a Write down the ratio of length : width : height in its simplest form.

b Which of the following cuboids have the same ratio of length : width : height?

   i   Length 3 m, width 1.5 m, height 1 m

   ii Length 90 cm, width 45 cm, height 20 cm

   iii Length 1.2 m, width 60 cm, height 40 cm

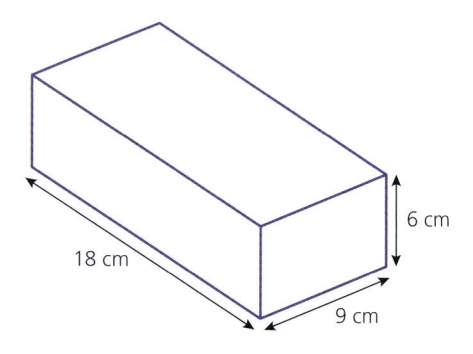

17 Look at these two angles on a straight line. They add up to 180°.

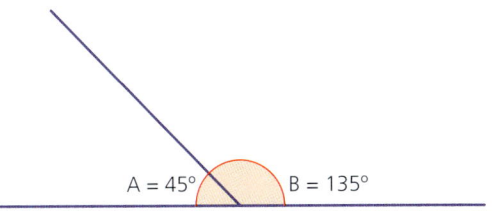

A = 45°   B = 135°

a What is the ratio of angle A : angle B in its simplest form?
b What fraction of the total does each angle make?
c Angle A is made 5° smaller and angle B is made 5° bigger.
What is the ratio of their sizes now in its simplest form?
d If, instead, angle A is made 5° bigger and angle B is made 5° smaller, what is the ratio of their sizes? Give your answer in its simplest form.

18 The side lengths in shapes X and Y below are in the ratio 1 : 2.
The side lengths of triangle Y are double the side lengths of triangle X.

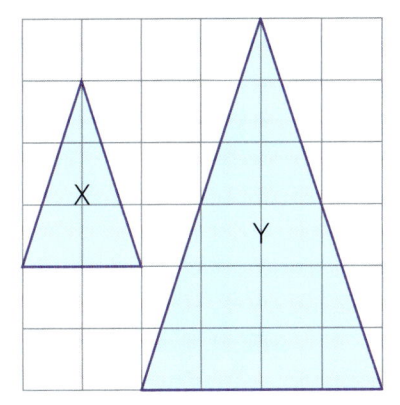

a For each of these pairs of shapes, what is the ratio of lengths in shape X to shape Y?

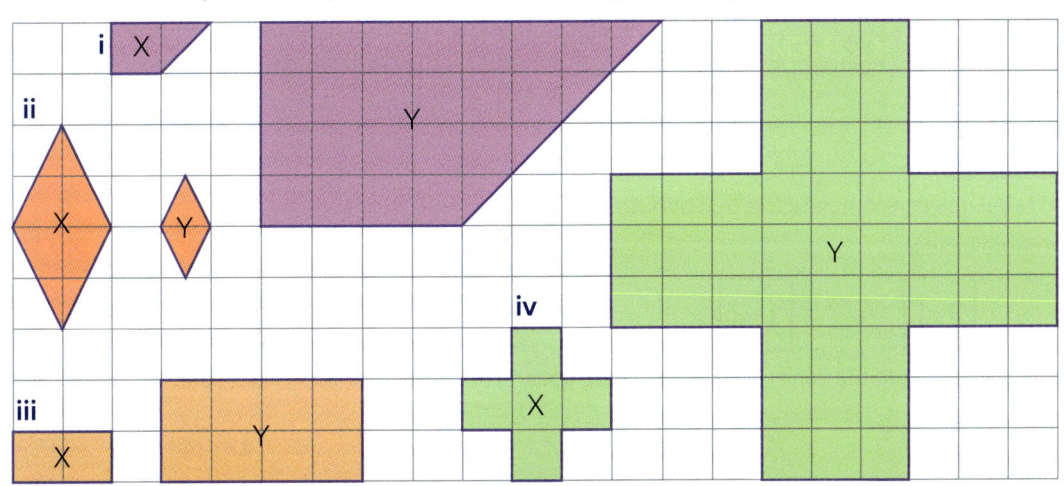

b For the two rectangles in part **iii**, work out the area of both shapes, X, and Y, by counting the small squares.
What is the simplified ratio of the area of X to the area of Y?
c Work out the ratio of the areas of shape X to shape Y in part **iv**.

19 The diagram shows the Saturn V rocket that took astronauts to the Moon.

The rocket is made up of three stages that carry the fuel and the crew modules at the top.

When the fuel in Stage 1 is used up, that stage falls away from the rocket.

The fuel in Stage 2 is used next and it then falls away.

Finally, the fuel in Stage 3 is used up, and it falls away.

Only the crew modules were left to travel to the Moon. These contained only a small amount of fuel.

The weight of each part of the rocket is shown in the table, as well as the amount of fuel each part holds.

	Stage 1	Stage 2	Stage 3	Crew modules	Total
Weight empty (tons)	130	40	13	47	
Weight of fuel (tons)	1800	400	99	1	
Total weight (tons)					2530

a Copy and complete the table.
b Find the ratio of the total empty weight to the weight of the fuel.
c Find the ratio of the total empty weight to the total weight.
d What fraction of the weight was fuel when the rocket was launched?
e What fraction of the weight is fuel after the first three stages have fallen away?

Crew modules

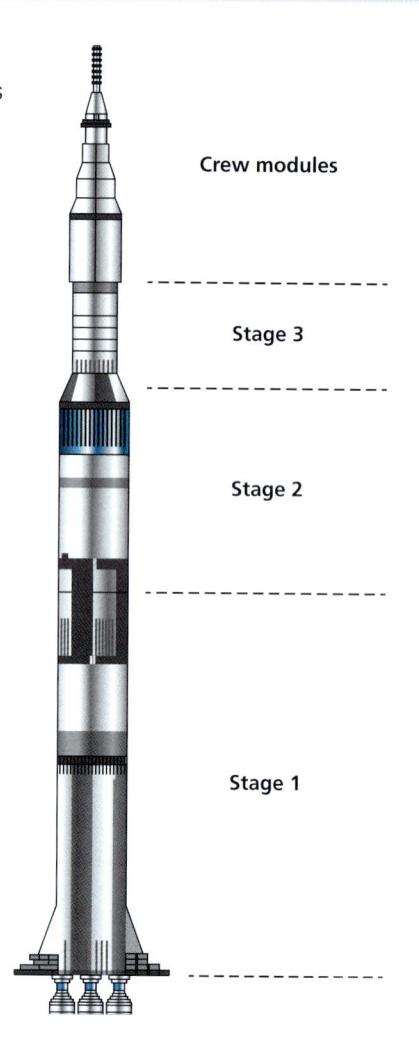

Stage 3

Stage 2

Stage 1

14.2 Sharing in a given ratio

Skill checker

Speed test! See if you can complete this in 2 minutes!

Copy these three boxes:

| 1 : 2 | | 2 : 1 | | 1 : 3 |

Put all these cards beneath the correct boxes. One card doesn't belong with a box – which one?

2 : 4	6 : 12	4 : 12	9 : 27	3 : 9	12 : 24	50 : 25
5 : 15	8 : 16	10 : 5	14 : 7	10 : 30	12 : 6	4 : 8
8 : 4	18 : 9	2 : 6	9 : 18	16 : 8	12 : 5	20 : 10

14 Ratio and proportion

▶ Sharing problems

In sharing problems, start by finding the total number of parts. Then decide how the parts are allocated.

Worked example

Kate and Gwenan buy a pizza costing £8.40 and share the cost in the ratio 3 : 4.
Find how much each of them pays.

Solution

The total number of parts is 3 + 4 = 7.
To find the cost of one part of the pizza, divide its price by 7.

$£8.40 \div 7 = £1.20$

One part costs £1.20.
Since Kate is paying for three parts, she pays:

$3 \times £1.20 = £3.60$

Gwenan is paying for four parts. She pays:

$4 \times £1.20 = £4.80$

So Kate pays £3.60 and Gwenan pays £4.80.

As a check, add the two amounts:
£3.60 + £4.80 = £8.40
This is the total cost of the pizza.

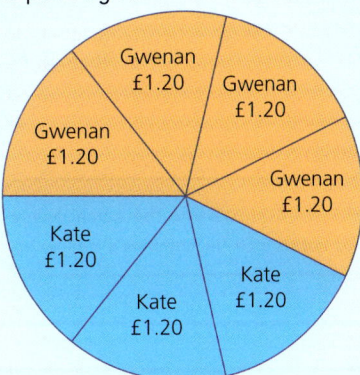

The total cost of £8.40 is divided by 7 to give £1.20. This is multiplied by 4 for Gwenan and 3 for Kate.

Worked example

Charlie and Jac go to a car boot sale and buy a box of old action figures for £10. There are 40 figures in the box.
Charlie pays £4 and Jac pays £6.
How many figures should they each keep?

Solution

Charlie and Jac pay in the ratio £4 : £6, so the figures should be divided up in the same ratio. Simplify the ratio:

$£4 : £6 = 4 : 6 = 2 : 3$

The figures should be shared out in the ratio 2 : 3.

You would get the same result if you used the ratio 4:6.

Add the parts:

$2 + 3 = 5$

Divide the number of figures by the number of parts:

$40 \div 5 = 8$

In each part there are 8 figures.
Charlie should get 2 parts: $2 \times 8 = 16$ figures.
Jac should get 3 parts: $3 \times 8 = 24$ figures.

Check that these add up to the total number of figures, 40.

40 figures		
1 part 8 figures		
Charlie gets 2 parts 16 figures		Jac gets 3 parts 24 figures

The total number of figures (40) was divided by 5 to give 8. This was multiplied by 2 for Charlie and 3 for Jac.

Worked example

This map shows four towns and the distances between them.

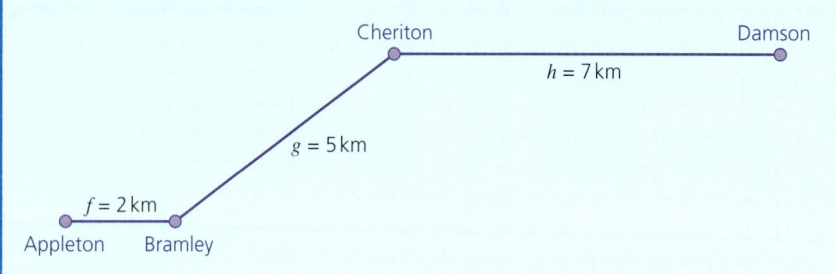

```
        Cheriton          Damson
           •─── h = 7 km ───•
          /
     g = 5 km
        /
f = 2 km
  •──•
Appleton Bramley
```

Find these ratios:

i $f:g$ **ii** $g:h$ **iii** $f:g:h$ **iv** $f:h$

Solution

i $f:g = 2:5$
ii $g:h = 5:7$
iii $f:g:h = 2:5:7$
iv $f:h = 2:7$

> Since these numbers are the same, these two ratios can be combined easily.

Worked example

The ratio $P:Q = 3:4$ and $Q:R = 8:11$.

Find these ratios:

i $P:Q:R$
ii $P:R$

Solution

$P:Q = 3:4 = 6:8$
and $Q:R = 8:11$

> Make the Q parts of the two ratios the same, so that the two ratios can be combined.

i $P:Q:R = 6:8:11$
ii $P:R = 6:11$

Activity

Can you crack the code to find the secret password?

There are seven clues below.

When you have the answer to a clue, read off the letter next to the answer.

The letters will spell the password.

Clue 1: A 3-metre plank is sawn into two sections. The sections are in the ratio $1:2$. How long is the first section?

Clue 2: An adventure course is made up of forest tracks, cycle paths and beach in the ratio $2:4:1$. The total length of the course is 21 km. How much of the course is cycle paths?

Clue 3: In class 7B there are 25 students. The ratio of those having school dinners to those having packed lunches is $3:2$. How many have school dinners?

Clue 4: A train travels from Newport to Cardiff and then on to Neath. The ratio of passengers getting off at Cardiff : getting off at Neath is $5:2$. If there are 315 passengers on the train, how many get off at Neath?

Clue 5: A car has a mass of 900 kg when empty. For a holiday, the car is packed with luggage and passengers. The empty mass and the full mass are in the ratio 9 : 10. What is the mass of the luggage and passengers?

Clue 6: A sunflower is 80 cm tall. Its height is made up of the stem and the flower in the ratio 7 : 3. How tall is the flower?

Clue 7: A mug and a jug are on the table. The mug holds 300 ml of liquid. The capacities of the mug and jug are in the ratio 3 : 5. How much more liquid does the jug hold than the mug?

A £8	B 100 kg	C 9.75 m	D 200 ml	E 90
F 3 kg	G 9.8 kg	H 15.2	I 18 litres	J 0.34 km
K 2 litres	L 9 m	M 0.5 kg	N 9.191 g	O 12 km
P £5.50	Q 68.9 kg	R 1 m	S 15	T 65 litres
U 24 cm	V 1.8 g	W 6	X 6.9 g	Y 30 cm
Z 1.5				

14.2 Now try these

Band 1 questions

1 Share out these amounts of money in the ratios given.
  a £50 in the ratio 1 : 4
  b £90 in the ratio 4 : 1
  c £65 in the ratio 2 : 3
  d £108 in the ratio 4 : 5
  e £36.50 in the ratio 3 : 2
  f £144 in the ratio 7 : 2

2 Share out these lengths in the ratios given.
  a 60 cm in the ratio 1 : 4
  b 80 m in the ratio 3 : 1
  c 57 inches in the ratio 2 : 1
  d 99 feet in the ratio 1 : 10
  e 1250 km in the ratio 3 : 2
  f 39 miles in the ratio 7 : 6

3 Copy this grid five times and use red and yellow to shade each copy in the ratios shown.
  a 1 : 1
  b 2 : 1
  c 3 : 1
  d 5 : 1
  e 5 : 3

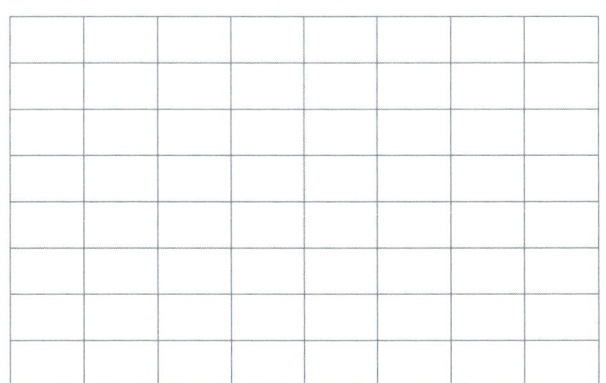

4 Colin and Olivia's nain gives them £240 to share in the ratio 1 : 3. How much money does each of them receive?

Band 2 questions

5 Heledd, her brother Dafydd and her sister Cara are given £240.

It is to be shared out in the ratio of their ages.

Heledd is 8 and Cara is 1, so the ratio of the children's ages is 8 : ☐ : 1.

When they share the money out, Cara receives £20.

   a How much money does Heledd get?

   b How much money does Dafydd get?

   c How old is Dafydd?

6 The three angles a, b and c shown add up to 180°.

The sizes of angles a, b and c are in the ratio 1 : 3 : 2.

What is the size of each angle?

7 A gardener plants six rows of onions. There are ten onions in each row.

The gardener knows that the ratio of red to white onions he has planted is 7 : 8.

Find how many red onions and how many white onions he will have.

8 Neha, the goalkeeper for the Ysgol St David's football team, has a good record of saving penalties.

This season, St David's faced 30 penalty kicks. The ratio of penalties saved to scored is 2 : 3.

   a Find the number of penalty kicks Neha saved this season.

   b What fraction of the penalty kicks did she save?

Grace, the rival goalkeeper at Ysgol Harlech, says she has a saved : scored ratio of 2 : 1.

Neha says, 'Yes, but you've only faced half the number of penalties!'

   c How many penalty kicks did Grace face?

   d How many did she save?

   e Which goalkeeper saved more penalties?

9 Rhian has a collection of stamps. She has twice as many foreign stamps as British stamps.

   a What is the ratio of foreign to British stamps in Rhian's collection?

   b If Rhian has 480 stamps altogether, how many of them are foreign?

10 Akiva has 35 socks. Some of them belong to a pair; some are odd.

The ratio of paired socks to odd socks is 6 : 1.

   a How many pairs of socks has Akiva got and how many odd socks?

   b The following week Akiva finds a sock that makes a pair with one of the odd socks.

      What is the ratio of paired socks to odd socks now?

Band 3 questions

11 Kristi is doing her homework on ratios, but she thinks she has gone wrong. Can you correct her work?

The question is: 'Share £300 in the ratio 4 : 1.'

Kristi writes:

> Add the number of parts: 4 + 1 = 5
> £300 ÷ 5 = £60
> 5 × £60 = £300
> 1 × £60 = £60
> The two amounts are £300 and £60.

14 Ratio and proportion

12 This is Sophie's bike lock. It can only be opened with the correct combination of three numbers.

Sophie can't remember the correct combination.

However, she does know that the three digits are in the ratio 1 : 3 : 2.

She also remembers that the 3 digits add up to 18.

Can you help Sophie find the correct combination for her bike lock?

13 **a** D and E are in the ratio 3 : 2.

E and F are in the ratio 2 : 7.

Find the ratios:

  i D : E : F   **ii** D : F

b X and Y are in the ratio 4 : 3.

Y and Z are in the ratio 6 : 7.

Find the ratios:

  i X : Y : Z   **ii** X : Z

c Two lengths, P and Q, are in the ratio 4 : 1.

The lengths Q and R are in the ratio 5 : 4.

Find the ratios:

  i P : Q : R   **ii** P : R in its simplest form

14 The areas of the UK and France are roughly in the ratio 10 : 23.

The areas of Norway and the UK are roughly in the ratio 13 : 10.

Find the ratio of the areas of Norway and France.

15 Two measuring jugs, A and B, have capacities that are in the ratio 3 : 2. The capacities of jugs B and C are in the ratio 4 : 5.

a What is the ratio of the capacities of jug A to jug C?

b The capacity of jug C is 100 ml. Find the capacity of jug A.

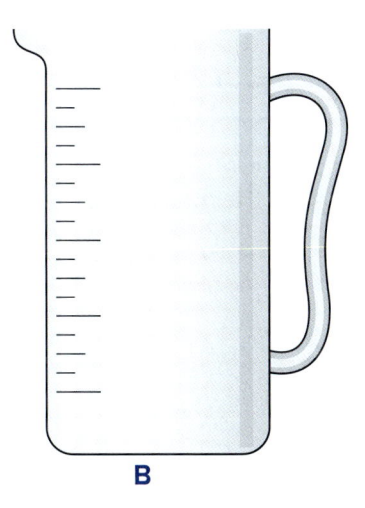

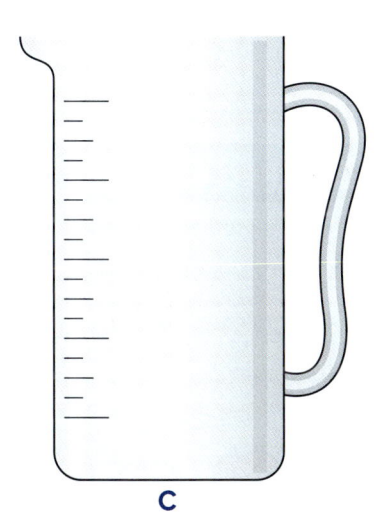

A   B   C

297

Curriculum for Wales **Mastering Mathematics: Book 1**

14.3 Proportion

Skill checker

How could you get from the first stepping stone to the second to the third?

To move from the first to the second, you need to divide by something.

To move from the second to the third, you need to multiply by something.

Question 1 has been done for you.

Don't fall in the water!

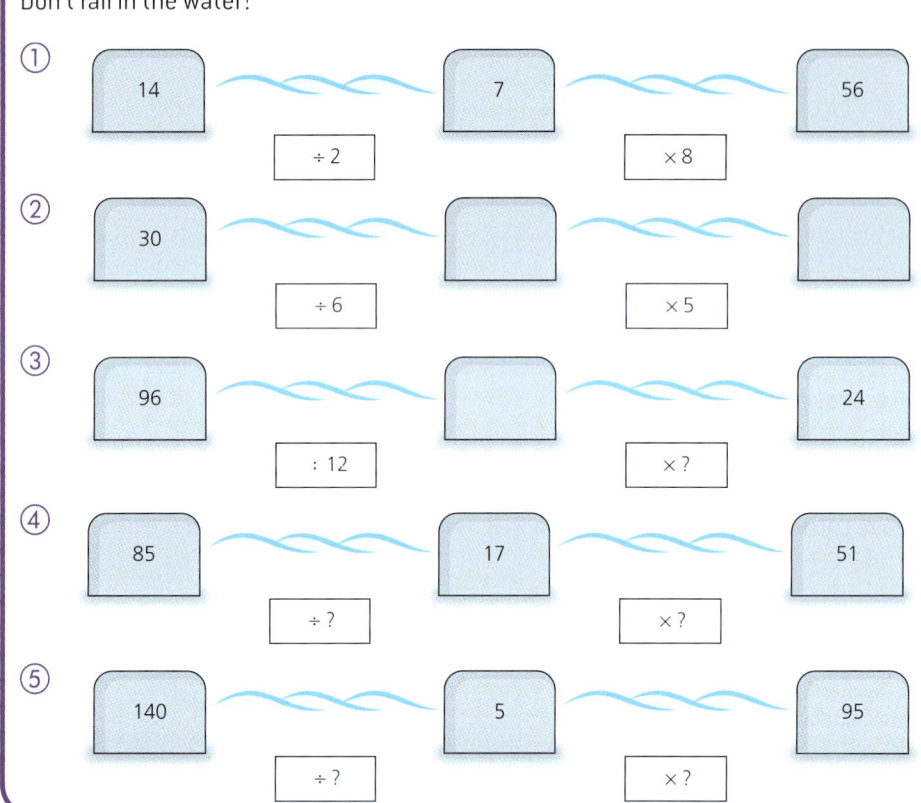

① 14 → 7 → 56
   ÷ 2   × 8

② 30 → ☐ → ☐
   ÷ 6   × 5

③ 96 → ☐ → 24
   ÷ 12   × ?

④ 85 → 17 → 51
   ÷ ?   × ?

⑤ 140 → 5 → 95
   ÷ ?   × ?

Worked example

These ingredients for apple crumble make enough for two people.

Apple Crumble (serves 2)
1 large cooking apple
25 g white sugar
$\frac{1}{4}$ teaspoon cinnamon
90 g wholemeal flour
40 g butter
75 g brown sugar

Inga needs to make an apple crumble for five people.
How much of each ingredient should she use?

Solution

This method is called the **unitary method**.

You first find the ingredients for one person and then multiply by 5.

Ingredients	For 2 people	For 1 person	For 5 people
Cooking apple	1	$\frac{1}{2}$	$2\frac{1}{2}$
White sugar	25 g	12.5 g	62.5 g
Cinnamon	$\frac{1}{4}$ teaspoon	$\frac{1}{8}$ teaspoon	$\frac{5}{8}$ teaspoon
Wholemeal flour	90 g	45 g	225 g
Butter	40 g	20 g	100 g
Brown sugar	75 g	37.5 g	187.5 g

Divide by 2 to find how much you need for one person.

Multiply by 5 to find how much you need for five people.

Worked example

An office manager wants to buy pen drives for the office staff. 40 pen drives cost £20.

a Find the cost of 50 pen drives.

b Find the cost of 24 pen drives.

Solution

You can use a ratio table to help you solve this type of problem.

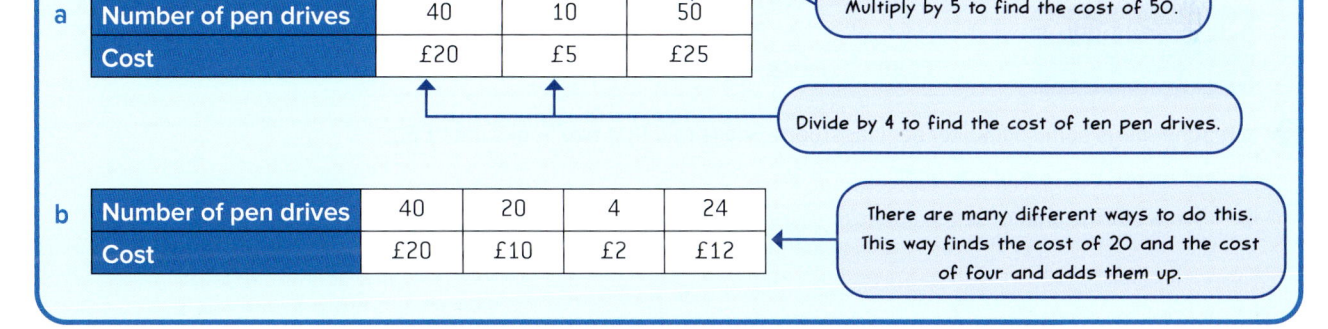

a
Number of pen drives	40	10	50
Cost	£20	£5	£25

Multiply by 5 to find the cost of 50.

Divide by 4 to find the cost of ten pen drives.

b
Number of pen drives	40	20	4	24
Cost	£20	£10	£2	£12

There are many different ways to do this. This way finds the cost of 20 and the cost of four and adds them up.

The pen drive example could be done using the **unitary method**, finding the cost of one pen drive first.

The cost is **proportional** to the number of pen drives.

In the apple pie example, the amount of flour used is **proportional** to the number of people. The same is true for all the other ingredients.

Curriculum for Wales **Mastering Mathematics: Book 1**

Activity

Hugo Fizzipop

Hugo Fizzipop is a very famous person, although nobody is quite sure why. He is so famous that people pay for his autograph.

One day Hugo Fizzipop comes to the town centre. People queue up to buy his autograph. Selina loves Hugo Fizzipop and she joins the queue.

Finally, Selina reaches the front of the queue. She introduces herself and asks Hugo for his autograph.

'Of course! That will be £24 please!' he says. 'It's a fixed amount for each letter of my name!'

'Oh', says Selina, disappointed, 'I only have £6.'

a Find how much Hugo Fizzipop charges for writing each letter of his name.

For a moment Selina doesn't know what to do. She is on the point of going home. But Hugo sees how disappointed she is. He suddenly has a great idea.

'Selina!' he says, 'I'll write as many letters as I can!'

b How many letters can Hugo write for £6? What does he write?

Selina is very happy with the word Hugo writes.

Then Hugo adds a free smiley face! Everybody is happy.

14.3 Now try these

Band 1 questions

1 It costs £1.60 for 2 hours' parking in a multi-storey car park.

This is a table taken from a sign in the car park, but some of the numbers are missing. Copy and complete it.

Number of hours	1	2		4	5		15	24
Cost		£1.60	£2.40			£8.00		

2 A teacher buys some books for her classroom. She is told that five books cost £80.
  a Work out the cost of one book.
  b Work out the cost of seven books.

3 Lowri usually gets paid £60 for doing 5 hours' work.
  a On Tuesday Lowri feels ill and leaves work after 3 hours.
     Find how much she gets paid.
  b On Wednesday Lowri stays longer than usual to make up for the pay she lost on Tuesday.
     She is paid £84. How many hours did Lowri work?

4 A photograph is 4 inches wide and 6 inches high.
  a The photo is enlarged so that its width is 10 inches. Find its height.
  b The photograph is shrunk to make a passport photo 2 inches high. Find the width of the passport photo.

5 Here is a recipe for lemon and raisin scones.

How much flour, milk, sugar and raisins would you need to make ten scones?

> 240 g self-raising flour
> 180 ml milk
> 30 g sugar
> 90 g raisins
> One lemon
> Makes 6 scones

Band 2 questions

6 Some Year 7 students are going on a school trip. Last year four teachers went with 32 students.

   a Find the ratio of teachers to students.

   b This year 56 students are going on the trip.

      Using the same ratio, how many teachers should go?

      Use a ratio table to help you organise your work.

7 The load that a steel beam can support is proportional to its thickness. A beam 40 cm thick can support 1000 kg of weight.

   a How much weight could a beam 50 cm thick support?

   b How thick would the beam need to be to support a weight of 800 kg?

8 The Davies family are driving to Scotland on the motorway.

Mr Davies drives at 60 miles per hour.

Number of hours in car	1	2	4
Number of miles travelled	60		

   a Complete this ratio table.

   b How far will the family have driven after $2\frac{1}{2}$ hours?

   c The journey is 250 miles altogether.

      Find how long it will take the family to reach Scotland.

9 Kelly has a new pencil, which is 12 cm long.

She reads on the internet that a 10 cm pencil could draw a line roughly 25 miles long!

How many miles of writing can Kelly do with her pencil?

10 On a large construction site, a wall 120 metres long is needed.

Five builders could complete 40 metres of the wall in a day.

   a How much of the wall could one builder, working on his own, complete in a day?

   b How much could 12 builders complete in a day?

   c How many builders would be needed to complete the wall in a day?

11 Ching is cooking spicy stuffed peppers for dinner. Here is the list of ingredients.

Ching is cooking for three people. She uses a ratio table to work out how much of each ingredient she should use.

> 4 red peppers
> 100 grams rice
> 1 large onion
> 1 tin of tomatoes
> 2 chilli peppers
> 60 grams cheddar cheese
> Serves 4 people

   a How much rice should Ching use?

   b How much cheese should she use?

   c Ching forgets to change the number of chilli peppers and uses the number in the recipe for four people.

      Will her stuffed peppers be spicier than usual, or less spicy?

Band 3 questions

Logical reasoning

12 Megan stacks 20 identical books on her desk. The stack of books is 70 cm high.

Megan removes three books.

How high is the stack of remaining books?

13 The Eiffel Tower in Paris is 324 metres high.

It has a square base measuring 125 metres on each side.

A tourist shop sells models of the Eiffel Tower in different sizes.

Copy this table and fill in the blank spaces to help the shop work out the missing height and width.

	Actual tower	Large model	Small model
Height	324 m	64.8 cm	
Width	125 m		12.5 cm

14 Pete is going fishing and needs some maggots to use for bait.

He goes to a fishing supplies shop with £5. This is one of the signs in the shop window:

> **Maggots**
> 1.2 kg £0.75

How many kilograms of maggots can Pete afford?

15 In a storm, Mark sees a flash of lightning.

Eight seconds later he hears the thunder.

Sound travels 343 metres every second.

a How far away was the lightning? Give your answer in metres.

b After another 10 minutes, the storm is 1500 metres away.

Find how long it takes for the sound of thunder to reach Mark now.

16 A prisoner sits in his jail cell.

He has been given 18 years in prison for stealing 24 gold bars from the bank.

The prisoner now regrets what he has done.

'If only I had only stolen 12 gold bars!' he thinks. 'I would have just 9 years in prison!'

Clearly, the prisoner thinks that the length of his jail sentence is proportional to the number of gold bars he stole.

a If the prisoner is correct, find how long his sentence would be for stealing four gold bars.

b How long would he spend in jail for stealing 36 gold bars?

c Do you think these things really would be proportional? Explain your answer.

Key words

Here is a list of the key words you met in this chapter.

Equivalent   Proportion   Ratio   Simplify   Unitary method

Use the glossary at the back of this book to check any you are unsure about.

Review exercise: ratio and proportion

Band 1 questions

1 Write these ratios in their simplest form.
   a 6:8
   b 9:45
   c 12:27
   d 45:25
   e 77:33
   f 68:17
   g 91:84

2 Copy and complete these equivalent ratios.
   a 5:2 = 25:☐
   b 5:☐ = 15:6
   c 2:7 = 16:☐
   d 18:6 = 9:☐ = ☐:1
   e 98:56 = ☐:4
   f ☐:66 = 10:11
   g 390:240 = ☐:8

3 A football commentator says the words, 'Oh my word!' 36 times during one football match. She says 'Quite extraordinary!' 45 times. What is the ratio of 'Oh my word!' to 'Quite extraordinary!' in its simplest form?

4 In a packet of balloons there are 36 round balloons and 12 long balloons.
   a Write down the ratio of round balloons : long balloons.
   b What fraction of the balloons are round?
   c What fraction of the balloons are long?

5 Five music downloads cost £25.50. How much would it cost for three?

6 In a field, 2700 kg of wheat is growing. The ratio of wheat eaten by birds : wheat harvested is 2:7.
How many kilograms of wheat do the birds eat?

Band 2 questions

7 Find the number that goes in each box to make an equivalent ratio.
   a 11:3:2 = 33:☐:6
   b 2:9:3 = 4:☐:☐
   c 25:16:9 = 75:☐:27
   d 32:14:8 = ☐:7:☐
   e 20:55:45 = ☐:☐:9

8 This is a section of tiling in a kitchen.
In this section, find these ratios in their simplest forms.
   a white:yellow tiles
   b white:red tiles
   c orange:yellow tiles

9 Red roses are priced at £9.60 for 12.
   a Use the unitary method to find the cost of:
      i three roses
      ii 16 roses.
   b Use a ratio table to find the cost of nine roses.

303

Strategic competence

10 Carrie is making a pumpkin pie for eight people.

Work out how much of each ingredient she needs using the information given.

> 1 egg for every four people
> 350 g pumpkin for every egg
> Half as much pastry as pumpkin
> 35 g of sugar for every two people
> 3 g of butter for each person
> 10 ml milk for every 20 g of pastry
> ¼ teaspoon of mixed spices for each person

11 One season a rugby team wins, draws and loses its games in the ratio 3 : 1 : 2. They won 18 games.

    a How many games did they draw?

    b How many games did they lose?

    c How many games did they play this season?

The following season, the team has a new coach. The team plays the same number of games and wins 20 of them. The team loses three-quarters of the remaining games.

    d Find the ratio in which the team wins, draws and loses games now.

Band 3 questions

12 Mr Frugal uses a teabag three times before he throws it away.

Mrs Thrifty uses a teabag twice before she throws it away.

They both drink six cups of tea per day.

    a Find, in its simplest form, the ratio of teabags used by Mr Frugal to teabags used by Mrs Thrifty each day.

    b Mr Frugal and Mrs Thrifty both buy boxes of 60 teabags.

       How many days does Mr Frugal's box last?

       How many days does Mrs Thrifty's box last?

    c Find, in its simplest form, the ratio of days Mr Frugal's box of teabags lasts : days Mrs Thrifty's box of teabags lasts.

13 The pie chart shows the colours of new cars bought last year.

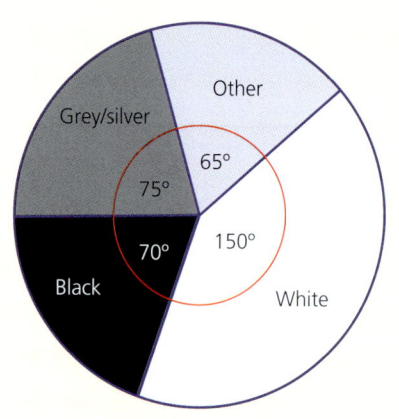

    a Find the ratio of black to white cars bought in its simplest form.

    b Find the ratio of grey or silver to 'other' cars bought in its simplest form.

    c If there were 140 000 black cars bought, find the number of grey or silver cars bought.

14. Mrs Cooper has one large red mat, and lots of small green mats and small blue mats on the floor, as shown.

    She asks her class whether it is possible to cover the large red mat using the green and blue mats, without rotating any of the mats.

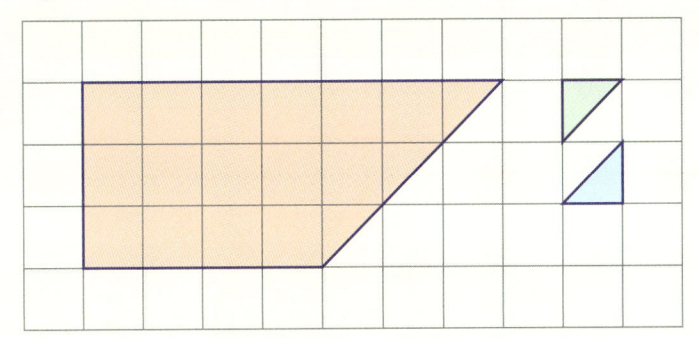

    a   Do you think this is possible? Don't worry – you won't run out of green and blue mats!
    b   If you think it is possible, find the ratio of green to blue mats that will be used, giving a simplified ratio as your answer.

15. Louise is allowed to claim expenses for using her car for work.

    One month she claims £68 for driving 170 miles for work.

    a   How much does she claim per mile?
    b   Louise's boss wants her claim to be no more than £50 per month.
        How many miles can Louise drive for work per month?

16. In the UK the use of renewables, such as solar power and wind power, is increasing every year to generate electricity.

    Last year, the ratio of renewables to fossil fuels to nuclear power was 4 : 5 : 3.

    If the total energy use was 360 million units, find the number of units of electricity generated using renewables.

17. a   The ratio of two even numbers is 7 : 2.
        What are the two numbers? There is more than one possible answer.
    b   Is it possible to find two odd numbers in the ratio 7 : 2? Explain your answer.

18. Mr Draper is painting his daughter Sally's bedroom. He has a paint 'recipe' for misty blue.

    > 3 tins navy blue paint
    > 4 tins elephant grey paint
    > 1 tin white paint

    This 'recipe' covers 32 square metres of wall space.

    Sally's room is only 16 square metres.

    a   How many tins of navy blue, elephant grey and white paint will Mr Draper use?
    b   How many tins of each does he need to buy?

19. On a small farm, a pig and a sheep have masses in the ratio 25 : 16.

    The sheep and a cow have masses in the ratio 6 : 11.

    If the pig has a mass of 150 kg, what is the mass of the cow?

20. There are between 60 and 70 tennis balls in a bucket.

    Gareth and Carys share all of the tennis balls between them in the ratio 2 : 9.

    How many tennis balls were in the bucket originally?

Consolidation 5: Chapters 12–14

Band 1 questions

1 Look at the picture of a mountain range.
  a What is the ratio of the heights of:
    i Mountain A to Mountain B
    ii Mountain B to Mountain D
    iii Mountain E to Mountain D?
  b The heights of which two mountains are in the ratio 2 : 1?
  Give all your answers in simplified form.

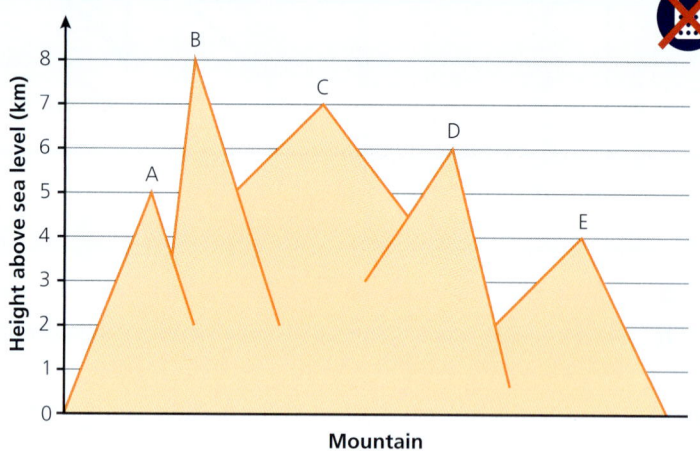

2 Look at these diagrams.

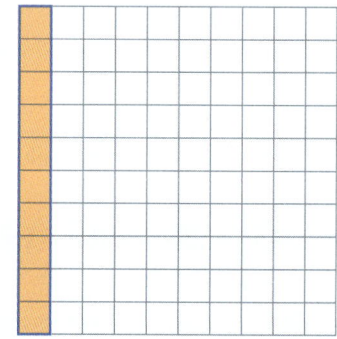

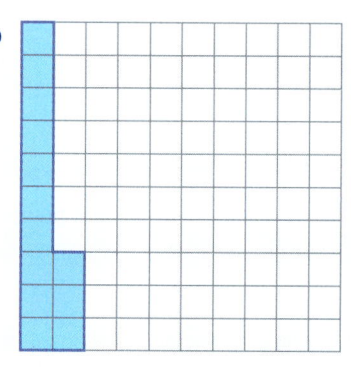

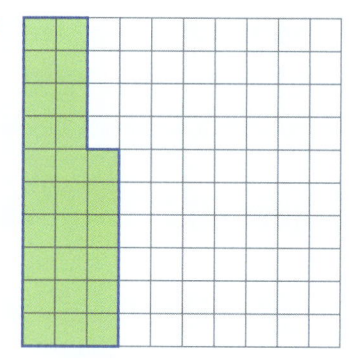

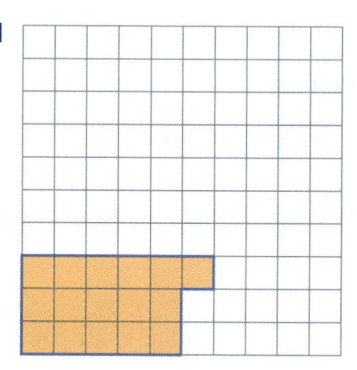

  a   b
  c   d

  i Express each shaded part as a percentage of the whole square.
  ii Write each of your answers a decimal.
  iii Write each of your answers as a fraction, simplifying your answers.

Consolidation 5

3 Look at the number 430.726.

The digit 7 is in the tenths column. It has a value of seven tenths or 0.7.

  a Write down the value of each of these digits:

    i 4   **ii** 3   **iii** 2   **iv** 6

  b Work out:

    i 430.726 × 0.01   **ii** 430.726 ÷ 0.1

4 For lunch, Gwilym goes to the café near to his office.
He buys a packet of sandwiches for £3.49, a carton of orange juice for £1.29 and a packet of crisps for 69p.

  a How much did Gwilym spend on his lunch?

  b Gwilym paid with a £10 note. How much change did he get?

5 Anna thinks that 0.381 is larger than 0.42.

Is she correct? Explain your answer.

6 Copy and complete these calculations.

  a 2 × 0.9 − 0.4 =   **b** 1.8 × 3 − 2 =   **c** 5 − 3 × 0.8 =

  d 7 − 0.6 × 5 =   **e** 0.9 ÷ 3 + 3.1 =

7 At Ysgol Harlech, 24 out of 80 students in Year 8 wear glasses.

  a What percentage do not wear glasses?

  b Convert this to a fraction and to a decimal.

Band 2 questions

8 By first converting all of these quantities to percentages, put them in order of size.

     0.795 $\frac{4}{5}$ $\frac{3}{4}$ 72%   0.81

9 For the school play Mrs Williams, the drama teacher, buys some equipment for the stage. She gets:

- ten light bulbs costing £0.87 each
- ten costumes costing £19.95 each
- one tin of paint for the set at £13.45.

Find how much Mrs Williams spends in total.

10 There are 126 houses in Spencer Street.

The houses are a mixture of bungalows, two-storey houses and three-storey houses, in the ratio 2 : 3 : 4.
Find the number of each type of house in the street.

11 Copy and complete the following:

12 ÷ 3 = 4   12 ÷ 0.3 = ____   1.2 ÷ 0.3 = ____   0.12 ÷ 0.3 = ____

307

12 35% of a football crowd are certain that Bala Town are going to win the game.
20% think that their opponents Cwmbran Town will win.
10% think the game will end in a draw.
The rest do not know what will happen.

   a What percentage of the crowd are not sure about the outcome of the game?

   b There are 2000 people watching the game. How many people think Cwmbran Town will win?

13 This bar chart shows the number of books taken back to the school library each day of one week.

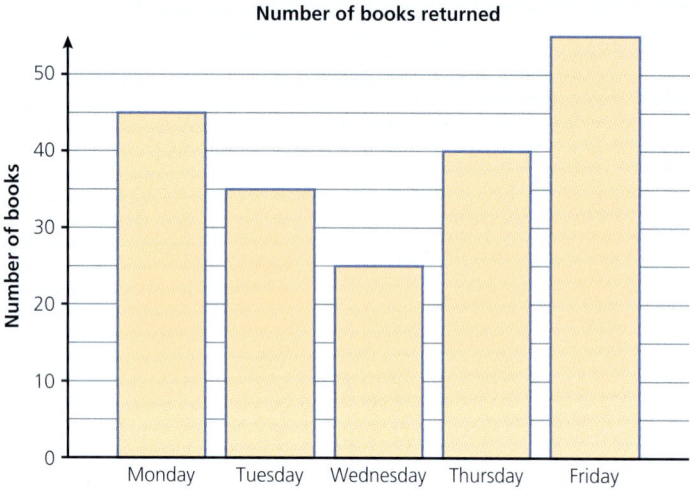

Number of books returned

(Bar chart: Monday 45, Tuesday 35, Wednesday 25, Thursday 40, Friday 55)

   a What percentage of all the books returned were taken back on

      i Thursday   **ii** Monday   **iii** Friday?

   b The librarian says, '25% of books were returned on Wednesday.' Is she correct? Explain your answer.

14 One day on the farm, Percy the pig ate:
- 90% of his own food
- 40% of the chickens' grain
- 30% of the ducks' eggs.

Percy's own food weighed 4 kg.
The chickens' grain weighed 1.25 kg.
There were ten ducks' eggs, weighing 0.15 kg each.
What weight of food did Percy consume?

Band 3 questions

15 Tristan asked all the students in his class what they liked to drink with their school dinner or packed lunch.

The results are shown in the pie chart, but Tristan has forgotten to put the numbers on the chart.

Tristan remembers that:
- he asked 20 students altogether
- the same number of students said fruit juice and fruit smoothie
- 15% said milk.

Find the number of students who said:

   a fruit juice   **b** fruit smoothie

   c milk   **d** water.

16 Marc, the doctor, is very behind with his paperwork.

He has 600 files in his room. Each file contains the notes of patients he needs to put on the computer.

    a On Monday, Marc types up the notes from 12 files.

       What percentage of his paperwork is that?

    b On Tuesday, he gets through another 5% of the files.

       How many files is that?

    c What percentage of Marc's paperwork does he still need to type up?

17 In a field there are 550 field mice, 50 blackbirds and 5 pheasants. Find these ratios, in their simplest form:

    a mice : blackbirds

    b blackbirds : pheasants

    c mice : pheasants

    d How many more field mice would make the ratio of mice : blackbirds 12 : 1?

18 A café is making cheese sandwiches for some of the lunchtime customers.

For every four slices of bread, they use five cherry tomatoes and 50 grams of cheese.

    a How much cheese will they use in ten sandwiches?

    b How many cherry tomatoes will they use if they have used 750 grams of cheese?

Note: There are two slices of bread in each sandwich.

19 Eddie is making cream of mushroom soup for his family of six people. The recipe is for four people.

Copy and complete the table to help Eddie work out how much of each ingredient he needs.

Ingredients	For 4 people	For 1 person	For 6 people
Mushrooms	240 g		
Stock	300 ml		
Small onion	1		
Plain flour	30 g		
Milk	400 ml		

20 King Henry VIII had six wives. The table shows what happened to them:

Name	For how long were they married?	What happened?
Catherine of Aragon	24 years	Divorced
Anne Boleyn	3 years	Beheaded
Jane Seymour	1 year	Died
Anne of Cleves	0.5 years	Divorced
Catherine Howard	1 year	Beheaded
Catherine Parr	3.5 years	Survived

    a What is the ratio of Henry's wives that suffered these fates:

       i divorced : beheaded   **ii** beheaded : died?

       Give your answers in their simplest form.

    b What are these ratios of lengths of marriages to Henry?

       i Catherine of Aragon : Anne Boleyn

       ii Catherine of Aragon : Jane Seymour

       iii Catherine of Aragon : Anne of Cleves

Strategic competence

㉑ Marios has an older brother and a younger sister.

The ratio of his brother's age to Marios' age is 3 : 2.

The ratio of Marios' age to his sister's age is 3 : 1.

   a   Find the ratio of the ages of Marios' brother and Marios' sister.

   b   If Marios' older brother is 18, how old is his little sister?

㉒ Aled has 200 marbles.

His marbles are blue, red and yellow.

The red and yellow marbles are in the ratio 7 : 5.

There are 45 yellow marbles.

How many blue marbles are there?

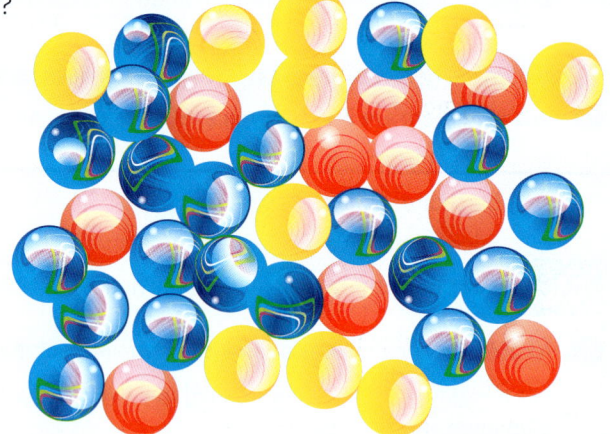

15 Measurements

Coming up...
- Understanding and converting between metric units of mass
- Understanding and converting between metric units of volume
- Using measuring scales

Multiplying and dividing by 10, 100 and 1000

1. Osian says that he can multiply any number by 10 just by putting a 0 at the end of it.
   Is he right? Can you write down a better rule?
2. Osian says that adding two 0s is an easy way to multiply by 100.
   What sort of numbers does Osian's rule work with?
3. Write down rules for multiplying by 10, 100 and 1000.
4. Write down a rule for dividing by 10, 100 and 1000.

15.1 The metric system

Skill checker

1. Multiply each of these numbers by 10.
   a 4   b 7.2   c 0.78
2. Multiply each of these numbers by 100.
   a 0.6   b 2.8   c 11.8
3. Multiply each of these numbers by 1000.
   a 3   b 0.8   c 23.6
4. Divide each of these numbers by 1000.
   a 7000 b 36.2   c 0.8

Activity

Rearrange each group of letters into a mathematical word, and then use them to complete the criss-cross puzzle.

AACCIPTY	AGIKLMOR	CEEIILNRTT	EILRT
ACELS	AGMR	EGHITW	ELMOUV
AGIOLKMR	AMSS	EIIILLLMRT	ENNOT

311

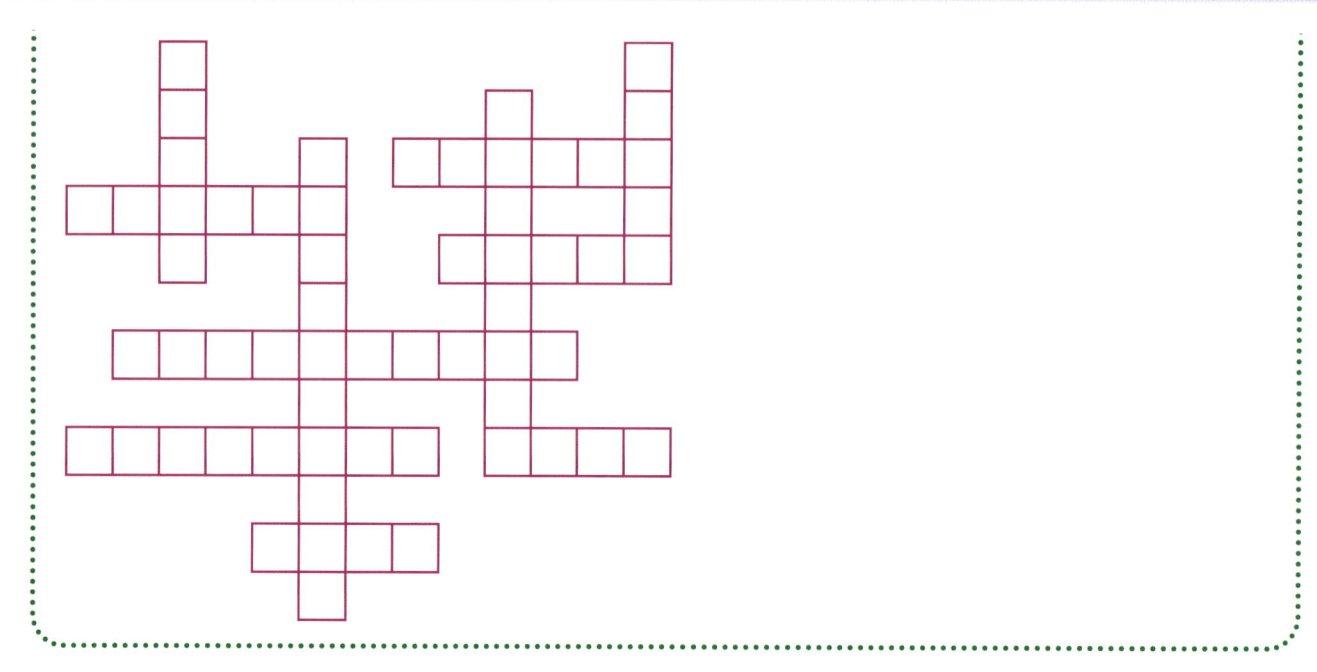

Curriculum for Wales Mastering Mathematics: Book 1

▶ Metric measures of volume

The units of volume are based on the litre (l).

Volume is sometimes referred to as capacity.

Half of a large water bottle is 1 litre.

1 litre = 1000 **millilitres** (ml)

Milli- means 'one thousandth'.

A **cubic centimetre** is exactly 1 ml.

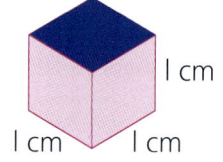

1 litre = 100 **centilitres** (cl)

Centi- means 'one hundredth'.

A teacher's whiteboard pen has a volume of about 3 cl.

You can measure the volume of a liquid using a measuring jug.

This measuring jug contains about 450 ml.

Remember

1 litre = 1000 ml

1 litre = 100 cl

1 cl = 10 ml

1 ml = 1 cm^3

312

15 Measurements

Worked example

Jathika is measuring the volume of liquids for a science experiment.
What is the volume of the liquid in each of these beakers?

a
b

Don't forget the rules!

millilitres → litres	÷1000
litres → millilitres	×1000
millilitres → centilitres	÷10
centilitres → millilitres	×10
centilitres → litres	÷100
litres → centilitres	×100

Solution
a The volume is 4 litres.
b The volume is 700 ml.

▶ Converting between volumes

Worked example

Here is the liquid for another of Jathika's experiments.

a What is the volume of liquid in this beaker?
b How many centilitres is this?
c How many millilitres is this?
d How many cubic centimetres is this?

Solution
a The volume is 3 litres.
b 3 litres = 3 × 100 cl = 300 cl
c 3 litres = 3 × 1000 ml = 3000 ml
d 3 litres = 3000 cm^3

Remember
1 ml = 1 cm^3

Worked example

The label on a packet of orange juice says 'Content 75 cl'.
What is this content in:

a millilitres
b litres?

Solution
a 75 cl = 75 × 10 = 750 ml
b 75 cl = 75 ÷ 100 = 0.75 litres ← You could also use the answer to part **a** and divide by 1000.

▶ Metric measures of mass

The units of mass are based on the **gram** (g).

A pen cap has a mass of about 1 g.

Mass is sometimes mistakenly referred to as weight. However, as it is in such common usage, some of the questions and examples in this book refer to weight rather than mass.

Kilo- means 'one thousand'.

1000 g is a **kilogram** (kg).
A litre of water has a mass of exactly 1 kg.

1 kg is 1000 **milligrams** (mg).
20 grains of salt have a mass of about 1 mg.

> **Remember**
> Milli- means 'one thousandth'.

1 **tonne** is 1000 kg.
A small car has a mass of about a tonne.

> **Remember**
> 1 tonne = 1000 kg
> 1 kg = 1000 g
> 1 g = 1000 mg

You need to have a rough idea of the mass of an object so that you can choose an appropriate **measuring instrument**.

This could be a scientific balance, kitchen scales or bathroom scales.

This papaya has a mass just under 400 g.

Worked example

Here are two scale readings.

Cai is measuring some bricks on one scale and a bean on the other scale.

a   What is the mass of the bricks?
b   What is the mass of the bean?

Solution

a   Look at the units given on the scales.

   You would weigh bricks in kilograms, so the scale on the left is weighing the bricks.

   The pointer tells you that the mass is 6 kg.

b   You would weigh a bean in grams, so the scale on the right is weighing the bean.

   The pointer is halfway between 3 and 4, so the mass is $3\frac{1}{2}$ grams.

Worked example

What is the most appropriate instrument to measure the mass of:

a   yourself
b   a bar of chocolate
c   a spider's egg?

Solution

a   Bathroom scales
b   Kitchen scales
c   Scientific scales

Don't forget the rules!

kilograms → tonnes	÷ 1000
tonnes → kilograms	× 1000
grams → kilograms	÷ 1000
kilograms → grams	× 1000
milligrams → grams	÷ 1000
grams → milligrams	× 1000

▶ Converting between masses

Worked example

Sioned's shopping bag has a mass of 4.3 kg.

a   Convert this mass into tonnes.
b   Convert it into grams.
c   Why would you not weigh a shopping bag in tonnes or grams?

Solution

a   4.3 kg = 4.3 ÷ 1000 = 0.0043 tonnes
b   4.3 kg = 4.3 × 1000 = 4300 g
c   0.0043 is too small so tonnes would not be an appropriate measure to use. 4300 is a big number, so you would avoid using grams in this instance.

315

Curriculum for Wales **Mastering Mathematics: Book 1**

> **Activity**
>
> With a 5-litre beaker and a 3-litre beaker (which have no markings), you can measure 2 litres by filling the 5-litre beaker and pouring as much as possible into the 3-litre beaker. 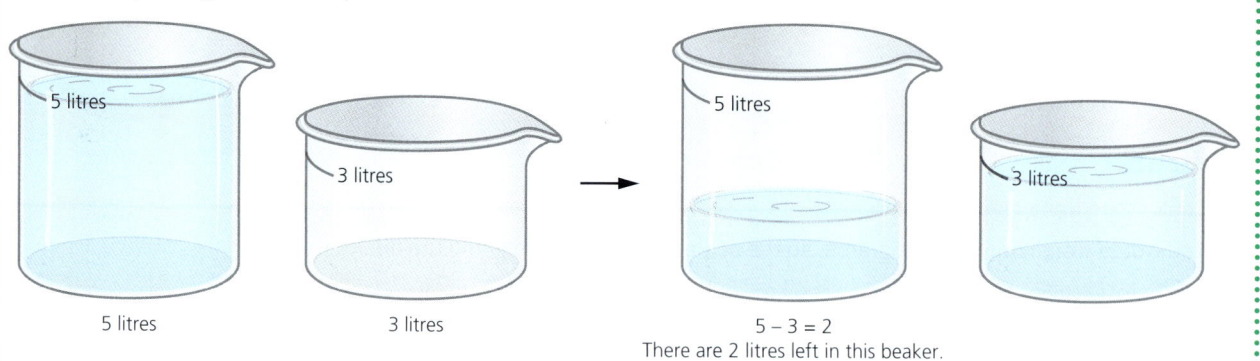
>
> 5 litres   3 litres   →   5 litres   3 litres
>
> 5 − 3 = 2
> There are 2 litres left in this beaker.
>
> 1. a How can you measure 1 litre using a 4-litre beaker and a 9-litre beaker?
>   b How can you measure 4 litres using a 3-litre beaker and a 5-litre beaker?
>   c Show how you can measure any whole number of litres from 1 litre to 7 litres using just two beakers which hold 2 litres and 5 litres.
> 2. Design a pair of beakers that could be used to measure anything from 1 to 10 litres.

15.1 Now try these

Band 1 questions

1 What is the mass shown on each of these scales?

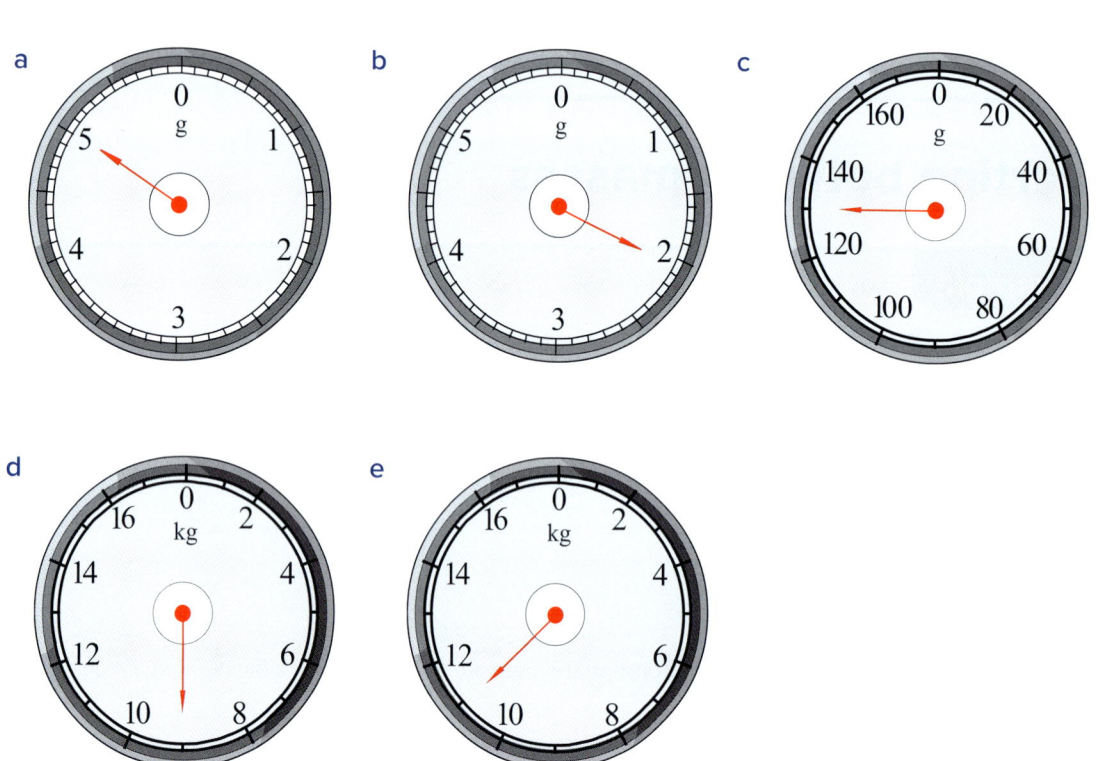

a, b, c (g scales 0–5)

d, e (kg scales 0–16)

15 Measurements

2 How much liquid is in each of these beakers?

a b 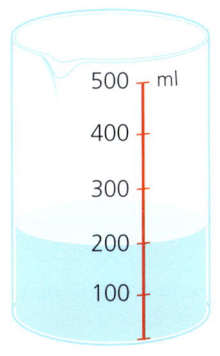 c 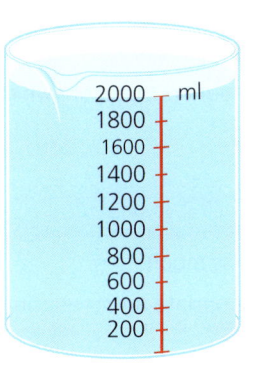 d

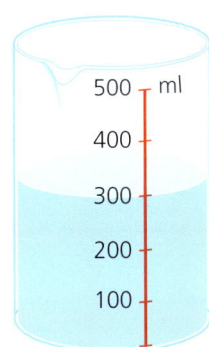

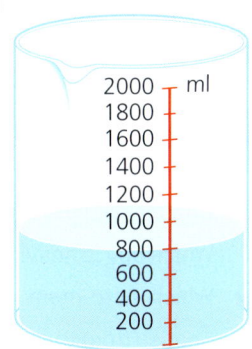

e Convert each of your answers into centilitres.

3 This cube is filled with water. The amount of water is 1 millilitre (1 ml).
What is the volume of water in each of these shapes?

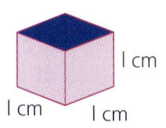

a 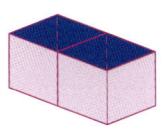 b 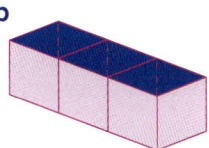 c

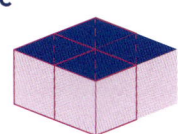

d Convert each of your answers into centilitres.

4 a Write these masses in grams.
  i 7 kg ii 30 kg iii 2.5 kg iv $\frac{1}{2}$ kg
  b Write these masses in milligrams.
  i 4 g ii 19 g iii 1.2 g iv 0.3 g

5 a Write these volumes in millilitres.
  i 3 litres ii 20 cl iii 2.1 litres iv $\frac{1}{2}$ litre
  b Write these volumes in centilitres.
  i 6 ml ii 2 litres iii 0.6 litres iv 15 ml

6 a Write these masses in kilograms.
  i 7000 g ii 2 tonnes iii 14.6 tonnes
  b Write these volumes in litres.
  i 3000 ml ii 60 cl iii 740 cm³

Band 2 questions

7 a How much water is in each of these beakers?
  i ii 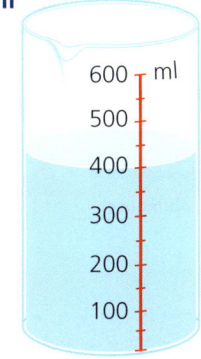 iii

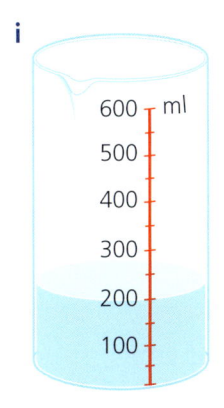

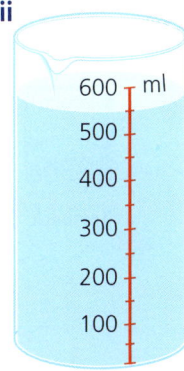

317

Strategic competence

   b How much water is there in total?

   c Angharad needs 2000 ml of water.

      i How many litres is this?

      ii Angharad has the amount of water shown in the jugs in part **a**. How much more water does Angharad need?

8 Elis has two dogs.

Max weighs 13 kg.

Gnasher weighs 11 000 g.

Which dog is heavier and by how much?

Logical reasoning

9 Which instrument is most appropriate for measuring the mass of each of the things below?

Choose from this list.

| scientific balance | kitchen scales | bathroom scales | industrial scales |

  a A lorry   **b** A child   **c** A grain of sand   **d** An apple

10 Which of these is most appropriate for measuring the volume of each of the things below?

Choose from this list.

| medicine spoon | measuring jug | the gauge on a pump | a 5-litre can |

  a The quantity of milk for a recipe

  b Petrol for your mower

  c A dose of cough medicine

  d The volume of petrol you put in your car

11 A bag of sugar weighs 1000 g (1 kg).

Copy and complete the table. Put the objects in the correct column.

Less than 1000 g (1 kg)	More than 1000 g (1 kg)

Tin of beans 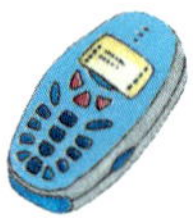   Mobile phone    Vacuum cleaner    Apple    Dog

Doll    Textbook    Computer    Pencil    Desk

15 Measurements

Logical reasoning

12 Look at the objects. Match each one to its possible capacity below.

- Bathroom sink
- Teaspoon
- Kettle
- Bath
- Mug
- Bottle of ketchup

| 5 ml | 400 ml | 80 litres | 15 litres | 250 ml | $1\frac{1}{2}$ litres |

Band 3 questions

Strategic competence

13 a How much liquid is in each of these beakers?

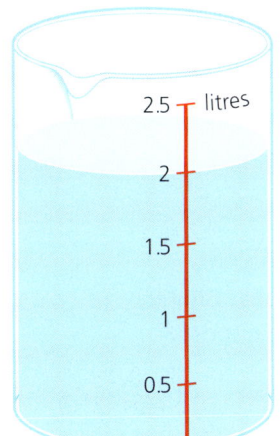

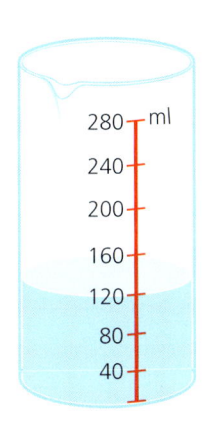

i (beaker marked in litres: 0.5, 1, 1.5, 2, 2.5)

ii (beaker marked in ml: 40, 80, 120, 160, 200, 240, 280)

b Asaph pours liquid from beaker **i** into beaker **ii** until it reaches the 280 ml level.

How much liquid remains in beaker **i**?

14 Look at this list of ingredients. It makes flapjacks for 12 people.

a Rajani is catering for a wedding.

She wants to make flapjacks for 600 people.

How much of each ingredient does she need?

Flapjacks
★★★★★

75 grams of sugar
75 grams of butter
50 grams of golden syrup
150 grams of rolled oats
35 grams of dried fruit

319

b Sion is catering for a school.

He wants to make 1800 flapjacks. He has the ingredients shown in this list.

   i How much of each ingredient does Sion need?

   ii How much more does he need to buy, or will he have some of each ingredient left over?

> 10 kg of sugar
> 10.3 kg of butter
> 4 kg of golden syrup
> 16.9 kg of rolled oats
> 450 g of dried fruit

15 The capacity of a car's fuel tank is 80 litres.

On average, the car uses 125 ml of fuel per mile.

a How much fuel does this car use when it travels 8 miles?

b How far can the car travel on a full tank?

When the amount of fuel in the tank falls to 6 litres, a warning light comes on.

c The warning light comes on. The driver says, 'I can still drive 50 miles'. Is he right?

16 It's a busy day in July at the airport and everyone is keen to get away.

Suitcases are crammed full of luggage and some people's suitcases are too heavy!

Any suitcase that weighs over the ticket allowance is charged as excess baggage.

Baggage allowance

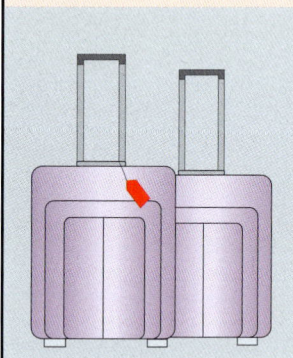

Number of bags: 1
Weight per bag: Up to 20 kg
Dimensions per bag: Up to 90 × 75 × 43 cm
Excess baggage: £5 per kg when paid online
£11 per kg at the airport

a The scales show the weight of baggage for five passengers.

How much did each of them pay online for excess baggage?

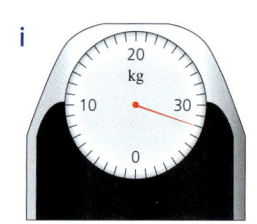

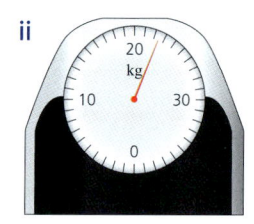

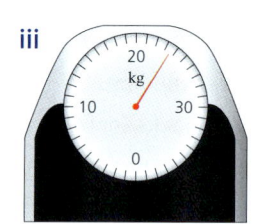

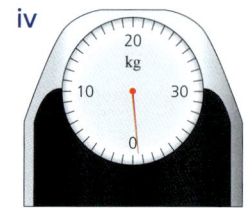

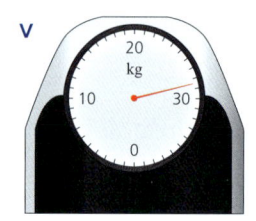

   i, **ii**, **iii**, **iv**, **v**

b How much did each passenger save by paying online for their excess baggage before they arrived at the airport?

c Is this a fair way to charge for luggage? What suggestions would you make?

d These charges are for short-haul journeys to places in Europe.

What would be a fair excess baggage charge per kilogram for a long-haul flight to Australia?

17 Rhodri has a jug which holds 750 ml of liquid.

He pours 20 jugs of water into his fish tank.

There were already 25 litres of water in the fish tank. The fish tank is now full.

What is the capacity of the fish tank?

18 The table shows the cost of posting parcels in Afonffordd.

Weight	Cost
Up to 0.25 kg	£1.00
0.5 kg	£1.50
0.75 kg	£2.00
1.0 kg	£3.00
1.5 kg	£4.00
2 kg	£5.00
3 kg	£6.00
Over 3 kg: £1.00 for every extra 1 kg or part of 1 kg.	

a How much does it cost to send this parcel?

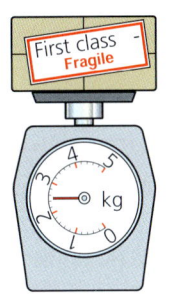

b How much does it cost to send each of these parcels?

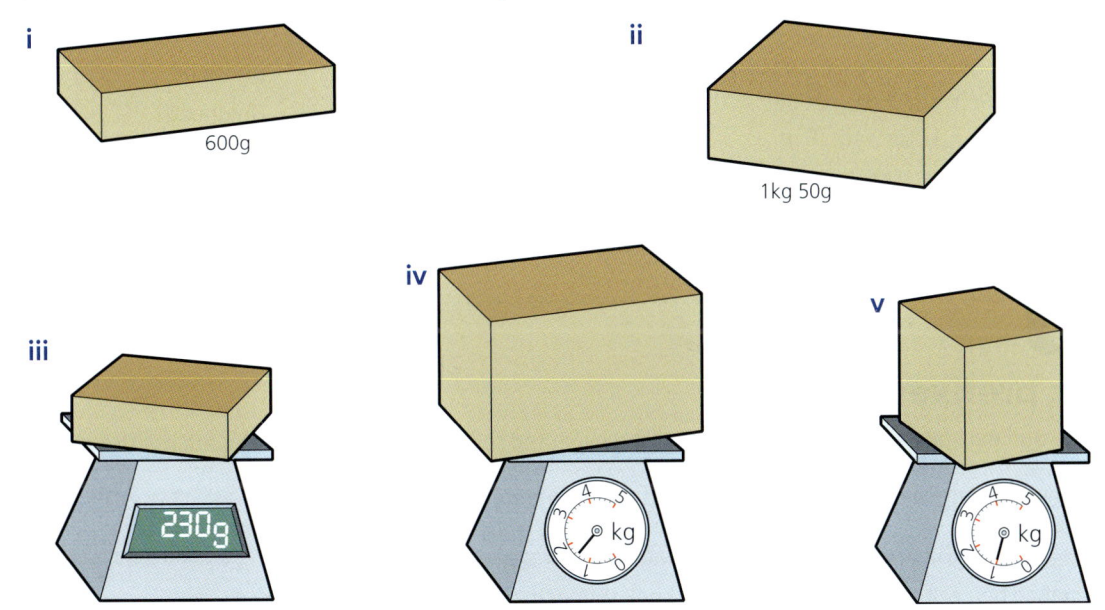

i 600g

ii 1kg 50g

iii 230g

iv

v

c All the parcels in part **b** are then wrapped together in one very large parcel.

　i How much does it cost to send them in this way?

　ii How much does this save?

d Put the parcels in part **b** together into two big parcels.

　How much does each parcel cost to post?

e Find the cheapest way of posting the parcels in part **b** as two big parcels.

15.2 Converting units of length

Skill checker

① How many millimetres are in 1 centimetre?
② How many centimetres are in 1 metre?
③ How many metres are in 1 kilometre?

▶ Converting units of length

Remember

1 km = 1000 m
1 m = 100 cm
1 m = 1000 mm
1 cm = 10 mm

Don't forget the rules!

kilometres → metres	×1000
metres → kilometres	÷1000
metres → centimetres	×100
centimetres → metres	÷100
metres → millimetres	×1000
millimetres → metres	÷1000
centimetres → millimetres	×10
millimetres → centimetres	÷10

Worked example

The width of a laptop is 38 cm.

a Write this measurement in:
  i millimetres   ii metres   iii km.
b Which of the above units would not be appropriate when measuring the width of a laptop?

Solution

a i 38 cm = 38 × 10 mm = 380 mm
  ii 38 cm = 38 ÷ 100 m = 0.38 m
  iii 0.38 m = 0.38 ÷ 1000 km = 0.000 38 km
b Kilometres would not be an appropriate unit to use.

Cross-curricular activity

In geography, you will sometimes need to find the distances between places. Calculate the distance as the crow flies between your house and the centre of:

- Bridgend
- Holyhead
- St Clears.

Write each of the distances in both kilometres and metres.

Activity

Metric prefixes

Kilo-, centi- and milli- are the only prefixes you will be expected to know in maths, but they are not the only ones.

You may have already met others and not realised they were metric measures.

① In what context have you heard the prefixes mega- and giga-? What do they mean?
② In science you will meet micro- and nano-. Look these up to find out what they mean.
③ Is there a difference between deci- and deca- ?

Communication using symbols

④ How many different metric prefixes can you find? Copy and fill in this table with the prefixes you find.

Metric prefix	Multiplication	Symbol
kilo-	× 1000	k
centi-	$\times \frac{1}{100}$	c
milli-	$\times \frac{1}{1000}$	m

15.2 Now try these

Band 1 questions

1 Copy and complete this conversion diagram.

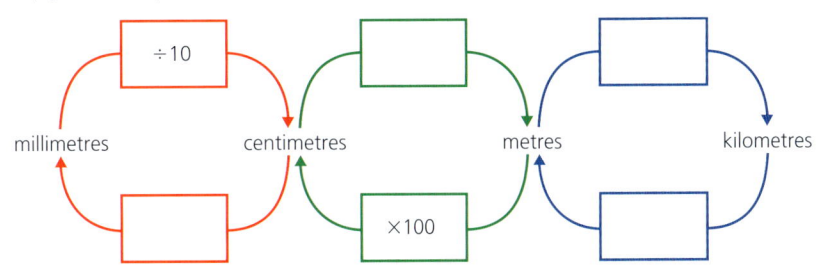

2 Write these lengths in millimetres.
- a 3 cm
- b 24 cm
- c 2 m

3 Write these lengths in centimetres.
- a 50 mm
- b 3 m
- c 24 m

4 Write these lengths in metres.
- a 400 cm
- b 1000 mm
- c 2 km

5 Write these lengths in kilometres.
- a 7000 m
- b 11 000 m
- c 500 m

6 Copy and complete these sentences.
- a 52 mm is the same as _____ centimetres.
- b 560 cm is the same as _____ metres.
- c 3200 m is the same as _____ kilometres.

Band 2 questions

7 Copy and complete these sentences.
- a 8 mm is the same as _____ centimetres.
- b 23 cm is the same as _____ metres.
- c 0.9 m is the same as _____ kilometres.

8 Ieuan thinks that 55 mm is longer than 6.5 cm because 55 is bigger than 6.5.

Explain why he is not correct.

Curriculum for Wales Mastering Mathematics: Book 1

9 Write down the longer length in these pairs of measurements.
  a 23 cm and 210 mm
  b 83 mm and 9 cm
  c 7 km and 8200 m
  d 123 cm and 2 m

10 Gruffydd says that multiplying by 1000 converts from kilometres to metres.
Becky says the rule should be divide by 1000 because metres are smaller than kilometres.
Who is right? Explain your answer.

11 Convert these lengths into more convenient units.
  a 30 000 cm
  b 0.000 04 km
  c 0.007 m

12 Copy these lengths and link the equivalent ones.
The first one has been done for you. There are five more links to be found.

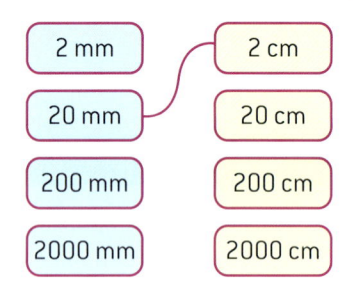

2 mm	2 cm	2 m	2 km
20 mm	20 cm	20 m	20 km
200 mm	200 cm	200 m	200 km
2000 mm	2000 cm	2000 m	2000 km

Band 3 questions

13 a How many centimetres are equivalent to 1 km?
  b How many millimetres are equivalent to 1 km?

14 This is the conversion rule from kilometres to metres: km $\xrightarrow{\times 1000}$ m.
Copy and complete these conversion rules.
  a km $\xrightarrow{}$ mm
  b cm $\xrightarrow{}$ km
  c km $\xrightarrow{}$ cm
  d mm $\xrightarrow{}$ km

15 Copy and complete these.
  a 2 km = _____ cm
  b 3.4 km = _____ mm
  c 56 km = _____ mm
  d 340 km = _____ cm
  e 7 cm = _____ km
  f 72 mm = _____ km
  g 3 mm = _____ km
  h 0.02 cm = _____ km

16 Write each group of four lengths in order of size, starting with the shortest one.
  a 832 mm   78 cm   4 m   1 km
  b 5000 mm   412 cm   3 m   2 km
  c 11 000 mm 8000 cm 54 m   0.3 km

17 Work out these length sums.
  a 4 cm + 13 mm = _____ mm
  b 23 cm + 50 mm = _____ cm
  c 4 m + 345 cm + 90 mm = _____ cm
  d 2 m + 570 cm + 3000 mm = _____ m

324

18 Work out these length subtractions.

a   2 m – 67 cm = _____

b   8 km – 580 m = _____

c   3 km – 29 m = _____

d   7 m – 235 cm – 1248 mm = _____

19 The height of a 2p coin is 26 mm.

Find the height of £3 worth of 2p coins.

Give your answer in metres.

20 Dyfrig is 1.4 m tall.

His friend Mari is 3 cm shorter.

What height is Mari?

Give your answer in metres.

Key words

Here is a list of the key words you met in this chapter.

Capacity	Centilitre	Centimetre	Gram
Kilogram	Kilometre	Litre	Mass
Metre	Milligram	Millilitre	Millimetre
Scale	Tonne	Volume	Weight

Use the glossary at the back of this book to check any you are unsure about.

Review exercise: measurements

Band 1 questions

1 Write these lengths in centimetres (cm).
   a   4 m
   b   13 m
   c   2.5 m

2 Write these lengths in metres (m).
   a   200 cm
   b   530 cm
   c   621 cm

3 a   How many centilitres are there in 1 litre?
   b   How many millilitres are there in 1 centilitre?

4 Convert these volumes from millilitres to litres.
   a   3000 ml
   b   1500 ml
   c   800 ml

5 Convert the masses shown on the packaging from grams to kilograms.
   a   Lentils 1200 g
   b   carrots 2400 g
   c   Margarine 500 g

6 Copy and complete these.
   a   14 cm = _____ mm
   b   350 mm = _____ cm
   c   8000 cm = _____ m
   d   7300 g = _____ kg
   e   6.4 litres = _____ ml
   f   4020 m = _____ km

Band 2 questions

7 a   Write the measurement 450 cm in:
      i   millimetres
      ii metres.
   b   There are 10 decimetres in 1 metre. Write 450 cm in decimetres.

8 Write down the larger value in each of these pairs of measurements.
   a   14 cm and 130 mm
   b   28 mm and 3 cm
   c   4 km and 3800 m
   d   76 cm and 1 m
   e   8100 g and 8 kg
   f   3 litres and 2900 ml
   g   990 mm and 1 m
   h   4100 g and 4 kg

9 Tommy says that the conversion from metres to millimetres is ×1000.

Ben says that the conversion should be done by first converting to centimetres (×100) and then converting the centimetres to millimetres (×10).

Who is right? Explain your answer.

10 Match each measurement in List A with the same measurement in List B.
Which two cannot be matched?

   A   a   34 mm × 10
       b   3.4 cm ÷ 10
       c   34 cm × 10
       d   3.4 m ÷ 100
       e   3.4 m × 10
       f   340 cm × 100

   B   i   3.4 km ÷ 10
       ii   3.4 cm × 100
       iii 3.4 km × 10
       iv   3.4 m × 10
       v   3.4 km ÷ 100 000
       vi   34 mm × 10

11. The length of Sam's pace is 60 cm.

    How many paces does she take in 3 kilometres?

12. A type of brick weighs 1250 g.

    Calculate the mass of 8000 of these bricks in tonnes.

Band 3 questions

13. The diagram shows part of a fence.

    Each post is 1200 mm high and weighs 1800 g.

    Posts are connected by a single bar 500 cm long.

    There are 301 posts.

    Calculate:

    a the total mass of the posts in kilograms

    b the total length of the posts in metres

    c the length of the fence in kilometres.

14. The metric prefix micro- means $\frac{1}{1\,000\,000}$.

    So there are 1 million micrometres in 1 metre.

    a How many micrometres are there in 1 millimetre?

    b How many micrometres are there in 1 centimetre?

    c How many micrograms are there in 1 gram?

    d In what context would such measurements be useful?

15. The metric prefix mega- means 1 million.

    So 1 megametre is 1 million metres.

    What is a common name for 1 megagram?

16. Convert these measurements to more convenient units.

    a 2 760 000 cm
    b 870 000 ml
    c 3 600 000 mg
    d 0.002 litres
    e 0.000 006 3 tonnes
    f 0.000 079 km

17. This is the conversion rule from kilograms to grams: kg $\xrightarrow{\times 1000}$ g.

    Copy and complete these conversion rules.

    a kg $\xrightarrow{}$ mg
    b mg $\xrightarrow{}$ kg
    c tonnes $\xrightarrow{}$ grams
    d grams $\xrightarrow{}$ tonnes
    e milligrams $\xrightarrow{}$ tonnes
    f tonnes $\xrightarrow{}$ milligrams

18. a How many milligrams are equivalent to 2.6 tonnes?

    b How many tonnes are equivalent to 734 mg?

19. Dafydd's bucket weighs 700 g.

    He fills the bucket exactly half-full with sand and the bucket now weights 2.8 kg.

    How much will Dafydd's bucket weigh when it is filled to the top with sand?

16 Area and perimeter

Coming up...
- Understanding and using perimeter of a rectangle
- Understanding and using area of a rectangle
- Understanding and using area of a triangle
- Understanding and using compound shapes

Triangle tangle

You can join dots on a 3 × 3 square to make different triangles like this:

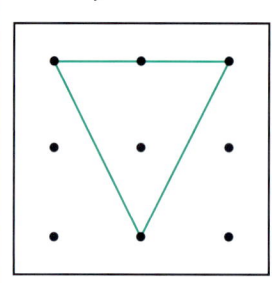

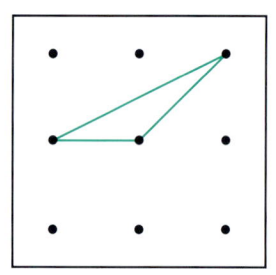

① Use square dotty paper or a nine-pin geoboard and an elastic band to find as many *different* triangles as you can.

② By counting squares, work out the area of each triangle.
One small square has an area of 1 cm².

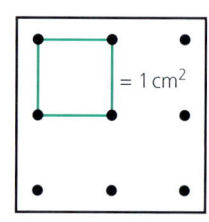

= 1 cm²

16.1 Area and perimeter

Skill checker

① a Draw a rectangle which is not a square.
  b Draw all the lines of symmetry on your rectangle.
② a Draw a square.
  b Draw all the lines of symmetry on your square.

▶ Area and perimeter

Area is the amount of space inside a two-dimensional shape.
It is measured in square units, such as cm² or m².
One way to find the area of a shape is to count the number of squares inside it.
1 m² is the space inside a square of side 1 m.
An area of 4 m² means an area equivalent to 4 × 1 m².

328

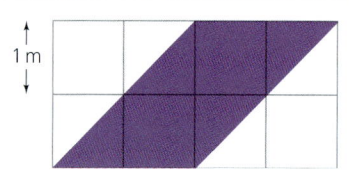

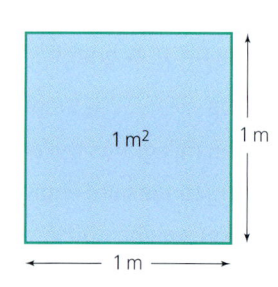

16 Area and perimeter

Worked example

Lewis covers a flat roof on his house with decking.

The roof is 9 metres long and 4 metres wide.

What is the area of the roof?

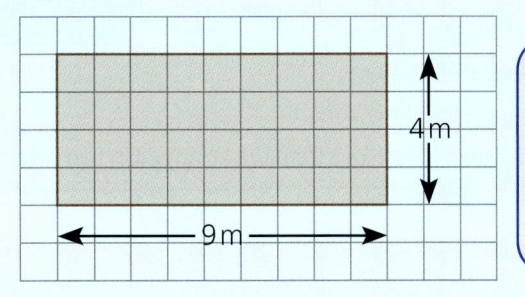

Solution

The roof is made up of four rows of nine squares.

So the area is 4 × 9 = 36 m².

This rectangle is nine squares long and four squares wide. So each square represents 1m². Say this as 'one square metre'.

It is not always practical to count the squares inside a shape to find the area.

A useful rule is:

area of a rectangle = length × width

Perimeter is the distance all the way around the outside of a shape.

Perimeter is measured in units of length, such as centimetres or metres.

Worked example

Calculate the perimeter of a rectangle with length 8 cm and width 5 cm.

Solution

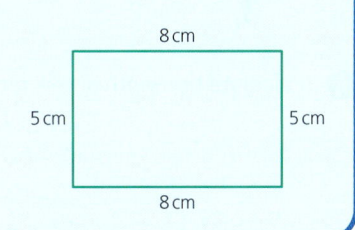

Starting at the top left corner and working clockwise around the shape, the side lengths are 8 cm, 5 cm, 8 cm and 5 cm.

The perimeter is 8 + 5 + 8 + 5 = 26 cm.

Maths in context

The word 'perimeter' in English, or 'perimedr' in Welsh, is from the Greek words 'peri', which means 'around', and 'metron', which means 'measure'.

16.1 Now try these

Band 1 questions

1 Calculate the area of each of these rectangles.

　a 7 cm, 4 cm

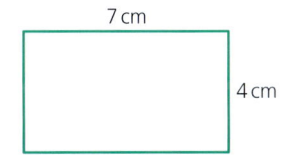

　b 10 m, 6 m

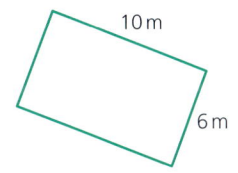

　c 15 mm, 11 mm

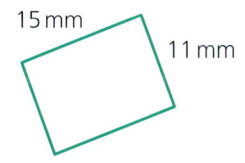

2 Calculate the perimeter of each of these shapes.

　a 8 cm, 8 cm, 8 cm, 8 cm

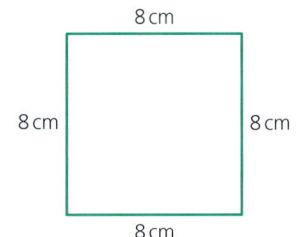

　b 9 mm, 15 mm, 15 mm, 9 mm

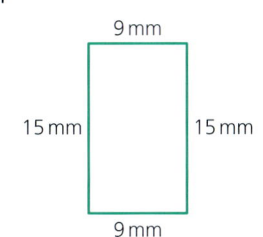

　c 5 m, 12 m, 12 m, 5 m

329

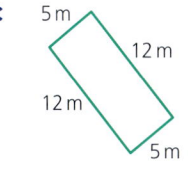

Curriculum for Wales Mastering Mathematics: Book 1

Fluency

3. Calculate the area and perimeter of this rectangle.

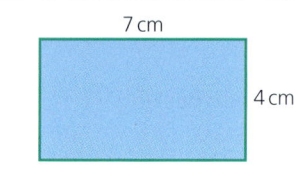

   7 cm
   4 cm

   Note: Remember to give the units with your answer.

4. A square has sides of length 11 mm.
   a Calculate the area of the square.
   b Calculate the perimeter of the square.

5. Ten square tiles with a side length of 15 cm are arranged in two rows of five. Calculate the total area of all ten tiles.

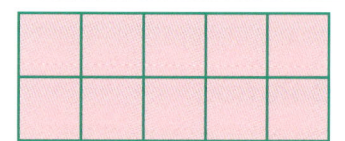

Band 2 questions

Logical reasoning

6. John says that the length and width of this rectangle have been labelled the wrong way around, because the length should go across and the width should be at the side.

   Is John right? Explain your answer.

   Width
   Length

Strategic competence

7. Calculate the length of this rectangle.

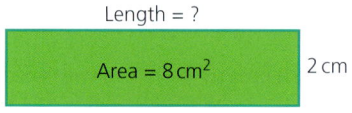

   Length = ?
   Area = 8 cm²
   2 cm

8. Calculate the width of this rectangle.

   6 m
   Width
   Area = 30 m²

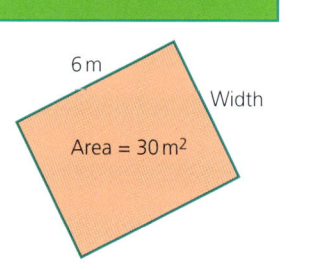

Logical reasoning

9. Mr Jones draws this rectangle on the board to assess his students' understanding of area and perimeter.

   Could there be a problem with this example?
   Explain your answer.

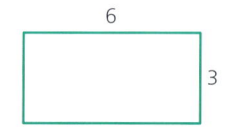

   6
   3

Strategic competence

10.
    2 m
    80 cm

    a Calculate the area of this rectangle.
    b Calculate its perimeter.

    Look carefully at the units.

Fluency

11. Tomos is painting a fence. He paints one side of each of five fence panels.

    The height of each panel is 1.5 m and their lengths are all 1.8 m.
    The posts don't need to be painted.
    Calculate the total area he will need to paint.

330

Band 3 questions

12 A rectangular field has length 50 m and width 30 m.
   a Calculate the perimeter of the field.
   b Calculate the area of the field.

13 Calculate the value of w shown on the diagram.

15 cm, w cm, Area = 135 cm²

14 The perimeter of a square is 40 m.
   Calculate the length of each side of the square.

15 This square has an area of 144 cm².
   Find the value of x.

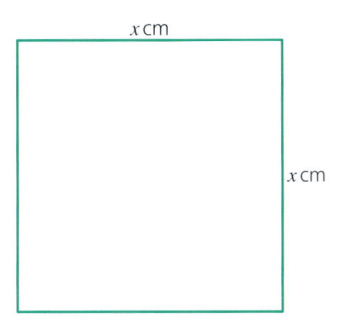

x cm, x cm

16 The area of a square is 81 cm².
   Calculate the perimeter of the square.

17 Each small square on this chessboard has an area of 9 cm².
   Calculate the perimeter of the whole chessboard.

18 The area of a rectangle is 24 cm². Its perimeter is 22 cm.
   Calculate the length and the width of the rectangle.

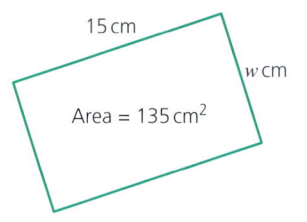

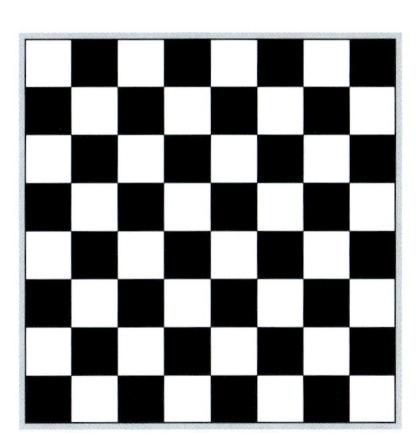

16.2 Area of a triangle

Skill checker

① a Draw an isosceles triangle which is not equilateral.
   b Draw all the lines of symmetry on your triangle.
② a Draw an equilateral triangle.
   b Draw all the lines of symmetry on your triangle.
③ Draw a scalene right-angled triangle.
④ a Calculate $\frac{1}{2} \times 5 \times 6$.   c Calculate $5 \times 6 \times \frac{1}{2}$.
   b Calculate $5 \times \frac{1}{2} \times 6$.   d What do you notice about your three answers?

Curriculum for Wales Mastering Mathematics: Book 1

Activity

On squared paper, draw a rectangle.

Using one of the sides of the rectangle as the base, draw a triangle inside the rectangle so that it reaches the opposite side.

Shade your triangle.

Cut it out, keeping the outer triangles.

Use the outer triangles to demonstrate that the area of the shaded triangle is exactly half the area of the rectangle.

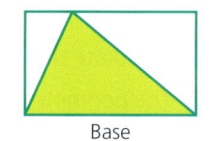

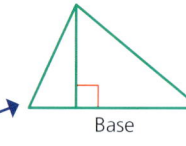

Area of a triangle = $\frac{1}{2}$ × base × height

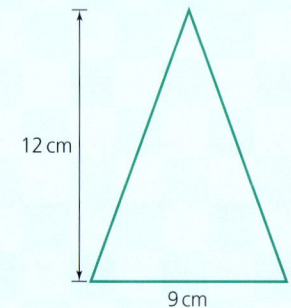

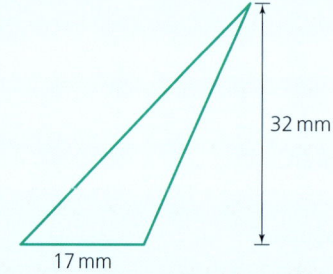

The base must be perpendicular to the height.

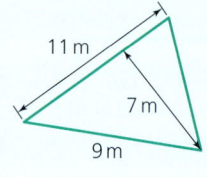

Worked example

Calculate the area of each of these triangles.

a 12 cm, 9 cm
b 32 mm, 17 mm
c 11 m, 7 m, 9 m

Solution

a Area = $\frac{1}{2}$ × 9 × 12 = 54 cm²

b Area = $\frac{1}{2}$ × 17 × 32 = 272 mm²

c Area = $\frac{1}{2}$ × 11 × 7 = 38.5 m²

16.2 Now try these

Band 1 questions

1 Calculate the area of each of these triangles.

a 8 cm, 5 cm

b 7 m, 10 m

c 16 mm, 23 mm

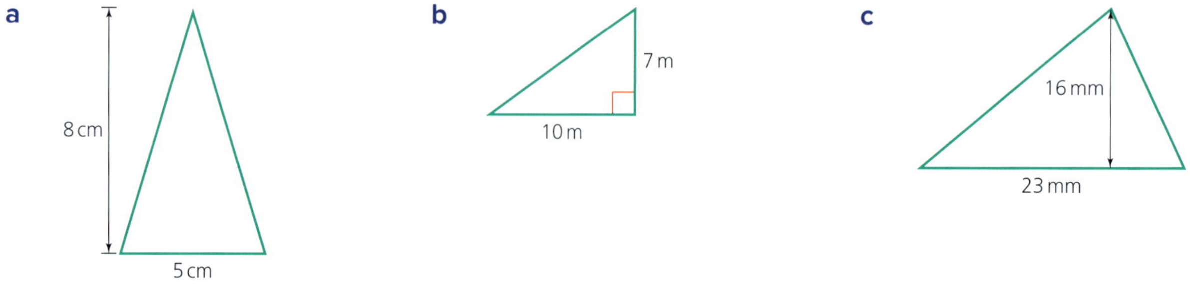

16 Area and perimeter

Fluency

2 Calculate the area of each of these triangles.

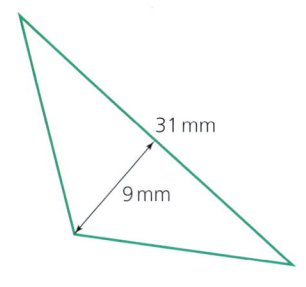

a) triangle with 31 mm and 9 mm

b) triangle with 7 m and 6 m

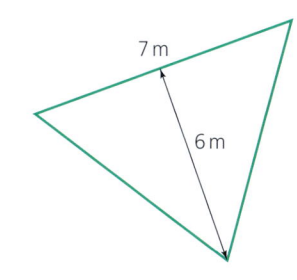

3 Calculate the area of each of these triangles.

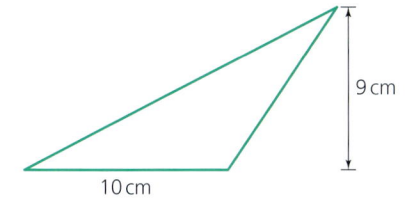

a) triangle with base 10 cm and height 9 cm

b) triangle with base 13 m and height 11 m

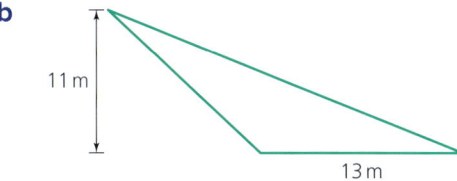

4 Calculate the area of each of these triangles.

One of the lengths in each of the triangles in question 4 needs to be ignored. You need to decide which one.

a) triangle with 8 cm, 10 cm, 12 cm

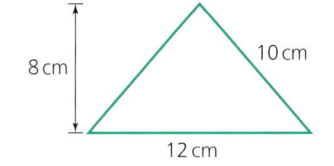

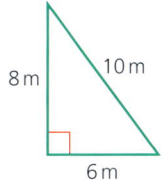

b) triangle with 8 m, 10 m, 6 m (right angle)

c) triangle with 13 mm, 10 mm, 12 mm

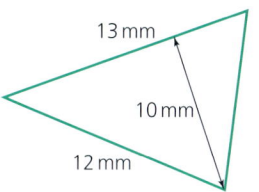

5 Calculate the area of this triangle.

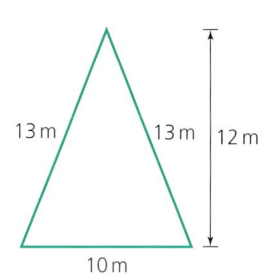

triangle with 13 m, 13 m, 12 m, 10 m

6 An equilateral triangle has sides of length 15 cm and a perpendicular height of 13 cm. Calculate its area.

Band 2 questions

Strategic competence

7 Calculate the perpendicular height (h) of this triangle.

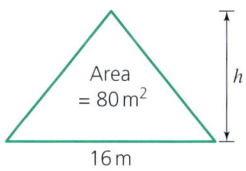

Area = 80 m², base 16 m, height h

8 This triangle has area 20 cm². It has a perpendicular height of 10 cm. Calculate the value of x.

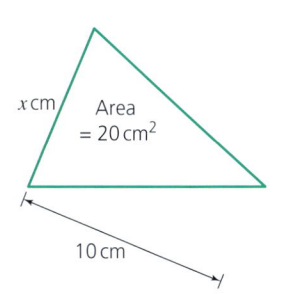

triangle with x cm, Area = 20 cm², 10 cm

333

9 Eleri asks this area question:

'Calculate the area of an equilateral triangle with sides 10 cm and height 12 cm.'

Rhys says that the question can't be answered. Is he right? Explain why.

10 Wil draws a 5 cm, 12 cm, 13 cm triangle.

There is a right angle between the 5 cm and 12 cm sides.

a Calculate the perimeter of the triangle.

b Calculate the area of the triangle.

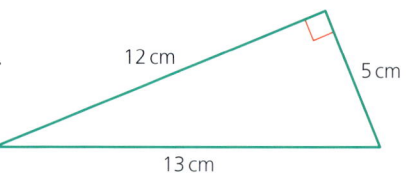

11 Alwyn, Tegan and Seren are explaining how to calculate the area of a triangle.

Alwyn says that you should first halve the base and then multiply by the perpendicular height.

Tegan says that you should first halve the perpendicular height and then multiply by the base.

Seren says that you should first multiply the base by the perpendicular height, and then halve the answer.

Who is right?

12 The area of an equilateral triangle is 390 cm². It has a perpendicular height of 26 cm.

Calculate the perimeter of the triangle.

13 Matthew tries to work out the area of this triangle.

Here is Matthew's calculation.

$\frac{1}{2} \times 10 \times 11 = 55 \, cm^2$

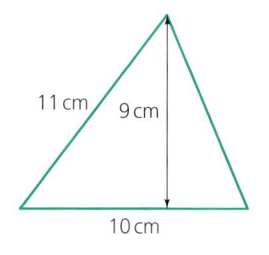

a Explain the mistake Matthew has made.

b Calculate the correct area of the triangle.

Band 3 questions

14 a Calculate the area of this triangle.

b Calculate the length, labelled x, of the perpendicular from the 12 cm side to the opposite corner.

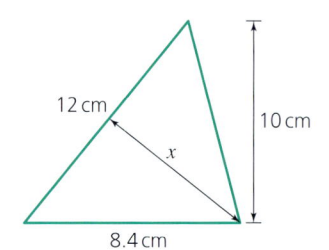

16 Area and perimeter

Strategic competence

15 Calculate the perpendicular height, labelled h, shown on this triangle.

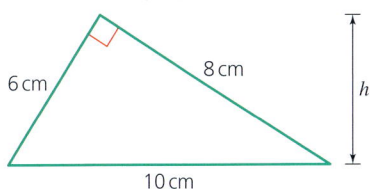

Logical reasoning

16 Three triangles are labelled A, B and C. The dashed lines shown are parallel.

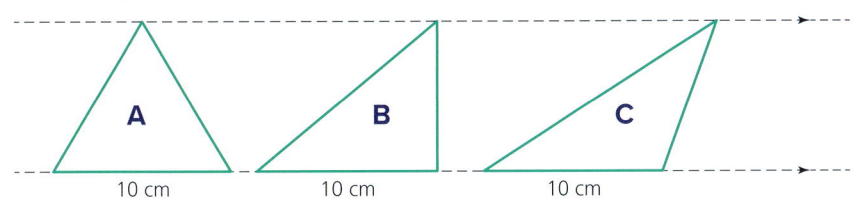

Mali says that A has the largest area and C has the smallest area.
Saul says that C has the largest area and A has the smallest area.
Anna says that all three areas are the same.
Who is right? Explain your answer.

Strategic competence

17 The area of this right-angled triangle is 6 cm².
Its perimeter is 12 cm.
Calculate the lengths of the other two sides.

18 The perimeter of this right-angled triangle is 40 cm.
Its area is 60 cm².
Calculate the lengths of the other two sides.

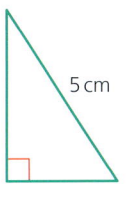

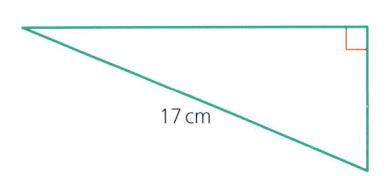

16.3 Compound shapes

Skill checker

① a Draw a parallelogram which is not a rhombus.
  b How many lines of symmetry does your parallelogram have?
② a Draw a rhombus.
  b Draw all the lines of symmetry on your rhombus.
③ a Draw a kite.
  b Draw all the lines of symmetry on your kite.
④ Draw a trapezium which is not a parallelogram.

▶ Compound shapes

Make sure that you include lengths for all the sections of the perimeter. They may not all be given.
In addition to the base, you need the perpendicular height of a shape to calculate its area. This may be different from the side length.
Perimeter is a length, but remember to use square units for area.

335

Curriculum for Wales Mastering Mathematics: Book 1

Worked example

Find the area of this shape.

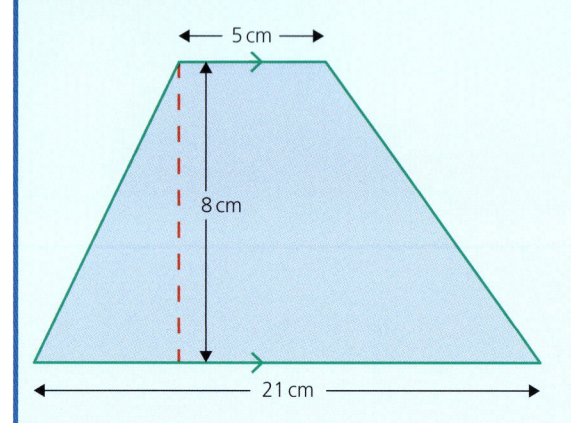

Solution

Area of rectangle = length × width
= 8 × 5
= 40 cm²

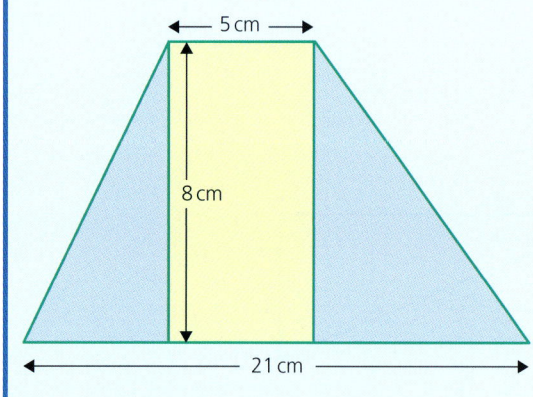

The two shaded triangles can be put together to make a bigger triangle with base 16 cm and perpendicular height 8 cm.

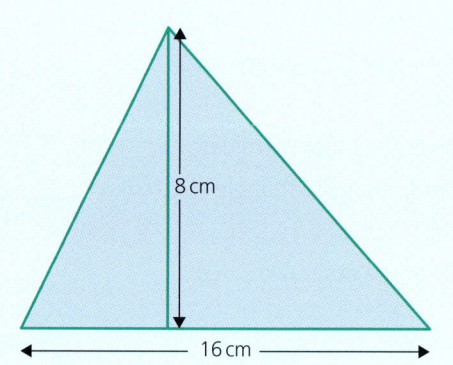

Area of triangle = $\frac{1}{2}$ × base × height
= $\frac{1}{2}$ × 16 × 8
= 64 cm²

Total area = 40 + 64
= 104 cm²

Worked example

Find the perimeter and area of each of these shapes.

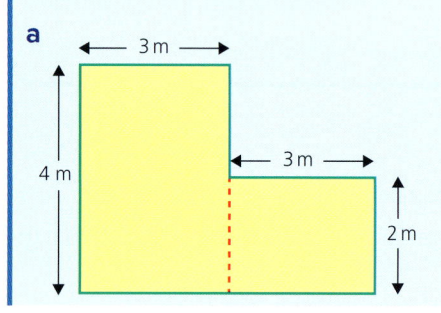

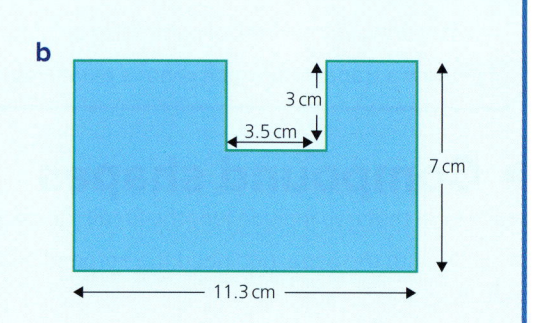

a

b

336

16 Area and perimeter

Solution

a Perimeter = 4 m + 3 m + 2 m + 3 m + 2 m + 6 m
    = 20 m

The shape can be divided into two rectangles.

Be systematic. Start at one corner and work your way around the shape.

Area of whole shape = area A + area B
    = (3 m × 4 m) + (3 m × 2 m)
    = 12 m² + 6 m²
    = 18 m²

b Perimeter = 7 cm + 11.3 cm + 3 cm + 3 cm + 7 cm + 11.3 cm
    = 42.6 cm

Area of whole shape = (7 cm × 11.3 cm) − (3 cm × 3.5 cm)
    = 79.1 cm² − 10.5 cm²
    = 68.6 cm²

You could think of this shape as a large rectangle with a small rectangle cut out.

Activity

① On squared paper, draw and cut out these four shapes.

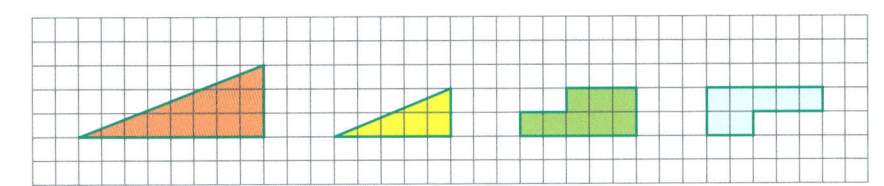

② Arrange the four shapes to form this 'triangle'.

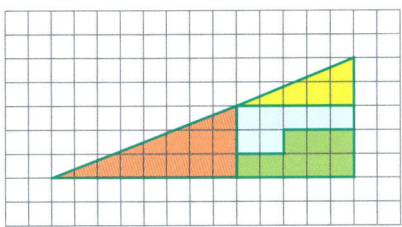

③ Calculate the area of your 'triangle'.

④ Now rearrange the four shapes to form this 'triangle'.

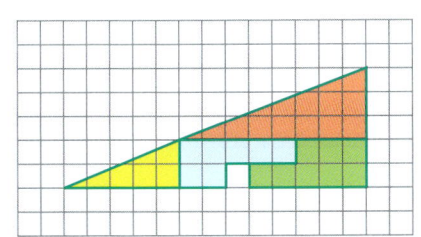

⑤ Calculate the area of your 'triangle' now.

⑥ Where has the missing square gone?

337

16.3 Now try these

Band 1 questions

1 A rectangle and a square are combined as shown.

Calculate the area of the compound shape.

11 cm, 7 cm, 4 cm, 4 cm

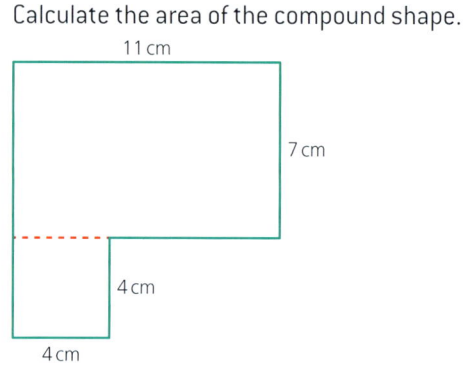

2 A rectangle and two squares are combined as shown.

Calculate the area of the compound shape.

12 cm, 9 cm, 3 cm, 3 cm

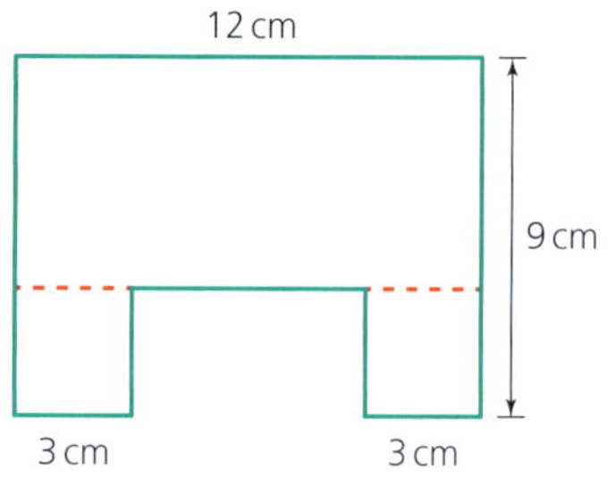

3 A rectangle and a right-angled triangle are combined as shown.

Calculate the area of the compound shape.

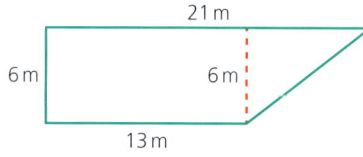

21 m, 6 m, 6 m, 13 m

4 A small rectangle is cut from the corner of a large rectangle.
   a Calculate the area of the remaining shape.
   b Calculate the perimeter of the remaining shape.

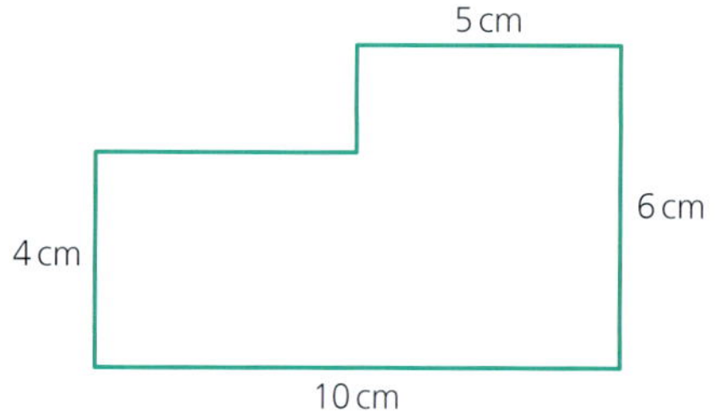

5 cm, 6 cm, 4 cm, 10 cm

5 A rectangle and an isosceles right-angled triangle are combined as shown.

Calculate the area of the compound shape.

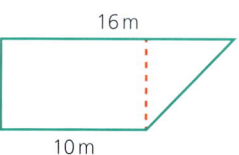

16 m, 10 m

6 A small rectangle is cut from a large rectangle as shown in the diagram.

Calculate the shaded area.

11 cm, 2 cm, 5 cm, 18 cm

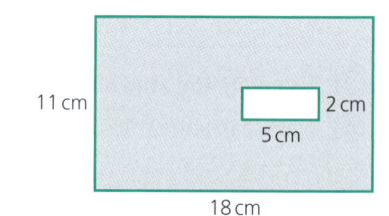

Band 2 questions

7 Sam draws a picture of the front of a house using a rectangle and a triangle.

The area of each of the four windows is 4 cm².

The area of the door is 12 cm².

The rectangle is 15 cm wide and 9 cm high.

The triangle is 4 cm high.

Calculate the shaded area.

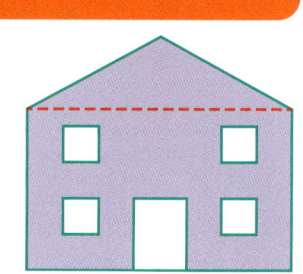

16 Area and perimeter

8 Two right-angled triangles are combined as shown.
Calculate the area of the compound shape.

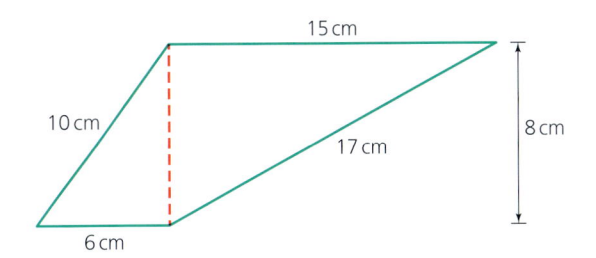

9 A 5 cm square and a 3 cm square are combined without overlapping.
   a Calculate the area of the compound shape.
   b Pedr says he can't work out the perimeter of the compound shape unless he sees a diagram.
       Is he right? Explain why.

10 The perimeter of a square is 20 cm.
A smaller square of area 4 cm² is cut from the corner of the larger square, as shown.
Calculate the remaining area.

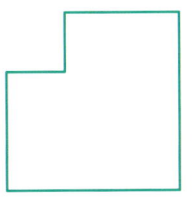

11 Brian measures the perimeter of a large rectangle.
A small rectangle is cut from the large rectangle, as shown.
Will the new perimeter be shorter, longer or the same?

12 Two congruent triangles and a square are combined to form a trapezium.
Calculate the area of the trapezium.

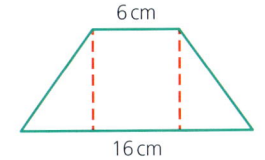

13 A straight line of length 16 cm is drawn between two corners of a quadrilateral.
The line divides the quadrilateral into two triangles.
The triangles have perpendicular heights 5 cm and 10 cm.
Calculate the area of the quadrilateral.

14 This trapezium has been divided into two triangles.

   a Calculate the area of each triangle.
   b Calculate the area of the trapezium.

Curriculum for Wales Mastering Mathematics: Book 1

Band 3 questions

Strategic competence

15. A large right-angled triangle has height 8 cm and area 52 cm².
    A smaller right-angled triangle of sides 8 cm and 4 cm is cut from the large triangle.
    Calculate the length marked x.

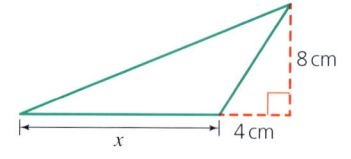

16. The dotted lines in this kite shape are 14 m and 8 m.
    They are perpendicular to each other.
    Calculate the area of the kite.

17. A rectangle has sides of length 10 m and 6 m.
    One corner of the rectangle is joined to the midpoints of two sides of the rectangle to form four triangles.
    Calculate the area of the shaded triangle.

18. Calculate the area of this parallelogram.

19. Calculate the area of this trapezium.

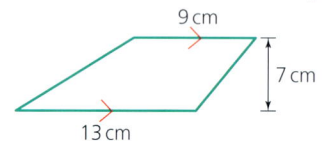

    Look back at Question 12 for a clue.

20. The area of this trapezium is 144 cm².
    Calculate its height.

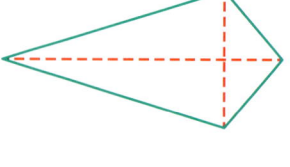

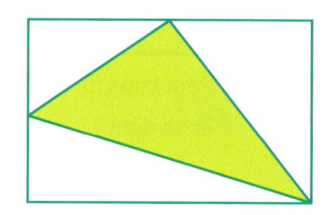

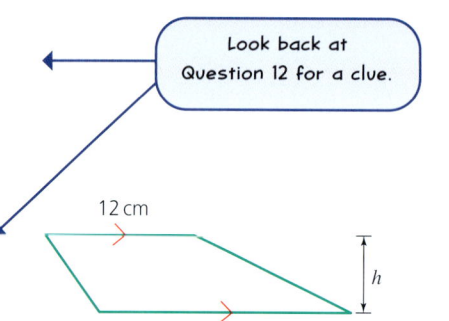

Key words

Here is a list of the key words you met in this chapter.

Area	Base	Congruent	Equilateral
Height	Kite	Length	Parallel
Parallelogram	Perimeter	Perpendicular	Quadrilateral
Rectangle	Right angle	Square	Square metre
Trapezium	Width		

Use the glossary at the back of this book to check any you are unsure about.

340

16 Area and perimeter

Review exercise: area and perimeter

Band 1 questions

1 A rectangle and a square are combined as shown.
  a Calculate the perimeter of the compound shape.
  b Calculate the area of the compound shape.

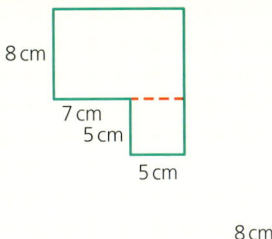

2 A small square and a large square are combined as shown.
  a Calculate the area of the new shape.
  b Calculate the perimeter of the new shape.

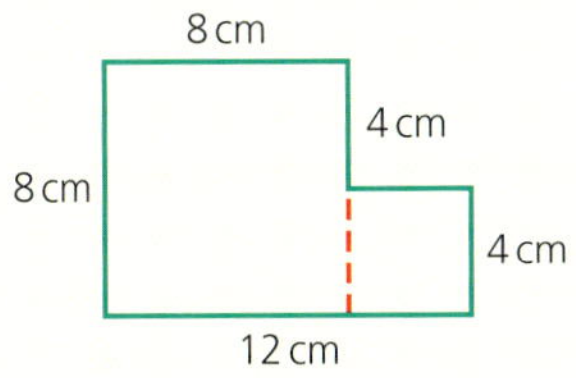

3 A rectangle and an isosceles triangle are combined as shown.

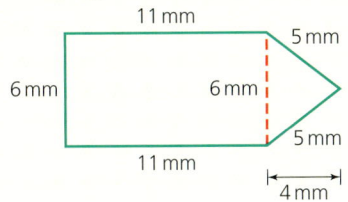

  a Calculate the perimeter of the compound shape.
  b Calculate the area of the compound shape.

4 Three squares are arranged so that their sides form a right-angled triangle as shown.
  a Calculate the perimeter of the compound shape.
  b Show that the sum of the areas of the two smaller squares equals the area of the largest square.
  c Calculate the total area of the compound shape.

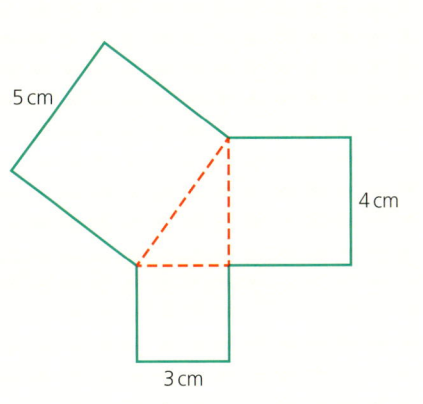

5 A square and a triangle are combined as shown.
  a Calculate the perimeter of the compound shape.
  b Calculate the area of the compound shape.

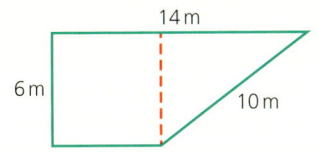

6 A regular octagon is divided into eight congruent triangles.
Each triangle has a base of 24 cm and a perpendicular height of 29 cm.
Calculate the area of the octagon.

Band 2 questions

7 A rectangle and two congruent squares are combined as shown.
  a Calculate the perimeter of the compound shape.
  b Calculate the area of the compound shape.

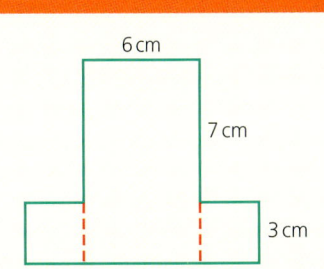

8 A 3 m square is cut from a 7 m square piece of paper.
Morgan says that he cannot work out the area of the remaining shape unless he sees a diagram. Is he right? Explain your answer.

341

Logical reasoning

9 An isosceles triangle is removed from the corner of this square.

Calculate the area of the remaining shape.

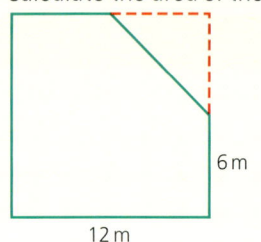

6 m
12 m

Fluency

10 Write down the area of this rectangle in terms of x.

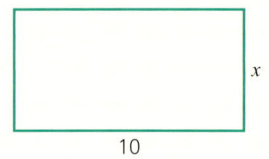

x
10

y
5
4
10

Strategic competence

11 Work out the area of this shape in terms of y.
All angles are right angles.

12 Four congruent isosceles right-angled triangles are cut from the corners of a square.

The sides of the large square are 10 cm.

Calculate the area of the small square which remains.

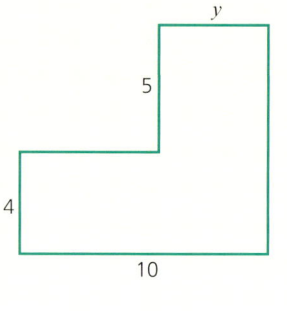

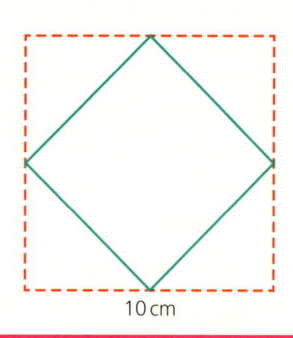

10 cm

Band 3 questions

13 The area of the blue triangle in the diagram is 60 cm².

Calculate the area of the rectangle drawn around it.

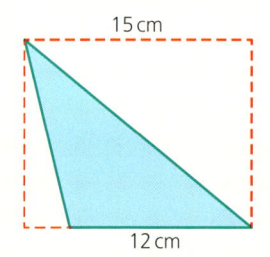

15 cm
12 cm

14 A small triangle is removed from a large triangle, leaving a trapezium.

Calculate the area of the trapezium.

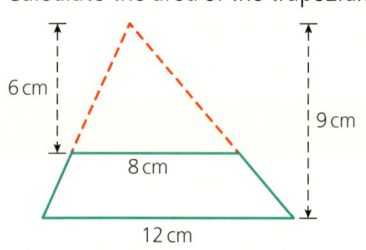

6 cm
9 cm
8 cm
12 cm

15 An isosceles triangle is drawn inside a square as shown.
Calculate the area of the shaded triangle.

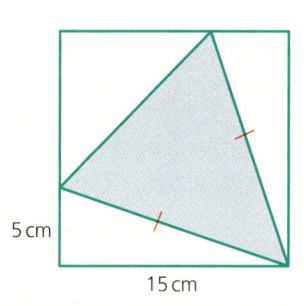

5 cm
15 cm

16 Area and perimeter

16) A square path of width 1 m surrounds a square pond.
The pond has an area of 25 m².
Calculate the area covered by the footpath.

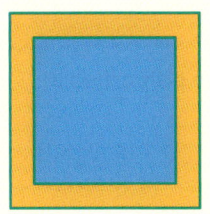

17) The dotted lines in this rhombus are 12 cm and 8 cm, and are perpendicular to each other.
Calculate the area of the rhombus.

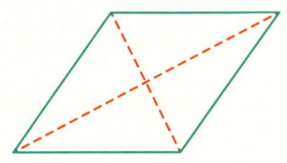

18) A 7 m square has four congruent triangles removed from its corners, leaving a smaller square.
Calculate the perimeter of the smaller square.

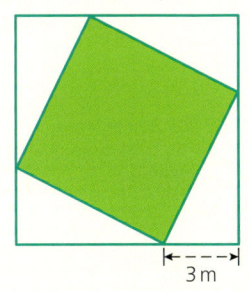

3 m

19) The area of the square is the same as the area of the right-angled triangle.
Calculate the perimeter of the square.

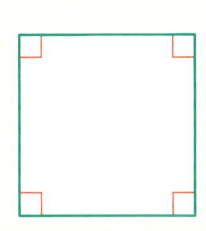

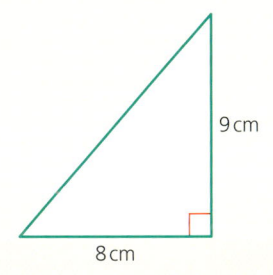

9 cm

8 cm

20) Mr Jones wants to plant some seeds at his farm in Pembroke. His field is shaped as shown.

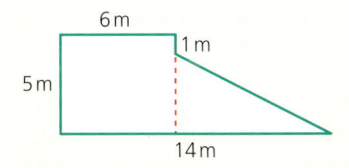

6 m
1 m
5 m
14 m

Each sack of seeds costs £7 and covers 10 m².
How much will it cost for him to cover all of his field?

343

17 Angles

Coming up...
- Understanding and using angle sum properties
- Understanding and using angle properties of triangles
- Understanding and using angle properties of quadrilaterals

The clock's ticking!

① What time does the clock show?
   What is the angle between the clock hands?

② Write down the angle between the hands at these times.

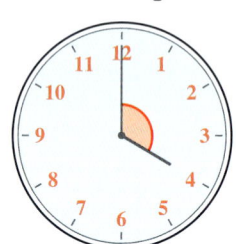

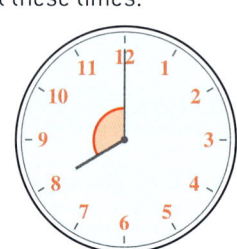

   a   b   c

③ a Sam says that the angle between the hands at 9.15 is 180°.
      Is Sam correct? Explain your answer.
   b Write down a time when the angle between the hands is 180°.

17.1 Angle facts

Skill checker

Copy and complete these sentences.

① An acute angle is less than _____ °.
② An _____ angle is between 90° and 180°.
③ A _____ angle is between 180° and 360°.
④ A right angle is exactly _____ °.
⑤ A half-turn is _____ °.
⑥ A _____ turn is 360°.

17 Angles

> **Activity**
>
> Without measuring, draw a random angle, for example:
>
> Each person estimates the size of the angle, hiding their estimates from the others in the group until all have finished.
>
> Then measure the angle with a protractor.
>
> Award points to each person depending on how close their estimate is.
>
> For example, in a group of five, award five points to the closest, four points to the next closest, and so on.
>
> Take turns to draw and measure the angle.
>
> Include obtuse and reflex angles when your confidence increases.

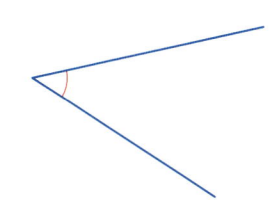

▶ Angles on a straight line

In this diagram, the three angles make a half-turn.

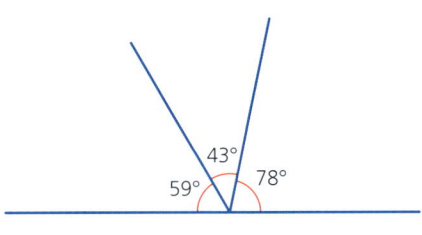

$59° + 43° + 78° = 180°$

A half-turn forms a straight line.

You can use this fact to find missing angles.

> **Remember**
>
> Angles on a straight line add up to 180°.

Worked example

Find the missing angle.

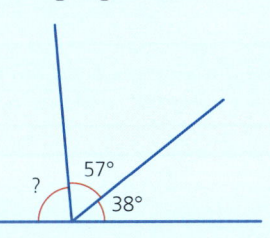

Solution

$57° + 38° = 95°$

So, the missing angle is $180° − 95° = 85°$.

It is sometimes easier to answer such questions by setting up an equation and labelling the missing angle x (or any other suitable letter).

For example:

$x + 57° + 38° = 180°$
$x + 95° = 180°$
$x = 180° − 95°$
$x = 85°$

> **Note**
>
> Look back at Chapter 6 for a recap of equations.

345

Curriculum for Wales Mastering Mathematics: Book 1

▶ Angles at a point

The angles at a point make a **full turn** (360°).

In this diagram, the four angles add up to 360°.

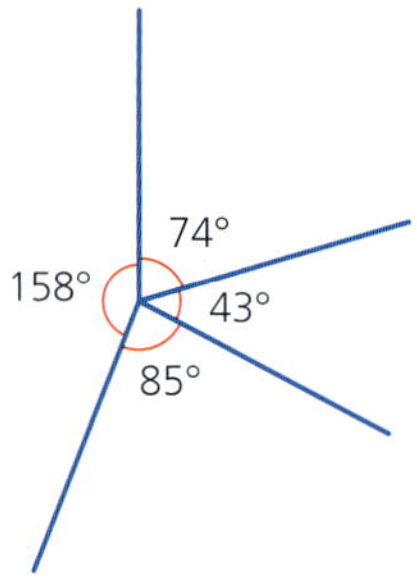

158° + 74° + 43° + 85° = 360°

Note

The angles in diagrams are sometimes deliberately drawn inaccurately to ensure that the missing angles are calculated rather than measured.

Remember

Angles at a point add up to 360°.

▶ Vertically opposite angles

Vertically opposite angles are formed where two lines cross.

Vertically opposite angles are equal.

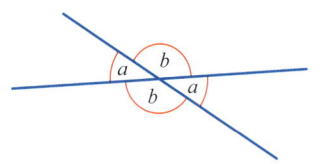

Worked example

Find the size of the lettered angles in this diagram.

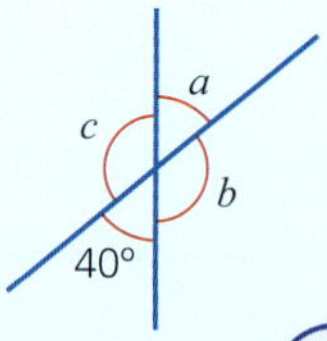

Solution

Vertically opposite angles are equal so $a = 40°$.

$b + 40° = 180°$ ← Angles on a straight line add up to 180°.

$b = 180° - 40° = 140°$

$c + 40° = 180°$ ← Angles on a straight line add up to 180°.

$c = 180° - 40° = 140°$

Alternatively, since c is opposite b you can say that $c = 140°$ without doing the calculation twice.

17.1 Now try these

Band 1 questions

1. Calculate the size of each lettered angle in the three diagrams.

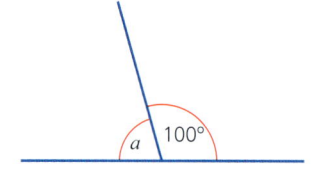

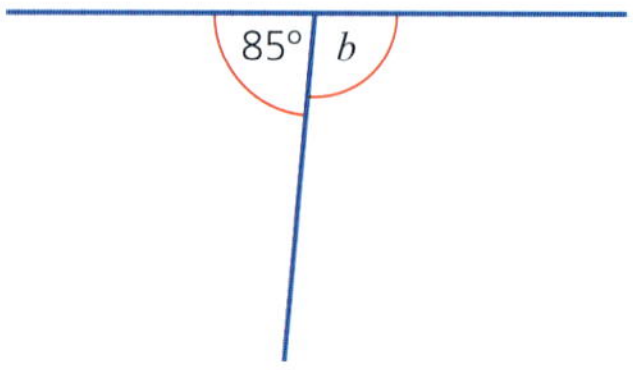

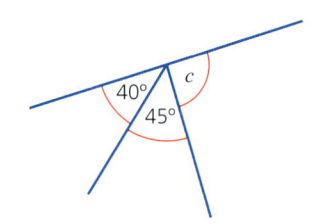

346

17 Angles

2 Calculate the size of each lettered angle.

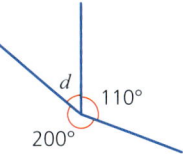

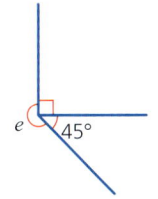

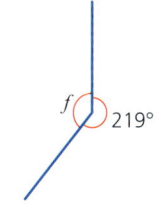

d = 110°, 200° shown; *e* with right angle and 45°; *f* with 219°

3 Calculate the size of each lettered angle.

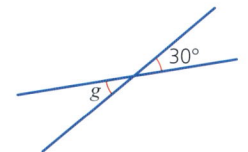

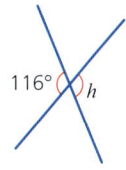

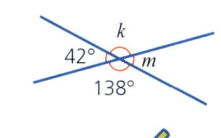

30°, *g*; 116°, *h*; *k*, 42°, *m*, 138°

4 A pipe is bent through 45°.
What is the size of angle *x*?

5 Copy these statements and fill in the missing words or numbers.
Four right angles make a _____ _____.
$4 \times 90° =$ _____
A whole turn is _____ degrees.

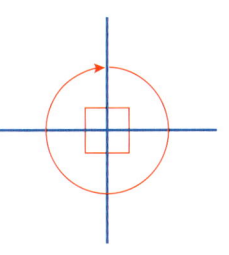

6 Find the size of each lettered angle in these diagrams.

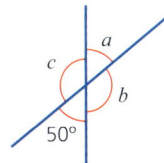

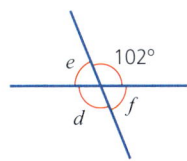

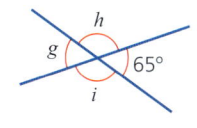

a, *b*, *c*, 50°; *d*, *e* = 102°, *f*; *g*, *h*, *i*, 65°

Band 2 questions

7 a Calculate the angle between the spokes on this car wheel.
b What assumption did you need to make?

8 Calculate the size of angle *a* and of angle *b* in the two diagrams.

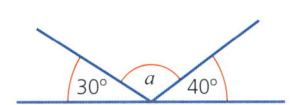

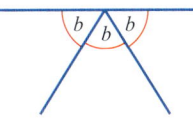

30°, *a*, 40°; *b*, *b*, *b*

9 In this diagram, angle $p = 30°$.
  a Use this to find angle *q*.
  b Use your answer to part **a** to find angle *r*.
  c Use your answer to part **b** to find angle *s*.
  d Show that $p + s = 180°$.
  e State which angles are equal.

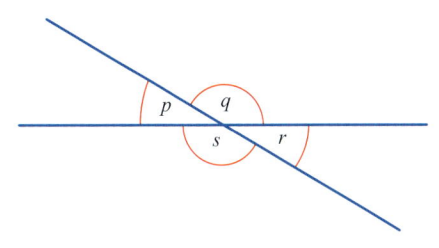

347

Curriculum for Wales **Mastering Mathematics: Book 1**

Strategic competence

10 This water wheel has 18 blades.
    Work out the angle between adjacent blades.

    Adjacent means 'next to'.

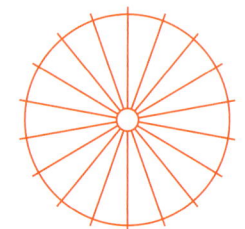

11 Work out the angle between the hands of a clock at:
    a 1 o'clock
    b 8 o'clock.

Logical reasoning

12 For each of the four diagrams, calculate the size of the lettered angle.
    Give a reason for each of your answers.

    135°, a
    72°, 214°, b
    45°, c, 45°
    d, 150°

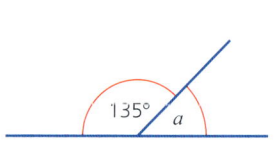

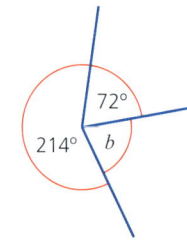

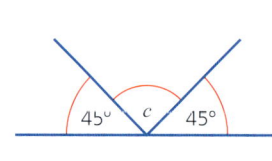

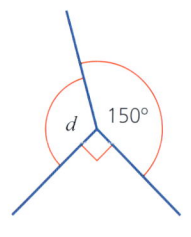

Band 3 questions

13 Alun is programming a robot. It can take steps forward and turn clockwise.
    His instructions are:
    a FWD 10   b TURN 245°
    c FWD 8   d TURN 100°
    e FWD 11   f TURN 120°
    g FWD 9

    Alun now wants the robot to face in the same direction as it was facing originally.
    What should his last instruction be?

Strategic competence

14 Dewi is designing a new fairground ride.
    His initial design is shown here.
    It has 20 viewing capsules equally spaced on a circle.
    a Calculate the angle between the adjacent spokes.
    b The ride takes 15 minutes to complete a full turn.
       When one capsule is at the top of the ride, calculate the time (in seconds) before the next capsule will reach the top.

15 Calculate the angle w shown in the diagram.

16 Calculate the size of angle x.

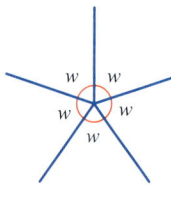

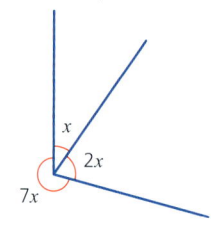

    x, $2x$, $7x$

348

17 AG and TC are straight lines.

Calculate the size of angles m, n and p.

18 Use all three diagrams to calculate the angles a, b, c, d and e.

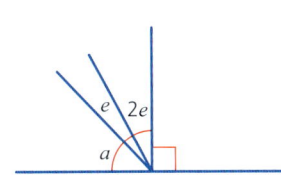

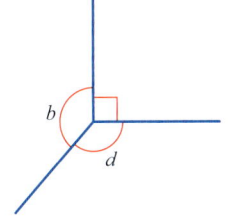

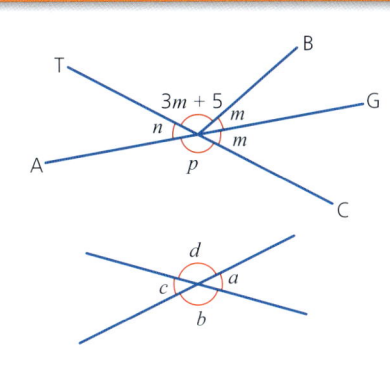

17.2 Angles in a triangle

Skill checker

Copy and complete these sentences.

① An _____ triangle has two equal sides and two equal angles.
② If one of the angles in a triangle is 90° then it is a _____ triangle.
③ A _____ triangle has three different sides and three different angles.
④ A triangle with three equal sides and three equal angles is an _____ triangle.

Activity

Draw any triangle on coloured paper.

Label the three corners.

Tear the triangle into three parts so that each part includes one of the corners.

Rearrange the three shapes so that all three angles are together.

The three angles should form a straight line.

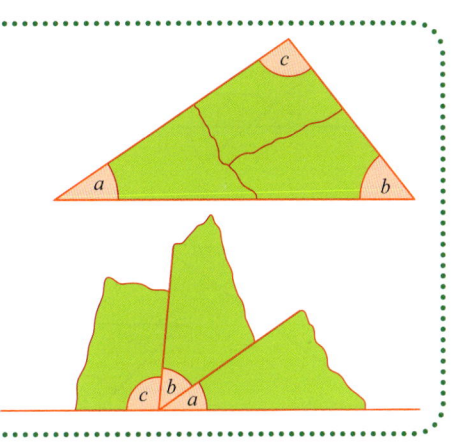

Worked example

Find the size of each unknown angle in these triangles.

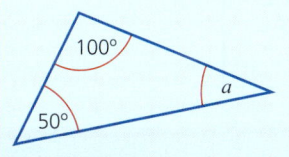

Remember

Angles in a triangle add up to 180°.

Solution

Angles in a triangle add up to 180°.

$a + 50° + 100° = 180°$

$a + 150° = 180°$

$a = 180° - 150°$

$a = 30°$

Angles in a triangle add up to 180°.

$b + 90° + 32° = 180°$

$b + 122° = 180°$

$b = 180° - 122°$

$b = 58°$

Curriculum for Wales Mastering Mathematics: Book 1

17.2 Now try these

Band 1 questions

1 Find the size of each lettered angle in these five diagrams.

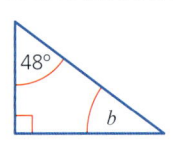

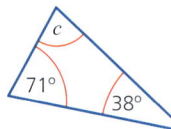

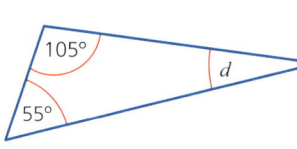

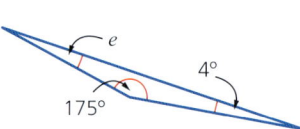

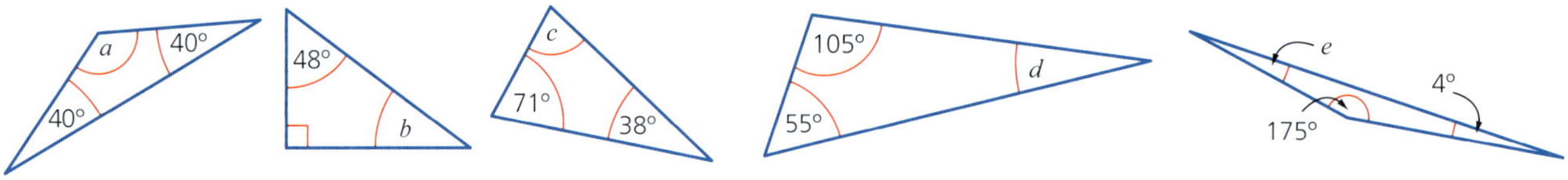

2
  a Calculate the size of angle m.
  b Calculate the size of angle n.
  c Add angle n to 67°.
     What do you notice?

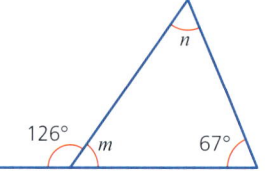

3 Find the size of each lettered angle in these five diagrams.

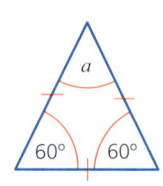

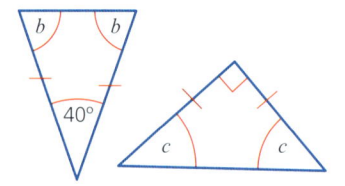

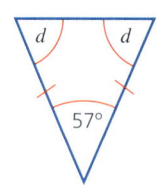

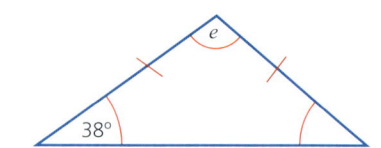

4 Find the size of each lettered angle in this diagram.

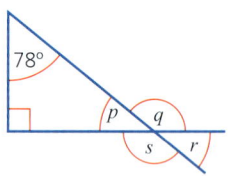

5 Find the size of each lettered angle in these five diagrams.

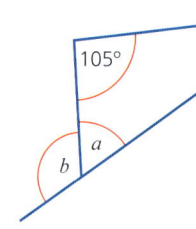

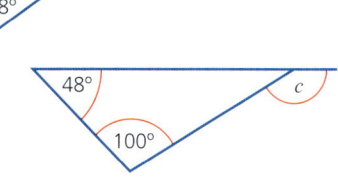

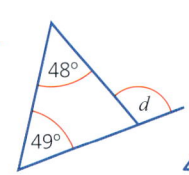

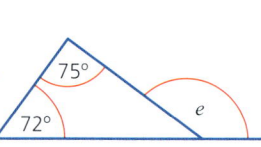

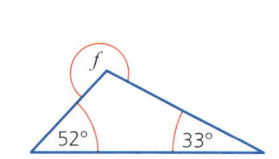

6 The diagram represents a ladder leaning against a wall.
   Calculate the size of the acute angle between the wall and the ladder.

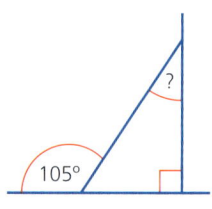

Band 2 questions

7 **a** Calculate the size of angle g.
   b Give the two reasons you have used to calculate your answer to part **a**.

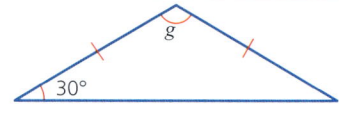

8 Tom says that all equilateral triangles are isosceles. Huw says that all isosceles triangles are equilateral.
   Who is right? Explain your answer.

17 Angles

9. Calculate the size of angle d.

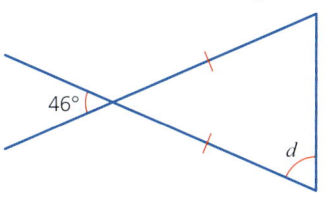

10. Calculate the size of angle v.

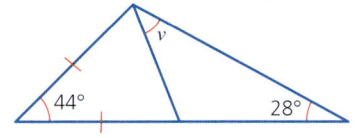

    Give a reason for each angle you calculate.

11. Here is a diagram of the end wall of a house.
    a   What is the value of angle x?
    b   What assumptions do you have to make to answer this question?

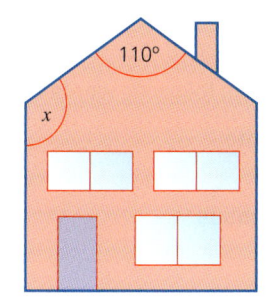

12. Calculate the size of:
    a   angle p
    b   angle q
    c   angle r.

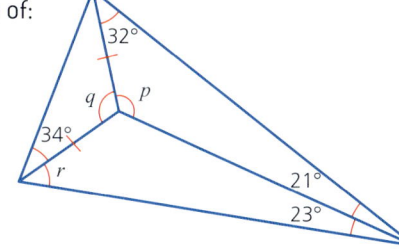

Band 3 questions

13. Calculate the size of angle x.

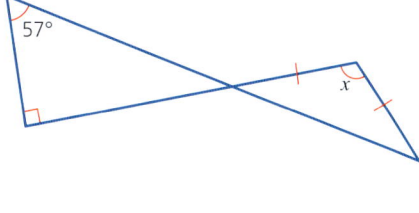

14. Calculate the size of angle f.

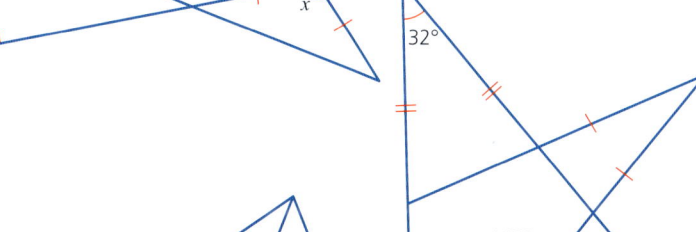

15. Calculate the size of angle m.

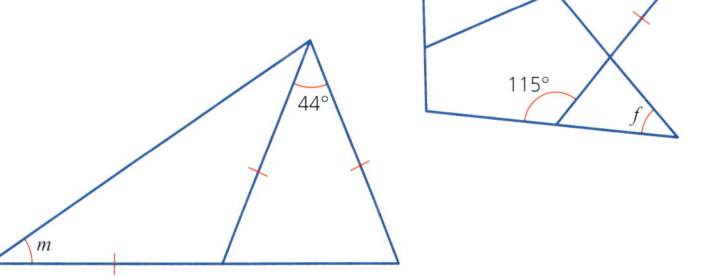

16. Calculate the size of angle w.

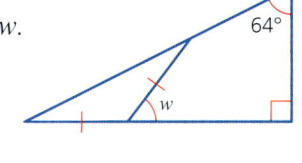

17. Calculate the size of angle a.

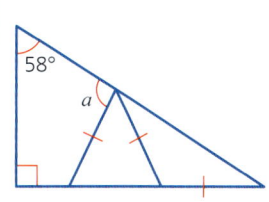

351

18 A large isosceles triangle, ABC, is divided into four smaller triangles as shown.

AC = BC, AQ = RQ, RP = BP, PQ = PC.

The three triangles in the corners are isosceles.

Bronwen says that the middle triangle PQR is also isosceles.

Is Bronwen correct? Explain your answer.

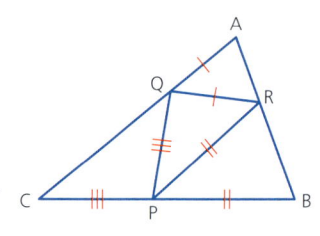

17.3 Angles in a quadrilateral

Skill checker

① Copy and complete this sentence: A **quadrilateral** is any shape with _____ sides.

② Link each of the following words with just one of the shapes below.

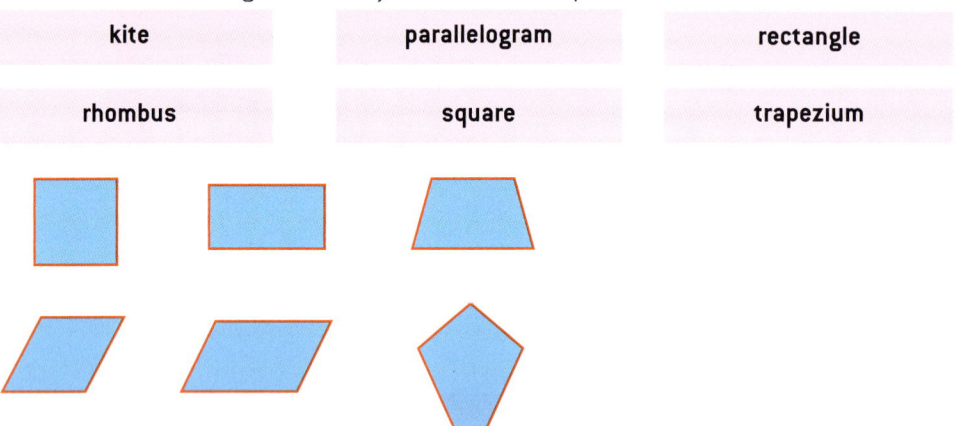

| kite | parallelogram | rectangle |
| rhombus | square | trapezium |

Any quadrilateral can be divided into two triangles. The angles in each triangle add up to 180°. So when the two triangles are put together to form a quadrilateral, the angle **sum** is 360°.

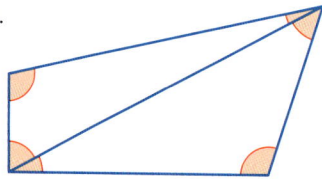

Remember

Angles in a quadrilateral add up to 360°.

Activity

Draw any quadrilateral on coloured paper.

Label the four corners.

Tear the quadrilateral into four parts so that each part includes one of the corners.

Rearrange the four shapes so that all four angles are together.

The four angles should form a full turn (360°).

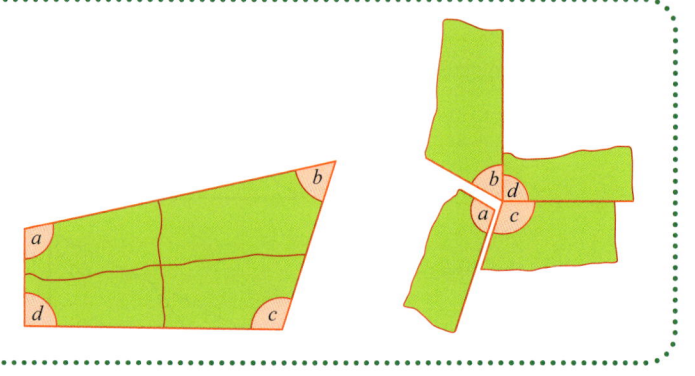

17 Angles

Worked example

Find the size of each unknown angle in these quadrilaterals.

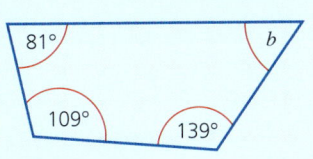

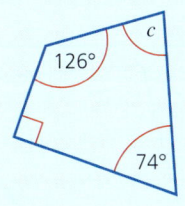

[Quadrilateral with angles 81°, b, 139°, 109°]

[Quadrilateral with angles 126°, c, 74°, 90°]

Solution

Angles in a quadrilateral add up to 360°.

$b + 81° + 109° + 139° = 360°$

$b + 329° = 360°$

$b = 360° - 329°$

$b = 31°$

Angles in a quadrilateral add up to 360°.

$c + 74° + 90° + 126° = 360°$

$c + 290° = 360°$

$c = 360° - 290°$

$c = 70°$

Discussion activity

Apart from Mathematics teachers, what other jobs do you think use angles? When do they use them?

17.3 Now try these

Band 1 questions

Fluency

1 Find the size of angles a to e.

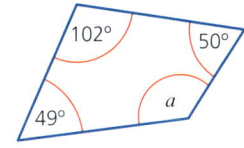

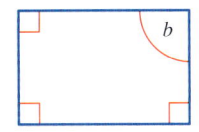

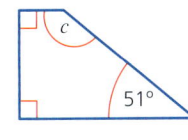

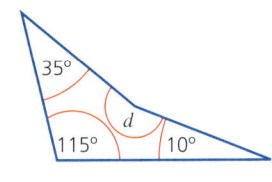

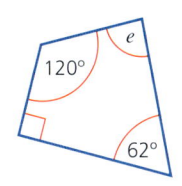

[Quadrilateral: 102°, 50°, a, 49°]

[Rectangle with angle b]

[Right-angled shape: c, 51°]

[Triangle: 35°, d, 115°, 10°]

[Quadrilateral: e, 120°, 62°]

2 Find the size of each lettered angle in these four diagrams.

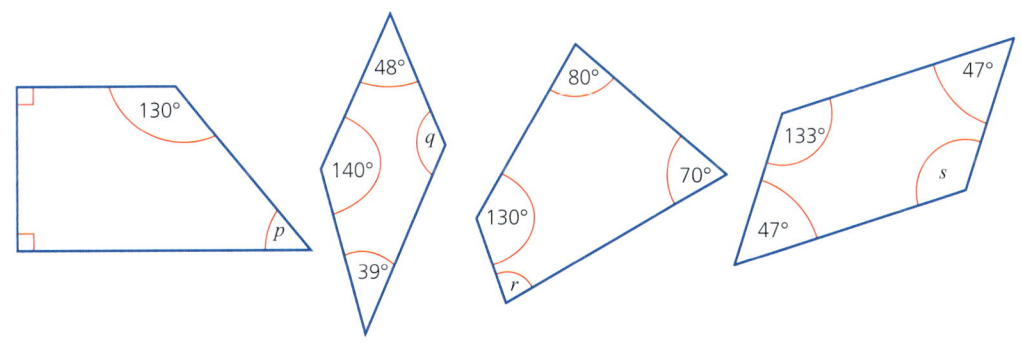

[Quadrilateral: 130°, p, with right angles]

[Quadrilateral: 48°, q, 140°, 39°]

[Quadrilateral: 80°, 70°, r, 130°]

[Parallelogram: 47°, 133°, s, 47°]

Logical reasoning

3 Ioan says that the size of angle a is 85° because the angles on a straight line add up to 180°.

Cerys says, 'I got the same answer, but I used a different method.'

What was Cerys's method?

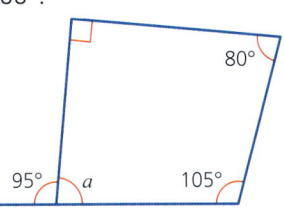

4 Copy and complete these sentences with numbers.

By drawing one line, any quadrilateral can be divided into _____ triangles.

The angle sum of each triangle is _____ °.

The angle sum of any quadrilateral is therefore _____ × _____ ° = 360°.

[Quadrilateral: 80°, 105°, a, 95°, with right angle]

353

Curriculum for Wales Mastering Mathematics: Book 1

5 Calculate the size of angle *v*.

6 Calculate the size of angle *b*.

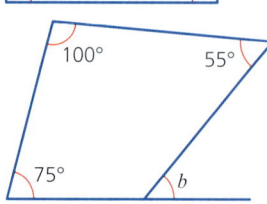

Band 2 questions

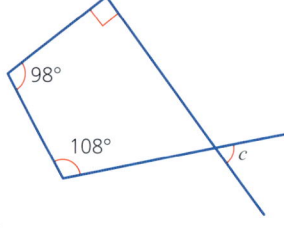

7 Calculate the size of angle *c*.

8 a Calculate the size of angle *d*.
   b Write down two reasons that you used to calculate the value of *d*.

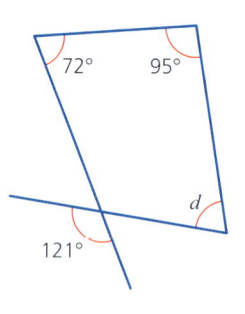

9 Calculate the size of angle *e*.

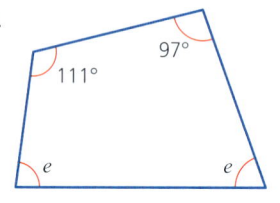

10 Ffion draws this diagram and writes this question to go with it.
Molly says that there is a problem with the question.

> Calculate the size of angle x.
> The diagram is not drawn to scale.

Is Molly right? Explain your answer.

11 Iwan calculates the size of angle *g* in this diagram.
His method is shown here. Copy Iwan's method and include the reason for each step.

> x = 360 − 88 − 112 − 85
>   = 75
> y = 75
> g = 180 − 75 − 74
> g = 31°

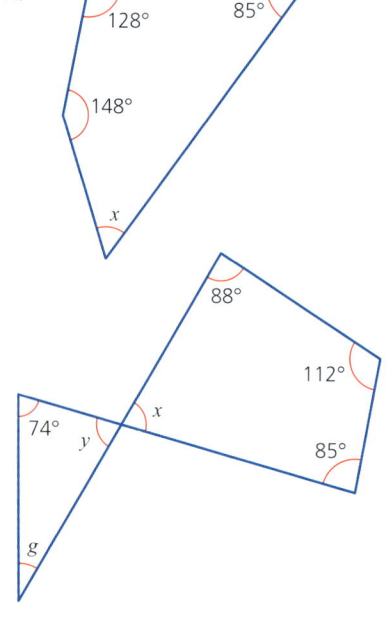

354

17 Angles

12 Calculate the size of angle m.

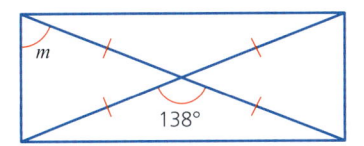

Band 3 questions

13 Calculate the size of angle f.

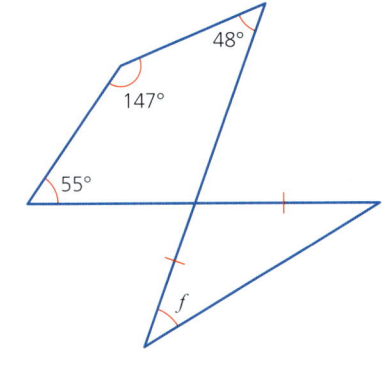

14 **a** Use this diagram to write down an equation for w.
   b Solve your equation to find the value of w.

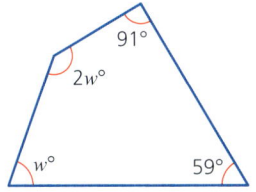

15 Calculate the size of angle h.

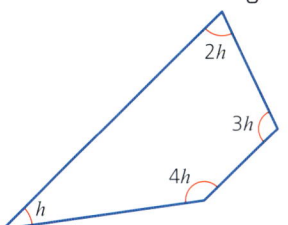

16 Calculate the size of angle n.

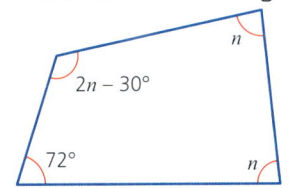

17 Calculate the value of m.

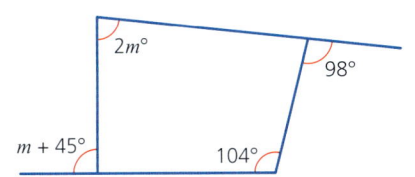

355

Curriculum for Wales Mastering Mathematics: Book 1

Logical reasoning

18 Calculate the value of t.

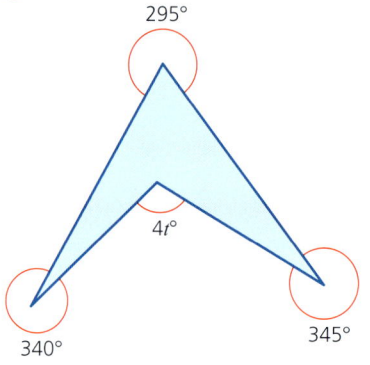

295°
$4t°$
340°   345°

19 ABCD is a quadrilateral as shown.

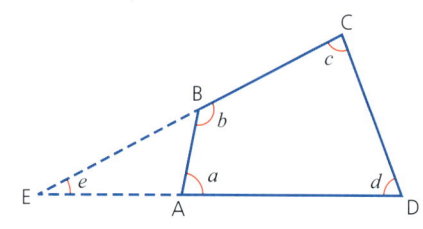

Lines CB and DA are extended until they meet.
The intersection point is labelled E.

> Produced means 'made longer'.

The angles in triangle CDE are c, d and e,
so $c + d + e = 180°$.

i What reason has been used to write this equation?

The angles in triangle BAE are $180° - b$, $180° - a$ and e.

ii What reason has been used to write angles $180° - b$ and $180° - a$?

You now have:
$180° - b + 180° - a + e = 180°$

iii What reason has been used to write this equation?

Rearranging $180° - b + 180° - a + e = 180°$
gives: $e = a + b - 180°$.
Substituting for e in $c + d + e = 180°$
gives: $c + d + a + b - 180° = 180°$.
So $a + b + c + d = 360°$.

Meic says this proves that the angles in all quadrilaterals add up to 360°.

Bethan says that there is one type of quadrilateral for which this proof does not work.

iv Who is right? Explain your answer.

Key words

Here is a list of the key words you met in this chapter.

Acute	Angle	Congruent	Equilateral
Isosceles	Kite	Line	Obtuse
Parallelogram	Quadrilateral	Rectangle	Reflex
Rhombus	Scalene	Square	Sum
Trapezium	Triangle	Turn	Vertically opposite

Use the glossary at the back of this book to check any you are unsure about.

356

17 Angles

Review exercise: angles

Band 1 questions

1 Find the size of each lettered angle in these eight diagrams.

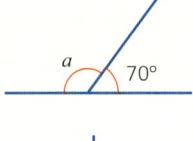

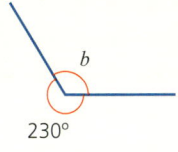

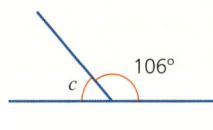

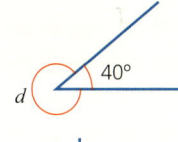

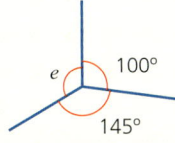

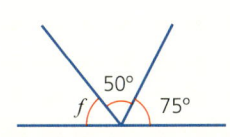

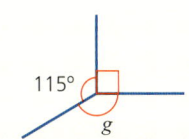

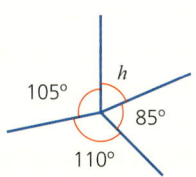

- a, 70°
- b, 230°
- c, 106°
- d, 40°
- e, 100°, 145°
- f, 50°, 75°
- g, 115°, (right angle)
- h, 105°, 85°, 110°

2 Calculate the size of angle x.

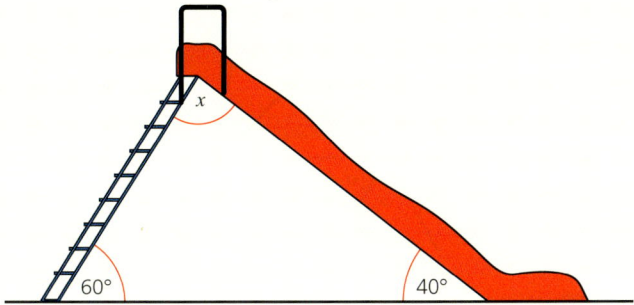

(60°, 40°)

3 Calculate the sizes of angles a, b and c.

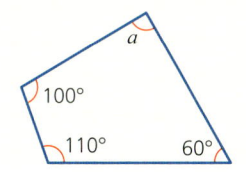

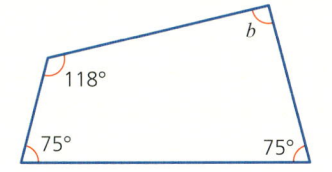

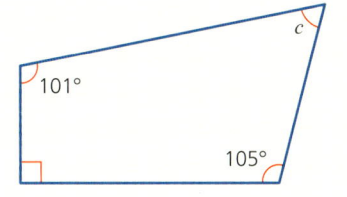

- Quadrilateral with angles a, 100°, 110°, 60°
- Quadrilateral with angles b, 118°, 75°, 75°
- Quadrilateral with angles c, 101°, (right angle), 105°

4 Look at the angles in this girder bridge.

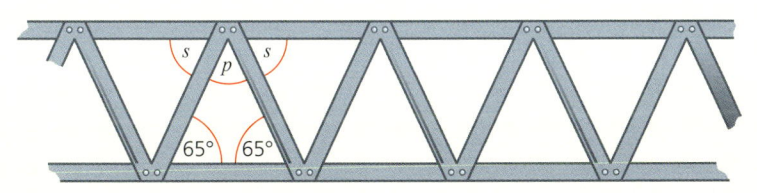

(65°, 65°, with angles s, p, s)

a Calculate the size of angle p.
b Calculate the size of angle s.

5 The diagram represents a tent.
Calculate the size of the angle at the apex of the tent.

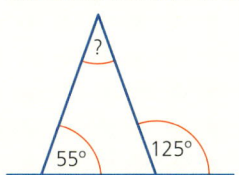

(?, 55°, 125°)

Curriculum for Wales Mastering Mathematics: Book 1

Strategic competence

6 A metronome produces a steady beat for music.
   These four diagrams show the swings for different tempos (speeds).

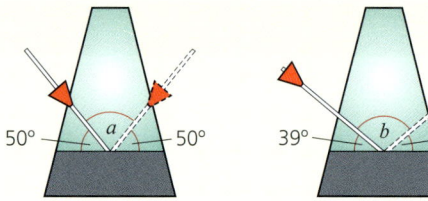

   Moderato — 116 beats per minute — 50°, a, 50°
   Largo — 50 beats per minute — 39°, b, 39°
   Presto — 208 beats per minute — 68°, c, c
   Adagio — 72 beats per minute — 92°, d, d

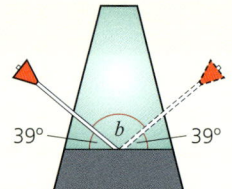

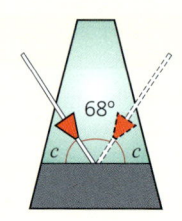

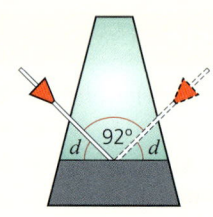

   a Calculate the size of each lettered angle.
   b Write down the tempos in order of speed, from slowest to fastest.

Band 2 questions

Logical reasoning

7 Calculate the size of each lettered angle in these five diagrams.

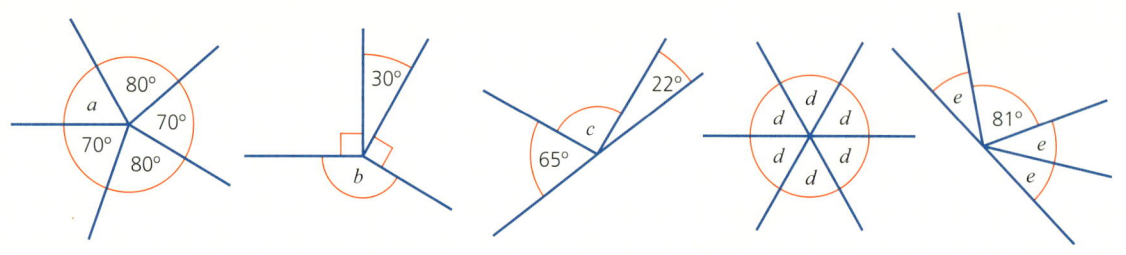

   (Diagram 1: 80°, a, 70°, 80°, 70°)
   (Diagram 2: 30°, b, right angle)
   (Diagram 3: 22°, c, 65°)
   (Diagram 4: six angles labelled d)
   (Diagram 5: 81°, e, e, e)

Strategic competence

8 Find the size of each lettered angle in these three diagrams.

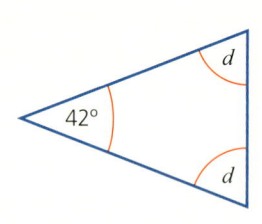

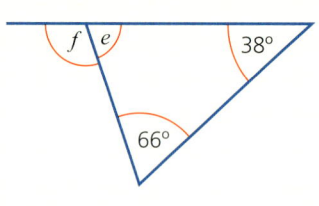

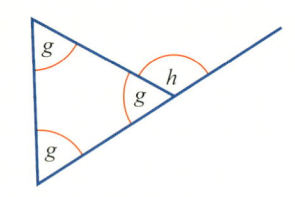

   (Diagram 1: 42°, d, d)
   (Diagram 2: f, e, 38°, 66°)
   (Diagram 3: g, g, g, h)

9 Each of the unknown angles in these triangles has a code letter in the table below.

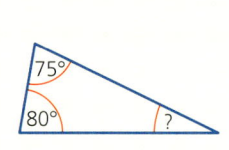

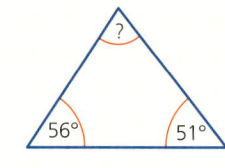

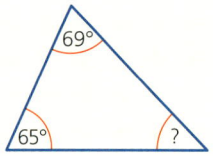

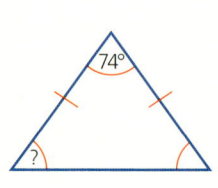

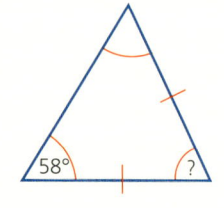

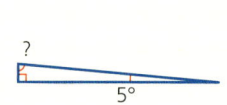

   (Triangle 1: 75°, 80°, ?)
   (Triangle 2: ?, 56°, 51°)
   (Triangle 3: 69°, 65°, ?)
   (Triangle 4: 74°, ?, ?)
   (Triangle 5: 58°, ?)
   (Triangle 6: ?, 5°)

   a Find the six code letters.
   b Rearrange the code letters to discover the code word.

n	e	g	i	s	m	a	r	o	l	q	y	w	u
82°	73°	66°	32°	53°	48°	25°	64°	21°	74°	46°	59°	33°	85°

17 Angles

10 This pattern is made by placing four equilateral triangles inside a rectangle.

Calculate the size of each angle in the pattern.

11 Saul is proving that in a rectangle like the one in the diagram, the angle marked w is always twice the size of the angle marked m.

Copy and complete Saul's method by adding the reasons.

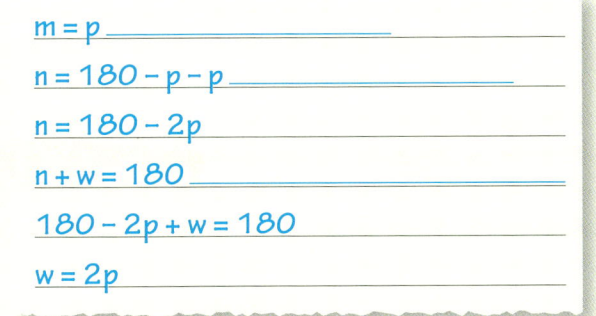

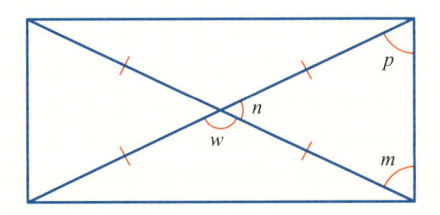

$m = p$ _____

$n = 180 - p - p$ _____

$n = 180 - 2p$

$n + w = 180$ _____

$180 - 2p + w = 180$

$w = 2p$

12 Triangle ABC is an isosceles triangle.

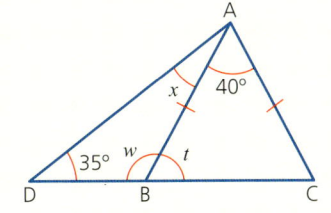

Show that Triangle ABD is also an isosceles triangle.

13 One of the angles in an isosceles triangle is 76°.

Write down the possible sizes of the other two angles.

___ and ___ or ___ and ___

Band 3 questions

14 Lloyd and Erin both correctly calculate the size of angle z, but they use different methods.

Lloyd says he used the same reason twice.

Erin says she used two different reasons.

   a   Write down Lloyd's reason.

   b   Write down Erin's reasons.

15 Calculate the size of angle r.

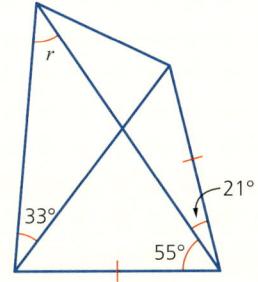

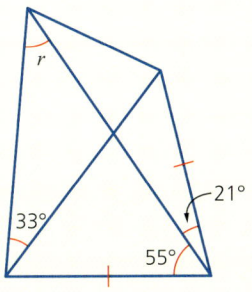

359

Curriculum for Wales Mastering Mathematics: Book 1

Strategic competence

16 Calculate the size of angle y.

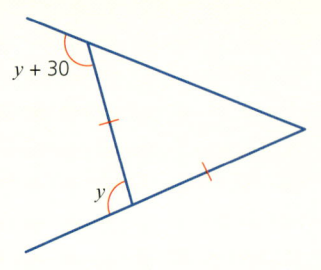

$y + 30$

y

Logical reasoning

17 This question shows you why the angles of a triangle must add up to 180°.
Follow through the steps yourself.

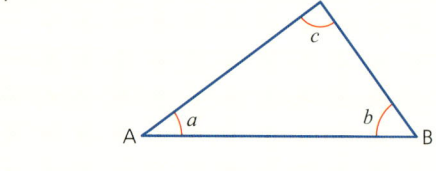

a   Start by drawing your own triangle ABC.
    There should be nothing special about it.
    Call the angles a, b and c.
    You want to show that $a + b + c = 180°$.

b   Now draw a rectangle around your triangle, like this. Call it AXYB.
    Mark in all the right angles in your diagram.
    The one at X is already done.

c   Now draw in the line CZ.
    It makes two more rectangles.
    Mark in the new right angles.

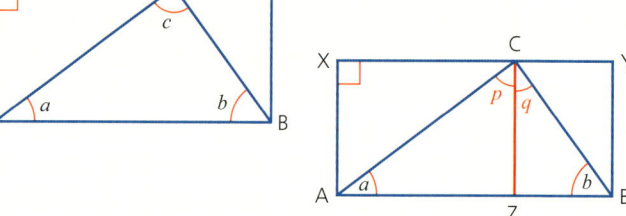

d   The line CZ divides the angle c into two parts, p and q.
    Copy and complete this statement.
    $p + $ _____ $= c$

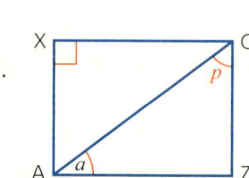

e   Now look at rectangle AXCZ, then copy and complete the statements about its symmetry.
    AXCZ has _____ symmetry of order _____.
    So triangles AXC and CZA are _____.
    Mark in the missing angles on a copy of the diagram using one of the letters a or p.

f   Look at the angle at a then copy and complete this statement.
    $a + p = $ _____

g   Now look at the rectangle ZCYB.
    Describe its symmetry, mark the missing angles, then copy and complete this statement.
    $b + q = $ _____

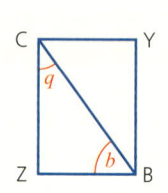

h   Now copy and complete these statements.
    $a + p + b + q = $ _____° + _____° = _____°
    $a + b + p + q = $ _____°
    $a + b + c = $ _____°

So the angles of triangle ABC add up to 180°.

360

Consolidation 6: Chapters 15–17

Band 1 questions

1. Write down the seven weights shown on these scales.
   a, b, c, d (scales shown)

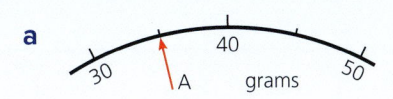

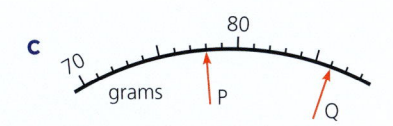

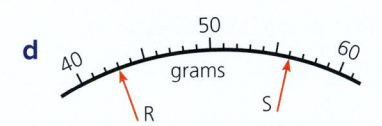

2. Look at this measuring cylinder.
   a. What is its capacity?
   b. What does one small division represent?
   c. How much liquid is in it?

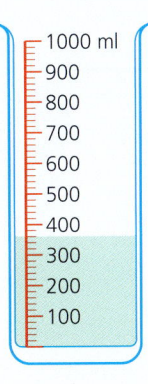

3. Calculate the sizes of angles a, b and c.

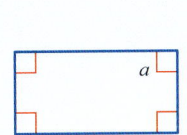

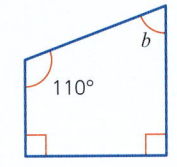

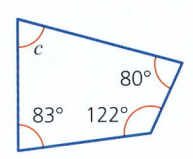

4. a. Calculate the area of a rectangle with length 8 cm and width 5 cm.
   b. Calculate the perimeter of a square with side length 10 m.

5. Convert these weights.
   a. 2000 mg = _____ g
   b. 3 kg = _____ g
   c. 7 tonnes = _____ kg

6. The length of a football pitch must be between 90 m and 120 m, and its width between 45 m and 90 m.
   a. Calculate the greatest possible area of a football pitch.
   b. Calculate the smallest possible perimeter.

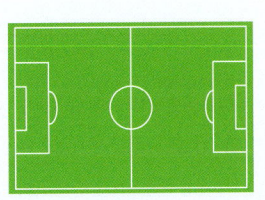

7. Calculate the perimeter and area of this triangle.

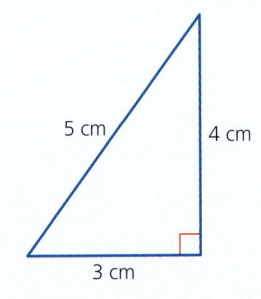

(Triangle: 5 cm, 4 cm, 3 cm)

8. The area of Twm's rectangle is 40 cm².
   The perimeter of his rectangle is 26 cm.
   What is the length and width of Twm's rectangle?

Band 2 questions

9. Calculate the sizes of angles d, e, f, g and h in the three diagrams.
   Write down the reason used for finding each angle.

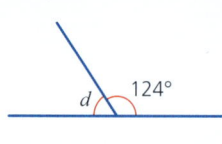

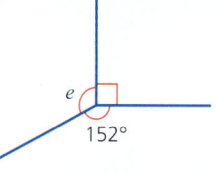

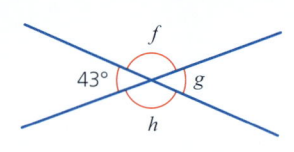

10. Convert these volumes.
    a   2.3 litres = _____ ml
    b   57 cl = _____ litres
    c   3.8 ml = _____ cl
    d   236 cm³ = _____ litres

11. Write these lengths using more convenient units.
    a   9200 m
    b   83 000 mm
    c   0.000 006 km

12. A rectangular hole measuring 4 cm by 2 cm has been cut from this shape.
    Calculate the remaining area.

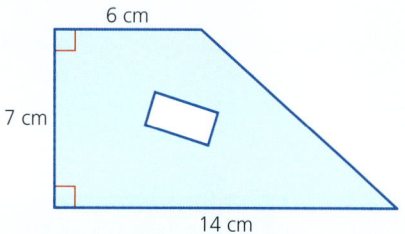

13. a   Calculate the size of angle m.
    b   Write down the reasons used in part a.

14. Write these weights using more convenient units.
    a   2 600 000 mg
    b   73 000 000 g
    c   0.000 006 tonnes

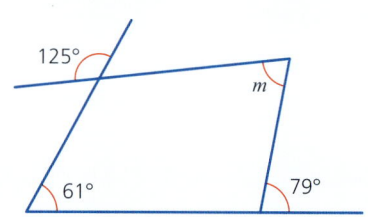